MANAGERIAL COMMUNICATION
Strategies and Applications

Larry R. Smeltzer
Donald J. Leonard
Arizona State University

IRWIN
Burr Ridge, Illinois
Boston, Massachusetts
Sydney, Australia

To Catherine
and Mary

 This symbol indicates that the paper in this book is made of recycled paper. Its fiber content exceeds the recommended minimum of 50% waste paper fibers as specified by the EPA.

Senior sponsoring editor: *Craig Beytien*
Editorial assistant: *Jennifer McBride*
Project editor: *Mary Vandercar*
Production manager: *Irene Sotiroff*
Marketing manager: *Kurt Messersmith*
Cover designer: *Maureen McCutcheon*
Art coordinator: *Heather Burbridge*
Art studio: *David Corona Design*
Compositor: *J.M. Post Graphics, Corp.*
Typeface: *10/12 Palatino*
Printer: *R.R. Donnelley & Sons Company*

Library of Congress Cataloging-in-Publication Data

Smeltzer, Larry R.
    Managerial communication: strategies and applications/Larry R.
Smeltzer, Donald J. Leonard.
        p.   cm.
    Includes bibliographical references and index.
    ISBN 0-256-12072-2
    1. Communication in management.   2. Business communication.
I. Leonard, Donald J.   II. Title.
HD30.3.S572/1994
658.4'5—dc20   93–18311

Printed in the United States of America
    3 4 5 6 7 8 9 0 DOC 0 9 8 7 6

Larry R. Smeltzer

Dr. Smeltzer is currently the chairman of the Department of Business Administration at Arizona State University. He has taught managerial communication at the undergraduate and graduate levels at Arizona State University and Louisiana State University as well as at the Helsinki School of Economics and Business and the Oslo Business School. His research focus is on managers as communicators. He has published in numerous journals and served as the executive editor of *Management Communication Quarterly*. He is also on the review boards of the *Journal of Business Communication* and the *Journal of Business and Technical Communication* as well as several other journals. In addition, he is co-author of *Management: The Competitive Edge*. In 1991, he received the Association for Business Communication Outstanding Researcher Award. Before joining academia, Dr. Smeltzer was employed by a Fortune 500 company; and throughout his career, he has been involved with numerous consulting projects.

Donald J. Leonard

Dr. Leonard is an associate professor of managerial communication in the Department of Business Administration at Arizona State University, where he has taught business and managerial communication for the last 18 years. Before that, he taught at Louisiana State University, from which he received his doctorate. In the summer of 1987, he served as visiting professor of business, managerial, and organizational communication at the Indonesian Institute of Management Development in Jakarta, Indonesia. He revised *Shurter's Communication in Business* and *Effective Letters in Business*, co-authored *Teaching Business Communication* (with Max Waters) and *Managerial Communication: A Strategic Approach* (with Larry Smeltzer and John Waltman), and co-edited *Readings and Materials for Managerial Communication* (with Patricia Murranka and Larry Smeltzer). In 1991, he received the Association for Business Communication Outstanding Teacher Award. He is currently a reviewer for the *Bulletin* of the Association of Business Communication.

iii

In the rapidly changing, complex organizational environment of the 1990s, managers must be able to analyze their environment and develop effective management communication strategies. But they must also be able to apply these strategies. *Management Communication: Strategies and Applications* is designed to prepare students to think strategically about communication and prepare appropriate managerial applications. A contingency approach is integrated throughout this text to remind students that few universally applicable guidelines are available; however, research-based guidelines are presented when appropriate.

Because managers must communicate in many different situations using a variety of techniques, both oral and written communication are covered at five levels: intrapersonal, interpersonal, group, organizational, and intercultural. To accomplish this task, we have integrated concepts from several academic disciplines including business communication, organizational behavior, organizational communication, composition, rhetoric, and linguistics. We have thoroughly reviewed the current research literature in our efforts to integrate these disciplines.

To assure that we were drawing on relevant literature and addressing appropriate issues, we visited with a number of managers as we wrote this text. We wanted to be sure we were addressing the current and future relevant communication needs of managers. Our teaching experience in executive management programs and consulting also provided valuable guidance while preparing this text.

In addition to being relevant, we wanted the book to be interesting and easy to read. Our combined 40 years of teaching has told us that the book must go beyond simply listing and explaining principles. Accordingly, we integrated actual managerial examples from a variety of organizations wherever appropriate. We hope this will make the book more enjoyable to read, and we are modestly confident that our experience in writing other books and articles has provided the required experience to make this book readable.

Organization

To cover both written and oral managerial communication at the different levels of analysis, we divided the book into five parts. Part I provides a historical and current overview of the environment faced by managers. The demand for quality, a concern for ethics, increasing diversity and greater job stress are mentioned as dynamics that will make managerial communication more challenging but more important as we move toward the year 2000. A model of managerial communication is presented in Chapter 2 and considerations for strategic analysis are presented in Chapter 3.

The second part covers written communication. We put this section early in the book so teachers could introduce students to writing projects early in the course. Both the process and product approaches are taken in the four chapters that make up this section. We first present a chapter that discusses the preparation required for writing; then we cover the essentials of writing in the next chapter. These two chapters are followed by a discussion of strategies for specific applications: letters, memos, and reports.

Part III presents three chapters on oral managerial communication. Strategies for making oral presentations is the first topic so students can possibly combine written and oral reports on the case studies presented throughout the text. The chapter on listening is a natural subtopic of oral communication, but some aspects of nonverbal communication apply to written communication while others apply to oral communication. However, we believe most nonverbal considerations fit more comfortably in this section on oral communication.

Part IV contains five chapters on interpersonal and group applications. It is difficult to classify topics strictly according to either a level or type of communication. But we believe the first 10 chapters of the book establish a solid foundation for the subsequent 7 chapters. For instance, competent interviewing requires listening, oral skills, nonverbal awareness, and often a written summary or letter. This is why we located interviewing in Part IV. Also, because of the importance of interviews, we dedicated two chapters to this topic. The first chapter covers strategies and applications that are appropriate for many interview situations. The second chapter discusses more specific applications that all managers face, such as employment interviews, performance reviews, and discipline.

Also included in Part IV is a chapter on group dynamics and meetings, followed by chapters on conflict management and negotiations. Separate chapters are dedicated to each of these topics because of their growing importance and because of the increased knowledge we have about both conflict management and managerial negotiations.

Part V presents two topics that apply to most other topics in the book and that probably are the most rapidly changing aspects of managerial communication. Technologically mediated communication is becoming more complex and a more valuable tool as computer uses increase. And as technological developments become more universal, the opportunities and necessities of communicating with diverse cultures both within the United States and around the world become more pronounced.

An appendix on the legal dimensions of managerial communication is included because research indicates many managers are not aware of the many legal issues they face. Awareness of the basic legal issues involving managerial communication should assist the readers to communicate within the legal constraints they face.

To Help Teaching and Learning

The ultimate purpose of this book is to assist its readers to become better managerial communicators in a rapidly changing environment. But what is true today may not be true tomorrow. Accordingly, we first present a strategic model and then look at the many ways it can be applied. To help with this strategic development and application, each chapter is followed by at least two cases or a series of exercises. Each of these cases is based on actual rather than hypothetical organizational events. In addition, a real-life scenario introduces each chapter. Many of the discussion questions at the end of each chapter ask the students to relate the concepts in the chapter to their own lives. Finally, where possible, examples from organizations are provided to show how the concepts apply to real organizations.

Instructor's Manual and Videos

An instructor's manual is also provided to assist with the teaching and learning. A number of teaching aids are included in the manual.

Transparency masters. Concepts from each chapter are supplemented with numerous transparency masters. Many of these masters are diagrams that are not in the book but help teachers present the material in the book. Over 100 masters are provided.

Test questions. Objective test questions for each chapter as well as for Appendix 1 are included. Many of these questions have been class tested.

Case notes. Key points are summarized for each of the end-of-chapter cases.

Comprehensive case. To supplement the shorter cases in the book, a longer, more comprehensive case with notes is included in the instructor's manual. This case involves each of the five levels of managerial communication and requires both a written and oral response.

Chapter outlines. Each chapter is outlined and additional readings are suggested that can provide additional information.

Possible syllabi. Potential syllabi for both quarter and semester courses are included.

Assignments and rating forms. Analytical memo assignments with detailed explanations are provided along with a sample report. An intercultural communication assignment is also provided. In addition, rating and grading forms for both written and oral assignments are included.

The Irwin Business Communication video series consists of self-contained, informative segments covering such topics as writing correctly and the power of listening. Presented in a clear and engaging style, every segment holds students' interest while presenting the techniques for sharpening their communication skills. More information about these videos may be obtained from your Irwin representative.

Larry R. Smeltzer
Donald J. Leonard

Acknowledgments

A typical question of a book author is, "How long did it take you to write the book?" But authors soon realize that most books have an indefinite beginning and end. The ideas presented in this book began to develop someplace in work history when we first experienced the power and influence of a good managerial communicator. The ideas continued to develop as we received feedback from the many students we have had during the years, had frequent conversations with our professional colleagues, and discussed communications with the hundreds of managers we have worked with. It would be difficult to say if a particular idea became clearer as we visited with a manager from Bombay, India, or were talking about a class assignment with an MBA student.

Several colleagues, however, have had an immediate impact on this project. First, we would like to acknowledge John L. Waltman from Eastern Michigan University. He wrote Chapter 10 for this book, and we thank him for his scholarly effort. In addition, he has had a major influence on our thinking in many other sections of the book. We are indebted to John for his willingness to work with us. Mary Jane Dundas, a professor of Legal and Ethical Studies at Arizona State University, prepared the Appendix on the Legal Dimensions of Managerial Communication. As a textbook author and lawyer, she provided extremely valuable insights that will be helpful to students.

Two former colleagues at Arizona State University have also influenced our thinking. Jeannette Gilsdorf, who is now at California State University,

Long Beach, and Gail Fann Thomas, who is now at the Naval Postgraduate Academy, have both influenced our thinking about managerial communication and encouraged our professional efforts.

A unique opportunity was provided to work at the Helsinki School of Economics and Business with JoAnne Yates of MIT and Annette Shelby of Georgetown University. This opportunity to share syllabi, exchange exercises, and generally compare ideas was most beneficial in developing the foundation for this book.

Our present colleagues in managerial communication at Arizona State University have also provided encouragement and support. For this we would like to thank David Lynch and Patricia Murranka. During their busy schedules, they frequently responded to our inconvenient questions.

Larry Penley, the dean of the College of Business at Arizona State University, has provided support by encouraging our faculty to develop communication competencies in business students.

Our list could go on as many colleagues in the Association for Business Communication, the Academy of Management, the Management Communication Association, and the International Communication Association have been helpful. Several people served as reviewers and have provided especially valuable feedback on this text.

Judi Brownell
Cornell University

Ruthann Dirks
Emporia State University

Robert Gieselman
University of Illinois

Robert J. Myers
Baruch College

Martha A. Nord
Vanderbilt University

Christine Kelly
New York University

Our appreciation also goes to the Irwin team, especially Craig Beytien who encouraged us to pursue the idea of a management communication text. In addition to Craig, others at Irwin who were helpful include Jeannie Warble; Mary Vandercar, Project Editor; Keith McPherson, Designer; and Irene Sotiroff, Production Manager.

Finally, we want to acknowledge the help and support of our spouses during this pursuit, Catherine and Mary.

L.R.S.
D.J.L.

B R I E F   C O N T E N T S

CONTENTS

PART II

STRATEGIES FOR WRITTEN MANAGERIAL COMMUNICATION

4 Preparing for Written Managerial Communication 91

PART III

STRATEGIES FOR ORAL MANAGERIAL COMMUNICATION

8   Strategies for Making an Oral Presentation   195

PART V

MANAGERIAL COMMUNICATION IN RAPIDLY CHANGING ENVIRONMENTS

16   Technologically Mediated Communication   417

I THE BASIS OF MANAGERIAL COMMUNICATION

The three chapters in the opening section of this book present a foundation for the understanding of managerial communication in contemporary organizations. The first chapter describes the historical evolution of managerial communication and suggests it will continue to evolve. Four factors that will profoundly affect this evolution are employee diversity, competitiveness and the drive for quality, job stress, and ethics.

The second chapter explains the five levels of managerial communication that are presented in this text. The chapter then presents a model of managerial communication, explains personality factors that affect communication, explains the role of metacommunication, and describes four critical errors in communication.

Chapter 3 presents a strategic model of managerial communication. This model is described using the metaphor of layers of an onion in that variables in the levels of the model have to be peeled off to develop the final communication strategy. The contingency approach is used when presenting this model. Finally, individual communication strategies and styles that managers frequently use are also described in this chapter.

1 MANAGERIAL COMMUNICATION IN TRANSITION

> *Clarence opened a farm supply store in Montana during the early 1900s. By the time he retired and his son, Jim, took over, the company had expanded to three stores in three cities and had 14 full-time employees. When Jim retired, his daughter, Kathy, took over the company that now has 23 stores with 228 employees in three states and one wholly owned subsidiary of 18 gas stations. Kathy and her husband/partner find themselves traveling extensively from the corporate office to the various stores. Finding time to manage everything is a problem, but they have a staff of 12 professionals in the corporate office to assist them. A computer network and fax machines help tremendously. Imagine how the communication requirements and styles were different for Clarence in the early 1900s and Kathy in the late 1900s.*

As we approach the mid-1990s, management communication is both challenging and exciting. It is challenging because organizations are becoming much more complex, and many new forces confront the manager. Greater competitive pressures, shorter product life cycles, increased demands for quality and service, increased regulatory constraints, greater concerns for cost containment, heightened awareness of environmental concerns, and renewed emphasis on human rights are just some of the pressures increasing the complexity of the manager's job. But these pressures also make managerial communication exciting. The contemporary manager has a greater opportunity than ever to make a significant difference in the success of the organization and increase the quality of work life for fellow employees. But herein lies the challenge. Effective managerial communication skills are becoming more complex and more critical, so, it is more difficult to master them.

The workplace is much more diverse and complex than it was just a few decades ago and it requires more sophisticated management communication skills. At the turn of the century, heavy manufacturing was the industrial base of western countries. Products changed little from year to year, and the work force consisted mainly of white males. But today, products and entire management systems change rapidly, and employees must adapt as quickly. For instance, consider the computer chip company Intel. In 1979, Intel had the luxury of concentrating on one computer chip design, the 285. But today, to remain competitive, the company must concurrently work on four generations of the computer chip, the 486, 586, 686, and the 786.[1] In addition, work teams are extremely diverse. At a company like Intel, it is not uncommon to have a design engineer from Singapore working with a purchasing manager from Ireland and an accountant from California. This means the manager must have the sophisticated skills required to communicate to a diverse work group in a rapidly changing environment.

Technology helps with this communication challenge, but it also adds new requirements. Advances in telecommunications have increased our communication capabilities, but we must learn how to best use these capabilities. In addition, the improved communication systems mean we have greater abilities to interact with multiple cultures, which requires that we become better intercultural communicators. Furthermore, as technical products and services become more complex, we must be able to communicate about more complicated concepts than in the past.

Organizations and communication within these organizations will continue to change. As a result, we must think about how communication will occur in the future. One way to understand the events that will lead us into the year 2000 and what this will mean for managerial communication is to look at the different stages through which managerial communication has already passed. As you read the following pages and note how managerial communication has changed during the past century, it is interesting and valuable to speculate how it will change during your career. Knowledge of the past will help us prepare for the future.

A Brief Historical Overview of Managerial Communication

Managers communicated with subordinates in markedly different ways in the past than they do today. To best understand these changes, it is helpful to review the eras of management thought diagrammed in Figure 1–1. After an overview of each era, the management communication strategies and techniques appropriate for that era are discussed.

TABLE 1–1 Historical Perspective of Managerial Communication

Era	Characteristics	Communication
Ancient and medieval	Initial efforts to organize commerce	Written records
Scientific management	Clearly defined job duties, time specifications for completing the task, adhere to rules	One-way communication, heavy reliance on written job instructions and rules
Administrative management	Emphasis on authority and discipline	Similar to scientific management: one-way communication
Human relations	Relationship among managers and workers is important	Listening and two-way communication
Behavioral	Complexity of organizational behavior and communication recognized	Difficult to apply theories
Empowerment	Distribution of power to everyone in the organization	Two-way communication; participation of employees
Contingency	Interdependence of jobs, organizations, and people	Communication strategy must be applied to the situation

Management Communication in Ancient Times

The earliest known example of managerial communication may be the record-keeping procedure developed by Sumarian priests around 5000 B.C. The Egyptians recognized the importance of putting requests in writing—a written code of conduct can be found circa 1750 B.C. with the Code of Hammurabi. The first committee may have been organized around 325 A.D. as Alexander the Great organized staff groups. (Do you suppose managers complained about meetings then as much as they do now?)

Venice, Italy, was a major center for merchants and economic exchange during medieval times. Merchants built warehouses and used an inventory system that required periodic reports for the city governing body.[2] These brief examples indicate that since the beginning of commerce, some type of managerial communication has been practiced.

The Industrial Revolution and Scientific Management

Although management communication occurred in ancient times, the systematic evolution of managers as communicators began with the Industrial Revolution. The philosophy most generally associated with the early industrial revolution is *scientific management*. This philosophy and set of methods and techniques stressed the scientific study and organization of work. During this era, it was believed that the greatest levels of efficiency could be obtained with extremely precise job instructions and that subordinates should not question the instructions. Managerial authority was not to be questioned.

The background to the scientific management philosophy helps us understand its relationship to communication. Frederick Taylor created scientific management. He was a supervisor at the Philadelphia Midvale Steel Company in the late 1800s when he became interested in ways to improve lathe work. Taylor studied the work of individual lathe workers to discover exactly how they performed their jobs; he identified each aspect of each job and measured anything and everything that could possibly be measured. He believed it was possible to develop a science that could indicate the most efficient and effective manner for performing a task and then this technique could be written in elaborate job designs and communicated to employees through extensive training. Taylor treated individual employees as another element in the scientific formula.[3]

Several disciples of the scientific management espoused by Taylor developed these concepts further. Frank Gilbreth developed the study of motion to the highest level of perfection. To assure precision, he invented the microchrometer, a clock with a sweeping second hand that could record time to 1/200 of a minute. Gilbreth's most famous accomplishment was a bricklaying study. After carefully analyzing the procedures followed by bricklayers, he reduced the number of motions from an average of 18 to 4 1/2 per brick on exterior brick and from 18 to 2 on interior brick. Can you imagine the reaction of today's workers if they were to be timed by a microchrometer?

A second disciple was Harrington Emerson who developed 12 principles of efficiency for the railroads. One of his most repeated principles was discipline, which included adherence to rules and strict obedience. In other words, he believed management's role was to establish a set of elaborate rules and assure that employees followed them.[4]

Scientific management attempted to systematize the work environment by reducing individual variance. This made the job easier for both managers and the workers because unique situations were eliminated. No deviations from the norm were allowed. The manager was simply required to communicate the job specifications and the related work rules.

Scientific management is most often associated with the manufacturing efficiencies of the Model T Ford. These efficiencies allowed every working person of the day to drive a car. But we also see heavy reliance on the scientific method today in such businesses as McDonald's. Ray Kroc used scientific management techniques to bring quality, service, cleanliness, and value to the fast-food industry. Every employee has a precise job description, each task is to be completed in a specified period, and there is strict adherence to rules. These procedures allow employees to be trained in a short time, and managers do not have numerous unique conditions to which they must adapt. Only limited strategic managerial communication is required.[5] Rules and job tasks are clearly explained, and employees are expected to follow them. No negotiations or conflict resolution is expected.

The Administrative Approach

While scientific management was receiving extensive attention, a second branch of early management thought was developing called *administrative theory*. Although this approach to management emerged during the same era as scientific management, its focus was quite different. Where scientific management was concerned mainly with the individual worker and efficiency at the operational level, administrative theory focused on broader issues facing all managers.

A key figure in developing this theory was Henri Fayol who developed 14 principles of management.[6] For our discussion of managerial communication, six principles are presented in Table 1–2. As you review these principles, note that two-way communication between the manager and subordinate is limited; the manager's authority is emphasized. The manager's role is to give orders and maintain discipline; little attention is placed on listening skills. Extensive use of groups and participative decision making is not integral to administrative theory. This approach is reminiscent of the traditional military in which the officers were extremely autocratic—no one provided feedback to them and the officers seldom listened. It is also comparable to the political system used in totalitarian governments.

The last of these principles, scalar chain, has special importance in our discussion of managerial communication. Fayol recognized the traditional organization hierarchy as important in establishing the chain of command. However, he also saw inefficiencies in the system when employees at the same level needed to communicate. Figure 1–1 shows how employee B would communicate with employee J according to prevailing thought at the time. The employee would have to send the message up the organization chain of

---

TABLE 1–2   **Six of Fayol's Principles**

---

1. Division of work. Efficiency requires that the total task be broken into small component parts assigned to workers who specialize in these limited tasks.

2. Authority. Managers have the formal authority to give orders. However, to be effective leaders, they must also possess personal authority deriving from their skill, experience, and character.

3. Discipline. Workers should willfully obey the rules and leaders of the organization.

4. Unity of command. Each subordinate should receive orders from only one supervisor.

5. Subordination of individual interest to general interest. The company's interest always takes precedence over the individual's interests.

6. Scalar chain. An unbroken line of authority runs from the top manager of an enterprise to the lowest levels of the organization. For giving orders and reports, this line should normally be observed.

FIGURE 1–1

Following the Hierarchy

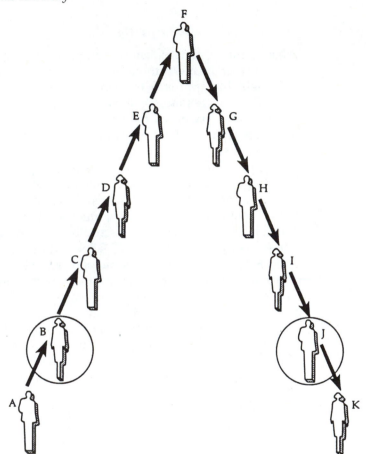

command to the top, and then the message would come down through another chain of command. The implications for inefficiencies and ineffectiveness are clear to contemporary managers.

To bypass these problems, Fayol developed what is now famously know as the gangplank theory. According to this theory, employee B would be allowed to communicate directly with employee J if each had permission from their immediate supervisors to do so and they kept the supervisors apprised of the communication. Informal networks and horizontal communication are diagramed in Figure 1–2. Gangplank theory was the first formal recognition of horizontal communication and acknowledged the importance of informal communication networks, which are now taken for granted in most contemporary organizations. But a strict chain of command is still used in some

FIGURE 1–2

Gangplank Theory

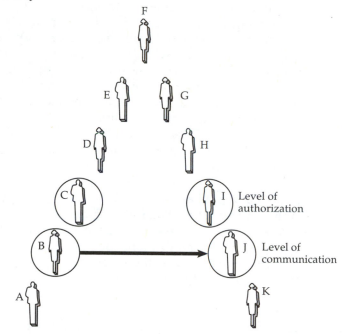

organizations. Throughout this book, we will discuss how organizations differ and how these differences must be considered when communicating. While working on this book, one of the authors attended a research meeting at the Pentagon in Washington, D.C. Several important points were brought up by the army officers in attendance; in response, the researcher mentioned he would like to discuss the ideas further. The Major in attendance immediately noted it would be best if all information was sent to him. In other words, all information should be funneled through him. Formal hierarchy is still followed to some extent in the military.

The Human Relations Approach

During the 1900s, the nature of management and the manager's job became the focus of attention. Little was being said about how the manager related to employees. But this began to change in the 1920s and 1930s as the relationship between organizational members began to receive attention.

Dale Carnegie

Dale Carnegie was one of the first writers to link communication skill with managerial effectiveness. He wrote extensively about the social and psychological aspects of "winning friends and influencing people."[7] Carnegie argued that gaining compliance from other people depends on interpersonal dynamics of attraction and influence. He offered his own prescriptions for influencing others by listening, showing an interest in their concerns, and gaining their confidence. Although his primary audience was not managers, his message to them was clear. Obtaining employee commitment to the organization does not depend solely on economic motivators or the authority of a manager's position. Commitment is gained through skills in interpersonal communication. This was a radical change to those who previously believed a manager could "buy" commitment.

Before Dale Carnegie's death in 1955, nearly 5 million people had purchased his book, and thousands of managers had flocked to Dale Carnegie seminars.[8] His seminars are still popular throughout the world.

Hawthorne Studies

About the same time that Dale Carnegie was presenting his seminars, a series of studies that became known as the Hawthorne studies was being conducted by a group of Harvard professors.[9] The studies were conducted at Western Electric Company's Hawthorne plant in Illinois, where management followed the scientific management principles in the production of telephones. Little personal communication occurred between managers and employees; job specifications and work rules were spelled out, and the manager's job was to enforce them through authority and discipline.

Originally, a group of industrial engineers designed the Hawthorne studies to show the effect on worker productivity of increasing the light in work areas. The engineers set out to find the optimum conditions by experimenting with the lighting, but the results of the study defied explanation. Productivity increased regardless of what the researchers did to the lighting. When light was increased, productivity went up. When light was held constant, productivity still went up. Even when the level of light was decreased, productivity continued to increase until workers could no longer see what they were doing.

The results of these illumination studies were disturbing to engineers schooled in scientific management principles. To further study why their principles failed, researchers isolated and studied a small group of workers. These studies included changes in compensation, rest periods, work schedules, and work methods. In general, productivity increased during the studies regardless of changes in the work conditions. The researchers finally concluded the *relationship* between the researchers and the workers accounted for the results. The researchers had shown a great personal interest in the workers as they consulted with and kept them informed about changes. The relationship established between the researchers and the employees was quite different from that of the managers and employees in other parts of the plant.

Because the results differed from what was expected, the industrial engineers continued to study working conditions. During the next phase, the researchers interviewed thousands of employees to discover their attitudes toward working conditions, managers, and work in general. This was probably the first time extensive interviewing was conducted in the workplace. Traditionally, scientific management advocates simply observed workers as the researchers sought the most efficient way to organize a job. Now the Hawthorne researchers were asking employees about their feelings. Questioning or interviewing became part of the work environment.

The interviews indicated people who work under similar conditions experience these conditions in different ways and assign different meanings to their experiences. The research concluded that employees' attitudes depend on the social organization of the groups in which they work and their positions in these groups. One of the primary researchers, Elton Mayo, recommended that managers be friendly in their relationships with workers, listen to worker concerns, and give workers a sense of participation in decisions so they could meet their social needs.[10] In many respects, both Mayo and Carnegie were similar in their advice, and both were in stark contrast to the scientific management philosophy.

Or were they? Did this human relations approach really differ from the scientific management approach? Some would argue that both Mayo and Carnegie were promoting highly manipulative, managerial communication strategies intended only to gain compliance from workers and to promote acceptance of managerial authority. The heart of the human relations approach is that attention to social needs and participation improves morale. In turn, this morale leads to greater compliance with managerial authority. In the human relations approach, managerial communication is seen as a tool for controlling organizational processes.

Although the general orientation of management during that era may have been manipulative, the human relations approach pointed out the importance of interpersonal communication. Because of the human relations approach, managing groups, listening, and interviewing are now all considered integral to managerial communication. In addition, the administrative approach highlighted the importance of organizational structures. Without the administrative and human relations orientations, the only focus of managerial communication would be recording of records, giving orders, and maintaining discipline. But managerial communication goes beyond these functions. Each era approaches communication differently but helps us better understand communication within contemporary organizations and the type of communication that may be appropriate in the year 2000. For instance, the gangplank concept is not totally accepted today in some organizations. Will it be accepted in the year 2000? What will be the acceptable rule for communicating with other employees?

The Behavioral Approach

The perspectives on managerial communication changed during the 1950s. Managers' behavior, including communication, received extensive attention. Economics, anthropology, psychology, and sociology were all applied to understanding communication on the job. The general orientation was to view organizational members as full human beings, not just as tools used to complete a job.

Many different theories emerged during this era, such as McGregor's Theory X and Theory Y, Maslow's hierarchy of needs, Likert's four systems of management, Blake and Mouton's managerial grid, and Herzberg's motivational model.[11] These theories have valuable information about what is required for effective managerial communication. Unfortunately, the theoretical explanations of managerial behavior became extremely complex, too complex for most managers to understand and apply. Many training programs were developed to help managers apply these theories, but often little benefit resulted.

While many theories were being developed on people's behavior at work, much also was being done in the area of communication theory. For instance, J. L. Austen developed the speech act theory, which maintains that certain communication conventions must be used to be effective, and David Berlo developed a model emphasizing two-way communication.[12] Also, attention was given to social influences on communication but, unfortunately, the social context of managers was given little or no attention.[13]

In addition, the nature of organizational structure received extensive attention. Organizations of the 1950s and 1960s were recognized as being different from the social organizations of the earlier 1990s. Karl Weick developed a theory of organizing that helped us understand the nature of organizations and how communication operates within them. Weick and others made it clear that organizations are not stable, static entities; rather, they are continually evolving. In addition, both internal and external communication networks are continually evolving, and they must be considered by managers when communicating. For instance, the importance of rumors and informal communication began to receive attention. Also, the types of information managers need change from day to day. Earlier, Fayol recognized the importance of communication networks and organization structure when he presented the gangplank concept. Now, entire organizations and their structure were receiving renewed attention.[14]

The nature of managerial and employee behavior, the study of communication, and an analysis of the nature of organizations all had important implications for managers as communicators. But as mentioned earlier, these studies resulted in a complex body of knowledge that was difficult for managers to use. But out of this behavioral approach, the contemporary era of employee empowerment has emerged.

Empowerment

The 1990s may be termed the era of empowerment. Empowerment is power sharing, the delegation of power or authority to subordinates in the organization.[15] In the traditional organization, all of the power to make decisions was vested in top management; but since the emergence of the behavioral approach, we have seen a major shift away from the centralization of power. Empowerment encourages employees to participate fully in the organization. We now see power being given to others in the organization so they can act more freely to accomplish their jobs.

As companies experience more intense global competition and rapidly developing technology in the 1990s, many top managers believe giving up centralized control will promote faster product development, flexibility, and quality. In a recent study, 74 percent of the chief executive officers surveyed reported they are more participatory, more consensus oriented, and now rely more on communication than on command. They are finding less value in being dictatorial, autocratic, or imperial.[16]

General Electric CEO's letter to the stockholders in the 1990 annual report provides an example of the empowerment philosophy. In this letter, the CEO asserts that in the 1990s, managers must learn to delegate, facilitate, listen, and trust. He talks about the sharing of ideas to develop one vision for the huge corporation.

Sharing a vision means sharing information. In the traditional organization, the top managers are frequently the only ones that know the financial condition of the company, but in organizations that attempt to empower employees, information is shared with everyone. For instance, at Springfield Remanufacturing Center Corp. in Springfield, Missouri, workers on the line know—and are taught to understand—almost everything the president knows about costs and revenues, departmental productivity, and strategic priorities.[17]

The empowerment movement can be seen in union-management relations; union members are becoming more involved in management decisions as management provides more information to them. In fact, information sharing is becoming part of contract negotiations.[18] Both management and union members can be found on work quality and productivity improvement teams.

But not everything has gone smoothly with attempts at empowerment. Caterpillar, Inc., the heavy equipment manufacturer, made employment involvement a near-religion in the late 1980s; however, when the industry met financial troubles, the employee involvement program became the victim of a bitter battle between the company and the United Auto Workers. An adversarial relationship between union and management returned; accordingly, one-way communication was more frequent than would be expected in an environment of empowerment that encourages two-way communication.

Although efforts to empower employees may run into problems, many different strategies for empowering employees are being attempted. Such strategies as autonomous work groups, self-leadership, work-out groups, and quality circles attempt to increase employee empowerment. But as mentioned in the discussion of the behavioral approach, some of the theories and programs for empowerment can become so complicated they are difficult to apply and are not suitable for every organization. As a result, it is important to consider the contingency approach, which is stressed throughout this book.[19]

The Contingency Approach to Management Communication

Managers must see the interdependence of the various aspects of jobs, organizations, and communication to be effective communicators. The basic idea of the contingency approach is that there is no one best way. The appropriate communication strategy varies from one situation to another. The most effective and efficient strategy depends on a number of factors; accordingly, a communication method highly effective at one time and place may be ineffective in another situation. The contingency approach recognizes the importance of matching different situations with different communication strategies. The scientific approach may be more appropriate in one situation, while extensive efforts to empower employees may be better in another setting.

For example, during a crisis, a manager may yell at subordinates and tell them exactly what to do because two-way communication might waste time. But during more tranquil times, discussion between the manager and subordinates may be appropriate. Time allows discussion. Each communication—a direct autocratic approach and the participative style—is appropriate in different situations.

The contingency approach has grown in popularity recently because of the complexity of organizations. There is no one best way of communicating; effective communication is contingent on the situation. During a military battle, one-way communication may be best. During peacetime, the same manager (officer) may use a participative, group decision process with the same employees (soldiers).

Managers in the 1990s and beyond must use a contingency approach to communication. Good ideas can be drawn from the scientific, administrative, human relations, behavioral, and empowerment approaches to communication. But as managers move to the mid-1990s, creative analysis is required to assure that communication strategies adapt to the varying needs of different situations.

Contemporary Dynamics Affecting Communication Contingencies

The nature of communication is discussed in Chapter 2, and a model of managerial communication is presented in Chapter 3. Each of these discussions presents various contingencies that should be considered when developing a strategy for managerial communication. But all possible contingencies cannot be reviewed because every manager faces so many unique situations. However, it is possible to review the major current events that may influence a manager's environment. The following discussion reviews major social and business influences that affect managerial communication contingencies, particularly, diversity, ethics, stress, and product quality.

Diversity

Today, everyone works with more diverse populations than just a few decades ago. This challenge, which is discussed throughout this text, means managers must be able to communicate with a greater variety of audiences. The contemporary manager should be particularly aware of three types of diversity that are becoming more predominant.

Gender Diversity

During the past two decades, much has been written about how men and women communicate differently. Attention has also been given to how women and men communicate with each other. Many questions have been asked: Are men more assertive than women? Do women show more social support and sympathy to colleagues? Do men and women provide different types of feedback? Do writing styles of men and women differ? Do women convey a different nonverbal message with the same gesture? Do men use space differently with other men than with women? Do men and women use different persuasive strategies?

In many cases, the answers to these and similar questions are not clear; furthermore, there is evidence that the answers evolve as general social changes occur. Sexual harassment is an example of evolving communication between the genders. Andre, who researches women's workplace issues, contends the definition of sexual harassment has been evolving since the early 1980s. She states, "There are people who haven't realized that behaviors that once were common are no longer acceptable." A management consultant states that when men think of sexual harassment they think of touching. However, to women, sexual harassment can be a tone of voice or other forms of nonverbal behaviors, such as their chest being stared at or sexual jokes.[20]

Acceptable communication between genders at work is changing in other countries as well. Traditionally, Japanese women were expected to be submissive to men; they were to be seen but not heard. If they worked, women were generally "office ladies" serving tea, making photocopies, and cleaning ashtrays. Their ideas were not solicited; they were told what to do. But this is changing. During the past 10 years, many Japanese women have joined the professional ranks and are becoming much more assertive. Practices accepted only 10 years ago would be considered sexual harassment today. And because of their newfound assertiveness, women are not afraid of charging men with sexual harassment.[21]

Because of the evolving nature of communication and the relationship between the genders, definitive answers on gender differences in communication are difficult. But strong arguments for differences have been presented. In a recent best-selling book, Deborah Tanner makes a strong argument for differences in communication styles of men and women. In doing so, she also presents some interesting reasons men and women have difficulty communicating with each other. These reasons include both inherited traits and learned behavior.[22]

The differences in communication between genders is important because of the increasing gender diversity of the work force. Both men and women will have difficulty succeeding if they cannot successfully communicate with each other. During the era of the industrial revolution when scientific management practices prevailed, women had certain types of jobs and men had another type. Women had either mostly routine, low-level manufacturing or clerical jobs; if they wanted to be a professional, their choices were teaching and nursing. Most frequently, they were housekeepers. Meanwhile, men had a greater variety of jobs such as management and engineering. In other words, men worked mostly with men, and women worked with other women or children.

But women have greater opportunities today and have access to most professions. Women represented 40 percent of the work force in 1976; their numbers are estimated to grow to 47 percent by the year 2000.[23] Also, the percentage of women in managerial positions in the United States has been growing steadily over the past two decades. Between 1966 and 1990, the percentage of managerial positions held by women increased from 15 percent to 40 percent.[24]

What does this mean? As mentioned earlier, a strong argument can be made that men and women communicate differently, and men and women have difficulty communicating with each other. This was highlighted in 1991 when Supreme Court nominee Clarence Thomas was accused of sexual harassment by Anita Hill. The extensive publicity of this case brought to light many examples of poor communication between men and women. Effective men and women managers of the year 2000 must be sensitive to gender differences and make special efforts to adjust their communication. Men cannot expect to communicate with women as "one of the boys," and women cannot communicate with men as "one of the girls." Gender sensitivity will be a key word for the coming years.

Cultural Diversity

Managers must be able to communicate with those of other cultures. Minorities will account for over 30 percent of the new entrants in the U.S. work force between 1993 and 2000. Hispanics are predicted to account for 27.5 percent of this net increase.[25] The concentration of minorities varies by geographic areas. For example, the populations of Mississippi, South Carolina, and Louisiana are more than 30 percent black, while approximately 32 percent of all Asians living in the United States reside in California. Further, more than half of all Hispanics in the United States live in California or Texas, and 38 percent of the population of New Mexico is Hispanic.[26] These trends are important because minority groups possess different work values and communication styles. As such, minority managers must learn to communicate with other managers and employees of the majority group and vice versa.

Managers must be able to work with diverse cultures both within their own organizations and from other organizations. Communication with employees and managers from other cultures will increase as transportation and telecommunications improve. A graphic demonstration of this development occurred in early 1992 when the CEOs of the three major U.S. auto firms and Japan's big five automakers met to discuss trade relations. They were accused of talking but not communicating on this international problem.[27] But even on a lower level, executives such as purchasing managers must be familiar with cross-cultural communication due to the increase of international business. International purchasing alliances too frequently fail because of poor communication.[28] This may be termed *cross-cultural* or *international communication*, which is thoroughly discussed in Chapter 17.

Age and Educational Diversity

America's population is living longer, and the average employee is getting older. The median age in the United States climbed from just under 28 in 1970 to 30 at the outset of the 1980s. The median age of the work force is projected to reach 39 by the year 2000. In addition, the education of the work force is changing. As of 1988, approximately 26 percent of the labor force had a college degree, a 12 percent increase from 1970. By 1988, 18.7 percent of all male workers had one to three years of college and 28.8 percent had four or more years.[29]

The worker who is 25 years old in 1995 has lived in a much different world than that of the worker who is 60. The 25-year-old, born in 1970, did not experience the national turmoil of the Vietnam War, has lived in an era of relative affluence, and is an avid watcher of MTV. Economic security is not a big issue. The 60-year-old remembers, albeit barely, the end of World War II, the Korean conflict, and the Vietnam War and has lived through the 13 percent inflation of the late 1970s. Economic and national security is probably a major concern for this person.

These differences in age and experiences may result in even greater communication difficulties than are normally caused by cultural differences. For instance, consider a woman of Korean descent and one of Hispanic descent who are 25 years old and were both born and raised in a suburb of Dallas, educated at the University of Texas-Dallas, and work in Dallas. These two women may have more in common and find it easier to communicate with each other than with either the 60-year-old Hispanic or Oriental women they supervise. Communication across these age differences can be a major challenge.

Greater educational levels also mean employees will readily question managers. In the scientific management era of Frederick Taylor, a manager could tell an educated employee what to do; however, in the 1990s, managers will probably find they have to consult with educated subordinates.

This tremendous gender, cultural, and age diversity increases the complexity of managerial communication; however, managers can find assistance with the problems they face. About half of the Fortune 500 companies now have diversity managers.[30] These managers have a variety of responsibilities;

but at such companies as Colgate-Palmolive and General Electric, they provide individual assistance and conduct specialized training programs. Most managers will probably be seeking such assistance with the increased challenges they face.

Competition and the Drive for Quality

In the late 1960s, the French journalist Jean-Jacques Servan-Schreiber received considerable notoriety for his book *The American Challenge*.[31] In this book, he warned Europeans that American industry was well ahead of the industrialized world and the United States was widening its lead. But in 1992, such books as *Quality or Else: The Revolution in World Business* emphasized that quality must be improved if the United States is to remain competitive.[32] Contemporary managers in the United States as well as in many other parts of the world are now accepting the idea that business is a globally competitive game and quality is the key to victory. *Competition* and *quality* are common words in business today. But what do the terms mean?

Competition may be considered as the effort of two or more parties acting independently to secure the business of a third party by offering the most attractive terms. A competitive environment means the organization must produce a product or service in a more efficient and effective manner than its competitors. Also, the service or product must possess greater value at the same or lower price. Little room exists for errors; defective parts must be minimal, few or no reworked parts can be allowed, few product repairs can be tolerated, and delivery cycles must be short. Continuous efforts are required to find new ways to improve the product or service while reducing costs.

What does this mean for managerial communication? Managers must be efficient and effective communicators in a fast-paced, highly competitive environment. Limited time exists to relax and contemplate communication strategies. For example, Motorola was attempting to bring new cellular radio technology to market before its Japanese competitors. Engineering managers were working long hours to beat the competition. Time was precious when exchanging information among work teams. No meeting time was available for bickering or wandering from the agenda, and agendas had to be clear and well organized. Project status reports had to be accurate and comprehensive; employees did not have time to ask questions and get additional interpretations if the reports were not clear. But at the same time, errors were not permissible if quality was to remain high. One reason Motorola has maintained its competitive edge in cellular radios is its emphasis on efficient and effective managerial communication.

To enhance their competitiveness, many organizations use cross-functional work teams in which employees learn a variety of tasks and work together. It is almost the direct opposite of the scientific management approach. When cross-functional work teams are used, managers must understand and coordinate a variety of activities. They must be able to communicate from a variety of perspectives.

Quality circles are another technique used to improve competitiveness. Quality circles are usually defined as small groups of volunteers who meet regularly to identify, analyze, and solve quality or other problems that could affect competitiveness. The success of these programs is well documented, but quality circle efforts do not always succeed.[33] One problem is that they require employees from different organizational levels to communicate in an equalitarian fashion. But ignoring status differences is difficult for some. Also, employees must learn how to effectively communicate in group problem-solving meetings. Again, this represents another set of challenges for management communicators.

Organizations use cross-functional work teams and quality circles to improve quality. But in many organizations, entire organizational cultures must be changed from one in which quality is of little importance to a culture that says, "Quality is Job One." This motto is used frequently by Ford Motor Company, but it represents the corporate culture changes that many companies are attempting. This means managers must be able to communicate a real interest in quality, and they must be willing to listen to employees about quality improvements. For example, a Ford automobile assembly worker believed he had a better way to mount the door mirror. After several discussions with the departmental manager, a better procedure was implemented.[34] If managers are not willing to listen about quality improvements, they will not be successful in implementing the necessary corporate culture.

Job Stress

Because everyone must manage greater differences among employees and because competitive demands are greater than ever before, stress is much greater in organizations today. Job stress is yet another dynamic that must be considered when managers are communicating. When we are under stress, we are short-tempered and have limited tolerance for errors. Managers must be aware of the potential effects of job stress and communicate accordingly; however, they must also be aware that communication can both cause and alleviate work stress.[35]

Managerial communication can create stress by causing managers to process so much information that it is difficult for them to decipher the critical facts. Any manager who has received a 40-page report containing complex information can understand the phenomenon referred to as *information overload*. Information overload is also created when two or three people are trying to speak to the same person at the same time. Humans can process only a limited amount of information, but in today's environment, extensive information is received from many sources at the same time. Stress results when a person tries to decipher all this information.

A second source of stress is inaccurate or incomplete information. When

FIGURE 1–3

Communication/Performance/Stress Cycle

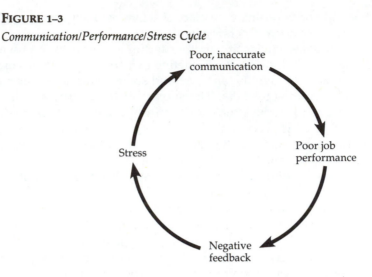

a manager does not receive complete or accurate instructions about a job, ambiguity results. The person must then attempt to decide what to do without clear directions. The anticipation of making the wrong decision can create stress. Also, when the resulting performance does not meet others' expectations, negative feedback results. Again, stress develops. This can result in a vicious cycle because the stress can cause additional poor performance and negative feedback. Consider Figure 1–3. Inaccurate communication can be a key factor in creating job stress.

While poor communication may create job stress, effective managerial communication may alleviate job stress. In particular, positive social support alleviates stress. This support can be provided through positive feedback on a specific job, or it can be in the form of encouragement. People feel better about themselves and experience reduced stress when they are told they are appreciated and their work is valuable.

Ethics

The ethics charges filed against the most visible executive officer in the United States—President Nixon—in the Watergate scandal brought about the fall of the highly esteemed diplomat and world leader. Other renowned managers have been charged with major ethics violations—Ivan Boesky, who was charged with violating insider trading laws; Michael Milken, who had problems with junk bonds; or Charles Keating, who apparently misrepresented millions of dollars of investments to retired citizens. Then there is Dennis Levin. On his release from federal prison in 1988, he returned to his Park Avenue apartment, put on the same $1,000 suits and the same million-dollar smile, and re-entered the same basic business in which, by his own admission, he had traded on inside information for much of his Wall Street career. Within a short time, he was facing more allegations of ethical misconduct.[36]

Ethical dilemmas and temptations face managers at all levels, not just the millionaires that receive the attention of journalists. Consider these examples of ethical issues in managerial communication.

- The supervisor of a travel agency was aware his agents could receive large bonuses for booking 100 or more clients each month with an auto rental firm, although clients typically wanted the rental agency selected on the basis of lowest cost. The agents worked on a commission basis. Should the supervisor "warn" his subordinates or should they be trusted to use their best judgment?
- The executive in charge of a parts distribution facility told employees to tell phone customers that inventory was in stock even if it was not. Replenishing the items took only one to two days; no one was hurt by the delay. Is it ethical for the company to omit this information?
- The project manager for a consulting project wondered whether some facts should be left out of a report because the marketing executives paying for the report would look bad if the facts were reported. What is the project manager's ethical responsibility?
- A North American manufacturer operating abroad was asked to make cash payments (a bribe) to government officials and was told it was consistent with local customs, despite being illegal in North America. Should the manufacturer make such payments?

Answers to these questions are not easy; and in today's atmosphere of cynicism and mistrust, little room for error seems to exist. Chapter 3 discusses the concept of communication climate and points out that trust is essential to developing a positive communication climate. Unfortunately, managers have difficulty developing trust when so many blatant examples of mistrust surface and individual managers face conflicting ethical demands.

No concrete set of ethical rules exists. There is no law to follow. Many behaviors have not been codified, and managers must be sensitive to emerging norms and values. Sensitivity to the nuances of ethical communication is the only way to maintain employee trust.

Because no rules exist, what one person or group considers ethical may be unethical to another. The question of taking bribes is a good example; they are quite ethical in one country but unethical and even illegal in another. Organizations are doing something to assist managers with the many ethical quandaries they face when communicating. Many companies are sponsoring ethics training for managers. A report issued by the Business Roundtable, an association of some 250 companies, indicates the vast majority were requiring managers to attend some type of ethics training. This type of training has helped Nynex managers resolve many of their ethical decisions after being faced with major ethical charges in the late 1980s.[37]

Another strategy many companies use to improve communication ethics is to develop a formal code of ethics. The code clarifies company expectations of employee conduct and makes clear that the company expects its personnel to recognize the ethical dimensions of corporate behavior and communication. A code of conduct may be broad or specific and most address managerial communication. For instance, the following is taken from Champion International's statement of corporate values.

> Champion wants to be known as an open, truthful company. We are committed to the highest standards of business conduct in our relationships with customers, suppliers, employees, communities, and shareholders. In all our pursuits we are unequivocal in our support of the laws of the land, and acts of questionable legality will not be tolerated.

Another possibility is an ethics committee or an ethics ombudsperson. With this approach either one executive or a panel of executives is appointed to oversee the organization's ethics and serve as a consultant to other managers. This provides an opportunity for a manager to go to one person or a group of people to seek advice when confronted with an ethical issue. The importance of such a position is demonstrated by Xerox where the ombudsperson reports directly to the CEO.

The Transition

This introductory chapter presents a historical overview of managerial communication, concluding that the contingency approach is the most appropriate, and it reviews four factors that affect contingencies. But organizational management and the corresponding communication are in constant transition. Managers do not communicate today as they did 15 to 20 years ago, and communication styles and strategies will continue to change. Our challenge is to understand management communication and begin to prepare for these changes.

In 1982, John Naisbitt wrote a widely read book titled *Megatrends*.[38] In this book, he presented 10 major predictions. Four of them are particularly pertinent to management communication. First, he stated we would be moving from an industrial society to an informational society. By 1994, this movement had definitely occurred with the tremendous influence of computer technology and global telecommunications.

The other three trends are highly related: Moving from centralized to decentralized decision making; participatory governance replacing representation; and, networking becoming more important than traditional hierarchies. Each of these trends implies that both written and oral managerial communication will become more frequent and intense. Evidence of these trends is increased communication training for managers, more emphasis on work groups, and managers at all levels having greater influence on decision making. During the past few years, these trends seem to have grown in importance. Eight years after the original book, Naisbitt and Aburdene wrote a follow-up to the original *Megatrends* titled *Megatrends 2000*.[39] In this later book, the authors again listed many of the same trends that appeared in the first book. In addition, intercultural communication was emphasized. Not only will managerial communication grow in intensity and importance, but it also will take on an increased international and intercultural significance. This book discusses the strategies and applications that will be required of effective managerial communications as we approach the year 2000. But as mentioned previously, not every contingency can be discussed. Managers must all remain creative and strategic as they communicate in many unique and challenging situations.

Summary

Management communication has gone through a number of changes since ancient and medieval times. Six separate eras are presented in this chapter: ancient and medieval, scientific management, administrative management, human relations, behavioral, and empowerment. During each of these eras, increasingly more attention has been given to managerial communication. Although valuable ideas can be obtained from each era, specific guidelines cannot be presented for each situation faced by a contemporary manager; consequently, the contingency approach, which says appropriate strategies vary from one situation to another, is presented in this text.

To better understand managerial situations, several contemporary dynamics affecting communication are presented. Different types of diversity are reviewed: gender, culture, age, and education. The work population will probably become more diverse in each of these attributes between now and the early 2000s.

The drive for improved product and service quality also affects communication. As a result, everything will occur in shorter time cycles, and less room for error will exist as a result of quality demands. Job stress is another consideration. Stress can result in a negative cycle. Inaccurate communication can cause poor job performance, which results in negative feedback and causes stress. This stress in turn will cause further inaccurate communication.

Ethics is another contemporary dynamic that must be considered. Although management ethics can create difficult communication decisions, organizations provide assistance with training programs and codes of ethics. In addition to these dynamics affecting contemporary communication, trends imply that communication will become more frequent, intense, and intercultural as it grows in importance.

Endnotes

1. "Inside Intel," *Business Week*, June 1, 1989, pp. 86–94.
2. C. George, *The History of Management Thought* (Englewood Cliffs, N.J.: Prentice Hall, 1972), chaps. 1 and 2.
3. Edwin A. Locke, "The Ideas of Frederick W. Taylor," *Academy of Management Journal*, January 1982, pp. 41–44.
4. William F. Muks, "Worker Participation in the Progressive Era: An Assessment by Harrington Emerson," *Academy of Management Review*, January 1982, p. 101.
5. "McRisky," *Business Week*, October 21, 1991, pp. 114–117.
6. Henri Fayol, *General and Industrial Management* (London: Sir Isaac Pitman and Sons Ltd, 1949), pp. 3–13.
7. M. Richetto, "Organizational Communication Theory and Research: An Overview," in *Communication Yearbook* 1, ed. B. D. Rubin (New Brunswick, N.J.: Transaction Books, 1977).
8. Dale Carnegie, *How to Win Friends and Influence People* (New York: Simon & Schuster, 1936).
9. F. L. Roethlisberger and W. Dickson, *Management and the Workers* (New York: John Wiley & Sons, 1939).
10. E. Mayo, *The Human Problems of an Industrial Civilization* (Boston: Harvard Business School, 1947).
11. Most of these theories are explained in comprehensive management principles textbooks.
12. J. L. Austen, *How to Do Things with Words* (Oxford: Oxford University Press, 1962): and David K. Berlo, "Human Communication: The Basic Proposition," in *Essay on Communication* (East Lansing, Mich.: Department of Communication, 1971).
13. Larry R. Smeltzer and Gail F. Thomas, "Managers as Writers: Research in Context," *Journal of Business and Technical Communication* (forthcoming).
14. K. Weick, *The Social Psychology of Organizing*, 2nd ed. (Reading, Mass.: Addison-Wesley, 1979).
15. Edwin P. Hollander and Lynn R. Offermann, "Power and Leadership in Organization," *American Psychologist* 45 (February 1990), pp. 179–89.
16. Thomas A. Stewart, "New Ways to Exercise Power," *Fortune*, November 6, 1989, pp. 52–64.
17. John Case, "The Open-Book Managers," *Inc.*, September 1990, pp. 104–5.
18. Stephenie Overman, "The Union Pitch Has Changed," *HR Magazine,* December 1991, pp. 44–46.
19. Robert L. Rose and Alex Kotlowitz, "Strife between UAW and Caterpillar Blights Promising Labor Idea," *The Wall Street Journal*, November 23, 1992, p. 1
20. Susan B. Garland and Troy Segal, "Thomas vs. Hill: The Lessons for Corporate America," *Business Week*, October 21, 1991, p. 32.
21. U. Lehner and K. Graven, "Japanese Women Rise in their Workplaces, Challenging Tradition," *The Wall Street Journal*, September 6, 1989, pp. A1, A13.
22. Deborah Tanner, *You Just Don't Understand* (Ballantine Books, New York, 1990).

23. Howard N. Fullerton, Jr., "New Labor Force Projections, Spanning 1988–2000," *Monthly Labor Review*, November 1989, pp. 3–12.
24. R. Y. Hirokawa, R. A. Kodama, and N. L. Harper, "Impact of Managerial Power on Persuasive Strategy Selection by Female and Male Managers," *Management Commmunication Quarterly*, August 1990, pp. 30–50.
25. Fullerton, "New Labor Force Projections," p. 10.
26. William Dunn, "Minorities: A Larger Part of the Population," *USA Today*, June 21, 1989, p. 1.
27. "Automakers Talking Past Each Other," *Fortune*, February 10, 1992, p. 90.
28. Michiel R. Leenders, Harold E. Fearon, and Wilbur B. England, *Purchasing and Materials Management*, 10th ed. (Homewood, Ill.: Richard D. Irwin, 1993), p. 480.
29. Fullerton, "New Labor Force Projections."
30. Julie Amparano Lopez, "Firms Elevate Heads of Diversity Programs," *The Wall Street Journal*, August 8, 1992, p. B1.
31. Jean-Jacques Servan-Schreiber, *The American Challenge* (New York: Atheneum Publishers, 1968).
32. Lloyd Dolyns and Clare Crawford-Mason, *Quality or Else: The Revolution in World Business* (New York: Houghton-Mifflin, 1992).
33. Ricky W. Griffin, "A Longitudinal Assessment of the Consequences of Quality Circles in an Industrial Setting," *Academy of Management Journal*, June 1988, pp. 338–58.
34. James R. Healey, "U.S. Steel Learns from Experience," *USA Today*, April 10, 1992, p. B1.
35. Eileen Berlin Ray and Katherine I. Miller, "The Influence of Communication Structure and Social Support on Job Stress and Burnout," *Management Communication Quarterly*, 1991, pp. 506–27; and E. B. Ray, "Supporting Relationships and Occupational Stress in the Workplace," in *Communicating Social Support*, ed. T. L. Albrechy and M. B. Adleman (Newbury Park, Calif.: Sage Publications, 1987), pp. 172–91.
36. "Ah, Mr. Levine, Your Usual Hot Seat," *Business Week*, October 21, 1991, p. 126.
37. "Nynex Unplugs its Raucous Image, Dials New Number," *The Wall Street Journal*, May 5, 1992, p. B4.
38. John Naisbitt, *Megatrends* (New York: Warner Books, 1982).
39. John Naisbitt and Patricia Aburdene, *Megatrends 2000* (New York: William Morrow and Co., 1990).

Additional Readings

Frohman, A. L., and L. W. Johnson. *The Middle Management Challenge: Moving from Crisis to Empowerment*. New York: McGraw-Hill, 1992.
Gordon, Jack. "Rethinking Diversity." *Training*, January 1992, pp. 23–30.
Kelly, Joe, and A. Bakr Ibrahim. "Executive Behavior: Its Facts, Fictions and Paradigms." *Business Horizons*, March–April 1991, pp. 27–36.
"Quality: Small and Midsize Companies Seize the Challenge—Not a Moment Too Soon." *Business Week*, November 30, 1992, pp. 66–70.

"31 Major Trends Shaping the Future of American Business." *The Public Pulse*, 2, no. 1 (1991), pp. 1–8.

Weiner, Edith. "Business in the 21st Century." *The Futurist*, March–April 1992, pp. 13–17.

Discussion Questions

1. A company can use management principles drawn primarily from one or more eras. Consider Burger King, the fast-food franchise. From which era are most of its practices drawn?

2. Discuss the statement, "Most attempts to improve management communication are really attempts to improve manipulation of employees."

3. Because you are reading this book you are probably taking a course at a university. Does the university use the gangplank theory to any extent? Explain.

4. How does the behavioral approach differ from the contingency approach to management communication?

5. Provide an example in which you have seen a manager attempt to empower employees.

6. This textbook states that it is not possible to review all possible contingencies. Elaborate on this statement.

7. In which ways do you believe women communicate differently than men?

8. Why do you think men and women may have difficulty communicating with each other?

9. In your own experiences, which culture do you believe is most difficult for you to understand? Why?

10. Give a specific example in which a demand for greater quality also increases the demand for more efficient communication.

11. Describe a situation that may be stressful for you and how this may alter your communication style.

12. Why would inaccurate communication cause job stress?

13. Describe a situation that may have caused a manager to be unethical in which the problem was more one of poor communication than of ethics.

14. What is meant by the statement that networks are replacing hierarchies?

15. What major changes in management communication do you expect between now and the year 2000?

CASE 1–1
GENERAL MOTORS' NEW TOP BUYER

In the spring of 1992, Ignacio Lopez de Arriortua hit Detroit like a storm. General Motors was in trouble and needed help, so the company's president appointed

Lopez as the vice-president of global purchasing. He had saved the company millions of dollars in its European operation and set out to do the same for the entire corporation. His goal was to save the company $5 billion in purchasing costs in 1993 alone.

Lopez approached his mission like a military commander. He dubbed his employees "warriors" and moved a group of young managers into key positions. He convened a series of intense meetings steeped in the rhetoric of war. At these meetings, he insisted that the western world is under attack, adding that saving GM was tantamount to saving western civilization. Attendees reported being overwhelmed by scores of slides that Lopez projected overhead to support his points. "It's a message that's as crafty as it is captivating," suppliers say. "He knows how to pounce on the emotional needs of an audience," said Donald C. Trausch, president of Borg-Warner Corp.

Lopez created upheaval. He immediately sent a directive to all GM suppliers that costs had to be cut by as much as 10 percent. Contracts were canceled and suppliers had to resubmit proposals. He said he would work with suppliers only if they guaranteed to cut prices every year. Some suppliers were extremely angry, while others were happy about the chance to do business with the huge auto company.

Lopez received considerable attention because he was responsible for purchasing billions of dollars worth of parts. However, some of the attention and maybe even enemies were caused by his communication style. For example, when he arrived in Detroit, he issued a 44-page health manifesto titled "Feeding the Warrior Spirit." He told his employees they would have to follow his diet to remain competitive in his purchasing organization. In addition, he told everyone, including the company president, to wear their watches on their right hands to remind them of the trouble faced by GM. And his Basque accent can be perplexing, as he frequently catches people off guard. At one interview, he replied, "I laugh at your question," as he unnerved the journalist. He tears into people as he demands performance. He responds to allegations that he may be too tough by saying, "It is tough, but it is fair."

Although some were extremely critical of Lopez, others were complimentary. "Lopez comes through and hits you over the head with a 2-by-4 and starts you bleeding. Then he puts on a bandage and helps you heal," said one manager. A vice-president for GM in Europe says, "Lopez has been tremendously misunderstood. The bottom line is that his teams get in and do it." When accused of possibly causing too much stress in the organization, Lopez simply shrugs, "We do not have the time. If we had three years, we could make everything comfortable and no one would be fearful."

Comment on Mr. Lopez's style in relationship to what has been discussed in this chapter. From which era of management thought does he borrow the most? Does he attempt to empower employees? What is the role of cultural diversity in the reaction to Mr. Lopez? How does he create job stress?

References

Stertz, Bradley A., and Joseph B. White, "GM's New Top Buyer Shakes up Detroit with 'Warrior Spirit.'" *The Wall Street Journal,* June 18, 1992, p. 1.
Maynard, Micheline. "GM's Lopez is driven by Cost-Cutting Mission." *USA Today,* November 24, 1992, p. 5B.

CASE 1–2
A 120-YEAR DIFFERENCE

A historian has said this about Gen. George A. Custer: "Generals who led men were rare; generals who won battles were rarer. It is no wonder that he was idolized from President Lincoln down. All the world loves a winner." On June 26, 1874, Custer's 261 soldiers were killed at the Battle of the Little Bighorn. Another historian asks, "Was Custer a hero or a fool?"

On February 27, 1991, the allied coalition forces of Operation Desert Storm led by Gen. H. Norman Schwarzkopf overcame the armies of Iraqi's Saddam Hussein in a victory that quickly became known to the world as "The 100-Hour War." Shortly before that war, Schwarzkopf is quoted as saying, "I told my family that during the first month of any military campaign, the guy in charge is a hero, and it's downhill after that."

We don't normally think of military leaders as managers, but they are responsible for the actions of numerous subordinates in critical times. They must be effective communicators to carry out this mission. Generals Custer and Schwarzkopf are mentioned here because they help demonstrate the differences in managerial communication that have occurred during the past 120 years.

General Custer led his 261 men on horseback in southeastern Montana. Compare this to General Schwarzkopf as you think about him stepping quickly toward the podium in a fourth-floor ballroom at the Hyatt Regency hotel in Riyadh to address 200 reporters from around the world. No doubt these two managers had different communication support systems, but they also had different responsibilities. General Custer was managing an operation of 261 horse soldiers. Schwarzkopf was coordinating a half-million-strong international military force including the U.S. Air Force, Navy, and Army as well as the first Tank Division of the United Kingdom and corps from Egypt, Saudi Arabia, and France.

What a difference! But in some ways their training was quite similar. Both were educated at West Point, went through army war colleges at Fort Leavenworth, were stationed at Fort Riley, and had frontline battle experience. Both had experienced defeat and victory.

Compare the management communication systems of these two managers. How are the basics similar? What is the role of technology? Which of the two generals had the easier job? Consider this question carefully because Custer had a much smaller group of men, but Schwarzkopf had sophisticated technology and organizational structure. Which of the two managers required more advanced training in management communication? Why? How would you compare these two generals to business managers during the same era?

References

Pyle, Richard. *Schwarzkopf: In His Own Words.* New York: Signet, 1991.

Anderson, Jack and Dale Van Atta. *Stormin' Norman: An American Hero.* New York: Zebra Books, 1991.

Kinsley, D. A. *Favor the Bold.* New York: Holt, Rinehart and Winston, 1968.

Frost, Lawrence A. *Custer Album.* Seattle: Superior Publishing, 1964.

2 THE MANAGERIAL COMMUNICATION PROCESS

Bill Waters just returned from a two-day, university-sponsored seminar on current management techniques where topics such as cost control, performance improvement, and computer technology were discussed. But it seemed that references to communication accompanied every topic. The speaker used such phrases as "open lines of communication," "mutual understanding," and "open-door policy" throughout the seminar.

This emphasis concerned Bill. During his last performance review, he learned that a key to advancement in the company was communication and that he needed improvement in this area. He was hoping the management seminar would help; but, once again, he heard only about the importance of communication. What precisely does he need to know about communication? It seemed obvious to him he would not be able to improve unless he could study the basic process of communication.

Bill decided to ask his manager to explain what she considered to be the most important elements of communication. After all, the manager had said Bill needed the improvement. Unfortunately, the only explanation Bill got was that he should consider the other person's point of view and that continuous effort is required to be an effective communicator.

How would you explain the communication process to subordinates as you asked them to improve their communication skills? What are the most important elements of the communication process that a person should consider when developing communication skills?

Whether working for a hospital, manufacturer, or service firm, more than 75 percent of a manager's time is spent communicating. Considering the amount of information for which a manager has responsibility, this is not surprising.[1] Effective communication is the key to planning, leading, organizing, and controlling the resources of the organization to achieve its stated objective.

29

Communication—the essential process that managers use to plan, lead, organize, and control—is not easy. Understanding of a manager's message is based on the receiver's perception and message interpretation. The process becomes more complex when communicating to a group of people because of the variety of perceptions and interpretations possible.

In the communication process, symbols, such as words or gestures, comprise messages; and understanding depends on a common meaning or frame of reference for those symbols. When sending a message, a manager may have the meaning of the symbols clearly in mind, but if someone receiving the message attributes a different meaning, the message is misunderstood. The process is made even more complicated because the symbols' meanings differ not only between people but also change as the experiences of the people involved change.

In this chapter, we examine those aspects of the process of developing and exchanging symbols that relate to managerial communication, and we analyze the human factors that aid or hinder understanding. To achieve this goal, we examine a model of managerial communication, followed by a discussion of six factors that affect the process. In this model, the ability to communicate is determined by competence in using mutually understood symbols. If all parties give mutual meaning to the words and have similar frames of reference, effective communication and mutual understanding will develop.

Levels of Managerial Communication

Managerial communication can usually be thought of as occurring at one of five different levels: intrapersonal, interpersonal, group, organizational, and intercultural.[2] Figure 2–1 diagrams these five levels. One level is not more important than another. Communication may occur at any or all of these levels simultaneously. They are simply different ways of categorizing the communication process for discussion purposes.[3]

The intrapersonal is the first level of communication. It focuses on internal behavior such as observing, listening, reading, speaking, and writing. Most of these activities involve the seeking of information; consequently, this communication level is extremely important for managerial decision making and problem solving because effective decisions require accurate information. Intrapersonal communication occurs as a manager peruses a complex report to determine if a capital investment can be justified or reads *Fortune* magazine while on the train to work.

The second category is the interpersonal level of communication. At this level, two or more people exchange thoughts. They may be sharing information, providing feedback, or simply maintaining a social relationship. The manager contemplating a capital investment may not be able to obtain all the necessary information without exchanging ideas and obtaining feedback from other managers. This process is interpersonal communication.

FIGURE 2–1

Managerial Communication Levels of Analysis

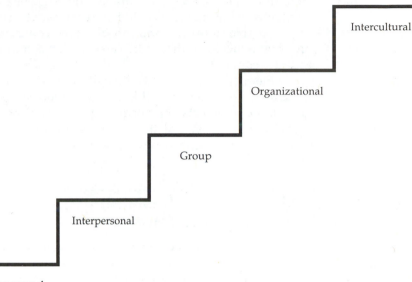

The most frequent form of group communication is meetings, which may be either formal or informal. The various types and functions of formal meetings are discussed in Chapter 13. The organizational level of communication operates within the networks that link organizational members. For instance, American Airlines has a weekly newsletter describing general business news that is distributed to all employees. Organizational communication is also concerned with how a group of tasks is linked to complete a job. Before an accountant can complete a monthly cost report for a city government, she must obtain information from the car pool to determine the number of miles driven in city vehicles. This requires organizational communication.

The intercultural level of communication concerns interactions among people of different cultures. As discussed later in this chapter, intercultural communication is occurring more frequently due to improved telecommunications and transportation.[4] Because of its importance, Chapter 17 is dedicated to intercultural communication.

These five levels can be demonstrated in a hypothetical situation at Chrysler. In January 1991, *The Wall Street Journal* reported Chrysler was cutting back on its production of minivans even though they had been one of its best sellers. The decision could have occurred something like this. First, a vice-president of marketing could have been reading about the war in the Middle East and growing more concerned about the state of mind of the consumers (intrapersonal communication). Next, this manager could have called a major market analyst to discuss the market forecast (interpersonal). Next, the vice-president might have called a meeting (group) of marketing, production, labor, and finance managers to discuss the possibility of a production cutback. The results of this meeting could have been sent to many employees throughout the organization (organizational). This communication might have involved employees with a variety of national, ethnic, and religious backgrounds (cultural).

As mentioned earlier, it is difficult to place communication activities into neat categories. However, this categorization system helps to explain the many different aspects of management communication. But regardless of the communication level and the problems with categorizations, the model of communication described next applies.

A Model for Understanding Managerial Communication

Many different models of managerial communication exist; however, many of the models reported in academic writing assume a scholarly rather than a managerial orientation.[5] As noted in Chapter 1, they can become impossible to apply because of their complexity. Businesspeople need a model that is complex enough to accommodate different business situations and provide insights to problems, and it must contain enough elements so that users can relate their personal experiences and training to the model.[6] But it must not become so complex that practitioners find it impossible to understand. We believe the following model meets these requirements.

The model presented here is a simplified description of a complex process. Unfortunately, a simple model loses much of the dynamic nature of communication. A map of the ski runs at Aspen cannot convey the exhilaration of the wind against your face as you float through the fresh powder on a beautiful winter morning. Nor can a model of managerial communication fully depict the richness of communication.

A map lets us know where to turn so we don't get lost. A communication model helps us understand the basic components so we can discuss the process without getting lost in the complexities. Unfortunately, a simplified model of managerial communication may give the impression that communication is a matter of simply exchanging messages. But a communication transaction is not just sending and receiving messages. It is a sharing of feelings, ideas, and symbols. It is an ever-developing process that changes as it occurs. It is not even possible to isolate when one communication transaction has occurred; many symbols are exchanged and created concurrently.

Unfortunately, some managers believe communicating is like shipping a load of lumber. Loading the lumber onto a truck and sending it with a driver is like sending a message. Just as the lumber arrives in the same condition that it was sent, the message is presumed to arrive just as it was sent—

understood and unchanged. For instance, while discussing strategies for announcing an employee layoff, an executive stated, "I don't see the problem. We announce the layoff and the employees will understand."[7] This manager believed communication is a simple matter of sending out the message and receiving it unchanged.

A danger in the following model is that communication may be perceived as a static process—messages are simply sent through a conduit.[8] But as you study the following model, remember that communication is an evolving process. It is a result of social reality, but it also creates a new reality.[9] Just as the study of a map helps us understand a country, the following model helps us understand managerial communication. But we must remember that both the map and the model are simplified pictures.

Elements That Make the Communication Model Work

The four elements of the model needed to develop an effective communication transaction are channel, encoding, decoding, and feedback.

Channel

The channel is the method used to convey meaning among people. The type of channel used depends on the message and the approach used to exchange ideas. A sudden angry gesture, such as pounding on a desk, uses sight and sound as channels. A poster with a picture showing a recommended safe behavior uses sight only, whereas a dictated message relies on the channel of sound. A variety of channels may be used such as face to face, written computer mail, voice mail, bulletin boards, and video recorded presentations.

We send messages via channels, but channels also affect the message. For example, a high-level executive might visit an office area to convey support for the employees' hard work. But if she seldom walked around in that area, her presence would probably cause anxiety. The interpersonal approach would thus alter the message she was trying to convey. Research also indicates that a written channel can convey a more serious formal message than a face-to-face channel.[10] Channel selection has become more complex with the development of new technologies such as voice mail, e-mail, and fax. Managers are frequently confronted with difficult decisions when deciding which communication channel to use. Technologically mediated communication is discussed further in Chapter 16.

Encoding

The next element in the communication model is encoding. People encode when they choose the best symbols to represent their thoughts and feelings.

They seek the symbols they think have the greatest chance of being understood by the person receiving the message. Symbols in a face-to-face encounter may include words, voice, gestures, and facial expressions. Their meaning is not inherent; rather, the meaning lies in the significance the encoder attributes to the symbol. And the receiver of the message will also give meaning to that symbol (see Figure 2–2). The greater the agreement between two people as to the meaning of the symbols, the greater the probability of mutual understanding.

Managers must choose the symbols that best express the idea they wish the other person to understand, and they must be sure the meaning they give the symbols will be the same meaning the receiver gives them. For example, suppose a manager said to her secretary, "Gene, call a nice restaurant and make a dinner appointment for Nicole Uerges and me." If Gene is not familiar with the manager's terms, the instructions could be easily misunderstood. The word *nice* can have a different meaning to Gene who may have a significantly smaller budget or different tastes from the manager's. Does *nice* mean a place that has white tablecloths and requires a coat and tie, or does it mean a place that serves quickly and is not too noisy? What if the manager is new in town and cannot cite specific examples to use as a guide for Gene? Choosing a clear symbol is not simple, and poor choices can easily result in poor understanding.

Consider an example that was even more abstract but had great ramifications. Barron Hilton, chairman of Hilton Hotels, stated in a press interview designed to discuss general corporate strategy, "We will work very closely with any state or city that wishes to explore the benefits gaming can bring."[11] Was he encouraging gambling at hotels? Would he help with local and state lobbying efforts to change gambling laws? Was the company attempting to change its image? Many conflicting interpretations resulted from this message.

Choosing the correct symbol when encoding is the most challenging aspect of communication. Finding the correct symbols for this text is easy com-

FIGURE 2–2

Encode–Channel

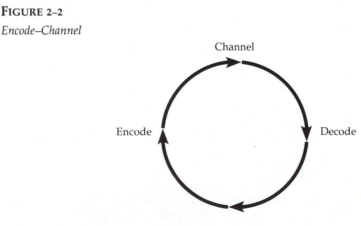

pared with some of the challenges managers face. How does a manager tell employees that she trusts and believes in them but is disappointed in their performance? Choosing the correct verbal and nonverbal symbols is what makes a manager productive and effective.

Thus far, we have seen the importance of selecting the correct channel and of choosing appropriate symbols. These two factors have to be considered together to ensure accurate communication. For example, a word such as *dear* may take on a different meaning with two carriers. It surely means one thing when written in a letter but another when said to someone in person. Also, the tone of voice (carrier) can change the meaning of a word, as can body language. The word *dear* used by two people hugging one another means something different from what it would mean if a person were yelling, "Look, here, dear!" Effective communicators are aware that the meaning of a symbol can change when it is used in different channels.

Decoding

Once encoders have chosen and translated the symbols that represent their thoughts, the communication receiver must decode the message. Two steps occur in the decoding process. The person must first perceive the message, and then he or she must interpret what has been perceived. Sending a message does not guarantee that someone will receive the intended or even a comparable message. Numerous other message stimuli might affect a receiver at any given time; consequently, the receiver may miss all or part of a particular message.

Because so many different messages can confront listeners, people have to decide which to attend to and which to ignore. Human nature being what it is, people will attend to what is pleasant and helpful to them and ignore the uncomfortable and distasteful; in other words, people practice selective attention. Similarly, employees select what they want to hear and see, not necessarily what the manager wants them to hear and see.

Everyone exposed to advertising has probably experienced selective attention. When people need or want a particular product, they pay attention to the advertisements for that product. However, once they have bought the product or have fulfilled their needs, they are less likely to pay attention to the ad. Similarly, political partisans often hear nothing but good about their candidates and nothing but bad about the opposing candidates.

After a person has attended to a particular message, the next step is to interpret it. Interpretation, the second step in decoding, finds the receiver giving meaning to the perceived symbol, such as *dinner* and *nice* in the earlier example.

How should the word *nice* be interpreted? One dictionary gives the word seven meanings.[12] Furthermore, the term could have hundreds of different meanings based on nuances reflecting different people's experiences. This is why semanticists have long maintained that "words don't have meanings, only people do" and neuro-linguistic programmers maintain "the meaning of a message is the response it elicits."[13]

When interpreting, the receiver must often read between the lines to determine what a person means by a certain symbol. A receiver may ask, "What experience does this person have with a 'nice restaurant'?" The process may break down if the interpretation given by the receiver differs greatly from that given by the speaker.

For example, a problem once arose when a manager asked if a subordinate would like to work overtime the next Saturday morning. Several other employees could have worked just as well on Saturday; however, the manager believed the subordinate he asked would appreciate the opportunity to earn the extra income. Unfortunately, even though the subordinate had special plans for Saturday, he interpreted the offer as a demand and canceled his special plans to work. His misinterpretation of the manager's symbols was caused by poor communication.

Feedback

Improving understanding is not so difficult for those who apply the right effort. The best way to increase the understanding of symbols is through feedback. Feedback allows the sender to determine how the message was interpreted and, if necessary, provides an opportunity to modify future messages.

Feedback, the connecting link in the two-way communication process, binds the sender and receiver together so they are truly communicating with each other. Unfortunately, some managers are poor communicators who attempt to communicate to, rather than with, people. These managers fail to use feedback.

A manager may use one-way rather than two-way communication for several reasons, even though the one-way approach is less effective. One reason is simply that communication without feedback is considerably faster than two-way communication. A manager may believe feedback (and, hence, accurate communication) takes too much time.[14] A second reason for not using feedback is that the sender may feel under attack by a receiver who does not understand a message and lets the sender know it. It takes self-confidence to admit a message is not always clear! Third, two-way communication with feedback can be relatively noisy and disorderly. Feedback may interrupt the speaker's thinking and cause the sender to have to start the message over again, making the communication look disorganized. On the other hand, one-way communication, even though it is less accurate, often appears neat and efficient to observers.

Feedback is always present, but it can be ignored. Feedback is not always obvious, and it may often be ambiguous. For instance, when a manager is giving instructions to subordinates, the subordinates may say they under-

FIGURE 2–3

Decode–Feedback

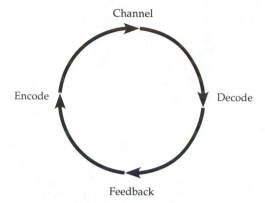

stand, but their facial expressions may say something different. They may not be paying attention to important feedback.

Feedback is essential for every planning, leading, organizing, and controlling function in business today to ensure that messages are complete.[15] Imagine an accounts receivable manager who did not receive feedback from subordinates to determine if they had sent out all the billing statements correctly; employees could be making major errors and the manager would not know it. The job would lack any organization or control, and the manager would be able to do little to resolve the problem.

Consciously attending to feedback is critical for effective communication; without the two-way circular process, effective managerial communication is impossible. Figure 2–3 diagrams the model as it appears with feedback.

As we have noted, the type of communication channel used depends on the message and the approach used to send it. The same is true for feedback, which also uses a channel. Managers need to know the different channels to use in both sending messages and receiving feedback. For instance, a manager may ask if all the requisitions for a project have been completed and filed correctly. The subordinates may respond with a yes (verbal channel), but the expression on their faces (nonverbal channel) may say otherwise. The manager may obtain further feedback by actually checking the forms (written channel). Sending a message and receiving feedback are parallel situations in that the message channel must be considered in both. In fact, sending a message and receiving feedback can be almost simultaneous. While a person speaks to others, she can immediately observe the feedback by noting the nonverbal, face-to-face channel. However, feedback can even be received quickly with written channels now because of technologically mediated formats such as electronic mail.

Noise

Noise, which can be external or internal, is any breakdown in the flow of communication that blocks or distorts a message and understanding. For effective communication, managers must minimize noise.

External noise occurs within the communication environment and interferes by either distracting the communicators or blocking the message. Examples of external noise are machine noise, another person, the hard seat of a chair, or a blinking light. Internal noise occurs within the sender and/or receiver. Examples of internal noise are hunger, a headache, a sore foot, or fatigue.

Noise is anything that gets in the way of clear communication. For instance, a person may use many obscenities in conversation. This may not bother some people; however, if one person reacts negatively to obscenities, the speaker has generated unnecessary noise for that person. The same may be said for a typographical error in a memo. If it distracts from the message, it is noise.

While it is impossible to eliminate noise, one can minimize its effect on communication. Awareness is the best way to deal with the problem of both internal and external noise. As Figure 2–4 shows, whatever the source, the manager needs to be on the alert for noise in the communication process so it can be controlled.

Internal Personality Factors

Communication involves people—an obvious but often forgotten fact. The fact that people are dynamic and unique makes the world interesting, but

FIGURE 2–4

Noise

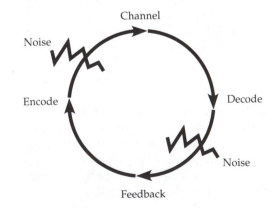

FIGURE 2–5

The Complete Model

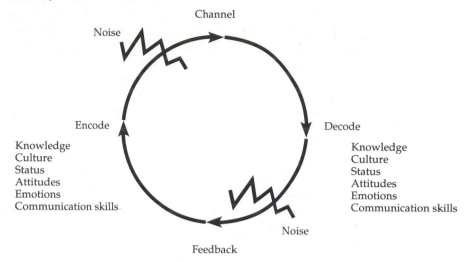

communication difficult. Because people are unique, each views the world differently. Even those who have much in common see important events quite differently. In 1992, IBM was in the midst of a major reorganization. John Akers, the president, was quoted as saying, "The business is in crisis." But George Conrades, the head of IBM's U.S. operations, believed the company was doing well in a changing market. Obviously, the two executives saw things differently and made conflicting statements to the press. As a result, Akers "removed" Conrades from his responsibilities.[16] The two executives were having difficulty communicating with each other and were sending inconsistent messages to others.

Messages go through receivers' mental filters—all the things in the mind that will influence the interpretation of symbols. Filters are what a person is and has been. They are comprised of all that a person knows and thinks, as well as emotions, opinions, attitudes, and beliefs. Each filter is unique because no two people have identical experiences. We will examine six factors that create unique individual filters and affect communication: (1) knowledge, (2) culture, (3) status, (4) attitudes, (5) emotions, and (6) communication skills. Understanding these can improve managerial communication skills.

When these factors are added to the managerial communication model, it looks complex. This model involves all those ideas already discussed, plus the factors that make up the filters. A brief study of Figure 2–5 shows the many different components required for effective communication. To understand this process better, let us review each of the individual components.

Knowledge

The sender's and the receiver's knowledge of the subject under consideration affects the level of understanding achieved. Greater knowledge is not necessarily the key; rather, the knowledge the sender and receiver have in common is important. The more knowledge two people have in common, the greater the probability of achieving understanding. Thus, the sender and receiver must first find areas of common knowledge and then build on those areas to improve communication.

A person in field sales probably does not have the same knowledge of a product as a production supervisor who builds the product. Each person has extensive knowledge of the product but in different ways. The sales representative knows how the customer can use the product, and the supervisor knows the methods used to produce the product.

Before communicating about the product, these people must define their common knowledge of the product and use it for understanding. To determine this definition, both have to want to share and to ask questions, listen, and be willing to admit their knowledge is limited.

When communicating with someone who has a different knowledge level, the communicator's use of technical terms plays an important role. The manager who is familiar with certain specialized words may forget that others do not understand them. The words do not even have to be technical. People in Chicago know what the *el* (the elevated train) and *loop* (a downtown area) are, but neither term would be useful when giving directions to someone from Seattle trying to drive through Chicago. Probably every department, company, or city has certain jargon that is not understood by outsiders.

Knowledge differences can act as communication barriers, but managers can minimize the barriers by doing three things. First, they must ask the other person questions to determine areas of common knowledge. Second, they must be willing to admit limits to knowledge. Third, they must communicate in the areas of commonality and use explanations when going outside these areas. A brief example should clarify.

> *Manager:* Bill, I'm not sure how we are presently recording the maintenance expenses for the avionics division. It's been a long time since I've looked at them. Could you quickly tell me how it's done?
> *Bill:* It looks like we record them just like any other expenses.
> *Manager:* Which accounts are we putting them in?
> *Bill:* We credit account 107 and debit 203.
> *Manager:* Let me see, 106 is the . . . .

In this example, the manager has extensive accounting experience, but she has not worked with these entries for some time. She needs to know more about the specific entries. But Bill has just transferred to the accounting department; consequently, the manager does not know how much terminology Bill has had time to learn. Besides getting the information originally sought, the manager has also found that Bill understands the maintenance accounts and the concepts of debit and credit.

Culture

Culture refers to the way in which a group of people thinks, acts, lives and communicates. A person working and living with a group of people shares some of the trademarks of the group's culture. Our American culture shares many trademarks. Apple pie, baseball, hamburgers, cars, and TV are all trademarks of American culture.

The more common the culture between two people, the greater the chances of achieving understanding. When two people do not understand each other's trademarks, communication is all the more difficult. Remember the manager asking the secretary to make a reservation for dinner. The secretary and manager could come from different socioeconomic backgrounds, which could influence the meaning of *nice* and *dinner*. The intended meaning could be misinterpreted because of the lack of shared cultures.

Cultural differences exist not just among countries; they can occur within a country or even a company. Workers who have been members of a trade union throughout their careers live according to a set of cultural factors different from people who have been members of management. Members of these two groups must be aware of their cultural differences to communicate effectively. The members of either group must try to understand what the others enjoy, believe, and value.

A person can never completely understand another group's culture because it is not possible to live another's life completely. However, managers must attempt to understand the culture of others while remembering that theirs is not the only culture. Much more is said about culture in Chapter 17.

Status

A person's status in an organization does not need to affect communication, but it usually does.[18] Status affects communication mainly because people play psychological games. A barrier to effective communication develops when people at higher status levels intimidate those below them. They may intimidate by using complex terms, not allowing two-way communication, not communicating common knowledge, or simply not listening.

Status is a barrier for those at a lower level who are intimidated solely because they are aware of their lower status. They may not ask appropriate questions for fear of appearing less knowledgeable, or they may act as if they understood the message when they really do not.

Mid-level managers can be caught in a bind when dealing with status. While nonmanagement employees challenge and test the manager's status, higher management may also try to intimidate the middle manager through omission or distortion of information.

Current Emotional State

Emotions are a large part of our work environment.[19] *Emotion* refers to the psychological and physiological state at the time of communication. It can even be called the "now" factor. For example, just after a machinist came to work, the manager asked him how he was doing on the Eastern Machines job. The machinist snapped at the manager, saying he was "tired of all the pressure and harassment lately; everything around here is just rush, rush, rush!" This is not like him at all.

What happened to this machinist? He tripped and bruised his shoulder as he left the house, and he had to change a flat tire on his car on the way to work; and now the manager has asked (pressured) him about the Eastern job. The emotional state, or what is happening now with the sender and receiver, is important in communication. Everyone has days of emotional trials. Employees may be reprimanded at work when they are already upset about something. It can be a vicious cycle. Because of his unsettled emotional state, the machinist now goes home and explodes at his wife, who, in turn, yells at their daughter. The poor girl does not know what to do, so she throws her toys on the floor in anger.

This example shows what can happen with emotions. Emotional barriers to effective communication may occur in two ways. First, emotions may be carried into a situation where even a minor event may trigger them. This is what happened in our example. Second, a verbal or nonverbal signal may trigger emotions. A comment inspired by bigotry or a racist epithet may trigger emotions that hamper the rest of the communication.

Clearly, emotions, the "now" factor, can block communication from time to time. A skillful manager will recognize that emotions exist and, when they flare, take action to cool the emotional intensity. The action chosen depends on the person involved, the intensity of the emotions, and the manager's ability to avoid the temptation to become equally emotional. When the manager becomes as emotional as the employee, an argument or a "don't we have it terrible" conversation develops. Two highly emotional people seldom produce constructive conversation.

The manager who feels emotions building must avoid shouting back, since this adds fuel to the fire. Instead, the manager can leave the immediate situation causing the emotions and release the pressure by engaging in physical activity such as a brisk walk or by shouting in private.[20] Since emotions get in the way of communication, managers need to be on the alert for them. Highly related to emotions is work stress, which is becoming a greater concern in communication strategy as it becomes more prevalent.

Attitudes

Attitudes are another element of the mental filter. The attitudes that people hold about things, people, and themselves affect how they react and communicate. If people have a strong attitude against something, they may not want to discuss it, thus blocking any possible communication. For example, a manager who strongly dislikes preparing budgets probably would not be a good communicator on the topic. The manager would probably neither listen effectively nor concentrate on sending clear messages when discussing the topic.

Prejudice can also be a major barrier to effective managerial communication. The manager who has a negative attitude toward another person will feel uncomfortable around that person, and this discomfort will probably obstruct communication, especially since it leads the manager to prejudge anything the other has to say. The manager concentrates more on the discomfort than on communication. One way of avoiding the uncomfortable feeling is to avoid communicating with the other person, which only worsens communication, especially when it is required.

Managers' attitudes about themselves can also have a tremendous effect on communications. People who have a poor self-image and believe they are poor communicators often confirm their self-perception by communicating poorly. After all, they want to prove themselves right. Also, they are not likely to attempt to become better communicators.

Of course, nobody is ever perfect, whether a truck driver, brick layer, lawyer, or manager. All the same, managers need to believe in themselves and realize they may be effective but never perfect. Self-confidence, a realistic understanding that "I'm OK but not perfect" enables people to work at understanding their attitudes and those of others. Such an attitude lets a person take advantage of the power of positive thinking.

As much as possible, a manager needs to understand attitudes and be alert to their effect on communication while preventing them from blocking understanding. Also, managers must remember that attitudes about themselves, others, and even things can change. Alex Haley described in *Roots* the change in his own self-perception as a black person from second-class citizen to an individual with self-respect. This occurred when he discovered the African ancestral practice of holding an 8-day-old child up to the stars and saying, "Behold the only thing greater than yourself."[21]

Communication Skill

The final internal factor, communication skill, is a combination of all the other aspects of communication because it refers to one's overall ability to communicate for mutual understanding. It requires the ability to encode, decode, receive feedback, and adjust to noise as well as understand all internal personality factors involved.

Optimum communication occurs when both sender and receiver are skilled communicators. However, a manager can rarely afford to assume the other person is similarly skillful. Managers are ultimately responsible for the effectiveness of the communication. In fact a major reason for their being managers stems from their superior communication skills.

Each of the personality factors we have just examined—knowledge, culture, status, emotions, attitudes, and communication skills—influences a manager's ability to plan, lead, organize, and control the resources of the organization. Consider the manager who has been made responsible for a special product planning task force. How this manager communicates with other members of the group depends on his or her product knowledge. If the manager has a design engineering background, but others have a production orientation, differences in the perceived goal of the task force may arise. Likewise, if status differences exist, organizing the group may be complex; and emotions may become a factor when parties express highly dissimilar viewpoints. When communicating, managers must consider the relationship of all these factors.

Metacommunication

Metacommunication is a word used to describe the nonverbal process. The prefix *meta* is from the Greek and means "beyond" or "in addition to." Hence, metacommunication is something "in addition to the communication."[22] Metacommunication is anything relevant to our interpretation of what another is saying or doing beyond the manifest content of what is being said or done.[23]

We have already touched on the "meta" aspect in our discussion of the communication model. For instance, the phrase "nice place for dinner" illustrated that context can change meanings. However, the concept of meta is given special attention here because of its importance and complexity.

The definition of metacommunication says it is something in addition to the communication. An additional definition may be that it is a message that, although not expressed in words, accompanies a message expressed in words. These unworded ideas have characteristics that all managers should consider.[24]

1. Unworded messages cannot be avoided. Both written and spoken words communicate messages other than those contained in the words. All actions, and the lack of action, have meaning.

2. Unworded messages may have different meanings for different people. If a person yawns during another's presentation, one manager may think the person is bored, another may think the individual is tired, while still another may consider it a habitual behavior and pay no attention to it.

3. Unworded messages may be intentional or unintentional. "That is a good idea" may be intended to mean just that: it is a good idea. However, it could be said in such a manner that it sounds like, "That's the first good idea you've ever had."

4. Unworded messages may get more attention than worded messages. A letter that contains wordy phrases and grammatical errors may convey a message that the writer is unprofessional or incompetent.

5. Unworded messages provide clues about the sender's background and motives. For example, a well-dressed person who is always neat may be someone who is well organized and holds a professional position.

6. Unworded messages are influenced by the circumstances surrounding the communication. Assume that two people (Jerry and Bill) work together and are always friendly and smiling at each other. However, if Jerry receives a promotion, he may see Bill's subsequent friendly behavior as an attempt to gain favors.

7. Unworded messages can contradict the accompanying worded message. During an employment interview, an applicant may say she really likes her present job but is seeking a position with more opportunity. However, the nervous expression and tone of voice may indicate this is not the case.

8. Unworded messages may be beneficial or harmful. This is substantiated by the previous examples. Unintentional messages that do not substantiate the written or spoken word may be harmful; however, metacommunication may augment the spoken or written message when it coincides with the unwritten message.

Discussions throughout the book demonstrate the importance of metacommunication. The discussion on written correspondence concerns the importance of neatness, format, tone, and style as communication "between the lines." A misspelled word in a letter says the writer does not pay attention to details. Because metacommunication is so important, one chapter in this book deals with nonverbal messages. That discussion covers the importance of listening to the meta factors of facial expressions, posture, gestures, paralanguage, and spatial messages. It also discusses nonverbal leakage, a form of nonverbal communication especially important in interviews. The discussion of presentations also reviews certain elements of metacommunication that managers should consider. Metacommunication is clearly an integral component of all aspects of managerial communication.

Critical Errors in Communication

The communication process, then, depends on the personalities of those involved and the environment in which they operate. This process creates a dynamic interaction; and as the model shows, this interaction is not perfect. In short, communication is not perfect. It is not the highly precise activity many managers would like to believe it is.

Even when people believe they are communicating what is real, they are communicating only what is reality in their own minds. No perfect correspondence exists between what is real in the world and the reality perceived by the mind because of the mental filters. This imperfect correspondence is manifested in a person's attempt to communicate real events of the world. These critical but common errors arise from problems in the mental filters: the assumption-observation error, the failure to discriminate error, and the allness error.[25]

Assumption-Observation Error

An assumption occurs when people accept something as valid without requiring proof. Every day we must act on some assumptions. For example, we assume the food in the cafeteria is not toxic (despite our persistent jokes to the contrary), the ceiling in the office will not fall, and numbers being used in a report are valid. Assumptions are essential and desirable in analyzing materials, solving problems, and planning.

When we drop a letter in the mailbox, we assume it will reach its destination in a reasonable time. But is this assumption completely accurate or safe? Evidence suggests the letter may be lost, delayed, or even destroyed. Nevertheless, we take a calculated risk, and the act seems to be relatively safe. But if the same envelope contains something valuable, we insure the envelope's contents.

At what point is insurance necessary? That is, when is an assumption safe and when is it a risk? Strategic communication continually addresses this question. Strategic communicators must avoid assumptions that may be incorrect and unreliable and that result in miscommunication. Consider the following example.

The manager of the quality control department noticed that Bill, a new chemist, was extremely conscientious. Bill remained after work at least a half-hour every night to check all the figures. The manager was so impressed with Bill's commitment that she wrote a special commendation letter for his personal file. Later, the manager discovered Bill was really having a lot of difficulty with the tests and was remaining late to correct the many errors he normally made.

While the assumption in this example was not particularly harmful, in some situations a disastrous decision may be made about a statement based on assumption instead of fact. For example, a purchasing clerk made a costly error when he canceled an order for copper plates because he saw that a shipment of copper plates had arrived at the receiving dock and he assumed this was the back-ordered shipment. Unfortunately, this was not the case, and it took an additional two weeks to obtain the required copper.

To avoid the assumption-observation error, we must determine the extent of risk that is safe or acceptable in a specific situation. Once done, the resultant communication should be stated as either a fact or an assumption. For instance, "I see we got a shipment of copper [fact]." On the other hand, expressions like "In my opinion," "It looks to me as if," and "I am assuming" can help us to differentiate between fact and assumption. Just as these phrases can help managers to clarify in their own minds when they are using assumptions, they also give the receiver a clearer understanding of the message.

Failure to Discriminate

The failure to discriminate is the failure to perceive and communicate significant differences among individuals or changes in situations. This failure to make clear distinctions or to differentiate can lead to the neglect of differences and the overemphasis of similarities. One of the consequences of the failure to discriminate is what William Haney calls "hardening of the categories." To quote Haney,

> Most of us have a penchant for categorizing—for classifying. Show someone something he has never seen before and one of his first questions is likely to be: "What kind is it?" We meet a new person, and we are uneasy until we can pigeonhole: What is she? How is she classified? Is she a salesperson, plumber, farmer, teacher, painter? Is she Protestant, Catholic, Jew, atheist? Democrat, Republican, independent? Lower, middle, upper "class"?[26]

This hardening of categories can result in stereotypes because people may apply their set image of the group to any individual in the group; consequently, inappropriate labels may be applied. One common example concerns managers who are interviewing job applicants. An applicant may have attended a school whose graduates the interviewer categorizes as undesirable. Therefore, the interviewer does not fully listen to the applicant. The hardening of categories can also cause a person to communicate in terms of general categories rather than specifics and thus lose valuable information. For example, "Joyce is a union member" omits the fact that she is the most qualified inspector in the department.

The potential danger is that those who put everything into a category are usually not aware they are doing it. This blindness makes failure to discriminate an extremely difficult tendency to overcome. However, Haney provides two valuable suggestions.[27] The first is to internalize the premise of uniqueness, that is, to develop a sensitivity to all the differences in the world. No two things have ever been found to be exactly the same. A second technique is to index evaluations. This means each person, thing, or situation should be indexed according to some unique characteristic. This can soon lead to the conclusion that everything and everyone is unique and, in turn, provide sensitivity to differences.

Polarization is a special form of indiscrimination involving "either-or" thinking. Of course, some situations are true dichotomies that can be stated in terms of either-or: an employee is either absent or present; a person is either over or under 6 feet tall; the light is either on or off. However, we cannot accurately describe many situations in either-or terms: a product is not either good or bad; a person does not work either fast or slow; and a picture is not either pretty or ugly. In this second test of examples, many classifications fall between the two extremes on the scale. Polarization occurs when a person deals with a situation involving gradations and middle ground in strict either-or terms. A person making an either-or statement may include herself as well as others. Thus, someone may state he will either succeed or fail in a job and may truly believe that no middle ground for success exists; consequently, the person will either meet all the criteria established or consider himself a failure. Conversely, if a person is told the only options are either success or failure, the person may begin to believe that in-between possibilities do not exist. The net result is that part of the real world is being eliminated from the person's sense of reality. Few true dichotomies exist, and most events can be seen as occurring on a continuum. When managers are wary of either-or statements, they can more accurately distinguish the degree of differences between two items and more accurately perceive the world.

Frozen evaluation is another failure to discriminate. It occurs when people disregard possible changes in persons, places, or things. Because everything in the world changes, evaluations cannot remain static. However, while it is easy to say that change is a major aspect of business, it is often difficult to adapt to that continuous change. In fact, change is such a prevalent aspect of the business environment that it is frequently ignored. Even as a person adjusts to the tick of a clock to the point that it is no longer noticed, so is it possible to adjust to change to the point that it is no longer noticed. Unfortunately, such an adjustment can result in an inaccurate perception of the world, and management errors may result.

Language also contributes to the error of frozen evaluation. Such statements as, "We tried it once and it didn't work," "We've always done it this way," and "We have had to change this before; why worry about it now" imply that the environment has not changed. Both the sender and receiver of such a message may actually believe no change has occurred.

Frozen evaluation can be so inordinately affected by communication that Alfred Korzybski, a noted student of language use, suggested that all references to people and things should have a date subscript.[28] For example, "The marketing department (1991) investigated the product possibilities . . . ," "I checked with Mary (February 10, 1993)," or "I really liked Boston when I visited there (May 1992)." While this practice has not been adopted in managerial communication, it is easy to see how it could aid in developing clear communication and make frozen evaluations much less likely.

The key to avoiding frozen evaluations is to remember that all things change. While it is easy to assume permanency, the manager who continually asks when and what has changed since then will avoid assuming that events are static.

The failure to discriminate can result in inaccurate communication of the real events of the world. Of course, other errors must also be avoided to ensure that communication is accurate.

Allness and the Process of Abstraction

Another error a manager must conscientiously avoid is that of allness. People commit this error when they structure communications as if all there is to know about a subject is being stated. The astute person knows that reality is too complex for anyone to know all there is to know about something. However, the error is still made. Haney states that allness is the result of two false beliefs: (1) it is possible to know and say everything about something, and (2) what I am saying (or writing or thinking) includes all that is important about the subject.[29]

Normal communication patterns contribute to the problem of allness because people abstract as they speak. Abstracting is the process of focusing on some details and omitting others. When communicating, we need to select some details and omit others. The very process of abstracting, however, can conceal that we have selectively omitted certain data. As a result, the listener, and in some instances the speaker, has no warning that certain information is being left out. Sometimes the more that is omitted, the harder it is to recognize that one has left out anything.

As Herta Murphy and Charles Peck state:

> A conspicuous example is that of the high school sophomore chatting with a man who (unknown to the student) was a distinguished scientist devoting his lifetime to studying botany. The smug sophomore commented, "Oh botany? I finished studying all about that stuff last semester." As Bertrand Russell stated, "One's certainty varies inversely with one's knowledge."[30]

Almost everything we do involves some level of abstraction, so the solution to the allness error is not simply to omit abstraction. Rather, it is important to be aware of the level of abstraction occurring. Once the person is aware of the level of abstraction, the message can be phrased accordingly: "as far as I know," "according to the information I have," "this is what I consider to be the critical information." To help overcome the allness error when listening, ask, "What has been omitted?" Also, if it is possible to put the phrase *et cetera* at the end of a sentence, ask what the et cetera would include.

Errors in Communication and the Managerial Process

In this now classic book, *Language in Thought and Action,* S. I. Hayakawa states:

> To be able to read and write, therefore, is to learn to profit by and take part in the greatest of human achievements—that which makes all other achievements possible—namely, the pooling of our experiences in great cooperative stores of knowledge, available . . . to all.[31]

In reading and writing, we exchange symbols—words. Words are the symbolic tools of managers. According to Hayakawa, again, the first of the principles governing symbols is this: the symbol is not the thing symbolized; the word is not the thing; the map is not the territory it stands for.[32]

The exchange of symbols that closely approximate the real world makes communication a difficult, challenging, and exciting process. Knowledge and skill are necessary to achieve this goal. Just as reading requires specialized training and practice, so does managerial communication. It does not come naturally.

This chapter presented the model for understanding managerial communication and critical communication errors largely from the perspective of the intrapersonal and interpersonal levels of communication. Readers generally find it easier to understand the managerial communication process when it is explained at the intra- and interpersonal levels. However, management communication seldom operates at just the intra- or interpersonal levels.

Managers communicate at numerous levels, and the process may become more complex as more people become involved. In a meeting, the three communication errors discussed earlier exist, and specialized problems inherent in groups must also be considered. Or when a manager of one department is communicating with a group in another department, organizational-level dynamics become involved. In each of these cases, the basic errors presented in this chapter can occur, and specialized types of potential errors must be considered also. More is said about the group and organizational levels of communication in the next chapter, which presents a strategic approach to managerial communication. In addition, Chapter 13 is dedicated to meetings and group dynamics, while Chapter 17 addresses intercultural communication.

Summary

Managerial communication can occur at one of five different levels: intrapersonal, interpersonal, group, organizational, and intercultural. Each of these levels is considered in this text within the framework of a simplified model of communication.

To master the complex communication process, managers must continually concentrate on all the concepts presented in the managerial communication model. The four main elements of the model that lead to an effective communication are channel, encoding, decoding, and feedback. The channel is the method used to carry the message from one person to another. People encode successfully when they choose the best symbols to represent their thoughts. After encoders have chosen symbols to represent their thoughts, the receiver must interpret, or decode, the material received. The last element in the basic model is feedback. From the receiver, feedback allows the sender to determine how the message was interpreted and provide an opportunity to modify future messages, if necessary. Noise is any breakdown in the flow of communication that either blocks or distorts a message.

Because communication involves people, the communication messages go through mental filters. Filters are all the things that exist in the mind that influence the interpretation of symbols. Six factors that create unique individual filters and affect communication are (1) knowledge, (2) culture, (3) status, (4) emotions, (5) attitudes, and (6) communication skills.

Metacommunication is a message that, although not expressed in words, accompanies a message presented in words. Metacommunication deserves special attention in all aspects of managerial communication due to its importance and complexity.

Because of the nature of the basic communication model, filters of the mind, and metacommunication, critical errors in the communication process can result. The most common include (1) the assumption-observation error, (2) the failure to discriminate, and (3) the allness error. The assumption-observation error results when a manager communicates something as real when no observable evidence is present; although assumptions are often correct, errors result when the assumption is incorrect or treated as fact. The failure to discriminate is the failure to perceive and communicate changes in events or significant differences between things; this failure can cause a manager to communicate in terms of general categories rather than specifics and, thus, lose valuable information. The error of allness occurs when a person structures communication as if it states all there is to know about a subject; the allness error results from the process of abstraction, which involves focusing on some details while omitting others. Abstraction is such a natural process that the allness error is difficult to overcome.

Endnotes

1. Henry Mintzberg, *The Nature of Managerial Work* (Englewood Cliffs, N.J.: Prentice Hall, 1980), pp. 38–39.
2. Lee Thayer, *Communication and Communication Systems* (Homewood, Ill.: Richard D. Irwin, 1968).
3. Steven H. Chaffee and Charles R. Berger, "Level of Analysis: An Introduction," in *Handbook of Communication Science*, ed. C. Berger and S. Chaffee (Newbury Park, Calif.: Sage Publications, 1987), p. 143.
4. Harry C. Triandis and Rosita D. Albert, "Cross-Cultural Perspectives," in *Handbook of Organizational Communication*, ed. F. Jablin, L. Putnum, K. Roberts, and L. Porter (Beverly Hills, Calif.: Sage Publications, 1987), pp. 264–95.
5. A review of the models is presented in Joel Bowman and A. S. Targowski, "Modeling the Communication Process. The Map is not the Territory," *Journal of Business Communication* 24, no. 4 (1987), pp. 21–34.
6. Dwight A. Haworth and Grant T. Savage, "The Channel-Ratio Model of Intercultural Communication," *Journal of Business Communication* 26, no. 3 (1989), pp. 231–54.
7. Larry R. Smeltzer and M. F. Zeiner, "Development of a Model for Announcing Major Layoffs," *Group and Organization Management* (forthcoming).

8. S. R. Axley, "Managerial and Organizational Communication in Terms of the Conduct Metaphor," *Academy of Management Review* 9 (1984), pp. 428–37; and R. V. Rasmussen, "A Communication Model Based on the Conduit Metaphor: What Do We Know and What Do We Take for Granted," *Management Communication Quarterly* 4, no. 3 (1991), pp. 363–74.

9. Linda L. Putnam, "The Interpretive Perspective," in *Communication and Organizations: An Interpretive Approach*, ed. L. L. Putnam and M. E. Pacanowsky (Beverly Hills, Calif.: Sage Publications, 1983), pp. 31–54.

10. R. E. Rice and D. E. Shook, "Relationships of Job Categories and Organizational Levels to Use of Communication Channels, Including Electronic Mail: A Meta-Analysis and Extension," *Journal of Management Studies* 27 (1990), pp. 195–229.

11. "Can Hilton Draw a Full House?" *Business Week,* June 8, 1992, p. 88.

12. *Webster's New World Dictionary*, Third College Edition, 1988.

13. Joel P. Bowman, "Letter to the Editor," *Journal of Business Communication* 26, no. 1 (1989), p. 14.

14. L. Smeltzer, "Barriers to Effective Communication for the First-Line Supervisor: Implications for the Instructor of Business Communication," *Proceedings,* American Business Communication National Convention, Atlanta, Georgia, 1979.

15. C. A. O'Reilly and C. Anderson, "Trust and the Communication of Performance Appraisal Information: The Effect of Feedback on Performance and Job Satisfaction," *Human Communication Research* 6 (1980), pp. 290–98.

16. David Kirpatrick, "Breaking up IBM," *Fortune,* July 27, 1992, pp. 44–58.

17. R. Brislin, K. Cushner, C. Cherrie, and M. Young, *Intercultural Interactions: A Practical Guide* (Newbury Park, Calif.: Sage Publications, 1986).

18. Chester I. Bernard, "Functions and Pathology of Status Systems in Formal Organizations," in *Industry and Society*, ed. William F. Whyte (New York: McGraw-Hill, 1946), p. 69.

19. Vincent R. Waldron and Kathleen J. Krone, "The Experience and Expression of Emotion in the Workplace," *Management Communication Quarterly* 4, 3 (February 1991), pp. 287–309.

20. Karl Albrecht, *Stress and the Manager: Making It Work for You* (Englewood Cliffs, N.J.: Prentice Hall, 1979), p. 113.

21. Alex Haley, *Roots* (New York: Dell, 1976), p. 368.

22. R. D. McPhee, "Formal Structure and Organizational Communication," "in *Organizational Communication: Traditional Themes and New Directions,* ed. R. D. McPhee and P.K. Tompkins (Newbury Park, Calif.: Sage Publications, 1985), pp. 149–78.

23. Thayer, *Communication and Communication Systems,* p. 118.

24. William C. Himstreet and Wayne M. Baty, *Business Communication: Principles and Methods,* 9th ed. (Boston: Kent, 1991), p. 18.

25. Much of this discussion is drawn from William V. Haney, *Communication and Interpersonal Relations: Text and Cases,* 6th ed. (Homewood, Ill.: Richard D. Irwin, 1992).

26. Ibid., pp. 359–81.

27. Ibid., p. 368.

28. Alfred Korzybski, *Science and Sanity: An Introduction to Non-Aristotelian Systems and General Semantics*, 3rd ed. (Garden City, N.Y.: Country Life, 1948), p. 381.

29. Haney, *Communication and Interpersonal Relations*, pp. 320–57.

30. Herta A. Murphy and Charles E. Peck, *Effective Business Communication*, 3rd ed. (New York: McGraw-Hill, 1980), p. 20.
31. S. I. Hayakawa, *Language in Thought and Action*, 4th ed. (New York: Harcourt Brace, 1978), p. 11.
32. Ibid., p. 25.

Additional Readings

Cooley, C. H. *Human Nature and the Social Order.* New York: Charles Scribner's Sons, 1992.

Smith, Alvie L. *Innovative Employee Communication.* Englewood Cliffs, N.J.: Prentice Hall, 1991.

Targowski, A. S., and J. P. Bowman, "The Layer-based Pragmatic Model of the Communication Process." *Journal of Business Communication* 25, no. 1 (1988), pp. 5–25.

Thayer, Lee. *Organization Communication Emerging Perspectives.* Norwood, N.J.: Ablex Publ. 1986.

Van Hoorde, Johan. "The Targowski and Bowman Model of Communication: Problems and Proposals for Adaption," *Journal of Business Communication* 27, no. 1 (1990), pp. 51–70.

Discussion Questions

1. Why is the circle used for the model of communication? What is meant by communicating to someone and not with someone?
2. Give an example of a channel. What channel is used by a restaurant to tell you the price of a meal?
3. What are three reasons for a person not to bother with feedback?
4. Give several examples of selective attention.
5. List three types of internal noise and three types of external noise that you may find on your job.
6. Give an example of a filter you have regarding baseball that your spouse or friend does not have.
7. List several words you use all the time for which others may not know the meaning.
8. Give an example of a filter's content that a person age 65 may have that someone age 16 does not have.
9. What are three things you can do to minimize knowledge differences as a barrier to effective communication?
10. Is there a cultural difference between people who have worked in a hospital and manufacturing plant all their lives?
11. Give an example of status distorting the communication process.
12. What causes you to become emotional? Give examples of several situations in which you saw emotions block effective communication on the job.

13. When you start to feel yourself becoming emotional, what are some strategies you use to keep from becoming more emotional?

14. Give an example of metacommunication that you have observed in a written message and another in an oral message.

15. Cite several examples of critical errors in communication that you have observed. How could they have been avoided?

CASE 2–1
DEVELOPING A BROCHURE

Mitch Finley, a 29-year-old with a degree in finance, began working as a loan officer at a bank two years ago. Later, he began consulting for other businesses in financial planning. His career goal has been to begin his own business.

Recently, Finley started The Suite Thing, a development company using one of his original business ideas—the construction of two large hotel-like buildings containing suites (living room, bedroom, kitchen) rather than single rooms.

The hotels are located in two cities that are important regional centers for the oil industry. Instead of renting the suites, he is selling them to large oil companies to meet entertainment and tax planning needs.

Finley had been using a brochure his architects had put together, but he was not pleased with its presentation. He had collected other company brochures that he liked and decided to call an advertising firm to design a new brochure and logo for his company.

In the initial meeting, Finley told the advertising representative he needed a new company logo and a brochure folder that would hold his leaflets. Most important, the logo and kit had to be completed as soon as possible, because time was money to him. The advertising representative (very new to the job) acknowledged that his company could do logo and brochure layouts. The representative then asked Finley a few general questions about his two projects—what they involved, where they were located, and their surroundings. The agency rep said he would return within one week with his ideas.

Two-and-one-half weeks later, Finley called the advertising agency and wanted to know if it had developed the materials. The representative came by later that afternoon with his idea. The agency's approach centered on a hard-sell theme of "Beat the Hotel Game with the Suite Thing." Finley, frustrated by the response delay and the inconsistency between the advertising agency's offering and his own image of the project, said, "No, that's not at all what I want." The advertising representative, taken aback, sat in silence for a time before responding in a frustrated voice, "Well, what do you see your project as being?" and reminded him of the time constraints Finley had given. Finley said he did not see hotels as his competitors, and he wanted a brochure and logo that used soft sell to introduce his idea to top-level executives as an investment.

The next day the advertising representative returned with a more conservative, soft-sell piece. Finley said, "That's *kind of* what I want . . . but not really."

Finley cannot understand why he did not get what he wanted the first time because "that's their business and they should know how to do it."

Questions

1. What are some possible causes of Finley's communication problem? Of the advertising representative's?

2. Identify how assumptions caused communication problems in this case.

3. What actions would you recommend to the advertising representative to assure this did not happen again?

4. Do you believe there is a communication deadlock? If so, what should the participants do to resolve it?

CASE 2–2
WHY IS JONES CHANGING?

The Finance Investment Company is located in Houston, Texas. The company is only two years old, but it has made the headlines in regional magazines as "the company to watch." It is staffed with three investment analysts and four secretaries. The firm occupies a fairly small space with the secretaries in the front office and the analysts' offices adjacent to the front office.

Mr. Jones, a top-notch analyst, is very unfriendly. He runs the company with an iron fist. Jones is the first one at work and the last one to leave. Promptness is his motto.

The women working in the office think the middle-aged Jones is attractive. One secretary commented to another, "I wonder what it's like to be married to him. He's so good looking, but he's such a stuffed shirt. He couldn't be that much fun to be married to." Jones never talked to them; it seemed as if business was the only thing on his mind.

Recently, Jones began coming in late, taking long lunch hours, and leaving earlier. One of the secretaries commented, "Boy, what a change in Mr. Jones. I wonder what's going on?" Another secretary replied, "You're right; I've noticed a change in him also. He started all this about the time that new woman began working here."

The secretaries did not like the new woman in the office. She was tall, blonde, and beautiful. She talked little, could hardly type, and knew little about computers. The other secretaries just wrote her off as a "dumb blonde."

One secretary commented to another, "Old Jonesey is not only coming in from lunch late, but lately he's been in the best moods. He even talked to me today!" Another said, "I noticed that, and I also saw his secretary coming in the door right after he did. And a woman calls about 6 P.M. every afternoon for Mr. Jones, but he has been leaving the office at 4:30 and cannot take the call." The other secretary said, "Well, I can put two and two together. Can't you?"

Answer each of the following questions as true (T), false (F), or questionable (?) Do not reread the story before answering the questions and do not change any of your answers.

1. Financial Investment Company is located in Houston, Texas.   T   F   ?
2. Financial Investment Company is the fastest-growing company in Houston.   T   F   ?
3. The building has four offices.   T   F   ?
4. Jones is unfriendly.   T   F   ?
5. Jones is very prompt.   T   F   ?
6. Jones owns the company.   T   F   ?
7. Jones has an iron fist.   T   F   ?
8. Jones is about 45 years old.   T   F   ?
9. Jones is married.   T   F   ?
10. Jones hired a new secretary.   T   F   ?
11. The new secretary is a gorgeous blonde.   T   F   ?
12. The new woman types well.   T   F   ?
13. Jones returns to the office in a good mood.   T   F   ?
14. The secretaries in the office think Jones is having an affair with the gorgeous blonde.   T   F   ?
15. Jones is having lunch with his secretary.   T   F   ?
16. Jones is not going home after work.   T   F   ?
17. A woman calls Jones every day at 6 P.M.
18. Jones' wife is probably looking for him.   T   F   ?
19. Jones is going through his midlife crisis.   T   F   ?

Which critical communication error is demonstrated with this exercise? Explain.

3 STRATEGIES AND STYLES OF MANAGERIAL COMMUNICATION

You have been a supervisor for more than eight years, and Shirley has been a fellow supervisor for the past three years. The two of you have developed an excellent work relationship and have been able to discuss any problems that developed between your departments. Cooperation between departments is critical because the employees all work together on many important projects. Both you and Shirley are respected in the company for your supervisory capabilities and product knowledge. It is not uncommon for employees to come to you with questions even if they do not report to you. You are both seen as up-and-coming young managers, even though you are about five years older than Shirley.

During the past six months, you have noticed that Shirley is generally less enthusiastic about her job. She is frequently unwilling to work with you on projects, and employees in the two departments seem to be having more disagreements. Just yesterday one of your subordinates came to you and hinted that perhaps you should talk with Shirley. She has been much more negative and criticized both you and your employees on several occasions. You have decided to have a talk with Shirley. It is important that you do this soon because you will be working on a new product for which both departments will be interacting with several newly formed departments. What strategic factors should you analyze before initiating the communication in this critical situation?

Communication begins at birth and is a behavior we engage in throughout life and often take for granted. Adults may reach a managerial position, yet never deliberately analyze their communication because it has become such common behavior. Some people communicate the way commuters often drive. Commuters drive on the same road to work day after day; they do not need to plan their route to work anymore. Driving may actually become a semi-conscious act as they turn left, right, or apply the brakes. Unfortunately, because they no longer make strategic decisions, a lackadaisical attitude can develop, which can cause serious problems when a critical situation suddenly occurs on the road.

Similarly, a lack of strategic decision making can cause communication problems for a manager. Unconscious decisions, effective for many types of communication, cannot succeed in critical managerial situations that call for strategic communication decisions. Just as a complex fiscal transaction triggers many different accounting decisions, a communication situation should trigger strategic communication decision making. The accountant does not intuitively enter a transaction as a debit or credit. She makes a series of analytical decisions to ensure that every transaction is correct. Unfortunately, the same accountant may communicate in a critical situation in a style that seems correct without making a similar strategic analysis.

This text emphasizes that effective managerial communication requires strategic decisions, or choices. But a framework is required to make choices. Communication choices cannot be made unless all the relevant variables are analyzed, considered, and compared.[1] This chapter reviews these variables and their relationships to each other.

Before reviewing these variables, let's consider another example of making strategic choices. After the invasion of Kuwait on August 2, 1990, many U.S. leaders were fearful that our military was not ready for a major confrontation. On several occasions, spokespersons, such as Secretary of Defense Cheney or Major Johnson of the Marines, stated they did not know the type of decisions our soldiers would make under fire. Extensive rehearsal occurred before the initial attack on January 16, 1991, where many choices had to be made by individual pilots, soldiers, and others. Managers also make many choices under fire, and they must also rehearse before going into the battle of business. This chapter establishes a framework for these choices.

A Strategic Approach

The following discussion analyzes separate elements of a strategic approach to communication. But these variables do not actually occur separately, nor can they be analyzed separately in the managerial context. They are highly interdependent and affect each other concurrently. For instance, the power of the person sending the message, the intended receiver, the message's purpose, and the organizations involved are all interrelated. Each strategic component is reciprocally interdependent. Although the following discussion considers each of the components separately, remember that each variable is affected by the others.

The strategic approach may be compared to an onion. The strategy is at the very core of the onion, but one must peel away the different layers to get to the core. But as the discussion proceeds, remember that communication strategy development is not a linear process moving from one layer to another. It is a recursive process in which we move among variables, backtrack, and reconsider. The onion analogy is used only as a model. The outer layer of the onion, which we will examine first, can be compared to the cultural environment of the people involved in the communication event.

The First Layer

The first layer consists of communication climate as well as culture.

Communication Climate

The first layer in our model includes the communication climate of an organization. Past communication, such as whether employees and managers have been trusting and open or closed and defensive, has a cumulative effect.[2] A trusting, open climate makes it much easier to communicate in an organization, and there seems to be a positive correlation between communication openness and trust.

Success breeds success. Effective communicating results in trust and openness, which generally improve job performance.[3] In turn, future effective communication will get easier because of the trust and openness that has developed. This communication cycle is demonstrated in Figure 3–1. However, after only one or two critical errors, a positive environment can quickly change to one of distrust and closed communication. Unfortunately, this makes future communication more difficult. This is why the skills and principles discussed in the following chapters are so critical—managers must avoid communication errors that may result in a negative climate.

FIGURE 3–1

Communication Climate Cycle

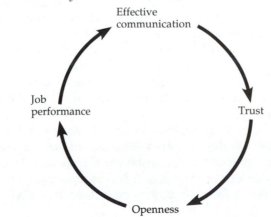

Effective communication

Trust

Openness

Job performance

The communication challenge that a manager faces may be compared to that of a trial lawyer. As the lawyer develops a successful reputation, more clients seek the lawyer's services—an enviable position. However, the lawyer must always be prepared for court and alert to the legal issues at hand. The jury is not going to be swayed by reputation, and one major trial loss may severely damage the lawyer's reputation. The same is true of the manager. A victory definitely helps build a positive climate and productivity, but the manager must always be on the alert to avoid defeats. Reputation or the power of one's title alone are not enough to maintain a positive climate and high level of performance.

In summary, the first factor a manager should consider when developing a communication strategy is communication climate.[4] Does a trusting, open climate exist or does a closed, defensive climate prevail? But cultural environment must also be considered.

Cultural Environment

All communication occurs within a culture. Culture is the social glue that binds members of nations and organizations together through shared values, symbols, and social ideals. Culture generally remains below the threshold of conscious awareness because it involves taken-for-granted assumptions about how one should perceive, think, and feel. But it is ubiquitous.

To a large extent, national culture determines how we communicate. Obviously language differs among cultures, but managers need to beware of many more subtle conventions. For example, an American manager may perceive his British associates as reserved but his Italian connections as outgoing.

Organizational culture also affects how managers communicate. In some organizations, a common value may be to put every request or suggestion in writing, whereas in another organization writing is a waste of time. Extreme formality is the norm at IBM, so formal business attire is expected at all meetings. But at Intel, casual slacks and polo shirts may be seen at high-level meetings. Autocratic management is acceptable in India, while a more participative approach is expected in the United States.

These are just a few examples of the importance of culture and its effects on managerial communication. But because of the impact of both national and organizational culture, this subject should be a primary consideration when developing managerial communication strategy. Accordingly, culture is the first layer of the onion that must be peeled away before developing a strategy.

A cultural analysis does not provide definitive answers, but it gives an understanding of generally accepted values. These values must be related to communication. For instance, if independence is valued, a persuasive approach rather than a demanding approach may be required. If formality is valued, a formal typed memo rather than a telephone call may be necessary.

FIGURE 3–2

The First Level of the Model

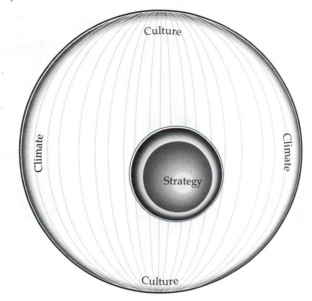

If extensive technical details are part of the organizational culture, all reports may require technical elaboration.

Culture is discussed in a number of different contexts in this book because advancements in transportation and communication are creating more contact among diverse cultures. Also, immigration is becoming a bigger factor. In the 1980s alone, 8.7 million people came to the United States.[5] Accordingly, multicultural diversity is becoming a major issue in organizations throughout the world.[6] These numerous cultural concerns have resulted in a separate field of study termed *polycultural communication.*[7]

Because culture provides generally accepted patterns of communication, it is depicted as the outer layer of our analysis. Or, to use our analogy, it is the outer layer of the onion, as depicted in Figure 3–2. This layer must be analyzed and peeled away before developing the strategy.

The Second Layer

In addition to reviewing cultural aspects of the communication situations, managers should consider the sender, receiver, and the purpose of the communication. Figure 3–3 shows these three variables at the second layer of the onion. Note that the relationship of the three variables is circular rather than linear. Each affects the other concurrently; one does not necessarily come

FIGURE 3–3
Sender—Receiver—Purpose

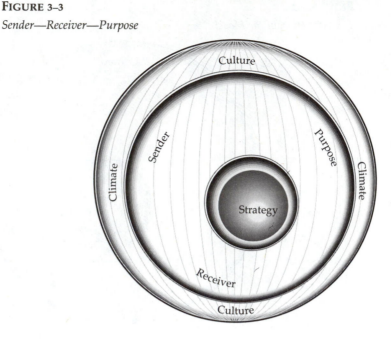

before the other. To simplify our discussions, the manager will be considered as the encoder.

Sender (Encoder)

The manager encodes a message's meaning depending on his or her personality and experiences. A grocery store manager may encode a 3 percent profit margin as highly profitable, while a chemical company manager may encode it as a low return. Managers must analyze their own frames of reference to determine how their perceptions may affect the outcome of the communication.[8]

Self-Analysis

Managers must first analyze how they best communicate. Answers to the following self-analysis questions will help to prepare a manager to communicate effectively in critical situations.

1. In which situation do I feel the most *comfortable* communicating?
   With just one other person.
   With a group of people.
   When giving a formal presentation.
   When writing.

2. How *skillful* am I as a communicator?

Do I have trouble with pronunciation?

Does grammar present a problem?

Am I often at a loss for words because of self-consciousness?

Can I usually find the right words to express myself in difficult situations?

Can I use nonverbal communication effectively (facial expression, hand gestures, posture, etc)?

Can I accurately read another's nonverbal communication?

3. How does my *personality* affect my communication?

Am I generally an introvert or an extrovert (withdrawn or outgoing)?

Am I uncomfortable asking questions?

Do I use humor effectively?

Am I a domineering person who tries to control the situation?

Am I a submissive person who generally agrees with others?

Do I speak up or remain quiet when I disagree with the speaker?

Am I a patient listener?

Do I talk more than listen?

Do I value personal relationships more than productivity?

4. How much *power* is there in my position in the organization?

Can I make demands of others?

Do I generally have to persuade others?

Do people generally respect my position?

5. What are my areas of greatest *knowledge?*

Do I have a great deal of technical knowledge?

Do I have to rely on other people's ideas a great deal?

Do I use a lot of technical terms?

The answers to these questions will help managers determine the most appropriate communication technique in critical situations. For instance, what strategy is best when persuading a work group to accept a new procedure? While answering the self-analysis questions, a manager may have realized he is most comfortable with just one person, has trouble with grammar but can usually find the right words, is a patient listener, and holds a company position that makes it difficult to place demands on others. Consequently, the manager decides it would be best to meet with employees individually in a fact-to-face setting to persuade them to accept the new procedure. The manager has strategically analyzed his role in the communication situation.

Receiver (Decoder)

Now we can add the second element to this layer: the receiver, or decoder. Senders must continually adapt communication to different receivers to be effective. Just as a husband and wife discuss between themselves the problem of controlling the household budget in much different terms from those used with their young children, an effective manager discusses a topic differently with various members of the organization.

For instance, Sidney Jones, the undersecretary of the Treasury in President Bush's administration, has made numerous presentations on U.S. economic conditions. But he once commented that each receiver of these presentations must be analyzed separately. Even though he has frequently made presentations to U.S. presidents and top CEOs, he always analyzes the differences among the individuals.

Several characteristics of the receiver require analysis: personal relationship of the receiver to the sender, status, interest in the message, feelings toward the message, knowledge about the subject of the message, and the communication skills of the receiver. A review of these items indicates the types of strategic communication decisions a manager must make relative to the receiver.

Relationship

Participants in a friendly relationship tolerate error and initial misunderstanding more than do those in a neutral or hostile relationship.[9] Friendly participants need less time and concentration when communicating than is required in a hostile relationship. For instance, suppose that a manager is discussing a report with a colleague who finds a certain table difficult to read. A friendly colleague will be more tolerant and more willing to ask for clarification than will a hostile one who might criticize the report but not seek clarification or provide constructive criticisms.

Status Difference

Status differences between senders and receivers also deserve attention. Status may require that certain customs or traditions be integrated into the communication. For example, the manager may need to refer to certain people as sir, Mr., Ms., doctor, or chief in some organizations to avoid offending the receiver. Also, the manager may need to remain standing when addressing a person of higher status, but it may be appropriate to sit down with a person of equal or lower status. People at different status levels may easily interpret words and gestures differently.[10] Suppose a manager says, "If you could have the report done by Friday, I would appreciate it." The statement may be either a request or a demand, depending on the emphasis placed on the words. The speaker may emphasize the word *if* with a higher-status person and *have the report done* with a lower-status person. Similarly the simple statement, "Could I meet with you for a few minutes?" may be a request or a demand depending on the receiver. Obviously, verbal emphasis needs to be adapted to different audiences.

Audience Interest

The interest of receiver is another strategic consideration.[11] If the receiver has low interest, some persuasive elements may be appropriate to get the person's attention even when the ultimate goal of the message is to inform. Audience interest level may affect the objective of the communication. Managers must adapt the nature of the message to fit the interests of the receiver rather than just the managers' personal interest.

Receiver's Emotional State

The receiver's emotional state at the time of communication may affect how the message is received. A receiver upset about something requires a different communication strategy from that used with a relaxed person. When a receiver is upset, the sender needs to deal first with the feelings and attempt to relax the individual to allow him or her to be more receptive to the main message.

Managers should consider the feelings of the receiver toward a specific message as well as feelings in general. For instance, if an employee is calm and relaxed, but the manager is about to discuss work assignments (a potentially emotional topic), the manager should be ready to deal with an emotional person. The manager should keep an open mind and listen to the employee. Strategic analysis of the possible emotional reaction makes it possible to be on guard without getting caught up in the emotion.

Receiver's Knowledge

Remember that technical words and examples are appropriate in a message if everyone understands them; unfortunately, technical concepts may only add confusion if not all understand them. Would it be appropriate to ask, "Have you checked the FAR on the VOR at LAX?" How many technical terms may one use with this particular reader or listener? Will certain concepts need explaining? Incorrectly assuming the receiver has considerable knowledge may result in a communication breakdown. But assuming too low a level of knowledge may waste time and insult the receiver. A receiver's level of knowledge can be gauged quickly by asking questions and receiving feedback. The answer given to an open-ended question on a specific topic is often the best indication of a receiver's level of knowledge.

Receiver's Communication Skills

The receiver, as well as the sender, must be a competent communicator.[12] Can the receiver communicate clearly? Does the receiver get nervous in communication situations? If the receiver cannot express concepts clearly or gets nervous when communicating, a manager needs to exercise patience and assist or even relax the person as much as possible. It is possible to put receivers at ease by asking them about subjects they consider important and easy to talk about. Recent personal achievements, hobbies, sports, and children are examples of such topics. Simply asking how a person is doing is not enough.

Thus, a manager should consider six characteristics of the receiver before communicating: personal relationship, status, interest in the message, feelings, knowledge, and communication skills. Managers have few set techniques or guidelines to apply because they must assess each situation individually; however, this discussion can provide a strategic communication framework. First, the manager needs to analyze the purpose of the message for effective communication in critical situations.

Purpose of the Message

Unless managers analyze their goals, the resulting communication may waste time and effort. And before reviewing the purpose of a communication, managers should first determine whether it is best to verbalize a message at all. Just as a properly timed silence contributes to the effectiveness of a symphony, silence at some points in managerial communication can make a significant impact. Silence may be best when emotions are high, when the purpose of the communication is not clear, when the message is uncertain, or when the message may result in immediate confrontation. In certain situations, no deliberate communication may be the most effective technique. A typical example is a merger negotiation between two firms. In case negotiations are not successful, it would probably be best not to announce the pending negotiations to employees. It may only create unnecessary anxiety among employees.

In addition to not communicating at all, some situations call for ambiguous communication. The concept of *strategic ambiguity* refers to situations where complete, open communication may be harmful.[13] Legal ramifications of terminating employees, for example, make it difficult to explain why some are dismissed while others are retained; consequently, partial information may be better than complete disclosure.

A manager has five major reasons for choosing to communicate. First, the mere act of communicating with a fellow worker may be enjoyable. Communication does not always have to mean business, although one should not confuse working with socializing. At work, some socializing by managers can contribute to employee morale, but employees need to delineate socializing and working so that socializing does not become excessive.

Second, managers communicate to present information and, third, to gain information. Ironically, not all managers make a distinction between gaining and presenting information. Many managers tend to do all the talking when they are trying to gain information. While it seems to be human nature to tell others everything one knows, managers must resist this tendency if they wish to gain information.

Fourth, managers communicate to persuade.[14] Managers with persuasion as a goal must develop an appropriate persuasive strategy. Would a rational-logical approach be best, or should it be an emotional appeal? This question of goals can become complicated since goals may be combined. For instance, a goal may be to inform a subordinate of a new procedure while also persuading her to accept the procedure. In these situations, managers need to identify goals clearly and develop appropriate strategies; otherwise, they may achieve neither goal.

The final reason to communicate is to defend one's self.[15] On critical issues, managers often feel defensive and will attempt to defend their positions. This happens when managers feel threatened, or do not want to take responsibility for their actions, or do not possess self-confidence in a situation.

Unfortunately, defensive communication may be filled with emotional, even irresponsible, interactions. It may block efforts at problem solving by restricting the manager's ability to get at the root of a problem. To quote Jack Gibb,

> The person who behaves defensively . . . devotes an appreciable portion of his energy to defending himself . . . he thinks about how he may win, dominate, impress or escape punishment, and/or how he may avoid or mitigate a perceived or an anticipated attack. Such inner feelings about outward acts tend to create similarly defensive postures in others, and, if unchecked, the ensuing circular response becomes increasingly destructive.[16]

The challenge to a manager who perceives defensive communication is to try to remain objective and listen to the information presented. Such objectivity is difficult, but it separates the effective manager from the ineffective one.

The communication goal or purpose often defines the strategy appropriate for a given situation; consequently, effective managers are keenly aware of their communication goals. Subsequent chapters explain how the strategy relates to the audience and the goal and present several examples. For instance, in our discussion on memos and letters, we explain why a deductive rather than an inductive approach should be used in certain situations.

The Third Layer

Now that we have looked at the two first layers of analysis, we can move to the next layer. Managers must consider four more elements in determining an effective communication strategy.

1. The specific content of the message.
2. The message's channel.
3. The time the communication occurs.
4. The physical environment in which it occurs.

Figure 3–4 presents the complete strategic managerial communication model. These four elements appear on the most inner layer because they depend on the sender, receiver, and purpose of the message, as well as culture and climate. For purposes of discussion, we review each component separately. But again, remember that in reality a manager needs to consider all interrelationships when developing a communication strategy. Neglecting any one component when analyzing a critical situation may result in a communication failure.

FIGURE 3–4

The Complete Model

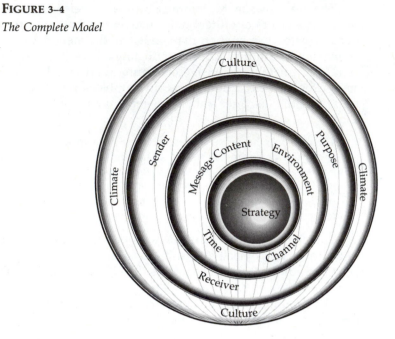

Message Content

We can simplify our discussion by classifying the content of a message according to six categories. Of course, rigidly classifying the content of a message can create difficulty because the content may fall into more than one category; however, it is possible to delineate the major differences with the classification system.

First, will the receiver perceive the message as positive, negative, or neutral? When the message is positive, the best strategy is to present the good news immediately; however, with a negative message it is best to present neutral information before the negative news.[17] To determine whether the message is positive or negative, consider the receiver's perspective. What may seem positive to a manager may be negative to the receiver.

For example, the manager of an accounting firm was ecstatic as she announced a new contract with a growing firm. No doubt this would result in a large year-end bonus for everyone. But staff members were unhappy with the news. They all felt overworked and didn't see a potential bonus as good news.

Second, does the message deal with *fact* or *opinion*? A fact may be established with concrete information, but opinion is largely based on assumption. The manager should critically analyze the objective basis of his message because he may feel so sure about his opinion that he will present it as a fact. When the manager presents opinions as facts, the receivers may feel deceived when they later determine the information was actually an opinion. Misunderstanding can result in bitter feelings, even though the sender never intended to misrepresent the fact. If the senders feel any uncertainty about a message, they need only attach a qualifier such as, "In my opinion . . . ," or "I believe. . . ."

Third, to what extent is the message *important* to the receiver? If the message is important to the manager, but not to the receiver, the manager has to emphasize attention-getting techniques. She would structure such a message according to the needs of the receiver rather than those of the sender. A manager needs to determine how to make the content of the message important to the receiver and then integrate that importance into the information. For instance, an announcement of a staff meeting to be held at 2 P.M. may not capture an employee's interest; however, if the notice states one of the items on the agenda is a possible new incentive program, employees are more apt to pay attention. When a message is inherently important to the receiver, the sender may move directly to the critical information.

Fourth, to what extent is the message *controversial?* A controversial message calls for neutral words that can reduce the emotional response. In these situations, phrases such as "Surely you realize . . . ," "Everyone else believes . . . ," "Can't you see . . . ," or "You have to understand . . ." can make the receiver defensive and create conflict.

Polarization should be avoided in a controversial message since a polarizing message implies an either-or alternative. For instance, a polarized message presents every component of a proposal as needing to be either accepted or rejected and implies that no room exists for compromise. Polarization may quickly lead to conflict when the content of the message is already controversial.

Sixth, to what extent does the message deal with *facts* (or ideas) versus *feelings?* In many situations, feelings may be more important than facts. The fact that a person is late with a report may not be as important as the disappointment expressed by the manager. Likewise, a subordinate complaining of being bypassed for a training program may actually be expressing frustration with her overall job situation. Sometimes managers tend to ignore feelings because of the emphasis put on factual content. However, it is important to be aware of ideas and feelings so that one or the other may be emphasized at the appropriate time.

Effective managerial communication requires analysis of these content factors—negative versus positive messages, fact versus opinion, importance to the receiver, controversiality and polarization, and facts versus feelings. Consider these factors simultaneously with the sender, receiver, and purpose, because they all affect one another when developing strategic managerial communication.

Channel of the Message

With the advent of sophisticated telecommunications and overnight delivery, the question of how the message is to be sent becomes increasingly complicated. Also, with ever-increasing salaries and the volume of information exchanged, costs have grown significantly. Habits further complicate channel selection. Managers find ways of communicating that are comfortable for them and continue to use the same methods, even when they are inappropriate. For instance, some managers may shy away from memos because of their dislike for writing, whereas others, who have a habit of putting everything in writing, avoid oral communication. Both modes have an appropriate time and place, so managers must make individual decisions for each situation.

Which channel is appropriate for which message? Written communication (memos, letters, and reports) provides the opportunity for permanent records and may be precise and clear; however, it usually does not provide the opportunity for immediate feedback. Electronic mail is less permanent and is often hastily written, but it has the advantage of immediacy. Thus, in choosing channels, managers must decide whether feedback or clarity is important. In addition, it may be more difficult to persuade an individual in a written message than in an oral one. Since so many factors are involved, it is difficult to declare one technique invariably preferable to the other.

The question becomes one of minimizing costs while maximizing communication effectiveness. Consider just these basic options: (1) oral, (2) written, (3) oral and written, and (4) visual. Now subdivide these further into formal and informal approaches. Table 3–1 presents some of these options.

TABLE 3–1   Channels of Communication

	Informal	*Formal*
Oral	Personal contacts Interviews and counseling Telecommunication Employee plant tours (orientation)	Staff meetings Public address system Conferences Order giving and instructions Briefings
Written	Bulletin boards Daily news digests	Company policies Management newsletters Company magazines Company reports
Both oral and written	Face-to-face contact between superior and subordinate where written information is exchanged	Company meetings where reports and data are presented
Visual	Sound-action exhibits Closed-circuit TV	Motion pictures Slides Chart talks

But let's complicate the options even further by adding technologically mediated communications such as video teleconferences, electronic mail, and fax. It quickly becomes apparent that the correct channel choice is not simple. This is why Chapter 16 presents an extensive discussion on communication channels mediated by some form of technology.

The telephone, another channel of communication, can be quick, but it generally provides no permanent record of the conversation. Also, while it provides oral feedback, the participants can observe few nonverbal messages. And one of the greatest disadvantages of the telephone is that one never knows what distractions are interfering with the conversation on the other end of the line. Is the receiver really paying attention? Once again, a manager needs to analyze the situation to determine the appropriate communication channel.

Should the message be presented to one individual at a time or to a group? While individual communication allows the manager to adapt the message to each person, group communication is quicker and cheaper. The manager needs to decide if individual adaptation is necessary or if the time saved with group communication is more important. The chapter on meetings will detail this later.

The question of individual versus group also relates highly to persuasive communication. In some situations, it may be easy to persuade a group of people; however, in other situations, one-to-one communication may be more effective. The manager must strategically analyze all the factors to determine which would be best in a given situation.

Not surprisingly, cost affects all questions regarding channel selection. Managers do not often analyze the dimension of communication cost because it does not show up as a special entry in the income statement. However, when one considers the time and people involved, communication is costly. A letter requires time for drafting and typing. A group meeting requires many different individuals to commit their time, and that pooled time can be expensive. These costs need to be balanced with the fact that groups allow for input and feedback from different employees. A telephone call may be quick, but long-distance rates can add up. A formal report may be extremely time consuming to put together, but others may refer to it again later, whereas an oral report is temporary. Thus, managers balance cost and time factors when selecting the appropriate channel for their communication.

Physical Environment

The environment in which communication occurs has a clear effect. Just as communication between a husband and wife changes when in a public or a private setting, managerial communication strategies should also change in different environments. Ask four questions when you analyze the environmental factors in strategic communication:

1. Is it a public or private situation?

2. Does it involve a formal or informal setting?
3. What is the distance between the sender and the receiver?
4. Is it a familiar or unfamiliar environment?

The answers to each of these questions can significantly affect the communication strategy.

Privacy

A congratulatory comment may be best in a public forum, while a sensitive question is best asked in a private setting. Some choices between public and private settings are obvious, but others are more difficult. For instance, should a group's performance problem be discussed with each person individually or should the discussion be held with all members in a public forum?

Formality

The formality of the setting affects the wording of the message as well as the opportunity for feedback. Thus, while official titles may be appropriate when presenting a formal oral report, they may restrict communication in an informal group discussion. Also, feedback is often more difficult to obtain in a formal setting because questions may seem inappropriate or the questioner may be shy. Finally, people are generally more reserved in their nonverbal behavior in a formal setting, which makes their feedback more difficult to read.

Physical Distance

A third variable to consider is the physical distance between the sender and receiver. In oral communication, physical distance mutes the variations in the voice's tone and loudness and in the participants' gestures and posture. Thus, it is less effective to use these strategies for emphasis when distance is great. In written communication, distance also affects feedback and time. The quality of feedback for a report mailed from Ohio to California may be less timely (and, consequently, less useful) than it is for a report exchanged in one building. A manager can expect less comprehensive feedback as distances increase. Distance also makes persuasion more difficult because opposing arguments cannot be answered immediately. A manager may have to decide if it is better to wait until a face-to-face opportunity is available or if the persuasive efforts should occur over a greater distance for the sake of timeliness.

Familiarity

The final factor to consider when discussing environment is its familiarity. This concept needs to be analyzed in terms of the manager as well as the receiver. A familiar environment allows the participants to be relaxed, which is important when controversies or feelings are involved. When communicating in an unfamiliar environment, a manager should anticipate the distractions that may occur. Distractions that we might be accustomed to in our own environment can be unnerving when we encounter them in unfamiliar surroundings. Something as seemingly simple as heavy traffic outside an office window can be a distraction when we aren't used to it.

Thus, managers must strategically analyze privacy, formality, distance, and familiarity when considering the environment of a communication event.

Time

Time affects all elements of management, and it has a ubiquitous effect on communication. Clearly, the adage that "time is money" is appropriate here. Managers need to consider the amount of time spent in preparing to communicate and the amount of time spent in the process. Consider the time of both managers and receivers to obtain cost and communication efficiency. Thus, while a meeting may at first seem advisable because it allows for questions and feedback, it may not be efficient because of the time required to assemble people. Consequently, a memo may be more efficient in certain situations. This effort is the type of strategic time decision a manager must make.

Remember also that time is power and time is status. People with busy schedules are perceived as more important than those with whom you can make an appointment at any time. Also, while the subordinate must make an appointment to see the manager, the manager, who has higher status, can drop in on the employee without notice. Status is also communicated by the amount of time a person is kept waiting.

The actual timing of the communication is also an important consideration. Communication behavior appropriate at one time may be inappropriate or even detrimental at a different time. It is not appropriate to try to get the attention of someone immediately before an important meeting. Also, it is highly unlikely that a report will receive much attention if it arrives late on a Friday afternoon. As another example, consider the timing of an announcement made at a large urban hospital consisting of several buildings. For several years, landscaping improvements were being installed to improve water runoff. The grounds were beautiful on completion. But, as the project was completed, layoffs of hospital staff were announced. It appeared the landscaping was done at the expense of jobs. Understandably, many employees were bitter.

Feedback and Measures of Effectiveness

Integral to a strategic management communication approach are feedback and measures of effectiveness. These variables are not included in the model (Figure 3–4) because they are so pervasive. They are inherent in each variable and cannot be separated. Feedback is important in two ways. First, it should be continually obtained to determine how changing events may affect the overall strategy. For instance, a manager determined that a memo about a new procedure was not as clear as he thought because many questions were being asked. Based on this feedback, he quickly called a meeting to clarify the procedure. In this case, the channel was changed to improve the communication strategy.

Second, feedback may be obtained to determine if the strategy was effective even though it may be too late to change it. Unfortunately, many managers may avoid this feedback because they believe nothing can be done about it. For example, an advertising agency submits a proposal for an ad campaign. When the contract is given to another agency, the tendency is not to evaluate the effectiveness of the written proposal. After all, nothing can be done about it now. But this is the opportunity to thoroughly evaluate all aspects of the proposal, including such items as an analysis of the receiver, writing style, and timing.

Obtaining feedback and measuring effectiveness may be extremely difficult. In one case, a regional insurance manager was disappointed in sales. She wrote a number of letters, made phone calls, and personally met with her independent sales agents to motivate them. Sales continued to slide. She contracted a management consultant to determine how she could improve her motivational strategies. But it could not be determined if poor sales were the result of communication with the sales agents or the insurance products themselves. Managerial communication is so interrelated with other factors that it is often difficult to determine effectiveness.

Another example demonstrates the importance of feedback and its relationship to measures of effectiveness. A bank was forced to lay off a number of employees. The executive group was initially going to announce the layoff

FIGURE 3–5

Analysis—Strategies—Styles

in a press release and a formal memo to all employees. But after discussing options, the executives decided this would be too formal and insensitive in a corporate culture that supported personal contact and informality. As a result, they decided to announce the layoffs in small management meetings. But feedback indicated numerous inaccurate rumors were circulating throughout the company before half of the management meetings were completed. Due to the feedback, the strategy was quickly changed. The meetings continued, but the CEO also issued a formal memo explaining the details. Did the executive group initially select the wrong strategy? Were they ineffective? Although the ultimate effectiveness of either strategy separately would be difficult to determine, feedback helped the management team adjust.

Thus far, we have discussed an approach for strategic analysis required for effective managerial communication. Next, we will discuss types of communication strategies and then communication styles. Figure 3–5 presents their relationship. Because analysis, strategies, and styles are contingent on each other, the relationship is presented as a circular model.

Communication Strategies

Strategy is the result of skillful planning.[18] Strategic managerial communication requires analytical planning of the components involved: culture, sender, receiver, purpose, message content, channel, environment, and time. Communication can rarely be intuitively implemented; rather, it must be planned and strategically implemented. This planning integrates all the factors discussed thus far, but one may become more important in any given situation.

Different situations require different strategies. A controlling strategy is appropriate in one instance, while a relinquishing strategy may be best another time. An effective manager knows how to analyze all the factors presented in the strategy model (Figure 3–4) and select the best communication strategy or combination of strategies.

Jerry Wofford and others have presented various communication strategies that may be appropriate in different situations.[19] Table 3–2 summarizes six strategies, their major communication characteristics, and the situations in which they may be most appropriate. A more detailed description follows the table. Although these strategies are discussed from an interpersonal perspective, they can also be applied at the group or organizational level.

The Controlling Strategy

In controlling strategy, the manager constrains and directs the actions or thoughts of others. The communication in this strategy is essentially one way, with any feedback being basically for clarification. Managers using the controlling strategy often formulate their ideas before communicating and then

TABLE 3–2 **Communication Strategies**

Strategy	Communication Characteristic	Possible Appropriate Situation
1. Controlling	One way Dictate	Emergency Unskilled subordinates
2. Equalitarian	Two-way	Reduce resistance to change Knowledgeable employees
3. Structuring	Precise guidelines	Clarification needed Routine tasks
4. Dynamic	Brief Action oriented	Fast-moving environment Challenge employees
5. Relinquishing	Comply with other's request	Highly competent employees Delegate
6. Withdrawal	Ignore or change subject	Avoid conflict High emotions

gain the compliance of others. By virtue of their power, the communicators dictate what others will or will not do. If direct threats or promises do not apply or are not effective, the manager using this strategy may manipulate the receiver into the desired action.

The controlling strategy may be most useful in an emergency when time is crucial and the manager needs uncontested power. For instance, assume a leak just developed in a toxic gas pipeline. No time is available for exhaustive two-way communication, and only basic feedback can be acquired. The manager must use the power inherent in her managerial position to communicate the directions and priorities in this situation.

The controlling strategy may also be effective with a new and inexperienced employee. Since the job is unfamiliar for the new person, he usually accepts direction and instructions readily. Although the orientation is toward a controlling strategy, managers alert to changing competency of their employees can adjust their communication strategies to suit the rising level of employee competence.

When a manager must deal with dependent or unmotivated employees, the controlling strategy may also be effective. These persons may prefer to take a receptive role in communication and need a dominant and informed leader to provide the security and stimulation they lack.[20]

Managers should use the controlling strategy carefully because it can lead to negative reactions. It may bring about resistance or create rebellion from employees who resent direct control. A strategy that demands compliance and thus omits two-way communication may detract from, rather than facilitate, goal attainment.

The Equalitarian Strategy

The equalitarian strategy is characterized by a two-way flow of information in which the influence flows back and forth between people. The manager does not assume the role of expert but, rather, receives information as well as gives it. Rather than being unilateral in their decision making, the managers often base their decisions on a consensus. As a result, an atmosphere of mutual understanding and personal interest develops.

The equalitarian strategy serves most effectively in situations that are almost directly opposite to those calling for the controlling strategy. The equalitarian approach is effective for managers who wish to build teamwork and to strengthen the closeness and understanding between themselves and those with whom they work. It is used to draw out the other person and to improve understanding. This approach is effective for a wide range of situations, and it is especially useful for those desiring a participative style of management. It is also beneficial when a group of knowledgeable employees face a complex problem.

Not surprisingly, the equalitarian style is not effective for communicating with people who lack experience, knowledge, or competence. In addition, the equalitarian style is inadvisable for communicating with either highly dependent or authoritarian people. The style is also ineffective in crisis or emergency situations or for communications addressed to a large group. Instead, the equalitarian style works best with small groups, particularly when the parties have time for thorough discussion and decision making.[21]

The equalitarian strategy is also effective in overcoming resistance to change. In a now classic study, Coch and French concluded that the equalitarian strategy is best when attempting to change employees' job behaviors. Conversely, they found the controlling approach brought resistance to change. Employees who were permitted to discuss changes freely and to help determine their nature showed a marked improvement in output following the change.[22]

The controlling and equalitarian strategies are quite different, but either may be appropriate in different situations and cultures. The most extreme examples are that a controlling strategy is appropriate in an emergency, whereas an equalitarian strategy is best when a deadline is not pressing.

The Structuring Strategy

The structuring strategy is used by the manager who is oriented toward establishing order, organizing, scheduling, and structuring through the communication process. When using this strategy, the manager influences others by citing the standards and procedures that apply to a situation. Managers direct communication toward clarifying the structure or establishing structure for a problem.

This strategy works best in a complex environment or where clarification is needed. It helps to bring order into a complex situation by establishing goals, making work assignments, encouraging employees to meet deadlines, and explaining precisely what they should accomplish. Routine tasks can also best be managed with this strategy.

The structuring strategy is not advisable when the message involves a highly sensitive or emotional topic, since a wise manager does not hide behind rules and policies in an attempt to avoid issues. Also, managers should minimize the structuring approach when tasks are relatively simple and the environment stable. The manager who is too strongly oriented toward structure may waste time and energy.

The Dynamic Strategy

Managers using the dynamic strategy are brief and to the point. The message content is pragmatic and action oriented. The communication is not deep and philosophical, but oriented to the immediate programs the manager confronts. This approach is rarely used with plans or strategies dealing with the distant future.

The dynamic strategy is most appropriate for managers operating in a fast-moving environment. Managers who deal with frequent crises and are competent to handle the problems should use the dynamic strategy. It differs from the controlling strategy in that the manager presents a brief and enthusiastic position statement and then delegates the authority to make decisions and take action to the other employees. The controlling strategy does not allow employees the freedom of the dynamic strategy. Used correctly, the dynamic strategy challenges employees and stimulates them to action. The controlling strategy generally does not develop the same level of employee motivation as the dynamic strategy.

The dynamic approach requires competent employees operating in an environment of trust. When these characteristics are not present, it is best to use one of the other communication strategies.

The Relinquishing Strategy

When implementing the relinquishing strategy, a manager submits to the desires of another and complies with the other person's point of view. Responsibility for communication shifts from the manager to the other person involved.

This strategy is often used when the purpose of the communication is to counsel or to boost confidence. It is also valuable when managers are tempted to take over a conversation because of superior knowledge or when they wish to delegate responsibility for a project. Of course, the relinquishing style works only when the other person is willing and able to assume responsibility.

A manager should be sure not to use this strategy just to avoid responsibility. Moreover, when a manager relinquishes communication to employees who are extremely dependent or insecure, frustration and resentment may develop. Dependent employees may describe a relinquishing manager as weak and indecisive. As with any other strategy, it must be used at the right time with the right people.

The Withdrawal Strategy

The final strategy, withdrawal, is used by a manager trying to avoid a subject. Indications of the withdrawal strategy include quickly changing the topic, joking about the subject, acting as if a statement were not heard, or even avoiding the person. Because withdrawal solves few problems, it is effective in only limited situations. When an unauthorized person requests confidential information, withdrawal may be a solution. Also, when emotions are high and little of value is to be accomplished at that moment, the withdrawal strategy may be effective. Although withdrawal will not solve a problem or improve a condition in the long run, an astute manager can use this strategy at times.

Managers approach communication situations from different strategic approaches. Just as investors differ—some prefer risky market innovations and others prefer stable, predictable markets—managers approach communication strategies differently. Probably no two managers approach the many different situations they face in exactly the same way.[23]

Communication Style

Thus far, we have reviewed the strategic elements of managerial communication and six strategic approaches. As mentioned, effective managers will fit the strategy to the situation. The same is true with style. The typical way an individual communicates is termed *style*. Each manager develops his or her own style.[24] The goal of the communication should determine the choice of communication style. Unfortunately, too many managers develop standard or habitual ways of responding to different situations.[25] Thus, although most people could respond in a variety of ways, they often choose to fall back on the way they have found most comfortable in the past.

Managers should identify their personal communication style and adjust it for different situations. Although many different ways to communicate exist, managers may apply an inappropriate style in a given situation simply because they are accustomed to using the style in other situations. Every style is effective in some specific situation or another; for a manager to be most effective, his style must match the situation at hand. Strategic analysis helps a manager to understand and adapt his style to each unique situation.

Style is highly related to one's personality. As people think about their communication style, it may be helpful to relate back to the internal personality factors presented in Chapter 2. Our knowledge, culture, status, attitudes, emotions, and communication skills in relation to those with whom we communicate affect our communication style.

Another way to understand communication style is to use the categories developed by Virginia Satir.[26] The five basic styles she describes include;

1. The blaming or aggressive style.
2. The nonassertive style.
3. The computing or intellectual style.
4. The distracting or manipulative style.
5. The leveling or assertive style.

As is the case when discussing communication strategies, these styles are presented from an interpersonal perspective. However, they also apply at the group or organizational level of managerial communication.

The Blaming or Aggressive Style

A manager using the blaming or aggressive style acts in a demanding fashion with others. Blamers find fault and are critical of others. They act in a superior fashion, and others describe them as bossy. Ultimately, blamers can become tyrannical as they attempt to get their way at any cost—even at the expense of the rights and feelings of others. Blamers send messages implying that anyone who does not agree with them is ineffective. They win, but often by humiliating or overpowering other people who are too weak to express and defend their rights.

Unfortunately, the immediate consequence of blaming and aggressive communication is that it often provides emotional release and a sense of power for the blamer. The blamer gets what she wants without experiencing negative reactions from others. Subordinates may fear a blaming manager and be motivated through scare tactics. A blamer usually fails to establish close relationships, feeling a need to constantly guard against other people's attacks and possible retaliation. The blamer may rely on written rather than interpersonal channels, may be inconsiderate of others' time, and may generally communicate in a negative environment.

The Placating or Nonassertive Style

Placaters always try to please and ingratiate themselves with others. They apologize constantly, seldom disagree, and talk as though they could do almost nothing for and by themselves. Placaters often ignore their own rights, needs, and feelings or are unable to express them in a direct manner. When they do express their feelings or thoughts, they usually do it in an apologetic way so that others tend to disregard them.

Because placaters degrade themselves, others often exploit them. By showing lack of respect for themselves, placaters teach others not to respect them. The basic goal of placaters is to avoid conflict at all costs. Nonassertive managers have difficulty refusing their employees' requests and end up trying to please everyone, which ultimately pleases no one. They fear hurting others' feelings and worry that saying no or standing up for their own rights will cause others to dislike them.

The Computing or Intellectual Style

Computers are people who tend to use calculations when dealing with communication situations. This style requires an appearance of being calm, cool, and collected. Feelings simply must not show. A person using this style believes emotions are best kept hidden because feelings distract from the work at hand. Since this type does not trust feelings, he requires logic and rationality. This type generally presents a distant, aloof facade.

The Distracting or Manipulative Style

Managers who employ the distracting style do not deal directly with situations requiring communication. They avoid threatening situations and develop strategies to manipulate themselves out of unpleasant encounters. For instance, when confronted with a unique situation requiring a definitive reply, many managers will change the subject rather than responding. If they cannot avoid the encounters, their communication style may include manipulating other people's feelings. They often use anger, hurt, and guilt as manipulative devices to get others to do what they want. Such a manager can get employees to work overtime by appealing to their potential guilt feelings with such communication ploys as, "How could you let the company down after the way it has taken care of you?"

The Leveling or Assertive Style

Levelers are able to stand up for their rights and express their feelings, thoughts, or needs in a direct, honest, clear manner. Actions match words, and assertive managers follow through on what they say they will do.

When communicating in an assertive manner, managers will not stand up for their own rights at the expense of another employee's rights. Respect for self exists alongside respect for others with room for compromise or negotiation. The basic message of leveling is, "This is what I think" or "This is how I see the situation." At the same time, one does not become aggressive or defensive if other employees do not happen to see things the same way.

The goal of leveling is accurate communication. Whenever conflicts over rights or needs arise, the object is to solve them together with the other employees involved. Although leveling and communicating assertively do not guarantee that a manager will always accomplish his desired goals, it does have positive consequences. It usually increases the manager's self-respect and results in greater self-confidence. When people can say what they feel and think without fear, they will feel good about having done so. Anybody who has asked for a raise can relate to this. A supervisor may not grant a raise just because it was requested. However, if the individual has explained clearly and directly just why she deserves a raise, a feeling of satisfaction results. She has done what she believed to be worthwhile, whatever may come of it. The placater who does not bring up the subject for fear of being turned down, the manipulator who complains constantly to others about the unfairness of management, and the aggressive person who engages in heated and loud arguments with the supervisor may all develop strong feelings of resentment in addition to not getting the raise.

Clearly, the leveling or assertive style is the most preferred, but assertion requires flexibility to fit different situations. Michael Maccoby, the social psychologist and author of the *Gamesman*, emphasizes this by saying the contemporary manager is more flexible than his predecessors.[27] It is important to thoroughly assess the situation and use the most appropriate style.

When managers understand strategic communication and use an effective strategy and style, a supportive communication climate results. Lee Iacocca provides an interesting example of how effective managers adapt their managerial communication style and strategy to the situation. At most times during his career, he used an equalitarian but assertive strategy, such as when he was chairman of the Statue of Liberty Fund. When Chrysler was having serious troubles, however, he used a controlling strategy. At other times, he is reported to have used a computing or intellectual style.

Summary

We have presented a model for strategic managerial communication that may help managers reduce errors in critical situations. While it is not possible to present concrete rules that will serve in every instance, we have explored factors the manager should review before communicating.

These factors are presented as three layers. The first layer includes climate and culture. The communication strategy must be consistent with the national and organizational cultures. The second layer involves the sender, receiver, and the purpose of the message—the fundamental considerations to be reviewed. However, individual analysis is not possible since the factors are all interrelated. The same message may take on a different meaning when two receivers are involved, or a change in purpose may require a different approach for the same receiver. Communicators must consider all these factors as parts of an integrated system.

The third layer includes the message, channel, environment, and time of communication. The appropriate strategic implementation of these factors depends highly on these three layers of variables and once again all the factors are interrelated. In addition, feedback should be considered so the communication process may be adjusted.

As managers analyze all the variables, they may use six different strategies: controlling, equalitarian, structuring, dynamic, relinquishing, and withdrawal. Each is appropriate in different situations. The critical skill is to match the strategy to the situation.

A personal style of communication develops in managerial communication situations. The five basic styles are (1) blaming or aggressive, (2) nonassertive, (3) computing or intellectual, (4) distracting or manipulative, and (5) leveling or assertive. The leveling or assertive type is the most preferred in the United States, but managers must learn to be flexible.

Endnotes

1. Annette N. Shelby, "A Macro Theory of Management Communication," *Journal of Business Communication* 25, no. 2 (1988), pp. 13–28; and Priscilla S. Rogers, "Choice-Based Writing in Managerial Contexts: The Case of the Dealer Contact Report," *Journal of Business Communication* 26, no. 3 (1989), pp. 197–216.
2. M. S. Poole, "Communication and Organizational Climate: Review, Critique, and a New Perspective," in *Organizational Communication Traditional Themes and New Directions,* ed. R. D. McPhee and P. K Tompkins (Beverly Hills, Calif.: Sage Publications, 1985), pp. 79–108.
3. Raymond L. Falcione, Lyle Sussman, and Richard P. Herden, "Communications Climate in Organizations," in *Handbook of Organizational Communication,* ed. F. Jablin, L. Putnam, K. Roberts and L. Porter (Newbury Park, Calif.: Sage Publications, 1987), pp. 195–227.
4. P. R. Monroe, "The Network Level of Analysis," in *Handbook of Communication Science,* ed. C. Berger and S. Chaffee (Newbury Park, Calif.: Sage Publications, 1987), pp. 239–70.
5. Marlene G. Fine, "New Voices in the Workplace: Research Directions in Multicultural Communication," *Journal of Business Communication* 28, no. 3 (1991), pp. 259–75.
6. "The Immigrants," *Business Week,* July 13, 1992.
7. Rosita Daskal Albert, "Polycultural Perspectives on Organizational Communication," *Management Communication Quarterly* 6, no. 1 (1992), pp. 74–84.
8. John Petit, Jr., and Bobby C. Vaught, "Self-Actualization and Interpersonal Capability in Organizations," *Journal of Business Communication* 21, no. 3 (1984), pp. 33–40.
9. Joseph N. Cappella, "Interpersonal Communication: Definitions and Fundamental Questions," in *Handbook of Communication Science,* ed. C. R. Berger and S. H. Chaffee (Newbury Park, Calif.: Sage Publications, 1987), pp. 184–238.
10. C. L. Hale and J. G. Delia, "Cognitive Complexity and Social Perspective-Taking," *Communication Monographs* 43 (1976), pp. 195–203.

11. Kitty O. Locker, "Theoretical Justifications for Using Reader Benefits," *Journal of Business Communication* 19, no. 3 (1982), pp. 51–66.
12. Gary F. Soldow, "A Study of the Linguistic Dimensions of Information Processing as a Function of Cognitive Complexity," *Journal of Business Communication* 19, no. 1 (1982), pp. 55–70.
13. Eric M. Eisenberg and Marsha G. Witten, "Reconsidering Openness in Organizational Communication," *Academy of Management Review* 12, 3 (1987), pp. 418–26.
14. Mohan R. Limaye, "The Syntax of Persuasion: Two Business Letters of Request," *Journal of Business Communication* 20, no. 2 (1983), pp. 17–30.
15. William H. Baker, "Defensiveness in Communication: Its Causes, Effects, and Cures," *Journal of Business Communication* 17, no. 3 (1980), pp. 33–43.
16. Jack R. Gibb, "Defensive Communication," *Journal of Communication*, September 1961, pp. 141–48.
17. Mohan Limaye, "Buffers in Bad New Messages and Recipient Perceptions," *Management Communication Quarterly* 2, no. 1 (1988), pp. 90–101.
18. Kenneth R. Andrews, *The Concept of Corporate Strategy*, 3rd. ed. (Homewood, Ill.: Richard D. Irwin, 1987), p. 13.
19. Jerry C. Wofford, Edwin A. Gerloff, and Robert C. Cummins, *Organizational Communication* (New York: McGraw-Hill, 1977).
20. Warren Bennis and Burn Nanus, *Leaders: The Strategies for Taking Charge* (New York: Harper and Row, 1985).
21. Robert P. Vecchio, "Situational Leadership Theory: An Examination of Prescriptive Theory," *Journal of Applied Psychology* 72, no. 3 (1987), pp. 444–51.
22. L. Coch and J. R. P. French, Jr., "Overcoming Resistance to Change," *Human Relations* 1 (1948), pp. 512–32.
23. David A. Bednar, "Relationships between Communicator Style and Managerial Performance in Complex Organizations: A Field Study," *Journal of Business Communication* 19, no. 4 (1982), pp. 51–76.
24. R. Norton, "Foundation of a Communicator Style Construct," *Human Communication Research* 4 (1978), pp. 99–112.
25. "Good Leaders Aren't Perfect," *INC*, January 1992, p. 76.
26. Virginia Satir, *Peoplemaking* (Palo Alto, Calif.: Science and Behavior Books, 1972).
27. Michael Maccoby, *The Gamesman* (New York: Simon & Schuster, Inc., 1976), pp. 2–3.

Additional Readings

Ashforth, B. E. "Climate Formation: Issues and Extensions." *Academy of Management Review* 10 (1985), pp. 837–47.

Fine, M. G., F. L. Johnson and M. S. Ryan. "Cultural Diversity in the Workplace." *Public Personnel Management* 19 (1990), pp. 305–19.

Johnson, Wendell. "The Fateful Process of Mr. A Talking to Mr. B." *Harvard Business Review*, January–February 1953, pp. 43–50.

Pearce, W. B., and F. E. Cronen. *Communication, Action, and Meaning: The Creation of Social Realities*. New York: Praeger, 1980.

Johnson, Wendell. "The Fateful Process of Mr. A Talking to Mr. B." *Harvard Business Review*, January–February 1953, pp. 43–50.

Discussion Questions

1. Briefly describe yourself as a communicator following the checklist presented.
2. Describe a situation in which an emotional persuasive strategy is appropriate. Tell why it is appropriate, given the nature of the sender and receiver.
3. Give several examples of how a change in the sender, receiver, or purpose will affect the other two components.
4. List several phrases that are likely to add fuel to the fire when discussing an emotional issue.
5. Give an example of polarization that you have observed.
6. What are the advantages and disadvantages of the following communication channels: letter, telephone, meeting, face to face?
7. Give an example of when the message may vary between a formal and informal setting.
8. Why is the adage "time is money" pertinent to communication? Discuss specific ways in which this is pertinent.
9. How are the concepts of time, timing and timeliness different and how are they similar in relationship to communication?
10. Why is there a greater margin of error in some communications than in others? Discuss the implications of this concept.
11. What is meant by "an integrated communication system"?
12. Give several examples of when feelings toward a message affected the communication strategy.
13. Give an example of when a high-status and a low-status person may interpret the same gesture differently.
14. How is it possible to determine a person's level of knowledge on a subject?
15. What do you consider to be the most important strategic communication decisions?

CASE 3–1
KATHY SPRINGER AND THE VICE PRESIDENT

Kathy Springer has been a branch manager for Northeastern Bank for three years. She is proud of this position because she was the first female branch manager among the 14 branches. She has worked hard in this position and believes she has been doing an outstanding job. Her perception was confirmed four months ago when the director of branch operations took a four-week medical absence and Springer was named the temporary director. She received every indication that she had done a good job during the four weeks.

Two weeks ago, the director of branch operations retired because of a continuing medical problem. Springer was immediately optimistic that she would be considered for the job. Her background of 10 years with Northeastern (3 of these as a branch manager) would seem to qualify her. One drawback may be that she does not have a college degree; however, she expects to receive a degree in management within a year by attending evening classes.

Springer is upset because Larry Oates, the executive vice president, has been interviewing outside candidates for this position. One of the candidates is an acquaintance from another bank who confirmed to Springer that he was being considered for the position. It appears to Springer that she is not even being considered, which angers and frustrates her. She has decided to talk to Oates about the situation.

The conversation with Oates will be difficult for several reasons. First, he is an extremely cold, formal person who is difficult to approach. Second, he has always seemed to ignore Springer, even when she was acting director of branch operations. Third, she has never before initiated a formal meeting with him, even though they have both been at Northeastern for 10 years. Fourth, he is a highly educated person (MBA) with over 25 years of experience and appears to talk down to subordinates in certain situations.

Questions

1. List the sender, receiver, and purpose factors that Springer should consider before meeting Oates.
2. List the channel, environment, content, and time factors that Springer should consider.
3. Springer is making the appointment to meet Oates through his secretary. What should Springer say is the purpose of the meeting?

Case 3–2
Resigning from the TV Station

Jane Rye is a student of advertising at State University and will graduate at the end of the next term. She had a part-time job in the sales department at a local television station. When hired, Rye thought she was very lucky to have a job there, not only for the money but also for the work experience.

Pat Trent, the sales manager who hired her, was Rye's immediate supervisor. Rye was doing a very good job and received considerable support from Trent. In fact, the sales manager had nothing but praise for Rye's work when reporting to top management. Trent often told her subordinate that her work was exceptional and Trent would like to hire her on a permanent basis after graduation to head a new media research department for the station. The job seemed to promise a challenging and rewarding career.

While Rye was flattered by the offer, she was not interested in the position because she found her present job unsatisfying. However, she never told Trent her feelings about the job or the possible appointment. Because Trent had trained Rye and had promoted her to everyone, Rye had become very loyal and grateful to her sales manager. Thus, Rye thought she would betray Trent if she were to refuse the job. After six weeks, however, Rye decided to quit and work part time at the university, but she did not know how to approach her boss.

Rye, unable to say anything to Trent, let time pass until the day she was ready to quit to start her new job. When Rye got to work that day, the sales manager was scheduled to leave early that morning for a weekly meeting. Rye was forced to go into Trent's office while two other people were there discussing their problems. Trent asked Rye what she wanted, and Rye replied, "I am resigning." The sales manager was taken completely by surprise and asked Rye why and wondered what was to be done with the project Rye was handling. Rye apologized for such short notice and said maybe she could help clear up the matter when Trent returned from her meeting.

When Trent returned later that afternoon, Rye explained that she was taking a part-time job at the school starting tomorrow. Trent, very disappointed in her subordinate, said, "If you had told me sooner, I could have phased out the project to someone else—now I'm in a bind." As the months passed, Rye began to interview for permanent work and was afraid of getting a bad recommendation from Trent despite her work accomplishments.

Questions

1. How should Rye have handled her resignation?
2. Where, when, and how do you think Rye should have resigned? Do you think Trent would have understood under different circumstances?
3. How did Trent foster Rye's reluctance to communicate?

II SRATEGIES FOR WRITTEN MANAGERIAL COMMUNICATION

This section contains four chapters that discuss the written communications managers must compose. Chapter 4, "Preparing for Written Managerial Communication," reviews writing apprehension, planning, the product and process approaches to writing, collaborative writing, and factors that make the writing of managers different from that of people in other professions or discourse communities.

Chapter 5, "Essentials of Written Managerial Communication," lists and illustrates 12 principles that contribute directly to clarity and ease of comprehension. The first seven principles deal with effective word choice, while the last five relate to the organization of words for effect.

Chapter 6, "Strategies for Letters and Memos," stresses audience adaptation and reviews the direct and indirect approaches in general. It then examines specific types of directly and indirectly organized letters. The discussion of memorandums includes memo format, a review of their major uses, types of memos, and political uses of memos in offices.

Chapter 7, "Strategies for Management Reports," reviews the report writing process, strategic decisions about format and organization, memorandum and letter reports, elements of formal reports, and visual aids. Receiver analysis, as discussed in Chapter 3, is stressed as an important part of making strategic report writing decisions.

4 PREPARING FOR WRITTEN MANAGERIAL COMMUNICATION

You have been away from your office for the past two days, and you fear returning to your desk for several reasons. One is that you'll need to write a report to the director of engineering about the seminar on energy conservation you just attended. Another is that you'll also have to write a memo to all the production supervisors recommending energy saving changes.

Then you have the job reclassification matter your secretary asked you to undertake. Over a week ago, you explained to him that a higher classification could not be given for his job. Nonetheless, you still have to write an official rationale for the personnel file. For some reason, you just keep putting it off.

Besides these known writing projects, you suspect that others will be pending after a two-day absence: inquiries to be answered, requests to be made, notices to be sent, and acknowledgments to be made. Furthermore, most of these tasks will probably have some stated or implied deadline that will require you to work overtime.

You wish writing came easier to you and you could be better at it. How can you improve your writing so that you do it more quickly, clearly, comprehensively, and professionally? This chapter provides guidelines for accomplishing those objectives.

Mangers spend about 75 percent of their time communicating;[1] and the higher up managers go in the managerial hierarchy, the more time they spend communicating. While much of this communication involves oral, face-to-face interaction, some require written communication: memos, letters, and reports. All have the potential to play a critical part in the success of the manager and the organization.

Given the time and effort required to put things in writing, readers may wonder why managers would prefer to write a message rather than communicate it orally. Written managerial communications offer several strategic advantages: economy, efficiency, accuracy, and official permanence.

Writing is usually more economical than long-distance phone calls and much more economical than long-distance travel. Furthermore, it provides immediacy, in that the manager can write the message whether or not the receiver is immediately available to receive it.

Writing is efficient because the manager can work independently and use words selectively. Additionally, written electronic mail allows receivers to read messages at their convenience and thus avoids the time wasted in telephone tag.

Accuracy is another advantage of writing; writing permits greater control of words and message organization than does oral communication. Accuracy, in turn, often eliminates confusion, assures clarity, and further contributes to economy and efficiency.

Finally, writing provides an official record that can be retained for recall and review. In our increasingly litigious society, the importance of documentation cannot be overstressed. The difference between a legal judgment for or against organizations and their managers is becoming more often a matter of adequate documentation.

Writing Apprehension

Given the many advantages of written communication, it may be difficult to understand why some people have an aversion to putting anything into writing. Such people will try anything to get out of writing and will put off as long as possible the things they simply cannot avoid writing. This aversion has been termed *writing apprehension* and has been found in many writers, regardless of their managerial experience, educational background, or writing proficiency.

Causes

One possible explanation for writing apprehension points to a person's earliest writing experiences. If those early writing efforts met with severe criticism, the seed of apprehension may have been planted. Then, expectations drop, and the writer ultimately faces writing assignments with a defeatist attitude. As the writing becomes more muddled and incoherent, the apprehension is reinforced by subsequent negative evaluations.

Another possible reason for writing apprehension might relate to the first. Apprehensive writers may have never been taught to plan to write and thus approach the task in a very disorganized and disoriented state. In a survey of 254 managers and executives from a variety of organizations, Pearl Aldrich found that the majority of these adult writers "seemed not to know the value of deciding in advance of writing what their purpose, audience, and point would be." They thus experienced anxiety, defensiveness, and reluctance to approach writing tasks until the last minute. As a result, they produced disorganized and ineffective writing.[2]

Results

In terms of slowed productivity, confused instructions, inexact reports, and defaulted contracts, the costs to business of inept writing have been estimated to be in the millions.[3] Also, because the apprehensive writer is not going to volunteer ideas in writing, we can add to the preceding costs the value of good ideas that were never offered for consideration.

The individual bears a cost, too. That cost manifests itself in diminished confidence, dashed hopes, unfulfilled ambitions, and possibly even health effects. One researcher recently noted that writing causes a significant increase in blood pressure.[4] Though yet unproven, one might infer that people who experience unusually high anxiety at the prospect of writing might also experience unusually high blood pressure.

A less obvious side effect of writing apprehension is the impact it might have on career choices. A study of 500 employees from two large manufacturing firms revealed that those with high writing apprehension held positions that were significantly less writing intensive than were the positions of people with low writing apprehension. In other words, apprehensive writers held jobs that did not require a lot of writing in a short time; they were not engaged in many different types of writing; and they were not subject to deadline or audience pressure.[5] Unfortunately, employees may be restricting job opportunities unnecessarily.

Finally, the overall performance evaluations of apprehensive writers may be colored by the negative evaluation of their communication ability. One study found that communications competencies were good predictors of overall performance ratings. A high or low rating in four communication competencies taken together predicted a high or low overall performance evaluation 89.6 percent of the time.[6] Whether good communicators are also good performers overall, or whether performance in one area affects the superior's perception of performance overall, we don't know. But fair or not, the connection is there.

Correctives

Is the writing apprehensive person doomed to a life of criticism and diminishing self-confidence, to a career of limited choices based on the writing requirements of jobs available, to a series of performance evaluations assigning undue weights to communication abilities? Not necessarily.

Several approaches may be taken to reduce and ultimately eliminate writing apprehension. Kaye Bennett and Steven Rhodes suggest using workshops and seminars designed to systematically desensitize employees with writing apprehension.[7] The trick is to get these people writing and to build their confidence with a series of successful writing experiences.

Another approach can occur in a workshop or seminar or in a private tutoring session. Its goal is to convince people with writing apprehension that they are not alone. Many people face this same problem. However, because people do not readily discuss this problem, those who suffer from it sometimes see themselves as uniquely troubled. Often, the awareness that others have faced the problem and have dealt with it gives apprehensive writers the courage to do something about their problem.

Another approach apprehensive writers might take, especially when in the throes of writer's block, is to start writing at any place in the message they feel like writing. Often, the toughest place to start a message is at the beginning, yet that is the place people often feel obligated to begin. If a general plan of presentation has been mapped out, we can start in the middle or even at the end. Once the rest of the message has been written, the beginning might come more easily.

When apprehensive writers start to write any place in the message, they should not worry about errors. Often the fear of making mistakes, added to the fear of writing, stalemates writers. Mechanical errors can be caught and corrected later in the editing and revising stage. The primary concern should be to get thoughts down on paper, to show some evidence of progress.

The final approach recommended for an apprehensive writer is to seek evaluation from a supportive person and remain open to constructive feedback. Others may be able to point out certain aspects of a message that need improvement, improvement that might not be apparent to the writer. Writers are rarely good self-editors because they often read into a message what they wanted to say in the first place. It sometimes takes an objective "other" eye to see that something is missing or needs change or clarification.

On the last point mentioned, managers have an opportunity to perform a valuable service for employees. Managers should not only write effectively, but they should also help subordinates do so. For the apprehensive writer, the manager can assume the role of the supportive person and provide constructive feedback. With this ongoing constructive feedback and practice, the apprehensive writer may ultimately conquer the apprehension.

Planning

As noted earlier, some writers may be apprehensive because they were never taught to plan the writing process. Unfortunately, a lack of planning also hurts the writing of many managers who are not apprehensive. Both parties turn out disorganized and largely incoherent letters and reports.

The planning process for a managerial writer is a lot like the one journalists are trained to use. The parallel is logical, since both might be characterized as professional writers. Both spend a significant amount of time at work writing. Thus, both might be expected to determine the five Ws—who, what, when, where, why—and perhaps how. Managers might determine the five Ws in a slightly different order; but they ought, nonetheless, to have a clear understanding of each before committing a word to paper.

What?

The "what" question deals with the nature of the message. A definitive answer to this question may have to wait until many of the other questions have been answered. Even so, a manager should have a fairly clear idea of what needs to be communicated early in the planning stages. Does he need certain information? Is she granting or rejecting a request? Is he informing subordinates of a policy change? Is she trying to secure the cooperation of workers in implementing certain procedures?

Any time readers see a message that seems to bounce from one side of an issue to another, any time readers are forced to wade through a message that rambles on endlessly and incoherently, any time readers wonder, "What is this person trying to say?" the chances are good that the writer *didn't know* exactly what he was trying to say or what purpose he was trying to accomplish.

Why?

The answer to the "why" question is probably just as important as the answer to the "what" question. Furthermore, the answer should be just as clear to the recipient of the message as it is to the sender. Unfortunately, many miscommunications occur because the sender does not know why a message is being sent or does not bother to share with the receiver the reason for the message.

Many corporate policies, procedures, and rules, for example, are imposed on employees without any accompanying justification. Personnel would probably be much more receptive to these directives if they understood why the directives were necessary. Human beings are complex creatures who like to deal with cause and effect. When an effect is imposed and the cause is withheld, one likely result is resistance.

Who?

One of the most important elements of the planning that should precede any managerial communication is the answer to the "who" question. The person or people receiving the message will likely have an impact on the answers to the other planning questions.

Characteristics such as age, sex, education, subject knowledge, political and religious affiliations, and job title may provide some indication as to how the reader will interpret a message. Within an organizational setting, however, these characteristics fall short of telling us about the writer-reader relationship and about the characteristics of the organization and the department that may be pertinent to successful message transmission.

To engage in a truly thorough reader analysis and to be fully attuned to the reader's likely reception of a message, a writer should consider the following points:

1. The relative power position between the writer and the reader.
2. The communication requirements the corporation exerts on the reader and the writer.
3. The business functions the writer and reader work in.
4. The type of perceptual and problem-solving mind-set the reader has developed as a result of his or her business function.
5. The frequency of communication between the writer and the reader.
6. The types of messages they typically send.
7. The reader's reaction to past messages from the writer.
8. The timing of the message.
9. The relative sensitivity of the message.[8]
10. The reader's general attitude toward the subject, the sender, and the sender's department.

In the early years of a person's career, the time spent on reader analysis may vary with the relative importance of the message. For very important messages, a novice may scrutinize all the information available to determine the best wording, the most appropriate organization, the right medium, the best timing, and the best source and destination for the message. As time goes on, however, many of these areas of inquiry in reader analysis become second nature to the conscientious managerial communicator.

When?

The importance of the answer to the "when" question may vary with the routineness and/or importance of the information being conveyed. Many routine messages, such as sales reports, are distributed periodically. No actual decision has to be made as to when they are sent, because dates have already been set. Likewise, information of a casual and relatively insignificant nature is likely to be received in the same way regardless of timing.

For a nonroutine message, however, the decision on when to send it may directly affect how the message is received. For example, some years ago, the managers of a textile mill had to tell employees they were not going to get a pay raise even though the company had shown a profit the preceding quarter. Management chose to convey this message in letter form just before the employees went on vacation. Not only did this timing likely ruin the vacations of many employees, but it also probably encouraged a number of them to spend their vacations looking for another job.

On the subject of timing, managers need to keep in mind that it is possible to send messages too early as well as too late. For example, the agenda for a meeting and supporting material could be sent so early that the recipients forget the meeting by the time it is scheduled to occur. But if the material is sent too late, participants might not have time to get fully prepared for the meeting. Five to ten days' notice is a generally safe range; but the longer the meeting and the greater the amount of supporting material to be distributed, the longer the lead time needed.

Where?

The "where" question sometimes has to be addressed at both ends of the communication spectrum: from where should the message come and to where should it be directed? Should the message come from a manager at a particular level, or should it come from a person higher in the organization, so as to carry the additional weight of authority?

At the other end of the spectrum, even if we know who will receive the message, we may have to decide where they should be while receiving the message. To illustrate, some companies have grappled with the problem of company newsletter distribution: whether to send it to employees' homes or distribute it at the work site. Sending it to the homes might get the families interested, but it might also be viewed as an infringement of employee privacy or personal time.

How?

The "how" question is largely a matter of media selection. Even when managers decide to put it in writing, they are still faced with a number of written media options: letter, memo, report, e-mail, pamphlet, brochure, newsletter, policy manual, or even bulletin board. The choice of medium is determined at least in part by how personal the message needs to be and how widespread its distribution needs to be.

Additionally, managers should remember a rule of thumb that applies to media selection in general. Specifically, if a manager regularly uses one particular medium, the choice of a different medium might communicate a sense of urgency or importance. If, for example, a manager regularly communicates with subordinates in person, a memo might suggest something unusual and worthy of extra attention. More is said about media selection in Chapter 16.

Though the preceding planning areas were discussed separately and in a particular order, they are all interdependent and should not be treated in isolation. The good managerial communicator learns to see the interrelationships among the planning areas and to treat the areas as a decision package.

Overcoming writing apprehension and adequately planning will go a long way toward getting a manager prepared to write. Other factors, however, must also be considered as managers prepare to write in contemporary organizational environments. Some of these factors are the product and process approaches to writing, collaborative writing, and the uniqueness of managerial writing. These topics are the subject of the remainder of this chapter.

The Product and Process Approaches to Writing

In the last decade, one of the most controversial issues addressed by teachers of business and managerial communication has been the product and process approaches to writing. Initially recognized and developed in the field of composition, the process approach has challenged the traditional product approach in the fields of business and managerial communication as well.[9] Knowledge of the two approaches is important to managers as well as teachers because it helps them to better understand their own writing.

Definitions

The traditional *product approach* focuses on the message in terms of how it should appear and what it should contain in its final form. Most business communication textbooks and teachers, for example, advise that good news messages should begin with the main point, state supporting details in the message's body, and end on a note of goodwill. These teachers and textbooks then show examples of good news letters and memos with parts that accomplish the goals stated.

The newer *process approach*, on the other hand, focuses on the stages through which a writer ought to proceed in creating a message. Though the number and nature of stages may differ by author and teacher, the following list is exemplary: planning, gathering, writing, evaluating, getting feedback, revising, editing, and proofreading. Promoters of the process approach note that writing is a recursive, rather than linear, activity much more suited to the process approach. Furthermore, they argue that expression is discovery and the process approach is much better than the product approach in facilitating discovery.

Advantages and Disadvantages of the Product Approach

One advantage of the product approach is that it puts emphasis on the message, the sender, and the receiver[10] which is where it should be in many people's opinions. Another advantage is that the product approach is effective and efficient for practical business writing, short letters, and memos. The boilerplate approach is thought to be quite useful for most managerial writing.[11]

Opponents of the product approach argue that it puts too much emphasis on the end result without giving adequate attention to how a writer is supposed to get there. Additionally, the product approach is thought to stifle creativity as it encourages writers to produce mirror images of what they have been told are good pieces of writing.[12]

Advantages and Disadvantages of the Process Approach

One of the major advantages of the process approach is that it forces people to learn how to face their writing tasks and how to evaluate the writing itself.[13] Another major advantage is the emphasis given to prewriting activities. Before the process approach, prewriting activities were either neglected or haphazardly presented.[14] Generally, the process approach is thought to be a much more thorough approach to learning how to write, one that encourages creativity rather than mimicry.

While opponents accept that the process approach is useful for expressive writing and self-discovery, they argue it is too cumbersome and time consuming for practical managerial writing.[15] They note, too, that the process approach may not be workable for all writers. Different writers write in different ways, one just as effectively as the next. Furthermore, there is no evidence to support the belief that the process approach leads to better business writing.[16]

Though the proponents of the two approaches seem to have painted themselves into opposite corners, we take a contingency view that each can be useful in its own time and place. For shorter, more routine written messages, the product approach is likely to be the most effective and efficient. For longer reports of a nonroutine nature, however, at least some of the stages in the process approach would be worthwhile.

One other major development in the modern corporate world is the emergence of collaborative writing. It is becoming more prevalent because of the increased emphasis on teamwork. Also, frequently these teams consist of people with unique specialties that they bring to bear toward the successful completion of major projects.

Collaborative Writing

Though it may assume any of many different forms, collaborative writing is entrenched in contemporary professional writing. In personal interviews with 200 business people in two states, one team of researchers found that 73.5 percent of their respondents sometimes collaborate with at least one other person in writing.[17] Another research team found that 87 percent of their respondents sometimes wrote as members of a team or group.[18] At America West Airlines, most of the reports are collaboratively written. The same is true at Anderson Consulting.

Collaborative writing comes in a number of different guises. Sometimes a supervisor has a staff member research and write a document after which the supervisor edits it. Sometimes the collaboration comes in the planning of the document, which is drafted and revised by an individual. Other times, an individual does the planning and drafting of work that is revised collaboratively. Peers often critique one another's work. And there are times when the collaboration pervades the entire writing process from start to finish.[19]

Advantages of Collaborative Writing

Collaborative writing is becoming more popular largely because of the advantages of group decision making. It often works better than an individual effort because of the additional minds and perspectives being applied to creating the document. Furthermore, the understanding of and the motivation to carry out the directives of the document are greater among those who actually contributed to developing the document.

Collaborative writing is also thought to be particularly advantageous when the size of the task and/or time limits call for the labor of more than one person, when the scope of the job calls for more than one area of expertise, or when one of the task goals is the melding of divergent opinions.[20]

Gebhardt notes that the theoretical underpinnings of collaborative writing are "the rhetorical sense of audience; the psychological power of peer influence; the transfer-of-learning principle by which (people) gain insights into their own writing as they comment on the works of others; and the principle of feedback through which (people) sense how well their writing is communicating."[21]

Terry Bacon has found that collaborative writing socializes employees in several fundamental ways. It helps to acculturate newcomers by teaching writers about the corporation's capabilities and history and by modeling the corporation's values and attitudes in the actions of the experienced members. It also helps break down functional barriers, and it fosters the informal chains of communication and authority through which the corporation accomplishes its work.[22]

Finally, and perhaps most importantly, collaboration can improve writing quality.[23] People, without outside direction, can respond to each other's drafts with sharply focused and relevant comments.[24]

Disadvantages of Collaborative Writing

Some of the disadvantages of collaborative writing are also those associated with group decision making. Some members do not do their fair share. Coordinating schedules for meetings can be complicated and vexing. Personality conflicts can all but stall the group's progress. And some people believe that one person acting alone could probably complete the chore in much less time than it takes a group to do so. Finally, though one person may do a poor job on part of the project, everyone is held responsible for the entire end result.

Respondents in one study noted that the two major costs of collaboration were time and ego. One commented that in collaboration you had to "check your ego at the door," you had to be "confident in your own abilities and yet able to take criticism."[25]

Another surveyed group of professional writers cited several problems associated with collaborative writing. They spoke of difficulty in resolving style differences; the additional time required to work with a group; inequitable division of tasks; and the loss of personal satisfaction, ownership, or sense of creativity.[26]

Probably the most serious problem associated with collaborative writing is ineffectively dealing with conflicts that arise. Some people see all conflicts as bad and try to ignore them or sweep them under the carpet. They do not realize that some conflicts are functional and can help the group to come to a more creative resolution of its problem.

Characteristics of Effective Collaborative Writers and Groups

In their extensive research into the collaborative writing of people in a number of professions, Lisa Ede and Andrea Lunsford came up with the following profile of effective collaborative writers:

> They are flexible; respectful of others; attentive and analytical listeners; able to speak and write clearly and articulately; dependable and able to meet deadlines; able to designate and share responsibility, to lead and to follow; open to criticism but confident in their own abilities; ready to engage in creative conflict.[27]

Generally, this profile depicts people who are able to work with others, people who are going to be in greater demand as collaboration becomes more the norm than the exception.

Nancy Harper and Lawrence Askling studied the difference in the communication of small groups engaged in producing multimedia messages. They found that successful groups had certain characteristics and behaviors that clearly distinguished them from their less successful counterparts.

In the successful groups, the leader would establish clear deadlines, schedule meetings often, and deal with any conflict that developed in the group. Members of successful groups listened to criticism and came to important decisions together, and they knew the group's goals. Finally, they had a higher proportion of members who worked actively on the project. And they even found ways of using members who did not like to work in groups.

By contrast, in the less successful groups, the members did not know what they had to do and had to ask the leader. They met less often; and when conflicts arose, they tried to ignore them. Subgroups often made decisions and then told the other members what had been decided. They had a smaller proportion of active members and always had some members who contributed little to the final product.[28]

Guidelines for Effective Collaborative Writing

In addition to the advice implicit in the preceding characterizations of effective collaborative writers and groups, there are other ways to achieve successful collaborative writing experiences. A basic guideline is to make sure the work is divided equitably among group members. Nothing is surer to destroy a person's morale than to begin feeling overworked compared to others in the group.

Some authorities encourage each group member to write a private journal focusing on group interaction. They contend these journals facilitate group interaction by encouraging group members to think and write about the interaction process, how it influences their written products, and how they can improve their own communication skills. Such journals allow a supervisor to monitor group interaction as it affects group progress and would provide cues to the need for intervention.[29]

Some experts recommend forming groups on the basis of common blocks of free time—as shown on schedules that employees submit. This basis of organization facilitates the group process for employees who take many trips, work at different sites, and have certain weekly obligations. They also recommend a group size of three or four as most effective.[30]

Collaborative writers must also realize that conflict can be constructive. If there is too much respect and good feeling among members of a group, members may become reluctant to challenge one another, and group creativity may suffer. Mutual admiration is not always the best approach. Conflict should be seen as a necessary part of collaboration.[31]

All collaborative writing groups should have a team leader, even though the person may not have any formal authority. The leader should be responsible for coordinating the team's collaborative efforts, shaping the team's vision, and resolving conflicts among individuals and functional departments. The latter task usually requires good interpersonal skills if the leader has no formal authority.[32]

The last guideline we will discuss addresses a common complaint of students facing a collaborative writing assignment: Why do we all have to get the same grade? Beard, Rymer, and Williams recommend an alternative assessment system based on the instructor's (1) observing group meetings, (2) collecting a complete paper trail (working papers), (3) assigning a confidential journal, and (4) distributing peer-evaluation forms. Using all this information, the grade components are as follows:

- Group report—50 percent. All group members receive the same grade on the written product.

- Oral interaction—25 percent. Members receive an individual evaluation of their participation in the group process.
- Composing process—25 percent. Members receive an individual evaluation of their contribution to the writing.[33]

Though no one can guarantee that all collaborative writing experiences will be problem free, we are confident that anyone who follows the preceding guidelines will encounter fewer insurmountable problems and will attain greater success in group writing projects.

Implications for the Future

As technological advances make collaborative writing in various shapes and forms easier and more accessible, we can expect to see more of it in all types of organizations. And as it becomes more common, we will see the need for more research to answer the many questions that will arise.

By the mid-1980s, collaborative composition research had already studied several issues. Researchers were looking at authority in collaborative groups, and they had also begun to examine the impact of "difference"—class, ethnicity, gender, and race—on collaborative writing. They had also recognized the need to extend research beyond the classroom setting. They had introduced new theoretical constructs for understanding collaboration, and they were debating meanings of the basic term *collaborative writing*.[34]

Yet many other topics and issues await research studies. For example, what leadership styles are best for collaborative groups, and will the style vary by writing task or group membership? Is the writing task itself related to the collaborative approach used? Does the organizational setting (government, industry, military) affect the nature of the collaboration that occurs within it?[35]

When, why, and how do groups choose to write collaboratively? What interpersonal skills and group writing strategies enhance collaborative processes and products? What differentiates newly formed groups from those that previously have worked together? Do collaborative writing groups go through any definable stages of development? Is there an ideal group size for different kinds of collaborative writing jobs? What constitutes the most productive collaborative processes and the highest quality products?[36]

Though much research has been done and is being done toward developing a scholarly framework of knowledge in collaborative writing, a great deal of work remains to be done. But one point is clear: Managers must be sensitive to cultural diversity and group dynamics. Knowledge of these areas will enable managers to work much more effectively in collaborative environments.

Managers as Writers

In recent years, the various fields addressing composition have given much attention to discourse communities. A *discourse community* is a group of people who think in similar ways about how to communicate, subjects to be dealt with and how to approach them, and what makes up legitimate knowledge. These communities may be large or small, and any organization may contain a number of discourse communities.

Are managers in a particular firm or industry, or managers in general, members of a discourse community? Though different people may answer that question differently, we believe managers serve in sufficiently common roles and work in sufficiently common contexts to make them members of a unique discourse community. We see managers as people who plan the organization's objectives, organize the functions of the organization, lead people in the accomplishment of those objectives, and control activities to make sure they are proceeding in the right direction.

Equally important in defining the discourse community of managerial writers is the context in which they do their work. Stratman and Duffy label context as the most powerful variable affecting what writers in organizations do, and how these writers perceive, interpret, and value their own activity. They note that context potentially affects everything—the writer's underlying attitude toward the apparent organizational functions served by writing; the actual phrasing used in finished texts; and the decisions about what activities are (or are not) seen as part of the writing process.[37] The following paragraphs examine several aspects of the unique context in which managerial writing occurs.

One of the most critical aspects of the context of managerial writing is the fragmented nature of a manager's workday. Most people think of managers, especially higher level executives, as having meticulously organized days overseen and protected by a secretary or administrative assistant. Henry Mitnzberg found the opposite to be true. As he and colleagues recorded the activities of a number of managers, he found their days to be filled with interruptions. On the average, they had a full half hour of uninterrupted time only once every four days.[38] Most people faced with a writing task like to go somewhere quiet and work in sizable blocks of time. Such luxury is rarely available to managers.

Another aspect of the managerial writing context is the extent of collaboration and delegation that takes place. As was noted earlier in this chapter, collaborative writing is becoming more common in business and requires managers who can work well with others. Additionally, managers have the option of delegating some of their more routine writing chores.[39] This delegation, however, presupposes the manager's knowledge of various subordinates' abilities to handle the assignment.

The size and culture of the organization are also important elements of the context of managerial communication. Small companies can communicate many things orally; but the larger a company gets, the greater is the need to put things in writing for the record. With size also comes a tendency for greater formality in many written documents. With regard to culture, bureaucracies thrive on formality, while more participative organizations lean toward informality.

Authority and politics play a significant role in the context of managerial writing. Max Weber described three types of authority: traditional, charismatic, and legal.[40] How managers communicate messages is greatly influenced by the type of authority they are perceived to have. Also, business organizations must be viewed as political systems.[41] Managers who forget to consider the political forces at work in the company may soon find they are no longer at work in the company.

In the increasingly litigious society in which we live and given the ever-increasing role of government in business, legal concerns represent another important element of the managerial writing context. Managers are considered legal agents of the organization in many types of writing they do. They must be ever conscious of such things as libel, slander, privacy, and equal opportunity.

Though much research remains to be done on the nature of managerial writing and the factors that influence it, we believe that, for the reasons reviewed above, we can differentiate managers from other types of professional writers. We further believe that the problems and challenges of managerial writers should be studied separately from those of other professional writers in the true context in which they exist.

For managers, the phenomenon of a discourse community means they face a unique writing environment. They must carefully analyze the organizational culture in which they work, they must find the best time and place to write, and they must always remember that writing has a unique role in the manager's job.

Summary

Written managerial communication has several strategic advantages: economy, efficiency, accuracy, and official permanence. Unfortunately, despite these advantages, some people suffer from writing apprehension, resulting in lower productivity and self-esteem, limited career choices, and lower performance evaluations. Seminars, tutors, and mentors are a few of the approaches that might reduce writing apprehension; but adequate planning is probably one of the best ways of reducing it. This planning involves identifying what, why, who, when, where, and how.

Writing scholars still debate the values of the product and process approaches to writing. The traditional product approach focuses on the final document, its appearance, and content. The process approach stresses the stages through which a writer should proceed in creating a message. Though each approach has its advantages and disadvantages, we recommend the product approach for shorter, routine business documents and the process approach for the longer, nonroutine business documents.

Collaborative writing is fast becoming a fact of modern organizational life. In addition to the advantages of group decision making, it also socializes employees in several ways and can improve the quality of the writing. In addition to the disadvantages associated with group decision making (e.g., domination and reluctant contributors), time, potential ego damage, style differences, and conflicts can work against effective collaborative writing.

Despite the potential pitfalls, we can identify effective collaborative writers and groups. Good writers are flexible, respectful, attentive, articulate, responsible, and confident people who work well with others. Good groups establish clear deadlines, meet often, deal with conflicts, make decisions together, and have a high proportion of members who work actively on the project.

Guidelines for effective collaborative writing include dividing the work equitably among members. Also, having members keep a journal can be advantageous. Conflict should be viewed as potentially constructive. The group's leader should coordinate efforts, shape the team's vision, and resolve conflicts. Finally, for classroom collaborative writing, teachers might give some thought to alternative assessment systems that do not give everyone the same grade for the project.

Finally, the chapter addressed the question of whether managers should be considered members of a discourse community. We believe that their roles (planning, organizing, leading, and controlling) and the contexts in which they write are sufficiently similar for them to be considered a discourse community. Among the aspects of the managerial writing context considered were the fragmented nature of their time at work, the extent of collaboration and delegation, the size and culture of the organization, the authority and politics they must deal with, and the legal considerations of which they must remain aware as they communicate on the job.

Endnotes

1. Henry Mintzberg, *The Nature of Managerial Work* (Englewood Cliffs, N.J.: Prentice Hall, 1980), pp. 38–39
2. Pearl G. Aldrich, "Adult Writers: Some Reasons for Ineffective Writing on the Job," *College Composition and Communication* 33, no. 3 (October 1982), pp. 284–86.
3. Ibid.
4. William Sharbrough, "A Study of the Effects of the Act of Writing on Blood Pressure," *Proceedings,* 1988 National Association for Business Communication Convention, Indianapolis, p. 339.
5. Kaye Bennett and Steven C. Rhodes, "Writing Apprehension and Writing Intensity in Business and Industry," *Journal of Business Communication* 25, no.1 (Winter 1988), p. 37.

6. Joseph Scudder and Patricia J. Guinan, "Communication Competencies as Discriminators of Superiors' Ratings of Employee Performance," *Journal of Business Communication* 26, no. 3 (Summer 1989), p. 224.

7. Bennett and Rhodes, "Writing Apprehension."

8. James Suchan and Ron Dulek, "Toward a Better Understanding of Reader Analysis," *Journal of Business Communication* 25, no. 2 (Spring 1988), p. 33.

9. Janet Emig, "The Composing Process of Twelfth Graders," *National Council of Teachers Research Report*, no. 13 (Urbana, Illinois: NCTE, 1971).

10. Vanessa Arnold, "The Concept of Process," *Journal of Business Communication* 24, no. 1 (Winter 1987), p. 34.

11. Peter Bracher, "Process, Pedagogy, and Business Writing," *Journal of Business Communication* 24, no. 1 (Winter 1987), pp. 43–50.

12. Robert Waxler, "On Process," *Journal of Business Communication* 24, no. 1 (Winter 1987), p. 41.

13. Paula J. Pomerenke, "Process: More than a Fad for the Business Writer," *Journal of Business Communication* 24, no. 1 (Winter 1987), p. 39.

14. Steve Anderson, "Process in Business Writing Texts," *Journal of Business Communication* 24, no. 1 (Winter 1987), pp. 73–74.

15. Bracher, "Process, Pedagogy, and Business Writing."

16. Thomas G. Devine, "Caveat Emptor: The Writing Process Approach to College Writing," *Journal of Developmental Education* 14, no. 1 (September 1990), p. 3.

17. Lester Faigley and Thomas P. Miller, "What We Learn from Writing on the Job," *College English* 44, no. 6 (October 1982), p. 567.

18. Lisa Ede and Andrea Lunsford, *Singular Texts/Plural Authors* (Carbondale, Ill.: Southern Illinois University Press, 1990), p. 60.

19. Nancy Allen, Dianne Atkinson, Meg Morgan, Teresa Moore, and Craig Snow, "What Experienced Collaborators Say about Collaborative Writing," *Journal of Business and Technical Communication* 1, no. 2 (September 1987), p. 71.

20. Ibid., p. 85.

21. R. Gebhardt, "Teamwork and Feedback: Broadening the Base of Collaborative Writing," *College English* 42, no. 1 (September 1980), p. 69.

22. Terry R. Bacon, "Collaboration in a Pressure Cooker," *The Bulletin.* (June 1990), p. 4.

23. A. M. O'Donnell, D. F. Dansereau, T. R. Rocklin, C. O. Larson, V. I. Hythecker, M. D. Young, and J. G. Labiotee, "Effects of Cooperative and Individual Rewriting on an Instruction Writing Task," *Written Communication* 4 (1987), pp. 90–99.

24. Rebecca Burnett, "Benefits of Collaborative Planning in the Business Communication Classroom," *The Bulletin*, June 1990, p. 10.

25. Allen et al., "What Experienced Collaborators Say about Collaborative Writing," pp. 82–23.

26. Lisa Ede and Andrea Lunsford, *Single Tests/Plural Authors: Perspectives on Collaborative Writing* (Carbondale, Ill.: Southern Illinois University Press, 1990), p. 62.

27. Ibid., p. 66.

28. Nancy L. Harper and Lawrence R. Askling, "Group Communication and Quality of Task Solution in a Media Production Organization," *Communication Monographs* 47, no. 2 (June 1980), pp. 77–100.

29. Jone Rymer Goldstein and Elizabeth L. Malone, "Using Journals to Strengthen Collaborative Writing," *The Bulletin*, September 1985, pp. 24–25.

30. Meg Morgan et al., "Collaborative Writing in the Classroom" *The Bulletin*, September 1987, p. 22.
31. Allen et al., "What Experienced Collaborators Say about Collaborative Writing," pp. 81–82.
32. Terry Bacon, "Collaboration in a Pressure Cooker," p. 5.
33. John D. Beard, Jone Rymer, and David Williams, "An Assessment System for Collaborative-Writing Groups: Theory and Empirical Evaluation," *Journal of Business and Technical Communication* 3, no. 2 (September 1989), pp. 33–35.
34. Janis Forman, "Collaborative Business Writing: A Burkean Perspective for Future Research," *Journal of Business Communication* 28, no. 3 (Summer 1991), p. 234.
35. Allen et al., "What Experienced Collaborators Say about Collaborative Writing," pp. 87–88.
36. Forman, "Collaborative Business Writing," pp. 244–47.
37. J. F. Stratman and T. M. Duffy, "Conceptualizing Research on Written Management Communication: Looking through a Glass Onion," *Management Communication Quarterly* 3, no. 4 (1990), p. 430.
38. Henry Mintzberg, *Mintzberg on Management: Inside Our Strange World of Organizations* (New York: Collier Macmillan, 1989), p. 8.
39. Marie Flatley, "A Comparative Analysis of the Written Communication of Managers at Various Organizational Levels in the Private Business Sector," *Journal of Business Communication* 19, no. 3 (Summer 1982), p. 40.
40. Max Weber, *The Theory of Social and Economic Organization*, translators A. M. Henderson and Talcott Parsons and ed. Talcott Parsons (New York: The Free Press, 1947), pp. 324–86.
41. James G. March, "The Business Firm as a Political Coalition," *Journal of Politics*, 24 (1980), pp. 662–78.

Additional Readings

Bazerman, C. and J. Pardis. *Textural Dynamics of the Professions.* Madison, Wis.: University of Wisconsin Press, 1991.

Doheny-Farina, S. "Writing in Emerging Organizations." *Written Communication* 3, no. 2 (1986), pp. 158–85.

Liggett, S. "Speaking/Writing Relationships and Business Communication." *Journal of Business Communication,* 22, no. 2 (1985), pp. 47–56.

Lunsford, Andrea and Lisa Ede. *Singular Texts/Plural Authors: Perspectives on Collaborative Writing.* Carbondale, Ill.: Southern Illinois University Press, 1990.

McClelland, Ben W. and Timothy R. Donovan, ed. *Perspectives on Research and Scholarship in Composition.* New York: The Modern Language Association of America, 1985.

Mumby, Dennis K. *Communication and Power in Organizations: Discourse, Ideology, and Domination.* Norwood, N.J.: Ablex Publishing Company, 1988.

Volard, S. V., and M. R. Davies. "Communication Patterns of Managers." *Journal of Business Communication* 19, no. 1 (Winter 1982), pp. 41–54.

Yates, Douglas, Jr. *The Politics of Management.* San Francisco: Jossey-Bass, 1987.

Young, Art, and Toby Fulwiler. *Writing Across the Disciplines: Research into Practice.* Upper Montclair, N.J.: Boynton/Cook Publishers, Inc., 1986.

Discussion Questions

1. What are some advantages of written over oral communication?
2. Breakdowns in the written process are less difficult to locate than are breakdowns in the oral process. Discuss this statement.
3. Give an example of where two written messages on the same topic may have to be different to meet the needs of two different audiences.
4. We all suffer writing apprehension at some time. Give an example of your experience with this phenomenon.
5. What are some results of writing apprehension that go unchecked?
6. What methods might a person with writing apprehension use to overcome the apprehension?
7. In planning to write a document, what questions must a manager ask before putting words on paper? Should they all receive equal emphasis?
8. What is the difference between the product and process approaches to writing?
9. What are the advantages and disadvantages to the process and product approaches to writing? Do you favor one over the other? Why or why not?
10. What are some forms of collaborative writing you are likely to encounter in business?
11. Give five guidelines for effective collaborative writing. Which one would you consider the most difficult? Why?
12. Note several aspects of the context of managerial writing that make it unique.

CASE 4–1

Because you are known to be a good writer, the director of human resources has asked you to put together a seminar on written communication for employees in your company who think they need help. The seminar would cover basic concepts of written communication, letters and memos, and formal business reports.

Would you use the process or product approach or a combination in developing your seminar? What factors would you consider in making your choice or choices?

CASE 4–2

Richard Matherne has worked for you for a little over a year. During that time, his reports, letters, and memos have become increasingly delayed; and when they finally get done, their disorganization and sloppiness make it clear he spent little time on them. It would appear that you have a case of chronic writing apprehension on your hands.

What might you do to help Richard overcome this apprehension?

CASE 4–3

Assume you and two other classmates are working for a company that is about to purchase a fleet of 50 cars. The three top contenders are the Ford Taurus, the Honda Accord, and the Toyota Camry. Your group has been given the job of studying these three cars and recommending which to purchase.

Develop an outline that lists the major factors and subfactors you would consider and note who would do the research and writing of the various parts of the report. This outline should also serve as the table of contents for the report.

5 ESSENTIALS OF WRITTEN MANAGERIAL COMMUNICATION

You have been head of the consumer loans department at your bank for the past five years. Luck dealt you a nice hand when you took over this department. It was staffed by a group of intelligent experienced people who knew their jobs well and needed little direction.

Employee attrition and bank growth have changed all that. You recently had to hire four new employees. These new people are young, bright, and energetic; and you think they will probably work out well. There is, however, one problem that you are going to have to address soon.

The problem is how they communicate in letters and memos. Their writing is often cloudy and muddled. They seem to prefer long, abstract words and jargon. They often say things in very roundabout ways, and their tone is often stilted and impersonal. Their sentences are long and passive, and their paragraphs are also long and often poorly organized.

Since they all suffer from these writing ailments, you decide you might as well deal with them all at the same time through a two- or three-hour seminar. What are some of the pointers that you should try to impress upon these new employees to make them better written communicators? What are some of the characteristics of good, clear written managerial communication? These are the subjects that we will be dealing with in this chapter.

Dealing with apprehension, planning, deciding on the product or process approach, collaborating, and recognizing the unique world of the managerial writer are all important aspects of the preparation that should go into good written managerial communication. Once these preparatory functions have been carried out satisfactorily, the manager is ready to begin building the message that will accomplish the purpose to be served. More specifically, words need to be chosen with care and organized in a clear, comprehensive, and coherent fashion. These are the topics to be treated in this chapter.

Selection of Words

As discussed in Chapter 3, words are symbols that define the content of a message; thus, words should be carefully selected so the overall content will accomplish the communication's goal. Each word carries the potential for contributing to the effectiveness of the message, and each carries the potential for causing misunderstanding. Great care should therefore be taken to assure message effectiveness and avoid misunderstanding. The following principles should help writers accomplish their goals.

Principle One: Choose Words Precisely

While some areas of writing in business (contracts, job offer letters, personnel appraisals) may call for high levels of precision, managers would be wise to exercise care in choosing words in all their writing. And as they strive for this precision, they should remember that words can have both denotative and connotative meanings.

Denotative meanings are objective; they point to; they describe. Most people think of dictionary definitions as denotative meanings because these definitions are compiled from the common usages associated with a word. In other words, most people agree on the denotative definitions of terms—that is, they agree as long as there are no words similar in sound or appearance to confuse the issue. For example, can you pick out the correct word in each of the following sentences?

> The advertising agency that we just bought should profitably (complement, compliment) our manufacturing and distribution interests.
>
> My computer printer has operated (continually, continuously) for the last five years.
>
> The manager assured us that he had (appraised, apprised) his superior of the shipping problem.
>
> The secretary made an (illusion, allusion) to what had taken place in the cafeteria.
>
> To persuade upper management to take this action, we will need the testimony of an expert who is completely (uninterested, disinterested).

The confusion of one word for another when the two look or sound alike is called a *malapropism*. The term was coined for a character, Mrs. Malaprop, in Sheridan's book *The Rivals*. She was known for such confusing allusions as to "an allegory on the banks of the Nile." Along the same lines, consider the following excerpts from letters written to a government agency.

"I am very much annoyed to find that you have branded my son
illiterate. This is a dirty lie as I was married a week before he was
born."

"Unless I get my husband's money pretty soon, I will be forced to lead
an immortal life."

Gracie Allen and Norm Crosby built comedy careers on the use of mala-
propisms, but in business writing, a malapropism can produce embarrassing
humor at best and considerable confusion at worst. Neither is likely to provide
a boost to a manager's career.

Connotative meanings, on the other hand, are subjective. They can be
different for different people because they are determined largely by a person's previous experiences or associations with a word and its referent.

Consider the name of your school's library for a moment. What kinds of
mental association does it bring forth? Does it conjure up thoughts of hours
of research drudgery with frustration at every turn: volumes missing, articles
torn from journals, badly needed books checked out? Or does it rekindle the
excitement of discovering genuinely interesting and valuable information that
allowed you to develop one of the best term projects you've ever put together?
It's all a matter of individual experience and the resultant perceptual set.

Though connotations are subjective, people can manipulate the language
so as to try to bring forth either positive or negative connotations. An expression with intended positive connotations is called a *euphemism.* The words
slim and slender are much more euphemistic than are words like skinny,
scrawny, and underweight.

Many years ago, both the United States and Russia entered cars in a
European automobile show. For one particular event, Russia and the United
States were the only two countries with entries. The U.S. entry won. The
Russian newspapers described the results of this event in the following way:
The excellent Russian vehicle came in second, while the United States vehicle
came in second to last.

As advertisers and other interested parties try to portray life in the most
pleasant way possible, euphemisms have become a stable part of American
life. We thus hear talk of "senior citizens" and the "dearly departed." Men
are portly, and women are pleasantly plump, and fat around the waist becomes love handles. Such examples are relatively harmless, as they represent
slight make-overs of reality.

When, however, euphemisms are used in an effort to veil or gloss over
major human and environmental tragedies, we must recognize the language
abuse and the feeble cover-up. When an army accidently kills a number of
its own troops and officials use the expression "friendly fire" to explain the
tragedy, we should question the description. When "collateral damage" is
used to describe the deaths of innocent civilians in war, we must wonder at
the value assessed to human lives by the people using these descriptions.

Managers, as well as people in other careers, bear a responsibility to their constituents to use the language as accurately as possible. Managers should strive to communicate accurately and honestly and to avoid insulting the message recipients' intelligence. Additionally, they should try to act as responsibly as they can in using words as control tools and instruments of change.[1]

Before leaving the subject of precision, we should recognize the evolving nature of language. It doesn't stand still. It grows and it changes. Expressions that might once have been considered unacceptable become acceptable with widespread usage. For example, 20 years ago, the following expressions would have been frowned on:

Feel as a synonym for *think* or *believe,* as in, "I feel that you should accept the Smith offer." The thinking was that the word *feel* should be used with reference to touch or in describing one's physical or mental state.

Anxious in place of *eager,* as in, "I shall be anxious to see you Saturday." Does this mean you are going to experience great anxiety at the thought of seeing me?

Quote as a noun instead of just as a verb, as in, "He used a quote from Henry Clay to end his speech." Some would still say that *quotation* is the only noun form.

These usages are now being recognized in many of the most recent editions of widely accepted dictionaries. Language purists cannot rest on the learnings of 20 or 30 years ago. They must recognize the evolutionary nature of language and adjust to the changes.[2]

Principle Two: Use Short Rather than Long Words

Winston Churchill once said, "Big men use little words and little men use big words." People who are genuinely secure generally feel quite comfortable using simple words that are easy to understand. On the other hand, people who are relatively insecure can often be found groping for a string of difficult words to impress others with their vocabulary.

In general, short words are less confusing than long words. Long words, especially when strung out in the company of several other long words, can produce a communication barrier between writer and reader. Readers do not like to have to consult a dictionary repeatedly to understand the content of a business communication.

Written business communications should be economical and efficient. The following lists provide alternatives for some of the many longer words used and abused in business writing.

Instead of Using	Use
abundance	plenty
accumulate	gather
advise	tell
ameliorate	improve
approbation	approval
approximately	about
commence	begin
compensate	pay
conveyance	car, bus, etc.
demonstrate	show
expectancy	hope
explicate	explain
encounter	meet
locality	place
modification	change
subsequent to	after
utilize	use
utilization	use
terminate	end
unavailability	lack

We are not suggesting that the use of any words in the left-hand column will condemn a message to ambiguity and obscurity. The occasional use of a multisyllable word may even inject a little variety into a piece of writing. The caution here refers to the overuse of long, difficult words. When overused, they tax a reader's powers of comprehension—and patience—and create an unnecessary barrier to effective communication.

Principle Three: Use Concrete Rather than Abstract Words

In discussing a topic, a writer can choose from a range of words. This range, or continuum, might be thought of as a ladder that the writer might climb. This ladder moves from concrete (specific) words on the lowest rungs to the more abstract (general) words on the highest rungs.

Concrete words tend to be specific; they create clear pictures in the reader's mind. Abstract words are less specific and produce wider, more general interpretations of meanings. The ladder moves from something easily visualized to something that is more abstract, even vague, as shown by the examples in Figure 5–1.

The level of abstraction or concreteness depends in part on the reader's background, needs, and expectations. Abstract words and phrases threaten some readers and generate mistrust and confusion. They give rise to questions that the text may or may not answer: when? how many? who? how much?

FIGURE 5–1 **Abstraction Ladders**

| Levels
of
Abstraction | High ↑

Low ↓ | transportation
surface transport
vehicles
trucks
18 wheeler | environment
resources
wood
writing device
pencil |

---

which one? Notice the differing amounts of information in the following pairs of expressions:

Abstract	*Concrete*
She was a good student.	She earned the highest semester total in a class of 68 students.
. . . in the near future.	. . . by Friday, June 19.
a significant profit.	a 28 percent markup.
a noteworthy savings.	50 percent off the normal price.
very pure.	99 and 44/100 percent pure.
a high level of accuracy.	pinpoint accuracy.

Concrete words and phrases frequently create sharp, vivid images and stimulate reader interest. Forming concrete phrases may take more time and thought, but they are more efficient and stay with the reader longer than do abstract phrases.[3] Additionally, it has been shown that concrete writing takes less time to read, produces better message comprehension, and is less likely to need rereading than abstract writing.[4]

Principle Four: Economize on the Use of Words

Joubert once said, "Attention has a narrow mouth; and we must pour into it what we say very carefully and, as it were, drop by drop." Alexander Pope delivered a related admonition when he said, "Words are like leaves; and where they most abound, much fruit of sense beneath is rarely found."

The scientist, Pascal, wrote a 20-page letter to a friend in 1656. In a postscript, he apologized for the letter's length, saying, "I hope you will pardon me for writing such a long letter, but I did not have time to write you a shorter one." Pascal was testifying to the fact that conciseness, or economy of word choice, takes time and effort. But if we want to deliver as much "fruit of sense" as possible to our reader, we must carefully pour our words into attention's narrow mouth "drop by drop."

A practical, bottom-line reason exists to strive for word choice economy.

Wordiness costs companies money. Unnecessary words take valuable time to compose, dictate, type, read, and understand; and they waste paper and resources. Consider the following two versions of a business message.

> Enclosed please find a check in the amount of $82.56. In the event that you find the amount to be neither correct nor valid, subsequent to an examination of your records, please inform us of your findings at your earliest convenience.

> Enclosed is a check for $82.56. If a look at your records proves the amount incorrect, please let us know.

The second version takes 20 words to say the very same thing said by the first version in 41 words—a reduction of over 50 percent. Imagine how much more productive American businesses could be if everyone spent 50 percent less time writing and 50 percent less time reading.

Readers may wonder why people in business continue to be so wordy when such reductions are possible. Two likely reasons stand out. One is that writers often use wordy phrases out of habits that developed when they had to write 1,000-word essays in school. Such assignments may have led the essay writers to conclude that quantity was equal to quality.

The other reason is that untrained business writers often look to the files for a model when faced with an unfamiliar writing assignment on the job. When the files are filled with jargon and wordy and/or redundant expressions and when the novices mimic these writing patterns, the tradition of **verbal** waste continues. Note in the examples that follow how the wordy/redundant expressions on the left can be replaced by the more economical alternatives on the right.

Wordy/Redundant Phrases	*Alternatives*
due to the fact that	because
for the purpose of	for
for the reason that	since, because
the reason is because	one, not both
in order to	to
in the event that	if
with reference to	about
pursuant to your request	as requested
subsequent to	after
along the lines of	like
sole and only purpose	sole, only
true facts	facts
necessary steps required	requirements
even more complete	complete
manufactured in the past	manufactured, made
still continues	continues
same identical	identical
basic principles	principles
	(continued)

Wordy/Redundant Phrases	Alternatives
exactly equal	equal
surplus left over	surplus, remainder
enclosed herein	enclosed
look forward with anticipation	anticipate
consensus of opinion	consensus
a new innovation	innovation
advance planning	planning
past history	history
past experience	experience
absolutely finished	finished
personal opinion	opinion
from the point of view of	from
in as much as	since, because
in accordance with	as
in the case of	in
on the grounds that	because
at a later time	later (or a time)
within a period of one year	within one year
take into consideration	consider
agreeable and satisfactory	one, not both
demand and insist	one, not both
basic fundamentals	basics, fundamentals
a check in the amount of	a check for
for which there was no use	useless
that could not be collected	uncollectible

If today's emphasis on controlling costs is to be applied to business writing, the habits illustrated in the left-hand column will have to be broken and replaced by the alternatives in the right-hand column.[5] Though word-choice economy is admittedly time consuming and toilsome initially, it eventually becomes a relatively easy habit to apply.

Principle Five: Avoid Overused or Hackneyed Phrases and Jargon

Overused or hackneyed phrases are also referred to as trite expressions or cliches. Their appeal lies in the assumption that they have an accepted meaning; however, these words yield dull messages that lack creativity. Readers may understand what is written, but the message appears impersonal since the writer has injected nothing original into it.

Additionally, trite phrases often go out of style quickly; so a writer runs the risk of misunderstanding on the part of a reader not familiar with the time-worn expression. The following lists present some overused phrases to avoid and their alternatives:

Overused Phrases	Alternatives
white as a sheet	pale
busy as a bee	busy, working
smart as a whip	intelligent
follow in the footsteps of	pursue the same career
get it all together	get organized
	resolve the problem
stretches the truth	exaggerates, lies
clean as a whistle	sanitary, clean
rock of Gibraltar	reliable, dependable
really down to earth	realistic, honest, sincere
as luck would have it	unfortunately, luckily

The last of the preceding examples illustrates a significant shortcoming in the use of these hackneyed phrases. They can have more than one meaning. Furthermore, sometimes they are simply vague, and sometimes their logic can be questioned. These weaknesses are illustrated in the following examples:

"... *At* an early date" or "... *At* your earliest convenience."

Such phrases usually follow a request for information or for a favor of some sort. They are normally used by people who do not want to appear pushy. Such people don't realize two things. One is that the reader's "earliest convenience" may end up being something quite different from what the writer had in mind. The second is that businesspeople deal with deadlines all the time. They are not likely to take offense when asked for something within a range of time, if the writer concisely and courteously states the reason for the time range, for example:

"So that we may complete our report within two weeks, may we hear from you soon?"

or

"So that we may fill your order as quickly as possible, would you please send us this information by March 21."

Two other hackneyed expressions some readers interpret as presumptuous are

"Thanking you in advance ..." and "Permit me to say. ..."

Besides being time worn, mechanical, and impersonal, the first expression seems to say, "I fully expect you to comply with my request, but I don't want to have to take the time to thank you later, so I'll do it now." The second expression seems to seek permission, but the writer says what he or she wants to say before getting that permission. The second expression would be better left unsaid, and the first might be replaced by a conditional expression of appreciation that doesn't take the reader for granted, for example:

"I would genuinely appreciate whatever help you can give me in the matter."

Jargon is the technical language or specified terms that become part of the everyday vocabulary of an organization or discipline. Insiders know what the words mean, but outsiders may not. Jargon includes technical terms, acronyms, and terms used in special ways. When writing to readers outside the organization, managers should avoid using jargon. Rather, they should choose the layperson's version whenever possible to reduce the likelihood that the reader will misunderstand the message.[6] Additionally, some organizations are so large that the people in one part may not understand the jargon of other parts. Some caution might be exercised under those circumstances. The following lists illustrate how some of the jargon used in business might be simplified for the layperson:

Jargon	*Layperson's Version*
accounts receivable	firms or people owing money to the company
HVI bonus	extra pay for selling high-volume machines
maturity date	date that final payment is due
feedstock	raw materials used for manufacturing in the petrochemical industry
duplexing	photocopyist's term meaning copying on both sides of a sheet of paper
FAA	Federal Aviation Administration
abstract	history of the property
per diem	daily
assessed valuation	value of the property for tax purposes
current ratio	ratio of current assets to current liabilities

Readers may note that, with only one exception, the descriptions on the right are wordier than the jargon on the left. If these wordier versions assure understanding and prevent inquiries aimed at clarification, then the extra effort and words used will have been worthwhile. This is a decision managers must make when writing. Is the added clarity worth the additional words and potential for wordiness? No general answer is possible, so the manager must analyze each situation.

Finally, on the subject of jargon, note that acronyms can be particularly troublesome. In some situations, an acronym may be perfectly appropriate, while in other situations, it may cause a problem. For instance, in one division of EXXON, a DHR is the director of human resources; but in other divisions, it is a by-product of the chemical scrubbing process.

Principle Six: Use Positive Words that Convey Courtesy

As stated earlier, written communications present stimuli and generate responses. Generally speaking, the more positive the stimuli, the more positive the response. Conversely, the more negative the stimulus, the more negative the response. Behavioral scientists, for example, tell us that subordinates will either live up or down to the expectations communicated by their managers.[7]

Whether a manager is dealing with subordinates, superiors, peers, customers, suppliers, or others, she is likely to want her message to be well received. The positive wording of a request, of information, or even of bad news should increase the probability of a positive or at least neutral reaction by the receiver.

It should be stressed that the difference between positive and negative wording is not a matter of content, but of emphasis. Negative messages emphasize the least desirable aspects of a situation. As such, they are likely to arouse defensive or antagonistic responses from the reader.

The sender of an effective communication must establish credibility and goodwill with the receiver, and positiveness and courtesy aid the manager in developing these aspects of successful communication. The following examples illustrate the different impacts that can be generated by positive and negative wordings of messages:

> I cannot have the report ready by tomorrow morning.
>
> I can have the report completed by 3:00 P.M. Wednesday.

> You should not use Form A to file the weekly sales report.
>
> Form B is the weekly sales report form.

> Our customer representative cannot see you before Friday.
>
> You may see our customer representative at 9:00 A.M. Friday.

> We regret to inform you that we must deny your request for a promotion because you haven't earned enough continuing education credits.
>
> As soon as you earn six more continuing education credits, we can further process your request for a promotion.

> You were incorrect in thinking that the computer made an error in calculating your fines. The amount stated on your original notice is correct.
>
> As you requested, we checked the calculation of your fines. We find, however, that the sum reported on your original notice is correct.

In each of the alternative statements in the preceding examples, the writer has minimized negative information by stating it positively. The writer states what can be done or what has been done rather than what cannot be done or what has not been done.

Some phrases, because they seem discourteous, are likely to irritate readers. Avoid them to ensure a positive and courteous climate. Although we cannot (in fact, should not) totally avoid negatives, we need not overemphasize them. Words and phrases like "inexcusable," "you claim that," "your insinuation," "you failed to," and "obviously you overlooked," harp on the negative and should be avoided if at all possible. Chapter 6, on letters and memos, will explain this point further.

Being positive and conveying courtesy in word choice also involves non-sexism in language. The trend of recent decades away from sexual discrimination dictates that communicators must treat men and women as people, not just as members of one sex or the other. Furthermore, the language must reflect the existence of both sexes in most walks of life, since gender is rarely a prerequisite for an occupation.

Consequently, human resource managers use new, gender-neutral terms to describe jobs and thus avoid arbitrary stereotyping of people on the basis of gender. Also, pronouns and nouns that refer to one sex when both are being described (manpower) are now largely unacceptable. Likewise, expressions that belittle the behavior or qualities of one gender should be avoided. The following listings present unacceptable and acceptable terms.

Terms to Avoid

man (when referring to the species)	steward, stewardess
man-made	homemaker
manpower	dirty old man
grow to manhood	fairer sex
businessman	weaker sex
cameraman	old man, breadwinner
fireman	career woman
foreman	male nurse
salesman	lady doctor
	female realtor
	little woman

Acceptable

wife	mature
husband	business executive
state career (e.g., doctor, lawyer, editor)	camera operator
humanity, human beings, human race, people	firefighter
	supervisor
person	sales representative
human power, human energy, workers, work force	salesperson, salesclerk
	flight attendant

On the subject of sexism in writing, one particularly thorny problem is the generic or universal pronoun *he*. Until about 20 years ago, the standard practice had been to use he in impersonal constructions where both sexes were to be included: "Each person has his own problems to resolve." "In industry, a worker knows he needs skills." "Each person votes his own way." Authorities have noted that such constructions, when widely used, can make women feel ignored in the business world.

Fortunately, conscientious managers wishing to avoid sexist writing have several options available for avoiding such pronoun use. One is the use of plural nouns accompanied by plural pronouns. Instead of "A manager should motivate his employees," one could write "Managers should motivate their employees."

Another option is the use of "he and she," "his or her," "he/she," or "his/her." Though not entirely graceful, this option is considered acceptable. Writers should be careful, however, not to use this option too often, for it could hinder style and readability when overdone.

Another technique, one used widely in this book, is to alternate masculine and feminine pronouns. One paragraph may use *she* as the generic pronoun, while the next might use *he*. Naturally, if one paragraph deals with a subject addressed in the previous one, it would be logical to keep the same pronoun as that used in the first. While this technique avoids the generic *he*, it does not sacrifice style the way *he or she* sometimes does. Furthermore, traditional usage is spared, at least in part.

The last nonsexist technique we shall discuss is one that is not entirely satisfactory to strict grammarians. It uses plural pronouns for traditionally singular antecedent references such as *each, every, everyone, everybody*, or *anybody*. An example would be, "Everyone has their problems to resolve." Though not in accord with traditional rules of usage, this technique merely legitimizes what many people do as a matter of course.

Principle Seven: Use a Conversational Style

Sentences communicate effectively when they use everyday language, that is, when the words are those that would be used in face-to-face communication. A conversational style involves writing with words from a person's speaking vocabulary. Of course, the words should not include colloquialisms, slang, or jargon; but they should be the language most people would use in conducting everyday business.

A conversational style is particularly important in the writing of business letters, as it aids in developing the "you viewpoint." The you viewpoint involves consideration of a communication situation from the reader's point of view. It helps a writer to personalize letters, something most readers appreciate in business correspondence.[8]

Before writing, the sender identifies who will receive the information. He considers the reader's need for the information and, as much as possible, her knowledge, expertise, interests, culture, and value system. In effect, the writer "speaks" to the reader in the letter that results.

Some readers may be wondering if a conversational style and the you viewpoint are as applicable today as they might have been 10 to 20 years ago. Such a question might stem from the communications technology available today, a technology that makes form paragraphs and letters so easy to use. For many reasons, the answer is yes.

Even form paragraphs and letters can be written with a category of reader in mind, people who might have certain common concerns that have to be addressed. And even form paragraphs and letters can be written in a conversational style, as though they were composed by a human being rather than a jargon-stuffed computer. And finally, rather than rendering the you viewpoint obsolete, the technology available today makes it easier than it has ever been to alter and personalize a form paragraph or letter.

These first seven principles have focused on the selection of words. Since each word can influence the total message, each word deserves attention. The professional manager also needs to analyze the combination and organization of words strategically to ensure effective communication. The remaining principles will address the ways in which words might be grouped for best effort.

Organization of Words for Effect

The next five principles discuss organizational concepts to consider when putting words together to convey a message. The comprehension of a message is largely determined by the extent to which the writer uses these principles when writing.

Principle Eight: Keep Sentences Relatively Short

An anonymous member of President Warren G. Harding's cabinet once described the president's speeches in the following way:

> When he stands up to speak, battalions of words march out of his mouth and scour the countryside in search of an idea; and when they find one, they immediately trample it to death.

This quotation aptly describes many of the long-winded sentences we sometimes encounter in business writing. These seemingly never-ending constructions stem from a number of possible causes. One cause mentioned earlier is the need to impress. Some people shun the simple expression of simple thoughts in favor of dressing up simple thoughts to resemble the intellectually sublime. Consider the following example from a government report.

> It is obvious from the difference in elevation with relation to the short depth of the field that the contour is such as to preclude any reasonable development potential for economic utilization.

One would have to study the preceding message long and hard to figure out that the writer was, in fact, saying:

The field is too steep to plow.

On the other hand, some people engage in these lengthy, roundabout sentence constructions to avoid appearing forward or pushy, as in the following example.

During the past two weeks, we have been wondering if you have as yet found yourself in a position to give us an indication or whether or not you have been able to come to a decision on our offer.

Most businesspeople, who face deadlines daily, would not be offended if they were asked a question more to the point.

Have you decided on the offer we made you two weeks ago?

Another possible cause for unnecessarily long sentences is a combination of two writing maladies. One is the need to say everything that can be said about a topic in one sentence. The other is a lapse of memory regarding the value of the period as a punctuation mark that signals a rest stop for the reader. Note the confusion created by the following example and the improvement in the alternative version that follows it.

Although 17 people from our department (purchasing) attended the workshop, 9 of them, including Jerry Stoves, had no background for the topic of the workshop (advanced negotiating techniques) offered by the Purchasing Association of Chicago.

Last week 17 people from our purchasing department attended a workshop on advanced negotiating techniques. The Purchasing Association of Chicago offered the workshop. Of the 17 who attended, Jerry Stoves and 8 others lacked the necessary background.

Unnecessarily long sentences require readers to spend more time than necessary to understand the message. And the more time and patience required to understand a message, the less likely is the reader to look positively on the objective of the message.

Effective written communications are usually easy and quick to read. Studies show that most effective business sentences have an average length of 15 to 20 words. They also use no more than 10 long (three-or-more-syllable) words in every 100 words.

Effective sentences express one main point. Any connected phrases or clauses should complement or explain that point. When we place two or more important ideas in the same sentence, we reduce the importance of each and often confuse the reader.

Principle Nine: Prefer the Active to the Passive Voice

The active voice presents the parts of a sentence in the normal order expected by English-speaking people. The subject of the sentences is the actor and is acting in a way portrayed by the verb, and the action is directed toward the object. The following sentences illustrate the active voice.

David Leeper directed the meeting.
Donald Hebert enforced the policy.
Ridley Gros promoted the university.

The passive voice reverses the order of the parts in such a way that the subject is being acted on by the object in a way depicted by the verb.

The meeting was directed by David Leeper.
The policy was enforced by Donald Hebert.
The university was promoted by Ridley Gros.

Besides the reversed order and the slight additional length, the passive voice weakens the sentence construction by making the doer of the action the object of the "by" phrase. Furthermore, the passive voice carries the hazard of luring the writer into longer, more roundabout expressions.[9] For example, instead of writing,

The new president reorganized the administration.

we see

A reorganization of the administration was effected by the new president.

Though managerial writers should favor the active voice in the majority of the sentences they construct, they should remain open to the occasional use of the passive voice. It should be used occasionally for variety, if for no other reason. A long string of active-voice sentences eventually takes on a certain dullness that can be broken by the insertion of the passive voice.

Another reason to consider the passive voice is diplomacy. Notice that by eliminating the "by" phrase from a passive-voice sentence, we eliminate the doer of the action. At times, we may not want to identify the doer of the action, as in the case of delicate or guilt-inducing matters—especially if the doer of the action is higher up in the organization than we are. Note the following transformation for purposes of diplomacy:

Active: The director of purchasing has been soliciting bids from unauthorized vendors.
Passive: Bids from unauthorized vendors have been solicited by the director of purchasing.
Passive minus the "by" phrase: Bids from unauthorized vendors have been solicited.

With the preceding exceptions, managers should prefer the active voice when possible. It is more direct and to the point, and it gives appropriate emphasis to the actor and the action.

Principle 10: Develop Effective Paragraphs

Paragraphs serve a major function in written communication. They bring separate thoughts together and arrange them to convey a single important idea. A paragraph is a device to combine sentences to form messages: alone, these sentences might seem illogical and would not make the same point.

Six guidelines can help writers to develop effective paragraphs. First, present one major idea in a paragraph. A structured paragraph presents one major idea and whatever support is necessary for the development of that idea.[10] This paragraph quality is commonly referred to as unity. Writers who try to get more than one major thought into a paragraph generally create confusion.

Second, determine if a deductive or inductive pattern is appropriate. Deductive paragraphs present the main idea in the first sentence and the supporting ideas in the sentences that follow. Inductive paragraphs begin with the details or the support and end with the main idea. The deductive pattern is the most commonly used, but the inductive pattern is useful for persuasion.

Third, use a variety of sentence structures in a paragraph. A paragraph that contains all simple sentences can cause tedious reading; interest builds when a combination of sentence structures is used.

Fourth, structure paragraphs to emphasize important points. Emphasis can be accomplished in a variety of ways:

- Place important ideas at the beginning or end of the paragraph.
- Repeat key concepts.
- Place vital information in independent clauses and use complex sentences to provide supporting information.
- Use attention-getting words.
- Use mechanical devices to show emphasis, as is done by the "bullets" in this paragraph. Other techniques include framing, underscoring, using quotation marks, or numbering.

Fifth, keep paragraphs relatively short. Short paragraphs are easy to read and give more emphasis to the information they contain. Readers need visual and mental breaks so they can assimilate the message; short paragraphs help to achieve these breaks. In business letters and short memos, paragraphs usually average 5 to 6 lines in length; in reports, they average 8 to 10 lines. Exceptions, however, will sometimes be justified by the need for emphasis (shorter paragraphs) or by the complexity of the material (longer paragraphs).

Sixth, use transitions within well-organized paragraphs. Transitions help the reader to move from one idea to another. Place transitional words and phrases wherever they help develop smooth movement within the paragraph. Some common transitional words are *therefore, next, also, in addition*, and *finally*. Principle 11, on coherence, further develops this point. These six points are summarized in Table 5–1.

TABLE 5–1 Developing Effective Paragraphs

1. Present one major idea in a paragraph.
2. Decide if a deductive on inductive pattern is appropriate.
3. Use a variety of sentence structures in a paragraph.
4. Structure paragraphs to emphasize important points.
5. Keep paragraphs relatively short.
6. Use transitions within well-organized paragraphs.

Principle 11: Develop Coherence

With coherent writing, the relationship between sentences is clear. Sentences flow from one to another easily and smoothly. This movement from one thought to another is accomplished through transition, which is sometimes described as a bridge that connects thoughts. Transitions may be natural or mechanical.

Natural transition occurs when the content of the thoughts is such that the second flows naturally and smoothly from the first. Note the smooth movement from the first thought to the second in the following opening paragraph to a job application letter.

> Now that the Dillon Pharmaceutical Company is expanding its Western region, won't you need trained and experienced sales representatives to call on accounts in the new territory? With a degree in marketing and eight successful years in pharmaceutical sales, I believe that I am well qualified to be one of those representatives.

The first sentence introduces the ideas of training and experience, and the second sentence builds on that introduction.

At times, however, a writer cannot rely on the content of thoughts to show a clear connection between them. In such cases, the writer may have to use specific means to show that connection. These means are referred to as mechanical transition, and they can assume various forms. To show that connection, a writer can (1) repeat key words, to show the reader that the same subject is still being addressed, (2) use pronouns and synonyms, to avoid being too repetitious, or (3) use transition words, words that are used to connect thoughts and show a particular type of relationship between them. Table 5–2 lists some frequently used transition words.

In addition to making sure the thoughts within a paragraph flow smoothly, writers should be concerned that this quality of coherence pervades entire documents, including letters, memos, or longer reports.

More specifically, paragraphs, like sentences, need to be clearly related. Sometimes this relationship is shown through the use of transition devices such as those discussed above. At other times, an entire sentence at the beginning or end of a paragraph will be used to show the relationship of that paragraph to the one that precedes or follows it.

TABLE 5–2   Frequently Used Transition Words

but	accordingly	even so
next	again	on the other hand
thus	consequently	furthermore
then	otherwise	in summary
finally	besides	similarly
hence	conversely	as a result
still	to illustrate	in contrast
also	in addition	subsequently
and	however	for example

As we move into longer and more involved documents, the task of assuring coherence becomes more involved. For example, a 5-page section of a 25-page report may need an introductory paragraph to show what is to come in that section. It may also need a concluding paragraph or two to *tie up* the section and show how it relates to the larger purpose of the entire report.

Before we leave the subject of coherence, a word of caution may be in order. Though the transition devices discussed here can go a long way toward showing relationships to readers, we must recognize that a logical organization is the foundation of coherent writing. Writers must clearly understand why information is being arranged in a certain way. They must have a logical plan of presentation, for transitional devices cannot show relationships that don't exist.

Principle 12: Edit and Rewrite

The step of editing and rewriting is perhaps the most important to practice. Few writers possess the skill to write clear copy in one sitting.[11] The multitude of writing principles, approaches, and grammatical rules requires all writers to check their work.

Editing involves (1) reading what has been written; (2) examining it for clarity, concreteness, correctness, and conversational tone; (3) determining grammatical accuracy; and (4) organizing to assure coherence.[12]

Rewriting means rewording awkward sentences and phrases. It may even involve rearranging content and adding illustrations. Writers should not assume their prose is satisfactory after only one or two drafts. Few people write that well.[13]

The amount of editing and rewriting necessary will depend on the individual writer's skill. However, all good writers edit and rewrite. They even sometimes have someone else read their work before finalizing it. Others can often detect errors or confusing statements that writers miss because writers read into their messages what they want to communicate.

Though editing and rewriting may seem like time-consuming, tedious tasks, the results are worth the effort. By making the message clearer and easier to understand, editing and rewriting benefit the reader and reduce the likelihood of requests for later clarification. In the long run, they save time and money.

Summary

A writer who is ready to select words and arrange them for proper effect would want to keep certain strategic concerns in mind. The following principles provide guidance in the selection and arrangement of words for message clarity, comprehension, and coherence:

Selection of Words:

Principle one: Choose words precisely.

Principle two: Use short rather than long words.

Principle three: Use concrete rather than abstract words.

Principle four: Economize on words used.

Principle five: Avoid overused or hackneyed phrases and jargon.

Principle six: Use positive words that convey courtesy.

Principle seven: Use a conversational style.

Organization of words for effect:

Principle eight: Keep sentences relatively short.

Principle nine: Prefer the active to the passive voice.

Principle 10: Develop effective paragraphs.

Principle 11: Develop coherence.

Principle 12: Edit and rewrite.

The application of these principles does not come naturally and does not come automatically after an introduction. A good writer reviews the basics from time to time as a reminder of the qualities that contribute to effective written communication. Readers might likewise do well to keep these principles in mind as they read the next two chapters on business letters, memos, and reports and as they construct these larger business documents.

Endnotes

1. Barbara Czarniawska-Joerges and Bernward Joerges, "How to Control Things with Words: Organizational Talk and Control," *Management Communication Quarterly* 2, no. 2 (November 1988), pp. 170–93.

2. Donald J. Leonard and Jeanette W. Gilsdorf, "Language in Change: Academics' and Executives' Perceptions of Usage Errors," *Journal of Business Communication* 27, no. 2 (Spring 1990), pp. 137–58.
3. Sarah Ellen Ransdell and Ira Fischler, "Effects of Concreteness and Task Context on Recall of Prose among Bilingual and Monolingual Speakers," *Journal of Memory and Language* 28, no. 3 (June 1989), pp. 278–79.
4. James Suchan and Robert Colucci, "An Analysis of Communication Efficiency Between High-impact Writing and Bureaucratic Written Communication," *Management Communication Quarterly* 2, no. 4 (May 1989), pp. 454–84.
5. "Weak Writers," *The Wall Street Journal*, June 14, 1985, p. 1.
6. Peter Crow, "Plain English: What Counts Besides Readability," *Journal of Business Communication* 25, no. 1 (Winter 1988), pp. 87–95.
7. Sterling Livingston, "Pygmalion in Management," *Harvard Business Review*, September–October 1988, pp. 121–30.
8. Kitty Locker, "Theoretical Justification for Using Reader Benefits," *Journal of Business Communication* 19, no. 3 (Summer 1982), pp. 51–65.
9. Pamela Layton and Adrian J. Simpson, "Deep Structure in Sentence Comprehension," *Journal of Verbal Learning and Verbal Behavior* 14 (1975), pp. 658–64.
10. Thomas L. Kent, "Paragraph Production and the Given-New Contract," *Journal of Business Communication* 21, no. 4 (Fall 1984), pp. 45–66.
11. Larry Smeltzer and Jeanette Gilsdorf, "How to Use Your Time Efficiently When Writing," *Business Horizons*, November–December 1990, pp. 61–64.
12. Larry Smeltzer and Jeanette Gilsdorf, "Revise Reports Rapidly," *Personnel Journal*, October 1990, pp. 39–44.
13. Jeanne W. Halpern, "What Should We Be Teaching Students in Business Writing?" *Journal of Business Communication* 18, no. 3 (Summer 1981), pp. 39–53.

Additional Readings

Bogert, Judith. "Improving the Quality of Writing in the Workplace." *Management Communication Quarterly* 2, no. 3 (February 1989), pp. 328–56.

Dulek, Ron, and John Fielden. *Principles of Business Communication*. New York: Macmillan Publishing Company, 1990.

Gibson, Jane, and Richard Hodgetts. *Business Communication*. New York: Harper & Row Publishers, 1990.

Gilsdorf, Jeanette. "Executive and Managerial Attitudes Toward Business Slang: A Fortune-List Survey." *Journal of Business Communication* 20, no. 4 (Fall 1983), pp. 29–42.

Harcourt, Jules, A. C. "Buddy" Krizan, and Patricia Merrier. *Business Communication*, 2nd ed. Cincinnati, Ohio: South-Western Publishing Co., 1991.

Hilton, Chadwick, William H. Motes, and John S. Fielden. "An Experimental Study of the Effects of Style and Organization on Reader Perceptions of Text." *Journal of Business Communication* 26, no. 3 (Summer 1989), pp. 255–70.

Himstreet, William C., Wayne Murlin Baty, and Carol M. Lehman. *Business Communication*, 10th ed. Belmont, Calif.: Wadsworth Publishing Company, 1993.

Lesikar, Raymond V., John Pettit, and Marie Flatley. *Basic Business Communication*, 6th ed. Homewood, Ill.: Richard D. Irwin, 1993.

Limaye, Mohan, and Richard Pompian. "Brevity versus Clarity: The Comprehensibility of Nominal Compounds in Business and Technical Prose." *Journal of Business Communication* 28, no. 1 (Winter 1991), pp. 7–22.

Locker, Kitty O. *Business and Administrative Communication*, 2nd ed. Homewood, Ill.: Richard D. Irwin, 1992.

Lutz, William. *Double Speak*. New York: Harper & Row Publishers, 1989.

Mendelson, Michael. "Business Prose and the Nature of Plain Style." *Journal of Business Communication* 24, no. 2 (Spring 1987), pp. 3–18.

Stevens, Kevin T., Kathleen C. Stevens, and William P. Stevens. "Measuring the Readability of Business Writing: The Cloze Procedure Versus Readability Formulas." *Journal of Business Communication* 29, no. 4 (1992), pp. 367–82.

Suchan, James, and Ron Dulek. "A Reassessment of Clarity in Written Managerial Communication." *Management Communication Quarterly* 4, no. 1 (August 1990), pp. 87–99.

Discussion Questions

1. What are some advantages of short words over long words?
2. Give examples of some recent obvious euphemisms used by people in advertising, public relations, or government.
3. Give several examples of abstract words you have observed causing vagueness or obscurity.
4. What are some disadvantages of using hackneyed phrases and jargon?
5. What is some of the most common sexist language you have observed?
6. What are some advantages of conversational writing? Give an example of conversational writing that you have observed.
7. What is the difference between deductive and inductive paragraph organization? Give an example of each.
8. List some linking devices that may be used to develop coherence in a paragraph. Give an example where linking devices are used effectively.
9. What is the you viewpoint and how is it related to a courteous tone in your writing?
10. What are the average lengths for good, coherent paragraphs in business letters and memos and in business reports?

Exercises

5–1 Rewrite the following sentences to eliminate confusing, long words.

1. Bill received excessive remuneration for his promulgated work according to his professional colleagues.
2. What form of personal conveyance shall we solicit between the airport and the hotel?
3. The best operative unit for this interaction is the computer-assisted storage system.
4. Extrel, the computer company, has an inordinate influence on our purchasing agent.

5. The company terminated their contract with the city as a consequence of their ineffectual payment procedures.

6. The audience was demonstrating engrossment with the audio-visually mediated presentation.

7. We received approbation from the executive committee.

8. This antiquated procedure could be liquidated with a new word processing system.

9. Last year's profits were exorbitant in that division.

10. Our assets cannot be utilized to the maximum due to the unavailability of trained human resources.

5–2 Rewrite the following sentences using concrete words.

1. We received a lot of responses to our survey.

2. The personnel department has expanded in the last several years.

3. Profits are up throughout the industry.

4. If we don't receive the order pretty soon, we will have to cancel it.

5. Please send your reply as soon as possible.

6. We would like to receive as many bids as possible.

7. We need the shipment by sometime next month.

8. Extel is a large company.

9. Is it possible to meet next week?

10. We are expecting a rapid rate of inflation.

5–3 Reduce the length of the following sentences.

1. Record sales were set by the top division, from $48.2 million to $51.4 million; the home appliance division decreased from $67.2 million to $58.4; the big shock was in the electronic division, which saw a drop from $17.2 million to $14.9 million; but in all top management was generally pleased.

2. Management attributed the decline to several significant business environment economic factor conditions including higher borrowing interest rates.

3. At this point in time pursuant to your request we find it difficult to meet your stated requests as made in your letter.

4. The task force has been given the special responsibilities to accomplish the goals as stated in the letter sent yesterday by the executive vice-president to the task force chairperson who was assigned the position.

5. On the grounds that this action could be completely finished in a period of one year, it was not seen as a totally practical action to take.

6. The past history of the new innovations indicates that the product innovation department should be terminated and ended.

7. We received your recent inquiry of last week regarding our new products we just came out with.

8. For the reason that all the information was not completely available, no immediate decision could be made then.

5–4 Rewrite the following sentences to eliminate trite expressions and improve clarity.

1. Enclosed please find a check in the amount of $40.

2. Please be advised that your order will be shipped within a short period of time.

3. I enclose herewith an order to which you will please give your earliest attention and forward, with as little delay as possible, as per shipping instructions attached.

4. Your letter dated July 25 has been duly received and noted.

5. Referring to your letter of the fifth, we wish to state that there has been an error in your statement.

6. With reference to your letter of the tenth, permit me to state that there will be no interference with the affairs of your department.

5–5. Use more courteous words in the following sentences.

1. We cannot deliver all 100 units by Friday, March 6.

2. We don't provide second mortgages.

3. We are sorry that your total deposit on the trip cannot be refunded.

4. No. An extension will not be permitted.

5. We do not feel that you qualify for the excessive request that you made.

6. You are not qualified for this position.

7. The competition provided a much more favorable bid, and they have a reputation for fine service.

8. Sorry, but the product you requested is no longer available.

9. We are turning down your request for an extended vacation.

5–6 Give a nonsexist term for each of the following words.

businessman	airman
congressman	manpower
mailman	manmade
foreman	mankind
insurance man	salesman

5–7 Clarify the following message by using paragraphs and transitions and by generally following the guidelines presented in this chapter.

Most managers would agree that there are advantages to both the telephone and letters. Letters are more effective in some situations whereas the use of the telephone is best in others. So now the question is, "What are the advantages of each?" The telephone has the advantages of speed, immediate feedback, consuming less time, and cost. The advantages of the business letter is that a hard copy is available. Also, future reference can be made to it for legal reference. Also, enclosures can be included. One of the disadvantages of the telephone is that the conversation cannot be filed for future reference. Another advantage of the letter is that it can be circulated to other people who may be involved with the topic involved. Another disadvantage of the telephone is that you may not know if you are disturbing the receiver at a busy time during the day. The letter can be read when the receiver is ready to read it. All of these advantages and disadvantages must be considered when strategically determining the most effective communication tool. The greatest mistake may be to communicate via the most "convenient" media without considering the alternatives. Analysis of the situation is required to assure that the most effective technique is used.

6 STRATEGIES FOR LETTERS AND MEMOS

Sue Latimer, office manager for a branch of a nationwide real estate firm, has just returned from a three-day vacation. Now sorting through her in box, she finds that she has several letters and memos to write.

The office manager from the Houston office wants to know about the word processing software that Latimer has recently begun using at her office. Additionally, applicants for the vacant word processing position in her office have written to her, and she needs to request more information from several of them.

A colleague from another department sent her a memo while she was away requesting some procedural changes in her office that would make his life a lot easier. Unfortunately, the impact of these changes on her life and her department warrants a refusal of his request. She'll have to write him a tactful memo.

The vice-president of human resources wants her to send him a memo explaining her implementation of the company's vacation policies and procedures. It seems that someone from her office has made some anonymous inquiries suggesting she has not been following the company's guidelines as closely as she might have.

Finally, in addition to several inquiries she must make, she must prepare a letter refusing a claim made by the former office cleaning service whose work she found unsatisfactory. Her morning's work is cut out for her.

As earlier chapters have emphasized, written communication is an important part of a manager's job. One study of 837 business school graduates with varying years of experience found that they spent from 23.2 to 28.4 percent of their time at work writing.[1] And of all the different types of writing they do, letters and memos are certainly the workhorses of written managerial communication.[2] Another study (of 118 participants in a writing seminar) revealed that 63.1 percent of the managers surveyed wrote letters daily and 76.3 percent wrote memos daily.[3]

Letters and memorandums are probably the two forms of written communication that benefit most from the strategic considerations we have discussed in this text. The conciseness of letters and memos and the relatively detached atmosphere in which managers usually write them can help to ensure that the principles of reader adaptation and strategic analysis are carried out.

Unlike telephone conversations or oral presentations that require quick thinking and immediate response, the contents of letters and memos can be revised and refined until the proper style and tone are achieved. Finally, letters and memos lack the ponderous bulk that can make a report (especially a formal one) so hard to manage strategically.

Unfortunately, too many managers take letters and memos for granted. Perhaps because managers write so many, letters and memos frequently become impersonal things that convey information in a lifeless manner. Rather than being responses to a specific communication situation, many letters merely respond to types of situations. Thus, some managers write stock answers to claims and ignore, or at least discount, the factors making the claim unique and calling for adaptation.

Additionally, because they are such common and relatively informal media, managers often relax their guard in terms of the quality of their messages. One study of correspondence in 13 industries found punctuation errors in 43.7 percent of the correspondence surveyed, word usage errors in 52.2 percent, and sentence construction mistakes in 45.3 percent.[4]

Perhaps because letters and memos are so bound by conventions of format, the language used in them poses another problem. These media can easily become choked with stock phrases and cliches that turn the message into a ritual utterance: "as per your request," "reference your letter," and "herewith acknowledge receipt." Such letters and memos may sound right to some people, but they often communicate very little.

This chapter takes a strategic approach to letter and memo writing, emphasizing ways in which a writer can adapt correspondence to fit as nearly as possible the needs of the intended reader. The chapter also offers two general patterns for correspondence to fit as nearly as possible the needs of the intended reader. The chapter also offers two general patterns for correspondence situations you are likely to face as a manager and gives specific types of letters you can use for guidance in certain cases. Of course, use these models as a foundation only; as suggested in Chapters 2 and 3, each letter or memorandum a manager writes needs to be adapted to fit the audience and the situation.

Audience Adaptation

Audience adaptation is the first area we will consider. In many letter writing situations, a writer may not know the reader of the message very well. The writer may have only a claim letter or a letter of inquiry to respond to or may not know the reader at all. All the same, managers must carefully consider the strategies of letters they send to achieve the maximum benefit. Fortunately, we can recognize some letter writing strategies that suit most correspondence situations. The following discussion reviews some of these strategies.

You Attitude

The "you" attitude is the basis for the organizational strategies this chapter details for letters. Letter writers who have this attitude prepare messages matching their readers' interests. They do this by putting themselves in the reader's place. A letter writer with the you attitude begins by asking herself, "How would I feel if I were this person in this situation?"

The you attitude requires empathy, the ability to understand another's feelings; we show empathy when we say to a colleague who is having trouble solving a problem, "I know what you mean" or "I know what you're going through." It does not require sympathy, which requires experiencing the same feelings as another. Thus, a person can empathize with the writer of a claim letter without sympathizing with him by feeling his anger.

Basis of the You Attitude

The you attitude, which is reader oriented, grew out of an awareness that most people, especially when they are involved in business matters, are likely to be looking after their own interests. In reading a letter, they want to know how they can gain, or at least how they can minimize a loss. Writers having the you attitude keep this point in mind. Thus, when communicating in a positive situation, they seek to increase the positive impact of the news. In a negative situation, they seek to reduce negative impact while stressing reader benefits.

Few people have trouble using the you attitude in positive situations, but some balk at using it in negative ones, fearing that the you attitude requires that they show weakness. They think the reader might see the gentle denial of a request as weakness. This view is a misperception.

Anticipating Questions

To be effective, letter writers should anticipate the questions a reader might have. Thus, as they write the letter, they ask themselves just what the reader might be uncertain about and then answer the uncertainties so no additional correspondence is needed. A good measure of the success of a business letter is that it doesn't require a second letter to clarify points it attempted to make. Remember the five Ws: who, what, when, where, and why. Of course, it is also best not to forget the big one that applies to so many letters dealing with money to be paid or refunded: How much?

Stressing Reader Benefits

With the you attitude, the writer always strives to show the reader how she or he benefits from the letter. This is not to say that the writer gives in to the reader in each letter written. Rather, the writer designs the letter either to capitalize on or overcome the reader's attitudes about the writer as well as the issue at hand. Readers are shown that the situation benefits them as well as the sender of the letter.[5] Thus, a businessperson trying to collect on a past-due account might stress that the reader needs to pay the account balance to retain credit privileges at the store as well as an overall good credit rating. The potential for success in this case is far greater than if the credit manager had stressed only the company's interest by writing of its need for payment.

Avoiding Negatives

Avoid negatives and words with negative connotations, especially in negative situations. These words have a way of jumping off the page when read in a letter. While you can soften them with a concerned expression in a conversation, no such nonverbals are available in a letter. Watch especially words like *claim, allege, problem, damage,* and *regret.* A negative word can affect a reader's perceptions so much that he won't be able to read the rest of the letter objectively. Much of the positive efforts expended on letters can be lost with careless negatives in the final draft.

Metacommunication and the You Attitude

The you attitude shows itself in a variety of ways, some more obvious than others. One of these ways is metacommunication. Without reading a word, an individual receiving a letter can tell a lot about the sender and the sender's attitude toward the reader.

Stationery and Typing

Both the stationery chosen for correspondence and the typing job send messages to readers. A positive letter marred by smeared printing, stains, or hand corrections, or one typed on a cheap grade of paper creates static in the communication channel. While the written message says the writer cares, the physical elements of the medium suggest indifference at best. On the other hand, error-free letters with crisp black print on white, high-rag-content bond paper suggest professionalism and concern for the reader's feelings. Both letters may have the same wording, but both are not likely to achieve the same effect because they really do not say the same thing.

Tone

A second aspect of metacommunication is tone. The tone chosen for a letter should be friendly and sincere and, thus make the reader receptive to the idea presented in the letter. A conversational tone is appropriate in most letter writing situations. The writer, again showing the you attitude, visualizes the reader and writes as he might talk to the reader in that situation.

If the reader's feelings are not considered, a letter's tone can easily suggest irritation, resentment, superiority, or impatience. Of course, one can also lapse into flattery, bragging, and preaching, which can be just as irritating to a reader.[6]

Diction

The you attitude also influences a letter's wording. If the reader's interest is of central concern, show this by making the reader central as well. If the reader is saying, "What's in it for me?" she will have a hard time determining that if you write the letter in the first person with *I, me, mine,* or *we, us, our, ours.* A better focus is on *you, your, yours.* Thus, rather than saying, "We are sending the samples of the ads we worked up for Reality Industry's new pumps," a writer could easily substitute, "You will soon receive three samples of the magazine ads for your new pumps." The revision makes the reader rather than the writer the focus of the attention.

Jargon

Business jargon is another language problem that can cripple a letter. Someone who receives a business letter written in impersonal jargon may think he is corresponding with a machine that spits out words and phrases simply because they seem to belong regardless of their relevance to the situation. The writer is actually using these expressions like rubber stamps. A list of rubber-stamp cliches from business includes the following:

Enclosed herewith	Enclosed please find
I wish to advise	The above-referenced material
This is to inform you that	Said matter
Please be advised	Reference your letter
As per your request	We regret to inform

Instead of writing, "It is recommended that said matter be pursued," one would do better to write, "You should continue to market your product in that area."

Active Voice

The previous sentence, a clear improvement over its original, is also written in the active rather than the passive voice, another language consideration to keep in mind. As you may remember from Chapter 5, in the active voice, the subject does the acting. On the other hand, in the passive voice, the subject is being acted on. The passive voice is frequently impersonal; no one person or thing is mentioned as acting.

Expletive Constructions

Another language problem in letters lies in expletive constructions: "It . . . that" and "There is . . ." or "There are . . ." An expletive has no grammatical antecedent in a sentence, and it often diffuses the focus of the message by displacing or even eliminating people in the sentence. For example, in the sentence, "It is thought that interest rates will fall," the word *it* has no antecedent, yet *it* gets the main emphasis. The person who holds this opinion is unclear or unknown. A better wording would be, "I think that interest rates will fall." Naturally, a writer may find times when she wants to use "it . . . that" constructions to temper a suggestion: "It is suggested that you rewrite this proposal." Even there, however, "Please rewrite the proposal" is more acceptable.

Generally, "there is" and "there are" constructions merely waste the reader's (and writer's) time.[7] Rather than saying, "There are three options from which you can choose," say "You can choose from three options."

Strategies

Thus far we have looked at a variety of ways in which a manager can personalize messages to make them better understood and received by readers. Letters that have a conversational tone, focus on "you," avoid jargon, use the active voice, and avoid expletives help to convince readers they are dealing with considerate writers. However, one key element remains: overall strategy. The suggestions given so far for signaling concern for the reader will fall short if you do not organize the message in a manner that anticipates reader reaction. Let us look then at two basic strategies that, when used properly, can appropriately address anticipated reader reaction. The strategies deliver the message while promoting a positive image of the letter writer.

Direct Strategy

The direct strategy is used for letters conveying good news or neutral information. Someone receiving good news in a letter is pleased after reading it and appreciates having the good news as quickly as possible. However, if the letter's main idea is buried in the middle or is located near the end of the letter, the reader, who probably began the letter with some enthusiasm, loses interest and becomes frustrated at wasting valuable time searching for the main point. This frustration can affect the reader's attitude toward the letter writer: "Why can't he come right out and tell me?" Thus, such a letter in a positive situation with lots of potential for building goodwill can, instead, weaken and even destroy the positive impact of the letter.

Opening

A better strategy is to put the main point of the letter very early. A brief introduction might be needed to orient the reader, but this introduction should not delay the presentation of the main point.

Body

A letter using the direct strategy then provides the necessary supporting details: the reasons for the decision or the procedures the reader needs to follow. Of course, these details promote the letter writer or the company he represents, especially when the letter grants a favor.

Ending

A direct letter has a positive ending. Among the choices can be an offer to help, a statement of gratitude, or a repetition of any further action the reader needs to take.

Indirect Strategy

Unfortunately, not all letters communicate good news or even neutral information. Often, requests are denied, proposals are rejected, and job applications are turned down. The readers of such letters are naturally not pleased, but the letters need to be written. Obviously, negative letters have the potential for building resentment against the writer. The reader may believe his or her claim is valid, or proposal brilliant, or job application impressive; but the manager who received them must respond otherwise. The effective bad news letter conveys its information while creating a minimum of resentment. If possible, it should help to build goodwill for the company.

However, in too many negative situations, letter writers apply the wrong strategy. At the opening of the letter, when the reader's hopes are likely to be highest, these writers quickly reveal the bad news.[8] The reader's disappointment colors the rest of the message. In fact, an abrupt statement of the bad news may make the writer seem careless and even inconsiderate of the reader's feelings. Such an impression erodes goodwill.

A better strategy for negative situations is the indirect one. Using this strategy, a letter writer leads the reader logically to the bad news. By the time the reader reaches that point, she is convinced the letter represents the writer's best efforts. Successfully developed, the letter minimizes the reader's negative reactions and even builds goodwill. A comparison between the direct and the indirect approaches is presented in Table 6–1. Not all indirect letters convey bad news, of course. The persuasive letter is a specialized type of indirect letter that will be detailed later in the chapter because it differs in several respects from the typical indirect letter.

TABLE 6–1   The Direct Compared to the Indirect Approach

Direct	Indirect
Opening	**Opening**
Main point	Neutral buffer
Body	**Body**
Supporting information	Explanation and negative news
Ending	**Ending**
Positive close	Goodwill building

Opening

The indirect letter begins with a buffer, some neutral or positive statement that clearly relates to the letter's purpose or that both reader and writer agree on. The beginning might be agreement with a point in the reader's letter; it might express appreciation for the reader's candor in writing; or it might assure that the points the reader raised have been carefully considered.

The buffer is there to provide a neutral or even positive note, but it must not mislead the reader into thinking that good news follows. A good opening begins to let the reader down gently. Ideally, it would subtly set up the explanation that follows in the body of the letter. As we saw with the good news strategy, the reader expects things to go his way. When the indirect beginning fails to reinforce that expectation, the stage is set for the denial or bad news to follow.

Body

Next, the letter analyzes the circumstances or provides details on the facts that led to the bad news being conveyed. The challenge here is to be convincing. If you cannot be convincing, perhaps the bad news is not justified. The tone of this part of the letter is cooperative. The writer does not have to say, "Let's look at the facts," but the reader should have that feeling. Cooperation here is far better than a confrontation of the sort: "That was your version, here's mine."

Next, one implies or directly expresses the negative information. Naturally, a writer should not be so subtle in implying the negative news that the reader is left hanging. But any direct statement should be tactful and not blunt. The best approach is to subordinate the actual point where the bad news is stated in the middle of a paragraph, rather than allow it to appear at the beginning or end of one.

Ending

The next step is important: at the end, strive to rebuild goodwill. Depending on the situation, several options are available. One is to suggest another course of action open to the reader. In response to claims for goods, suggest others that are more durable or more appropriate for the reader's use. A letter rejecting a proposal might give another outlet for the idea. The discussion of specific letter types will detail these endings later.

Close the indirect letter on a positive, friendly note. Often, the effort at building goodwill is enough. Sometimes a little more is necessary. A manager might want to offer services or information. For example, a letter written to an old customer might have a catalog enclosed and end by looking forward to the reader's next order.

Handling Negatives

Since an indirect letter conveys bad news, it is potentially very negative. To minimize the damage to a company's goodwill, good writers generally avoid negative words in such letters. Although the task is a challenge, avoiding negatives pays off in the long run because the practice helps to keep the overall tone of the letter positive. The following three rules hold the key:

1. Place negative information at points of low emphasis.
2. Avoid *no* or *not* when possible.
3. Avoid words with negative connotations.

De-emphasize negative facts by placing them in a subordinate structure (a dependent clause, a parenthetic expression, or a modifier) rather than in a main clause of a sentence. In a paragraph, negative information should not be placed in a prominent position. Compare the following two short paragraphs telling a job applicant that the company has no job openings in his area.

> We do not anticipate any openings in the Baytown Company anytime soon since we have been laying off people in your field. You might apply at Rumfield and Company or Bennington, Inc., since they are adding to their staffs.

The writer could easily have softened the negatives by placing them in a less prominent position.

> I suggest that you apply for one of the engineering positions now opening at Rumfield and Company or at Bennington, Inc., rather than at Baytown Company. Currently Baytown's personnel needs are in other areas.

The second suggestion for avoiding negative writing (avoiding *no* and *not*) is easier to follow than it seems at first, and it usually leads to much more positive writing. In the revision in the following examples, the writer emphasizes what she *can* do, not what she *cannot* do.

> We cannot fill your order until you tell us what size grill your restaurant currently uses.

> We can fill your order as soon as you let us have your restaurant's grill size.

Please specify your grill size so that we may fill your order as quickly as possible.

The third suggestion (avoiding words with negative connotations) is one of the most important. Whereas *claim* and *state* might have very similar denotations, their connotations are widely separated. Writing to a person and saying, "You next claim that . . . " makes it sound as if the reader's is only one side of the story. Numerous words are likely to irritate or even inflame when they appear in bad news letters:

allege	argue
failure	mistake
claim	damage
regret	error
careless	broken

Specific Types: Direct

The direct and indirect strategies are useful for most letter writing situations managers face. Nevertheless, because some situations are so frequent (for example, the letter of inquiry) and because some are so sensitive (for example, negative responses to claim letters), several specialized versions of the direct and indirect patterns have developed. Table 6–2 lists the specific versions reviewed here.

The patterns suggested here are not absolute. After strategic analysis, a manager may determine that a different approach is appropriate. That kind of adaptation is to be encouraged since it helps to prevent following a mechanical pattern. First, we look at letters using the direct pattern; then we consider those following the indirect. Remember to use direct letters for good news and neutral, informative messages.

Letters of Inquiry

Perhaps the most common direct letter is the inquiry. Managers in all areas of business routinely need information to conduct their affairs. A manager might need to know about the performance of a product; another might want credit information about a client or wish to know about the qualifications of a job applicant. Since most readers see these requests as routine and reasonable, readers are likely to respond to them willingly.

If you project yourself into the position of a reader receiving an inquiry, you'll see why the direct approach is so appropriate. You are probably busy with other matters and need to know quickly what is required of you. When you receive an inquiry, you appreciate your reader's efforts to be direct and to let you know from the start what he or she wants.

TABLE 6–2 **Types of Direct and Indirect Letters**

Direct	*Indirect*
Letters of inquiry	Negative responses to inquiries
Favorable responses to inquiries	Refused claims
Claim letters	Persuasive messages
Positive responses to claims	

Opening

Make the inquiry clear from the start. One effective method is to begin with a question that summarizes the letter's objective. For example, an inquiry about a potential employee could begin with, "Would you please comment on Mary Keynes's qualifications to become a management intern? We at Infovend are considering her for the position, and she has given your name as a reference." The question beginning makes the purpose immediately clear.

Body

In many cases, the next step in the letter of inquiry is an explanation of the inquiry's purpose. In the example just given, the writer quickly made it clear that he is considering Keynes for a job. The amount of information a writer gives naturally depends on the situation. In an inquiry about the potential employee, the writer also probably would want to assure the reader that her response will be kept confidential.[9]

The main body of the inquiry needs to be efficiently organized; it cannot simply be a "fishing expedition" for information. Even after the purpose is clear, the reader usually needs guidance to answer the inquiry satisfactorily. Given as much of the sample letter about Mary Keynes as we have so far, it might be answered several ways depending on how the reader projected the writer's needs—or it might not be detailed at all. Thus, the next part of the letter should set out the areas requiring information, plus any necessary additional information. Numbering the questions may also help the reader respond.

Ending

The close of the letter of inquiry is friendly and builds goodwill. In some cases, it is appropriate to offer similar services. In situations where a purchase might follow, the writer might ask for a speedy reply.

Let us look at the complete letter written about Mary Keynes. Note that in this inquiry about a person, the author has emphasized confidentiality, an advisable practice in this kind of letter.

Dear Professor Renton:

Would you please comment on Mary Keynes's qualifications as a management intern? Infovend is considering her for the position, and she has given your name as a reference. Of course, whatever information you give us will be held in strictest confidence.

1. How well does Keynes manage time? Is her work punctual?
2. Did you have a chance to observe her under pressure? If so, does she manage well or does pressure adversely affect her performance?
3. How well does she relate to her peers? Please comment on her relationship with them: Is she a leader or a follower, gregarious or shy, and so on?

I look forward to hearing your comments on Keynes's qualifications and will appreciate whatever insights you can share with us.

Sincerely,

Tom Inman

Favorable Responses to Inquiries

Inquiries naturally need answers. The favorable response to an inquiry is a direct one, as the reader is pleased to get the requested information or item.

Opening

The letter begins by identifying the request to which it responds. This identification appears in the subject line or in the first sentence of the letter and is just enough to jog the reader's memory. The letter opening also makes it clear the reader's request is being granted.

I found Mary Keynes, the subject of your June 5 inquiry, to be one of the most promising students I have ever taught.

As-Best-As Filing Cabinets have all the features you mentioned in your March 4 letter and several more you might be interested in knowing about.

I am pleased to answer your September 14 inquiry about our experiences with the M-102 Security System.

The writer can begin directly answering the most general of the questions originally asked (as in the first two examples) or, less directly, by agreeing to respond to the question originally posed (as in the third example).

Body

The way in which you organize the letter's body varies depending on the original inquiry. For an inquiry that asked one main question, the details in response appear in order of importance. If the letter responds to a series of questions, it normally answers them in the order asked. If the original is really a request (for example, "May we use your facilities for a club meeting?"), the body gives necessary conditions for use.

Not all responses to inquiries are all good or all bad news. Thus, although a manager is willing to answer most questions, some topics are confidential. In these cases, the denial is subordinated and appears after the writer explains why. For example, the response to the inquiry about a company's experiences with the M-102 Security System may withhold some details for security reasons.

Close

The positive response to an inquiry continues to be positive in the close. Note these closes to the letters whose beginnings we gave earlier:

> If I can help you with any other information about Mary, please call me or write to me.

> If you need any other information on how As-Best-As Filing Cabinets can meet your storage needs, please let me know.

> If I can help you by answering any other questions about our experiences with the M-102 Security System, I'd be delighted to. I think you'll be pleased with the system.

Claim Letters

Another type of direct style letter is the claim letter. Many people are surprised to find it in the direct category. Once again, project yourself as manager and consider how you would feel receiving a claim letter. Here you have a consumer or client who is not satisfied with your company's products or work. This dissatisfaction leads not only to a loss of goodwill and revenue, but it also reflects badly on your ability as a manager. Naturally you would want to find out quickly what the problem is and resolve it.

Opening

Everyone appreciates a letter that comes straight to the point of the problem. Even though the claim letter deals with something negative, it is written using the direct form. From the writer's perspective, directness strengthens the claim. In fact, some readers may interpret indirectness as lack of confidence in the claim being made. Indirectness would thus be a strategic error.

Early in the claim letter, a writer should include details about the faulty product, service, or sale. One place to present this matter is the subject line. Which details to include would depend on the situation, but they may include invoice numbers, dates, and product identification or serial number.

Stating the problem at the start relays assertiveness. Another good tactic that makes the letter convincing is to include the significance of the problem to the letter writer or his business. For example, a warehouse manager whose new intercom system failed might write:

> The new intercom system you sent us (Invoice #16789) has broken, thus considerably slowing the processing of orders in our company warehouse.

Body

The next step is logical: the facts of the case need detailing. In the intercom example, the writer discusses how the system broke down and the possible cause. Naturally, the writer does not need to be an expert analyst; but the more facts she includes, the more convincing the argument. If appropriate, she may also wish to detail the damage that resulted.

Of course, detailing the problem requires tact and forbearance. The letter writer feels justified in writing about the problem, but she refrains from attacking the person who sold or installed the product or its manufacturer. Name calling or accusations do little, if any, good and may create reader resentment, which usually precludes a favorable settlement. Abusive letters are best left unsent.

The next part of the letter states what the reader wants: What will set things right? Unfortunately, some letters end before this point. An unhappy writer complains and then forgets to say what he wants. Specifying the action or amount of money needed for satisfaction is usually preferable. Occasionally, the settlement can be left up to the reader if the situation is routine.

The writer may also wish to include a deadline for action on the matter. Naturally, a deadline needs something to back it up. One authority recommends that the writer make a threat that he is willing and able to carry out if the situation is not resolved.[10] Weigh threats carefully. They can be counterproductive. For consumers, these last two tactics might be more appropriate, although a manger might want to threaten to see a lawyer or may threaten to withdraw business.

Close

All that remains is to close the letter. Once again, avoid negativity. If the writer threatens to take his business elsewhere, the reader may lose any motivation for cooperation. End by expressing confidence in the good faith of the reader or by expressing intended gratitude for the early resolution of the problem.

Let us look at the rest of the claim letter about the faulty intercom and see how it illustrates these points.

Dear Mr. Packard:

The new intercom system you sent us (Invoice #16789) has broken, thus considerably slowing the processing of orders in our company warehouse.

Although the system worked fine immediately after installation, we began to notice problems with it during stormy weather. When it rained, static garbled many of the messages. Finally, during one heavy downpour, the main transmitter stopped working and began smoking.

We are shipping the transmitter to you via Brown Trucking. We would like it either repaired or replaced. Your prompt attention will help our warehouse to return to normal.

Sincerely,

Patricia Murranka

In this letter, the manager detailed the problem her department faced, yet she resisted accusatory language. She set out her experience with the system and provided enough information for the manufacturer to diagnose the problem. The ending is positive, yet assertive.

Positive Response to a Claim

The next direct letter is the positive response to a claim. While the use of the direct order is unquestionable, this type of letter still challenges the writer who is aware of the unpleasantness the reader experienced. The reader may have lost sales or may have been uncomfortable or inconvenienced. The challenge here is to rebuild goodwill and, in many cases, restore faith in the product. The reader who does not believe in the product will buy elsewhere next time. Occasionally, especially when dealing with angry customers, the letter responds to a very unpleasant or accusatory missive. The writer must not rise to the bait.

Opening

Begin the adjustment grant with the good news. The reader needs a reminder to recall the situation, but this reminding should be done quickly. Thus, the letter responding to the claim letter about the faulty intercom might begin:

> Your transmitter is now in working order and should arrive in Cedar Rapids by truck in the next few days.

Body

After the good news, the development of the rest of the letter depends on the situation. Routine cases need little explanation. In many cases, however, the reader needs more. It is usually necessary to explain what went wrong, and it is often a good idea to stress that the problem is corrected and will not recur.

Occasionally, you will need to explain the proper use of the product to a reader who unintentionally misused the product. In such cases, the reader's goodwill is worth the cost. This explanation needs to be tactful and is most effective when presented impersonally, as in the second example that follows.

> You left the valves open on the unit. As a result, your heater was on constantly and wore out.

> The valves leading out to the unit must be kept tightly closed to reduce the demand on the heating unit.

In the explanatory material and the close, avoid apologies. Common courtesy seems to dictate an apology, but it often serves to open old wounds:

We are so very sorry for all the problems we must have caused you.

Now the reader remembers all the inconvenience he endured, and the goodwill is erased.

Close

The closing of an adjustment grant is positive. It anticipates continued good relations with the customer or client and may include information on other products or services the company offers. Look at the response to the claim on the intercom system. Note how the writer builds goodwill by discussing the advantages of the product. He also refrains from stating the fault was the electrician's rather than the manufacturer's, although he has taken steps to protect the equipment in the future.

Dear Ms. Murranka:

Your transmitter is now in working order and should arrive in Cedar Rapids by truck in the next few days. Please call your electrician when it arrives so his installation will protect the warranty.

You reported that the system had static in it during rainstorms and that it smoked when the system stopped working. I've checked the new patented fusible ground lead and found that it had melted, as it was designed to do, and protected the transmitter and you from electrical shock.

When your electrician installs the transmitter, have him check the unit's grounding. At present, when it rains, the unit is shorting out because of incomplete grounding.

You might be interested in our new security alarm system that hooks into the existing intercom system. The enclosed pamphlet gives you the details. We will be glad to discuss its installation with you.

Sincerely,

Robert Packard

Specific Types: Indirect

Most managers cannot comply with all of the requests made of them and still find enough time to do a good job and make a profit for the company. In those situations where a writer cannot grant a request to a reader, the response is best organized according to the indirect plan.

Negative Responses to Inquiries

The strategy for constructing negative responses to inquiries requires thought and planning. When requests need denying, use a bad news strategy. Reasons appear first, followed by the refusal.

Opening

The opening of the letter needs to remind the reader of the original request but in such a way that the bad news is not given away. Remind the reader by a subject line reference or by making an initial statement that clearly recalls the request. This initial statement should also serve as a buffer that does not imply either a positive or negative answer. Furthermore, a truly effective opening leads logically into the presentation that follows.

Suppose, for example, you received a letter from a researcher inquiring into the population sample used to determine your company's marketing strategies. Since such questions deal with proprietary information that the company keeps confidential, you must deny the request. At the same time, you do not want to refuse directly. Your response might begin as follows:

> The results of your study of population samples should prove interesting, as most companies protect these data because they are so central to their marketing strategies.

This introduction gives no false hope for a positive reply, yet it does not deny the request yet. However, it lays the basis for that rejection. The rest of the letter develops the approach.

Body

From this beginning, the letter moves into a discussion of why the request cannot be granted. The writer considers the reader and chooses examples or reasoning likely to convince the reader that the writer's is the only viable solution. For example, in the letter referenced above, one could appeal to the reader's own experience as a researcher who has spent hours developing ideas. Similarly, after great expense, your company had developed ideas that it applies to its own needs.

Once the writer has given the reasoning, he can state the refusal, unless it has been clearly implied. At the same time, a refusal should be final. Occasionally, writers refuse requests so vaguely that the reader still sees hope for his request. The well written refusal letter reasons the reader out of the original request. However, the reasoning does not suggest the original request was unreasonably ill advised or misdirected.

Close

Close the letter positively to build goodwill. The close can be a wish for success in the reader's work or a suggestion for some other sources of information the reader could use. Avoid apologies, however; they might suggest the door is still open.

In the letter refusing the request for information on marketing strategies, note how the writer implies the refusal rather than states it. Note also that he makes no apology for his refusal.

Dear Ms. Leeper:

The results of your study of population samples should prove interesting, as most companies protect these data because they are so central to their marketing strategies.

At Flo-Sheen Fabrics, we develop our marketing strategies only after our test market has had a chance to examine our new fabrics. Before we settle on any one strategy, we test out all market options using the group as well. As a researcher, you can surely appreciate the countless hours that go into any marketing campaign.

Our test market provides us with valuable feedback on our products and planned strategies, both of which we alter before marketing nationwide to reflect their needs.

We keep the population sample used for our marketing analysis confidential both to protect their privacy and to help us keep our competitive edge. Our competition would have an unfair advantage over us if they were able to know in advance what products we planned to introduce or what strategies we would use.

If your interest in population samples is general, you might look into any text on statistical sampling. That will give you the considerations managers must take in selecting population samples.

Sincerely,

Sheila Hebert

Refused Claim

A greater challenge than the negative response to an inquiry is the refused claim. In most cases, the person making the claim believes she is justified; her interests have been damaged by what she sees as bad products or services. However, for whatever reason, the writer has determined that he must reject the claim.

In doing so, the writer must avoid negatives and build goodwill. The key is empathy. How would the writer want to be treated in this situation— probably reasonably. To respond in an authoritarian or a condescending fashion would be foolish. The language of the letter must be positive and selective. Most likely, the reader will be sensitive to any possible nuances.

Opening

The claim refusal must begin as would any other negative letter: with a buffer. This buffer can refer to the reader's original claim as its subject, or it can be an expression of appreciation for the reader's frank letter—some opening that brings the reader and writer together neutrally.

The effective opening also indicates the line of reasoning to be followed in the letter. Take, for example, the opening sentence, "Whitlow Co. does guarantee its sump pumps for 18 months against breakdown in normal operation or under normal circumstances." The reader is reminded of the original claim and is introduced to the line of reasoning developed in the letter: "normal operation" and "normal circumstances." Another letter opening might be the following: "Your recent letter shows that you are a person who appreciates being treated fairly and openly. You will be interested in what we have found in our investigation into your questions."

Body

The body of the letter details the writer's findings. This explanation should be objective and convincing, but it should avoid a my-side, your-side dichotomy. One effective tactic in some situations is to describe the effort that went into investigating the matter. For example, a negative response to a warranty claim may emphasize the laboratory tests made on the broken part. This detail is useful because it projects a caring image; the decision made is not just some automatic response.

The refusal should be given once the reasons are clear. Of course, the refusal should appear at a point of low emphasis. If the refusal is based on company policy, the policy should be clearly explained.

Close

Most claim refusal letters close with an effort at resale. If the customer has been treated fairly in a reasonable manner, she may stay with the product since the company was not at fault. Frequently, it is a good idea to get off the immediate topic by mentioning an upcoming sale or by sending a recent catalog. Apologies do not belong in the close, though. If the action is justified, why apologize? Doing so may only invite further correspondence on an issue that should be settled.

Dear Ms. Clark:

Whitlow Co. does guarantee its sump pumps for 18 months in normal operation under normal circumstances. After your recent letter, we looked closely into the questions you raised.

Our laboratory examined the returned pump and found that the entire unit had been submerged for some time. This submersion was in keeping with the newspaper accounts of heavy flooding in your town last month. Apparently the area where your unit was located was also inundated. While the pump is designed to take care of normal seepage, it is mounted at least 18 inches above the basement floor to protect the housing and pump. Like most motor-driven appliances, the pump must be kept totally dry, as it is in normal circumstances.

You might be interested in another model pump we offer, the SubMerso. Its waterproof housing withstands even prolonged immersion. The enclosed pamphlet details its capacities. We'll be glad to answer any questions you might have on it.

Sincerely yours,

Lionel Naquin

Persuasive Messages

The persuasive message is another place where the indirect strategy is appropriate. A manager uses the indirect persuasive strategy when trying to persuade others to do things they might not ordinarily wish to do. A manager might need to write a persuasive letter to convince a reluctant client to pay his bill. Another might write a persuasive memorandum to gain a colleague's support on a project.

The persuasive strategy is indirect because the reader needs to be convinced the author's goals are his goals before the reader can be asked to cooperate with the author.

Opening

The persuasive letter opens by catching the reader's interest.[11] One effective way of doing this is to show the reader that her goals are your goals. The best way to show this identity of goals is to show her that the letter deals with matters the reader is interested in. At the same time, since the message must catch the reader's interests, the opening must be brief.

Body

The body of the letter consists of several parts. First, it must set out the problem the writer and reader share. Then, it must reveal the solution to the problem—the solution that the writer wants the reader to embrace. This section reflects careful strategy, since the reader's possible objections must be anticipated and answered. In this section (which can consist of several paragraphs), the writer must stress the benefit accruing to the reader as a result of the solution.[12]

Close

The ending of the persuasive letter is important. The effective persuasive letter does not end after the proposed answer is revealed. At the end, after the reader's interest has been aroused, that interest must be channeled into action. Otherwise, interest will wane with nothing resolved. The call for action should be specific: a meeting, an order, a payment, an interview, a change in procedure. An action must be prompt. Delay only lessens the probability of action.[13]

The following job application letter illustrates the implementation of the persuasive strategy.

Dear Mr. Harris:

Now that Lynch's is about to open its third department store in Jonesboro, won't you need a sufficient staff of part-time employees to supplement your full-time workers? I believe I have the background and motivation necessary to become one of your most productive part-time workers.

As a junior marketing major at State University, I am this semester beginning to take my required marketing courses. I could apply what I learn over the next two years to my sales work at Lynch's. The job references listed on the attached resume will all attest to the fact that I am very energetic in and enthusiastic about my work.

Another reason I think I would make a good part-time worker for you is that I am very much interested in pursuing a career with Lynch's upon graduation. I would thus see these two years as a testing period to prove myself, and you would have the two years to decide whether or not you would be equally interested in me.

If I have described the kind of part-time salesperson you want at Lynch's, may I have an interview to further discuss the position? I can be reached at 992-8403, and I can be available at a time convenient to you.

Sincerely,

John Morris

Memorandums

While letters are the most frequently used medium of communication between firms, memorandums are the most frequently used within an organization.[14] The memo is an efficient, straight-forward kind of communication. However, because the reader of a memo is only human, the writer needs to adapt strategically. This is especially true when one is writing to employees at a different level within the organization, or who possess a less specialized knowledge of the subject, or when the memorandum deals with sensitive matters.

Memorandums, while useful, do tend to proliferate in some organizations to the point that they cease to be effective. Too much communication may create a negative image in the minds of the recipients. One authority calls the tendency to shower others with needless memorandums *memoitis*.[15] The tone of memorandums is usually less formal and more personal than it is with letters.[16] At the same time, it is important to show respect where needed;

one shouldn't be so informal with higher level managers that they are offended.

Format

Memorandum formats differ from one another in minor details; but they generally have four standard headings: *To, From, Subject,* and *Date.* The "from" line offers few problems. However, if needed, a writer can add to her authority by adding the names of others here as well—assuming she has their agreement.

The subject line has obvious value in situations requiring directness. However, when used properly, the subject line can serve as a buffer in situations where the reader is likely to feel disappointed or might need persuasion. Keep the subject line to a reasonable length. Eliminate unnecessary words. Using key words in the subject line will often aid in the memorandum's later retrieval from computer files.

The date is a key feature as well, since it can protect your interests by showing when the ideas in the memorandum were shared.

Just as with face-to-face interactions, memorandums sent in an organization typically have a set protocol one should respect. This means paying attention to the format generally used as well as noting any subtleties related to whom the memorandum or its copies are sent.[17] Often, by noting at the bottom that the memorandum is being sent to a superior, one sends the message that one has access to that superior. This may not be your intent, or this may not be the way you want it read. Similarly, be sure that you copy in your immediate superior when contacting his or her superiors.

Occasionally you will be called in on special projects that require you to report to an individual at a higher level. Here it is often wise to copy in your superior to keep him or her aware of what is going on. Even in cases where that individual is not immediately involved, he or she appreciated knowing about events.

The final format element to note is the need for either your initials or signed name on the memorandum. What is used varies from one group to another; use the practice common with your employer.[18]

Uses

Memorandums serve a variety of uses within an organization. We have listed the most common below. You may see other practices where you work as well.

Communicating to Groups

Managers find the memorandum useful for communicating the same information to several individuals at once. The memo not only saves time over talking, but it also ensures that each person has the same information.

Fixing Responsibility

The memorandum can be a valuable management tool in other ways. For example, it can fix responsibility for actions. A manager who uses memos for giving assignments has a written record if questions of responsibility arise later.

Communicating with Opponents

Managers quickly learn to appreciate the memo as a way of communicating with those they cannot get along with. Personal dislikes crop up in any organization from time to time, but memos bridge the gaps that may ensue. The message gets delivered without one's having to bring the two factions together.

Communicating with the Inaccessible

The memo is handy for dealing with people (especially supervisors) who are hard to reach. Sometimes, those who are too busy to see a subordinate can be reached by memo. A series of memos can also be proof of past attempts to contact a superior if problems arise.[19]

Memorandum

TO: All Salaried Employees

FROM: Alan Reynolds, Director of Human Resources

DATE: October 3, 1993

SUBJECT: Changes in Payroll Practices

We've made a couple of changes in the payroll procedures that should alleviate some of the bottlenecks that have delayed paychecks in the past few months.

First, paychecks will no longer be mailed out. You will be given your check for the month on the last working day of that month. Direct deposits will still be made to your checking or saving account provided you use direct deposit for only one account. Multiple deposits will no longer be made.

All travel and expense reimbursements received before the twentieth of each month will be included in your monthly paychecks. Those requests received after the twentieth will be paid in the next month's paycheck. Requests for reimbursement will no longer be paid by individual checks as they have been in the past. Of course, these expense reimbursements will not be taxed.

These changes in payroll should help to guarantee that the delays we've seen before will be a thing of the past.

Types of Memorandums

Memorandums tend to fall into two groups: notifications and requests. Both these general types can be directed to large groups within a firm (especially notifications), and both can be directed to individuals.

Notifications

Notifications concern policy changes, meetings and conferences, and personnel changes (including promotions). Other types of notifications include status reports, for example, progress and periodic reports. The following memorandum is a typical notification.

Memorandum

TO: Sam Bruno, Assistant Controller

FROM: John Pettit, Controller

Date: July 23, 1993

Subject: Developing Procedures for Spending Cuts

At its quarterly meeting, the board of directors mandated a 15 percent reduction in overall expenditures in the company during the next fiscal year. The controller's office is to hep determine where these cuts can be made.

Please develop a procedure for determining where the company can make cuts during the next fiscal year without radically affecting production and our public image. This procedure should include input from all levels of the organization. Be sure that our own office gives detailed suggestions!

I would like your recommended procedure by a week from next Friday so that I can report back to the chairman by the next Tuesday. If you have any questions, see me.

Requests for Action

The nature of the request-for-action memo dictates organization. When a manager requests action that typically falls under her jurisdiction, direct order is appropriate and the memo begins with a clear subject line. When the requested action may meet with resistance, a less specific subject line and a more persuasive strategy are appropriate. Direct or indirect, these memos often require enumeration of steps and careful wording for successful implementation. Naturally, written requests for action are inappropriate for minor tasks that can be accomplished through verbal directions. Note that in addition to being a notification, the preceding memo also requests action from a subordinate.

Form Memos

Occasionally, a particular type of memorandum may be used so frequently that a form is developed. The one most widely seen is the "While You Were Out" phone message record. Forms can also be used to report on routine problems or activities within an organization. The writer merely fills in the necessary blanks.

Another form is the "Memorandum to the File" or the "Memo for Record." It records information about meetings, telephone conversations, impressions of people, observations of potential problems, and ideas that might occur to the writer. While not usually intended for general circulation, this memo is useful later when facts need to be recalled. If innovations are recorded, they can be reviewed later and developed and implemented where appropriate.

Political Uses in Offices

The memorandum is a much more strategic tool than first meets the eye. In fulfilling its ostensible task of communicating announcements and requests for action within an organization, it is often put to other strategic uses. The uses are detailed in the paragraphs that follow, but they are not necessarily recommended as models for behavior; some practices are reprehensible, but managers should be aware of them.

The memo can be of great value in a manager's career, or it can be a stumbling block. As Auren Uris notes in his *Memos for Managers,* "In countless interoffice memo files are stored the evidence of the animosities, pains and pleasures, the courage, imagination, creativity, and energy of human beings at work together."[20] Uris comments in detail on the politics of the memo, and some of his observations are of value not only for sending memos but also for understanding those that cross one's desk.

Copying In

One device of interest is the copy list as a pressure tool. Some high-level executives will, as a matter of practice, include favored subordinates on the routing lists for memos. When someone falls out of favor, his or her name is dropped from the list.

Taking Credit

Another memorandum practice is shady but more widely used than many think. A manager might write a practice memo recapitulating a meeting. While the memo is ostensibly "for the record," its recording of the meeting or conversation is decidedly in favor of the writer who lays claim to ideas that were not necessarily hers. Such a memo might be of value to that person later in proving ownership of an idea.

Cover Memos

Still another shady or cagey tactic is to attach a covering memo to that of a colleague. The original memo usually reflects badly on the writer, and the practice serves to spread negative impressions. The covering memo is ambiguous, of course, "Just thought you'd be interested in what Allen is up to these days."[21] A conscienceless colleague can do the same to you if your memos are muddled and riddled with error. The results can be devastating—for the poor writer.

This latter point underscores a valuable lesson managers too often learn too late. Putting something in writing may make it more permanent than one intends. Think twice before committing yourself to paper in controversial situations.

Summary

Letters and memorandums can benefit greatly from strategic considerations. However, they are frequently mere impersonal messages written automatically. One of the key considerations for audience adaptation in letters and memos is the you attitude. The writer with this attitude projects himself into the reader's place and prepares communications to suit that reader. Some of the factors affected by the you attitude include metacommunication (including typing and tone) and diction (including jargon, voice, and expletives). The you attitude also influences the letter's order: direct order is appropriate for letters bearing good news and neutral information; indirect, for bad news messages. Direct order places the main point first in the letter; indirect, last.

Negatives must be handled carefully in correspondence. A writer should de-emphasize the negative by using subordination, by avoiding *no* and *not*, and by avoiding negative wording or words with negative connotations.

One direct letter is the letter of inquiry, which indicates the nature of the letter in an initial question and follows with the reasons or necessary details. Another direct letter is the positive response to an inquiry, which gives the good news first followed by any necessary detail. Another is the claim letter whose directness adds to the assertiveness of the claim. The problem is identified early in the letter, and the body gives the reader's view of what happened. A positive response to a claim first gives the good news and then explains what happened. Negatives and apologies are inappropriate in this type of letter.

Indirect letters include the negative response to an inquiry, which first details why the question asked cannot be answered or why the favor requested cannot be granted. This letter (and all indirect letters) subordinates the *no*. The refused claim letter begins neutrally and then explains why the reader's claim cannot be granted. It reasons the reader into agreeing with the writer. The letter avoids negatives and apologies.

Memorandums are the most frequently used written communication within many organizations. The memorandum is an efficient, straightforward communication that requires some strategic considerations in its writing. It has several uses for a manager, including communicating to groups, fixing responsibility, communicating with opponents, and communicating with the inaccessible. It falls into two categories: notifications and requests for action. Form memos are occasionally developed for frequently used types of memos.

Memorandums are occasionally used in office politics in one of several ways: one is copying in (or out) with the copy list, another tactic allows the writer to take credit for ideas not necessarily her own, and a third is to circulate memos of others, usually for a negative purpose.

Endnotes

1. Gilbert C. Storms, "What Business School Graduates Say About the Writing They Do at Work," *Bulletin of the Association for Business Communication* XLVI, no. 4 (December 1983), pp. 13–18.
2. JoAnne Yates, "The Emergence of the Memo as a Managerial Genre," *Management Communication Quarterly* 2, issue 4 (May 1989), p. 486.
3. Mary K. Kirtz and Diana C. Reep, "A Survey of the Frequency, Types, and Importance of Writing Tasks in Four Career Areas," *Bulletin of the Association for Business Communication* LIII, no. 4 (December 1990), pp. 3–4.
4. Edward Goodin and Skip Swerdlow, "The Current Quality of Written Correspondence: A Statistical Analysis of the Performance of 13 Industry and Organizational Categories," *Bulletin of the Association for Business Communication* L, no. 1 (March 1987), pp. 12–16.
5. Kitty Locker, "Theoretical Justification for Using Reader Benefits," *Journal of Business Communication* 19, no. 3 (Summer 1982), pp. 51–65.
6. Michael C. White, "The Tone Scale: A Five-part Activity for Measuring and Adjusting Tone in Business Correspondence," *Bulletin of the Association for Business Communication* LI, no. 1 (March 1988), pp. 21–23.
7. James Suchan and Robert Colucci, "An Analysis of Communication Efficiency Between High-impact Writing and Bureaucratic Written Communication," *Management Communication Quarterly* 2, no. 4 (May 1989), pp. 454–84.
8. Robert J. Aalberts and Lorraine Krajewski, "Claim and Adjustment Letters: Theory versus Practice and Legal Implications," *Bulletin of the Association for Business Communication* L, no. 3 (September 1987), pp. 1–5.
9. Stephen B. Knouse, "Confidentiality and the Letter of Recommendation," *Bulletin of the Association for Business Communication* L, no. 3 (September 1987), pp. 6–8.
10. Marlys Harris, "Gaining Through Complaining," *Money*, May 1982, pp. 174–75.
11. Mohan R. Limaye, "The Syntax of Persuasion: Two Business Letters of Request," *Journal of Business Communication* 20, no. 2 (Spring 1983), pp. 17–30.
12. Chadwick B. Hilton, William H. Motes, and John S. Fielden, "An Experimental Study of the Effects of Style and Organization on Reader Perceptions of Text," *Journal of Business Communication* 26, no. 3 (Summer 1989), pp. 255–70.
13. Jeanette Gilsdorf, "Write Me Your Best Case For . . . ," *Bulletin of the Association for Business Communication* LIV, no. 1 (March 1991), pp. 7–12.

14. Marie E. Flatley, "A Comparative Analysis of the Written Communication of Managers at Various Organizational Levels in the Private Business Sector," *Journal of Business Communication* 19, no. 3 (Summer 1982), pp. 35–50.
15. Thomas O. Kirkpatrick, *Supervision, a Situational Approach* (Boston: Kent Publishing Co., 1987), p. 293.
16. Jo Anne Hennington, "Memorandums—An Effective Tool for Management," *Bulletin of the American Business Communication Association* XXXXI, no. 3 (September 1978), pp. 10–14.
17. Charles T. Brusaw, Gerald J. Alred, and Walter E. Oliu, *Business Communicator's Handbook,* 3rd ed. (New York: St. Martin's Press, 1986), p. 390.
18. Ibid., p. 395.
19. Max Rose, "A Memorandum About Memos," *Supervisory Magazine*, March 1980, pp. 6–8.
20. Auren Uris, *Memos for Managers* (New York: Thomas Y. Crowell, 1975), p. ix.
21. Ibid., pp. 40–44.

Additional Readings

Campbell, Kim Sydow. "Explanations in Negative Messages: More Insights from Speech Act Theory." *Journal of Business Communication* 27, no. 4 (Fall 1990), pp. 357–76.

Dumaine, Deborah. *Writing to the Top: Writing for Corporate Success.* New York: Random House, 1989.

Elbow, Peter. *Writing with Power.* New York: Oxford University Press, 1981.

Fruehling, Rosemary T., and N. B. Oldham. *Write to the Point!* New York: McGraw-Hill Book Co., 1988.

Harrison, Teresa M. "Frameworks for the Study of Writing in Organizational Contexts." *Written Communication* 4, no. 1 (January 1987), pp. 3–23.

Hirokawa, Randy Y., Rachel A. Kodama, and Nancy L. Harper. "Impact of Managerial Power on Persuasive Strategy Selection by Female and Male Managers." *Management Communication Quarterly* 4, no. 1 (August 1990), pp. 30–50.

Morris, John O. *Make Yourself Clear.* New York: McGraw-Hill Book Co., 1980.

Price, Jonathan. *Put That in Writing.* New York: Penguin Books, 1984.

Salerno, Douglas. "An Interpersonal Approach to Writing Negative Messages." *Journal of Business Communication* 25, no. 1 (Winter 1988), pp. 41–52.

Scott, James Calvert, and Diana J. Green. "British Perspectives on Organizing Bad-News Letters: Organizational Patterns Used by Major U.K. Companies." *Bulletin of the Association for Business Communication* LV, no. 1 (March 1992), pp. 17–20.

Shelby, Annette N. "Applying the Strategic Choice Model to Motivational Appeals: A Theoretical Approach." *Journal of Business Communication* 28, no. 3 (Summer 1991), pp. 187–212.

Shurter, Robert L., and Donald J. Leonard. *Effective Letters in Business.* New York: McGraw-Hill Book Co., 1984.

Discussion Questions

1. Cite examples of letters you have received that were merely impersonal communications. What led you to believe this?

2. Using a letter you recently received from someone you do not know, note some of your characteristics that the writer obviously knew about.

3. Describe the you attitude for letter writers.

4. What is the basis of the you attitude?

5. What elements of metacommunication can you as a letter writer use?

6. What are the direct and indirect orders, and when is each appropriate?

7. When writers use the indirect order to convey negative news, what are they trying to accomplish?

8. Which strategy should be used when the writer is uncertain of the reader's reaction?

9. Write a different buffer beginning for one of the indirect letters in this chapter.

10. Why should apologies be avoided in most negative situations?

11. How can a letter writer de-emphasize the negative in letters?

12. What are some of the tactics one should avoid in writing an initial claim letter?

13. What strategy would you suggest for building goodwill in an adjustment letter? Why?

14. How can goodwill be built in a refused claim? What dangers exist in offering an unexplained compromise?

15. Why is reader adaptation needed in memorandums?

CASE 6–1

You are sales manager for a furniture manufacturer and have just received a strongly worded claim letter from Hyram Blalock, who owns a large hotel in a nearby city. Mr. Blalock has been refurbishing his hotel and had placed a special order with you for 115 headboards to fit specifications he sent.

He ordered headboards an inch and a half narrower than conventional double-bed size. He also specified a finish different from that normally used in this grade of headboard. Finally, he wanted his hotel's logo imprinted on each headboard. You completed this order and shipped it to him about a week ago.

He ordered the mattresses directly from a manufacturer that has since gone out of business. They did, however, deliver his mattresses before going bankrupt, just a week before your headboards arrived. The problem is that all these mattresses were manufactured in the conventional dimensions, rather than the narrower ones for which the headboards were designed.

Blalock is asking you to take back the current shipment and either change the dimensions to fit the conventional mattresses or to send a different set (which would, of course, have the finish he specified and his hotel's logo on them).

Obviously, you cannot comply with his request. Write an appropriate strategic claim refusal. Of course, the facts are on your side—he ordered the headboards in the size and finish that he received. However, the challenge is to tell him so without lecturing or using negatives. If you do choose to alter the headboards in the original order, feel free to do so—but be sure to charge him.

CASE 6–2

You are the assistant human resource manager for a small insurance company whose territory includes your state and three surrounding states. Your company has recently revamped its retirement and employment benefits packages, and you have been assigned the task of communicating these changes to all employees.

Since some of the changes are complex, you will be traveling to four sites in your region to meet with the company's agents and their personnel. You need to arrange hotel accommodations at each of the sites for the personnel, and you will need a meeting room with video equipment and full-screen projection capabilities.

Since the company has had a very good year, management wants the employees to enjoy their stay at the hotels. Hence, you also need to inquire into the recreational facilities available.

Write a letter of inquiry to the Hotel Beacon in a major city in one of your surrounding states. The letter should elicit the information you will need to decide if the hotel is the right one for your meeting.

CASE 6–3

You are the administrative assistant to R. D. Spenser, president of Flo-Sheen Fabrics. Flo-Sheen employs over 300 people in its mill and corporate offices. Each year, these employees contribute generously to the city's annual fund-raising drive. Spenser also has developed a volunteer program that allows some employees to work on charitable projects on company time.

On your desk today you found a letter that was sent to Mr. Spenser from a statewide youth organization requesting permission to conduct a fund-raising drive in your plant for a new project it is developing. The organization wants to establish a scholarship fund for its brightest members.

Mr. Spenser jotted a note at the bottom of the letter asking you to deny the request. Do so, but build up goodwill. Be positive, yet assertive; do not leave the organization wondering if the request is denied.

7 STRATEGIES FOR MANAGEMENT REPORTS

> *Rod Battle did not expect to write so many reports in his new job as assistant manager of human resources. It seems that everyone wants a report on something from him.*
>
> *For every person interviewed, he collects data to fill in reporting forms for the government. For every white-collar employee hired, he must prepare one report for the vice-president in charge of the new employee's division and one for the employee's immediate supervisor. For all employees terminated, he must prepare a report for the legal office.*
>
> *He also prepares reports on recruitment expenses, employee benefits, sick leave, and taxes withheld. And just today, he has discovered he was supposed to write a quarterly report on the human resources department. It was due yesterday. Rod is learning a great deal about written communication.*

Reports are among an organization's most important communications. They appear in a variety of forms, carry out a number of functions, and ensure the efficient transfer of data within an organization. Managerial reports are usually well organized and objective, and they transfer verifiable information that addresses some purpose or problem.

Evidence indicates the importance of reports in business is not likely to diminish soon. In one study of recent business graduates, 65.6 percent of respondents noted that they frequently wrote informational reports, while 31.3 percent replied that they sometimes wrote these reports. In the same study, 40.6 percent responded that they frequently wrote analytical reports and 43.8 percent replied that they sometimes wrote these reports.[1]

In another larger study (837 respondents) of recent business graduates, 74 percent of those responding either sometimes, often, or very often wrote short reports. For that same study, 42 percent of the respondents either sometimes, often, or very often wrote long reports.[2] Another researcher found that report writing in private-sector firms differed by level—with middle-level managers writing a bit less than lower level managers and upper level managers writing less than middle-level managers.[3]

In their role as report writers, managers appreciate how reports can contribute to the management functions. Reports are essential to management's ability to control organizational actions. Management is required to plan, organize, execute, evaluate, and correct; and it needs some medium for carrying out these tasks. Reports are a means to some of those ends.

While some reports depict current status or progress toward a goal, others convey the results of previous management decisions; still others relay a manager's evaluation of results and performance and give suggestions (or orders) for changes in current policies and procedures to bring about greater effectiveness and efficiency. Common to all these diverse report writing settings, however, is that managers must have the know-how to approach problems, solve them, and communicate the findings.

The Report Writing Process

Typically, managers write reports for one of three reasons. The most common is simply that someone has asked them to. A higher level manager who sees an area where information is lacking or a problem that needs solving will ask a subordinate to fill that gap or solve that problem. A report may also be part of a company's regular business. Thus, writing progress or periodic reports may be one of the manager's regular duties. Finally, a manager may also write reports spontaneously, perhaps to fill gaps he has found on his own or to share information with the rest of the staff.

Groundwork

Of course, managers do not just sit down and write reports one after another. Typically, they must lay the groundwork for the report. This preliminary effort often takes more time than actually writing the report and can intimidate some writers.[4]

Defining the Problem or Objective

After accepting a report writing assignment, a manager must make sure the process leading up to the report will yield optimum results. The writer's time is valuable not only to the company but to the writer as well. Valuable hours spent following blind leads waste personal energy and resources.

First, then, the report writer must determine the problem under study or the objective. What does the person who authorized this report want from her effort? The problem may be nothing more than an information gap—someone needs data or demographics on taste, for example. The problem may also be one requiring analysis. Thus, the report writer must choose from among several options and recommend a plan of action.

Establishing Hypotheses

In analytical reports, once the problem and purpose have been determined, the next step before gathering data is to set up hypotheses to be tested. This process involves formulating possible reasons for the phenomenon under study.[5] For example, productivity in a plant has dropped and a manager needs to determine the cause (or causes) and propose a solution. Possible hypotheses might be raw material shortages, equipment malfunctions, abuse of sick leave, or a host of other possible causes and/or combinations.

Once these hypotheses are formulated, the researcher tests them to see which (if any) might be the cause. The technique used for testing hypotheses varies from situation to situation, of course, and relates to the manager's own problem-solving skills.

Seeking Data

Once the manager has established hypotheses for the problem analysis or has determined the information needed for the informative report, she needs to know where she can find the data needed to complete the report. Where she looks will be guided by what is sought. Most of the data needed for business reports are primary data, that is, data the writer collects from interviews, surveys, experiments, and observation. Occasionally, writers draw from secondary research data, that is, material already published—but only occasionally.

Once a writer settles on the best sources for data, the next step is to plan how to tap that data. What information is needed first? The answer to that question may depend on prior understanding of other material. By being aware of informational gaps, a writer helps to ensure that the collection and storage of data for the report are orderly and involve a minimum of duplicated effort.

Classification of Reports

Knowing what form the final report will assume helps writers gauge the effort needed to prepare the report and thus helps in the budgeting of time and resources.

Various systems exist for cataloging groups of reports, but only one is general enough to cover all report writing situations that managers might encounter. The other systems fall within this scheme, but they are not broad enough to cover the wide range of reports possible. They frequently overlap, too, and make distinctions fuzzy with their classifications by time, by frequency, and by subject matter.

Probably the most effective classification system is the informal versus formal, which places reports on a continuum based on the degree of formality (or informality) of the report. This continuum starts with the most informal reports, which find a manager filling in several blank spaces and, in some cases, providing the briefest narrative or description.

Next on the continuum is the letter or memo report. Although either of these may be several pages long (10-page letter reports are not unheard of), at a certain point, the short report with its title page becomes appropriate.

Next on the continuum, the report becomes increasingly more formal, that is, dressed up. Thus, the writer may add a letter of transmittal for a report slightly more significant than a short one and a summary for one even more significant. This process can continue until the full formal report is reached with its cover, title fly, title page, letter of transmittal, table of contents, summary, formal introduction, body, conclusion, and appended parts. Later in the chapter, we describe what goes into those elements of the report.

Strategic Considerations

As with all other communications undertaken by managers, reports should reflect careful strategic decisions. These decisions fall into a number of areas, many of which are subtle but important.

Format

The format of a report reflects the report writer's careful strategic decisions. Generally, the more significant the contents of the report, the more formal it is. Nevertheless, obvious exceptions exist. The wise report writer considers all the elements discussed in the paragraphs that follow and balances them in deciding on the report format.

Audience
A report's intended audience guides, at least partially, the degree of formality. A manager preparing a report recommending the purchase of one component over another might choose memorandum form for the company controller but a short report form (with a title page) if the same report is to go to the chief executive officer. Just as we might dress more formally for an interview with the CEO than we might for subordinates, our reports similarly get more or less dressed up to match their readers.

Effort
Another significant factor in determining the report format is the amount of time spent researching and preparing the report. Usually related, of course, is the actual size of the report, which often reflects the effort expended. The

report that requires a couple of phone calls and a half hour for the writing calls for less dressing up than does one resulting from several weeks of careful planning, the administration and evaluation of testing instruments, and several days of writing. The extra effort merits more formality.

Value

We also must consider the value of the findings the report shares. Some findings are more important than others. For example, a report on options for a new janitorial service might conceivably reflect as much effort as one recommending an executive jet. However, the significance of the second calls for a dressier treatment than that of the former.

Original Assignment

Of course, a report writer should use any clues given in the initial assignment. It might be unwise to prepare a fully formal report if the original assignment from one's manager was to "shoot me a memo when you've found the answer." If on another assignment, that same manager indicated a different report might be forwarded to top management, you might give it a dressier treatment.

Precedent

Precedent is also relevant to the format a report will assume. A new manager is advised to learn what format is traditional for certain types of assignments. Many companies, such as Exxon, Honeywell, and Andersen Consulting, specify guidelines. Often the best guidance comes from a secretary who has worked for the company for some time. Precedent is especially relevant with periodic reports, which are expected to look like previous periodic reports.

Order

Another strategic decision that report writers must make is the order of the information appearing in the report.

Direct Order

As the last chapter showed, direct order puts the main point first, followed by the details. In letters conveying good news or neutral information, direct order is appropriate. Similarly, with short reports, when the reader is likely to agree with the writer's main point, direct order is often best.

Most reports are received neutrally; and since recommendations are needed for deciding on actions to take, the sooner the reader gets to them, the better. Direct order is especially appropriate when the reader trusts the writer's work. If the reader needs to check on any point, the specifics are in the text.

Indirect Order

At the same time, the indirect order is often more favored for long reports, even for those conveying good news. The traditional inductive organizational pattern of introduction, body, and conclusion is still common for such reports. And the indirect approach is unquestionably called for when the reader is likely to interpret the main conclusions as bad news. Then, too, new writers may find that management doesn't always unquestionably accept their conclusions. They should lead the reader logically to the conclusion with the indirect order.

Organization of the Body

Whether a writer uses direct or indirect order to organize the overall report, the body of the report also needs organization. The body, the part that gives the reasons for the conclusions and recommendations, needs unifying elements to ensure that the material is in its clearest, most useful form.

The organizational plan chosen is situational and depends on the problem under study, the nature of the information being reported, and the reader's needs. The most common organizational plans are by time, place, quantity, and criteria (or factors). The plan chosen should be the one that moves the reader smoothly from the body's beginning to its end through a series of clearly interrelated parts.[6]

Time

Time organization is obviously appropriate for chronologically sequenced material. Any report that narrates events uses this pattern. For example, a quarterly report might have main divisions for each of the three months covered. Chronological organization works to the advantage of the writer since she can work either forward or backward through the time period being detailed. Once the writer chooses this order, questions about what comes next are easily resolved.

Place

Organization by place is more complex than is organization by time. This pattern would be appropriate for an activity report dealing with simultaneous but separate events (for example, a monthly report on the activities of several branch offices of a company). It is also appropriate for descriptive reports. Using spatial organization in complex reports dictates some order in which to proceed. Regions of the United States, for example, could be covered in a clockwise fashion.

Quantity

Organization by quantity is another option that is relevant when the data lend themselves to quantification. For example, a report discussing a city's household characteristics might be best organized by the number of individuals per household or by the incomes of the household heads. A writer discussing cities might organize by population ranges.

Factors or Criteria

The final category, organization by factors (or criteria), is a catchall. It is also the most useful since it is so broad. Here, the report's body is organized by the relevant factors that led to the conclusions. In an informational report, these factors are the categories into which the information falls. For example, a report discussing the characteristics of a sales market that is largely homogeneous might deal with the income, age, education, and tastes of the market.

In an evaluative report, the conclusions and recommendations are based on a set of criteria. Criteria are really nothing more than the factors on which a decision is based. For example, a writer may prepare a personnel report recommending the selection of a job candidate. He might divide the report by the optimum characteristics of an employee filling the position. Thus, a secretary might be evaluated in terms of typing skills, loyalty, education, and competence in office practices.

We have focused on overall and major division organizations so far. At the same time, material within each of the major divisions needs to be organized following a clear plan. At the second and third levels of division, the organization plans chosen do not have to be the same as the one selected for the major divisions. For example, a report recommending the fleet purchase of a particular car might have its major divisions deal with the criteria used, such as safety, comfort, financial considerations, and dependability. The second level might deal with subdivisions of the major criteria. For example, financial considerations might be broken into purchase price, operating expense, and trade-in values. At the third level of division, the report might be organized according to the particular three or four cars under consideration. With such an organization plan, the information the reader needs to compare is in one place. For example, the purchase prices would probably be presented on one page of the report. They wouldn't be physically separated by numerous pages, as would be the case if the cars had been chosen as the major subdivisions of the report.

Headings

All business reports (not just formal ones) benefit from the use of headings. Headings indicate to the reader the relative degree of significance of the material that follows. The higher the heading, the more significant is the material. Headings are also useful signposts to guide the reader through the report. Additionally, if the table of contents suggests something of particular interest to the reader, he can easily find it by turning to the appropriate page. Finally, headings help provide white space in reports, which contributes appreciably to their visual appeal. The following paragraphs provide useful guidelines to keep in mind in developing report headings.

Principle of Division

Outlines are built on the principle of division, and headings reflect a report's outline. The principle of division dictates that you cannot divide something into one. Thus, if you use a heading in a part of a report, you must have another heading at that level following it. Otherwise, the heading does not reflect division at all.

Headings and Transitions

Use other transitional devices besides headings. In moving from one major section to another, a writer should have one transitional paragraph (even a short one) to show the change. In moving from one subsection to another, a brief sentence should signal the shift and help the reader see the flow of ideas. A good rule of thumb for judging transitions is to see if the text reads well without the headings. If it does, then the reader is not likely to get lost or confused in working through the text.

Content

Write headings with the reader in mind. They should be descriptive of the content to follow but relatively short. Generally, seven words (or fewer) are appropriate for first-level headings, and even fewer than seven are usually needed for other level headings.

The report writer can choose from a variety of heading systems. One style may be too complex for a simple report, while another may be too simple for a complex report. The heading system described in the following paragraphs is one of the many available, one that is suitable for most needs.

First-Degree Headings

The first-degree heading is used for all major divisions of the report, including headings for some prefatory parts (executive summary, table of contents), the introduction, the major divisions of the body of the report, and the closing sections. To indicate its major importance, it should be centered and typed in all caps. Some writers underline and/or bold strike it to make it further stand out from the text. When reports are double spaced, first-level headings will sometimes be triple spaced from the text. The writer may choose any variation but must apply it consistently. First-degree headings should be treated in the same way throughout the report.

Second-Degree Headings

The second-degree heading indicates material subordinate to the main divisions of the report. The material so identified corresponds to the A and B divisions under the roman numeral headings in an outline. These headings begin at the left margin, are underscored and/or bold struck, and have the initial letters of important words capitalized. The typist then double spaces to begin the text below the heading.

Third-Degree Headings
Generally, the third-degree heading is as far as a report writer needs to go. This heading corresponds to the 1 and 2 below the A and B in an outline. Indent the heading, underscore and/or bold strike it, and capitalize the initial letter of only the first word (unless proper nouns appear in the heading). Follow the heading by a period and continue the text on the same line after skipping at least two spaces.

Paper and Typing

The final preparation adds to the effectiveness of your report. The paper chosen for reports should be high-quality, watermarked bond (preferably 20-pound weight) both for appearance's sake and for durability. For the best effect, use a letter-quality printer.

The margins are usually one inch on all sides, unless the paper is to be bound. Then the left margin is a half inch wider. Occasionally, pages with visual aids are bound facing the text. In this case, the right margin of that page is a half inch wider.

One other exception to the one-inch margin occurs on the first page of the report's body. Here a writer should space down two inches from the top before typing the title of the report. The extra spacing gives the beginning of the report the proper dramatic emphasis it deserves.

Now that we have discussed strategic decisions on format, order, organization, headings, and paper, we are ready to talk about the content of some of the more common types of business reports: letter reports, memo reports, and formal reports.

Memorandum and Letter Reports

The first specific types of reports we examine are the memorandum and letter reports. They tend to fall toward the informal side of the formal-to-informal continuum for business reports.

Memorandum Reports

In addition to being the most informal type of report in an organization, memos are efficient and suggest a no-nonsense approach. They invariably have some form of headings—*To, From, Subject,* and *Date*—at the top for efficient routing and a quick understanding of purpose. The comments made about subject lines in the last chapter apply here as well. In an indirectly ordered report, the subject line should not give away the conclusions.

Introduction

The memo report begins with a brief introduction that usually tells the purpose of the report and who authorized it. One way to accomplish this objective is with a formal statement: "This report, which you authorized on June 8, evaluates three copying machines and recommends the purchase of one." Often preferable, though, is something less formal, "Recently you asked me to look into the purchase of a new copier."

Whenever writing a report at the request of another, one should make sure the authorization is stated. If the value of the assignment is questioned by others, the report writer can always point out that she was asked to do it.

It is also appropriate to indicate how the writer derived the information: "I called sales representatives from three manufacturers," or "I examined sales materials supplied by three companies." A statement of the scope, that is, how widely the research into the problem ranged, is appropriate as well, although it is often obvious.

Close to the beginning, a direct report indicates the conclusions and/or recommendations reached in the report. In the example on copiers, the writer using direct order might end the first paragraph with her choice of copier.

Body

Whether the overall report uses direct or indirect order, the body of a memo report will detail the findings that led the writer to the conclusions the report makes. For the sake of efficiency, headings often set off this material. Either centered or marginal, these headings guide the reader through the contents; he can tell at a glance what a given section discusses.

The list is another highly appropriate organizational tool in the memorandum report. Lists must be introduced by the writer, but that introduction is often no more than a sentence. Lists help to cut down on prose, and their simplicity can improve reader comprehension and retention of the material. Finally, to maximize reader comprehension, lists should be constructed in parallel grammatical form. For example, in the report on copiers, the writer might state:

My evaluation of the copiers sought to determine four things about each unit:

1. its use of energy
2. its cost of operation
3. its speed of operation
4. its frequency of repairs

Writers must be careful not to let the memo degenerate into a mere catalog of lists. The report needs to be businesslike and efficient without being a challenge to interpret.

In a memo report, a manager may also choose to use visual aids (discussed later) to help the reader. However, the effort required to derive and evaluate the data for a graph or table may justify a slightly more formal format than the memorandum supplies.

Ending

The end of a memo needs planning. If the memorandum uses indirect order, the last paragraph would give the conclusions and recommendations reached. On the other hand, a report using direct order easily ends on the last point. The writer might wish to introduce the last paragraph with some transitional device that indicates the approaching end: "Finally, I evaluated the ease of operation of the copiers. I found. . . ." Often this aesthetic transition is enough to signal the end.

Letter Reports

The letter report is similar to the memo report, but three essential differences exist: form, tone, and audience.

The differences in form are products of necessity (the inside address, for example) and convention (the salutation and complimentary close). The inside address is necessary since the report is to be mailed to someone outside the organization (as opposed to the memo, which is delivered within the organization).

Another subtle difference between the two is tone. Since the letter report goes outside the organization, it greets an audience different from that of the memorandum report. It is accordingly a potential tool for building goodwill, and goodwill means increased business. Thus, the letter report stresses reader benefits more than the memorandum and is likely to close with a goodwill statement that promises continued cooperation.

Organization

The letter report may use direct or indirect order, although most prefer indirect order since the reader's reaction might be difficult to gauge at a distance. Of course, when the findings are unquestionably positive, direct order is advisable. In these cases, a clear subject line can orient the reader to the nature of the problem and solution addressed in the letter report.

Introduction

Like the memorandum report, the letter report needs a brief introduction. The opening acquaints the reader with the purpose of the report. Often, the purpose and authorization (or reference to the request being granted) can be dealt with in a single sentence. For example, one manager reporting to another on her experiences with a maintenance service company might begin her report, "As you requested in your letter last week, here is a report on our experiences with Ace Maintenance Service." If appropriate, the scope of the report and the methodology used for developing the details can be included, although these may be clear from the discussion.

Body

The letter report has no set length, and it is not unheard of for such a report to reach 8 to 10 pages. A memorandum report intended for internal circulation might take on more formal characteristics before it gets that long, but the letter report merely continues growing while still retaining letter form.

Headings are appropriate in a letter report since they quickly guide the reader to whatever sections might be of special interest. Since managers write some letter reports in response to a series of questions submitted by the reader, the headings can reflect those questions. In fact, a manager should be pleased to have such an organizational plan suggested; it will save time in the drafting of the report. As with memo reports, lists are appropriate for the letter report.

Ending

If conclusions and recommendations are reserved for the end of the report, they precede the last short paragraph. The last paragraph of a letter report is usually a statement of goodwill. Readers appreciate the writer's personal involvement, and writers appreciate a standard form for ending the report.

The last type of report to be examined here is the formal report. Though we will review all the parts associated with fairly long, formal reports, intermediate stages along the way to a formal report will add one or more of the parts detailed here. Remember that as reports get longer, they tend gradually to pick up the trappings of formality.

Elements of the Formal Report

The formal report has a number of elements. Though you may not often be called to write long, formal reports, when the situations arise, you'll want the resultant reports to look right. We will first discuss prefatory parts and then review parts of the report proper.

Prefatory Parts

Prefatory parts are report parts that come before the report itself. They tend to be directly associated with report length and formality. The longer and more formal a report is, the more prefatory parts it is likely to have. Since prefatory report parts include some repetition of report contents, however, writers must be sensitive to the possibility of becoming overly redundant and irritating readers.[7]

Title Fly

Some formal reports (generally the longest) begin with a title fly on which only the report title appears. The title is set up in the highest order of heading used in the report and placed slightly above the page's vertical center. If necessary, the title may appear in more than one line with each successive, shorter line centered below the preceding line.

In constructing the report title, writers should strive to make it a concise but complete description of the report's nature. As guides, writers might consider the journalists' five Ws and how. Most, if not all, of these elements ought to be treated in the title. Because of their charge of completeness, titles of business reports tend to be longer than titles of other literary works.

Title Page

The title page is the first page for most formal reports. Generally, it consists of three main components: the title and the complete identifications of the recipient and author. That complete identification includes the person's name, position, organization, and city and state. The identifying blocks of information are generally preceded by expressions such as "presented to" and "prepared by." If the organization and/or city and state are the same for recipient and author, they need not be repeated under the author's name and position. These blocks of information should be spaced evenly down the page with margins of about one and a half inches at the top and bottom of the page.

Letter of Transmittal

The letter of transmittal is the next item found in most formal reports (although some writers actually clip it to the cover of the report). It is usually set up as an actual letter on letterhead stationery, although within organizations a memo is more appropriate. Generally, it replaces the conversation the writer would have with the reader if the report were being handed over in person.

The first paragraph serves three purposes. First, it transmits the report to the recipient with wording like, "Here is the report. . . ." It also briefly states the nature of the report and mentions authorization details. Note that all three purposes might be accomplished in one sentence, as in "Here is the report on cost cutting options you requested in your memo of July 10."

The content of the transmittal's body may vary with the circumstances. Generally, it is viewed as an opportunity to make helpful comments, anything that might help the reader to read, interpret, and use the report. Also, it is here that the writer might wish to acknowledge people who helped her do the research and compile the report. Finally, in reports of intermediate length (10 to 20 pages), the synopsis is sometimes sandwiched into the letter of transmittal. In such cases, it would follow the helpful comments and acknowledgments.

Typically, the transmittal closes with a goodwill gesture. It thanks the recipient for the assignment and looks forward to continued service. To some, the idea of thanking someone for giving them work might sound strange. Such skeptics should remember that report writing assignments present chances to showcase analytical abilities and communication skills, abilities and skills that might be carefully viewed and valued when promotional opportunities arise.

Table of Contents

The table of contents follows the letter or memo of transmittal. It can take several forms. Some set it up in outline form with roman numerals, capital letters, and arabic numerals. Others use the same order of entries as in the report but without the mechanics of the outline.

In both cases, it is advisable to indicate through the form of the entries the level of significance they represent in the text. One way is to parallel their form in the text. For example, if a main entry is set up in the text in all capital letters, it would appear that way in the table of contents. Another way to show the relative significance of the entries in the table of contents is to indent five spaces for each successive level.

To facilitate their use by readers, the entries should use wording identical to that in the text. Also, to connect an entry to its page number, use leader dots (made by alternating periods and spaces on the line, aligned for all the entries). The page numbers should have their right digits aligned.

A long table of contents looks best single spaced. However, if all material will fit on one page, double spacing is permissible. A writer might also double space between levels and single space within levels of the table of contents that don't have subdivisions.

Lists of Tables and Figures

The lists of tables and figures is an optional feature appropriate to a report with three or more visual aids. If needed, and if there is room, the list begins several spaces below the end of the table of contents. It is headed by the title "List of Tables and Figures" and is set up like the table of contents. Most report writers usually divide the list into tables and figures. The table or figure number is followed by its title and is separated from its page number by leader dots.

Synopsis

Another prefatory element found in formal reports is the synopsis. Also called the epitome, review, brief, digest, or executive summary, it provides a quick overview of the report.[8] Managers who are only the secondary audience of a report may be interested only in the report's highlights. The synopsis serves these readers well. The challenge to the report writer is to shrink the report down to its major facts, analyses, and conclusions.[9] The synopsis should be brief (about one eighth the length of the report) and businesslike, with a focus on the report rather than on the writer. As was mentioned earlier, for reports of intermediate length, the synopsis is sometimes sandwiched into the letter of transmittal. When this option is selected, the synopsis simply follows the helpful comments and acknowledgments and precedes the final goodwill paragraph.

The Report Proper

It is in the report proper that the writer presents the findings of her research. It begins with an introduction and ends with the summary, conclusions, and/or recommendations. The following paragraphs detail the content of the various parts of the report proper.

Introduction—Required Elements

The first page of the body of the formal report contains the introduction, which may or may not be identified as such with a first-degree heading, depending on the writer's taste. The introduction contains a number of elements, some of which are necessary in all cases and some of which are optional. No hard rule sets the order in which the elements may occur, although the order in which they are discussed in the paragraphs that follow might be appropriate for most circumstances.

One element appropriate to any introduction is the purpose of the report. Generally, the purpose statement indicates the problem addressed in the report.[10] You can state the purpose as simply as, "The purpose of this report is to. . . ." On the other hand, you can word it more artfully: "This report recommends a new procedure for. . . ."

Though it may not be treated as a separate section of the introduction, another element necessary to most reports is the authorization. It can usually be stated quite simply as in, "This report, which you requested on December 10, is . . ." or "This report, which Mr. Bruce Ferrin authorized on March 5, shows why. . . ." The authorization is valuable because it established a clear chain of responsibility. The authorization shows justification for the time, effort, and resources that went into the preparation of the report. The only time it is not needed is when the writer developed the report on his own.

A statement of methodology is another element frequently included in reports. Readers usually want to know how a writer arrived at his data because knowing that may indicate the degree of authority the contents possess. If the report used library research, the writer needs only to mention that secondary research was used. If, on the other hand, the material arose from primary research, the writer should describe the technique used for gathering data in sufficient detail to allow the reader to judge the quality of the research.

The last necessary item, and almost always the last item in an introduction, is the plan of development in which the writer tells the reader what steps will be used to develop the body of the report. This invaluable element of the introduction signals a major transition and sets the order of the report's organization firmly in the reader's mind. The plan of development is usually quite simply written: "This report first . . . then . . . and finally. . . ." The report then follows the precise order set out in the plan of development.

Introduction—Optional Elements

The introduction also might include other elements, depending on the writer's needs. For example, a statement of limitations details external factors that may have limited the range of exploration in developing the report. The most typical constraint is fiscal; report writers often work on limited budgets that prohibit extensive travel or detailed samplings of populations. Time is another common limitation. Deadlines often limit the depth in which one might research a problem.

Another optional element of the introduction is the scope. In preparing a scope statement, a writer might ask herself what the reader might reasonably expect in such a report. If any inconsistency exists between these expectations and the report content, the writer would delineate briefly those areas that are and are not covered. For example, in the scope statement for a report recommending a new plant site, the writer might note that the report covers only the top four sites and that architectural and engineering details are available elsewhere.

Definitions are another element required in some introductions. If several key terms used throughout the report are unfamiliar to the reader, they should be defined in the introduction. On the other hand, if only a few unfamiliar words are used only a few times, they should be defined the first time they appear in the text. If numerous terms need defining, a glossary should be used.

Sometimes circumstances call for a brief statement about the background of the report problem. Some writers detail background in the introduction; others put it into the report. A short background statement fits better as part of the introduction than as a main section of the body.

Body

The body of the report follows the introduction. Since most formal reports are set up using indirect order, the conclusions and recommendations appear at the very end of the report proper (but before any appended material). If the report is written using direct order, those conclusions and recommendations will appear right after the introduction.

The information in the body of a formal report is usually set off using some sort of heading or caption system, either that given earlier in this chapter or another. Remember that the heading is not usually enough of a transition. If necessary, repeat the information in the heading as part of the transition into that section.

The report's body should be well organized, using one or more of the bases of organization discussed earlier. It should also be coherent, allowing the reader to move smoothly from one part to another. Appropriate transitions should be employed where necessary, connecting the major and minor parts of the report.

The report body should employ the right degree of objectivity. Generally, persuasive reports, such as proposals to potential clients, are not as coldly objective as informational and analytical reports. In all reports, however, writers need to distinguish between facts and assumptions and inferences. Assumptions and inferences need to be recognized with words like, "Assuming that . . ." and "The figures suggest that. . . ." One assumption or inference treated as a fact could jeopardize the credibility of the entire report.

The report body should also use the correct time perspective. The time perspective deals with the tense used in presenting the report's findings and the tense used in making cross-references to other parts of the report. The present time perspective is suitable when the data are current, as in the case of a recent survey. The finding might be presented as follows, "Fully 68 percent of our employees *believe* that their benefits are adequate." Using this perspective, a writer would also use the present tense to cross-reference other parts of the report: "Table II, in the previous (or next) section, *presents* the responses to questions 4, 5, and 6 of the questionnaire."

When the data are not current, as in the case of secondary research referencing studies years old, the past time viewpoint is appropriate. Here the findings are presented in the past tense: "In the Gifford study, 51 percent of the respondents *reported* dissatisfaction with their benefits." For consistency, the writer uses the past tense in referring to earlier parts of the report and the future tense in cross-referencing parts of the report yet to come.

Summary, Conclusions, and/or Recommendations

The final elements in most formal reports are the summary, conclusions, and/or recommendations. A strictly informational report would end with just a summary. An analytical report might end with a conclusions or with a conclusions and recommendations section.

The conclusions section does nothing more than list the results of the writer's investigation. If he were researching alternative sites for a new plant, he might conclude that site A is the least expensive and the most accessible, whereas site B is the largest, closest, and safest for the company's needs.

Recommendations move a step beyond. To prepare recommendations, the writer has to make a decision about the problem. Occasionally, the person authorizing the report may want conclusions but not recommendations. That is, she may want to know the results of the investigation, but she may want to reserve the decision making for herself. Young managers may find this is often the case at the start of their careers. Later, their recommendations may carry more weight.

The conclusions should not introduce any new material; the text should support anything found in them. Frequently, writers will introduce new facts (or worse, new qualifications) that change the whole picture. These belong in the text. Of course, the recommendations will be new material, but they should arise from the conclusions. The evidence should not point in one direction while the conclusions point in the other.

The direct order formal report contains the conclusions and recommendations at the beginning of the report. A summary is an appropriate ending for this kind of report, or one might begin the final section with some kind of statement that makes it clear it is the last section of the report.

The last, upcoming section of this chapter reviews the more common types of visual aids found in business reports and guidelines for their most effective use.

Visual Aids

Visual aids are a common and usually very effective means of illustrating trends and relationships in business reports that are not easily understood in verbal form. The great majority of the research done on visual aids shows that tables and graphics can boost the comprehension of material.[11] In fact, visual aids, particularly computer-generated graphics, are thought to be instrumental to the survival of decision-making managers now being inundated with computer printouts.[12]

Visual aids can appear in a report of any length or degree of formality, but they are most likely to be used in formal reports. Visual aids take a number of forms including tables, graphs, bar charts, component bar charts, pie charts, and pictographs. The choice a report writer makes depends on the nature of the material under discussion and the audience.

Audience adaptation can best be explained by placing visuals on a continuum that ranges from dramatic to informational. In general, less sophisticated audiences and those not familiar with the workings of a business will appreciate dramatic visual aids. Thus, a pictograph might be effective in an annual report comparing a company's production figures for the past three years. A glass company might use small drawings of bottles to represent millions of units produced. While such a dramatic visual aid gives a clear idea of any significant rise or fall in production, it may not accurately portray smaller changes. The fractions of a bottle needed to represent fractions of a million are difficult to interpret precisely. Of course, the exact quantities or percentages can be typed to the side to increase the informational impact.

On the other hand, a formal report submitted to upper-level management would use visual aids fitting the sophistication of the readers. For example, a comparison of several years of production figures broken down by products might appear in a table. The table, while providing large quantities of information, has very little dramatic impact by itself. The reader has to analyze the data and even after that may see little that is dramatic.

Midway on the continuum between dramatic and informative visual aids is the line graph, which can emphatically show trends. Using this graphic aid, readers can also determine fairly easily what specific production rate, interest rate, or income the graph is charting. They simply read across to the scale representing the amount.

General Rules

Several general rules apply to all visual aids. By following them, report writers create visual aids that are clear and strategically suited to their readers.

Appropriateness

First, visual aids should add to the section of the report in which they appear. The data they contain or symbolize should complement the text without duplicating it. The visual aid that merely repeats what the text has shown belongs in an appendix rather than in the body, which it merely clutters. Additionally, the type of visual aid chosen should be suited to the data being portrayed. Information in a line graph, for example, would not necessarily be suitable for portrayal in a bar chart.

Reference and Placement

Second, when using visual aids, writers should always refer to them in the text. The best approach is to make some reference to the visual aid just before it appears. This reference can be as simple as "see TABLE I" in parentheses or, preferably, something more graceful. When a visual aid is placed in a report without a reference to it in the text, the reader is frustrated at having to find the discussion to which the aid relates.

A writer, however, cannot always predict where she will be when she gets to the reference. It may be that only 6 lines of space are left on the page at that point, and the visual aid will take at least 12. In this case, the writer should put the visual aid on the top of the following page. She should be sure, however, to include the location in the reference to the visual aid.

Size

Third, the size chosen for a visual aid should be appropriate to its content. A simple graph showing the number of orders for a given product each month over the past year probably does not merit much more than a quarter of a page. On the other hand, a complex table detailing six factors for each of the 50 states may need to be done on long paper folded into the report. Though no hard and fast rules exist to dictate exact dimensions for visual aids, good judgment will usually indicate an acceptable range.

Content

Fourth, the content of the visual aid needs to relate closely to the current discussion. Do not try to pack too much data into a single chart or graph. Some of that data may apply to later sections of the report and may be used more appropriately at two or more points in the report.

Related to the need for relevancy is the need for simplicity. Strive to keep visuals, especially bar graphs, pie charts, and line drawings, simple. The content should unambiguously reflect the discussion. The use of abbreviations and standard symbols is also advisable for simplifying complex visuals. While symbols are usually not appropriate in the text, the need for compactness in visuals calls for such special references. A writer needs to make sure, however, that the reader understands the symbols and abbreviations used.

Conventions

Several conventions apply to visual aids. For one, writers have traditionally distinguished between tables and figures in reports, with figures being considered all types of visual aids other than a table. They make this distinction perhaps because the table is an extension of the typed text while figures require drafting. A related convention has tables and figures being counted as two separate series in a report. Thus, a report containing three tables and four figures would label them as follows: TABLE I, Figure 1, TABLE II, TABLE III, Figure 2, Figure 3, Figure 4. Note the additional distinction: All caps for table titles and roman numerals for tables.

A third convention places the titles of tables above the visual aid and that of figures below. In constructing the titles of visual aids, writers should keep two goals in mind: conciseness and completeness. In as few words as possible, a title should fairly accurately describe the information the visual conveys. Though we cannot cover every type of visual aid available to report writers, we can examine, in the following paragraphs, the ones most commonly used in business reports: pie charts, bar charts, line graphs, and tables.

Pie Charts

Pie charts are useful for showing proportional amounts of a unit. Their division into wedges representing the proportions makes a dramatic impact on a reader, but only when the differences are great enough to visibly affect the sizes of the divisions. Report writers can enhance this impact by using different colors or shading or cross-hatching in each of the divisions.

Writers can improve the pie chart's informational impact by having the typist insert what each segment represents in the segment itself along with the numeric or percentage significance. They can be entered horizontally, except where the material will not fit into a wedge. In that case, the information would be printed outside with a call-out, a short identifying arrow drawn to the wedge from the label. Figure 7–1 illustrates a typical pie chart.

Distribution of 1992 Sales Income XYZ Corporation

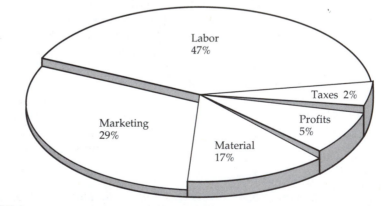

FIGURE 7–1
Sample Pie Chart

Bar Charts

The pie chart is very useful for symbolizing parts of one whole (for example, sources of income for a given year), but it is not good for comparing one total and/or its components with another. With the naked eye, it is difficult to judge the relative size of two more more circles and/or their slices placed side by side. The bar chart is more suited to that need.

The bar chart, in its simplest form, is useful for comparing totals over a period of time, distance, or quantity. The more complex component bar chart can compare totals as well as components of totals over time, distance, or quantity.

Simple Bar Charts

The bar chart should be constructed with the bars positioned either horizontally or vertically (generally the latter). The axis from which the bars rise usually measures time or place, and the opposite measures quantity. The units measured should be stated clearly on the quantity axis: "millions of dollars" or "thousands of units produced." Likewise, the bars should be clearly labeled.

Component Bar Charts

The component bar chart is one in which each bar (which represents a total) is subdivided into its component parts. This graph is handy for comparing totals and components of totals over several years or by places, for example, by region.

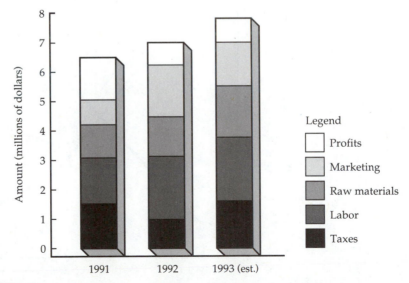

FIGURE 7–2

Sample Component Chart

To show the composition of new car sales for a given year, a writer could draw one bar representing the total new car sales and then divide it with each division representing one company. Clearly, this visual aid is preferable to a pie chart for year-to-year comparisons. The total differences would be easier to judge from a bar than from a circle, and components would be easier to compare as rectangles than as slices of pies.

Coloring, cross-hatching, and shading are also appropriate with a bar chart. When using any of these techniques, however, one should include some type of legend to aid in identifying components. In addition, writers can heighten the informational impact of the bar chart by having the amounts typed inside the segments where possible. Figure 7–2 illustrates a typical component bar chart.

Line Graphs

The line graph represents a fine balance between informational and dramatic impact. It conveys the overall advances and declines of amounts or trends while at the same time presenting specific dates and amounts. The line graph also allows the reader to compare the activities of several factors at one time. You can plot several lines (no more than four) within a single graph with each representing a different product or factor. Again, color often improves the reader's comprehension of the graph. If color is not feasible or desirable, a writer can always use different types of lines (solid, broken, dotted) to delineate the separate entries.

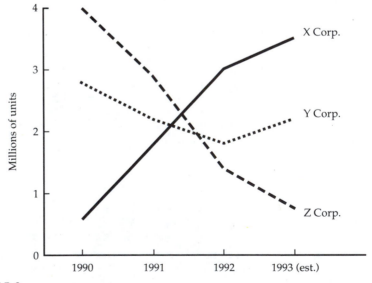

FIGURE 7–3

Sample Line Chart

TABLE 7–1 Tabor Company's Annual Product Sales for the Last Three Years
(in thousands of dollars)

	Year		
Product	*1990*	*1991*	*1992*
Heaters	632	716	805
Bread makers	231	367	592
Indoor grills	114	298	613

Line graphs must represent information accurately. The scales chosen for a graph should accurately represent the quantity symbolized. Graphs can be, and are, manipulated, though, so as to minimize or maximize trends. One manager may show new car sales statewide using units rather than tens or thousands of units along the quantity axis. Doing so exaggerates the point being made. Similarly, one might divide the quantity axis by hundreds or thousands to downplay the number of on-the-job accidents in a company. While no clear-cut rule can be given for scale divisions, common sense dictates that the scale should accurately represent any trends being reported. Figure 7–3 illustrates a typical line graph.

Tables

Tables, very useful visual communication devices, arrange data in a concise manner that permits easy comparisons of statistics. As mentioned earlier, they are informational and not as dramatic as other visual aids. Additionally, for making projections, they do not carry the credibility of line graphs.[13] Nonetheless, they assist the reader in grasping complex statistical or factual data far more easily than if the material appeared in the text.

Tables range from informal listings that appear without heading or ruling, and are intended merely to aid comprehension, to complex formal reference tables. Tables use columns and rows to illustrate relationships. Several rules apply to constructing a table:

1. Identify each reference table with a title and number (and source notation, if appropriate).
2. Use the left-hand vertical column, the stub, to list items detailed in the horizontal rows to the right. This row head defines its subject.
3. Use the column headings (listed horizontally at the top) to indicate the material in each vertical column below them.
4. Use rulings if necessary to set off column heads and stubs, but not so much that the table is cluttered.

5. Use abbreviations and symbols where appropriate.
6. Align figures on the decimal points; align figures with no decimals on the right.
7. Keep the tables as simple and uncluttered as possible leaving adequate white space.

Table 7–1 illustrates a typical tabular visual aid.

Summary

Reports, among an organization's most important communications, help managers to plan, organize, execute, evaluate, and correct. Managers write these reports as a matter of duty, or because they have been assigned to do so, or because they themselves see a need for one. In preparing to write a report, a writer must first define the problem to be addressed. Then, if the report is analytical, he must formulate hypotheses. The final step is to seek data needed either for information or to prove or disprove the hypotheses.

While one can classify reports using a variety of systems, perhaps the most useful is based on formality. How formal or informal a report is depends on several strategic considerations: the audience, the effort expended on researching and writing the report, the report's value, the original assignment, and the company policy.

The order chosen in a report is significant. Direct order is appropriate in most report writing situations, especially those dealing with good news or neutral information. It places the main conclusions and recommendations at the beginning of the report. Indirect order, best for reports delivering bad news and for formal reports, puts the main points last. The material with the body, however, may be organized by time, place, quantity, and factors.

The care that goes into solving a formal report problem should be reflected in the paper, the typing, and the arrangement of the final report. Reports use headings to guide the reader through the report. The typing and placement of the headings generally indicate the relative significance of the material they cover.

The memo report is the most common informal report within an organization. The material in its body can be set off using headings and tabulation, as necessary. Letter reports are similar but are intended for audiences outside the organization. They also usually attempt to build goodwill, a characteristic that is not as significant with memo reports.

The formal report typically consists of a number of elements, which may be broken down into prefatory parts (they precede the report itself) and the report proper. Prefatory parts include the title fly, title page, letter of transmittal, table of contents, list of tables and figures, and synopsis. Usually, the longer and more formal the report becomes, the more prefatory parts a reader is likely to find. The report proper includes a formal introduction, the major subdivisions that make up the report body, and the ending section made up of summary, conclusions, and/or recommendations.

Visual aids exist on a continuum ranging from dramatic to informational. The choice of visual aids depends on the audience's knowledge of the subject. The visual aid should be appropriate to the text, placed close to its first reference, and given an appropriate size. Pie charts are useful for showing proportional amounts of a unit. Although largely dramatic, their informational impact can be enhanced. Bar charts are also dramatic, but they can clearly represent information as well. The component bar chart is particularly useful for making proportional comparisons between (or among) different totals. The line graph strikes a balance between informational and dramatic impact, but it must be constructed with care to be accurate. Tables arrange data concisely, permitting readers to compare statistics. Though not as dramatic as other visual aids, they still make their content much easier to understand than the same information presented in the report's text.

Endnotes

1. Anita S. Bednar and Robert J. Olney, "Communication Needs of Recent Graduates," *Bulletin of the Association for Business Communication* L, no. 4 (December 1987), pp. 22–23.
2. C. Gilbert Storms, "What Business School Graduates Say About the Writing They Do at Work: Implications for the Business Communications Course," *Bulletin of the Association for Business Communication* XLVI, no. 4 (December 1983), pp. 13–18.
3. Marie Flatley, "A Comparative Analysis of the Written Communication of Managers at Various Organizational Levels in the Private Business Sector," *Journal of Business Communication* 19, no. 3 (Summer 1982), pp. 35–50.
4. Patricia Dorazio, "Preparing Technical Proposals: Planning and Prewriting Considerations," *Bulletin of the Association for Business Communication* LV, no. 3 (September 1992), pp. 49–52.
5. Marvin Swift, "Writing a Problem-Centered Report," *Bulletin of the Association for Business Communication* XLVI, no. 3 (September 1983), pp. 19–23.
6. James Van Oosting, "The 'Well-Made' Report," *Bulletin of the Association for Business Communication* XLV, no. 4 (December 1982), pp. 9–10.
7. Carol S. Lipson, "Theoretical and Empirical Considerations for Designing Openings of Business and Technical Reports," *Journal of Business Communication* 20, no. 1 (Winter 1983), pp. 41–54.
8. Frank Weightman, "The Executive Summary: An Indispensable Management Tool," *Bulletin of the Association for Business Communication* XLV, no. 4 (December 1982), pp. 3–5.
9. Claudia Mon Pere Isaac, "Improving Student Summaries Through Sequencing," *Bulletin of the Association for Business Communication* L, no. 3 (September 1987), pp. 17–20.

10. F. Stanford Wayne and Jolene D. Scriven, "Problem and Purpose Statements: Are They Synonymous Terms in Writing Business Reports?" *Bulletin of the Association for Business Communication* LIV, no. 1 (March 1991), pp. 30–37.
11. Becky K. Peterson, "Tables and Graphs Improve Reader Performance and Reader Reaction," *Journal of Business Communication* 20, no. 2 (Spring 1983), pp. 47–56.
12. Steve Golden and Michael Lynn, "Computer Graphics: A Survival Tactics for Managers," *Bulletin of the Association for Business Communication* XLVIII, no. 4 (December 1985), pp. 11–13.
13. Jeremiah J. Sullivan, "Financial Presentation Format and Managerial Decision Making: Tables Versus Graphs," *Management Communication Quarterly* 2, no. 2 (November 1988), pp. 194–216.

Additional Readings

Barabas, Christine. *Technical Writing in a Corporate Culture: A Study of the Nature of Information.* Norwood, N.J.: Ablex Publishing Co., 1990.

Barton, Ben F., and Marthalee S. Barton. "Modes for Power in Technical and Professional Visuals." *Journal of Business and Technical Communication* 7, no. 1 (January 1993), pp. 138–62.

Bowen, Richard W. *Graph It! How to Make, Read, and Interpret Graphs.* Englewood Cliffs, N.J.: Prentice Hall, 1992.

Bowman, Joel P., and Bernadine P. Branchaw. *Business Report Writing,* 2nd ed. Chicago: The Dryden Press, 1988.

Golen, Steve, C. Glenn Pearce, and Ross Figgins. *Report Writing for Business and Industry.* New York: John Wiley and sons, 1985.

Hagge, John. "Review Essay: Research in Technical Communication: A Bibliographic Sourcebook. *Journal of Business Communication* 24, no. 2 (Spring 1987), pp. 29–33.

Kuiper, Shirley, and Cheryl M. Luke. *Report Writing With Microcomputer Applications.* Cincinnati: South-Western Publishing Company, 1992.

Olsen, Leslie A., and Thomas N. Huckin. *Technical Writing and Professional Communication,* 2nd ed. New York: McGraw-Hill, Inc., 1991.

Sides, Charles H., ed. *Technical and Business Communication: Bibliographic Essays for Teachers and Corporate Trainers.* Washington, D.C., and Urbana, Ill.: National Council of Teachers of English and Society for Technical Communication, 1989.

Tufte, Edward R. *The Visual Display of Quantitative Information.* Cheshire, Conn.: Graphics Press, 1983.

Varner, Iris I. *Contemporary Business Report Writing,* 2nd ed. Chicago: The Dryden Press, 1991.

Discussion Questions

1. How can the format of a report reflect a writer's strategic consideration of the situation?
2. What is the direct order in report writing? When should it be used?

3. What is the indirect order in report writing? When is it appropriate?

4. Which is the most useful way to organize data in a report? Why?

5. What would be the best basis for organizing the major subdivisions of a site selection report's body?

6. How should the subject line be worded in an indirectly organized memorandum report?

7. What is an effective way to end a directly organized memo report?

8. Why is the indirect order often preferred in letter reports?

9. Explain the differences between dramatic and informational visual aids. Why is the line graph both dramatic and informational?

10. Where should visual aids be placed in the report text?

11. What size is appropriate for a visual aid?

12. What are the strengths of the pie chart? What are its weaknesses?

13. Briefly compare and contrast the uses of the pie chart and component bar chart?

14. What steps should one take to make sure a line graph accurately represents the data it plots?

15. How do headings in a report indicate the relative significance of the material?

16. What purposes does the letter of transmittal serve?

17. At a minimum, what elements should a writer include in the introduction to formal reports?

18. Find a visual aid in *The Wall Street Journal* or *Business Week* or in a company's annual report. Explain why they chose to use that type of visual aid.

Exercise 7–1

Assume you are a middle-level marketing manager in a large wholesale organization. This morning, your boss called you into her office and informed you that 126 cars in the company's sales fleet were ready for replacement. She asked you to do the research and write a report that would recommend a purchase to replace the cars about to be retired.

Pick four cars that are comparable—for example, the Ford Taurus, the Honda Accord, the Chevrolet Lumina, and the Toyota Camry. In selecting a particular type of car, you might want to make some assumptions about the products handled by your salespeople and whether they carry samples. For the purposes of this report, we will assume you considered other similar cars but the four you choose are the top contenders.

Your next task is to identify the criteria to be used in selecting the car to be purchased. Remember that the quality of your research and report will hinge largely on how thoroughly you identify the relevant criteria to be weighed. Once you have identified the criteria to be used and all subfactors of those criteria, you are ready to begin your research. You will probably find *Consumer*

Reports to be an invaluable source of information, but don't overlook other less obvious sources, such as dealerships.

After collecting and organizing your information, you will be ready to write your report. What format should that report take? Which strategic aspects ought to be considered in determining that format? If you choose to use a formal report format, which prefatory parts should you include? Which subsections should you include in the introduction? How should the body of the report be organized? What will the ending section of the report proper contain?

Exercise 7–2

Develop a questionnaire containing at least 10 statements about typical ethical dilemmas faced by businesspeople. Use "agree __disagree__undecided__" as response options. Possibilities might include, "It is acceptable for an American businessperson in a foreign country to bribe a public official if that practice is accepted and expected in that country." Another possibility might include, "It is acceptable to give a poorly performing employee a good reference to get rid of him or her."

At the end of the questionnaire, ask for some demographic information that might make the analyses of your findings more interesting. You might ask for gender, class status, age, business experience (yes or no, and perhaps years of experience), whether or not the respondent is a practicing member of a religious faith, and so on.

Next, circulate the questionnaire randomly on campus, perhaps at malls or at the student union building. Try to get at least 100 respondents. Remember that the larger your sample, the better your findings will be statistically. You might even consider having a ballot-like box with you to assure confidentiality.

After you have collected your data and analyzed your findings, you will be ready to put your information into a report to be presented to your instructor. What format will that report assume? What factors should you consider in determining that format? What parts will the report contain? Will you use the direct or indirect order? On what basis will the body of the report be organized?

An interesting twist on this report might be to circulate the questionnaire to businesspeople. In the demographic section, you could ask for level within the organization, rather than class status. And instead of asking whether they have had work experience, you could ask for years of experience. You might even ask for marital status and whether they have children. Additionally, you could ask for years of formal education.

If it were possible for you to circulate the questionnaire to people on campus and to businesspeople, you might then be able to compare the results overall.

III   STRATEGIES FOR ORAL MANAGERIAL COMMUNICATION

The three chapters in this section each analyze an aspect of managerial communication that is quite different from those in Section II; however, they are all related to the development of a managerial communication strategy. Chapter 8 reviews the many strategic considerations of oral presentations, such as the presentation plan and the use of visual aids. Each of these strategic considerations is contingent on audience analysis, which is also reviewed in Chapter 8.

The next chapter on managerial listening is so fundamental to effective management that it could have easily been situated earlier in the book. Listening to both informal and formal messages is discussed in this chapter as well as techniques for creating a productive listening climate.

Chapter 10 reviews another pervasive aspect of managerial communication: nonverbal communication. In addition to the traditional nonverbal communication topics of kinesics, proxemics, haptics, and dress, attention is given to nonverbal communication between genders and nonverbal leakage as cues to deception.

8 STRATEGIES FOR MAKING AN ORAL PRESENTATION

> *You are the marketing manager for the office furnishings division of a large furniture company. As you walked into the office this morning, the administrative assistant to the vice-president of marketing had a note for you that read, "Please have a short presentation on office trends in the 1990s ready for the executive group tomorrow morning."*
>
> *Your first reaction to this request is not printable. You are already facing a very busy schedule today, so you will have limited time to prepare this presentation. Furthermore, the vice-president is tied up with the executive group all day, so you will not have an opportunity to get a better description of what is expected.*
>
> *What is the purpose of the presentation? How can you find out more about the audience and what these people might expect? How can you best use your limited time for preparation? Should you use a flip chart, overheads, or slides? How long is "short"? These are a few of the questions you will need to answer as you develop your strategy for the presentation.*

Four steps to achievement: Plan purposefully. Prepare prayerfully. Proceed positively. Pursue persistently.

William Ward

Managers today find that presentation skills are important for a multitude of situations. At any time, they might be called on to present a product report, a marketing status report, a persuasive report to persuade higher management to accept a new product design, a financial report, or even an after-dinner speech to honor the winner of a cost-saving campaign.

For several reasons, the value of competency in presentational speaking is likely to grow.[1] First, as organizations become more complex, managers are often called on to present proposals and make explanations to large numbers of people. Second, products and services also are becoming more complex. The public may require detailed explanations of their function and/or design. Third, as organizations become more dependent on each other, it is necessary to share information in the form of public speeches and even TV presentations in some cases.

No matter what the topic, a presentation is a critical form of communication. It is generally given to a group of decision makers on an important topic. It is essential that these decision makers have timely and understandable information.[2] To be effective in making such presentations, managers need to understand the components of small-group dynamics, as well as the essentials of oral presentations. To assist readers in meeting these challenges, this chapter examines the purpose, preparation, delivery, and summation of an oral report.

Purpose

The first step in an effective presentation is to determine the purpose. The purpose is generally to inform or persuade the audience, but both purposes may be served at once. When, for example, an engineering sales representative presents a product design to a client's engineering management group, she might have two purposes in mind. She will want to inform the audience of the product's technical features, and she will want to persuade the group to order the product.

In some situations, the exact purpose is easy to determine; but in others, the purpose may be unclear. It may be unclear because the speaker and the audience have two different goals. For instance, the audience may want to know the most cost-effective location for a new manufacturing plant. The speaker, however, may want the audience to accept a certain location that has a special need for economic development. That is, the audience wants to be informed, whereas the speaker wants to persuade.

The purpose may also vary within the group. Consider an audience that consists of five people: a vice-president, a production superintendent, a director of finance, a marketing manager, and a personnel director. Suppose they were all attending a presentation comparing the relative success of two products introduced in a test market three months ago. What is "relative success" to each audience member? Each will look at the products from a different perspective because of differing functional responsibilities. The marketing manager may think in terms of market share, whereas the finance manager may look at only the cost factors. What type of information should the speaker emphasize?

The power and status of the different audience members can also influence the overall purpose. One member's viewpoint may initially differ from that of another member, but the more powerful person can quickly influence the less powerful member. In the previous example, the vice-president may simply say that the most important consideration is the expansion of production facilities required by the two new products. Suddenly, the definition of "relative success" has changed again. Though the goal of informing the audience has remained the same, the information required to meet this goal has been shaped by the audience.

The best way to ensure clarity of purpose is to write out a statement of the purpose and put a title on it. This act not only forces the speaker to think about the purpose, but also the written statement can then be presented to an associate or to likely audience members for their reaction. The feedback will help the speaker define the purpose clearly and accurately.

Preparation

Once the communicator has clearly established her purpose, the necessary preparation follows. She must consider cost and time throughout the preparation stage to determine what expense can be justified. One five-minute presentation might involve hundreds of hours and cost thousands of dollars; another could require a minimum of effort. As with any managerial communication, a manager must make some strategic decisions.

Preparation is generally the most time-consuming aspect of the effort. Unfortunately, the quantity of time spent preparing does not always guarantee proportionate quality in the presentation. The following suggestions, therefore, are aimed at helping presenters to prepare systematically and thoroughly for an effective and timely presentation.

Length of the Presentation

The first task is to plan the length of the presentation. Sometimes managers have no choice here, as when they are given a set amount of time, perhaps five minutes before the board of directors. In such cases, it is crucial to stay within the assigned time limit. The audience is probably listening to a number of such presentations. When many speakers exceed their time limits, the audience becomes less and less receptive to the proposals of the transgressors.

Even when speakers are given some choice on the length of the presentation, most make them too long rather than too short. Speakers should remember that it is difficult to hold people's attention beyond 20 to 30 minutes. When a presentation goes beyond 15 minutes, the speaker should divide it into major segments by using reviews, questions, or graphics.

Audience understanding does not necessarily last as long as the speaker's. Just because a speaker is eloquent for an hour does not mean others are listening and understanding. To improve effectiveness, the speaker needs to watch the audience for nonverbal and verbal feedback to evaluate comprehension.[3] This feedback will probably indicate it is best to keep the presentation short.

Audience Analysis

At the same time that effective managers analyze the purpose, they begin to analyze the audience. In any communication process, people naturally tend to become self-centered. Thus, a speaker may concentrate on his or her interests and the delivery and forget about the audience. One group of consultants on oral presentations noted that, time and time again, managers prepare messages that fail to tell the listeners what they want and need to hear but, rather, focus on the speaker's interests.[4]

The most successful presentations are prepared with a particular audience in mind and are organized to suit the knowledge, attitudes, likes, and dislikes of individual audience members. Many presentations are technically well delivered, but they fail because the speakers do not anticipate audience reaction.

Though audience analysis is part of the "pre-talk" preparation, a speaker should also be ready to analyze on the spot. During delivery, the presentation may be modified to reflect audience factors not available in advance. For instance, a speaker would need to alter her presentation if she found that a critical decision maker needing special information decided at the last minute to attend the presentation. Nevertheless, when a thorough audience analysis precedes a presentation, few last-minute adjustments should be required.

The audience analysis guide sheet provided at the end of this chapter is designed to assist readers in analyzing audiences. Each question on the guide sheet should be answered as thoroughly as possible. If all the questions cannot be answered with confidence, some investigative work is needed. Once all the questions have been answered, it might be beneficial to ask another person to answer them as well, to compare answers. This feedback is especially important when the presentation is critical but little is known about the audience.

If the speaker already knows the audience well, a thorough analysis is not necessary. For instance, an internal auditor who gives a quarterly report to a bank's board of directors may not need a separate analysis each quarter. However, a periodic review of the audience may remind the speaker about some of its special characteristics. It may be easy to forget that the interests, technical knowledge, or attitudes differ from one board member to another; thus, a quick audience analysis will help to reorient the speaker.

The Presentation Plan

The next step after audience analysis is preparing the plan of presentation. The plan is essentially the work sheet for the presentation and addresses two important concerns: how to organize the message and what kind of information to present. These two questions go hand in hand because the organization of the presentation will generally determine the information required.

Persuasive Presentations

As mentioned earlier, the purpose of an oral presentation can be stated as informative and/or persuasive. Howell and Borman discuss three patterns that provide meaningful strategies for persuasive situations: the scientific problem-solving pattern, the state-the-case-and-prove-it approach, and the psychological-progressive pattern.[5]

The first pattern, scientific problem solving, is most often effective in the discussion of a relatively complicated problem, especially if the audience is largely ignorant of the facts or is likely to be hostile to the message. With this approach, the speaker leads the audience through a systematic series of steps, which begins with a definition of the problem, then moves to an exploration of the problem (which includes an examination of causes and effects), then enumerates and evaluates representative solutions, and, when appropriate, recommends the objective selection of the best solution.

The manager using this plan must be especially well prepared on all aspects of the situation. The audience is probably not familiar with the problem, its causes, and potential remedies. The assumption is that the speaker possesses important information that will be shared on the way to an objective and logical discovery of the best solution. From there, the analysis of the problem must proceed with objectivity and candor.

The second pattern of organization for persuasion, state the case and prove it, is relatively simple. It entails the straightforward development of a central thesis with supporting arguments. Normally, each supporting element begins with a contention or topic sentence followed immediately by substantiation. Typically, the pattern consists of an introduction followed by a thesis statement; then each supporting contention has appropriate elaboration and support. The presentation closes with a summary reiterating the proposition.

Whereas the scientific problem-solving pattern is an inductive organizational approach, the state-the-case-and-prove-it approach is deductive. It begins with a general conclusion and then justifies it. This second approach is appropriate for organizing discussions of familiar, much argued topics. The audience familiar with a topic has no need to explore it gradually and comprehensively.

The third organizational strategy, the psychological-progressive pattern, involves five steps: (1) arouse, (2) dissatisfy, (3) gratify, (4) picture, and (5) move. Using this pattern, a manager first determines an appropriate attention-catching device. The next task is to demonstrate the nature of the problem, in a way that sets out the difficulties, tensions, or pathos of a specific situation of immediate concern. Then the speaker links the recommendation with the problem so the decision-making audience can understand the proposal as a viable solution.

It is not enough, however, that the audience simply understand the advantages of the recommended solution; the accepting audience usually needs to be moved both rationally and emotionally. Thus, the manager should focus on helping the audience to see how the recommendation will remedy the situation. Basically, the psychological-progressive pattern is a problem-solving approach to oral presentation that is ideally suited to presentations designed to innovate or effect change.

A city manager asking the city council for an additional $200,000 in the budget for snow-removal equipment gives a clear example of the psychological-progressive approach. The request was made during June because the new budget began July 1.

> Remember last February when we had to cancel our city council meeting because of the snow and ice on the streets! Not only did we cancel the meeting, but some of us couldn't get to work, children couldn't get to school, and in some cases it was even difficult to buy groceries (arouse).
>
> This was not only an inconvenience; it was a potentially dangerous situation. Emergency health care could have been a problem! Fortunately, no emergencies developed. Furthermore, it cost employees lost work time, and it made our city look inefficient. Our city works manager, who has been with us more than 15 years, was extremely demoralized at the inability to do anything about the situation due to the shortage of equipment (dissatisfy).
>
> This problem can be solved with the purchase of four additional plows! These plows have been offered at a special price from Kast Manufacturing in Minneapolis, which has more than 20 years of experience with snowplows. They also provide free delivery of the plows and a three-year warranty on all the hydraulic systems and an eight-year warranty on the main blade and all structural components. In other words, this purchase will take care of our needs for a long time.
>
> With this addition and the resolution of the snow-removal problem, this council will be identified as a group with vision and the ability for long-range planning rather than short-term reactions (gratify and picture).
>
> I am asking you to approve an additional $200,000 for next year's budget so that we can purchase four more snowplows. This would then become part of the city works equipment budget (action). This action will resolve our snow-removal problem next year and for many years in the future.

Persuasion Variables

As the preceding discussion indicated, different persuasive approaches are suited to different occasions or circumstances. To be a truly strategic attempt at persuasion, however, a person's efforts and ultimately his success should be moderated by a number of variables. These variables might be categorized under the labels of source, message, receiver, and context.[6]

Under variables associated with the *source* of the persuasion, probably the most significant variable is the source's credibility. Dimensions of source credibility include competence and trustworthiness; education, occupation and experience; the citation of evidence; and the position advocated (in other words, how much of a change in attitude the source is asking for). Whether or not the source is liked will probably affect how persuasive he is going to be. Also, the degree of similarity between the source and the people he is trying to persuade frequently affects success. Physical attractiveness has even been linked to persuasiveness in some studies. Finally, sex is apparently a factor, with most research indicating men are perceived as being more persuasive than women.[7]

A number of *message* variables can contribute to the success of a persuasive effort. The order of the information is one. Should a persuader be direct or indirect? Research indicates indirect approach is generally best. Another factor involves whether a person should be explicit or implicit in stating what is desired. Though most studies indicate that being explicit is generally best, some evidence supports being implicit for audiences that are highly intelligent and educated and/or familiar with the subject. Also under message content, should a persuader ignore or refute opposing arguments? It is usually best to refute them. On a related note, the persuader should address relevant obstacles. Finally, most studies conclude that concrete examples are more persuasive than statistical summaries.

Under *receiver* variables, one might consider the general persuadability of the person. Some people are simply more susceptible to persuasion than are others. Sex may also be a factor, with most studies finding women slightly more persuadable than men. Finally, are there personality traits related to ease or difficulty with which a receiver is persuaded? Research provides a very mixed answer to that question. For example, some studies show self-esteem positively related to persuadability, while others show a negative relationship. One possible explanation is that some personality traits provide effects that both enhance and prohibit persuasion. For example, intelligent receivers would be better able to understand persuasive messages, but they would also be better able to see weaknesses in a message and think up counterarguments. Much research remains to be done to uncover any stable relationships between personality traits and persuadability.

Context variables include primacy/recency effects, media, and persistence effects. In general, the order of a persuasive message (first or second) is not related to success. There is, however, some evidence that primacy effects are more likely to be found with interesting, controversial, and familiar topics, while recency effects are more common with topics that are relatively uninteresting, noncontroversial, and unfamiliar. With regard to the many media available today, research remains inconclusive as to their persuasion capabilities. To illustrate, if a company finds its TV advertising more effective than its radio advertising, do we conclude that the audiovisual medium is more persuasive than the audio medium? Or is the company's target market more likely to watch TV than listen to the radio? Or is that target just more likely to be watching the shows that feature the company's commercials?

The last context variable is the persistence of the persuasive message. Generally, persuasive effects will evaporate or decay over time. Thus, for maximum effectiveness, persuasive messages should be delivered as temporally close as possible to the point of decision or action. Thus, politicians usually spend the bulk of their advertising budget in the week before the election.

Though no one can prescribe a guaranteed plan for persuading people, we nonetheless recommend that managers seriously consider the variables described above as they develop their persuasive strategies. To the extent that they do, they should find that their rate of persuasive success increases appreciably.

Informational Presentations

Managers generally use the three approaches described in the preceding pages for persuasive situations. But what if the purpose of the presentation is simply to describe or inform? In these situations, it is best to organize the information in a definite sequence. Clarity may demand that a subject be presented one way as opposed to another, or the subject itself may suggest the best pattern or arrangement. Some of the arrangement possibilities are listed below.

Geographic region.
Political and economic categories.
Importance.
Time.
Advantages and disadvantages.
Differences and similarities.
Structure and function.

Whatever the division of the subject or the order in which it is to be presented, it is important to have a definite and strategic plan. And smooth transition is the key to the clarity of the plan's organization. A bridge or link must exist between one unit and another so the audience sees the organizational plan. As the speaker moves to a new unit, this link may take the form of a summary that simply states that a new unit will now be discussed or contrasts what has just been presented with that which is to follow. Another device is the repetition of key words or phrases for emphasis. Some examples of links appear below.

Now for the second major difference.
The next product, wood desks, differs from the last product, tables, in three ways.
Now for the present activities.
This geographic region includes Montana, Idaho, and Wyoming.
To begin . . . .
Not only . . . .
Also . . . .
Finally . . . .

Evidence

The type of information and corresponding research required for the presentation largely depend on which of the two types of evidence is required: fact or opinion. Evidence of fact is an objective description of something using empirical evidence without interpretation or judgment. Evidence of opinion is the application of interpretation and judgment.

Three types of opinions may be used in a presentation: personal, lay, and expert. While all managers probably support their presentations with personal views from time to time, success in using personal opinions for support largely depends on the manager's credibility with the audience. A manager uses lay opinion when citing the opinions of ordinary people (nonexperts). This source is prevalent in presentations on marketing or personnel problems.

A manager uses expert opinion when citing an authority to provide evidence. This form of evidence works well when objective facts are difficult to find. However, the expert chosen must be objective and possess actual expertise. A baseball player may be an expert in baseball but not on the quality of paint, advertising notwithstanding.

Different presentation strategies require different evidence. The psychological-progressive pattern generally requires less factual information and more psychological appeal. Consequently, it places more emphasis on personal opinion than on empirical information. The state-the-case-and-prove-it and scientific problem-solving patterns require extensive facts in most situations. Personal opinion is advisable in the latter cases only when the manager has a high degree of credibility, and expert opinion is valuable when there is no doubt about the authority of the expert.

The Introduction

The most crucial part of a presentation is the introduction. A presentation should begin with a clear statement of the purpose that captures the audience's attention. The more specifically the speaker states what she will present, the easier it will be for the audience to follow the main ideas systematically. They are, in effect, prepared for the report.

Humor or trite remarks in introductions are not appropriate if the speaker intends to maintain the focus on serious discussion. Too often, speakers begin with a humorous story that detracts from the substance of the report. For most business reports, speakers should just get down to business with the material.

At the same time, it is not necessary and may even be detrimental to begin with an apology. Beginning with "I know that you do not want to be here," or "I realize that it is late in the day," or "I am not much of a speaker," does little to enhance speaker credibility and may detract from the audience's perception of the meeting.

Instead, begin the report with a positive statement that has impact. Several strategies used in the introduction can clearly state the purpose, even as they catch the audience's attention:

1. A startling or shocking statement:

   If our costs continue to increase over the next five years at the rate they have in the past five, we will have to charge over $75 for our lowest-priced shirt. Today, I will present four strategies for reducing costs in . . . .

2. A hypothetical statement:

   What would happen if we could no longer obtain the silver we need to produce XY 115? I am going to show you a viable substitute for that metal.

3. Some historical event:

   It was just eight years ago this week that we purchased the Bordin division, our first major acquisition. This presentation will review the progress of our purchases.

4. A question or a series of questions (they do not always have to be answered; they can be used just to stimulate the audience):

   What will the inflation rate be in 1995? Will the energy problem continue? This presentation will outline the reasons we need a market projection plan.

5. Reference to some current event:

   On Tuesday, February 19, Millville had a chemical fire that killed 5 people and injured 15. To avoid that kind of disaster in our operations, we need to increase our budget for safety training.

6. A quotation:

   The national director of the health department has stated, "The number one health problem today is alcoholism. One in 10 Americans has a drinking problem." This serious problem is one of the many reasons we need an employee assistance program.

Whatever opening is selected, a speaker's main goal is the development of a dynamic, attention-getting opening statement.[8] Its success will set the tone for the rest of the presentation.

Audience Participation

Though audience participation can never be fully predicted, speakers, during the preparation stage, should decide on the general level of participation desired. Admittedly, the appropriate level of audience involvement varies from presentation to presentation. Even so, speakers need to keep two facts in mind. First, a speaker can achieve audience involvement with any size group; and second, involvement will generally facilitate the communication process.

The discussion of the managerial communication model in Chapter 2 emphasizes the importance of feedback, and the discussion of listening in Chapter 9 indicates the difficulty of maintaining attention on one topic for a long period. Audience participation is a valuable source of feedback and a useful way to maintain their interest.

In one effective technique for a large group (over 30 people), the speaker simply asks the audience to answer questions on a notepad. After they have had time to respond to the questions, the speaker presents answers audience members can compare with their own. This technique gets the audience involved.

A smaller group can be involved in many different ways. The speaker can ask participants for their reaction, offer to answer questions before the end of the presentation, and/or ask questions of members of the audience. The crucial element to remember is that effective speakers usually stay away from the "I talk, you listen" syndrome, which often is the best way to lose the interest of the group.

Visual Aids

Visual aids represent another way of maintaining audience attention and involvement. Since the spoken word is, at best limited in communication, and since its sound is transitory, the listener may miss the message, the opportunity to hear it again may never arise. However, visual support can help to overcome these limitations. Additionally, visual aids can add clarity to complex information.

Criteria

Good visual aids make a positive impression on the audience and justify the time spent in their preparation. An effective aid is one designed to fit the speaker, the audience, and the room. Three criteria for an effective visual aid are:

1. *Visibility.* The visual aid must be easy to read. Some speakers attempt to make visual aids from printed material; these are generally poor because lettering on visual aids must be larger and bolder than normal typewriter or printer lettering. Also, technical drawings cannot easily be used; lines on many of the drawings are lost because they are so faint. Little is more irritating to an audience than to be told there is something important on the visual aid that they cannot see. Have the artwork drawn to eliminate unnecessary lines and to make essential lines heavier on the drawing.

2. *Clarity.* Clarity refers to what an audience understands from a visual. Make the main points easy to identify. Color is a good way to focus the audience's attention on the important parts of the visual. Though statistics show that audiences remember only 20 percent of

what they hear but 80 percent of what they see, they must be able to understand what they see to remember it.[9]

3. *Simplicity.* After determining the content of a visual aid, look for ways to simplify it. Nothing should appear on the visual aid except the content relevant to the specific ideas to be communicated. Do not use a graphic just because it is handy when it was really prepared for some other purpose.

Keep several rules in mind when preparing a visual aid. These are not magic formulas, but they are helpful guidelines. First, no visual aid with words should contain more than seven lines. Second, no line should contain more than seven words. To meet these first two rules, a speaker may need to use more than one visual aid or design overlays to build a more complex visual.

Third, rows or columns of data should be shown a single line at a time by using an accentuation technique to keep the audience's attention on the point of discussion. Simple accentuation techniques include pointing with a pencil or using a piece of paper to reveal only the items under discussion.

Types

The criteria for effective visual aids are universal, but a speaker must still choose a particular type of visual aid. Though the choice will be influenced by the size and type of audience, the choice for many speakers is the overhead transparency. Because the room lights are left on and the speaker faces the audience, the overhead projector allows the maximum relationship with the audience. Additionally, several techniques ensure flexible presentation of the material: covering the visual and gradually revealing certain parts during the presentation, using overlays for added detail, and moving the transparency.

The blackboard is an impromptu speaking tool to be used only when there is insufficient time to prepare anything else. The speaker writing on the blackboard has to face the board while writing and must erase frequently. While the speaker's back is turned and eye contact is eliminated, the audience's attention may dwindle. A flip chart is better than a blackboard. One can use different colors for emphasis, and the tool presents a professional image. Both standing and table flip charts may be used. A related option is the electronic whiteboard. A speaker can use a felt-tip pen to write on a whiteboard and, with the push of a button, can generate a hard copy of what has been written.

While slides can be very colorful and professional looking, they have traditionally had two major disadvantages: the lead time for preparation was long and the room had to be darkened, distancing the speaker from the audience. Today's technology is doing much to eliminate those disadvantages. Many photo labs now offer one-hour processing, and color film recorders now make it possible to prepare color slides directly from computer output, in effect providing a picture of what is seen on the computer screen.[10] Additionally, modern hardware and software make it possible to show slides without darkening a room.

Whether speakers choose to use slides or transparencies, they should weigh the many advantages of computer-generated presentation graphics. The hardware and software now available allow presenters to produce professional, interest-arresting graphics with great ease, speed, and economy. One survey found 78.7 percent of responding firms making presentation transparencies in-house and 56.0 percent of those respondents making slides in-house.[11] In fact, companies are now incorporating presentation graphics software into their day-to-day internal communications and into their decision-making process, as well as into the graphics department.[12]

Along with ease of use, audience size, visibility, clarity, and simplicity, the timing of the visual aid contributes to its effectiveness. Since the visual aid is a graphical message intended to complement the verbal message, both messages should be presented at the same time. An aid should not be visible until it is used, and it should be removed after it has been discussed so it does not distract the audience. A common mistake of many managers is to leave a flip chart open or keep an overhead projector on after the need for the visual has passed.[13]

Distributed materials (handouts) are another optional form of visual aid. These written materials are different from the other visual aids because each member of the audience receives a copy, which may be used for reference during and after the presentation. Handouts are particularly valuable when the subject calls for such items as complicated charts and graphs, detailed regulations, points of law, or company policy. Often the material can be distributed to the participants before the meeting, so less time need be spent during the meeting for preliminary briefing. It is then possible to go directly to the discussion phase of the presentation.

When planning to distribute materials during the meeting, limit the information to what is required and do not distribute it until it is needed. Too many materials in front of the audience may distract them from the verbal message. The audience will be tempted to review the handout for one topic while the speaker is discussing a different one. Naturally, this reduces the impact of the message.

Delivery

Now is the time for the real test: delivering the message. Thorough preparation will allow concentration on a number of elements that require attention during the delivery. A well-prepared speaker will have analyzed the audience and will have an idea of what to expect from the various members. The opening statement is ready, and the message is organized. Visual aids are prepared, and the speaker has developed a plan for audience participation.

But what about stage fright? It might be consoling to know that about 60 percent of all speakers experience anxiety to some degree before speaking. A survey of 3,000 Americans revealed that the prospect of giving a speech brings forth the greatest fear that people possess; they fear it even more than dying.[14] On this very subject, George Jessel, the late entertainer, once said, "The human brain is a wonderful organ. It starts to work as soon as you are born and doesn't stop until you get up to deliver a public speech."

Stage fright doesn't limit itself to people who only occasionally speak to audiences. It has been known to haunt some very well-known people who make or made their living in front of audiences. Sir Laurence Olivier, perhaps the greatest actor to have ever graced stage and screen, had stage fright. He called it "the dreaded terror." Hugh Downs had such mike fright during the first 10 years of his radio career that he had to grab his lapels to keep his hands from shaking so he could read the script. Edward R. Murrow is quoted as having said, "I always develop some nervousness before speaking. The moisture in the palms of my hands is the sweat of perfection."

The best solution to anxiety is preparation. As people become better prepared to perform a task, their confidence generally increases, which, in turn, reduces anxiety. Rehearsal of the entire presentation is advisable when anxiety is particularly high. The speaker should become more comfortable with each rehearsal.[15]

But no matter how well prepared a person might be, some anxiety may remain. A small amount of tension or anxiety is good because it keeps a speaker alert; however, several techniques may be used when anxiety is so great that it may interfere with the presentation's effectiveness.

First, speakers should consider the value of the presentation and remember that the material is important. They must believe that the audience is there to listen and that they have an opportunity to provide a valuable service. A second technique for reducing anxiety is to find an isolated place to review the major characteristics of a presentation in general and those of the presentation in particular.

Third, it helps to sit with the eyes closed and to make a few deep breaths. With hands relaxed and dangling to the side, the head might be slowly rotated while the person concentrates on an especially pleasing thought (a mountain valley with beautiful flowers; soothing, fluffy clouds floating across the sky; waves breaking on a beach).[16] One minute of relaxation can be worth an hour of frantic preparation.

Another way to reduce anxiety is to memorize the first few remarks in the presentation. By the time these memorized comments have been presented, some of the initial anxiety should have subsided. Even though this part of the presentation has been memorized, it may be a good idea to have notes available just to increase confidence.

Selected, planned bodily activity can also help to reduce anxiety. Strategic movements during the delivery can be used to control the higher level of energy produced by the anxiety. This movement may take the form of appropriate gestures or of walking to a projector, flip chart, board, or screen.

Notes

How can notes be best arranged and used to support a managerial presentation? Traditionally, some people have advocated a precise outline following all the "proper" rules; others have maintained that 5-by-7-inch cards are essential. However, each person must find what works best for him or her.

A well-organized outline will help the speaker channel his efforts toward effective delivery. Notes written in a clear, concise manner make it easy to maintain eye contact with the audience. The need to maintain eye contact with the audience supports the recommendation that 5-by-7 or 4-by-6 cards be used. Regular-sized paper can be rather awkward to hold, and speakers might have trouble finding their place. Cards any smaller than recommended may be too small.

Outlining a speech on cards has three main advantages: (1) the cards are easy to hold; (2) they allow for the easy addition, subtraction, or rearrangement of material; and (3) they force the speaker to prune the speech down to an outline so it cannot be read word for word.[17]

Although notes can be a valuable source, they can easily become a psychological crutch. To make sure they do not become a crutch, keep the following don'ts in mind.

- Do not twist, bend, or fold the notes in an aimless way as a result of nervousness. This behavior does nothing to relieve a speaker's anxiety, and it may increase the anxiety of the audience.
- Do not glance at the notes out of a feeling of insecurity. Looking down to keep from looking at the audience can get to be a bad habit that physically and psychologically separates the speaker and the audience.
- Do not try to hide from the audience the fact that notes are being used. Why play games with the audience? The best procedure is to use notes openly, but only when absolutely necessary.

Nonverbal Aspects

Several nonverbal aspects of communication need to be considered during the delivery of a presentation, including eye contact, facial expressions, posture, gestures, and movement. Speakers are integral parts of the messages they convey, so how they present themselves affects the messages directly.

The nonverbal components of listening discussed in Chapter 9 can apply to the speaking as well as to the listening role. For instance, just as eye contact is important when listening for the total message, eye contact can be used to complement the delivery of a message. By looking at different members of the audience, effective speakers use eye contact to involve the audience in the presentation. Speakers can also use the rest of their faces to show concern or excitement about the message. A smile, a puzzled frown, a grimace—all complement the verbal message.

Posture, gestures, and body movement may also add to the spoken word. A forward-leaning posture may signify advancement or involvement, an open palm on the table may be used for emphasis, and walking toward a member of the audience may psychologically involve that person in the communication. The most important thing to remember is that body movements have meaning, and they should not be used indiscriminantly.

One aspect of nonverbal communication that has not been mentioned in the context of presentations may be the most important: the use of spatial arrangement. Few would question the speaker's need to stand when the audience includes more than seven or eight people; however, many managerial presentations involve audiences of fewer than seven people in a conference room. This latter situation calls for managers to analyze the group, the purpose, and themselves to determine whether to stand or sit.

When the manager and audience are equal in status, when the audience is extremely small, when the speaker reviews many technical charts, or when the speaker wants to develop an informal atmosphere, it may be best to remain sitting. Standing is probably the better choice when the manager's status is lower than that of the audience, when he wants to keep control of the situation, when certain items need to be pointed out on a chart or overhead projector, or when the manager wants to develop a formal atmosphere.

The speaker can also stand and sit at different times during the presentation. For instance, a manager may stand while presenting the body of the information but sit while fielding questions. When managers sit, they indicate it is time for two-way dialogue. Conversely, a manager may move from a sitting to a standing position to gain control or indicate it is time to close the presentation.

Voice Quality

Other nonverbal aspects important to the delivery of a presentation reside in the quality of the voice. The three major considerations are voice speed, pitch, and loudness.

The correct speed at which to speak is not easy to determine because no concrete answer exists. Generally, one should present parts that are potentially difficult to comprehend at a slower rate than that used in conveying parts that are easy to understand. Additionally, a speaker might slow down to emphasize an important and/or primary point and speak faster when presenting secondary information. If a speaker is feeling nervous, he should make a special effort to slow down, since nervousness usually speeds up a speaker's speech rate. Also, out of consideration, a speaker might slow down for an audience that may have difficulty understanding the language. Finally, variation can be used to keep the attention of the audience; a voice that never changes speed can become boring.

Speakers who talk at a constant pitch will also find it difficult to hold the audience's attention. Speakers should use the wide variations in pitch open to them. Usually, failure to vary pitch is a habit that one can break through special effort. Read the following sentence aloud three times, raising the pitch on the underlined word each time. It is easy to see that understanding can be drastically affected by pitch.

I never said he promoted *her*. (Give him some credit. He has better insight than that.)

I never said *he* promoted her. (I just said she got promoted, perhaps by her dad, the CEO.)

I never *said* he promoted her. (But I might have implied it in a number of ways.)

Robert McCloskey, a member of the State Department in the Nixon administration, would often give a four-word answer to questions from members of the press. Depending on how the answer was delivered, however, he could render three different meanings to the same statement.

I would not speculate. (Spoken without accent, this statement means the department did not have an answer to the question.)

I would not speculate. (With the accent on the I, it meant, "I wouldn't, but you may—and with some assurance.")

I would not *speculate*. (The accent on the speculate meant the questioner's premise was probably wrong.)

The third voice quality, loudness, can add to a presentation by making it lively and easy to follow. The correct volume depends on group size and the physical surroundings; however, regardless of the situation, changes in volume improve emphasis and add variety. Keep in mind one special warning about volume: a speaker does not gain attention or make stronger emphasis merely by being loud. In fact, an effective speaker may lower her voice during distractions so her audience is forced to quiet down to hear her. Changes in volume are more effective than a constantly loud voice.

Speakers can use several exercises to prepare their speaking voice. One simple but effective technique is to read a few paragraphs from a book aloud as though they were giving a presentation. This tactic draws attention to the voice quality. Speakers who determine that more extensive practice would help may turn to any number of speech tests.[18]

Practice

The cliche "practice makes perfect" definitely applies to presentations. Practice is essential for managerial presentations because they are neither memorized recitations nor verbatim readings. Unfortunately, many managers skip practice because they believe that they are either too busy or that practice is not important.

Even in the case of busy executives, however, practice is essential. It allows speakers to increase self-confidence and poise and to improve wording so the speech flows naturally and spontaneously. Additionally, practice permits speakers to identify any flaws or gaps in the presentation, to deal with distractions, and to make sure the visual aids are smoothly integrated.

Lee Iacocca once said that perfect practice makes perfect.[19] Practice doesn't mean simply reviewing the basic outline while sitting at a desk. Rather, it means rehearsing it aloud in a situation that simulates the actual situation as nearly as possible. Also, it means applying all the guidelines available for good presentation development and delivery. A dull presentation delivered in a lifeless manner is going to be a dull presentation delivered in a lifeless manner, regardless of how many times a speaker rehearses it.

An assistant or a colleague who plays the role of the audience and even asks questions can provide an invaluable service in spotting problem areas or gaps. Generally, whatever effort is expended in practice could make the difference between a mediocre presentation and an outstanding one.

Whenever possible, speakers should use the actual room and all the planned visual aids during the practice session. Doing so allows for an opportunity to develop the desired room arrangement. For example, though a semicircular arrangement would permit easy eye contact with all the participants, the room may dictate a theater-style arrangement. Knowing such things ahead of time would allow a speaker to make adjustments and avoid last-minute anxieties.

A practice session with the visual aids also helps one evaluate timing in relationship to the rest of the presentation. One can then also determine such simple things as where to plug in the projector and where a light dimmer is located. Such precautions can help to prevent disaster after hours and hours have gone into preparing a presentation. For example, after a slide presentation has been carefully and repeatedly rehearsed, a speaker doesn't want to discover that the projector cord will not reach the electrical outlet.

Finally, practice will help the speaker to arrange notes for maximum benefit. Managers who are completely familiar with their subject do not need notes, but disaster looms for the person who *thought* notes were not necessary. A rehearsal helps to settle the number of notes required and how detailed they should be. Also, additional notes can be made for words that need to be said slowly, loudly, or more clearly.

Questions and Ending

When the purpose is clearly defined, the preparation thorough, and the delivery effective, the response to questions and the summary are the final touches to an excellent managerial presentation.

Questions

Speakers solicit questions after the presentation to allow for appropriate additions and clarifications. In a situation where the group may be inhibited, but questions are important to open the dialogue, the speaker may want to ask one member of the audience to be ready with a question to stimulate further questions.

Several suggestions are helpful when answering questions:

1. If the original question was not loud and clear, repeat it for the rest of the group.
2. Do not allow one person to ask all the questions.
3. Select questions from all areas of the room, not just from one section.
4. Do not evaluate one question by saying, "That's a good question." Such a response could be inadvertently telling others that their questions are not good.
5. Do not answer with responses such as "as I said earlier," or "well, obviously," or "anyone would know the answer to that." Such responses can be quite demeaning.
6. Look at the whole group when answering a question, not just the person who asked it.
7. Do not point a finger at the audience while speaking. It is a scolding pose and it may appear authoritarian.
8. Do not put your hands on your hips while answering questions. This pose may also appear authoritarian.
9. If one has no answer to a question, it is best to admit it.
10. Allow sufficient time to answer questions.

Closing

The end of the presentation should contain a brief summary of the points covered in their appropriate order of importance. Once the presentation is finished, make sure it is finished. Do not present any new information or leave a question unanswered. If some action is to be solicited from the audience, the speaker's expectations should be made clear. Whatever the specific nature of the ending, it should strongly and clearly communicate that the speaker is ending. Too often, speakers just trickle off to a "Well, that's all" ending.

A Special Situation: Speaking before a Camera or Radio Microphone

The camera and microphone appear everywhere! A manager needs to learn to use these devices to maximize their potential. Unfortunately, many managers still take a defensive posture toward these audio and video presentation possibilities. Most people do not want to get involved in games for which they do not know the rules; thus, they shy away from the camera or mike.

Why learn the rules? The media offer many possibilities, from public service announcements to internal informative or motivational messages to employees. Managers sometimes receive requests for either informative or persuasive presentations for local radio or television stations. While television and radio are different forms of presentations, they can be rewarding and valuable media.

To take advantage of these media, managers need to know the special rules that apply to both the microphone and the camera. The first rule is to speak as though the audience were right there in the booth. Think of the microphone or camera as a friendly, trusting person. This approach reduces the likelihood of insincere, inappropriate alterations in communication style.

A second rule is to use the face, hands, and body as in ordinary conversation to keep the presentation as natural as it would be in person. Normal gesturing helps to communicate honesty, and it can complement the ideas being expressed. Some caution, however, should be exercised. Oversized grins, frowns, grimaces, and sweeping gestures are seldom appropriate in front of a camera.

The third rule is to use a script. What may seem to be an ad lib presentation by a professional performer is probably the result of an extensive script. A script is a means of coordinating the audio, visual, time, content, and human variables. In addition to the words for the show, it also contains instructions about production matters for crew members, enabling them to visualize how to integrate their responsibilities with the overall show. It helps establish the show's structure, organization, and timing. In other words, the script helps all parties know the show's sequence—how it will begin, move, and conclude.[20]

The fourth rule is closely related to the third: prepare and practice. We have already seen the importance of practice in relation to the regular presentation; however, practice is even more important for a television or radio interview. The unfamiliar environment is one compelling reason for extra practice. All the strange new stimuli make it difficult to concentrate on the task, so be prepared for distractions.

Another reason for the extra practice is the strict time limitations imposed on the presentation. Such a limitation is probably the one thing that can disturb the otherwise unperturbable speaker. The normal presentation has time limits set in terms of minutes, but the television or radio presentation has to be implemented in terms of seconds. Everything is scheduled tightly. In reaction to the tight scheduling, the novice media speaker should resist the tendency to speak rapidly and thus appear nervous.

Another reason for extensive practice is the higher level of refinement required for a television or radio presentation because the general public is less accustomed to observing nonprofessional speakers. Instead, it has as a standard of comparison a local or even a national newsperson. An unpracticed, nervous, and awkward manager does not fare well against such competition.

The fifth and final rule relates to the dress appropriate for a television appearance of a video-recorded presentation. The obvious recommendation is to wear what you want others to see you in, but you'll also want to feel at home in your clothes. If you wear a suit to work, wear one to the studio. Here are some additional tips to keep in mind:

1. Do not wear large patterns. They have a stroboscopic effect and appear to be moving.
2. Do not wear clashy or loud colors (especially red). They can be easily distorted on the monitor.
3. Wear a dark suit, but avoid black and white. Black absorbs too much light and white reflects it.
4. Avoid too much jewelry. Wedding rings and watches are OK, but exercise caution beyond that.
5. Don't wear something new. If you must, test it first for comfort and for how you look in it.
6. Women should maintain a modest skirt length, and men should wear knee-length socks. No exceptions.[21]

These five rules should assist managers to take full advantage of the opportunities presented by the camera and radio microphone. Such appearances can be challenging but enjoyable experiences that provide a valuable service to the company while offering a tremendous opportunity for professional self-development.

Summary

To ensure an effective presentation, a manager should thoroughly analyze the purpose, complete all necessary preparations, and use appropriate delivery techniques. A thorough analysis of the purpose means the speaker should determine if everyone involved has the same goal for the presentation. If the speaker perceives the presentation to have a goal different from that of the audience, or of individual members of the audience, misunderstanding will result.

Once the goal has been clearly established, the necessary preparations must be completed. Preparation includes an audience analysis, a presentation plan, the selection of an introduction, and the organization of the visual aids. An audience analysis includes all the social and psychological characteristics of the audience and the relationship of the audience to the speaker. A complete analysis allows the speaker to design the message content to fit the attitudes, needs, and knowledge of the audience.

The presentation plan, which determines how the message should be organized and what kinds of information (facts or opinions) should be presented, depends on the purpose of the presentation. Regardless of the organization, transitions are important to ensure that the audience can follow and understand the message.

The introductory statement should capture the audience's attention and clearly state the purpose of the presentation. Once the attention of the audience is ensured, visual aids help to maintain it and accurately communicate the message. Visibility, clarity, and simplicity, as well as timing, are important to ensure that the visual aid complements the verbal communication.

Both nonverbal and verbal characteristics of the speaker are important for an effective, professional delivery. Eye contact, facial expressions, posture, gestures, and movement all need to be considered. Voice speed, pitch, and loudness affect the verbal quality of the presentation.

A speaker should schedule sufficient time for questions and answers at the end of the presentation. When this part of the presentation is well managed, feedback and two-way communication develop. Also, a strong summarizing and/or concluding statement can help the presentation to end on a high note, rather than with a thud.

A special presentational situation that more and more managers face today involves speaking before a camera or radio microphone. Most of the rules that apply to a normal speaking situation apply also to this form of a presentation. However, several different rules dealing with nonverbal cues and the use of a script will help a manager to present an effective message via the electronic media.

Audience Analysis Guide Sheet

1. How many do I expect in the audience?
2. Are there one or two members of the audience who have more power than the others?
3. Is the knowledge level of all the members diverse or about the same?
4. What is their knowledge of the content area?
   - _____ High, may be higher than mine
   - _____ About the same as mine
   - _____ Less than my knowledge in the area
   - _____ Probably do not have even the basic knowledge
   - _____ Varied, some will have high knowledge, some low
   - _____ Not sure, need to find out
5. What will impress this group?
   - _____ Technical data
   - _____ Statistical comparisons
   - _____ Cost figures
   - _____ Historical information

_____ Generalization

_____ Demonstrations

6. Will different members of the group be impressed with different things?

7. What is the group's attitude toward the subject?

_____ Exceptionally positive

_____ Somewhat positive

_____ Neutral

_____ Somewhat negative, reluctant

_____ Definitely negative

_____ Group varies, some positive and some negative

_____ Not sure, need to get more information

8. What is the group's attitude toward me as the presenter?

_____ See me as credible and knowledgeable

_____ Neutral, probably do not have an opinion

_____ See me as having little knowledge and credibility

_____ Not sure

9. What is the group's attitude toward the organization I represent?

_____ See the organization as reliable and trustworthy

_____ Neutral

_____ Might question its capabilities and reliability

10. What will be the group's disposition at the time of my presentation?

_____ Will have listened to many other presentations similar to this one, could be tired

_____ Will have been sitting in one place for a long time, may need a minute to stretch

_____ This presentation will be unique, so it should be easy to grab their attention

_____ This is an early item on the agenda, they should be fresh

11. What is the audience's status compared with mine?

12. Summarize the *most important* audience characteristics that you should consider in your presentation.

Endnotes

1. S. Clay Willmington, "Oral Communication for a Career in Business," *Bulletin of the Association for Business Communication* LII, no. 2 (June 1989), pp. 8–12.

2. Robert J. Olney and Anita S. Bednar, "Identifying Essential Oral Presentation Skills for Today's Business Curriculum," *Journal of Education for Business* 64, no. 4 (January 1989), p. 161.

3. Carol A. McFarland, "Teaching Students the Elements of Oral Business Presentations," *Bulletin of the Association for Business Communication* XXXXIII, no. 1 (March 1980), pp. 15–17.

4. Ernest G. Borman, William S. Howell, Ralph G. Nichols, and George L. Shapiro, *Interpersonal Communication in the Modern Organization* (Englewood Cliffs, N.J.: Prentice Hall, 1982), p. 197.

5. William S. Howell and Ernest G. Borman, *Presentational Speaking for Business and the Professions* (New York: Harper & Row, 1971), pp. 122–30.

6. Daniel J. O'Keefe, *Persuasion Theory and Research* (Newbury Park, Calif.: Sage Publications, 1990), pp. 130–88.

7. Sherron B. Kenton, "Speaker Credibility in Persuasive Business Communication: A Model Which Explains Gender Differences," *Journal of Business Communication* 26, no. 2 (Spring 1989), pp. 143–58.

8. Lawrence L. Tracy, "Taming the Hostile Audience," *Training and Development Journal* 44, no. 2 (February 1990), p. 35.

9. Donna Barron, "Graphics Presentations at Your Fingertips," *The Office*, July 1990, p. 32.

10. Ibid., p. 34.

11. Leone N. Johnson, "How Computers Enhance Visual Presentations," *The Office*, March 1990, p. 14.

12. Patricia L. Panchak, "Capitalizing on the Graphics Edge," *Modern Office Technology*, June 1990, p. 63.

13. James Wyllie, "Oral Communication: Survey and Suggestions," *Bulletin of the Association for Business Communication* XXXXIII, no. 2 (June 1980), pp. 14–17.

14. David Wallechinsky and Irving Wallace, *The Book of Lists* (New York: William Morrow, 1977).

15. Kenneth R. Meyer, "Developing Delivery Skills in Oral Business Communication," *Bulletin of the Association for Business Communication* XLIII, no. 3 (September 1980), pp. 21–24.

16. Mary Ellen Murray, "Painless Oral Presentations," *Bulletin of the Association for Business Communication* LII, no. 2 (June 1989), pp. 13–15.

17. Mary Munter, *Guide to Managerial Communication*, 3rd ed. (Englewood Cliffs, N.J.: Prentice Hall, 1992), p. 80.

18. Douglas Ehninger, Bruce E. Gronbeck, Ray E. McKerros, and Alan H. Monroe, *Principles and Types of Speech Communication*, 9th ed. (Glenview, Ill.: Scott, Foresman and Company, 1982), pp. 412–17.

19. Lee Iacocca, *Lee Iacocca Talking Straight* (New York: Bantam Books, 1988).

20. Evan Blythin and Larry A. Samovar, *Communication Effectively on Television*, (Belmont, Calif.: Wadsworth Publishing Company, 1985), pp. 92–96.

21. Jack Hilton and Mary Knoblauch, *On Television: A Survivor's Guide for Media Interviews* (New York: AMACOM, 1982), pp. 60–62.

Additional Readings

Filson, Brent. *Executive Speeches: 51 CEO's Tell You How to Do Yours*. Williamstown, Mass.: 1991.

Fridlund, Alan, Doug Green, and Denise Green. "Rapid-fire Presentations." *Info World*, November 19, 1990, pp. 63, 66, 79.

Iapoce, Michael. *A Funny Thing Happened on the Way to the Boardroom*. New York: John Wiley & Sons, 1988.

Miculka, Jean H. *Let's Talk Business*, 4th ed. Cincinnati: South-Western Publishing Company, 1993.

The Oxford Dictionary of Quotations, 3rd ed. Oxford: Oxford University Press, 1980.

Parkhurst, William. *The Eloquent Executive*. New York: Times Books, 1988.

Reardon Kathleen Kelley. *Persuasion in Practice*. Newbury Park, Calif.: Sage Publications, 1991.

Robbins Larry M. *The Business of Writing and Speaking*. New York: McGraw-Hill, 1985.

Sigband, Norman. "Coping Successfully with the Media." *Advanced Management Journal* 50, no. 1 (Winter 1985), pp. 50–56.

Spitzer, Michael, Michael Gamble, and Teri Kwal Gamble. *Writing and Speaking in Business*. New York: Random House, 1984.

Van Ekeren, Glenn. *The Speaker's Sourcebook, Quotes, Stories, and Anecdotes*. Englewood Cliffs, N.J.: Prentice Hall, 1988.

Woodall Marian K. *Speaking to a Group*. Lake Oswego, Ore.: Professional Business Communications, 1990.

Woodall Marian K. *Thinking on Your Feet: Answering Questions Well, Whether You Know the Answer or Not*. Lake Oswego, Ore.: Professional Business Communications, 1987.

Discussion Questions

1. Give an example in which each member of an audience may be trying to obtain a different goal from the same presentation.

2. Present and discuss at least five items in an audience analysis.

3. Present a situation where little audience information is available. What can be done in this situation?

4. Explain the three major presentation plans presented by Howell and Borman. Present three different situations and the appropriate presentation plan.

5. Which of the approaches discussed in Question 4 is more likely to use facts and which is likely to use opinions?

6. What are the two most important considerations in an introduction? Give an example of an effective introduction that you have heard.

7. Discuss some of the rules of thumb for a visual aid. Give an example of an effective visual aid and of an ineffective visual aid.

8. Discuss a situation in which handout materials would be effective. What are some of the disadvantages of the handouts in this situation?

9. What techniques do you use to reduce speaker anxiety? What other techniques may be appropriate?

10. Cite several examples in which you have observed the effective use of nonverbal communication in a presentation.

11. What is meant by voice pitch? Give two examples where pitch can change the meaning of a statement.

12. If you were making a presentation to two people, would you sit or stand? What factors must be considered before answering this question?

13. Give a specific example of where you observed a presentation in which the questions were poorly managed. What errors were made?

14. What are the most important elements in a conclusion?
15. Describe the appropriate attire when speaking before a camera.

Exercise 8–1

Create a 10-minute informative presentation for your class on the latest developments in office ergonomics. After analyzing your audience, decide on the subjects you will cover and their order of presentation. How will you introduce your subject so that you grab the audience's attention? What would be the best type of visual aids to use so as to maintain the audience's attention? What type of supporting information will most impress your audience? How will you encourage questions at the end of your presentation? What kind of closing should you use?

Exercise 8–2

Pick a presentation graphics package with which you are familiar. Assume you are a new sales representative for the company that developed this package. In three days, you will be making a sales presentation on the latest version of this package to a group of executives at a large company. Obviously, you will want to inform them of all the features offered by your package and of all its advantages over the competition. You will also want to persuade them to purchase the package. How would you accomplish your goals?

Exercise 8–3

Pick one of the following topics to use in the development of a persuasive presentation. After picking a topic, visualize an audience to whom you would speak on the subject. Of the three persuasive presentation approaches described in this chapter, which would be most appropriate for your presentation? Given the topic you have chosen and the audience you have visualized, what type of evidence would you use to persuade them to accept your point of view?

a. Lie detectors should (or should not) be used in the hiring of employees.
b. Lie detectors should (or should not) be used by businesses in attempting to deter employee pilferage.
c. Businesses should (or should not) be permitted to subject employees to drug testing.
d. Top executives should (or should not) be held criminally liable for illegal (or unethical) actions by their companies.

e. Social responsibility should (or should not) be a major concern of today's CEOs.

f. A manager should (or should not) be concerned about the personal problems of his or her employees.

g. Subliminal perception should (or should not) be permitted in advertising.

h. An international code of ethics should (or should not) be developed.

i. In a country where such practices are common, the bribery of a government official is (or is not) acceptable business behavior.

j. Unionization is (or is not) appropriate for today's white-collar worker.

Exercise 8–4

Pick one of the following scenarios and develop a 10-minute informative presentation:

a. For an either all-male or all-female audience of graduating seniors, discuss the topic of appropriate dress for employment interviews.

b. For an either all-male or all-female audience of business executives, discuss the topic of appropriate dress for television interviews.

9 MANAGERIAL LISTENING: THE KEY SKILL

Mark has just reminded you he needs the manual you have on the electrical system. Reminded! You cannot remember him telling you about it in the first place. Is it possible you were not listening? You remember how you were not listening in the last production meeting and missed some of the information. You justified this at the time by saying that more important things were on your mind.

Now this idea of listening is bothering you. You always tell the supervisors who report to you that listening is a critical skill, but now you are wondering about yourself. What specific things should you do to improve your listening ability?

During the past several decades, the essential role of listening in business and management has received increased attention. Over 35 studies reveal that listening is the form of communication that is

- Most important for entry-level positions.
- Most critical in distinguishing effective from ineffective subordinates.
- Most critical for managerial competency.

But interestingly, many of these studies report that employers find that listening skills are

- Seriously lacking in subordinates and managers.
- Most in need of training.[1]

A number of essential managerial skills involve listening. First, much of the data necessary for decision making comes through listening to employees, and poor listeners miss important information. Second, listening makes a person more dependable: People who listen well follow directions better, make fewer errors, say foolish things less often, and generally become the kind of person others will ask for advice or direction. Third, good listeners are more respected and liked by those they work with. Managers who listen compliment those they listen to, in effect telling them they are worthy people.[2] This trait can lead to harmonious labor relations since employees generally trust and support managers who "listen them out."[3]

Fourth, better listening enables a manager to be better informed overall and more sophisticated. Sophistication comes not from talking, but rather from learning about the world around us. Fifth, good listening spares a person many embarrassments. In many situations, people may miss a name because of poor listening, or they may need to have critical information repeated because of daydreaming. Worse yet, a direct question may be unanswered because of inept listening. Such embarrassing situations can quickly label a manager as unconcerned or even apathetic.

Ultimately, the major reason for developing effective listening is to promote understanding between people. All people need to be heard for their own emotional well-being and to create understanding among each other. Mutual understanding is required in any work group. The power of listening is highlighted in an article in *Fortune* magazine describing the phenomenal success of Gallo Winery. This article credits the Gallo brothers' competitive advantage to their ability to listen to customers and employees. By listening to customers, Gallo is able to be on the leading edge of changing wine tastes. By listening to employees, the winery is able to be one of the most efficient wineries in the world.[4]

Management at Bank of America emphasizes the importance of listening through formalized programs. The company has six programs to improve the listening skills of employees. This company believes listening improves the bottom line and that it is also essential for the general well-being of society.[5]

Listening is not just hearing, and the effective manager differentiates between the two. Hearing is mechanical, an automatic sort of thing often difficult to avoid. A horn blaring, heavy construction equipment groaning, children shouting in a playground—all these sounds, plus others, may be heard even though they are not listened to actively. Hearing usually requires little special physical or mental effort.

By contrast, listening results from a concentrated effort; it requires both physical and mental effort. Listening requires a special effort because physical and psychological factors work against the process. In this chapter, we review those physical and psychological barriers to listening and then analyze techniques to reduce these barriers.

Barriers to Listening

Communication doesn't occur in discrete units and the term *barrier* may remind us of something mechanical rather than an interactive, dynamic process like listening. As a result, the title *listening barrier* may misrepresent listening

---

TABLE 9–1 Barriers to Listening

---

1. Listening–speaking differential 25–75 problem
2. Motivation
3. Willingness
4. Internal distractions
5. Detouring
6. Debate
7. Time

---

somewhat; however, dynamic, interactive processes are easier to discuss when categorized and put in a list. Table 9–1 lists the listening barriers presented here.

One of the greatest barriers to listening arises from our own physical limitations. People speak approximately 25 percent as fast as they think. Thus, while most Americans speak at a rate of about 125 words per minute, they are able to think least four times as fast.[6] As a result, instead of listening carefully, some people think about other things and devote only a fraction of their capacity to taking in what is said. They become impatient with the slow rate of the spoken word and begin to concentrate on topics other than the words being spoken; consequently, our inability to speak more rapidly becomes a physical barrier in listening situations. This problem may be referred to as the listening–speaking differential or the 25–75 problem: a person requires only 25 percent of his mental time for listening while he spends the remaining 75 percent on unrelated ideas. No wonder some find it hard to get their attention back to the main topic. The listening–speaking differential, or the 25–75 problem, is listed first because it partially causes many of the other listening barriers.

A lack of motivation is another barrier to listening. Many people find maintaining the continuous motivation required for listening to be a challenge. Managers who should be listening may be daydreaming, making private plans, or even focusing on an emotional problem. During that 75 percent void, many things can overpower the 25 percent listening.

Researchers have long known that motivation or incentive is a prevalent problem in the listening process. Research completed almost 30 years ago demonstrated that people score better on listening achievement tests when they know in advance they are going to be tested than when they think they are just supposed to listen.[7] More recent research has also indicated that scores on listening tests rise as the incentive to listen increases.[8] Since listening is hard work, we can expect greater effort when the goal is known and listeners can observe a positive outcome of the effort. This is why the listening goal discussed later is so important.

A barrier related to motivation is lack of willingness. A manager may not *want* to listen. Before listening is even required, he may have lost any desire to listen. Since we have already discussed motivation as a barrier to listening, we must differentiate willingness from motivation. These concepts are closely related, but for this discussion, assume that a lack of willingness develops *before* listening even begins. This is why it may supersede all other barriers. If a person consciously or unconsciously decides not to listen, listening skills are of no advantage. Manny Steil, who does extensive listening training for companies such as Honeywell, often refers to the LAW of listening—Listening equals *A*bility plus *W*illingness.

Why would a manager lack the willingness to listen? Several reasons explain this unfortunate condition. First, most people would rather talk than listen; and even when they ask a question, they often break into the first sentence of the response with another question or an argument.[9] Second, the listener may quickly stereotype the speaker as one who talks a lot but has little to say; consequently, the listener believes the person has little of value to say. Third, a listener may lack willingness because she may not want to receive negative information. For the speaker who bears "bad tidings," what incentive is there to listen? Defensive behavior relates closely to this. Some managers consider the slightest attack on one of their opinions as an attack on them personally; consequently, they will rise, sometimes almost obsessively, to the defense. This defense often involves verbal attacks that preclude the possibility for listening.

Internal distractions that cannot be ignored are another barrier. Our autonomic nervous system involuntarily pays attention to certain events such as a headache, sore feet, or an empty stomach. It is difficult to divide attention between these internal involuntary distractions and concentrated listening. Noise that may compete with the main topic of interest is also a barrier. It is hard to listen to a subordinate who speaks softly in a noisy foundry or to a phone conversation mixed with static on the phone line. In these situations, separating the speaker's voice from all the surrounding noise can be exhausting.

Another barrier may be termed *detouring*. The listener may become distracted by a mannerism, phrase, or concept and detour toward the distraction. This distraction then stimulates thought on another subtopic more interesting than the central point of the message; consequently, thoughts detour to the more interesting topics. The *debate* represents a sixth type of barrier. A listener may suddenly find herself disagreeing with the speaker and begin to plan her rebuttal. As she plans the rebuttal, she blocks out the speaker and misses his message. For instance, a manager listening to complaints from another department might prepare a rebuttal as the other person explains the incident. As a result, the manager creates a defensive climate and misses the most important information.

Finally, time, an important factor in every manager's day, can also be a barrier to listening, especially for busy managers. "I just don't have time to listen to this" is a common reaction for managers. The saying, "time flies when you're having fun," is true; being involved in an interesting conversation can use more time than a person realizes. However, time is relative and seems to drag when people have to listen to something in which they have no interest. When listening appears to take too much time, managers tend to stop listening. One way some terminate listening is by making a hasty conclusion. This time pressure may lead to the tendency to judge, evaluate, approve, or disapprove a person's statement too hastily. To achieve real communication, it is important to resist the temptation to form hasty conclusions.

The preceding review is only a summary of the many barriers to listening. All those personal factors mentioned in Chapter 2—knowledge, culture, status, attitudes, emotions, communication skills—can also create potential barriers to listening. Nevertheless, research indicates we can improve listening skills. When managers strategically analyze the critical components of communication and apply the techniques suggested in the following section, their listening skills and effectiveness as managers will improve.[10]

General Techniques for Improved Listening Skills

Let us first look at the different types of listening to be able to adapt techniques to the appropriate situation. Figure 9–1 shows two types of listening (active and interactive) and three levels of listening intensity for both types.

For the purposes of this discussion, active listening occurs in situations in which a manager has little or no opportunity to interact verbally with the speaker. People in a large audience use active listening as do those listening to a recorded message or reviewing an audiovisual replay. People use inter-

FIGURE 9–1

Listening Types

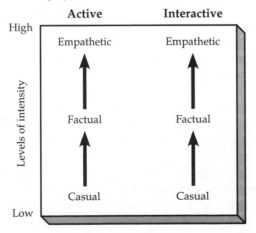

active listening when they have the opportunity to interact verbally with the speaker by asking questions or summarizing. Interactive listening occurs with a manager involved in a conversation with one other individual or in a meeting with many people.

The level of intensity at the side of Figure 9–1 reflects the relevance, the importance, or the significance of the information involved. Listening has basically three levels of intensity. Casual or marginal listening is used when the specific or technical information being discussed is not critical. Because no goal for specific information is established, a manager need not be as alert as in other situations. For example, casual listening occurs in social conversations or when listening to the radio. Although it is not as intense as many types of listening, it is nonetheless important. A manager can indicate social support by simply listening to an employee talk about a special event in her life. By listening, the manager is saying, "You are important as a person."[11]

A note of caution is important here. What one person considers casual another may consider critical information. The importance of the information is not inherent in the information itself. Therefore, in the same situation, different people could be listening with different intensities.

The next level of intensity, factual listening, is necessary when specific information needs to be obtained. Probably the most common type of listening in business meetings and conferences, factual listing is the level that most people probably think of when they consider the topic of listening. At this level, the listener should ask questions and receive feedback to ensure effective communication.

A manager uses the empathetic level of listening when he wants to understand another person from that person's own internal frame of reference rather than from his own frame of reference. The empathetic listener tries to get inside the other's thoughts and feelings. The listener expresses empathy when he verbally and nonverbally communicates such messages as, "I follow you," "I'm with you," or "I understand." The empathetic level of listening is not easy to achieve because we naturally tend to advise, tell, agree, or disagree based on our own view. It is well worth the effort to become an empathetic listener, however. A speaker who sees that a manager is really trying to understand her meaning will trust the manager and be more willing to talk and explore problems. Empathetic listening can be such a powerful form of listening that, even when it is only partially attained, the mere attempt can be enough to open up communication.

When listening, a manager should first determine the level of listening he needs to achieve. He can accomplish this by establishing a "listening goal," a specific statement of the purpose for listening. In the give-and-take of most communications, the need to adjust one's listening goal arises as the interchange develops.

But this is not always easy. Consider Andy Wilson who is a regional vice-president of Wal-Mart. He visits a different Wal-Mart store at least every week where he wanders around talking to customers, stock clerks, and store managers. One minute he may be listening to someone describe the weather in Salem, Oregon, and the next minute he may be discussing the drop in sales of bedding items. Soon after that he may be listening to a manager describe why she is so frustrated with her work. Within five minutes each of the different types and intensities of listening is required, so Andy Wilson must be quick to adjust.[12]

Once the manager has established the level of listening, it is important to prepare physically and psychologically to listen. He should complete the following steps during the preparation stage.

1. Pick the best possible place. While it is not always possible to change the place, the manager should not overlook better facilities when available.
2. Pick the best possible time. As with place, it is not always possible to change the time. However, the astute manager must be careful not to eliminate more favorable opportunities.
3. Think about personal biases that may be present.
4. Think about the physical and psychological barriers to listening.
5. Review the listening objectives.

A brief review of these five items shows why they are important in reducing the barriers to effective listening discussed earlier. First, selecting the best time and place helps one avoid internal and external distractions. In addition, since time influences the psychological barriers of motivation, emotion, and willingness, the choice of time may significantly alter the outcome of the conversation.

However, is it polite to tell another that one cannot listen at the moment? In a survey of more than 200 managers, respondents indicated they would not be offended if someone asked them to wait before discussing something for fear that important information might be missed. Of course, if time cannot be changed, it is important that the parties be aware of the barriers present and make a special effort to concentrate on the listening process.

A manager's biases may also have a drastic effect on the outcome of the communication. A manager unaware of personal bias may become selective and hear only what he wants to hear. The person may deal only with preconceived notions and even debate with the speaker on points of disagreement. For example, a manager who believes that women are unreliable may disregard any information indicating that a particular woman is reliable. The first step needed to control this psychological barrier of bias is awareness followed by recognition of the burden it places on the speaker–listener relationship.

Detouring, the psychological barrier that causes a listener to become distracted by a mannerism, phrase, or concept, is closely related to bias. A listener's negative bias toward a mannerism can distract from the content of the message. For instance, a speaker may place her hands over her mouth while speaking, or continually play with a pencil, or look away from the listener. Such mannerisms can distract, and one needs to recognize them as just that—distractions. Mannerisms should not get in the way of messages.

Emotional words or phrases can also trigger listener bias. Such phrases as "typical accountant," "it really isn't my job," "we tried that before, and it didn't work," or "all engineers think alike" can lead to emotional responses. The danger in such phrases is that they cause a listener to hear (or not to hear) different parts of a message. When a listener is caught by an emotional phrase, the internal response may overpower the content of the message. Once again, the listener should be aware of the possible emotional responses and not let them distract from the message. Finally, it is important to review and be aware of the listening objective. Without the objective in mind, a manager may use casual listening when factual listening is required, or factual listening when empathetic listening would be more effective. The person who can state in one sentence the specific goal and the type of listening involved is well aware of the listening objective.

The manager who is physically and psychologically prepared to listen could use some specific techniques to improve listening. Let us look at some of these techniques that are appropriate for active and interactive listening.

Techniques for Active Listening

A person uses active listening in situations where interaction with the speaker is difficult or impossible. For example, a person who is sitting in a large audience or listening to a recording cannot interact. Since asking questions is generally not possible in these situations, a listener usually needs to have a clear and complete understanding of the message the first time around. An active listener should implement the following techniques.

Identify the Main and Supporting Points

A message usually has one or two main points with supporting information in the form of examples, figures, or descriptions. One good clue to the main points is the nonverbal techniques the speaker uses when giving them; she might raise her voice, speak faster, repeat key words, or use gestures. Later we will detail nonverbal aspects that can be invaluable when identifying the main and supporting points. In the following example, note the emphasis on main and supporting points in a speech:

> (President speaking at the annual meeting) The electronic division was pleased with the successful introduction of *four new products* (raised voice) in the last year. All four of these products sold at a better rate than projected. We were especially pleased with the temperature sensor that sold 14 percent above projections. This small sensor, which has many applications and is easy to install, should do as well or better next year.

Besides introducing four new products (pause), we expanded the western division's sales force by adding 16 high-quality salespeople. These salespeople were recruited from all over the United States, and we're confident of their ability to help us expand in the West. They all have a thorough understanding of the product and the changing nature of our industry.

No immediate changes are seen in the home implement division (lowered voice). It will be necessary to wait and see what happens with the entire housing industry. We're stable here since garage openers, intercom systems, and burglar protection devices are all holding their own. We developed a new burglar protection system that can be programmed by means of digital device. This has been an interesting project to watch as it developed.

The main points in this example are the four new products, expansion of the western division's sales force, and a stable home implement market; the remainder of the message is supporting information. Separation of main and supporting points helps the listener retain the critical information.

Outline the Message

Often, a speaker has some type of organization pattern that a listener may use to outline the message. For instance, a speaker may organize the message by pros and cons, advantages and disadvantages, likes and dislikes, similarities and differences, chronological events, or functional duties. Just as it is easier to remember the outline of a chapter rather than every word in it, it is easier to recall the outline of a spoken message rather than all the specifics.

Summarize the Message

Another listening device is the summary, which can take the form of a mental picture of the main points. The summary need not contain elaborate sentences and details; simple words or sentence fragments may suffice. Furthermore, summarization does not have to wait until the end of the message; it may be more efficient at major division points. The president's speech given earlier could be summarized in three phrases: (1) four new products in electronics, (2) 16 new salespeople in the western region, and (3) a stable home implement market.

The three techniques tested so far—differentiating between the main and supporting points, outlining, and summarizing—operate together for accurate listening. The effective use of a fourth technique assists in the development of the others.

Visualize the Message

Another tactic for active listening, putting the message into a picture, will help keep the listener's mind on the message. The beauty of this tactic is that it allows a person to use some of that 75 percent of the mental capacity not required to keep up with the message. Consequently, a person can commit more effort to listening, thus reducing the possibility of missing a major part of the message. Finally, the retention of the message improves because a picture can now be associated with it. In the annual meeting seen earlier, a manager might imagine the 16 new sales personnel in the western region as 16 little people running from different points of a U.S. wall map to California. Absurd as the device might seem, these 16 little people running across a wall map will help the manager remember the main point of the message.

Related to visualization is mnemonics. One mnemonic device is the acronym, a combination of letters, each of which is the first letter of a group of words essential to the message. For instance, suppose a person is presenting his main objection to taking additional training in computer programming. The objection may stem from the cost, the individual's ability, and the time involved. The mnemonic CAT—cost, ability, time—can be used to record these main ideas whenever the speaker refers to him. Mnemonics in general and acronyms specifically may be considered a type of visualization because it is easier to see and recall the acronym. Other types of memory games such as word association and riddles are also beneficial.

Relate the Message to Personal Experiences (Personalize)

Effective listeners are those who search a message for information that has special meaning for the listener. A topic is naturally more interesting and easier to concentrate on if it personally relates to the listener. In fact, those who relate the message to personal experiences ensure that the key elements of listening, willingness, and motivation are present. The managers listening to the president in the previous example may also personalize the message by asking questions of themselves: "How will these four products affect my job?" "Will continued expansion of the electronic group affect me?" "Will those 16 new salespeople increase my work load for the western region?" "How will the stable market in the home implement group affect our division?" In answering these questions, the managers find how the message personally relates to them. Then, their incentive to listen to the message increases.

Take Notes

All these techniques are strengthened when the listener takes notes. College students generally do not have to be convinced of the importance of notes, but they often lose this good habit once they leave the classroom. A listener can easily make short notations to help visualize and personalize a message. Not only do notes provide a written record of the communication, but they also can provide valuable feedback that tells the listener just how well she is listening. If the notes are not well organized with main and supporting points, the listener probably has not mentally organized the message. If a quick review indicates no notes have been taken for some time, the listener may find that his attention has been wandering.

Another way that notes benefit a listener is that they keep her physically involved. Listening is a predominantly mental activity; consequently, people who are accustomed to being physically active get restless or impatient when listening for long periods. This urge for physical activity might be channeled into note taking, which keeps a person involved with the business at hand.

Of course, note taking can be a problem for people who overdo it. Not every word needs recording, and long sentences are not necessary. In fact, one can concentrate on the notes to the extent that major components of the message are missed. Instead, jot down key words and phrases in outline form using abbreviations when possible.

A final thought on notes. The listener who takes notes indicates a sincere interest in both the message and the speaker. Notes require involvement, so the speaker will have a greater degree of confidence that listeners are paying attention to the message. The fact that it is important to demonstrate effective listening is discussed in more detail later.

Each of these techniques—identifying the main points, outlining, summarizing, visualizing, personalizing, and note taking—is useful in either active or interactive listening. However, the techniques are especially critical in situations where the ability to ask questions and observe nonverbal messages is limited. When questions are possible, the ideal is to ask questions of the speaker for clarity without using questions to replace the five techniques just discussed. The next section discusses situations in which it is easy to ask questions. We refer to this as interactive listening.

Interactive Listening

The skillful use of questions adds immensely to a manager's ability to communicate and is the key ingredient in interactive listening. This book recommends several areas when questioning techniques are appropriate: listening, interviewing, conflict resolution, and coaching. Questions are important because they provide the two-way process of communication that Chapter 2 discusses. Without the use of questions, feedback and mutual understanding are severely curbed.

When the meaning of a message is either unclear or incomplete, it is important to ask questions. When key words, phrases, or concepts are vague or when inconsistencies or contradictions appear, questions help to develop clarity. Listeners are not the only ones to benefit from questions. Questions may also help a speaker clarify his thoughts. A speaker might not be aware of an omission or distortion in a message until asked a question. When questioned, the speaker may be forced to reanalyze his own communication to the listener's benefit.

A manager must strategically determine the most appropriate questions for different situations to ensure mutual understanding. Three classifications of questions are appropriate to this discussion: open–closed; primary–secondary; neutral–directed.

The phrasing of an open-ended question gives the respondent an open choice of possible answers. At the other end of the spectrum is the closed question, which permits a narrow range of possible answers. An example illustrates this point. Suppose a frustrated subordinate describes to you a major problem with a new project. In her agitation, the employee jumped from one point to another while describing the problem. Naturally, this disorderly description makes it difficult to listen, so you ask questions for both clarity and completeness of information. The following list includes open and closed questions that you might ask the employee for clarification.

What do you think are the major causes of the problem? (open)

What more can you tell me about it? (open)

Did you check the steam gauge? (closed)

Where do you think we should go from here? (open)

Would it be a good idea to wait until tomorrow? (closed)

While open questions may generate additional information, they also allow possible digression. Closed questions are more direct and help one to focus on the problem. Nevertheless, the lack of openness may cause valuable information to be omitted since the answer is so narrow. Managers must use strategic analysis to determine the best choice of questioning style in each case.

Two other options open to managers are primary and secondary questions. A primary question is the first question that seeks clarification or more complete information on a topic. A manager may choose to follow up with a secondary question that probes to obtain still more specific information after the primary question has been answered. A secondary question is not merely an additional question; it seeks to get at a deeper level of information than the first or primary level. The following dialogue shows the strategic use of primary and secondary questioning.

Manager: Do you think you'll be able to have the analysis done by Wednesday? (primary)

Employee: That shouldn't be any problem if everything goes right for a change.

Manager: What would you be afraid of going wrong? (secondary)

Employee: The accounting information is hard to get sometimes.

Manager: What specific part is hard to get? (secondary)

Notice that each secondary question seeks further information on the preceding answer.

Managers use the secondary question when they think they have not obtained sufficient information through the primary ones.

The third classification involves neutral versus directed questions. While a neutral question seeks information without attempting to lead the speaker to answer in a certain way, the directed question seeks to lead the speaker to a response the inquirer desires. A directed question, often referred to as a leading question, tries to pull the answer in a predetermined direction. Directed questions open with such phrases as "Doesn't it seem logical that . . . ," or "Wouldn't you agree that . . . ," or "Wouldn't you say. . . ." Directed questions may be used to obtain confirmation or clarification on one specific point, whereas the neutral question will obtain a more general response.

The use of an appropriate question adds clarity to communication because of the active two-way process that develops. Listening is clearly not a passive activity; rather, it requires the active involvement of the manager through the use of questions and other means.

Listening to Informal Communication

So far this discussion on listening has emphasized situations in which a formal speaking–listening situation is established. But informal, casual listening can also be extremely important—what began as casual listening can quickly become factual or empathetic listening. The manager must know what to listen to and what to ignore. In other words, managers must know how to listen to the rumors that circulate on the grapevine. At times, these rumors can provide important information; at other times, it may be important to attempt to alter the content of the rumor; and at still others, it may be best to ignore the rumors.

The term *grapevine* has an interesting history. The term arose during the Civil War when intelligence telegraph lines were strung loosely from tree to tree in the manner of a grapevine. Because the messages from the line often were incorrect or confusing, any rumor was said to be from the grapevine.

What causes rumors in modern organizations? To answer this question the following formula is helpful:

$$\text{Rumors} = \text{Ambiguity} \times \text{Interest}$$

Rumors are created when the available message is ambiguous. If all possible information were available and clear, no rumors would be created. But the information must also be interesting. When the message is ambiguous and interesting, rumors will result.

This relationship has an important implication for managerial communication. Management can determine what is interesting to employees by listening to the rumors. For instance, a vice-president recently resigned from a computer company. But the rumors in the grapevine do not address the replacement; rather, the social life of a man and woman seem to be the major topic. This would imply that the employees are relatively secure about the management team and one replacement will probably not rock the boat. Compare this to a company where the president suddenly retired. All that was discussed during lunch or anytime people gathered was the latest rumor about the replacement. Obviously, this matter was of great concern to the employees.

Research indicates information transmitted via the grapevine in organizations is approximately 70 percent accurate; in some organizations, the level of accuracy may reach 90 percent. However, some amount of distortion always exists.[13] This core of truth along with the degree of distortion is often what makes a message on the grapevine believable, interesting, and durable.

As information proceeds from person to person in the grapevine, it tends to undergo three kinds of change. The first is leveling, the dropping of details and the simplifying of context and qualifications. This process is especially prevalent when the rumor is extremely complex. It must be made rather simple to pass on to the next person. The second kind of change is sharpening, the preference for vivid and dramatic treatment of data. Employees work to make a story better and more entertaining as it is passed from one person to another. Third is assimilation, the tendency of people to adjust or modify rumors, to mold them to fit their personal needs. This makes the rumor more interesting to those on the grapevine.[14]

Effective managerial listening requires that managers critically assess informal communication to determine the extent to which leveling, sharpening, and assimilation has occurred. To what extent is the rumor accurate? To answer this question, managers must listen to informal communication and ask appropriate questions.

As mentioned earlier, valuable information can be detected from the grapevine. In early 1991, American Airlines was having extensive labor relations problems and many pilots called in sick rather than reporting for their scheduled flights. The company ultimately had to cancel many flights because of the shortage of pilots. It is possible that if managers would have listened to the rumors, they would have heard that the pilots were going to stage the walkout. Corrective action may have been possible.

Inaccurate rumors can also call for action. In one manufacturing plant, rumors maintained that a massive personnel layoff was about to occur because of the new machinery being installed. Management heard these incorrect rumors. Members of the management team met with employees to assure them no layoffs would occur. Listening to rumors helped prevent a loss of employee morale. As one manager once said, it is important to listen to "the talk on the street."

Listening to the Total Environment

This chapter primarily discusses listening to the spoken word. Chapter 10 discusses nonverbal communication. Managers must listen to spoken and

FIGURE 9–2

Three Dimensions of a Message

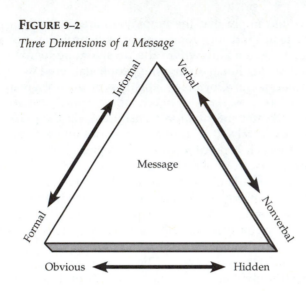

nonverbal messages both separately and jointly in formal and informal settings. Strategic managerial communication requires listening to messages that aren't always obvious. Figure 9–2 graphically demonstrates the three possible aspects of a message: formal to informal, verbal to nonverbal, and obvious to hidden. The three different possibilities are displayed an a triangle with equal sides because all three aspects should be considered equally.

The cover of a national magazine recently read, "How Safe is Your Job: The Warning Signals."[15] This title implies it is necessary for managers to keep their eyes and ears open for all kinds of signals in the organization and its industry.

When a person is aware of the signals of a forthcoming event, it is possible to take corrective action—but first the manager must listen to be aware. This article discusses signals of potential layoffs, such as employees who voluntarily quit but are not replaced, increased debt, layoffs at other companies in the industry, rumors, and departures of top executives. It is possible that most employees could know about pending layoffs long before they were formally announced.

Of course, layoffs are a drastic action. It is important that managers watch and listen to many other events in the company that can affect their careers. For example, which departments seem to be getting the best budgets? Employees in these groups will probably have the greatest opportunities for advancement. Although it is not always possible to determine budget allocations, it is possible to watch for the results of greater allocations. Hiring of additional support staff, purchasing of newer and better computer equipment, acquisition of new office furniture, and more frequent traveling to professional conferences can each signal a favored department.

The main point is that managerial listening goes beyond listening to the obvious words. It requires listening to nonverbal behaviors and the continuous signals that occur in the person's environment. Much is said about the "good ol' boys network" and how this is where a person *really* learns what is going on in the company.[16] Conversations that start out about the football game may end up reviewing the latest production problem. Again, this is why it is important to listen informally to employees and find out what is on their minds.

Demonstrating a Listening Climate

In addition to actually listening carefully, managers must also seem to be listening and establish a climate that demonstrates receptivity. Without this climate, the communication environment in an office can become like that in many homes:

Parent: Why don't you ever tell us what you are doing?
Child: I do, but you don't listen. You're always so busy.
Parent: We're never too busy to listen to you, but you just don't seem to want to tell us anything.

Are the parents too busy to listen, or do they just appear too busy? The same question may be asked of many managers. Is it possible that they appear too busy to listen? A manager may unintentionally establish a nonlistening climate by subtle behavior that says to the subordinate, "Why talk if nobody is listening?"

While a manager is responsible for a tremendous amount of information and spends as much as 50 percent of the working day listening, it is not possible to listen if nobody is talking. Managers need to demonstrate a listening climate to motivate people to open up. Consequently, managers should strive to eliminate listening habits that discourage communication. Table 9–2 lists 20 irritating listening habits.[17] A listener demonstrating these behaviors is not exhibiting a positive communication climate; consequently, the speaker may not believe he is being listened to. This list can serve as a personal checklist for managers to see if they demonstrate any of the irritating behaviors.

Two levels of the listening climate require attention. The first is the micro level or the one-on-one situation. The second level is the macro or total environment. First we will review the micro level.

Micro Listening Environment

A research study asked employees to indicate which of the poor listening habits in Table 9–2 they found to be the most common.[18] Two items seemed to stand out.

When I'm talking, he finishes sentences for me.

When I come in, he doesn't put down what he is doing and turn his attention completely to me.

This finding is especially revealing. Clearly, the listener needs to give undivided attention to the speaker, who does not want to be rushed to complete the message. This fact relates to the 25–75 speaking–thinking differential discussed earlier. The listener's mind moves so much more rapidly than the spoken word that the listener's impatience may show as she attempts to complete the speaker's sentence. Even though the listener is paying attention, this impatience to complete the speaker's communication may develop a negative listening climate. The same is true when the listener works on something else while attempting to listen. The speaker may soon get the feeling that the message being delivered is not very important.

TABLE 9–2   Irritating Listening Habits

1. He doesn't give me a chance to talk. I go in with a problem and never get a chance to tell about it.
2. He interrupts me while I'm talking—never lets me complete more than a couple of sentences before interrupting.
3. He never looks at me while I'm talking. I don't know for sure whether he's even listening or not.
4. He constantly fidgets with a pencil or a paper, studying it rather than listening to me.
5. He never smiles. I'm somewhat apprehensive about talking to him.
6. He always gets me off the subject with his questions and comments.
7. Whenever I make a suggestion, he throws cold water on it. I've quit trying to give him suggestions, ideas, or help.
8. He's always trying to anticipate what I'm going to say next and jumps ahead of me to tell me what my next point is.
9. He rephrases what I say in such a way that he puts words into my mouth that I did not mean.
10. Occasionally, he asks a question about what I've just told him that shows he wasn't listening.
11. He argues with almost everything I say, often even before I've had a chance to state my case.
12. When I'm talking, he finishes sentences for me.
13. He acts as if he's just waiting for me to get through talking so he can interject something of his own.
14. When I have a good idea, he always says, "Yes, I've been thinking about that too."
15. He overdoes trying to show me he's following what I'm saying—too many nods of the head, yeahs, uh-huhs.
16. He tries to insert humorous remarks when I'm trying to be serious.
17. He frequently sneaks looks at his watch or his clock while I'm talking.
18. When I come in, he doesn't put down what he's doing and turn his attention completely to me.
19. He often acts as if I'm keeping him from doing something "important."
20. He asks questions that demand agreement with him. For example, he makes a statement and then says, "Don't you think so?" or "Don't you agree?"

It is particularly important to demonstrate a positive climate when a manager is involved in empathetic listening. As discussed earlier in this chapter, an empathetic listener tries to understand the speaker's inner feelings. Most people have a very difficult time expressing their feelings, so an encouraging, supportive, receptive environment needs to be established. Feelings of elation, sadness, or fear are more easily and willingly expressed when received in a congruent manner by a receiver whose behavior demonstrates "I'm with you."

Unfortunately, incongruent listener behavior is too often the norm. For instance, an employee enters a manager's office and says she has a major problem to discuss. Meanwhile, her manager is shuffling papers around on his desk while saying, "Go ahead. I'll be listening while I get these forms finished." What kind of an impression will the employee receive? The employee obviously thinks her problem is important, but the manager acts as if his forms are as important, if not more so. As a result, he has established a negative listening climate with no demonstrated empathy. The manager should give full physical and psychological attention to the speaker by maintaining eye contact, leaning slightly toward the speaker, changing facial expression in relationship to the message, and taking notes. All of these behaviors demonstrate a positive listening climate.

For a valuable exercise, review the list of irritating listening habits and watch for them in your own behavior throughout a week. This form of personal feedback should provide insights for improving your personal listening climate.

Macro Listening Environment

Managers must take responsibility for ensuring that those who work around them are free to exchange information in a timely and accurate manner.[19] They must develop a general atmosphere that promotes rather than hinders the opportunity to communicate. This macro level of listening is demonstrated by the manager's general demeanor and style. For instance, much has recently been said about managing by wandering around.[20] When managers are physically available and not locked away behind closed office doors, they are creating an atmosphere that says, "I am here to listen to you."

In his popular book *Thriving on Chaos*, Tom Peters presents a number of suggestions that create strong listening environments.[21] First, it is suggested that opportunities to listen be built into managers' daily routines. This can be done by visiting the cafeteria or being available in the coffee shop when most people take their break. Unfortunately, many managers do not work these activities into their schedules because of time pressures. They believe they do not have the time to visit the lunchroom or coffee shop. Unfortunately, many managers do not realize this is an integral and critical part of their jobs.

Another technique is to have informal meetings. Spontaneously gathering a few people together to discuss a problem rather than scheduling a meeting with a formal agenda indicates the manager wants and needs to listen to employees' ideas. Another technique is to keep official titles and symbols of authority to a minimum. People are more willing to talk when they don't feel inferior to another.

The open-door policy expressed in many companies provides an example of a positive compared to a negative macro listening environment. Managers often pride themselves on announcing an open-door policy. They tell their employees to stop by anytime—the office door is always open. Some managers go so far as to mention the policy in memos and even put it in company manuals. But managers become frustrated when employees do not avail themselves of the open door.

Why is the open-door policy not used? A negative listening environment probably exists. First, it may be necessary to make an appointment with a secretary before the door is opened. As the secretary flips through the appointment calendar, every impression is given that the manager is probably too important to listen to the employee's "little" concern. Second, the office may be so formal that it inhibits open, candid communication. Wouldn't it be better to be available in a spontaneous manner by frequently walking around the work area? This would be a positive open-door environment. A junior supervisor in a large organization once remarked somewhat sarcastically, "If they have to announce an open-door policy, it probably means that there really isn't one!"[22]

Mention was made of the "good ol' boys network" earlier when discussing the importance of listening to the total environment. This concept of the total environment applies to macro level listening and the open-door policy, not just to the good ol' boys network. The importance of the total environment was aptly demonstrated by Celeste, a first-line supervisor in a foundry. Her company, on the far south side of the Chicago suburbs, was dominated by men. But Celeste was probably one of the most respected supervisors. She gained respect by always being available to the employees. For instance, one Saturday the company rented a bus and arranged for employees to attend a Chicago White Sox baseball game. Celeste was one of the first to sign up. During the bus trip and at the game, she was part of the group even though she was the only female manager present. She did not act as if she were superior to the others. This is probably one of the reasons her employees truly believed that Celeste always had an open door when it was time to discuss a problem. She demonstrated a positive listening climate.

A number of elements influence employees' perceptions that managers are willing and good listeners.[23] Employees' work and personal backgrounds, the organizational culture, the employees' roles within the organization and the little symbolic behaviors of the manager all affect the listening climate. Managers would do well to take a periodic audit of their personal listening behavior and their environment to assure they have established an environment that says, "Yes, I am willing to listen." Managers must be good listeners and take pride in this skill. Dr. Clyde Wright testifies to the importance of listening. He is an M.D. but found great personal satisfaction in management;

consequently, he became a manager of CIGNA Healthplan. In an interview, he related that being a manager requires a person to listen to people above all else; he firmly believes that development of this skill can be a challenge but also a reward.[24]

Summary

Managers must exert an active, concentrated effort to overcome listening barriers. One of the primary barriers is that people think about four times faster than they can speak; consequently, because verbal stimulation is frequently inadequate, the mind tends to wander. Motivation and willingness are highly related barriers. Willingness develops before listening even begins whereas poor motivation is largely caused by the 25–75 problem. Other barriers to listening include internal distractions, detouring, debate, and time.

To be an effective listener, a manager needs first to be physically and psychologically prepared to listen. Preparation includes setting the best possible time and place, being aware of personal biases and barriers to listening, and reviewing objectives. The manager who prepares to listen can apply certain techniques. For best results, it is important to identify the main and supporting points and then to outline, summarize, visualize, or personalize the message.

All these techniques are important in active listening, but in interactive listening, it is also possible to use various questioning strategies. Three major categories of questions are available: open–closed, primary–secondary, neutral–directed. Since each type of question is effective in developing mutual understanding only in certain situations, the manager must analyze the message to determine the appropriate question.

In addition to listening in formal situations, it is necessary to listen to informal communication. This includes rumors on the grapevine. Rumors are a result of the ambiguity and interest in a message. While passing from one person to another on the grapevine, rumors may be leveled, sharpened, or assimilated.

A positive micro listening climate can be either developed or destroyed through subtle behaviors. When the listener demonstrates such behaviors as ending a sentence for the speaker or failing to give full attention to the speaker, a negative climate may develop. A listener can develop a positive climate by maintaining eye contact, leaning slightly toward the speaker, and changing facial expression in relationship to the message.

At the macro level, listening can be improved by wandering around. This may include such activities as stopping by the coffee shop for a chat or having informal meetings. Also, the listening environment is improved when official titles and symbols are kept to a minimum.

Endnotes

1. C. G. Coakley and A. D. Wolvin, "Listening Pedagogy and Andragogy," *Journal of the International Listening Association* 4 (1990), pp. 33–61.

2. Judi Brownell, "Perceptions of Effective Listeners: A Management Study," *Journal of Business Communication* 27, no. 4 (Fall 1990), pp. 401–15.

3. B. D. Sypher and T. E. Zorn, "Communication Related Abilities and Upward Mobility: A Longitudinal Investigation," *Human Communication Research* 12 (1986), pp. 420–31.

4. Jaclyn Fierman, "How Gallo Crushes the Competition," *Fortune*, September 1, 1986, pp. 24–33.

5. A. W. Clausen, "Listening and Responding to Employees' Concerns," *Harvard Business Review*, January–February 1980, pp. 101–14.

6. Philip V. Lewis, *Organizational Communication: The Essence of Effective Management*, 3rd ed. (New York: John Wiley & Sons, 1987), p. 146.

7. Franklin H. Knower, D. Philips, and F. Koeppel, "Studies in Listening to Informative Speaking," *Journal of Social Psychology* 40 (1945), p. 82.

8. Larry R. Smeltzer and Kittie W. Watson, "Listening: An Empirical Comparison of Discussion Length and Level of Incentive," *Central States Speech Journal* 35, no. 3 (1984), pp. 166–71.

9. R. N. Bostrom, *Input! The Process of Listening* (Northbrook, Ill.: Waveland Press, 1988).

10. L. R. Smeltzer and K. W. Watson, "A Test of Instructional Strategies for Listening Improvement in a Simulated Business Setting," *Journal of Business Communication* 22, no. 4 (Fall 1985), pp. 33–42.

11. Edward E. Lawler, *The Ultimate Advantage* (San Francisco: Jossey-Bass, Inc., 1992).

12. Bill Saporito, "A Week Aboard the Wal-Mart Express," *Fortune*, August 24, 1992, pp. 77–84.

13. Hugh B. Vickery, "Tapping into the Employee Grapevine," *Association Management*, January 1984, pp. 59–64.

14. Lewis, *Organizational Communication*, pp. 46–48.

15. *Newsweek*, November 5, 1990.

16. Joe G. Thomas, "Sources of Social Information: A Longitudinal Analysis," *Human Relations* 39, no. 9 (1986) pp. 855–70.

17. Eugene Raudsepp, "Is Anybody Listening," *Machine Design*, February 24, 1977, p. 7.

18. Larry R. Smeltzer and Kittie Watson, "Barriers to Listening Comparison Between Business Students and Business Practitioners," *Communication Research Report* 1, no. 1 (December 1984), pp. 82–87.

19. E. H. Schein, *Organizational Culture and Leadership* (San Francisco: Jossey-Bass, Inc., 1985).

20. T. J. Peters and R. H. Waterman, Jr., *In Search of Excellence: Lessons from America's Best Run Companies* (New York: Warner Books, Inc., 1982).

21. T. Peters, *Thriving on Chaos* (New York: Alfred A. Knopf, 1988).

22. Charles E. Beck and Elizabeth A. Beck, "The Manager's Open Door and the Communication Climate," *Business Horizons*, January–February 1986, pp. 15–19.

23. Marilyn H. Lewis and N. L. Reinsch, Jr., "Listening in Organizational Environments," *Journal of Business Communication* 25, no. 3 (Summer 1988), pp. 49–67;

and J. Brownell, "Listening Environment: Critical. Aspect of Organizational Communication," Working Paper, Cornell University, 1992.

24. Angela Gonzales, "Clyde Wright: Profile," *Business Journal*, February 24, 1992, pp. 12–13.

Additional Readings

Barker, Larry. *Listening Behavior.* Englewood Cliffs, N.J.: Prentice Hall, 1971.

Brownell, J. *Building Active Listening Skills.* Englewood Cliffs, N.J.: Prentice Hall, 1986.

Colburn, William C., and Sanford B. Weinberg. *An Orientation to Listening and Audience Analysis.* Chicago: Science Research Associates, 1976.

King, P. E., and R. R. Behnke. "The Effect of Time Compressed Speech on Comprehension, Interpretive, and Short-term Listening." *Human Communication Research* 15 (1989), pp. 428–44.

Papa, M. J., and E. C. Glenn. "Listening Ability and Performance with New Technology: A Case Study." *Journal of Business Communication* 25, no. 4 (Fall 1988), pp. 5–15.

Rankin, Paul T. "The Importance of Listening Ability." *English Journal, College Edition* 17 (October 1928), pp. 626–30 (a classic article on the subject).

Steil, L., L. L. Baker, and K. W. Watson. *Effective Listening.* Reading, Mass.: Addison-Wesley, 1983.

Sypher, B. D., R. N. Bostrom, and J. H. Seibert. "Listening Communication Abilities and Success at Work." *Journal of Business Communication* 26, no. 4 (Fall 1989), pp. 293–303.

Watson, K. W., and L. L. Barker. "Listening Behavior: Definition and Measurement." In *Communication Yearbook 8.* Ed. R. N. Bostrom. Beverly Hills, Calif.: Sage Publications, 1984.

Weaver, Carl. *Human Listening.* Indianapolis: Bobbs-Merrill, 1972.

Wolff, F. I., N. C. Marsnik, W. S. Tacey, and R. G. Nichols. *Perceptive Listening.* New York: Holt, Rinehart and Winston, 1983.

Wolvin, D., and C. G. Coakley. *Listening,* 3rd ed. Dubuque, Iowa: Wm C. Brown, 1989.

"Killing a Rumor Before it Kills a Company." *Business Week,* December 24, 1990, p. 23.

Discussion Questions

1. What is the difference between hearing and listening?
2. Provide an example where you or someone else probably lacked the willingness to listen.
3. Provide an example where you detoured or debated while listening.
4. According to the discussion presented in this chapter, what is the difference between interactive and active listening?

5. Give examples where you would use casual listening, attentive listening, and empathetic listening.

6. What are five things a manager should do to become physically and psychologically prepared to listen? Discuss each of these.

7. Give an example of a message that was organized according to the pros and cons of a subject.

8. Give an example where you made an attempt to personalize a message.

9. Give a sample of two questions for each of the three types of questions discussed in this chapter.

10. Differentiate between formal and informal listening. Provide an example in which you have participated in both types of listening within the last day.

11. How would you explain the 70 percent accuracy of the grapevine? Assume a company had three vice-presidents and two of them quit the company at the same time. Of course a number of rumors about the cause would circulate throughout the company. Do you believe that leveling, sharpening, or assimilation would be the most prevalent?

12. Provide an example in which you have seen someone develop a positive micro listening environment. Now give an example of a negative micro listening environment.

13. Assume you were a consultant in a large corporation. What would you do to encourage the managers to develop a more positive macro listening environment? Provide details.

14. What does the university at which you study do to encourage or discourage an open-door policy?

15. Describe a situation in which poor listening was the cause of a problem. What should have been done to have prevented this problem?

CASE 9–1
HOLGATE'S LISTENING PROBLEMS

John Holgate, a section manager in a chemical plant, has several engineers reporting to him. As part of his job, Holgate attends meetings during any given day with some of his junior engineers as well as with people outside his immediate group. Occasionally, people higher up in the company (the technical director or vice-president, for example) attend these review meetings.

The engineers who work for Holgate believe he often misrepresents them—the engineers believe Holgate doesn't listen to what is being said. He often interrupts the speakers and completes the sentence for them. Since the engineers do not want to disagree with their boss openly, they do not contradict him in front of higher management. Holgate has a habit of completing sentences with either subordinates or higher level managers.

Naturally, this habit results in confusion, wasted time and effort, and poor morale. When members of higher management return for their next review, they usually find that the work they requested has not been done. In fact, they occasionally find that unrequested tasks have been carried out. As they listen to Holgate's project status review, management has lately been wondering what is going on. This doubt reflects not just on Holgate but on his subordinates as well. The subordinates' morale and productivity have been slipping.

Questions

1. Why does Holgate complete the speaker's sentences?
2. How can Holgate improve his listening skills?
3. Assuming you are Holgate's subordinate, how could you point out this problem to him? Write the statement that could be used to begin such a discussion. Assuming you are his supervisor, again write the statement that could be used to begin the discussion about this problem.

CASE 9–2
PARDON ME!

Bob Pierce, a kindly man of about 50, is the president of ABC Construction Company. The company is considered the most progressive and innovative in highway, bridge, and dam construction in the area. Pierce has served in different functional areas of the company, is fairly well educated, and is oriented toward engineering.

Before becoming ABC's vice-president of field operations, Walter Horton was the chief engineer of a rival firm. He has a reputation for being a very good project manager and for knowing intimately the details of ABC field operations.

Pierce has just returned from sick leave. His bad cold is still slowing him down. It is now noon, and Pierce, who has finally caught up with the backlog of work, is preparing to go to lunch. Just then, Horton walks into his office. Horton has been trying to get in touch with Pierce the past few days for his decision about the construction plan for the new dam. Horton spreads his blueprints on the president's desk and starts his presentation.

After the presentation, the following conversation occurs.

Horton: Well, how do you feel about the plan?
Pierce: (somewhat absently) Well, uh, pretty good. . . .
Horton: (a little too quickly) Is there anything I haven't made clear?
Pierce: Mmm . . . no. . . .
Horton: OK, good. Now I would like to present the plan to the board of directors and maybe. . . .
Pierce: Board of directors? Wait a minute. You're moving pretty fast.

Horton: You agreed the plan's a good one, didn't you?
Pierce: (not with it at all) Well, yes.

Questions

1. What are the physical and psychological listening barriers Pierce faced during the presentation?
2. What assumptions is Horton making about Pierce's ability to grasp the situation?
3. What could Pierce have done to prevent the situation?
4. What are Horton's shortcomings as a communicator that would complicate the situation for anyone listening to him?

CASE 9–3
HEARING BUT NOT LISTENING

Cedar's Furniture and Appliance is a chain of five stores, two located in Youngstown, two in Akron, and one in Cleveland. Cedar's main office is in Akron.

Jane Pyle is the office manager at the main office. She supervises four word processing operators. Three of Pyle's employees are efficient and thorough. She tells them what she wants done once, and it is done. However, the fourth employee, Harriet Enders, seems to get little done right. She finishes her daily work, but she always has to redo it, thus putting an extra burden on the other three operators. They have to make up the work Enders hasn't time for because she is redoing her original work. The other three employees are beginning to complain to Pyle about the problem.

Pyle doesn't want to terminate Enders because Pyle knows her subordinate can be a hard worker. When she does follow directions, Enders is the first of the four word processing operators to finish. The office manager wonders why Enders doesn't understand directions while the other three people always seem to. She is almost sure that, although Enders is hearing, she is not listening. Enders' problem is preventing the office work from running smoothly.

Questions

1. Write the dialogue Pyle can use to open the discussion with Enders about this problem.
2. What environmental factors might be responsible for Enders' difficulty in listening?

10 EFFECTIVE NONVERBAL COMMUNICATION IN MANAGEMENT

> *Jackson is dean of the college of business in a midwestern university. Through luck, politics, and a lot of hard work, the college has a new building ready to be occupied. He worked hard to preserve the quality features of the building as the university faced budget cuts during the years it was being constructed. One area is of particular pride: faculty offices. He has been able to provide one for each of the permanent faculty. Now he faces a dilemma. How does he allocate those offices? What should he consider to ensure the office assignment nonverbally reflects the assigned person in terms of rank, experience, and preference? What signals do location, propinquity, and design send to others? He has the blueprints before him once again as he faces one of the biggest challenges of the project.*

Understanding the importance of nonverbal communication is often difficult because it is such a natural part of any managerial interaction. To appreciate the contribution nonverbal communication makes to managerial communication, imagine yourself at a meeting with six others discussing an upcoming event—say the opening of a new facility for your company. It is a meeting like any number you have attended before, yet it is radically different because you cannot see the others. Something keeps you from this. It could be a fabric veil, a fog, beige panels, you decide. Your location is also a puzzle. Is it the boardroom for the corporation, or is it a meeting room just anywhere? How important is this meeting in the whole scheme of things? Your environment provides no clues. In addition, you cannot really hear the others very well. All voices have been altered by the device used during investigatory reports on television. You can hear the words, but the voices have little or no character. The words are slowed down and slurred to some extent.

You are all seated in the same room, but because of the room's setup, you cannot see who is seated where—who is at the head of the table (perhaps you are), and who is at the sides, not even who is seated next to whom. While you and several others flew in to attend the meeting, you have not had a chance to shake hands before the meeting began. In fact, today you have not seen the others or what they are wearing. Are they dressed as well as you are, or are they dressed informally. The only communication possible during the meeting is what you can get from you and the six others talking.

Unfortunately, even that part of the communication process is a challenge. You verbally trip over each other as the meeting proceeds since you have no efficient way to signal whose turn it is to speak. In addition, because speakers must identify themselves before speaking, the interactions take longer than usual. Furthermore, you must keep these verbal identities in mind as you listen because you have no visual, tactile, or olfactory cues to go on. As the meeting progresses, whenever you contribute, you are unsure of the reactions of any but the verbal respondents because you cannot see the shrugs, posture shifts, or expressions on the other faces.

The interaction is also lengthened by the need to evaluate each remark for intent. Did he mean that ironically? Was she being sarcastic? Was that last remark meant as a joke? The audio scrambler makes quick judgments on these fine points nearly impossible. And while you can hear the voices, which voice belongs to whom? Someone suggests that all the employees in the store dress up as clowns. You are just about to say "ridiculous" when you check yourself—be careful, maybe the boss said that.

You know the meeting is scheduled to last two hours, but because you had to surrender your watch at the door, you have no idea about the time, although it seems an eternity. You know the agenda for the meeting, but are you going to be able to cover all of the items in the time allotted? Are you giving enough time to each item? Are you going to get out of the meeting and find that only half the time has elapsed? Whatever the case, you wish you were out of the meeting now.

Importance of Nonverbal Communication

Nonverbals are clearly a crucial element of managerial communication. Without nonverbal communication as a source of information, most of the richness and much of the meaning in messages would be lost. In many cases, conversations would be complicated by the need to repeat messages for clarity, and the time required would multiply enormously.

Nonverbal communication accompanies oral and, by logical extension, written messages, while consisting of the signals delivered through means other than verbal. In short, it includes everything but the words. Managers send, receive, and interpret nonverbal messages in the same sense as they send, receive, and interpret verbal ones. The same communication dynamics come into play as the sender intends (although often unconsciously) to send a message and chooses some medium through which to do so (a gesture, for example), which receivers perceive and interpret just as they do with verbal messages. Nonverbal communication may bear a clear meaning in itself, but often it serves as an adjunct to the spoken words, adding nuance in one place and clarity in another. At other times, this complex source of messages may even contradict the words being spoken.

Nonverbal communication is an important part of our daily managerial interactions.[1] While the extent of the nonverbal aspect varies from interaction to interaction, one set of oft-cited statistics shows that 55 percent of a message comes from the facial expressions and posture of the speaker, while vocal aspects (vocalics) deliver 38 percent, and the actual words deliver only 7 percent.[2]

Nonverbal communication is a rich and complex source of communication data, and this chapter provides an overview of the areas relevant to the managerial function. But first, three generalizations about nonverbal signals should be stressed here. While the first two apply to most other signals, it helps to keep them in mind when interpreting nonverbal communication. First, with the exception of so-called emblems, nonverbal signals rarely have one set meaning. Rather, they usually add to the message's meaning as shown later in this chapter.

Second, nonverbal signals vary from culture to culture, region to region, in their meaning. Nonverbal signals derive from experiences within the communication environment (cultural, regional, or social) and are generally dispersed throughout it.[3] It is not enough merely to translate the verbal language; the nonverbal must be expressed as well.[4] The Japanese, for example, usually present a noncontroversial demeanor and are excessively polite by North American standards. In negotiation, the accompanying nonverbals can create confusion across cultures.[5] In cross-cultural situations, in fact, while the verbal takes on greater importance, knowing and using basic nonverbal signals—for example, bowing in South Korea—can communicate respect.[6]

Third, when nonverbal signals contradict verbal ones, the nonverbals are usually the ones to trust. When verbal and nonverbal disagree, credibility can suffer.[7] As this chapter will show, nonverbal signals can provide valuable clues to the truth of a message.

Telling people how to dress, talk, and even move is a far easier task than putting it all into play in one's life. While we can read about smiling behavior, for example, how much is too much? For women and men aspiring to be managers, an excellent source of models of appropriate nonverbal behavior is readily available. A variety of television shows regularly show excellent models for nonverbal behavior, especially in the people chosen for interviews on talk shows specializing in business. To get the maximum impact of the nonverbal elements in the conversations, with the exception of vocalics, watch these shows with the sound turned off. Not only do they show the kinds of gestures leaders make, but they also generally reflect current appropriate dress.

The Functions of Nonverbal Cues

Nonverbal communication is a broader concept than many realize. It is far more than just gestures and eye contact. One simple definition might be that in managerial interactions, nonverbal communication is everything but the words. A more precise definition is that offered by Harrison who said it is "the exchange of information through nonlinguistic signs."[8] These nonlinguistic signs are like any kind of sign in communication in that they are something tangible capable of bearing meaning, just as linguistic signs are. They differ in that they are nonword, that is, nonverbal.

Unfortunately, nonverbal communication can result in frustratingly inexact interpretation. Scholars have carefully studied nonverbal communication, but have only scratched the surface of the topic in many areas. If placed in the proper perspective, it can be a valuable source of cues in communication situations.

Burbinster sees six functions for nonverbal communication:[9]

1. Complementing.
2. Accenting.
3. Contradicting.
4. Repeating.
5. Regulating.
6. Substituting.

Nonverbal signals that complement the verbal message repeat it. Typically, these signals accompany what is being said. For example, a technician explaining the varying gap widths in faulty components in a heating system might hold up her thumb and index fingers and vary the gap between them as she discusses the problem. Or a supervisor welcoming a subordinate back after a lengthy illness might give a warm and long handshake to stress how pleased he is at the other's return.

Those nonverbal signals that accent call our attention to a matter under discussion. A common example is a person pounding on a desk as she makes an important point. People may also use vocalics, the nonverbal aspects of the voice itself, to highlight a point. Someone differentiating between one choice and another might say "I want *this* one and not *that*."

The nonverbal signals that contradict are less obvious. These are usually sent unintentionally by the subconscious to say nonverbally the *opposite* of what is being said verbally. Either subtly or obviously, nonverbal cues will often tell the careful observers the truth when the verbal cues don't. This complex area of nonverbal communication will be discussed later under the heading of nonverbal leakage of deception.

Repeating occurs when we have already sent a message using one form of communication and wish to emphasize the point being made. It differs from complementing in that it is not done simultaneously with the verbal comment.

Regulating, the fifth purpose Burbinster suggests, is a subtle and important one. Regulating occurs during conversations to signal to our partner to "slow," "stop," and even "wait your turn" and let the other person know when we are ready to listen or to speak. Watch an ongoing conversation and you will quickly spot a variety of these cues. A speaker who is not finished with his point but is being interrupted might speak louder or faster to keep his turn (thus using vocalics). Another might hold up her hand and say "not yet, let me finish."

Substituting is a less common nonverbal signal than the others. When we can't send a message by verbal cues, we might choose to use nonverbal ones—especially emblems, which will be discussed later—to get the point that we are making across to our receiver. A supervisor visiting a loud factory might use the "OK" sign to signal an employee. This will likely be more effective than something shouted.

From a theoretical perspective, nonverbal communication also serves another important function: Communication redundancy. This concept refers to the phenomena built into any language system that combats the effects of noise. It simply means that much of the meaning of a message can be deduced from other elements in the message that have already appeared. The TV show "Wheel of Fortune" is an example of redundancy in that not every word or letter must be on the game board before one can guess the correct phrase.

While part of a message delivers new information, much of it exists to ensure the points being made are understood. Far from being a negative phenomenon, communication redundancy is vitally important because it helps ensure that our message gets past the various barriers that environmental, organizational, or interpersonal elements erect. When a message is made more redundant, when the information in it has been made more predictable to the receiver, the message has a greater chance of transferring the meaning the sender intends it to convey.

Every communication system is redundant. Verbal languages build in redundancy through a variety of means including grammar and syntax. Most of the functions served by nonverbal communication serve in some way as redundancy. Thus, as we discuss an issue with another, we will use nonverbal signals to complement, accent, repeat, and even substitute to get a point across. This may be done without even thinking about it. Even when a nonverbal signal contradicts the verbal, additional nonverbal signals are likely to follow to underscore the contradiction.[10]

This chapter now explores several key areas of nonverbal communication and suggests how managers can use them to their advantage. It also looks at gender differences and how nonverbal leakage of deception can be detected through careful observation.

Kinesics

Say "nonverbal communication" to most people, and they probably think of movement, which is technically kinesics. Nonverbal communication consists of far more than just one general category, but kinesics is the most studied of the categories. It includes gestures as well as posture.

Gestures may include emblems, illustrators, affect displays, regulators, and adapters.[11] While people usually use gestures without thinking, a conscious awareness of them can help a manager communicate more efficiently. An understanding of and training in effective signals can open up the possibility of our strategic, conscious usage of them.

Earlier, we noted that nonverbal signals usually suggest meaning; they do not give direct meaning. Emblems are an exception in that they actually stand for something else. The OK sign cited earlier is one example and another is the "time out": one palm held at a right angle to the other.

Illustrators serve to complement verbal communication by providing an example of or reinforcing what is being said. When a person is trying to explain an item that is not present, what is more natural than drawing it in the air?

Regulators are a set of gestures that both subtly and obviously control what a speaker says. They arise from a variety of sources including the hands as, for example, when one holds up the hand palm outward to keep another from interrupting. We need to be able to regulate to draw some speakers out and rein others in.

The affect display is more complex than most gestures and involves several parts of the body. For example, suppose you are talking to someone who has a scowl on his face as he sits up straight but turned slightly away from you. His arms cross his chest, and you have little doubt this person doesn't like the idea under discussion. The affect display signals to another person what we are feeling and can show pleasure as well as anger, boredom as well as interest. Reading such a nonverbal signal from others is rarely a problem. The challenge lies in regulating these within ourselves in some situations. We may not always want to show what we are feeling, so we must regulate, particularly if it could affect our current communication strategy.

The adapter may be the least appreciated source of kinesic messages; however, it can be quite important. In many situations, when one behavior might be inappropriate, the body will adapt by sending signals that would provide a solution, if one could only possibly implement it. For example, the person wishing to leave, but unable to do so, might start to shake his crossed leg in imitation of walking. Another person under stress may begin to twist the paper clip she is holding as a socially acceptable substitute for what she would like to do with the person she is reprimanding. That employee being reprimanded may wrap his arms around himself as a sort of substitute hug to provide the comfort he needs at that moment. Adapters often appear as a pattern of seemingly irrelevant nonverbal signals, but to the careful observer, their presence may suggest discomfort. Similarly, in stressful situations when projecting an image of self-control is crucial, be aware of the nonverbal signals you may be sending. Looking outwardly calm while clenching the fists may reveal more than intended.

Proxemics

Proxemics refers to the space around us and how we and others relate to it. Proxemics can reveal much and merits careful attention. Most people hearing "proxemics" think only of personal space, the personal "bubble" surrounding a person. That is a good place to start, but the concept encompasses far more than just that.

Proxemic Zones

Edward Hall studied use of personal distances and determined that Americans have four arbitrarily established proxemic zones, described in Figure 10–1, in which we interact.[12] Strategic managers are aware of these zones and appreciate how they and others react when their spaces are invaded.

Our language suggests we all are aware of personal space to some degree. We talk about someone "keeping his distance," or complain when we perceive others "invading our territory" or say "they are crowding me on this issue" when in fact what they are doing has little to do with territory. When someone is pressing another on an issue, the other person may respond, "Give me breathing room," or less politely, "Keep out of my face."

In the North American culture, businesspeople generally operate within four zones: intimate, personal, social, and public. In the discussion that follows, keep in mind that the figures are averages. They reflect the culture in general as well as the relationship between the parties. A number of other factors enter into any interpersonal relationship to change the details. These can include personal appearance, physical attractiveness, gender, and age. Thus, we may react differently to a tall than a short person and may draw nearer to an attractive person than to another less attractive.[13]

North Americans' intimate zone ranges from physical contact to roughly 1.5 to 2 feet. It is reserved for those who are psychologically close. When it is invaded by others, especially for more than a moment, a person usually feels uncomfortable and is likely to react, although often without knowing why. The people involved may attempt to put more space between them or they may put up some kind of barrier.

FIGURE 10–1

Proxemic Zones

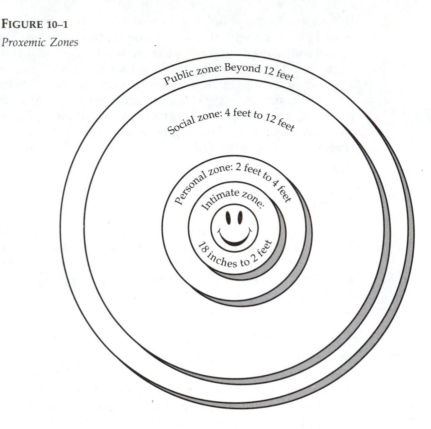

The personal zone extends from the edge of the intimate zone out to roughly four feet. Americans reserve it for close friends, but permit others to enter it temporarily during introductions. Watch as two strangers come together for an introduction. As they shake hands, they will often stand with one leg forward and the other ready to back up. Then, when the greeting is over, both will usually retreat into the next zone.

The next area is the social zone. It extends from about 4 feet to 12 feet and is the space in which we would like to conduct much of our daily business. Relationships between managers and their employees might begin in this area and continue for a time, but will often move into the personal zone once trust has developed, but this takes time.[14]

The North American public zone extends beyond 12 feet and reflects the distance at which most would like to keep strangers. Little communication of a business nature takes place in this zone. Perhaps the only spoken communication that occurs would be the public speech. We see the formal institutionalized reflection of this distance in the arrangement of public auditoriums or even in the layout of many political rallies. Even if the latter is not too crowded, the audience will often keep its distance.

For managers, the value of understanding proxemic zones is clear. An observant communicator can gauge the relative warmth that exists in a relationship by the distances individuals keep during interactions. As trust grows, distances should predictably diminish. If they do not diminish, then some other factor may be involved. Let's consider some of these.

Differences in Zones

Proxemic zones vary from culture to culture. For example, South Americans and Arabs typically interact with people at far closer ranges than do North Americans. Often when people from North America interact with individuals from either of these two cultures, the varying proxemic zones expected by the two groups create confusion unless one of the participants is aware of the need to adapt to the needs of the other. That is, either the North Americans give up some of their ground, or the others extend their distance. When two people from varying cultures interact, a curious backwards dance frequently develops as the one invades and the other evades a space.

Men tend to maintain larger personal space bubbles than do women. Women are more likely to allow men or other women to come closer than men, and women will be more tolerant of temporary violations of their own space.[15] Some of the adverse reactions of these and other differences in gender-specific behavior will be explored later in the chapter.

Naturally, circumstances may artificially affect our use of zones. The classic example of this is the crowded elevator where people sharing clearly defined sets of proxemic zones allow one another, even complete strangers to invade personal and intimate zones. Here, though, people will try to adapt to the invasion by other nonverbal means including blocking, that is, by folding the arms across the chest or putting up their briefcases as a short of shield. Some people may experience stimulus overload and attempt to prevent others from invading their field of vision. Like city dwellers who become aloof and isolate themselves whenever the opportunity arises, people will stare at the clock seemingly unaware that others are within inches. Real, tangible personal space is not available, so one creates it in the mind.[16]

When traditional proxemic zones need to be ignored for an extended period, people will stake out some territory. One way is to create even spacing between participants as when seated around a meeting table with movable seats. In other situations, people will erect some sort of barrier to signal the limits of their own space. Watch at meetings around a conference table as people unconsciously arrange notebooks, pencils, coffee cups, and other business artifacts around the other perimeters of their territory. They are signaling where the boundaries of their limited personal space lie in that crowded environment. Similarly, students in a class typically occupy the same seat day after day throughout the term. Should someone take that seat one day, the person feels uncomfortable, even slightly violated—his or her territory has been invaded.

FIGURE 10–2

(Fixed and Semifixed Space in the Same Office)

Semi-fixed space   Fixed space

Conference table   Executive's desk

Territoriality, our tendency to defend an area of space as our exclusive preserve, can be classified into fixed-feature and semifixed-feature. Fixed-feature territory has clear, unmovable boundaries. Probably the most obvious example is the office desk. On the other hand, semifixed-feature space has movable objects, as in the example of the meeting room.[17] It is easy for the "owner" to defend fixed space since it has clearly been labeled as belonging to that person, but semifixed feature is less so (see Figure 10–2).

Managerial Implications of Proxemic Zones

Managers should be aware that intruding into another's territory without invitation can be an annoyance or even a threat no matter what one's rank. Recognizing the boundaries of both fixed- and semifixed-feature spaces communicates respect to the individual. Artifacts belonging to another individual should be regarded as personal. The use of another's chair or telephone without permission can be perceived as arrogant.

Good managers recognize that those with little territory of their own should have that space respected as well. While one may have relatively little power within an organization, one still needs to have a place that is one's own. Secretaries are probably the most obvious example of this (although many secretaries wield tremendous power and others' cautious treatment of their territory shows that). Talk to many secretaries about territoriality, and they will share their annoyance at having their desk drawers rifled for writing implements or having the edge of their desk serve as a sort of couch for people stopping to chat. You can usually spot signs of intended territoriality with a little careful observation. An example is a receptionist whose desk was located in a public area. The receptionist put family pictures along the front of the desk and small figurines on the window separating the desk from another area to stress what was personal territory.

One of the skills possessed by experienced workers is the ability to read the environment for nonverbal clues. With just a little training, one can quickly scan an area and tell much about the rank of the individual holding control over the territory, the personal habits she practices, as well as her attitudes about others with whom she interacts. Similarly, managers should be aware that others are reading these same signs in the manager's environment.

The amount of space allotted to another, the amount of privacy that space entails, and where in the building that space is located can also speak volumes about how the organization sees the individual. Generally, more is better than less, bigger is better than smaller, new is better than old. Similarly, one can read much by relative distance from the center of power, so-called propinquity. Generally, the closer people are to the organization's leaders, the more power they enjoy or at least they are perceived by others to enjoy. In fact, some will even sacrifice space for propinquity to gain what they see to be closeness to power.[18]

A few examples illustrate these generalizations. More is better than less shows through with the number of telephone lines a person has, and even the number of secretaries available. Individuals new to a job may find the furniture in their offices suddenly replaced by smaller, cheaper versions that suit the lower rank of the new occupant. U.S. Civil Service regulations elaborately set out just what rank gets what furniture and in what quality. Some organizations even have a cleaning hierarchy that goes with the organizational hierarchy. At lower levels in the hierarchy, offices are cleaned once a week, while at higher levels the offices may be cleaned daily.

Haptics

Nonverbal communication goes beyond gestures, space, and proxemic zones. Haptics is another area of nonverbal communication and is concerned with touching behavior. Seasoned managers know that touching is sometimes a necessary part of interpersonal relations. But with the growing awareness of sexual harassment, the significant questions have become who, when, how much, and how often. Of course, haptics is not necessarily affectionate; watch a group of children for any length of time to support this statement. Typically, though, haptics focuses on affectionate behavior and falls into five categories:[19]

1. Functional to serve professional purposes.
2. Social to answer the needs of politeness.
3. Friendship to build warmth.
4. Love to create intimacy.
5. Sexual to arouse.

Each level in this progressive series can lead to the next, and not always in a clear way. Professional touching can lead to social touching, which can lead to friendship, and so on.

When a haptic category is exceeded, it may be done to communicate a message about the state of the parties' relationship. It is either warmer than it had been, or one of the parties wishes it so. Conflict can arise when the two parties involved do not agree on an acceptable haptic level for the relationship.[20] Anyone aware of the sensitive issue of sexual harassment can see that the division between the categories must be scrupulously respected if one is to retain a professional relationship. Recent court rulings that apply the "reasonable woman standard" to harassment show that what is acceptable to men may not be acceptable to women, and the latter would prevail. The cultural aspect is also crucial. For instance, the touching among friends of the same gender in the Midwest might seem frigid in the South. The key is to use discretion and common sense.

As with any learned behavior, watch respected leaders from within that culture and follow their behavior. At the same time, keep in mind that haptics and dominance are often related. The person in power is more likely to touch a subordinate than to be touched by subordinates.[21]

Dress

What we wear says much about who we are, or at least who we want to be perceived to be. Dress is an integral part of the first impression we form on meeting another and is often the key to initial credibility.[22] Consequently, managers should pay close attention to what they wear in order to send the right message to others. This section will focus on *general* suggestions for effective dress since clothing styles are so changeable. What is fashionable one year might look absurd only two years later. Specific details on dressing for success can be found in the latest editions of the various books now available for both men and women. One piece of advice is enduring, though. Be neither the first nor the last the adopt a fashion. Many businesspeople see the person who is always "with it" in terms of fashion as too concerned with outward appearances. Then, too, fads do not always catch on. In that case, rather than being a trendsetter, one is perceived as merely being out of step with accepted practices.

The greatest amount of dressing advice has probably been written for women. Theorists have pondered just why women have such a problem in advancing in many businesses, and men see dress as an important element, if not the most important one.[23] Some argue that the image women portray is, in large part, a result of poor choices in dress. It has been said that the woman who wishes to control subordinates and exert authority needs to avoid dressing in a way that portrays her as weak and indecisive. Unfortunately, much that is traditionally "feminine"—bows, flouncy skirts, and frilly blouses—may defeat efforts at being viewed as forceful.[24]

For women, the most common piece of advice is not to wear anything "sexy" to the office. Instead, women are advised to tailor their clothing to the demands of the job and the company. The old advice to dress as well as the person at the next level would be appropriate here (and for men as well as women). As one writer put it, "If you look the part, you get the part."[25] Similarly, both men and women should be aware of how status differences are conveyed through dress within their own office environments.[26] If short-sleeved shirts are worn by managers below but not above a certain level, one should be aware of that distinction and not dress down by wearing them. If shirts and ties are worn without coats at one level, but with coats at a higher one, then dress according to the level to which you aspire.

Like much of the information available on dress, the issue of which colors are "in" and which are not is subject to the vagaries of fashion. However, several colors have weathered well over the years, chiefly natural ones like navy, medium gray, camel, black, and some browns. Similarly, some colors are regularly condemned including many pastels, bright colors, green, purple, and orange. With color choice, when a manager is genuinely interested in making the right impression, the issue is not so much in choosing what the manager likes as in what is perceived by others as creating an authoritative or responsible image. At the same time, a person's achieved position has an impact on the perceptions. Thus, for women, the higher the rank, the more option she has for color variety. At the same time, even at that rank, "screaming" colors should be avoided.[27]

Paralanguage

The final source of nonverbal signals this chapter will focus on is paralanguage, or vocalics. The spoken word contains more than linguistic cues. Paralanguage concerns itself with the nonverbal aspects of vocal delivery including the pitch, tone, onset, and duration of messages. These cues are among the least obvious to most listeners with the likely exception of tone, yet can be as important, or even more important than the actual words used.[28] All the same, as we listen to others, the pitch of their voice, the onset of the message—that is, the time that it takes between the person's taking the turn and the message's beginning—and the length of the message send subtle messages.

Here is an example. If we are querying someone about a serious issue and the person's responses come almost too quickly, we might suspect he is not serious or has rehearsed the responses. Similarly, when someone takes far longer to answer a question than called for, we begin to wonder if all that is being said is true. And, as the discussion later in this chapter on nonverbal leakage of deception shows, we even monitor pitch and can read meaning into changes of it.

The importance of paralinguistic cues to managers is obvious in sending as well as receiving. It is important to monitor the signals being sent, particularly for tone, to ensure that the intended communication strategy is not being undermined by subtle nonverbal cues.

This chapter closes with two practical applications of the material discussed earlier. First, based on the research available, we will examine some recommendations for effective nonverbal signals for women. The next section details nonverbal communication and the leakage of deception.

Women in Business and Nonverbal Signals

With increased awareness of gender bias, experts have come to study women and the impact their nonverbal signals have in a male-dominated business world. Of course, it is possible to fairly argue the other side of the issue; that is, why should women have to adapt? In fact, a trend is beginning to emerge that recognizes the unique skills enculturated in women. This trend is seen as a reaction to the 1970s practice of encouraging women entering management positions to adopt the language, methods, and dress of the men in charge.[29] However, based on the assumption that old perceptions about nonverbal signals are still valid in the business world, the focus of this section is on achieving an image that will help in the present, admittedly flawed world. Obviously, the other side of the issue is to raise the consciousness of others about these differences.

Quasi-Courtship Behavior

In terms of nonverbal communication, both sexes rate women higher than men in both encoding and decoding abilities.[30] Yet it may be said that women often send the "wrong" signals in business situations and men often misinterpret the signals that are sent. In other words, if a female manager needs to send a nonverbal, authoritative message to subordinates, much of her acculturation might be working against her, at least in the traditional male-dominated business environment.[31] This is especially the case with the nonverbal phenomenon of "quasi-courtship behavior."

Courtship behavior invites a romantic relationship and has a role in the wider culture. Quasi-courtship behavior carries those roles into the business context. There it is more subtle, but it emphasizes sex role differences between men and women and creates confusion over expectations. Experts perceive its impact on women as a negative one, which holds back women in business. Not only do the cues sent in quasi-courtship behavior indicate a person's gender, but some also see them to be making a statement about her power and status relative to men, which could lead to miscommunication.[32]

Quasi-Courtship Cues

Quasi-courtship cues are sent in a variety of ways. One example was given earlier in this chapter under proxemics when noted that women tend to tolerate a violation of their personal space more than men. Not only do these cues indicate gender differences, but they may also serve subtly to undermine a person's power and status within the organization. This perceived ease of accessibility may send a message that says "don't take me seriously."

Men tend to take up more physical space than women, and not just because of generally larger size. To verify this, watch a situation with men and women sitting together. The men will tend to sprawl out more with legs spread wide, while the women will usually sit with arms and legs closer to their bodies, even when wearing informal clothes. While the "shrinking" behavior may be in part related to the need for modesty, these signals by women can be seen as signals of perceived weaker status or power and may even hurt their standing in the organization.[33] Those with higher position power will typically give greater credibility to body size in evaluating others.

Earlier, we also examined haptics, touching behavior. Gender differences exist here as well that could be interpreted as quasi-courtship cues. The gentle handshake traditionally given when a man was presented to a woman in social settings has given way to a firm but comfortable handshake in business situations.[34] Studies have shown that during conversations, men tend to touch women as much as twice as often as women will touch men. Generally, the initiator of impersonal touching, such as a pat on the back, possesses greater power and status than the recipient. This touching behavior could not only pose a threat to power and status, but could also endanger the business nature of a relationship.[35] Recall how haptics moves through various levels of increasing intimacy. Intentionally or unintentionally, gender tolerance difference may be misinterpreted by the unwary aggressive individual initiating contact.

Theorists argue that another source of quasi-courtship cues is smiling. In conversations, women tend to smile more than men, and women also laugh and giggle more. Theorists report that men might interpret this behavior in several ways, including that it is more appropriate to a social rather than a business setting or that it is the sign of a less-effective manager.[36] Others see excessive smiling as having the potential of being read as a sign of lower status and power. Limiting smiles is recommended for women to help create an image of seriousness and help reinforce the business nature of the relationship.[37] Ironically, some male and female managerial associates will resent a woman who doesn't smile frequently and label her as hard-nosed and humorless. How can a woman win! Still, the misperceptions arising from too much smiling seem to pose the greater potential problems.[38]

Even in eye contact, quasi-courtship cues have been detected. Cohen notes that women tend to keep eye contact longer than men, but men perceive this as a sign of affection. She recommends that women monitor the amount of eye contact in order to stress that the conversation is strictly business. At the same time, one should not be inaccessible to the other's eyes—doing so sends a signal of hostility.[39] Generally, those listening to another should maintain contact, while the speaker looks away now and again.[40]

Nonverbal Leakage of Deception

In many situations, managers must evaluate other employees to determine if the data they work with are accurate. While the facts and figures set out in a hard-copy report can usually be tested objectively, information derived from interpersonal interactions like disciplinary and pre-employment screening interviews frequently offers little opportunity for immediate objective verification. Fortunately, some nonverbal signals can help managers assess the veracity of verbal statements. While the nonverbal signals usually complement verbal ones and serve as needed reinforcement to reduce the uncertainty in communication, they may also unintentionally contradict the verbal ones they accompany.

When contradictory nonverbal signals betray deception, they are called *leakage*. During deception, certain types of nonverbal signals often escape from the deceiver despite attempts at control. Speakers' subconscious apparently betrays them through this nonverbal leakage. People also often unconsciously read and interpret these signals. The individual who reports, "I've got a funny feeling after talking to that guy" may be reacting to nonverbal leakage perceived unconsciously. With a little training and caution, managers can learn to spot nonverbal leakage of deception.

Several patterns of nonverbal behavior crop up during deception.[41] Since some sources of nonverbal signals can be controlled in deceptive situations better than others—for example, looking another in the eye while deceiving—we will focus on leakage signals that are difficult to control consciously. These include movement, dress, proxemics, and paralanguage.

Remember that nonverbal behavior usually *suggests* meaning rather than having a one-to-one correlation with a specific word or concept. The meaning of nonverbal signs may vary much, and a gesture might be motivated by something besides what is suggested here. In applying the concepts discussed here, consider the whole context of the communication situation to ensure accurate interpretation. Care can repay the effort expended.

To detect possible nonverbal leakage of deception, it is important to be in the right place. Often, interviewees are seated in such a way that significant clues can go undetected. The face, always likely to be visible, can be a poor source of deception clues (although hand-to-face contacts are valuable clues). Interview seating arrangements often allow few nonverbals other than facial to be seen since the interviewee is often seated behind some kind of barrier like a table or counter. These barriers may be called signal blunders.[42] Similarly, when you are seated at a desk you may also provide a barrier since the desk may block your view of the interviewee. The solution is simple. When necessary, seat the other person in the open such as in an open chair facing you. Nonverbal leakage from the hands, trunk, legs, or feet then will be more evident.[43]

Baseline

Since leakage consists of behaviors that differ from normal nonverbal inter-actions, you also need to know what behavior is normal for that individual. Researchers have found that when observers see an individual giving honest answers before the person is seen lying, the observers' ability to detect dis-honesty increases significantly over situations with no behavioral baseline.

The behavioral baseline needs to be established for each individual in each different situation. A situation may be naturally tense and responsible for fidgeting; however, it may suggest deception under less tense circum-stances. In a tense situation, it may represent simple nerves. Even an innocent person might have shaking hands and a quaking voice under investigation. Employment interviews fall into this category as would a visit from a tax auditor.

The individual's baseline is also invaluable because one person might behave differently from others in identical circumstances. A baseline allows one to gauge if nervous behavior reflects the overall situation or is a reaction to the question being asked. Even experienced deceivers may betray them-selves through leakage that will contrast earlier, less stressful responses.

In the job interview, a baseline is relatively easy. During the small talk making up preliminary dialogue, ask questions about nonthreatening facts drawn from the résumé before moving into the unknown. Watch for non-verbal cues. An investigatory interrogation could use the same pattern. Small talk serves its traditional primary purpose of putting the other at ease and a secondary one of providing a behavioral baseline.

Kinesics

Manual gestures and trunk movements, part of the broad category of kinesics, are probably the most valuable source of nonverbal leakage of deception. Perhaps the most common deception-related gestures are the hand-to-face movements, and the most common of these is the mouth cover. The hand covers the mouth, and the person talks through the fingers as if hiding or trying to keep the words from escaping. More subtle is the single finger to the mouth, or, with men, the moustache stroke. A variant of the mouth cover may be called "Pinocchio syndrome." When he lied, the wooden puppet's nose would grow; in many cases, a deceiver's nose itches! Before answering a question, an interviewee may slightly rub or scratch the nose with a finger, and thus suggest deception or annoyance at the question, annoyance that must be masked.[44] Another hand-to-face gesture suggesting deception comes as no surprise—nail biting. Lip biting may also be a red flag that a person is under stress.[45]

Conversational gestures vary as well. Generally, when one is comfortable with honest responses, gestures are open, outward ones. During deception, people both limit their gestures and keep them closer to the body. And, while smiling decreases and the frequency of gestures used to illustrate conversational points slows down in deception, the gestures suggesting deception increase. One of these is the hand shrug emblem. Researchers have found that deceptive speakers will shrug their hands—turning the palms up from palms down position—twice as frequently as in nondeceptive messages. This signal suggests a subconscious pleading for the listener to believe what is being said.

Some authorities also believe that an increase in leg and foot movements may indicate deception.[46] Foot tapping, leg rocking while the legs are crossed, and frequent shifts in leg posture are examples of this kind of activity. A rhythmic "walking" motion with one crossed leg has long been recognized as an intention gesture suggesting the person would like to walk away so he uses this gesture to compensate. But keep in mind the need to compare behavior with the baseline.

As the remainder of this chapter indicates, signals of deception are not confined just to the body. They can involve dress, proxemics, and paralanguage.

Dress

With clothing, nonverbal leakage mainly shows up in the manipulation of dress, which may suggest a respondent feels threatened with a given question. A male interviewee may suddenly close and button up his coat or begin to tug nervously at his pants leg. This may betray a fear of having some deception uncovered. This behavior is a literal nonverbal cover-up for the ongoing verbal one. Other signals for men would include collar straightening, collar tugging, and tie smoothing. A woman wearing a blouse with an open top might close it or toy with the top button. If she is wearing a dress, she might tug at the hem as she shifts her posture.

Interviewees may also start picking at lint or spots on clothes or begin to brush the clothes. Some see these tidying actions as betraying a subconscious desire to be symbolically purged of the guilt brought on by deception. Others suspect it to be an attempt to direct attention away from the interviewee's comments. Still others see this as a displacement gesture for getting rid of an annoying questioner.

Proxemics

Proxemics, relating to the distance that one keeps from others as well as one's relation to the surrounding environment, may be a rich source of leakage cues. Someone in a foreign environment, the interviewer's office, for example, can usually do little to alter the environment. One option, though, is for the people to move their chair. An interviewee might shift the chair's position or might suddenly lean back on the chair's back legs. Moving away from the interviewer may show a lack of cooperativeness or be a feeble attempt to put distance between interviewee and interviewer by altering the environment. Often, when a person physically backs up, the other person comes closer. In informal conversations occurring while standing, the interviewee may lean back or step back during a deceptive response even while "blocking" by folding the arms across the chest.

An interviewee who has been relaxed may shift under pressure. For example, deception may leak out when the person suddenly crosses the arms and legs and leans back. The vulnerable forward posture is less comfortable when facing the fear of discovery. Conversely, an interviewee might "open up" during a response, suggesting openness and honesty in the verbal response. An interviewee may also try to erect "signal blunders" to hide behind. These may be such subtle activities as placing a purse or briefcase in the lap as a barrier.

Paralanguage

Voice is another rich source of cues. As previously mentioned, nonverbal characteristics of voice are called vocalics, or paralanguage. Most relevant in detecting deception are the voice's pitch, tone, and volume, as well as the response's onset and duration. Authorities have long known that deceptive answers have a slower onset that honest ones. Faced with a threatening question, a respondent may hesitate or even pause before a deceptive response. Contrasted with quick answers to other questions, this behavior might suggest deception. At the same time, however, one may not be as quick to respond to a question because it is thought-provoking. Rather than showing deception, it might be showing reflection. Here, other cues should be sought to judge the response.

In addition to frequently having a slightly slower onset, deceptive answers are likely to be longer and less specific than honest ones. The deceiver may be attempting to fill in the gap with needless material. Some see length as an attempt to make a deceptive answer more elaborate and thus more convincing than the deceiver knows it is. The answer's length may also reflect the pauses and hesitations needed as the interviewee stumbles through the answer.

The final source of paralinguistic leakage is pitch. When children are accused of wrongdoing, one can often hear the pitch rise as they deny the truth: "I didn't do that." Researchers have found that vocal pitch rises measurably in deceptive responses. While observers frequently could not say why they labeled such a response as deceptive, they knew it was, and research instruments could show the difference.[47] In many interpersonal, managerial interactions, nonverbal elements are the source of most of the message. While not everything communicated nonverbally is done so consciously or intentionally, the unintentional signals may be as valid as the intentional ones and potentially more useful. Keep in mind, though, the suggestions about establishing a behavioral baseline for each person in specific situations. In addition, if deception is suspected, use that as an impetus for further investigation or at least caution, not as the final word.

Summary

Everything but the words themselves may be considered the domain of nonverbal communication. Every managerial interaction has nonverbal elements that add to or qualify the interaction. It is difficult to put precise meanings to nonverbal signals and they vary from culture to culture; however, when nonverbal signals contradict verbal ones, the nonverbal signals are usually the ones to trust.

Nonverbal cues have six functions: complementing, accenting, contradicting, repeating, regulating, and substituting. In addition, nonverbal cues add redundancy to the verbal message and increase the probability that the verbal message will be understood as intended by the sender.

Kinesics is the study of movement, which includes gestures and posture. Gestures may include emblems, illustrators, affect displays, regulators, and adapters. Proxemics refers to the space around us and how we and others relate to it. Four proxemic zones are presented and discussed in this chapter, but care must be taken in interpreting them because zones may differ between genders and among cultures. It is important that managers observe and study the use of proxemic zones. Inappropriate use of zones may make a manager appear rude, while an accurate analysis indicates much about the power structure in an organization.

Haptics is concerned with touching behavior. Haptics indicates much about the relationship between two people. When considering dress, managers should pay close attention to what those higher up in the organization wear. A general adage is, "If you look the part, you get the part." Paralanguage is the final source of nonverbal signals discussed in the chapter. Paralanguage concerns itself with vocal delivery including the pitch, tone, onset, and duration of messages.

Special attention is given to the nonverbal communication of women in business. In particular, quasi-courtship behavior is discussed. Such behavior is particularly important in the environment of the 1990s as men and women interpret cues differently while the percentage of women in the male dominated workforce is continually increasing.

The first step to detecting nonverbal leakage is to establish a baseline. Once this has been accomplished, kinesics, dress, proxemics, and paralanguage can each be used to evaluate the potential for deception in an interaction. But in all managerial communication situations, it is important to remember that no dictionary exists for the meaning of nonverbal cues.

Endnotes

1. Carol Lehman and Mark Lehman, "Effective Nonverbal Communication Techniques: Essential Element in the Promotional Strategies of Professional Service Firms," *Journal of Professional Services Marketing* 5, no. 1 (1989), p. 17.
2. Albert Mehrabian, "Communicating Without Words," *Psychology Today*, September 1968, pp. 53–55.
3. Scott T. Fleishmann, *Employment Relations Today*, Summer 1991, pp. 161–62.
4. Roswitha Rothlach, "Anglo-German Misunderstandings in Language and Behavior," *Industrial and Commercial Training* 23, no. 3 (March 1991), pp. 15–16.
5. Om P. Kharbanda and Ernest A. Stallworthy, "Verbal and Non-verbal Communication," *Journal of Managerial Psychology* 6, no. 2 (April 1991), p. 49.
6. Larry H. Hynson, Jr., "Doing Business with South Korea—Park II: Business Practices and Culture," *East Asian Executive Reports* 13 (September 15, 1991), p. 18.
7. Sandra G. Garside and Brian H. Kleiner, "Effective One-to-One Communication Skills," *Industrial and Commerical Training* 23, no. 7 (July 1991), p. 27.
8. R. P. Harrison, *Beyond Words: An Introduction to Nonverbal Communication* (Englewood Cliffs, N.J.: Prentice Hall, 1974), p. 25.
9. S. Burbinster, "Body Politics," *Associate & Management*, April 1987, pp. 55–57.
10. John L. Waltman, "Communication Redundancy and Business Communication," *Journal of Business Communication* 21, no. 4 (Fall 1984).
11. P. Ekman and W. Friesen, "The Repertoire of Nonverbal Behavior," *Semiotica* 1 (1969), pp. 49–98.
12. Edward T. Hall, *The Hidden Dimension* (New York: Doubleday, 1966).
13. Loretta A. Malandro and Larry Barker, *Nonverbal Communication* (Reading, Mass.: Addison-Wesley Publishing Co., 1983), pp. 226–30.
14. Phillip L. Hunsaker, "Communicating Better: There's No Proxy for Proxemics," in *Readings in Business Communication*, ed. Richard C. Huseman (Hinsdale, Ill.: Dryden Press, 1981), p. 52.
15. Lynn Cohen, "Nonverbal (Mis) communication Between Managerial Men and Women," *Business Horizons*, January–February 1983, p. 15.
16. Malandro and Barker, *Nonverbal Communication*, p. 231.
17. R. Ardrey, *The Territorial Imperative* (New York: Dell Publishing Co., 1966), p. 37.
18. A. G. Athos, "Time, Space, and Things," in *Behavior in Organizations: A Multidimensional View*, ed. A. G. Athos and R. E. Coffey (Englewood Cliffs, N.J.: Prentice Hall, 1975), pp. 69–81.
19. R. Heslin, "Steps toward a Taxonomy of Touching," paper presented to the Midwestern Psychological Association, Chicago, May 1974. Cited in M. L. Knapp, *Essentials of Nonverbal Behavior* (New York: Holt, Rinehart and Winston, 1980).
20. Deborah Borisoff and David A. Victor, *Conflict Management: A Communication Skills Approach* (Englewood Cliffs, N.J.: Prentice-Hall, 1989), p. 74.

21. N. M. Henley, *Body Politics: Power, Sex and Non-verbal Communication* (Englewood Cliffs, N.J.: Prentice-Hall, 1977).

22. Lynn Pearl, "Opening the Door to Rapport," *Agri Marketing* 30, no. 2 (April 1992), p. 97.

23. Betty L. Harragan, *Games Mother Never Taught You: Corporate Gamesmanship for Women* (New York: Warner Books, 1987), p. 339.

24. Ibid., p. 436.

25. Srully Blotnick, "Loosen that Tie," *Forbes,* December 29, 1991, p. 124.

26. John T. Molloy, *The Women's Dress for Success Book* (New York: Warner Books, 1989), pp. 68–69.

27. Irene Pave, "Dressing for Success Isn't What It Used to Be," *Business Week,* (October 27, 1986), pp. 142–43.

28. Patricia Buhler, "Managing in the 90s: Are You Really Saying What You Mean?" *Supervision* 52, no. 9 (September 1991), p. 19.

29. Sherry S. Cohen, "Beyond Macho: The Power of Womanly Management," *Working Woman,* February 1989, p. 77.

30. Gerald H. Graham, Jeanne Unruh, and Paul Jennings, "The Impact of Nonverbal Communication in Organizations: A Survey of Perceptions," *Journal of Business Communication* 28, no. 1 (Winter 1991), p. 59.

31. Christine M. Baytosh and Brian H. Kleiner, *Equal Opportunities International* 8, no. 4 (April 1989), pp. 18–19.

32. "Nonverbal Communication: A Threat to Women Managers?" *Management Review,* May 1983, p. 56.

33. Cohen, "Nonverbal (Mis) communication," pp. 16–17.

34. Nancy K. Austin, "The Subtle Signals of Success," *Working Woman,* April 1991, p. 106.

35. Mary Williams, "Something as Simple as a Smile Could Make or Break a Female Manager," *The Wall Street Journal,* February 16, 1984, p. 37.

36. Ibid., p. 30.

37. William Griend, "Reading Between the Lines," *Association Management,* June 1984, p. 99.

38. Jacqueline Shannon, "Don't Smile When You Say That," *Executive Female,* March–April 1988, p. 18.

39. Cohen, "Nonverbal (Mis) communication," p. 17.

40. Robin Chandler, "Moving Towards Understanding," *Accountancy (UK)* 105, no. 2 (April 1990), p. 78.

41. Paul Ekman and Wallace V. Friesen, "Detecting Deception from the Body and Face," *Journal of Personality and Social Psychology* 29, no. 2 (1974), p. 295.

42. Desmond Morris, *Manwatching: A Field Guide to Human Behavior* (New York: H. N. Abrams, 1977), p. 106.

43. John L. Waltman, "Nonverbal Interrogation: Some Applications," *Journal of Police Science and Administration* 11, no. 2 (June 1983), p. 167.

44. Morris, *Manwatching,* p. 110.

45. John W. Kennish, "Finding the Truth," *Internal Auditor* 46, no. 12 (December 1989), pp. 29–30.

46. Charles J. McClintock and Raymond G. Hunt, "Nonverbal Indicators of Affect and Deception in Interview Situations," *Journal of Applied Psychology* 5, no. 3 (1975), p. 420.

47. Paul Ekman, Wallace Friesen, and Klaus R. Scherer, "Body Movement and Voice Pitch in Deception Interaction," *Semiotica* 16, no. 11 (1976), p. 26.

Additional Readings

Anderson, P. A. and Linda Bowman. "Positions of Power: Nonverbal Influence in Organizational Communication." in *Readings in Organizational Communication.* Kevin L. Hutchinson, ed. Dubuque, Iowa: Wm C. Brown Publishing, 1992, pp. 342–61.

Beffart, Mark. "The Visible Business Tool." *Working Woman*, November 1984, pp. 194–200.

Burgoon, J. K., T. Burk, and M. Pfau. "Nonverbal Behaviors, Persuasion and Credibility." *Human Communication Research* 17, no. 1 (Fall 1990), pp. 140–69.

Eakins, Barbara Westbrook, and R. Gene Eakins. *Sex Differences in Human Communication.* Boston: Houghton Mifflin Co., 1978.

Kelly, Joe. "Surviving and Thriving in Top Management Meetings." *Personnel* 64 (June 1987), pp. 24–34.

McCaskey, Michael. "The Hidden Messages Managers Send." *Harvard Business Review*, November–December 1979, pp. 135–48.

Rasbery, R. W. "A Collection of Nonverbal Communication Research: An Annotated Bibliography." *Journal of Business Communication* 16, no. 4 (Summary 1979), pp. 21–30.

Thompson, P. A., and B. H. Kleiner. "How to Read Nonverbal Communication." *ABC Bulletin*, September 1992, pp. 81–83.

Walbach, J. *Looks That Work.* New York: Penguin, 1988.

Discussion Questions

1. What sources of nonverbal communication other than those in the text can you suggest?

2. Provide at least one example (other than those in the text) for nonverbal signals showing complementing, accenting, and contradicting.

3. Identify and briefly define the four personal space zones in which people communicate.

4. During the next few days, observe how people around you use the personal space communication zones detailed in the text. If these zones are not utilized according to what is predicted in the text, what other factors might explain the discrepancies?

5. Explain how nonverbal communication is a part of the feedback system in communication interactions.

6. Provide at least one example (other than those in the text) for the kinesic categories of affect displays, adapters, and emblems.

7. Why are emblems different from the typical kinesic communication cue?

8. Evaluate the office or work area of an acquaintance using some of the proxemic clues detailed in the text. Review your findings with your acquaintance and see if they concur with you.

9. Evaluate an artificially crowded situation (for example, a classroom, a waiting room, or public transportation). What have people done to mark their territory? How effective has that been?

10. Cite examples of social (or polite) haptics that a businessperson is likely to encounter during a given day. If possible, determine who initiates the touching.

11. Explain the quotation "If you look the part, you get the part" as it relates to job interviews and promotions. Cite examples, if possible.

12. Over the next few days, observe and compare the differences, if any, between the sitting behaviors of men and women in public situations (for example, in offices, classrooms, or public transportation).

13. During the next few days, watch for signs of nonverbal leakage of deception on television. Two excellent places to watch for these are the news as well as interview shows. If possible, try to determine why the person would want to deceive the other.

14. Subtly test the dynamics of the personal space zones during the next few days and record the reactions of the other parties. You might want to use your roommate, a close friend, or strangers in line at a public place.

15. If possible, observe the nonverbal signals of two individuals at opposite ends of the same organization as they interact with each other and with their closest peers. As you do so, what differences do you note in terms of haptics, smiling, proxemics, and paralanguage?

CASE 10–1
FACING A SERIES OF INTERVIEWS

Hanna Jenson recently applied for a position that involves supervising the work activities of a large comprehensive insurance company. She has just received a letter notifying her to report for an interview for this position in four days. The letter indicates Jenson will be required to attend a series of interviews as follows:

9:00 A.M.	Rodney Custer, personnel manager
10:00 A.M.	Charles Rhodes, department chief
11:00 A.M.	Robert Kent, medical claims supervisor

If Jenson gets the job, she will receive a substantial raise in salary as well as her first opportunity to gain supervisory experience. Therefore, she wants the job very badly and is concerned about how to prepare for each of the interviews.

Although she has never worked in this particular department, Jenson has worked for the company several years. She knows Custer and Rhodes on a casual basis, but she has never met Kent. Custer is 38 years old, meticulous in dress, and obviously very proud of the managerial accomplishments he has made since he became personnel manager two years ago. Jenson's friends in the department believe Custer is sexist and tends to hire men in supervisory positions if possible.

Rhodes is an elderly, rotund gentleman who will be eligible for retirement in two years. He is somewhat unkempt in appearance, but his knowledge of policy and regulations has earned him the respect of managers throughout the company.

Jenson is especially concerned about the interview with Kent. If she gets the job, she will be working directly under Kent, yet she knows nothing about him.

Questions

1. What positive and negative suggestions would you give Jenson about her choice of dress for this interview?
2. What effective nonverbal signals would you suggest Jenson send during the interview given the profiles of the two individuals Jenson is to meet?
3. How could Jenson's strategy differ in each interview situation?

CASE 10–2
WHAT IS GOING ON HERE?

Art is the 45-year-old director of marketing research for a Fortune 500 consumer products company. He joined the firm 19 years ago after he received his Ph.D. in marketing. Because of his technical expertise, management skills , and outgoing personality, he was made director of this 50-person group four years ago. Six people report directly to him, but the management style is informal, so he frequently interacts with everyone in the department.

Two years ago, Art extensively recruited Leona who had just completed her Ph.D. in applied statistics. Art had a difficult time persuading her to join the company because she had many attractive offers. Although she was only 34 years old, she had outstanding experience in marketing research and a unique educational background. Leona came in and quickly made a number of significant contributions to the department. As manager of statistical analysis, she reports directly to Art but has nobody reporting to her. She is the only manager in the department who reports to Art but has nobody reporting to her. Soon after joining the company, Leona and her husband divorced. Many employees in the department believe her personal problems are why she has not been more sociable with other employees.

Leona and Art have always gotten along well and often have lunch together to discuss various projects. They seem to have much in common as they both understand the advanced statistics used in the research. Recently, the conversations have turned more personal as Art went through a divorce and seems to be seeking more social support. In particular, he seems to miss his two teenage daughters and needs someone to talk to about it.

But Leona sees a problem developing, and she recently talked to a human resource manager about it. She explained that she has a lot of respect for Art and enjoys visiting with him. But she notices a definite change in his behavior around her. The eye contact is more prolonged and the personal physical space between them is reduced. Leona feels uneasy about it and has tried subtly to change the trend. However, this only intensified what Leona saw as "pressure" to spend more time with Art. Today, Art asked Leona to have dinner with him so they could talk over a project. It seems they haven't had time to cover the project during working hours.

Discuss this case in terms of quasi-courtship behavior and other topics presented in this chapter. What are the implications of this situation?

IV INTERPERSONAL AND GROUP APPLICATIONS

This section includes two chapters on interviewing. Although the communication contingencies and barriers presented in Part I are applicable to interviews, Chapter 11 presents six unique barriers to successful interviews that are followed by eight contingency questions that will help managers conduct effective interviews. This chapter examines the manager as interviewee and as interviewer.

Chapter 11 presents a general overview of the interview process, and the next chapter examines three specific types of interviews common to managers: employment interviews, performance reviews, and constructive discipline and counseling interviews. Chapter 12 first analyzes the advantages and disadvantages of groups and then reviews six strategic decisions that are necessary for effective meetings. As is true with the other specific types of communication presented in the text, when considering meeting management, it is helpful to refer back to the model presented in Chapter 3.

The other two topics presented in this section are conflict management and negotiation. Although these topics are highly related, each is so important to the managerial process that a separate chapter is dedicated to each. Both chapters present a model to help understand the process followed by a discussion of that model as it relates to the concepts presented in Chapter 3. This is followed by a description of the various managerial strategies.

11   INTERVIEWING FOR EFFECTIVE DECISIONS

As you glance at your appointment calendar, you see that you will have another busy day. First, you will meet with Jim, the industrial engineering manager, to investigate possibilities for sharing several projects between your departments. After that you are meeting Mary, an engineer in your department, for her performance review. In the afternoon, you are interviewing an applicant for an administrative assistant position, and then you are conducting an exit interview with your assistant, who is leaving for another job. Later in the afternoon, your manager wants to meet with you to discuss annual budget requests.

This means you are involved in five interviews in one day. Consequently, you decide it would be a good idea to review the principles of interviewing by writing down several important interview skills.

A manager faces many different kinds of interview situations: performance appraisal, employment, persuasive, exit, problem solving, and possibly informational interviews on radio or television. No matter what the situation, the process is an intensive communication transaction designed to obtain or share certain predetermined kinds of information. But successful managers must learn to avoid the special communication barriers that accompany the process. Accordingly, this chapter examines interviews from the perspective of both the interviewer and interviewee. The discussion examines the special barriers present and then explores eight questions relevant to the interview process. But first we discuss the difference between an interview and a conversation.

When Is a Conversation an Interview?

Many definitions of *interview* exist, but most definitions agree on three basic points:

1. The interview is a form of conversation. Like good conversations, good interviews are interactive. That is, all participants in the interview will get and give information, and all will think they have benefited in some respect from the exchange.
2. Unlike casual conversations, interviews have a purpose other than, or in addition to, affording the participants enjoyment. In truly productive interviews, interviewers and interviewees share a sense of purpose.
3. Interviews have time limits. The participants should bring their conversations to a close at or before a time that is set in advance or agreed on near the start of the interview.[1]

Putting these three points together, we define an interview as any conversation that has a time limit and an identifiable purpose other than enjoyment. According to this definition, the term *interview* includes many everyday business interactions. For example, "interview" can apply to a luncheon with employees during which a manager discusses ways of dealing with a persistent company problem. Or it can describe a meeting between a manager and an assistant to decide how to better use their time. Each of these may be considered problem-solving interviews.

We have chosen this broad definition in hopes of encouraging managers to treat more conversations and meetings as interviews and to focus attention on three important aspects of all successful interviews—interaction, purpose, and time limitation. If managers consider more of their dealings with others as interviews and make each interview conform to the definition given above, they will find themselves developing several useful habits.

The first useful habit is that they will begin encouraging more exchange of information and become less inclined to view communication as one way. The above definition stresses the conversational or interactive nature of the interview. Greater efficiency is a second benefit of treating more conversations as interviews. An interview is a purposeful conversation, so viewing a conversation as an interview will help you identify and achieve some purpose. You will spend less time conducting seemingly endless and aimless discussions and more time gathering useful information. The third useful outcome of looking at more conversations as interviews is that limiting the time devoted to a given conversation helps participants get to important issues quickly.

With this definition, managers face many different interview situations during any normal day. But regardless of the situations, there is a unique set of barriers to effective interviews.

Barriers to Effective Interviews

All the communication dynamics discussed earlier in Chapters 2 and 3 are present in the interview, but six barriers are particularly relevant: (1) differing intentions of the people involved, (2) bias, (3) the fact–inference fallacy, (4) nonverbal communication, (5) effects of first impressions, and (6) organizational status.

Barrier 1: Differing Intentions

Managers cannot always assume all participants agree on the information that should be exchanged in an interview. In fact, rarely do both the interviewer and interviewee agree. One obvious instance is the employment interview. While the interviewer wants to know all the strengths and weaknesses of the applicant, the applicant (interviewee) wants to reveal only his strengths to the interviewer.

Differences in intention operate at one of three levels. First, both parties consciously may intend to have a clear and accurate exchange of information. However, unconsciously, they may not reveal certain items. This type may be particularly relevant in a performance appraisal interview. At the second level, one of the parties does not intend to disclose certain relevant information. This often occurs in exit interviews when the employee does not reveal the real reason for leaving. At the third level, both parties do not intend to disclose certain relevant information. This may happen when an employee interviewed for a promotion discusses the potential salary. The employee would probably not reveal the lowest acceptable salary, and the interviewer does not indicate the highest possible salary. Figure 11–1 depicts these three levels of intentions.

Skillful questioning, which is reviewed later in this chapter, helps to overcome this barrier. Listening to the other person and understanding her

FIGURE 11–1 Differing Intention

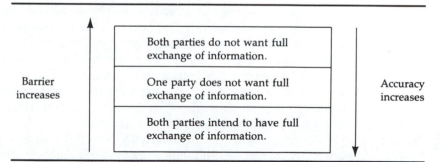

point of view also helps reduce this barrier. However, the key is to remember that the other person's goal may not always be the same as the manager's in the interview process.

Barrier 2: Bias

Bias is a barrier because it slants people's perceptions so they tend to see and hear only what they want to see and hear.[2] Biased people make a special effort to see what they consider to be the truth even if in reality it is not the truth. For example, to the fan at a ball game, the referee generally seems to favor the opposing team, but this is really only spectator bias. Such bias may be part of the fun in a ball game; but in an interview, it can prevent the interviewer from obtaining factual information.

The most prevalent type of bias is the so-called halo effect, which managers fall prey to when they allow the evaluation of one characteristic to be influenced by another characteristic or by a general impression.[3] One aspect of the job may affect the manager's impression of the employee in other areas. If an employee has a tendency to be late, for instance, the manager could let this shortcoming influence his impression of the employee on other unrelated characteristics such as technical skills. The bias creates problems in performance evaluation interviews since the reviewer cannot see beyond the effects of the one main characteristic.[4] Another type of bias is the recency effect. This occurs when the latest information disproportionately affects all the earlier information. Still other types of bias are leniency or harshness. In these instances, interviewers see everything as either positive or negative—they do not differentiate.[5]

Questions can also subtly bias an interview. For instance, one manager asked this loaded question: "Should the consumer group continue its generous support of the marketing research department when the research has proven to be of little value?" This question is obviously biased and would be difficult to answer in the affirmative. But drop the last part of the question so it now reads, "Should the consumer group continue its generous support of the marketing research group?" Bias now is much more subtle, but it is still present with the word *generous* used to describe the amount of support. Appropriate ways to phrase questions will be discussed later in this chapter.

New managers frequently find bias unwittingly introduced into their perceptions by co-workers who share their opinions of other workers. For instance, the following is the type of statement frequently heard: "You'll get nothing but trouble from Patrick, but you'll find Semkins a jewel to work with." Smart managers wait to form their own impressions of these subordinates. Otherwise, co-workers' irrelevant past experiences may shape the new managers' impressions of their colleagues.

Perhaps the best way to deal with personal bias is for a person to be aware of her own biases and then work to eliminate their effect on perception. Research has found that people who try hard can control their bias.[6] Thus, before entering the interview, the manager should try to review any bias that may interfere with her main objective of gathering information and then make a special effort to remain objective despite them.

Barrier 3: Confusing Facts with Inferences

Managers actually deal with very few facts in an interview. Rather, they must make inferences based on the words and actions of the interviewee. Sometimes, managers can be "almost certain" about their conclusions from an interview, but other times they are not too sure.[7] When they are not sure, however, problems can arise. Figure 11–2 reveals some problems caused by discrepancies among words, facts, and inferences in the interviewing process.

Managers need to be on the alert to determine when they are making plausible inferences and when they are jumping to unfounded conclusions. Many of the techniques discussed later in the chapter help to overcome this barrier. It is also helpful to use a simple form like that in Figure 11–3, which permits the manager to distinguish between "observations" in one column and "inferences" in the other. To a greater or lesser degree, all are subject to the fact–inference fallacy, but using this form will help achieve objectivity.

Barrier 4: Nonverbal Communication

A quizzical look, a frown, a smile, or a look of indifference are all important nonverbal messages, but those reading them from an interviewee must exercise caution before interpreting them. At the same time, during interviews,

FIGURE 11–2   **Facts and Inferences**

Words	*Facts*	*Possible Inference*
"I like selling office equipment."	The record shows that the person has been selling for two years but before that was unemployed for six months.	This is the only work the person is able to get.
(When asked to fully describe college activities) "I did well in college and was involved in some extracurricular activities."	The person tends to avoid discussion on these activities and changes subject when asked specifically about grades.	The person did not do well in academic work in college and had little involvement in extracurricular activities.
"I did not care for the atmosphere in that department" (by applicant for a job transfer)	The person received a poor performance review.	The applicant is a troublemaker.

FIGURE 11–3   Observations—Interpretations

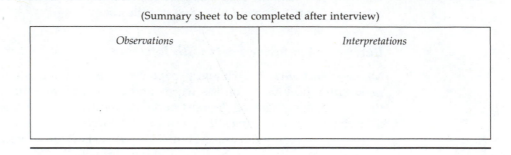

(Summary sheet to be completed after interview)

Observations	Interpretations

managers should be aware of the nonverbal signals they are sending. It may be that the interviewee is ill at ease as he reads what is being sent unintentionally by the interviewer.

Nonverbal information can be a problem in an interview because interviews are generally short and intensive.[8] The nonverbal communication is not the actual barrier; rather, the problem lies in interpreting the behavior. This is true for several reasons. First, it is easy to put on an act for a short time. If a job interview lasts only 20 or 30 minutes, an applicant can easily act alert and interested. In addition, the interviewee's manipulation of nonverbal messages can significantly affect the overall impact of the interview should the interviewer not be observant. If a person slouches in a chair for a few minutes during a 20-minute interview, this behavior is more noticeable than if he slouches for a few minutes during a four-hour meeting. In other words, because of the compact time span, obvious nonverbal signals have a great impact in an interview.

Accurately reading nonverbal signals in a compact time is complicated by the primacy effect—one piece of information overpowering all others. In a short period, one nonverbal cue can more easily overpower the others.[9] This is especially the case when one has no baseline of nonverbal signs for judging the candidate. The careful interviewer is also aware that she can use nonverbal signs from the interviewee to judge the honesty of responses. Since a person's nonverbal signals often tell an observer when the other is lying, these signals are worth exploring. Research has indicated that through training and practice, we can improve our ability to detect nonverbal deception.[10] This is further elaborated in the discussion of nonverbal leakage in Chapter 10.

Barrier 5: Effects of First Impressions

While first impressions can be accurate (and thus eliminate this as a barrier), such is not always the case.[11] A careless interviewer may form a quick first impression that colors what he sees during the rest of the interview. If the interview is short, this strong first impression may affect his overall impression since he does not have the time to find data to the contrary.

This barrier may also be referred to as "hypothesis testing," meaning the interviewer establishes a hypothesis early and then seeks information that supports it. The fear is that any information that doesn't support the hypothesis will be ignored.[12]

Since this barrier is so pervasive, managers must act to limit its impact. Part of the solution is simple: be cautious about making value judgments until evidence other than that available from first impressions has been considered. Then, too, be aware that short interviews encourage the manager to make a decision prematurely.

Barrier 6: Organizational Status

Perhaps the most pervasive communication barrier results from hierarchical rank.[13] In any interview situation, the parties involved know who holds the balance of power.[14] While a higher ranking person may encourage candor, the lower level person may fear such openness. It is only human to worry about the reactions of people in powerful positions, so candor frequently suffers.

The manager needs to be aware of this barrier and prevent it from distorting the message that gets through. Several suggestions can prevent it. For one thing, managers should recognize that employees will almost always want to make the best impression when communicating with higher level managers. Thus, the manager can judge the information in that light. In addition, the effective manager should try to create an open, supportive communication climate. Employees should not always fear saying the wrong thing. More is said about supportive climates in the next chapter.

Questions that Lead to Effective Interviews

Thorough analysis and planning are required for effective interviews, but few concrete guidelines are available because so many contingencies exist. However, we believe the numerous contingencies can best be managed by addressing the following eight questions.

Question 1: What Is the Interview Objective?

First, consider the interview objective. Are you trying to obtain general information, gather specific data, or persuade someone to accept an idea? The interview objective dictates the interview format. However, the objective is not always clear, or the interview may have more than one objective. Consider the employment interview in which a person is simultaneously trying to gather general information about the nature of the applicant and specific information about her skills. All the while, the interviewer is trying to sell the applicant on the benefits of joining the company. Because several goals may apply at one time, it is important to investigate the purpose of the interview.

Question 2: Where Is the Best Place to Conduct the Interview?

Time and place have an impact on the success of an interview. Managers should select a time convenient to themselves but consider the interviewee as well. Managers should also allow adequate time so neither party in the interview feels rushed. This is not just a courtesy; it is good interview strategy because it will help put the interviewee at ease.

Privacy is also a primary concern. It assures confidentiality and minimizes interferences. Many managers find they can best eliminate distractions by conducting the interview in a place other than their work area or office. Remember, though, that a neutral setting reduces the status barrier present in many interviews. Does the situation call for minimizing that?

A different approach to time and place occurs in the situational interview.[15] An interviewer may arrange an unusual situation and question the participant immediately following to see how he responds. This interview may also be conducted after a naturally occurring event. For instance, an employee may conduct a stressful negotiation with a foreign customer. Immediately afterward, a manager may interview the employee to get the employee's reaction to this type of work and determine if he would be a good candidate for an overseas assignment.

Question 3: What Is the Best Way to Begin the Interview?

This question and the next are closely related. The opening statements lay the foundation for the questioning to follow. The opening of an interview generally serves two purposes: (1) it establishes the communication climate, and (2) it explains the purpose of the interview.

The interview climate is established as soon as the interviewer meets the interviewee. At that point, nonverbal communication plays a crucial role. While a manager should not need to be reminded to begin with a friendly smile and a firm handshake, this is not always the case. The manager may be so busy or concentrating so hard on what to say first that a simple greeting or smile is forgotten.

An interview need not always begin with an exchange of pleasantries. In a disciplinary or appraisal interview, unnecessary chatter may be out of place. The interviewee may see this initial bantering as a delaying tactic. Anxiety grows as the interviewee asks himself "Okay, when's the bomb going to be dropped?" The same anxiety may grip the employee called in to see a manager without knowing the reason. In such cases, it is probably best to get directly to the point. An interviewer can still establish a positive communication climate without beginning with pleasantries.

One of the best ways of establishing that climate is to open with the interviewer's purpose. One can choose from a number of orientation statements, called starters.

1. Mentioning an incentive or reward for taking part in the interview.
2. Requesting advice or assistance.
3. Summarizing the problem.
4. Explaining how the problem was discovered.
5. Referring, if known, to the interviewee's position on an issue.
6. Referring to the person who suggested the interview.
7. Referring to the organization one represents.
8. Requesting a specific time commitment for the interview.

In addition to stating the purpose of the interview, an interviewer can establish a positive climate in some situations by asking for the interviewee's understanding of the purpose. This encourages a participatory attitude and may stimulate the other person's involvement in the interview. Thus, the opening, which may take the least time of all the segments in the interview process, is a crucial part of the whole interaction. Handled correctly, the session can begin on a proper note with both participants clearly understanding its purpose.

Question 4: What Is the Best Questioning Strategy?

Exact questions and their precise sequence cannot always be planned for an interview. However, developing a questioning strategy before the interview helps a manager reach the interview's goal. One strategy is the *structured interview* in which the interviewer writes out preliminary questions to use during the interview. This may be effective for inexperienced interviewers or for situations where each question must be repeated exactly the same way and in the same sequence with each interviewee.[16] Most of us have been stopped by an interviewer in a shopping mall. The person asks a series of specific questions such as how far you drove to get to the mall, what stores you shop in, and how much you have spent. These interviews are generally conducted by inexperienced interviewers who ask only those questions listed on their interview form. Because they do not ask any other questions, this is an example of a structured interview.

Because a structured interview restricts the interviewer's flexibility and makes it difficult to adapt to unique situations, certain cases require an *unstructured interview*. Here, the interviewer has a clear objective but has prepared no specific questions in advance. With an unstructured format, the interviewer initiates the discussion, letting the initial responses lead into the next question. The lack of a specific set of questions allows for the maximum flexibility many situations require. This type of interview is particularly valuable when it is important that the interviewer help set the direction—as in some appraisal interviews or certain counseling sessions.

The unstructured interview is not easy nor is it for amateurs. An undisciplined interviewer trying to remain unstructured will often meet few objectives. Often the interviewer becomes so interested in one subject that he slights other important information. However, important information could also be lost in the structured interview if the topics covered are not pursued adequately.[17]

A compromise between the structured and unstructured interview is the semistructured interview. In this format, the interviewer prepares certain questions and copies them on a checklist so the interviewer can simply check them off when covered. Following the specific sequence is less important than is covering the critical items. At the same time, on the checklist, the interviewee can note any additional subjects or questions arising during the discussion. The key is to cover the critical items.

A semistructured strategy works in most situations. With this strategy, the manager plans ahead by writing down some of the key questions to make sure she covers all important points by the close of the interview. Meanwhile, she maintains flexibility because the sequence of the questioning is not completely preplanned. Many consider this the most appropriate format for most situations faced by experienced managers.

Question 5: What Is the Best Sequence for the Questions?

For a semistructured interview, a funnel or inverted funnel question sequence is recommended. The funnel sequence opens with broad, open-ended questions and proceeds with increasingly restricted questions. The inverted funnel sequence begins with closed questions and gradually proceeds toward open-ended ones. Figure 11–4 shows these two sequences.

The appropriate strategy depends on the situation.[18] One consideration is the extent to which the manager wants specific or general information. The funnel sequence proceeds toward specific information, whereas the inverted funnel moves toward broad generalization. Another consideration is the sensitivity of the questions. If general questions are less sensitive, it may be best to begin with them before moving to the more specific, sensitive questions.

Question 6: What Is Appropriate Phrasing for Questions?

The various types of questions have already been discussed in Chapter 9 and are reviewed again in Chapter 12. However, the ability to select the appropriate question format is so important in managerial communication that we review these concepts here within the context of interviews.

FIGURE 11–4

Funnel Sequence

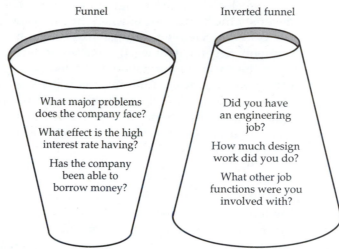

The advantage of the open-ended question is that it is generally non-
threatening. It allows the interviewee freedom of response, and it keeps the
interview progressing. However, the interviewer might not be able to obtain
the specific information he sought, and the interviewee may not be willing

Interview questions fall into three wording categories: open–closed, primary–secondary, and neutral–directed. Open and closed questions are best
explained using a continuum. An open-ended question is structured with
virtually no restriction on the type of response that is received. At the other
extreme is the closed-ended question, which is more restrictive. It limits the
possible answers elicited. Generally, questions can be answered with either
specific answers or a simple yes or no. Look at the following examples of the
two types of questions.

Open-Ended	*Closed-Ended*
1. How was your last job?	1. What exact part of your job did you dislike?
2. Tell me more about the Niles project.	2. What percentage of the Niles project is completed?
3. How is everything in the Denver Division?	3. Did you complete the quarterly report for the Denver Division?
4. Tell me about yourself.	4. Have you ever been in Los Angeles?
5. What do you enjoy doing?	5. Do you like to ski?

The advantage of the open-ended question is that it is generally non-
threatening. It allows the interviewee freedom of response, and it keeps the
interview progressing. However, the interviewer might not be able to obtain
the specific information he sought, and the interviewee may not be willing

to reveal sensitive or critical data even though the interview is generally nonthreatening.

The closed question offers three advantages in an interview. First, it is generally the best question when the interviewer needs specific information, since the interviewee is not that likely to ramble without ever answering the question. Second, it allows the interviewer to control and direct the interview since the specific information requested is obvious. Finally, the interviewer can receive the desired information faster with a closed-ended than with an open-ended question. The closed question has one major drawback: it often discourages dialogue as the interviewee may answer precisely what is requested and no more. If that one answer is all that is wanted, the situation is acceptable.

Unfortunately, managers often find themselves using closed questions when they would really like additional information and both the interviewer and the interviewee end up uncomfortable. They are uncomfortable because the interviewer would really like additional information, but does not know exactly how to obtain it, while the interviewee is not sure about the wisdom of offering additional (but unrequested) information.

The choice between open or closed questions does not need to be difficult. Managers need to ask themselves if they are looking for general information or need a specific answer. Are they trying to solicit additional information (open), trying to make the interviewee comfortable (open), or are they trying to get to a specific point as quickly as possible (closed)? The answers to these strategic questions help one decide when to use open or closed questions.

Although choosing the open or closed question need not be difficult, it is important to be analytical and consider all the important contingencies. Too frequently, managers do not concentrate on their communication so they ask a series of closed questions because such questions are easier. But this approach to asking questions does not lead to the desired information.

The second category of questions includes primary and secondary questions. A primary question introduces a topic in an interview while a secondary question seeks to add to the information gained from the primary question. The secondary question probes further into the response given in the primary question. A secondary question is most valuable when the primary question did not elicit all the desired information.

The following dialogue gives an example of the use of primary and secondary questions.

Interviewer: What did you do after entering the turbin group? (primary)
Interviewee: I supervised the AR Department.
Interviewer: The AR Department? (secondary)
Interviewee: Yes, that's the accounts receivable group that does all. . . .

In this example, the secondary question elicited additional information for the interviewer. Look at another example.

Interviewer: What don't you like about the job? (primary)
Interviewee: I guess it's all the paperwork that goes with the claims

department. It seems to be getting more and more complicated all the time.

Interviewer: What about it is more complicated? (secondary)

Interviewee: I'm thinking especially of these new interregional claims we're working on. I don't think people realize how much time they take, and we do a lot of them.

Interviewer: About how much time do they take? (secondary)

Secondary questions can be handled informally so they seem more like a normal conversation than an interrogation. A subtle form of secondary questions is a probe. Figure 11–5 presents seven types of probes. Again, notice that in a relaxed interview, although these probes obtain additional information, they may not appear to be questions but rather part of the conversation. They are subtle but effective.

Secondary questions help gain complete and accurate information, but also establish a positive communication climate in the interview. The effective use of secondary questions and probes can help demonstrate the manager is interested in listening. Initially, the interviewee may not know how much information is wanted, or whether the manager is really interested in her comments; however, the use of secondary questions and probes helps establish a willing and open atmosphere.

Neutral and directed questions, the third category, may also be considered in terms of a continuum with neutral questions at one end and directed questions at the other. Since the correct answer is not implied in the question, a neutral question does not lead the interviewee to answer in one particular way. The directed question, at the other end of the continuum, leads the interviewee or indicates he or she is supposed to give a particular answer. The classic example of a directed question is the courtroom ploy, "Didn't you say that . . . ?" or "Isn't it true that . . . ?" In reality, this type of extreme directed question may be considered a plea for agreement rather than a true question even when an interrogative tone is used.[19]

Examples of neutral and directed questions are listed to show the difference.

Neutral Questions	*Directed Questions*
1. What kind of car do your prefer?	1. Don't you think that foreign cars are superior to American cars?
2. What is your reaction to decentralization?	2. You are opposed to decentralization, aren't you?
3. What do you think of unionization?	3. Naturally, you are opposed to any kind of unions?
4. What was your reaction to the question?	4. Wasn't that a crazy question?
5. Do you feel we should hire more employees?	5. I don't think we should hire any more employees. What do you think?
6. Well, what do you think of the proposal?	6. Well, what do you think of the proposal?

FIGURE 11–5 Seven Probes

Probe	Definition of Probe	Illustration of Probe (Asterisk denotes probe applied)
1. Brief assertion of understanding	Anything A says that indicates interest and understanding, thus encouraging B to continue	"So, first I said to him, how'd you like a cup of coffee . . . sort of thought it would break the ice."
2. Neutral phrase	Any expression by A that elicits more information from B without affecting (biasing) the information	"I don't know . . . the kids today seem to be getting away with murder." "Uh-huh." "There doesn't seem to be the respect for things like there used to be." "Could you elaborate a bit on what you mean?"
3. Silence	A period of time when A does not speak and looks attentively at B. The period of time involved is under 10 seconds.	"Wow . . . what a day I've had." Silence—2 seconds. "I mean, I didn't have a minute to myself the way they kept me working."
4. Echo	A converting the last portion of what B says into a question . . . generally with almost all the words exactly the same as stated by B.	"I'm not sure that I can take anymore." "I understand." "No you don't . . . no one could . . . I'm at the end of my rope." "At the end of your rope?"
5. Clarification	An effort on the part of A to get a definition or further explanation about a word or phrase used by B that is not understood	"I'll tell you that lowering the voting age ain't all that its cracked up to be." "Oh . . . how so?" "Well, for one thing, it's going to increase the likelihood of political conspiracies."
6. Extension	A request for new information that is directly related to something already said.	"Chief, I'm really worried about the parade tomorrow." "How do you mean worried?" "Well I think we might be in for some rough stuff." "Oh . . . what indication do you have that we might have some rough stuff?"
7. Summary statements	A deliberate effort on the part of A to pull together the main points made by B during the past few minutes.	"And finally. Hank, there's the question of pay . . . we just don't get paid enough for the work we do." "Let me see if I have it straight, Ralph. First, you say the work is dirty, not carefully scheduled, and finally, you're underpaid for the work you do, correct?"

In the last question, the wording for both the neutral and directed question is the same. You can alter the question simply by changing emphasis from one word to another or by changing the tone of voice. Thus, "Well, what do *you* think of the proposal?" means something quite different from, "Well, what do you think of the *proposal*?" In the first question, *you* is the critical part as the interviewee's opinion is solicited implying that *your* opinion is particularly important or possibly quite different. But in the second question, the *proposal* is the important component, implying that the proposal must be somehow differentiated.

A person in a position of authority may ask a directed question when intending to ask a neutral question. Either slight, unintentional emphasis on a word or a minor change in tone of voice may imply the manager is demanding a certain response. The subordinate may exaggerate every change in emphasis or tone since he is aware of the power and status of the manager.

Harold Poling, chairman and CEO of Ford Motor, emphasized this point. He noted that early in his career, as he climbed to higher levels of responsibility, he became more and more aware that slight emphasis could be interpreted as major statements. In a discussion reviewing European marketing strategies, a manager mistook a question as a directive. Fortunately, he caught and corrected the misinterpretation. Poling believes he has had to become more skillful in the use of questions as he has moved into a major executive position.[20]

The skillful use of directed questions can be valuable since such questions can help keep the interview on track and be used effectively for persuasion. In persuasion, they point the interviewee in a particular direction and help him to think about the benefit of some concept. As with the other types of questions, the manager must be alert to determine the correct use of neutral and directed questions to fit the situation.

Question 7: Should I Take Notes During the Interview?

The decision to take notes depends on the interview objective and the type of information involved. If the parties exchange numerous facts, it is important to take notes to keep everything straight. Conversely, if only one or two facts are important, or if the objective is to obtain a general impression, notes generally are not necessary. When notes seem advisable, follow these guidelines:

1. First, ask if taking notes would make the interviewee uncomfortable. When made in a positive manner, this request may reduce some of the interviewee's anxiety.
2. Keep the notes brief; more thorough notes can be developed after the interview.
3. Keep eye contact with the interviewee as much as possible. Do not become so involved in writing that you forget the person involved.

4. Keep from doodling, which makes it appear you are not paying attention.

5. Avoid accentuating something the interviewee says by taking notes immediately afterward. If an interviewer eagerly takes notes after one statement, but then does not write anything for a long time, the interviewee will get the impression that certain information is more important than other information. Consequently, the interview could become slanted. Take notes at a consistent pace.

6. Review the notes immediately after the interview to organize them and elaborate on the important points.

Question 8: What Is the Best Way to Close the Interview?

When it is time to close the interview, as with many other communications, it is important to summarize the main information and ensure that all the relevant data are well organized. This provides the opportunity to arrange for any follow-up, if necessary, and to express appreciation to the interviewee. The closing needs to fit the interviewee, of course. For the employment interview, it might be best to let the interviewee know when he will next hear from you. For the performance review, it might be a genuine compliment that sums up the interviewee's accomplishments for the past term. Or if you interviewed someone to determine how she solved a problem, you may want to tell her how she helped you in solving your own problems.

The Manager as Interviewee

The interview is a two-way process. The preceding series of questions may seem to apply only to the manager as the interviewer; however, managers face many situations in which they are the interviewee.[21] Remember the comments made early in this chapter that the interview is like a directed conversation. When considering this perspective, a manager may be an interviewer and interviewee almost concurrently. But more specifically, the manager is an interviewee when he is the object of a persuasive effort, or is seeking a new position, or is involved in a performance review session.[22] Because of this dual role, it is worthwhile to review the same eight questions from the other side.

Question 1: What Is the Objective?

Too often, managers think that since they are being interviewed, all they have to do is show up. An interviewee must determine ahead of time what the interviewer wants to obtain during the interview. Without knowing the objective, your opportunity to gain and present important information may be lost. If the objective is not stated, try to determine it from the signals early in the interview.

Question 2: How Should I Manage the Time and Place Chosen for the Interview?

As interviewee, it will probably not be possible to control the place and time of the interview. However, the interviewee still should attempt to obtain the optimum place and time for an accurate exchange of information. If the original arrangements are not satisfactory, a tactful suggestion to the interviewer about place or time may remedy this. The manager might have more power as an interviewee than assumed.

Question 3: What Is the Best Way to Begin?

Whichever role one fills, an open communication climate needs to be established from the beginning along with a clear sense of purpose. An open climate may be at least partially fostered by the interviewee with such simple acts as a firm handshake, a smile, and a positive opening remark. One can obtain clear understanding of the interview's purpose through questions asked of the interviewer. The interviewee can repeat his understanding of the purpose of the interview so that both are on the right track.

Question 4: Which Questions Should Be Prepared Ahead of Time?

Managers are involved in an interview because they have an objective to meet: sharing and gaining information. The interviewee also often needs to ask certain questions to ensure a complete exchange of information. This is particularly obvious in the employment interview because the applicant should always know about the position and the company involved. It will probably be necessary to ask questions to ensure the objectives of the interview are met. Preparation is the key: write out potential questions before the interview.

Question 5: What Is the Sequence of Questions?

Listening is always important and takes on special significance in the interview. When managers interactively listen, they can determine the best time to ask particular questions. A short silence, a quick glance, or a nod of the interviewer's head may indicate a question would be appropriate. Interactive listening will also help to ascertain if the question was important to the interviewer and whether it is appropriate to pursue a topic further. Naturally, the interviewee should pay attention to the nature of the question—that is, is it an open or closed question? Is it primary or secondary? Such cues can be useful guides. Although the particular sequence of questions cannot be planned when one is the interviewee, interactive listening will help to determine the most appropriate timing of the interviewee's questions.

Question 6: How Should Questions Be Phrased?

The three categories of questions—open and closed, secondary and primary, neutral and directed—and probes are all appropriate when used by an interviewee. When asking questions, it is important to do so in a positive, non-threatening manner. This is why it is generally best to begin with neutral, open-ended questions. However, the manager needs to remain alert to determine the type of question that will achieve the desired objective at the right time.

Question 7: What About Taking Notes?

Just as communication is a two-way process, the interview needs to be a two-way process. This means that even when the person is the interviewee, she may need to take some notes. The guidelines presented earlier still apply. The interviewee must be alert to determine what is important and how extensive the notes should be. The interviewee is well advised to check and revise notes immediately after the interview.

Question 8: What Is the Interviewee's Role in Closing the Interview?

At the close of the interview, the interviewee should know clearly the main points that have been covered and what the interviewee is responsible for. A good way to do this is to orally summarize the interview and ask the interviewer if the summary is accurate. This will allow both parties to be clear on what transpired during the interview. If you are not clear on certain areas, ask questions.

Many of the strategies are the same whether a manager is the interviewer or interviewee. The important point is that the interviewee has definite obligations and must be a skillful and effective communicator. One should not assume the interviewee is in a passive position and cannot control critical aspects of the interview.

Summary

The term *interview* includes many daily interactions that have a time limit and an identifiable purpose. It is an opportunity to gain and share information, but it is important to be aware of special communication barriers that make this difficult. First, the interviewer and interviewee might have different intentions. Skillful questioning and listening will help to overcome this barrier.

Personal bias, the second barrier, results when people hear and see what they want to hear and see. The best way to deal with personal bias is to be aware of it so special efforts may be made to remain objective. The third barrier is the fact–inference problem. While this is always a concern, in an interview so few facts are available and presented that it is a special problem. Managers need to be aware of whether they are basing a conclusion on a fact or an opinion.

Nonverbal communication, the fourth barrier discussed, presents problems because the interview is generally a short, intensive communication interaction. One nonverbal behavior may take an unwarranted emphasis and result in faulty conclusions. The last two barriers are the effects of first impressions and organizational status.

To help overcome these barriers, eight questions should be asked by managers. The chapter discusses each question first from the perspective of the manager as interviewer and then from the interviewee's perspective. Also reviewed are critical elements relating to the purpose, time, place, and the techniques for beginning an interview.

A semistructured format is recommended. This means some of the questions should be established before the interview, but others will depend on how the interview develops. Either the funnel or inverted funnel sequence of questions may be used. The funnel sequence proceeds toward specific information, whereas the inverted funnel moves toward broad generalizations.

Three categories of questions are reviewed when discussing the phrasing of questions—open and closed, primary and secondary, neutral and directed—and each may be appropriate at the correct time. Seven types of probes also are presented. Strategic analysis is required to use the appropriate questions in different situations.

The appropriateness of notes depends on the objective and type of information involved in the interview. Guidelines are presented that may be used once a manager has decided to take notes. Finally, consideration is given to ending the interview. Both the interviewer and interviewee must be clear on the main points; this clarification may be obtained through summarization.

Endnotes

1. Geraldine Henze, "Interviewing Skills for Managers," in *The Handbook of Executive Communication*, ed. J. L. Degaetaxi (Homewood, Ill: Dow Jones-Irwin, 1986), pp. 635–50.
2. Susan T. Fiske and Steven L. Newberg, "A Continuum of Impression Formation, From Category-Based to Individuating Process: Influences of Information and Motivation on Attention and Interpretation," in *Advances in Experimental Social Psychology*, Vol. 23, ed. Mark P. Zanna (New York: Academic Press, 1990), pp. 1–74.

3. Kevin R. Murphy and Douglas H. Reynolds, "Does True Halo Affect Observed Halo?" *Journal of Applied Psychology*, May 1988, pp. 235–38.

4. Elaine Pulakos, Neal Schmitt, and C. Ostroff, "A Warning About the Use of a Standard Deviation across Dimensions within Rates to Measure Halo," *Journal of Applied Psychology*, February 1986, pp. 29–32.

5. Terry L. Leap and Michael D. Crino, *Personnel/Human Resource Management* (New York: Macmillan, 1989), p. 332.

6. Fran F. Kanfer and P. Karoly, "Self-Control: A Behaviorist Excursion into the Lion's Den," *Behavior Therapy* 3, no. 2 (1972), pp. 298–300.

7. James P. Walsh, "Selectivity and Selective Perception: An Investigation of Managers' Belief Structures and Information Processing," *Academy of Management Journal*, December 1988, pp. 873–96.

8. S. L. Ragan, "A Conversational Analysis of Alignment Talk in Job Interviews," in *Communication Yearbook*, Vol. 7, ed. R. M. Bostrom (Beverly Hills, Calif.: Sage Publications, 1983), pp. 502–16.

9. R. L. Birdwhistell, *Kinesics and Context* (Philadelphia: University of Pennsylvania Press, 1970), p. 97.

10. J. K. Burgoon, D. B. Buller, and G. W. Woodall, *Nonverbal Communication: The Unspoken Dialogue* (New York: Harper & Row, 1989), p. 76.

11. Susan T. Fiske and Shelley E. Taylor, *Social Cognition* (Reading, Mass.: Addison-Wesley Publishing, 1984), pp. 1–2.

12. M. Snyder and B. H. Campbell, "Testing Hypothesis About Other People: The Role of the Hypothesis," *Personality and Social Psychology Bulletin*, 1980, pp. 421–26.

13. H. J. Bernardin and Richard W. Beatty, "Can Subordinate Appraisals Enhance Managerial Productivity?" *Sloan Management Review*, Summer 1987, p. 69.

14. R. I. Lazar and W. S. Wilkstrom, *Appraising Managerial Performance: Current Practices and Future Directions* (New York: The Conference Board, 1977), p. 46.

15. G. P. Latham and L. M. Saari, "Do People Do What They Say, Further Studies on the Situation Interview," *Journal of Applied Psychology* 69, no. 4 (1984), pp. 569–73.

16. G. Johns, "Effects of Informational Order and Frequency of Applicant Evaluation Upon Linear Information-Processing Competence of Interviewers," *Journal of Applied Psychology* 60, no. 3 (1975), pp. 427–33.

17. R. L. Street, "Interaction Processes and Outcomes in Interviews," in *Communication Yearbook* 9, ed. M. L. McLaughlen (Beverly Hills, Calif.: Sage Publications, 1986), pp. 215–50.

18. C. D. Tengler and F. M. Jablin, "Effects of Question Type, Orientation, and Sequencing in the Employment Screening Interview," *Communication Monographs* 50, no. 2 (1983), pp. 243–63.

19. Charles Stewart and W. B. Cash, *Interviewing Principles and Practices*, 5th ed. (Dubuque, Iowa: William C. Brown, 1988), p. 21.

20. Personal conversation with Harold Poling after a presentation to the Deans Council of 100 at Arizona State University, September 29, 1992.

21. Keenan and A. Wedderburn, "Putting the Boot on the Other Foot: Candidates; Descriptions of Interviewers," *Journal of Occupational Psychology* 53, no. 1 (1986), pp. 81–9.

22. Paula Ancona, "Closely Examine Employer Before Accepting Job Offer," *Arizona Republic*, September 21, 1992, p. E6.

Additional Readings

Adler, Ronald B. *Looking Out, Looking In.* Orlando, Fla.: Holt, Rinehart and Winston, Inc., 1990.

Biegeleisien, J. L. *Make Your Job Interview a Success.* New York: Prentice Hall, 1987.

Drake, John D. *Interviewing for Managers.* New York: AMACOM, 1982.

Hergenrather, Edmund. "The 13 Most Critical Interviewing Mistakes." *National Business Employment Weekly,* June 3, 1990, p. 9.

Jablin, Frederick M., and Vernon D. Miller. "Interviewer and Applicant Questioning Behavior in Employment Interviews." *Management Communication Quarterly* 4, no. 1 (August 1990), pp. 51–86.

Karannich, Caryl Rae, and Ronald L. Krannich. *Interview for Success.* Manassas, Va.: Impact Publications, 1988.

Rafe, Stephen C. *Mastering the News Media Interview.* New York: Hapter Business, 1991.

Robinett, Judy M. "Advice to Interviewees: Hide Your Fatal Flaws." *National Business Employment Weekly,* September 17, 1990, pp. 9–19.

Discussion Questions

1. Give an example where you used an apparent casual conversation as an interview.
2. When would an interviewee and interviewer have different intentions? Give several examples.
3. Give examples of several biases that you may have that could interfere with the communication process. Explain how they could interfere with the interview.
4. Give examples of nonverbal behaviors that may indicate a person is interested in the interview. Give examples that may show lack of interest.
5. Describe an instance when you thought something was a fact but it actually was an inference.
6. How does the fact–inference fallacy affect the interview process?
7. What are some cues you believe create a positive first impression? A negative first impression?
8. Give an example where you have participated in an interview that had more than one objective.
9. What are the advantages and disadvantages of both the structured and unstructured interview format?
10. Supply a set of questions that provides an example for both the funnel and inverted funnel strategy.
11. Give examples of the three categories of questions that may be used in an interview.
12. When would each of the following types of questions be used: open-ended, closed-ended, secondary, and direct?
13. Give several examples of probes that you have used.

14. What should you consider when thinking about taking notes during an interview? What are your personal reactions to taking notes in an interview?
15. In what situations would you want to prepare answers to potential interviewer questions?
16. Do you believe communication is more critical for the interviewee or the interviewer? Discuss.

CASE 11–1
KAY AND THE QUIET NURSE

Kay is the director of the Corporate Safety Department for a large, multiplant manufacturing company in the Midwest. The company has six major manufacturing plants, and each has its own industrial nurses.

Twice a year, Kay has individual formal interviews with the nurses to find out if they have any major concerns or if Kay can help in any way. Since these nurses report to the personnel manager of each plant and not to Kay, this is not a performance review. Kay gets a lot of valuable information form the nurses through the interviews and seems to have developed a positive relationship with them. There is only one nurse, James, who does not really open up to Kay and say much. On several occasions, Kay has tried to get information from James, but generally when Kay asks a question, all she gets is a one-word response. When she does get more than a one-word response, it seems to be superficial.

For instance, several months ago all the plants instituted a new program for monitoring the number and types of visits to the nurses' offices. Kay asked James if everything was all right with the new program. James merely shrugged and said, "Yes." Earlier discussions had been just as limited. This worries Kay because James is a young nurse with only two years of experience and he probably has questions and could use some help. Kay has even asked some of the other employees in the plant if James was naturally quiet, but everyone said he was rather outgoing and easy to get to know.

Kay is getting frustrated, because in her 25 years of experience she has never had this much trouble getting someone to open up.

Questions

1. What are some possible incorrect interview strategies that Kay may be using?
2. What would you recommend to Kay?
3. Why are some people more difficult to interview than others? (Information in Chapters 2 and 3 may help with this answer.)

Case 11–2
Is It Harassment?

Jack Simpson, newly appointed as vice-president in charge of personnel for Geridan Contracting Corporation (GCC), has had an unusual morning. First on his agenda was an exit interview with Maria Johnson, the company president's departing personal secretary. Johnson informed Simpson she was quitting, for no apparent reason. Judging from her performance reviews over the last few years, Simpson believed her to be a competent, enthusiastic, and dedicated employee. Even though Simpson had little knowledge of her work load, he could see no obvious reason for the resignation. He had set up this exit interview hoping to find out why she had quit.

Next on Simpson's agenda was an interview with Ryan Ross, the president of GCC, who wanted to talk to Simpson before Simpson began interviewing later in the day for the secretary's replacement. Simpson had never conducted an interview for a president's secretary before, but he had planned on getting a good idea of what to look for during his talk with Johnson. He believed Ross would also advise him on what he expected for the secretary's replacement. At the outset, then, Simpson felt at ease about conducting these interviews.

However, when Simpson and the resigning executive secretary, Johnson, sat down in a secluded conference room at 8:30 A.M., the personnel director's ears began to burn. Johnson explained that for the last six months she was being sexually harassed by Ross and that she was considering suing GCC (and Ross in particular) for sexual harassment.

Simpson needs to know more about this accusation in case it does develop into a more serious situation. Also, the more facts he has, the better prepared he will be to discuss the situation with the president. What interview strategy should Simpson use with the president?

Questions

1. What type of questions would you recommend?
2. What do you think will be the major barriers in this interview? Why?
3. What can Simpson do to be sure he is getting the facts?

12 MAXIMIZING THE USE OF SPECIAL INTERVIEW SITUATIONS

You are aware of the dynamics of the interview process and the communication barriers that must be overcome. But now you are faced with several specific interview situations. First, the human resources department has scheduled you to interview three candidates for the cost accounting position in your department. Although the HR department reduced the applicant pool to the best three candidates, you are responsible for the final decision. Then you must conduct the annual appraisal interview with your administrative assistant. Although he has been with you seven years, this interview will be especially difficult because you have been slightly disappointed with some of his recent work. Then in the afternoon, you will meet with your senior accountant. For some reason, he seems to be making some silly errors lately.

What special concerns need to be considered for each of these interviews? What unique goals should be met? What special obstacles must be overcome? What is the best strategy for these different interviews?

A manager's typical routine includes a number of challenging interview situations. The last chapter gave an overview of the barriers to interviews as well as the most frequent questions managers ask about the interview process. This chapter builds on that knowledge by focusing on several specific interview situations managers face as well as the appropriate strategy for each.

The Employment Interview

Selecting the most qualified people available for a position is a major managerial responsibility. A variety of screening tools are used in employee selection, including formal application blanks and aptitude and personality tests, but the most common is the employment interview.

Problems and Types

While a member of the personnel department often conducts the initial screening of applicants, the applicant's future manager generally makes the final decision. The ability to match competent applicants with the correct job leads to the success of an organization. Managers have a responsibility to both the organization and the applicant to see that an applicant–job match exists. Without it, frustration, reduced self-esteem, stress, and poor performance result.

Yet, employment interviews are typically not used to their best advantage. While research shows that the interview is low in both reliability and validity,[1] no adequate replacement exists. It is the only technique that gives managers the chance to personally evaluate the candidate and to pursue questioning in a way that tests cannot. No test can provide the rich information available from facial expressions, appearance, nervousness, and the like.

In the employment interview, the manager's goal is to find ways to increase the reliability and validity of this selection tool. However, before examining specific techniques for improving the employment interview, we need to distinguish among the types of employment interviews. One way to do this is to determine the three distinct types or general purposes of employment interviews.[2] The first and most common is selection of the best applicant from a pool of applicants. In this case, seeking information is the goal. The purpose of the second type, the recruitment interview, is to sell the job or the company to the candidate who has already been selected as the preferred choice. Here persuasion is the goal. The third general purpose is to give applicants information about job opportunities or the organization. This is generally a preliminary step and provides information so the applicant can decide whether he wishes to be considered for the job.

Keep these three purposes in mind as you review the following information because an interview strategy needs to be adjusted according to the needs of the situation. Also, an interview takes on a different focus as it develops, so the strategy may need to be altered during the interview. Although employment interviews may have one of three purposes, most of the following discussion emphasizes selection.

Planning

The employment interview, like all communication situations, requires planning, but in a more specific way.

Characteristics of Position

A manager's first step is to ensure a clear understanding of the job's requirements. This effort helps to avoid putting too much weight on irrelevant information. An interviewer familiar with extensive details about the job to be filled (such as that provided by detailed job descriptions and job titles) enhances the reliability of employment selection decisions.[3] When no comprehensive job description is available, it may be necessary for the interviewer to complete a job analysis.

When reviewing the nature of the job, be careful not to compare the last *person* holding the job with present candidates. Doing so can inaccurately affect your impressions of a candidate. For instance, if the last two people to have a particular position were men who had backgrounds in engineering, then a woman with a background in math might not match the interviewer's image of the ideal candidate. Unfortunately, in this instance, the image has nothing to do with the characteristics required for successful performance; rather, the image is built by people who have held the job. Thus, it is important to review the job description rather than just think about the last incumbent. Also, many job incumbents change the nature of a position slightly to match their personal capabilities and interests. So what better time to analyze the present and future qualifications required for performance on a job than when personnel changes are made? The job description is a dynamic rather than static tool and is invaluable to the employment interviewer.

Time

Time and timing are also important parts of the planning process. The amount of time allocated for an interview varies. Certain applicants may be successfully interviewed in 15 minutes for some jobs, while other situations require several hours or even a complete day. Until one obtains adequate experience to determine accurately the amount of time that should be scheduled, it is better to allocate too much rather than too little time. Making a crucial employment decision is not an activity on which to try to save time.

Timing is important in the employment interview due to the contrast effect, namely the influence that earlier interviews may have on later interviews. The job candidate who is only average but follows a number of poor candidates will likely make a better impression than if she had followed other average candidates. Be aware of any potential contrast effect and plan accordingly. One way to reduce this effect is to avoid interviewing a long series of candidates without a break.

In addition, allow enough time between interviews and arrange your schedule so fatigue does not become a factor. Applicants interviewed when the interviewer is fatigued may receive lower ratings than other applicants. While these suggested strategies cannot eliminate the possibility of the contrast effect, they are valuable considerations when planning the interview strategy.

Applicant Preview

Interviewers worried about personal bias debate whether to review the application blank or the résumé before the interview, and no definite answer emerges. Viewing these may bias the interviewer. At the same time, either of these two tools may positively shape the direction of the interview.

Remember that the interview's objective is to get information that written material cannot easily reveal including motivation and personality characteristics. Clearly, time can be wasted if the interview covers the same material that the interviewer has already observed on the application blank. But you can also use the interview to clarify inconsistencies or fill in gaps left on written forms. It is best to integrate the written material and interview data to make effective decisions.

Legal Concerns of the Employment Interview

By now almost all managers are familiar with the Civil Rights Act of 1964, which was amended by the Equal Employment Opportunity (EEO) Act of 1972. Unfortunately, knowledge of the legal implications of employment interviewing is too often misapplied. Managers may become either too cautious in their questioning out of fear of the law and miss valuable information or they ignore the legal implications. Although the following paragraphs do not constitute a comprehensive discussion of the legal components of employment, several suggestions may help you in your employment interviews.

Probably the first thing that comes to managers' minds when discussing EEO is what is a legal or illegal question. To answer this, one needs to be aware of the concept of Bona Fide Occupational Qualification (BFOQ), which is any characteristic that is a valid criterion of job performance. Race, color, religion, gender, ethnic background, or marital status are *generally* not bases on which people may or may not be hired. The word *generally* is the key, because in rare cases, such as interviews for models or for parts in dramatic productions, gender or race may play a role in the decision process. Other rare examples may develop for race or religion.[4]

Firms with affirmative action programs are committed to ensuring that members of what are called protected groups (minorities and females usually fall into this classification) will be actively sought for employment.[5] Equal Employment Opportunity (EEO) and Affirmative Action (AA) are often confused because their goals have some similarities. However, EEO seeks a level playing field where all have an equal chance at gaining employment based on qualifications. A commitment to affirmative action is a commitment to make extra effort to identify and recruit individuals from protected classes.[6]

Generally, education, experience, and skills are the basic elements of BFOQs. Each job must be analyzed. In most situations, managers can follow guidelines that assure no condition of the Equal Employment Opportunity Act is being ignored. The best advice is to ask no questions that are not related to BFOQs or not directly related to making an objective employment decision.

Keep in mind, too, that casual conversations with job applicants should respect the guidelines set out here. For example, suppose a job applicant is

TABLE 12–1   Question Guidelines for Employment Interview

Focus on Question	Nondiscriminatory	Possibly Discriminatory
Name	Have you ever used a different name in other jobs?	What was your name before you changed it?
Birthplace and residence	Which state do you presently live in? How long have you lived in Cedar Falls (or a given state)?	Where were you born? In which country were your parents born? May I see your birth certificate (or similar papers)?
Physical characteristics including race and color	Do you have any distinguishing marks or scars?	Are you Asian descent? To what race do you belong?
National origin or ancestry		You're from Mexico, aren't you? Are you related to the Manuels from Hermossa (similarly, questions about descendants and parentage and questions about the nationality of parents and spouse)?
Sex, living arrangements		How many children do you have? Are you married?
Religion		Are you Jewish? What religious holidays will you be taking off if we hire you?
Citizenship	Are you a citizen? Does your visa allow you to work?	Are you a German subject?
Organizations	Do you belong to any charitable organizations?	Are you in the D.A.R.? Were you a member of the Catholic Students Club? Did you belong to the Hillel Organization (or similar questions whose answer would reveal race, creed, color, religion, national origin, sex, or ancestry)?
Arrest record and convictions		How often have you been arrested, and for what (unless related to job performance)?
Physical abilities or limitations	This job requires lifting and carrying; do you see any problems with that?	Are you handicapped (similarly, avoid questions about the type or severity of the handicap)?
Education	Have you received your CPM certification yet?	Do you have an MBA degree (or similar questions when educational achievement has no relation to the skills needed for a given job)?
Financial status		Have you ever had your wages garnished? What is your approximate networth? How much is your house mortgage?

being treated to lunch. Don't confuse this with a truly social situation and make small talk about spouses, family, or religion.[7] These could be misconstrued by the candidates as irrelevant, non-BFOQ questions and represent grounds for later disputes should the job not materialize.

Table 12–1 presents some useful guidelines regarding lawful and unlawful types of questions during the employment interview. These same considerations also apply to application forms. Discrimination occurs when an individual who has an equal probability of being successful on a job does not have an equal probability of getting the job.[8] A manager is responsible for seeing that discrimination does not occur.

After an applicant has been hired, many of the inquiries that were prohibited earlier can be made for a variety of purposes. For example, forms for medical examinations, insurance, and the like may ask about race, color, religion, and national origin. Photographs or other proof of national origin or race may similarly be needed for legal reporting purposes. All the same, this information must not be used for making promotion decisions.[9]

The Employment Interview Process

During the employment interview, the manager tries to find out as much as possible about a candidate that relates to potential job success. The best way to do this is to be aware of the various barriers and suggested strategies discussed in the previous chapter. Also, to be fully effective, managers should be familiar with certain conditions specific to the selection interview. The following guidelines assist managers in their efforts to increase the reliability and validity of the employment interview.

Know the Job Requirements

It bears repeating: Managers should know the requirements of the job being filled. Keep these requirements in mind during the interview process to ensure that the communication is on pertinent characteristics and not on irrelevant information. Research indicates the reliability and validity of the interview increases as the interviewer increases his knowledge about the job.[10]

Keep the Goal of the Interview in Mind

As stated earlier, an interview may have one of three different goals—selection, recruitment, and information. Not every employment interview is strictly designed to select the best candidate because situations arise in which the interviewee is one of the few candidates qualified for a position. In this case, one needs to sell the candidate on the merits of the company or at least provide information about the company. The goal may also change during the interview. Thus, the interviewer may decide an applicant is definitely the best candidate for the position and thus begin "selling." When the interviewer fails to observe that the interview's purpose has changed, a totally inappropriate strategy may follow and result in wasted time.

TABLE 12–2 Question Options

Openers
May I see your resume?
What can I do for you?
Why would you like to join our company?
Why do you feel qualified for this job?
What do you think you can offer us?
What attracts you to us?
Tell me about your experience.
What pay do you have in mind?

Determining Motivation
Does your present employer know that you're thinking of changing jobs?
Why do you want to change jobs?
What led you to enter this profession?
Why do you want to change your area of work?
Where would you like to be in your career five years from now? Ten years?
What do you see as the perfect job for you?

Determining Experience
How do you fit the prerequisites for this job?
What did you do while you were in the military?
How would you go about improving our operations?
Who or what has influenced you the most? Why?
What aspects of your last job did you like best/least? Why?
What are your greatest strengths/weaknesses for this position?
What are the greatest weaknesses you have found in past supervisors?
What kinds of people do you like most/least as work associates?
How many people have you supervised? What types? What kind of
  supervisory experience have you had?
What are your greatest achievements to date?
What equipment are you familiar with?
Why have you changed jobs so often?
Have you ever been fired or asked to resign?
What has been the biggest crisis in your career?
Why were you unemployed so long?
Why did you quit your previous employment?
Could I see examples of your work?

Evaluating Educational Background
Describe your education for me.
Why did you choose your major field?
What was your class standing?
What extracurricular activities did you participate in?
What honors did you earn?
What was your grade-point average? In your major?
Do your grades reflect your full ability? Why not?
What courses did you like best/least and why?
What special training have you had for this job?

Regarding Pay
What salary do you require?
What is the minimum pay you will accept?
What has been your pay record for the last five years?
Why do you believe you are worth so much more?
We can't pay the salary you request. Would you be willing to start at less and
  work up to that figure?
What salary do you expect to be earning five years from now?

The recruitment or informative interview requires that the interviewer know the company well and present a positive image to the applicant. The interviewer must also be ready to answer questions. The interviewer must know the opportunities for advancement, be informed about benefits, and have a thorough knowledge of the company. Clearly, the interview is not a one-way situation since the interviewee is probably also evaluating the interviewer.

Use Appropriate Questioning Strategy

Numerous research projects indicate the form and sequence of questions profoundly influence the outcome of the interview.[11] Most interviews open positively with the interviewer attempting to put the interviewee at ease. The résumé can be a useful guide for selecting some strong point from the candidate's background to help make the interviewee comfortable in the beginning.[12] The previous chapter detailed the difference between an unstructured and structured interview. It is generally best to use a semistructured interview that assures a definite direction is taken but also allows the opportunity to prepare additional questions as the interview proceeds. Table 12–2 presents a series of possible questions that you might use as an interviewer.

Open and Closed Questions

When designing the questions for the interview, remember the difference between open and closed, primary and secondary, and neutral and directed questions. Know the benefits and shortcomings of each of these types of questions so you can implement an effective questioning strategy. An employment interview generally uses open-ended questions, but it can also use closed and directed questions to obtain the correct type of information. Keep in mind that closed questions (often called dead-end questions) do not inspire detailed answers and may not provide the data needed.[13] Use leading questions only when they meet a specific purpose. The following dialogue demonstrates a typical questioning strategy in an employment interview.

> *Interviewer:* Tell me about your present job. (open-ended question)
> *Interviewee:* I spend approximately 75 percent of my time coding the production information to fit the cost accounting system that we use.
> *Interviewer:* What do you mean by "coding?" (secondary)
> *Interviewee:* Our entire cost accounting system is computerized, so it is necessary to take the forms submitted by the various production departments and translate the figures into our computer code.
> *Interviewer:* What kind of computer program is used? (closed)
> *Interviewee:* It's based on MS-DOS.
> *Interviewer:* To what extent have you used other computer programs? (Notice that this question is more open than "Have you used Lotus?" or a more leading question, "Do you like Lotus?" The open-ended question will probably provide more information than the closed or directed question in this situation.)

Interviewee: The only computer program that I'm familiar with is ABSTAT, but I did do a little work with SAS while I was in college.
Interviewer: So you have never used SPSS? (directed)
Interviewee: No, but I'm sure I could learn rather quickly. (In this situation a directed or leading question is used to gain confirmation, so it is appropriate.)

Mode of Presentation

Clearly, the interviewer must analyze the best use of questions since each type of question has a specific purpose. Besides the type of questions asked, it is important to take care with their presentation. First, give the applicant time to answer the questions. A series of rapid-fire questions may only confuse and frustrate the interviewee. A few seconds' pause between questions seems like hours sometimes, but the few extra seconds generally provide the opportunity for more accurate responses. Second, make sure the whole question is audible. Since the interviewee is likely to be a little nervous, it is important to communicate in a clear, articulate manner.

Third, do you use buzzwords or jargon that may be unique to your organization? Doing so makes it improbable that you will obtain the information sought and can embarrass the interviewee. Fourth, be aware of what you are communicating nonverbally by tone of voice, gestures, and eye movements. With these nonverbal elements, interviewers can lead the responses in a particular way without even knowing it. For instance, "What do you mean by *that*?" sounds as if the interviewer doubts the interviewee, when in reality she is only requesting more information. Finally, make the questions clear. Use trick questions only if you have a specific reason to do so. Unless an interview has been designed to create stress, don't play games with the interviewee. Also, most managers are not trained to evaluate the interviewee's responses to most stress or trick questions.

In summary, the structure and sequence of the interviewer's questions determine the effectiveness of the interview. Plan and develop the appropriate strategy realizing that each situation requires a different approach.

Avoid Premature Decisions

Survey findings indicate that many interviewers tentatively decide about an applicant within a few minutes, largely due to impressions founded on dress, physical appearance, eye contact, or other nonverbal cues.[14] Further, research indicates interviewers are influenced more by unfavorable than by favorable information, and the earlier in the interview the unfavorable information, the greater its negative effect.[15] In addition, it is more likely for the interviewer's impression to change from favorable to unfavorable than the opposite.[16]

These research findings show that interviewers must be careful to ignore initial stereotypes. Interviewers who are aware of their personal bias before interviewing are aware of the unrealistic influence that bias has on the interview; this awareness allows interviewers to control their personal bias.

Assume you were interviewing an applicant who had suffered several periods of unemployment. If you believe unemployment is generally due to poor personal habits such as laziness, tardiness, or lack of pride, your bias may lead to a premature negative conclusion. But if you think shifting labor trends cause unemployment, your initial bias may be different. In this latter instance, a premature decision would be less likely.

Premature decisions may cause a failure to perceive and communicate significant differences. Important information might be ignored. Once the early decision has been made, the remainder of the interview is relatively useless because the interview may be used only to confirm premature decisions.

Let the Interviewee Do Most of the Talking

In employment interviews, the interviewer is generally more talkative when reacting favorably to an applicant than when reacting unfavorably.[17] In other words, when an interviewer is impressed by the applicant, the interviewer is inclined to do less listening. Naturally, in doing this, the interviewer does not obtain as much information as he might by remaining silent, since listening is the key to obtaining information. Why then would the interviewer do more talking while interviewing a favorable candidate?

This phenomenon may arise because both the interviewer and interviewee are a little nervous during the interview and talking generally reduces nervousness. The interviewer is in the controlling position, so she may take the initiative and talk to reduce any nervousness or tension. Also, it may be that a decision is made early and the interviewer is supplying job information, or it could be that interviewers like listeners.

Whatever the reason, extensive talking is efficient only when attempting to sell a candidate on a position; information is obtained through listening, not talking. Thus, be careful not to talk too much. In fact, extensive speaking may indicate other interview errors such as a premature decision. Listen rather than talk.

Keep Records of the Interview

Given all of the information revealed during an interview, it is unrealistic to expect that it can be retained in one's head for any length of time. One study showed that half the interviewers could not accurately recall the most critical information produced in a 20-minute interview.[18] Thus, record notes or a summary of the interview immediately after its completion. One option is to use a rating in which you simply rate the applicant on various dimensions. This rating minimizes the possibility of erroneously making an early decision or letting one or two negative characteristics predominate because after the interview the interviewer reviews all the information gained during the review process. Another option is to have a routine form that reports on the same areas for each candidate interviewed. It might have a scale at the end to indicate overall rating of the candidate in relationship to the others interviewed.[19]

Another way an interviewer can ensure he has met the appropriate objectives is by writing out a series of questions before the interview. When the interview is over, the interviewer can write the responses to the questions. These written responses act as a record of the interview as well as a monitoring device to evaluate interview effectiveness.

Value of Training

This and the previous chapter both present many suggestions for improving the interview. But these are only suggestions. Training and practice increase both the reliability and validity of the interview process. Unfortunately, many managers believe that just because they have been interviewed and have conducted a few interviews, they understand the process. The employment interview is a highly concentrated, critical, and structured communication interaction requiring a strategic approach to achieve its maximum benefits. One effective training strategy is to have a practice interview videotaped and then to observe the effectiveness of both verbal and nonverbal behaviors. An easier approach is to take a few minutes after an interview to read back through the material just discussed in this chapter. Interviewers can then evaluate their own performance against the suggestions presented.

Performance Review Interviews

Placement interviews are not the only type of interviews that managers conduct. Periodically, they are called on to conduct performance appraisal interviews. Over 35 years ago, Maier cited several purposes for the performance review interview[20] and current objectives remain much the same.[21]

1. Let employees know where they stand.
2. Recognize good work.
3. Communicate to subordinates directions in which they should improve.
4. Develop employees in their present jobs.
5. Develop and train employees for higher jobs.
6. Let subordinates know the direction in which they make progress in the organization.
7. Serve as a record for assessment of the department or unit as a whole and where each person fits into the larger picture.
8. Warn certain employees that they must improve.

While the potential benefits of the performance review interview seem evident, its infrequent and ineffective use in organizations is widely recognized. This contradiction exists for several reasons, including that managers do not like to be put into the role of evaluator. Some managers may fear their working relationship with subordinates will be destroyed because of the discomfort created in both being evaluated and in evaluating.[22] Another reason may be that managers often are not adequately trained in conducting these interviews.[23] Knowledge of the following information should encourage managers to conduct performance appraisal interviews.

Purpose

The performance interview can meet two different purposes; (1) it can focus on the worker's past accomplishments or performance in an effort to determine growth, or (2) it can focus on future activities and involve setting goals that will lead to increased employee performance and development. A critical question is relevant here: Does a manager discuss goals, performance improvement, and personal development in the same interview as salary increases? Extensive review of the available research on this question makes it clear that one should not combine specific developmental topics and salary discussions in one interview. The importance of the salary review typically dominates the interview so neither the manager nor the employee is in the proper frame of mind to discuss plans for needed improvement in a positive manner.[24] Instead, two separate interviews would be more appropriate. This requires more time but generally yields a more positive response from the employee.

Types

Three types of developmental performance reviews are possible and vary according to the nature of the job and the employees.[25] Developmental appraisal interviews are used for high-performing, high-potential employees who have discretionary jobs giving them the opportunity to implement performance improvement. An accountant is an example of this type of employee, whereas an assembly operator who faces routine tasks is not.

The second type, the maintenance interview, is the most suitable for the majority of employees. Maintenance interviews are used for those who have performed at a steady, satisfactory level for some time and are not likely to improve due to constraints of ability, motivation, or the nature of their jobs. In this situation, the interviewee focuses on maintaining performance at the currently acceptable levels and on exceptions to established performance patterns.

The third type of interview, the remedial appraisal, is used for low-performing or marginal subordinates in an attempt to raise performance to acceptable levels. This category involves two processes: evaluation and development. First, evaluate the present and past performances, and then determine how they can be developed. Thus, sometimes the process is referred to as an evaluation interview and at others a performance review interview. For the sake of discussion, it is referred to here as a performance review.

Evaluation and Development

Each interview calls for a different degree of evaluation and development. More development is emphasized in the developmental and remedial interviews and more evaluation in the maintenance interview. The maintenance interview may seem to contradict the managerial notion that all people can be developed. The position taken in this discussion is that many managers become frustrated with attempts to develop subordinates who have probably reached their comfortable growth limits or are in positions that constrain further development. Exerting extensive development efforts with these employees has limited utility; it is better to exert the effort with individuals who will yield the greatest dividends.

A performance review interview does not always meet the same purpose; consequently, different communication strategies must be implemented to meet the established goals of either evaluation or development. In implementing the appropriate strategy, planning is required, just as it is in other interview formats.

Planning

In terms of the model presented in Chapter 3, the three main areas to be analyzed in the planning process are the timing, the environment, and the message—that is, when, where, and what.

Timing

Formal appraisals are most often conducted on an annual basis. But numerous cases can be cited where, although organizational policy dictates annual review interviews, the policy is not carried out by the manager. Often, managers believe the reviews serve no purpose. In other situations, logistical difficulties prohibit a manager from meeting with all subordinates. Another excuse often heard from managers is that employees know where they stand; "Why have a review?" Unfortunately, these excuses are inadequate. Set time aside to have a formal discussion with subordinates. Once a year seems to be a practical time frame; however, this should not preclude the feedback that should be provided to employees whenever needed.

Why have a formal review once a year when more frequent feedback is provided? For one thing, an annual review helps to overcome the various communication errors discussed in Chapter 2. A formal review also provides the opportunity to systematically review the possibility that different assumptions have developed between subordinates and managers. Also, the failure to discriminate—the failure to perceive and communicate significant differences between individuals or changes in situations—can be overcome by sharing concrete information during a performance interview.

The error of allness is also overcome with an effective performance interview that gives both parties a chance to appreciate one another's complexity. In this way, managers get a more accurate picture of the subordinates and establish a better communication climate. This process is more likely to be accomplished in a formal setting than in an impromptu interview; this is especially true for potentially negative information.

Also consider the receiver when analyzing the concept of time. Poor performers and new employees require more frequent reviews and appropriate feedback. Good performers require less frequent reviews. Also, certain situations, such as the completion of a major project or unusually poor performance, require formal feedback. Consider the entire situation when determining the best time for a performance interview.

Once the time is selected, inform the employee of the interview well in advance. The lead time required may vary from several hours to several weeks, depending on the employee and the type of job involved. If the employee is responsible for gathering statistics and facts regarding performance, several weeks may be required; but if the review involves a routine job and a steady performer with years of experience, a few hours may suffice. In any event, avoid the "stop by my office as soon as you get a chance" type of preparation, which deprives the employee of the opportunity to prepare psychologically for the interview.

Time spent in the interview is another consideration. Certain situations require more time than others, but both too little and too much time can affect the process. Too little time means the conversation is forced and critical points may be omitted. Too much time may mean the conversation wanders. Too much time is especially detrimental in a tense, highly volatile situation where feelings heat up and occasionally explode. It may be best to cut it short in these situations.

Environment

Once the necessary time and timing are determined, consider the best place for the interview. Managers tend to schedule the performance review interview in their own offices without realizing how potentially threatening this environment may be, especially when the subordinate is not accustomed to spending much time in the manager's office. Often, the best place for the interview is in a neutral territory where neither the subordinate nor the manager feels particularly uncomfortable. But, as with everything in communication, hard and fast rules do not always apply. If the review is being conducted with a particularly aggressive and difficult employee and deficient performance is being discussed, it may be better to garner all the leverage possible by using the manager's personal office where more power is manifested.

Wherever the interview occurs, try to guarantee complete privacy and freedom from even the most minor interruption; hold all telephone calls, and keep uninvolved persons from the area. Once isolated in the chosen room, be aware of barriers that fill the space between you and the employee. An intervening expanse of desk, especially one cluttered with papers, distances the worker physically and psychologically; side-to-side or corner seating is usually preferred.[26]

Content

Once the time and place of the interview are established, focus on the content of the session. Regardless of the specific interview purpose, review expectations and goals. To appreciate these fully, review the dimensions of the subordinate's job. As previously mentioned in the discussion on the selection interview, managers often believe they are familiar with a person's job responsibilities, but a review of the job description often provides valuable insights, even surprises. In addition to reviewing the job description, review notes from the previous performance review and recent job performance items. You may even want to solicit information from other managers who have observed the employee's performance. All these procedures allow a manager the opportunity to list specific items that must be discussed in the interview.

Give the subordinate the opportunity to prepare for the interview. One successful strategy is to give the employee a self-evaluation form before the interview. Managers can use the standard performance evaluation form or a separate form similar to that shown in Figure 12–1. If you use a positive, constructive tone of voice rather than a threatening one when asking a subordinate to complete a form, the situation is more likely to be seen as an opportunity for development than as a negative, obligatory chore.

The more opportunity an employee has to participate in the process, the greater the possibility that open and valuable communication will result. Studies show that performance appraisal discussions based on a self-review

---

FIGURE 12-1   Employee Self-Appraisal Checklist

The purpose of this form is to help you prepare for your performance review. Be ready to discuss any of your specific accomplishments or problems that have occurred since the last performance review.

Set aside some time and review your job since the last review so you can answer the following questions:

1. What are some unusually difficult problems you have solved?
2. What do you regard as your major strong points in *knowledge, skills,* or *experience*?
3. What do you regard as your weaker areas in *knowledge, skills,* or *experience*?
4. What are some working relationships you are pleased about?
5. What are some working relationships you feel need strengthening?
6. Did you carry out any special assignments with distinction or handle emergencies skillfully?
7. Is there an area where you need more help from your manager?
8. Determine one or two areas where you think you could improve something if you had the right assistance from your manager.

---

of performance are more satisfying than are those based strictly on manager-prepared appraisals.[27]

For the performance review interview to provide feedback to an employee and to establish goals, a trusting environment must be established. The next section describes the process that will lead to a trusting environment.

Process

The beginning of a performance review interview differs from a selection interview in that the parties involved already know each other and the purpose of the meeting is well established. However, it is still necessary to begin in a friendly, warm manner, and it is a good practice to state the purpose of the session to ensure mutual agreement.

Once the initial climate is established, choose one of three approaches: tell and sell, tell and listen, and problem solving.[28] The tell-and-sell approach is used to tell an employee what is expected without any discussion and then to sell the employee on the idea. Those using this style assume employees desire to correct weaknesses if they know them. Unfortunately, employees' defenses may be raised as a result, and any independent judgment on the subordinate's part may be suppressed. This style is often appropriate for the subordinate who has little knowledge about the job (such as a relatively new employee). However, the possibilities for this style are limited because most employees generally have something to say.

The second style, tell and listen, differs from the first in that it includes the element of listening. As Chapter 9 emphasizes, listening is the key skill to learning. Tell employees that they are doing a poor job, but listen to the reasons they give for such performance. The response probably indicates the cause behind the behavior.

The third strategy, problem solving, expands on the second approach. The problem-solving approach is based on the premise that two-way communication leads to a mutually acceptable plan for performance improvement. This approach allows subordinates more freedom and responsibility than the other two; however, the climate must be right for subordinates to express themselves. A manager establishes such a climate by providing a supportive environment in the appraisal process. But a supportive environment is not easy to establish because evaluation traumatizes many people. Expect employees to react defensively since a manager, in appraising a subordinate's performance, is automatically cast in the role of judge and the subordinate becomes the defendant.[29] Also, the discussion of personalities can lead to hostility and defensiveness, and in some situations, personalities will inevitably be discussed.[30]

Supportive Environment

Table 12–3 draws on Gibbs' classic work to differentiate the communication process that leads to a supportive rather than a defensive environment.[31]

TABLE 12–3 Communication Categories Characteristic of Supportive and Defensive Climates

Defensive Climate	Supportive Climate
1. Evaluative	1. Descriptive
2. Control	2. Problem orientation
3. Neutrality	3. Empathy
4. Superiority	4. Equality
5. Certainty	5. Provisionalism

Examples of communications from each of these categories assist in developing an effective communication strategy for the appraisal interview.

Evaluative	Descriptive
You simply have to stop making so many silly mistakes.	We're still getting more than three errors per run with the new system.
Betty, you're tactless and rude.	Betty, some people interpret your humor as rudeness.
You are too aggressive when dealing with co-workers.	Some employees consider you to be aggressive.
The delay was definitely your fault because you didn't follow instructions.	There seems to be some confusion about the instructions that were to be followed.
You just don't care about doing a good job.	Your work has the highest number of errors.

Evaluative versus Descriptive

Communication that blames a subordinate naturally leads to a defensive climate. Avoid statements that make moral assessments of another or that question an individual's values and motives. Descriptive communication provides specific feedback and does not judge the receiver. The above examples show the difference that might occur during a performance review interview.

Notice that the evaluative examples typically are less specific and make implications about the receiver's personality. These types of comments lead to nonproductive reactions.

Control versus Problem Orientation

Problem-oriented communication defines a mutual problem and seeks a solution. Controlling communication tries to do "something" to another person such as forcing him to change a behavior or an attitude. Controlling communication implies the receiver is doing something incorrect or even that the person is inadequate, so she must be controlled. The problem orientation conveys respect for the employee's ability to work on a problem and to formulate meaningful answers to the problem. Here are some examples of control and problem-oriented communication.

Control	Problem Oriented
Here is what you can do to reduce errors.	What do you think could be done to reduce errors?
You definitely have a problem with that project.	We've got a problem with this project.
Stop being so negative around here.	How do you think we could develop a more positive approach?
My instructions should be clear to you, so you can get back to work now.	How well do these instructions cover everything?
It looks as if the only solution is to move the typewriter to a different desk.	How do you feel about moving the typewriter to another desk?
Complete the first three reports by the 15th.	How should we schedule the reports?

The problem-oriented comments develop more opportunities for two-way communication by using open-ended questions and indicating a concern for solving the problem in a cooperative manner. Listening is also a productive by-product of the problem-solving approach.

Neutrality versus Empathy
Neutrality expresses a lack of concern for the well-being of the employee, whereas empathy shows that the manager identifies with the subordinate's problem, shares her feelings, and accepts the emotional values involved. Compare the following examples.

Neutrality	Empathy
Well, I really don't know what we can do about it.	I really can't figure out what to do. Where can we go for help?
That really isn't much of a problem.	Sounds like you're really concerned about it. Tell me more about the situation.
Everybody has had to face that at one time or another.	That can be a tough situation. I'll tell you how I've seen it handled before, and then you can give me your reaction.
I didn't know that. Oh well.	I wasn't aware of that. Let me see if I understand. . . .
Well, everyone is entitled to an opinion.	I get the feeling that we disagree. Let's discuss this further and compare viewpoints.

Managers show empathy in the appraisal interview when they are willing to listen, when they inquire how employees feel about something, and when they attempt to understand and accept the employee's feelings. Empathy cannot be developed when a person is hastily cut off from communicating any further or the listener demonstrates lack of interest in the message.

Superiority versus Equality

The less the psychological distance between the manager and the subordinate, the greater the probability of a productive assessment interview. Managers often inhibit subordinates by subtly indicating both verbally and nonverbally their superiority in position, wealth, power, intellectual ability, or even physical characteristics. Demonstrate equality by de-emphasizing differences in status (for example, don't meet in the manager's larger office), years of experience, and income levels. Following are examples of verbal communication demonstrating superiority and equality.

Superiority	Equality
After working on this kind of problem for 10 years, I know how to handle it.	This solution has worked before, so it should work here too.
I'm getting paid more than you so it is my responsibility to make this kind of decision.	It's my ultimate responsibility to make the decision, but I sure want your recommendations.
The type of problems I face shouldn't be of interest to people at your level.	I want to share with you the type of situations I'm involved with.
As a manager with higher visibility, I need to know what's going on.	I need to know what's happening so we can keep everyone informed.
The executive staff should know what's right, and this is their decision.	I want to let you know what the executive staff thought and why they made the decision they did.
I really don't have the time to get involved with these mundane problems.	I think you have the ability to work with the situation.

Managers demonstrate superiority or equality by nonverbal as well as verbal communication patterns. Sitting behind a big desk, putting your feet on the desk, looking uninterested, and acting too busy are all signs of superiority. People do not expect complete equality between a manager and subordinate, but an attempt to show superiority can only add to defensiveness and reduce two-way communication.

Certainty versus Provisionalism

This aspect of supportive communication relates highly to problem orientation versus control. Managers who emphasize certainty often phrase what they say as if the last word has been said and the decision cannot be changed. This dogmatic approach makes the employee feel that offering new ideas or a different solution is futile. Provisionalism demonstrates that a manager is willing to be challenged to arrive at the best possible solution. Provisionalism promotes enthusiasm and provides a challenge to employees, as these examples demonstrate.

Certainty	*Provisionalism*
I know what the problem is, so there isn't much reason to talk about it.	I have some ideas, but it would be good to talk about it.
I've considered all the options, so there isn't any reason to talk about it.	I've tried to think of all the options, but you can probably provide some insights.
This is the way it's going to be done.	Let's try it this way for a while and see what happens.
I want it to be absolutely completed by June 1.	What needs to be done to ensure that it's completed by June 1?

Managers are responsible for making decisions and holding subordinates to them; however, they must first listen to all sides of the situation. Provisional communication allows subordinates to participate in decisions made during the performance appraisal.

These five elements of an effective communication strategy—description, problem orientation, empathy, equality, and provisionalism—are major factors in reducing defensiveness and developing trust. Once a sense of trust has been developed, managers must provide feedback to subordinates. Providing feedback is especially difficult when it is negative. Providing feedback and developing trust are integral components of communication; one cannot be developed without the other. However, for purposes of discussion here, feedback is covered separately to show certain aspects of the process.

Providing Feedback

Clear instructions and expectations are critical in managers' efforts to provide a motivational climate. Performance evaluation gives feedback on past instructions and expectations related to the employee's past performances. The performance appraisal interview allows managers to motivate their employees to higher levels of performance through positive feedback. Subordinates can see feedback as constructive criticism rather than as negative criticism if managers keep in mind the following principles. These principles keep employees from becoming defensive and stopping listening.

1. **Identify concrete behavior.** Statements that identify specific, concrete behaviors are easier to accept than ambiguous, abstract statements. For instance, "You seem to have lost your self-confidence" is rather abstract. It is better to say, "You have not asked for any new projects since the hydraulic overhaul. I wonder if you're less sure of

yourself after all the trouble we had with that system. I'd like your reaction."

2. **Avoid inferences about motives, intents, and feelings unless you can cite specific behaviors to support these inferences.** The previous example on self-confidence deals with inference; however, the manager gives a specific reason and states it in a problem-oriented, provisional manner rather than a control, certainty manner. A statement such as, "You have lost interest in your job" is strictly an inference that does not lead to a constructive performance review interview.

3. **Focus feedback on a limited number of observable behaviors.** Employees can act on only a few feedback statements at a time. To flood people with an uncontrolled number of feedback statements at one time might only frustrate and discourage them. If one must deal with a large number of items, it is probably better to schedule several interview sessions.

4. **Time feedback to follow closely the behavior being discussed.** Immediate feedback almost always has more impact on the receiver than does delayed feedback. Accordingly, certain employees may require more than an annual review as it is difficult to relate to a specific behavior a year after its occurrence.

5. **Give feedback to help the employees rather than to make you feel better.** A manager may tell employees how he feels about their performance just to let off some steam, but such an evaluative approach is unlikely to help the employees change. Avoid giving feedback when feelings are not under control. The result in such a situation can make you feel better, but it will probably result in defensiveness from the employee.

The idea of a nondefensive environment and a positive approach to feedback may sound good in a textbook, but managers who experience difficult situations may ask, "What about the employee who receives extensive negative feedback? How can I continue to administer it in a positive environment?" Once again, the manner in which the feedback message is structured is important. Another factor to consider is that no matter how much negative feedback the situation calls for, positive comments can usually also be used; however, the once-fashionable "sandwich" approach is not necessarily recommended.

In the sandwich approach, a manager places a negative statement between two positive comments. However, most employees quickly recognize the manager's attempt to manipulate the situation; consequently, the strategy usually falls short of its intended purpose. The current recommended procedure is to dispense supportive feedback almost exclusively at the beginning of the interview. This tactic helps to establish an initial positive climate, and once aware that the manager duly appreciates past success, the subordinate becomes more receptive to a thorough analysis of those areas where room for improvement exists.[32]

Negative feedback need not be seen as criticism. In a positive climate, negative feedback can be stated in such a manner that subordinates perceive it as an opportunity for development.[33] Goal setting is a valuable process when structuring feedback in a positive manner. The following discussion points out several implications that need to be considered when establishing goals that help to build a positive climate.

Establishing Goals

The performance review interview ought to be constructive. Instead of dwelling on past failures, focus on the actions an employee can take to eliminate future performance deficiencies or continue to show improvement and development. Performance goals help to keep the focus on the future. The goals must be stated clearly so that when the manager and subordinate part, no possibility will exist for uncertainty or misunderstanding about the goals. When these goals are clear, the performance appraisal is positively related to subordinate satisfaction with the interview process.[34]

Managers clearly state objectives when they include the elements of time, quality, quantity, and priority. Consider the following example:

> During the next 60 days, you will be expected to set aside 20 minutes each day to meet with your crew and state what is expected in terms of their production and work schedules. Subordinates whose work schedules are not up to standard you will counsel on a daily basis. If your turnover rate continues to be the same, and you fail to counsel your employees, we will review your supervisory responsibilities.[35]

Notice that this activity is clearly stated: quality is stated in terms of production and work schedules; quantity is established in terms of turnover and the frequency of the meetings. These are important priorities for the supervisor because, if the conditions are not met, the supervisor could be demoted.

Frequently, managers will make vague generalizations that do not include specific conditions of time, quality, quantity, and priority. Stay away from such nonspecific phrases as:

- Reduce the number of complaints in the future. (How much of a reduction is expected? What is the "future?" Define complaint.)
- Stay on top of things better. (Although such a phrase is often heard, it is really not very specific.)
- Reduce the number of default loans. (Once again, how much of a reduction, what time span, and how important is this compared with generating more loan activity?)

- You seem to have a chip on your shoulder. Work on this. (Rather than leading to a solution, such a statement can actually create more problems.)

To ensure that the objectives or action plans are clear, write down the agreed-on activity. This allows both parties to review the statements and assure that all the meanings are mutually clear. The parties can also be sure the conditions of time, quantity, quality, and priority are included. In fact, most appraisal forms allow space for managers to record goals. But remember that clear writing is essential when recording goals.

Once the goals are established and agreed on, the manager's task is to conduct a follow-up session with the subordinate to monitor progress and problems involved in meeting the goals. These follow-up sessions may be formal or informal, but they are vital to the development of the worker and to the success of the appraisal system.

Constructive Discipline and Counseling Interviews

The performance appraisal interview is especially critical because it acts as a foundation for two other important managerial communication responsibilities: the constructive disciplinary interview and the counseling interview. Clear and positive feedback is essential in discipline, and empathy is especially important with the counseling interview. Brief comments on each of these situations follow.

Constructive Discipline

Communication during constructive discipline relates closely to the performance appraisal interview in that most of the same considerations about timing, environment, content, and process factors apply to both situations. Constructive discipline is also referred to as progressive discipline. The desired result is the same: replacement of an undesirable behavior with a desirable behavior. If constructive discipline does not meet the desired goal, the discipline must "progress."

Progressive discipline usually follows this sequence: (1) informal talk, (2) oral warning, (3) written warning, (4) layoff, and (5) discharge. Communication is important in each of these steps.

Informal Talk
When a good worker commits a minor offense, managers generally find that an informal talk clears up the situation. Here the manager simply discusses the employee's behavior and explains how it deviates from the expected standard. It is important that the intent of the discussion is clear. That is, when criticism is intended, it should be clear that it is criticism. Too often a

manager will fear offending the subordinate and phrase the comments in a way that masks the true purpose. In this situation, it is important that the manager listen and try to understand why the employee performed in such a manner. At the same time, the employee should understand that the offense should not be repeated. The manager should also express confidence in the employee's good work.

Oral Warning

The difference between an informal talk and an oral warning is not absolute, but a matter of degree. In both the informal talk and oral warning, the manager should listen to understand the facts behind the problem. One administers an oral warning because the informal discussion was not effective, so the warning needs to put more emphasis on the infraction and its consequences. If appropriate, clearly communicate each of the following to the employee:

- The exact rule violated.
- The problem caused by the broken rule.
- The kind of improvement expected.
- What will happen when the employee improves.
- What will happen if the employee does not improve.

Although negative information dominates this session, the manager should apply all the communication principles that develop a supportive environment—description, problem orientation, empathy, equality, and provisionalism. Remember to keep the focus on an *action* rather than a *person*. Communication that blames and threatens an individual at this stage of discipline generally creates a hostile reaction.

Written Warning

A written warning is the third stage of progressive discipline. An interview generally accompanies the written warning. Use the oral warning interview agenda for the written warning interview, making certain to tell the employee that a written warning is being given and will be forwarded to the employee's file. The written warning placed in the employee's file simply restates what was said in the interview. It should include nothing that was not made clear to the employee in the interview.

The written phase of progressive discipline is critical if the discipline is ineffective and the employee is ultimately discharged. While this point is discussed further in Appendix 1, two important points merit consideration here: To avoid any legal charges of discrimination when discharging an employee, a manager must (1) avoid vague and confusing language in the written warning and (2) document all performance appraisals.[36] In progressive discipline, managers need to use foresight to prevent legal difficulties.

Suspension

Some employees may not be impressed with warnings and may need a suspension without pay to convince them their behavior is a serious matter. Suspensions can last from one day to several weeks, even as long as a month, depending on the nature of the offense and the situation in which the offense occurred. A suspension is justified only if the recipient knows clearly the reason for it. To be fair and effective, the possibility of a suspension and its duration must be accurately communicated during previous phases of progressive discipline.

Discharge

Discharge is often called *industrial capital punishment*. Consequently, it is reserved for only the most serious offenses. The seriousness of this situation means such action needs to be reviewed by upper management before implementation. Be able to document your decisions. That is, be able to explain all pertinent factual details including the names of people who can verify those facts and be able to supply all relevant written materials. A strong, written case is required before discharge. Abstract or ambiguous statements lead only to confusion and possible bitterness and hostility.

General Communication Guidelines

Because progressive discipline can lead to discharge, follow these principles regardless of the stage of discipline. First, even if an infraction is serious, never lose your temper when administering discipline. Strategic communication is difficult when emotions are high. A cooling-off period is required.

A second guideline, prompt action, may seem to contradict the first principle. However, discipline, when delayed, loses much of its impact. Judgment is required to ensure that emotions are not excessively high without waiting too long to administer discipline. The third guideline to remember is that any disciplinary communication must be conducted in a private setting. A public reprimand builds needless resentment in the subordinate and in those who observed it. Contrary to what some may think, embarrassment does not help to make a point. Not only does public discipline humiliate the employee, but it hurts the morale of the entire work group. The only exception to this rule is the employee who challenges a manager's authority in front of other employees. Then the manager must act promptly and decisively to keep the respect of other employees.

Fourth, the disciplinary message must not be personal. Instead, direct it toward performance. Finally, give employees advance warning about what to expect. Every employee needs a comprehensive statement of work rules, policies, and procedures, and these statements must be carefully explained at the various stages of the progressive discipline procedure. As a result, employees know what to expect at each stage with no surprise.

When managers follow these five guidelines and maintain a positive, supportive environment, the possibility that discipline will be constructive rather than destructive increases tremendously.

Counseling Interview

The counseling interview, the final interview detailed here, differs from the performance appraisal interview only in emphasis. Counseling interviews focus on personal problems such as marriage difficulties, drugs and alcohol use, or the inability to cope with stress. Although personal problems may not have an immediate measurable impact on work performance, they can lead to serious organizational problems if unattended.

As a manager you are not expected to solve these problems, but it sometimes becomes necessary to confront the more obvious situations, lend a sympathetic ear, and know the procedures for referral to professional help where appropriate. A counseling interview demands a high degree of sensitivity, trust, and openness because extremely personal subjects are often discussed. It is not surprising that many managers prefer to ignore subordinates' personal problems, as if to say, "That's not my problem," when, in fact, it is.[37] Employee behaviors that would call for initial counseling include:

- A secretary starts to use abusive language, accusing the office staff of sinful behavior as she exhorts her fellow workers to adopt her religious beliefs.
- A manager makes abusive remarks to employees in the hall and refuses to communicate with anyone.
- An experienced, high-powered attorney begins to spend several hours a day sitting at his desk reading newspapers.

These behaviors challenge managers, but you can help by listening, by giving empathetic responses, and by providing guidance. Comprehensive books thoroughly outline counseling strategies, but you are not expected to be a professional counselor; rather, you should provide an environment that allows people to express their concerns freely. Doing so should improve the quality of their problem solving.[38] Use the communication skills discussed throughout this book: understanding communication strategies and styles, listening, questioning, summarizing, and encouraging. Of course, when a problem is more complex than you can handle, refer the subordinate to a professional counselor.

Summary

All managers conduct employment, performance appraisal, disciplinary, and selective counseling interviews during their careers; consequently, they need to be aware of several aspects of each of these interviews. The employment interview requires planning to ensure the manager clearly understands the job for which the applicant is being interviewed. Legal concerns are unique during the employment interview, so it is necessary to be aware of the general guidelines for lawful and unlawful pre-employment inquiries.

An appropriate questioning strategy is important, and the manager can draw on a large number of potential questions to evaluate the applicants' motivation, education, experience, and so forth. The important point is that each type of question has a specific purpose. The most common errors to avoid in the employment interview are making premature decisions about the applicant, talking too much rather than listening, and keeping inadequate records.

Performance appraisal interviews are critical for a number of reasons; unfortunately, they are often not conducted or are ineffective. The effectiveness can be increased by scheduling the interview at the appropriate time, conducting it in the correct place, and discussing relevant topics.

Strategic communication is essential when appraising performance; otherwise, defensive behavior may be aroused in the subordinate. Strategic communication allows the manager to develop a supportive, nondefensive environment that encourages a problem-solving approach. This communication should contain messages that are descriptive, problem oriented, empathetic, equal, and provisional. These characteristics should also be present in interviews giving feedback or setting goals.

Feedback in the interview is most valuable when concrete behaviors are identified and inferences avoided. Time feedback so it closely follows the behavior and focus on a limited number of behaviors. Clearly stated objectives include the elements of time, quality, quantity, and priority.

Constructive discipline contains many of the same elements as the performance appraisal interview. A progressive discipline sequence is the most successful, with both written and oral communication important elements along the way.

The counseling interview is the final form of interview discussed in this chapter. Counseling interviews focus on personal problems and, thus, require a high degree of sensitivity, trust, and openness. When the subordinate's problem is complex, he should be referred to a professional counselor.

Endnotes

1. Terry L. Leap and Michael D. Crino, *Personnel/Human Resource Management* (New York: Macmillan, 1989), p. 245.
2. Michael E. Stano and N. O. Reinsch, Jr., *Communication in Interviews* (Englewood Cliffs, N.J.: Prentice Hall, 1982), p. 121.
3. Michael M. Harris, "Reconsidering the Employment Interview: A Review of Recent Literature and Suggestions for Future Research," *Personnel Psychology* 42, no. 4 (1989), pp. 691–726.

4. *1986 Guidebook to Fair Employment Practices* (Chicago: Commerce Clearing House, Inc., 1986).

5. Jeanne C. Poole and E. Theordore Kautz, "An EEO - AA Program That Exceeds Quotas—It Targets Biases," *Personnel Journal*, January 1987, p. 103.

6. James R. Redeker, "The Supreme Court on Affirmative Action: Conflicting Opinions," *Personnel*, October 1986, p. 8.

7. Terry L. Leap and Larry R. Smeltzer, "Racial Remarks in the Workforce: Humor or Harassment?" *Harvard Business Review*, November–December 1984, p. 74.

8. "Employment Discrimination: A Recent Perspective from the 'Burger Court'," *Industrial Management*, September–October 1986, p. 3.

9. Richard D. Arvey and Robert H. Faley, *Fairness in Selecting Employees*, 2nd ed. (Reading, Mass.: Addison-Wesley Publishing, 1988).

10. John Langdale and Joseph Weitz, "Estimating the Influence of Job Information on Interviewer Agreement," *Journal of Applied Psychology* 57, no. 1 (1973), pp. 23–27.

11. Charles J. Stewart and William B. Cash, Jr., *Interviewing: Principles and Practices* (Dubuque, Iowa: Wm C. Brown, 1982), p. 133.

12. Fredric M. Jablin and Vernon D. Miller, "Interviewer and Applicant Questioning Behavior in Employment Interviews," *Management Communication Quarterly* 4, no. 1 (1990), pp. 51–86.

13. Donna Bogar Goodall and H. Lloyd Goodall, Jr., "The Employment Interview: A Selective Review of the Literature with Implications for Communication Research," in *Readings in Organizational Communication*, ed. Kevin L. Hutchinson (Dubuque, Iowa: Wm C. Brown, 1992), pp. 372–82.

14. John Hatfield, "Nonverbal Cues in the Selection Interview," *Personnel Administrator*, January 1978, pp. 30–33.

15. Loren Falkenberg, "Improving the Accuracy of Stereotypes Within the Workplace," *Journal of Management* 16, no. 1 (March 1990), pp. 107–18.

16. K. J. Williams, A. S. DeNisi, B. M. Meglino, and T. P. Cafferty, "Initial Decisions and Subsequent Performance Ratings," *Journal of Applied Psychology* 71, no. 2 (1986), pp. 189–95.

17. C. W. Anderson, "The Relation Between Speaking Times and Decision in the Employment Interview," *Journal of Applied Psychology* 44, (1960), pp. 267–68.

18. R. E. Carlson, D. P. Schwab, and H. G. Henneman III, "Agreement Among Selection Interview Styles," *Journal of Industrial Psychology* 5, no. 1 (1970), pp. 8–17.

19. M. E. Giffin, "Personnel Research on Testing, Selection, and Performance Appraisal," *Public Personnel Management* 18 (1989), pp. 127–37.

20. R. F. Maier, *The Appraisal Interview: Objectives, and Skills* (New York: John Wiley & Sons, 1958), p. 3.

21. Robert D. Bretz, Jr., George T. Milkovich, and Walter Read, "The Current State of Performance Appraisal Research and Practice: Concerns, Directions, and Implications," *Journal of Management* 18, no. 2 (June 1992), pp. 321–52.

22. R. M. Glen, "Performance Appraisal: An Unnerving Yet Useful Process," *Public Personnel Management* 19, no. 1 (1990), pp. 1–10.

23. B. Dugan, "Effects of Assessor Training on Information Use," *Journal of Applied Psychology* 73 (1988), pp. 743–48; Timothy M. Downs, "Predictions of Communication Satisfaction During Performance Appraisal Interviews," *Management Communication Quarterly* 3, no. 13 (1990), pp. 334–54.

24. Stano and Reinsch, *Communication in Interviews*, p. 101.
25. L. L. Cummings and C. P. Schwab, "Designing Appraisal Systems for Information Yield," *California Management Review* 20, no. 1 (1978), pp. 18–25.
26. W. E. Beveridge, *The Interview in Staff Appraisal* (London: Allen & Unwin, 1975), p. 57.
27. B. E. Becker and R. J. Klimoski, "A Field Study of the Relationship Between the Organizational Feedback Environment and Performance," *Personnel Psychology* 42, no. 3 (1989), pp. 343–58.
28. Maier, *Appraisal Interview*, p. 22.
29. C. Lee, "Poor Performance Appraisals Do More Harm Than Good," *Personnel Journal*, September 1989, pp. 91–97.
30. Stano and Reinsch, *Communication in Interviews*, p. 109.
31. Jack R. Gibb, "Defensive Communication," *Journal of Communication*, September 1961, pp. 141–48.
32. Douglas Cederblom, "The Performance Appraisal Interview: A Review, Implications, and Suggestions," in *Readings in Organizational Communication*, ed. Kevin L. Hutchinson (Dubuque, Iowa: Wm C. Brown, 1992), pp. 310–21.
33. Douglas Cederblom, "The Performance Appraisal Interview: A Review, Implications, and Suggestions," *Academy of Management Review* 7, no. 2 (1982), pp. 219–27.
34. M. M. Greller, "Evaluation of Feedback Sources as a Function of Role and Organizational Level," *Journal of Applied Psychology* 65, no. 1 (1980), pp. 24–27.
35. Judith Hale, "Communication Skills in Performance Appraisal," *Industrial Management*, no. 22 (March–April 1980), p. 19.
36. "Performance Appraisal Systems: An Empirical Study," *Personnel Journal*, September 1976, pp. 457–59.
37. John H. Meyer and Teresa C. Meyer, "The Supervisor as Counselor—How to Help the Distressed Employee," *Management Review*, April 1982, p. 44.
38. Norman C. Hill, *Counseling at the Workplace* (New York: McGraw-Hill, 1981), p. 3.

Additional Readings

Alder, Ronald B. *Looking Out, Looking In.* Orlando, Fla.: Holt, Rinehart and Winston, Inc., 1990.
Beigeleisien, J. L. *Make Your Job Interview a Success.* Englewood Cliffs, N.J.: Prentice Hall, 1987.
Hergenrather, Edmund. "The 13 Most Critical Interviewing Mistakes," *National Business Employment Weekly*, June 3, 1990, p. 9.
Krannich, Caryl Rae, and Ronald L. Krannich. *Interview for Success.* Manassas, Va.: Impact Publications, 1988.
Robinett, Judy M. "Advice to Interviewees: Hide Your Fatal Flaws," *National Business Employment Weekly*, September 17, 1990, pp. 9–10.

Discussion Questions

1. Why separate the last incumbent of the position from the job itself when reviewing the nature of the job?

2. Explain how the time and timing are important in the selection interview.

3. What is meant by BFOQ? Explain the assertion that there is no such thing as a legal or illegal question.

4. How does each of the three possible goals for an employment interview affect the communication strategy in the interview?

5. How can an interviewer avoid premature decisions?

6. Why should the interviewer emphasize listening rather than talking? How can this be achieved?

7. Discuss the three main planning components of the performance review interview.

8. List the communication categories that lead to a defensive climate; then list the supportive categories. Give an example of each category.

9. List some ways not mentioned in this chapter in which a manager may express superiority through nonverbal means.

10. What elements are needed to make feedback effective?

11. What is the "sandwich" approach to feedback? What is wrong with this approach? Give an alternative approach.

12. List several important considerations when communicating objectives. Give an example of an objective.

13. Why is a progressive system important to constructive discipline? Explain the progressive discipline system and the communication elements involved.

14. Explain the statement, "Discuss the action, not the person."

15. How does the counseling interview differ from the performance interview?

CASE 12–1
MOTIVATION AND THE PERFORMANCE REVIEW

Rex Jones has worked diligently for the same supervisor during the past three years in the accounting department of a local bank. During the period, he has never been reprimanded for any of the work he has done. In fact, only recently, he received his first, supposedly annual, performance review. Although he has received a raise in each of the two prior years, this was the first time he had been formally evaluated. The first year he received a slip of paper stating the amount of his raise from his boss as they crossed paths in the hall. The next year, his boss did not even contact him concerning a raise. Rather, Jones had to figure it out for himself from his paycheck stub.

After sitting through his first formal evaluation, Jones is stunned. His boss informed him his work effort is just average and he does not always show enough motivation in the tasks he undertakes. This is the most the boss has said to Jones concerning his work since Jones began working there over three years ago.

Jones' boss works on important matters alone in his office and shuts himself off from his employees' activities. Some of Jones' fellow workers see this as a sign the boss has faith in them to get the job done and to accept responsibilities on their own. But Jones believes his boss is just avoiding responsibility and is not interested in involving himself with his employees. Jones believes his boss thinks, "I've got my own problems, so don't come to me with yours."

Jones has healthy working relationships with several other supervisors in the bank, and they all have told him more than once that his performance is above average. Because of this, Jones feels hurt that his boss would call him "average." As far as motivation goes, Jones does not see what there is to be motivated about. He never receives rewards, verbal or otherwise, at the time that he does good work. Consequently, he is confused about what levels of effort and performance will lead to the recognition he feels he deserves.

Questions

1. What can the supervisor do to alleviate Jones' confusion? Be specific.
2. What can the supervisor do to get the most out of his performance evaluations?
3. What are some possible reasons that Jones' supervisor has not interviewed Jones in the past?
4. What, if anything, can Jones do to increase the flow of feedback from his supervisor?

CASE 12–2
A COUNSELING DILEMMA

Lance Leiter has worked as a registered nurse at a local chemical dependency treatment facility for about four months. He is still in the standard six-month probationary period for new employees; thus, his work performance has been carefully monitored. His behavior with patients shows an erratic pattern. Although no concrete data exist, the nursing supervisor believes Leiter may suffer from a personal chemical abuse problem.

The supervisor has decided to approach Leiter with the following observations. First, Leiter has demonstrated mood swings at work and does not consistently maintain a professional demeanor with the patients. He frequently utilizes the time spent with patients to discuss his personal problems and is, thus, not fulfilling the professional role of a registered nurse. Leiter also initiates discussions concerning his own home environment during therapeutic group sessions in a manner that demonstrates questionable motivation. Is he trying to help the patients, or is he seeking help for himself?

In addition, Leiter has received numerous phone calls during working hours from his estranged wife. After each call, he becomes morose and seeks advice and reassurance from other staff members. The nursing supervisor believes Leiter is using the treatment center as an indirect way to get professional help for himself and feels that Leiter's unsatisfactory work performance must not be allowed to continue.

The supervisor plans to conduct a counseling interview this afternoon. She intends to offer Leiter the services of the institution's Employee Assistance Program. If Leiter chooses not to accept a personal therapeutic program, the supervisor plans to sever his employment with the unit.

The supervisor wonders if she has prepared enough relevant data and is contemplating the best way to develop a sensitive, trusting environment for the interview. She wants to establish an empathetic climate that will encourage Leiter.

Questions

1. Discuss strategies that might be used to develop a supportive environment.
2. What are some general communication skills the supervisor should consider before conducting the interview?
3. What recommendations would you make for choosing the environment, timing, and content of this upcoming counseling interview?
4. Which element in Question 3 is more important to this case? Why?

13 GROUP DYNAMICS AND MEETINGS

After three years as a hospital maintenance supervisor in a 150-bed hospital, you just took a job as the maintenance manager in a 400-bed urban hospital. Not only is the hospital larger, but you will also be responsible for housekeeping and security. You have no previous experience in these areas. Unfortunately, you joined the hospital during the budget planning period, so you will have to meet with the appropriate people and start to plan your budget. This is going to be difficult because you do not know the people or understand the hospital budgeting process, and you know little about the functions in several of the departments. A series of meetings with the appropriate people is needed. What type of leadership should you use in these meetings? How many people should be in any one meeting? What is the best way to get people to participate in the meetings? What if conflict develops?

Meetings are a permanent organizational process that will probably grow in number and importance. Their need lies in the complexity and interdependence of tasks, which make it difficult for one person to have the knowledge to make decisions and solve problems in today's organizations. The contemporary regulatory environment illustrates this interdependence and high cost of decisions. Governmental regulations on how and what an industry can do often require that lawyers, industrial relations managers, tax specialists, and governmental relations experts discuss ideas before a decision is made.

Managers use meetings for several functions: informational, fact-finding, or problem-solving and decision-making. While a meeting may be termed staff, marketing, committee, ad hoc, or whatever, the actual meeting is designed to present information, obtain facts, solve a problem, or it may be a combination of all three.

Management uses informational meetings to tell employees about important new decisions, about company activities, or to persuade them to perform a desired task. The essential aim is to communicate a company point of view and have it accepted by employees. Such meetings succeed when they get the employees to identify their own interests with the company's.

Management conducts fact-finding meetings when it uses the expertise of several employees at the same time to obtain facts for planning and decision making. For example, a sales manager may call in all his sales representatives to find out about such matters as business conditions, competition, customer desires, and complaints. A production manager having trouble with a specific operation might meet with all the key people who have knowledge of a situation.

In problem-solving and decision-making meetings, employees pool their specialized expertise with the objective of developing a solution. This meeting goes beyond simply finding facts; it seeks to identify the issues and to discuss the probable gains and losses resulting from alternate actions.

Meetings are a way of managerial life; however, managers must use meetings prudently to maximize their benefits and minimize their costs.

The Group: Advantages and Disadvantages

Whether participating in a group or organizing one, managers should be aware of advantages and disadvantages to groups.

Advantages of the Group

One advantage is that a group decision may be of a higher quality than that made by an individual. But, before using a group, you must analyze the nature of the problem. Groups are better at solving problems for which there is no single correct solution or for which solutions are difficult to verify objectively.[1] Such problems require decisions that cannot be programmed. Nonprogrammed decisions are the result of infrequent situations that require creativity, insight, and sharing of ideas and perspectives on a problem.[2] Groups bring a greater variety of information and a wider choice of solutions.

A second advantage to a group is that when members have had an opportunity for discussion, they are more likely to be committed to the information presented or the decision made. In other words, they become "owners" of the decision. A classic study conducted by Coch and French over 45 years ago investigated workers' resistance to technological changes in their jobs. When workers participated in discussions regarding implementation of the changes, significantly less resistance resulted than that which occurred among workers excluded for such participation.[3] Each employee who participated in the meeting had increased ownership of the outcome, and the responsibility felt for making the solution or program work was enhanced.

Another advantage of a group meeting is that it may reduce the chance of communication problems. When a group of people hears the same message at the same time, the possibility of misinterpretation declines. Participants' questions can clarify the message, and each participant has the opportunity to hear the answer and ask additional questions. Feedback is increased and timing is reduced as a barrier to communication.

Disadvantages of the Group

Richard Hall put it well when he noted the "time spent on meetings is time not spent on other activities."[4] While the hourly cost of a meeting in terms of the base pay of the participants is already high, to determine the real cost, one must add payroll taxes, fringe benefits, and general overhead. The base pay would probably need to be doubled to determine the actual cost. Next time you attend a staff meeting, make a rough estimate of the expenses involved using Table 13–1 to help you.

Meeting costs often go unnoticed because they are not budget line items. Meetings are a hidden cost that can either impede or improve the effectiveness of a work group.

In addition to high cost as a disadvantage, the group may develop low-quality decisions. Pressures to conform, premature decisions, hidden agendas, extensive conflict, disruptive and dominant individuals, lack of planning, and poor leadership in the meeting can easily reduce effectiveness.[5] Later in this chapter we detail these factors and techniques for managing them.

A common disadvantage of meetings is their frequent overuse. Organizations often develop a "meeting" style of management. Management must meet for every little thing. Meetings generally are not necessary for routine or repetitive programmed decisions that can be handled by an established procedure. Unfortunately, meetings are too frequently used for programmed decisions. Overuse of meetings may cause employees to find them a nuisance so they avoid involvement if possible. Consequently, employees may miss

---

TABLE 13–1 **Estimate of the Hourly Cost of Meetings**

Annual Salary	Cost According to Number of Participants						
	10	9	8	7	6	5	4
$50,000	$481	$433	$385	$337	$288	$240	$192
40,000	353	346	308	269	231	192	154
30,000	288	260	231	202	173	144	115
25,000	240	216	192	168	144	120	96
20,000	192	173	154	135	115	98	77

truly important meetings or be unable to distinguish between a critical and a useless meeting and thus be psychologically ill-prepared for involvement.

Another problem is that the weekly staff meeting might become useless if the group is not required to gather facts before the meeting, make decisions at the meeting, or present information. The manager must analyze each meeting to determine need. Still another often useless meeting pattern finds the manager telling a group about a new event or presenting a progress report without providing an opportunity for questions or interactions. Those attending the session will not see the meeting as an opportunity for participation; as a result, it may be more difficult to get these same employees to participate later when participation is critical. Clearly, when a meeting can provide no meaningful interaction, it may be better to share information through a written report rather than a meeting.

Groupthink

After extensive analysis, Irving Janis wrote a book titled *Victims of Groupthink*.[6] Groupthink is the tendency of a group to conform to ideas simply because the general sense of the group has moved in a particular direction and the members of the group feel committed to continue in the same line of thought. Although the group may be pursuing an incorrect conclusion, the group does not alter direction for fear of offending a group member. It is the extreme form of cohesiveness and is especially likely when a group has a high sense of teamwork and desire for consensus or harmony.

Because groupthink has the advantage of harmony and cohesiveness, but the disadvantage of continuing toward a poor problem solution, it is given a special section in our discussion. But groupthink is especially important because of its potential disastrous effects. Some say the disaster of the space shuttle Challenger was a result of groupthink,[7] and many other disasters are partially attributed to groupthink.[8]

Based on Janis' concept, Von Bergen and Kirk describe symptoms of groupthink that managers should watch for.[9]

1. The illusion that everyone in the group holds the same viewpoint with an emphasis on team play.
2. The belief that the group can make no mistakes.
3. The belief that disagreements are to be avoided, faulty assumptions are not questioned, and personal doubts must be suppressed in favor of group harmony.
4. The tendency to comfort one another and to ignore or at least discount warnings that an agreed-on plan is either unworkable or highly unlikely to succeed.
5. The tendency to direct pressure on any dissenting group member who expresses strong challenges to the consensus opinion of the group.

6. The presence of inordinate optimism that predisposes members to take excessive risks.

When in a decision-making meeting, the effective manager is alert to groupthink symptoms and takes appropriate action. Or more appropriately, she takes actions to ensure that groupthink does not develop. Three actions help to avoid the tendency toward groupthink:

1. *Do not make an early decision.* Do not commit early or become locked into a position early in the problem analysis. When a manager begins a discussion by saying, "This is what I would like to see," or "This is the best solution . . . but I would like your comments," he is probably closing the opportunity for an open discussion and is setting the stage for an early unanimous decision.

2. *Be open to criticism.* This is easy to say but difficult to do. All are sensitive to what they consider to be a good idea, so they tend to defend it. Criticism of an idea should not be taken as criticism of another's self-worth. When criticism cannot arise within the group, it may be solicited from an outsider who will generally be less susceptible to status and conformity pressures. One need not always adhere to the criticism of an outsider, but even the process of discounting the information can be valuable.

3. *Use a "devil's advocate."* One member of the group voluntarily takes a viewpoint opposed to that expressed by the group. This will ensure that the group members review different alternatives. This procedure is the most effective when other members are clear that the dissenter is playing the advocate role; otherwise, they may consider the person to be an agitator who should be avoided rather than listened to. Also, the same person should not play the devil's advocate role in every meeting. Constantly stating opposing viewpoints not only puts pressure on the person, but also may result in a negative image of the individual.

Ample evidence is available that groupthink can be detrimental to managers; however, research indicates the techniques presented here are successful in controlling groupthink.[10]

A Series of Strategic Considerations

Meetings have advantages as well as disadvantages and groupthink adds to their complexity. But similar to many other types of managerial communication, no concrete guidelines can assure universal success. However, the following discussion of six strategic considerations, which are listed in Table 13–2, is provided to assist managers when considering the various contingencies.

TABLE 13–2 Strategic Considerations for Meetings

---

1. Should we meet
2. Premeeting arrangements
3. Leadership style
4. Meeting format
5. Managing disruptions
6. Follow-up

Strategic Consideration 1: Should We Meet?

"Maybe we should get together and talk about it," or "Let's call a meeting." These common lines often should be analyzed more thoroughly than they are. A manager who fears making a decision may request a meeting, or she may want to show others that she has the power to call people together, or she may merely want to be the center of attention. At the same time, people may attend a meeting for purely social or recreational reasons—as an opportunity to get away from the desk, to visit with Bill from accounting about the football game, or to be seen with some influential decision makers. Thus, although a meeting is at times an effective managerial tool, at other times a meeting may be detrimental. A key issue is whether or not a brief informal group conversation may be better than a formal meeting. A good way to handle the former is to hold the meeting with everybody standing up.[11] One way to encourage standing is by intentionally failing to include enough chairs for everybody or even removing the chairs. In this way, one benefits from some of the advantages of the group while avoiding the disadvantages.

Once having settled on conducting a formal meeting, the manager must attend to the premeeting arrangements.

Strategic Consideration 2: Premeeting Arrangements

Premeeting arrangements fit into three categories: determining whom to include, preparing the agenda and other appropriate materials, and arranging the physical environment.

Whom to Include

Before settling on whom to include, settle on a manageable group size. Remember the guideline that increasing the size limits the extent to which individuals want to communicate. Research shows that as a group grows, communication becomes distorted and stress between members increases. However, a decrease in group size may also be dysfunctional. Thus, small groups may engage in superficial discussion and avoid controversial subjects.

Members of small groups may be too tense, passive, tactful, or constrained to work together in a satisfying manner. They fear alienating one another.[12] Clearly, the group must have the needed skills or background to resolve the problem.[13]

So what is large, or small, or is there an ideal size? That depends on the purpose of the meeting, so no absolute numbers can be presented. The most important thing to remember is that the group membership should reflect the organizational members the problem affects. For instance, if the concern is a departmental one, then members of the department should be involved. If the problem is shared by two departments, group membership obviously should be drawn from both areas. When possible, membership should also include people with authority to grant organizational sanction to the group and provide the means to follow through on the chosen action with time, personnel, and financial resources. When necessary, then, group membership should reflect a cross section of people in the organization affected by the issues.

In addition, consider participants' potential functions within the group. When scheduling a problem-solving meeting, include employees who are versed in the different aspects of the problem. Also, include people who will actually carry out the solution to ensure implementation of the decision. Thus, the presence of knowledgeable people improves the quality of a decision, while including implementers improves the acceptance of the decision.

But the question of ideal size remains unanswered. What is the ideal size? Filley, who has conducted extensive research on work groups, believes the optimum size is generally about five. But when the problem is more complex, relatively larger groups—as large as 12 to 13 members—have proved more effective. But relatively smaller groups are often faster and more productive. Although it is always dangerous to generalize, five members is a good starting point before considering various contingencies.[14]

Most of the research deals with decision-making groups; however, if the purpose of a meeting is to inform a group of employees and provide an opportunity for questions, much larger sizes are possible. But size limitations still hold. Generally, the larger the group, the less inclined an individual group member is to ask questions to ensure accurate communication.

Sometimes, it may not be possible to limit the size of the group to five or seven employees. In such cases, a manager could break the large group into smaller subgroups. The improved decision or more accurate sharing of information may justify the time and effort required to coordinate several groups.

Determine What Materials to Prepare and Circulate in Advance
The agenda may be the first thing that comes to mind when considering materials for a meeting. More than a list of the meeting topics, the agenda is the foundation or working paper from which the meeting operates. As the cliche says, "What gets scheduled gets done." Consequently, the agenda

deserves the manager's special consideration. Careful planning is half the battle. However, be sure to follow the agenda during the meeting. When others try to introduce new elements during the meeting, refer back to the written agenda.[15]

Regardless of the type of meeting, the agenda needs to communicate the what, why, when, and who (the Ws) of a meeting. Frequently, one or several of the elements of an agenda are often omitted, yet each is important.

What

People first need to know the what, the topic under discussion, so they may understand exactly what is to be discussed. Let the agenda make this clear. A topic listed as "Maintenance" will not communicate as fully as one that reads, "Maintenance Status of the Emergency Generator." A more complete description enables participants to gather any special information or prepare questions relevant to the discussion.

Everyone knows that agendas are important, but it is not uncommon to attend meetings with no agenda. Maybe the extra effort of an agenda seems unjustified, or the lack of an agenda may merely reflect a lack of planning. It may also be that agendas are not the common practice in many companies. Agendas are often not needed in small informal meetings where two or three employees get together or when one obvious topic is the only point for discussion. However, some managers assume agendas are never needed for small meetings. Agendas require planning and time—two assets that ineffective managers rarely possess. Many managers would rather spend additional time in a poorly conducted meeting than take the time to plan. In many cases, a manager may wish to solicit input on the agenda from members. In these cases, it should be done in a systematic way to ensure orderly input. Few leaders like surprises at meetings.

Why

People attending a meeting need to know its goal. Describe this clearly so participants can prepare for it in different ways. Also, a clearly stated goal may reduce anxiety among participants. When people do not know why they are attending a meeting, apprehension arises.

When

Setting the time involves several strategic factors. First, what time of day is best for all the participants? A quick review of the organization may indicate that the first thing in the morning is bad if many other activities are competing for attention, whereas immediately after lunch may be a difficult time for people to maintain their alertness. Second, how long should the meeting last? If a meeting schedule does not allow sufficient time, critical issues may receive superficial coverage. But remember that people value time highly and resent its waste or misuse.

A standard time limit that applies to all meetings is impossible to set. The length of a meeting depends on the subject; however, some ground rules on length are possible. The most effective meetings last no longer than one and a half hours. At that length, a meeting may already be bordering on diminishing returns. After this long, people need to break for coffee or fresh air. Short, single goals can be met in less than an hour, and this should be the time span a manager aims for. Too often, meetings go on and on because no one has established definite time parameters.

"When" applies to the appropriate time to send out the agenda as well. The purpose of the agenda and any supporting material is lost if none of it arrives until the last minute. Neither should one send the materials with so much lead time that the participants forget about it. A rule of thumb is that the longer a meeting is (and, consequently, the more scheduling and preparation required by the participants), the greater the lead time required for the agenda and supporting materials. Yet, avoid too long a lead time, which could lead to forgetfulness.

Who

It is not a mere courtesy to inform the participants about the others who will be at the meeting. This knowledge allows the participants to complete their own audience analysis. Knowing who else will be present lets the participants prepare any material or information that others in the meeting may request.

A list of attendees also forces the meeting manager to think about possible group dynamics. For instance, will a verbally dominate person attempt to control the group? Will the correct mix of expertise be present? Is the correct number of people invited? Answers to these questions can influence the outcomes.

Attach Relevant Material

Sometimes it is advisable to include important material with agendas so the participants may study it beforehand. But often participants fail to study the materials. Few things are more frustrating than assuming participants will prepare, only to find out they have not even reviewed the material. The key is to get the participants' attention on the material, hold their attention until they have reviewed the material, and then hope they retain the information at least until the meeting. To meet this objective,

- Determine what material is the most important and of greatest interest to the participants.
- Limit the amount of information. If too much material is included, the mere volume will likely discourage a busy employee from studying any of it.
- Tell the participants why it is important to them that they review the material.
- Make clear and precise references to the material in the agenda to ensure the recipients know the purpose of the attachments.

- Indicate what the participants should obtain by reviewing the material. (It is always easier to find something when one knows what to look for.)

Physical Facilities

Once the participants have been selected, and the agenda, along with any supporting material, has been distributed, a question arises: Where is the best place to hold the meeting? What physical arrangements must be considered? Physical surroundings are important. Just as the game of golf is more enjoyable (and scores improve) on a well-groomed course, the same is true for meetings conducted in well-arranged facilities. A few simple guidelines will help to make a meeting productive:

- Use a room where the chairs and tables can be arranged to meet group needs.
- Match the size of the room with the size of the group. Meetings held in close, cramped rooms with the members jammed together around narrow tables make for an unpleasant conversational climate and hamper decision making. Tension, a prime breeder of conflict, builds in a closed-in and uncomfortable meeting room. At the same time, however, a room seating 45 can be cold and overwhelming to a group of 5.
- Check for comfortable chairs, ventilation, and lighting. Remember, though, that soft, overly comfortable chairs can affect concentration.
- Make sure space exists for visual aids if they are to be used. If you know you will be needing equipment, writing materials, and so on, be sure they are available. Keep the audience in mind. Thus, providing place cards may be useful if the participants are strangers.
- Above all, arrange to have the meeting in a meeting room since it will create an environment that emphasizes the participants are coming together for specific purpose at a specific time. The atmosphere created is one of urgency and seriousness, which helps keep the meeting on the topic. Also, the mere knowledge that the meeting is to be held in a designated room avoids the looseness and lack of preparation common in the "meet in my office" arrangement.

Seating Arrangements

After designating the appropriate facility for the meeting, managers should consider which of several possible seating arrangements to use. Depending on the situation, more than one arrangement may be possible; however, a few arrangements should also be avoided. The first arrangement to avoid is the long, narrow table that makes it nearly impossible for all participants to see one another. Eye contact can be used to gain attention or control a participant; consequently, such a seating arrangement works against the leader's attempts to use all the nonverbal techniques available.

A second arrangement to avoid is one that divides up sides. For instance, if two groups are in natural opposition (for example, cost accounting and production), they should not be put on opposite sides of the table. When opponents line up on opposite sides of the table, what could be more natural than a battle? The participants may believe strength lies in numbers, and the resultant united front may promote rigidity and entrenchment in preconceived ideas. Similarly, one should keep two hostile participants apart or in such a position they cannot easily see each other. The space between argumentative members will help the leader exert control.

Several seating arrangements lend themselves to effective meetings: the table with the leader at one end, the round table or circle, and the U shape.[16] When the leader sits at one end of the table, control of the meeting is easier to obtain because all communication will tend to flow toward the head. However, this arrangement loses effectiveness with a group larger than six or seven participants. As groups get larger, communication among individual members rather than among the entire group tends to increase, and eye contact is difficult to maintain.

When the size of the meeting becomes larger, to 10 or 12 members, a U-shaped arrangement is preferred. The manager sitting in the middle of the U can maintain eye contact with all the participants; at the same time, communication among subunits of the group is less likely.

The manager using the round table or circle arrangement has less direct control of the group than with other arrangements. Because the manager has a less dominant position, participants tend to address each other rather than the leader. A table is, in a sense, a kind of communication line, as the contour of the table establishes the flow of communication. Thus, the round table is best when seeking a true participative form of decision making and trying to minimize status differences. Figure 13–1 illustrates the different arrangements.

Whatever the seating arrangement, participants see the end of the room containing the easel or blackboard as the "business end" of the room. Thus,

FIGURE 13–1

Seating Arrangement

a manager should arrange the room so these presentation aids are near the manager or leader. More will be said about the use of the easel and blackboard when discussing the control of disruptions.

The use of visual aids is an important component of the physical arrangement, but each type of visual aid (flip charts, slides, overhead projectors) has definite advantages and disadvantages. It is advisable to review the material on visual aids in the chapter on oral presentations before using visual aids in a meeting.

In review, the three major types of premeeting arrangements require analysis: whom to include, what materials to prepare and circulate before the meeting, and what physical setting to use. The appropriate answers to these questions do not guarantee an effective meeting, but strategic analysis in these areas will help a manager prepare.

Strategic Consideration 3: Select an Appropriate Leadership Style

The problems facing organizations are so varied and complex that no one style of leadership suits all situations. Consequently, a manager must be flexible and diagnose the situation to determine the appropriate leadership behavior from one meeting to another. The leadership style may be either group or leader centered. With the leader-centered style, the leader tightly controls the agenda and group communication by frequently interrupting others and making concluding statements. With a group-centered style, the group members are given much more freedom in the direction they choose to take the discussion.

When diagnosing the situation to determine the most effective style, managers need to consider three factors: the group, the objective of the meeting, and the type of leadership behavior with which the manager personally feels most comfortable.[17] Figure 13–2 on the next page shows how these three factors operate together.

Each group differs but needs a leader with some degree of interpersonal orientation; therefore, tight control is generally inappropriate. Less control is required when the group is mature and knows the topic, whereas a new or immature group needs a leader who provides more control and direction.

A routine or structured decision-making meeting may call for more leader control and task orientation, but for a solution to an abstract problem, or one requiring a creative solution, a democratic or more laissez-faire approach may be required. A highly emotional task requires less control, while more control may be best for a nonsensitive topic.

Finally, a manager must be aware of the type of leadership behavior with which she is personally most comfortable. This awareness helps a manager to monitor her own behavior and remain flexible rather than use the same behavior repeatedly. Unfortunately, many managers use the behavior with which they are the most comfortable, even when the situation requires an adjustment.

FIGURE 13–2

Determining Leadership Style

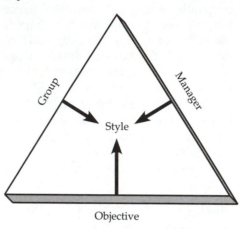

Strategic Consideration 4: Select a Meeting Format

A diagnosis of the task, group, and personal preference will help to determine the leadership style as well as the appropriate format or approach for the meeting. A formal plan is essential. Do not fall into the trap of believing that once the participants are together, everything will automatically fall into place. Both common experience and research suggest group members are haphazard and unorganized in their discussion and decision attempts when managers fail to use organizing formats.[18]

Five approaches to a meeting follow. The appropriateness of each of these is determined by the objective of the meeting, the participants in the meeting, and the manager serving as leader.

Traditional Problem-Solving Scheme

In 1910, John Dewey described the steps that rational individuals use to solve a problem.[19] Most know these as the six stages to problem solving: (1) determining the problem, (2) determining the cause of the problem, (3) determining the criteria that must be met to eliminate the problem, (4) determining the possible solutions, (5) determining the best solution, and (6) determining the implementation of the solution.

When following this process in a meeting, it is critical to take only one step at a time. People tend to begin to discuss solutions or even implementation of a solution before the problem has been precisely defined. However, it is critical to get everyone to agree on the problem being discussed. One way of doing this is to write the problem on a blackboard where everyone can see it. Doing so will keep everyone's attention on the definition of the problem and ensure that all agree on the problem under discussion. This same procedure can be followed for each step. Write the step on the flip chart or chalkboard, and then write the conclusions of the discussion. Since the material is directly in front of the audience, everyone should be at the same stage and agree on the discussion's conclusions.

Postproblem and Consensus

N. R. F. Maier developed a meeting technique in which the leader systematically polls the participants about the topic under consideration.[20] The purpose is simply to obtain a consensus from members on issues being discussed after which results are posted for all to see. The advantage is that the discussion remains on target, and everyone is aware of the progress being made. This system is similar to that recommended for use with the traditional problem-solving approach.

Brainstorming

Alexander Osborn, an advertising executive, first described brainstorming as a special technique for facilitating the idea-generating portion of the decision process.[21]

The object of brainstorming is to generate ideas rather than evaluate or analyze those ideas. A group can brainstorm successfully and produce a maximum number of ideas by adhering to three rules:

1. Ideas are expressed freely without regard to quality. All ideas, no matter how absurd, are recorded.
2. Criticism of the ideas produced is not allowed until all ideas have been expressed. Participants cannot use such phrases as "that will never work," or "we tried that one other time and it didn't work," or similar comments while ideas are being generated. These comments inhibit the free flow of ideas that is the initial purpose of the brainstorming.
3. Elaborations and combinations of previously expressed ideas are encouraged. The major strength of brainstorming is that one idea will create another. The ratio of high-quality ideas to the total number is not high, but often only one creative idea is needed for the solution.

Brainstorming has been an extremely popular approach since its inception due to the creative results achieved. Experiments have shown that brainstorming increases the production of new ideas.[22] However, in 9 out of 12 studies comparing brainstorming groups with individuals working independently, the individuals produced more ideas.[23] A number of reasons explain the apparent contradiction between the obvious advantages of brainstorming and the research results to the contrary. One may be the time limitation imposed on a group. Groups allowed to produce for longer work periods typically produce more ideas under brainstorming instructions than do individuals. Most groups continue to produce indefinitely, while individuals taper off.[24]

A second reason is that the members of a brainstorming group feel the pressure of conformity that is a part of any group's mechanics. Also, a trend may develop in a group that makes it extremely difficult to change the direction of the communication. Although brainstorming is highly recommended, managers must take precautions when developing a communication strategy to lessen the factors working against the process.

Two techniques allow a manager to maintain some of the benefits of brainstorming as well as the benefits of individual contribution. Let us look at these two techniques, the nominal group technique and the Delphi technique.

Nominal Group Technique

When using the nominal group technique (NGT), the meeting leader directs each participant to create separate lists of the advantages and disadvantages associated with the problem and solutions under discussion. After a predetermined time, the participants present their advantages and disadvantages, which are listed so everyone can see them. Then members are directed to work alone again to rank order all advantages and disadvantages from highest to lowest priority. After this, an average master list is compiled. The participants can then discuss the issue based on the information presented in the master list. When groups follow this procedure, they generate a basis for group discussion, which reflects all the participants' views that were individually developed by working alone.

The NGT has several advantages that a manager should consider when planning a meeting. One is that all participants can express their views without intimidation from more powerful or vocal group members. The procedure also ensures that each step in systematic problem solving is followed. Finally, it can save time because the meeting participants can generate their initial lists before the meeting. The NGT thus integrates the advantages of both group and individual creativity and is clearly a valuable process.[25]

Delphi Technique

The Delphi technique is a unique group problem-solving process that differs greatly from the typical meeting. Unlike the typical interacting meeting or NGT, which requires close physical proximity of group members, the Delphi technique does not require participants to meet face to face. This technique has been beneficial when knowledgeable individuals are geographically isolated or their schedules preclude a common meeting time. It is generally used with an ad hoc meeting of experts.

Delphi uses an initial questionnaire that elicits the participants' expert opinions on a topic. Once these opinions have been collected, all group members receive a second questionnaire listing others' contributions, and all are asked to evaluate each idea using several specified criteria. This step is then followed by a third questionnaire that reports the second-round ratings, a mean rating, and any consensus. The participants are then asked to revise their earlier ratings considering the average or consensus. A final question-naire includes all ratings, the consensus, and remaining minority problems.

The advantage of the Delphi technique is that it controls some of the possible disadvantages of group decision making. The most vocal or highest status person does not have an opportunity to control the group because everyone's comments are pooled. Also, the coordinator can guarantee the decision-making process does not omit any critical steps or ignore important comments.

The value of the nominal group technique and the Delphi technique was verified in a study conducted by Van De Ven and Delbecq.[26] They compared the effectiveness of group decisions when made with the traditional group discussion, with the nominal technique, and with the Delphi method. They also compared participant satisfaction with the three techniques. They concluded that the quality of decisions was higher with the nominal group technique and Delphi than with the traditional group discussion; however, participants preferred the group discussion technique. This preference has important implications for managers. It is possible that managers continue to use traditional group discussion because it is more enjoyable, not because it is more effective. Of course, it is important that participants enjoy the process. Also, in some situations, the Delphi technique cannot be used effectively because it takes too much time.

Strategic Consideration 5: Prepare for Possible Disruptions

One of the most aggravating occurrences in a meeting is when an individual seems continually to disrupt the communication flow. This person may be an extremely poor communicator in group situations or may be coming to the meeting with a personal agenda (that is, his own private objectives) that conflicts with the stated agenda. Disruptive behavior may include continuous clowning, dominating the conversation, attempting to change the topic, making accusations, or personalizing the conversation with emotional statements. These disruptions need resolution or the meeting can quickly deteriorate.

Disruptions can first be managed from a preventive point of view. John Jones suggests seven tactics that managers may use ahead of time when they believe a person will disrupt a meeting.[27]

1. Prior to the meeting, ask for the disrupter's cooperation.
2. Give the person a special task or role in the meeting, such as posting the viewpoints of others.
3. Work out your differences before the meeting (possibly with a third-party facilitator) to present a united front to all other members.
4. Structure the meeting to include frequent discussion of the meeting process itself.
5. Take all the dominator's items off the agenda.

6. Set the person up to be concerned about what might be the consequences of disruption. For example, "I have learned that a number of people are angry with you, and I am thinking about opening up their discussion in the meeting."

7. Set up other persons who will attend the meeting to support you in dealing with the disruptive behavior of the individual. For example, they can be asked to refuse to argue with the person, or they can agree to confront the dysfunctional behavior directly.

The assumption behind these tactics is that the disruptive behavior can be channeled into a productive effort. Prevention is preferable to meeting disruptive behavior with hostility or antagonism during the meeting.[28] However, if these methods are not feasible, a manager needs to have options available to keep control during the meeting. Neither hostility nor avoidance will control disruptive behavior. Here are some options for handling disruptions during a meeting.

If a person continually disrupts with questions, a manager can turn all the questions into statements. This strategy forces the person to take responsibility for expressing a point of view rather than merely blocking the process.

Clowning can be handled simply: the manager need only state that she does not understand the humor and ask the disrupter to explain it. Humor does not stand up well to dissection like this. Managers should also be careful about their own humor during meetings. What may seem humorous when one is alone with an individual may be seen as a putdown when done during a meeting.[29]

The person who tries to dominate can be asked to summarize the group discussion after 10-minute intervals. The summary process should keep the person occupied. For those who change the topic continually, it is often effective for the manager to act curious and ask how the latest comment relates to the discussion topic.

Emotional disruptions present a special problem to the meeting leader. When accusations and emotionally defensive statements prevail, address the emotions rather than the content. A statement like, "Bill, it appears that you're upset with Rae. If this is true, would you like to talk about that or deal with it later?" Such a statement brings the emotion to the surface. After this, the disrupter may choose to refrain from a discussion on the emotional issue; however, if the discussion proceeds in an emotional manner, the manager in charge must stay in charge. Do not deal with emotion unless it is relevant to the discussion.

When dealing with an emotional conversation, make sure only one person speaks at a time, paraphrase his statement to ensure accuracy before allowing anyone else to speak, and let the other parties know when they may speak. When conflict arises during a meeting, it creates barriers to communication. People focus on winning battles rather than sharing information. Above all, it is critical to maintain both verbal and psychological control of a group involved in an emotional discussion. One surprisingly effective technique is to move on to the next agenda item. One can return when tempers cool.[30] If it seems that control is fading, the manager can also stand and move to the flip chart or casually stand near the parties involved. This will help keep control in a nonverbal manner.

A less obvious disruptive influence occurs when participants do not get involved in the discussion. Of course, everyone should get involved to take full advantage of the group process. One way to ensure that participants become involved is to use the Delphi technique discussed earlier. When the participants need to have answers prepared for specific questions before the meeting, a manager can ask for these answers during the meeting and thus stimulate the discussion.

Another alternative is to ask participants to jot down answers on a notepad when sensitive issues are discussed. The leader can ask the participants to submit their written reactions anonymously to the leader, who then reads them to the group. Participants have an opportunity to present viewpoints in a "safe" manner when this process is used.

The use of written answers is an effective way to begin a meeting, but the strategic use of questions throughout the meeting helps to keep the participants involved. When worded correctly and addressed to the right audience, questions develop a participative climate. Questions have the greatest chance of soliciting participation when they are open ended, rather than when they require a simple yes or no answer. Questions should also be brief, easily understood, and immediately pertinent to the topic under discussion.

According to Lawrence Loban, a manager needs to consider four possible alternatives when addressing a question.[31] When an *overhead question* is asked by the leader, anyone in the group may feel free to answer. A good idea is to begin with an overhead question and continue until forced to change. Either domination or nonparticipation by certain individuals may require a change in question format. A *direct question* can usually overcome these problems. A direct question is simply one that is directed to an individual. However, keep in mind certain caveats about direct questions. Never start a meeting with one because it may sound like an answer is demanded before the participants have time to warm up. Also, try not to put a person into an uncomfortable position by asking a rhetorical question that really cannot be answered. With direct questions, do not put pressure on any one participant. Keep a balance instead of continually asking a verbal person or an assumed expert.

A *reverse question* is one originally asked by a group member to the leader who then directs it back to the person who asked it. The leader should do this when it is apparent the participant really wants to make a statement but is not quite sure that would be appropriate. The final alternative is the *relay question*, which is asked by a group member and is relayed by the leader to the group: "That's an interesting question by Mary. What would be a good answer to her question?" The relay question gives the leader an opportunity to keep the communication moving among all the members of the group rather than a select few.

A lack of participation is not only extremely frustrating in a meeting, but it also means the expertise of the different participants is not being used. Fortunately, an alert manager's use of appropriately phrased and directed questions can keep this from happening.

Strategic Consideration 6: Follow through with Follow-up

At meeting's end, the manager's responsibilities are completed once she has reanalyzed the original goals to assure she has met them, made appropriate follow-up assignments, and evaluated the meeting process to determine if and how future meetings could be improved. Since it is easy to lose sight of the original goal, it is important to reiterate the goal several times during the meeting. This tactic will help to keep the meeting going in the correct direction so the objective can be met. One way to determine if the goal has been met is to review the traditional problem-solving scheme to ensure each step was followed. If the group has defined the problem and has reviewed alternative solutions to this problem, it can be assumed the original objective has been met.

Another easy way to determine if the objective is met is to write out the decision or summarize the discussion in a few sentences. This clear statement allows the participants to review it and make sure they understand it. A summary of the decision reached will bring to the surface any individual misunderstandings or disagreements. This is not to say agreement must be unanimous at the end of the meeting; however, each member of the group should be clear about his position and the conclusions reached.

A good idea is to point out differences that exist at the end of the meeting. This recognizes that disagreement is not always bad; also, the disagreements will probably be vital to future discussions. A clear understanding of differences at the end of the meeting should make future meetings go more smoothly and help to prevent unnecessary meetings.

Appropriate postmeeting follow-up is also an important component of meeting management. Before closing the meeting, clearly set out the next steps each participant is to take. Also announce if another meeting will be necessary and when. But this is often not the end. The situation may require written confirmation of the decisions reached and any future actions to be taken by the participants. Such a memo serves as a reminder of the results and also informs other personnel who are interested but were not involved in this particular meeting.

Stress the positive when writing the follow-up memo so the participants

FIGURE 13-3   **Meeting Follow-up Memo**

Subject of meeting _____

Name of sender _____

Where held _____

Present _____

Major conclusions _____

Future actions _____

can see the fruits of their labor. A follow-up memo also sets a record of the meeting, assures follow-up, and establishes accountability for future action. Some companies have a standard form for the follow-up memo, as presented in Figure 13–3, that helps to keep it short, simple, and accurate.

In a meeting, much transpires that is lost forever. Members may require more detailed minutes when a follow-up memo is too short to record the important points in detail. Minutes are particularly valuable as a starter for future meetings on the same topic.

The final step in the management of a meeting is the evaluation of the meeting itself, an important self-development activity. One extreme form of evaluation is audio recording of the meeting and evaluating it step by step. This may be worthwhile when the same group plans to meet again to review critical issues. In fact, several companies require this of all project managers when they begin a project with a new team of specialists. At the other extreme is a quick self-evaluation to assess the dynamics of a meeting. When an experienced manager holds a noncritical, one-time meeting, a review lasting only a few minutes may be adequate. Regardless of a manager's experience, however, benefits can be derived periodically from an intensive review.

The evaluation sheet in Figure 13–4 represents one tool that could be used to evaluate a meeting. It could be adapted to meet the specific requirements of a manager.

This brief instrument is only a rough measure of a meeting's effectiveness because of the many dynamics involved. However, it can be a valuable tool when used by a manager, or it can also be completed by the participants. Participant feedback can be an invaluable source of ideas for the improvement of future meetings.

FIGURE 13–4 **Evaluation Sheet**

Listed below is a series of statements about a meeting. Circle the number of the scale that best describes the meeting in which you just participated.

1. The objective of the meeting was clearly defined.

Strongly agree   5   4   3   2   1   Strongly disagree

2. A systematic approach was used to solve problems.

Strongly agree   5   4   3   2   1   Strongly disagree

3. All the participants were involved in the meeting.

Strongly agree   5   4   3   2   1   Strongly disagree

4. Disruptions were effectively managed.

Strongly agree   5   4   3   2   1   Strongly disagree

5. An appropriate format was established for the meeting.

Strongly agree   5   4   3   2   1   Strongly disagree

6. Appropriate premeeting details (agenda, room, etc.) were arranged.

Strongly agree   5   4   3   2   1   Strongly disagree

7. Time was well managed.

Strongly agree   5   4   3   2   1   Strongly diagree

8. The stated objectives could have been met without a meeting.

Strongly agree   5   4   3   2   1   Strongly disagree

9. The objective of the meeting has been met.

Strongly agree   5   4   3   2   1   Strongly disagree

Summary

Meetings have advantages and disadvantages, including groupthink, with which managers should be familiar. To make effective use of meetings, a number of contingencies need to be reviewed. The first and most obvious consideration facing a manager is the stated objective. If the objective is a programmed decision, or if a commitment does not present a special problem, a meeting may not be required.

Once it is clear that a meeting should be conducted, it is important to consider the premeeting arrangements. These involve four aspects: who should be included in the meeting, what should be on the agenda, which additional materials should be attached to the agenda, and what should be the physical arrangements for the meeting. Overlooking any one of these questions may cause an omission that reduces meeting effectiveness.

After the arrangements have been prepared, managers need to consider meeting formats. However, before deciding on the precise format, select the appropriate leadership style for the situation. A group- or leader-centered approach may be used, but every group needs an interpersonally oriented leader to some extent. The selection of the appropriate leadership will assist in the format choice.

This chapter presents five approaches to a meeting. The traditional problem-solving approach is a separate approach, but to some extent, it should be integrated into each of the others. Postproblem and consensus, brainstorming, and the nominal group technique all involve group interaction, but the Delphi technique can be used without getting people together physically. Each of these approaches has inherent advantages and disadvantages, so the correct format needs to be selected to fit the situation.

Regardless of the format selected, disruptions can occur during a meeting, but they can be prevented if a manager takes precautions, including talking to potential disrupters ahead of time or planning special activities for them during the meeting. Once a disruption occurs, strategic communication can control it; hostility or antagonistic remarks by a manager only add to the disruption. Finally, a manager's responsibility as the leader of a meeting is complete only when the postmeeting follow-up has been completed. This follow-up may take the form of a short memo and an effort to ensure that various commitments have been met. Also, personal evaluation of the meeting helps to determine if there is any way a similar meeting could be improved in the future.

Endnotes

1. H. Simon, *The New Science of Management Decision* (New York: Harper and Row, 1960).
2. P. S. Goodman, E. Ravlin, and M. Schminke, "Understanding Groups in Organizations," in *Research in Organizational Behavior*, vol. 9, ed. I. B. M. Staw and L. L. Cummings (Greenwich, Conn: JAI Press, 1987), pp. 121–73.
3. Lester Coch and John R. P. French, Jr., "Overcoming Resistance to Change," *Human Relations* 1, no. 4 (1948), pp. 512–32.
4. Richard H. Hall, *Organizations*, 5th ed. (Englewood Cliffs, N.J.: Prentice Hall, 1991), p. 180.
5. M. E. Gist, E. A. Locks, and M. S. Taylor, "Organizational Behavior: Group Structure, Process, and Effectiveness," *Journal of Management* 13, no. 2 (1987), pp. 237–57.
6. I. L. Janis, *Victims of Groupthink* (Boston: Houghton Mifflin, 1972).
7. G. Moorhead, R. Ference, and C. P. Neck, "Group Decision Fiascoes Continue: Space Shuttle Challenger and a Revised Groupthink Framework," *Human Relations* 44, no. 4 (1991), pp. 539–50.

8. T. Hensley and G. Griffin, "Victims of Groupthink: The Kent State University Board of Trustees and the 1977 Gymnasium Controversy," *Journal of Conflict Resolution* 30, no. 4 (1986), pp. 497–531.

9. C. Von Bergen and R. J. Kirk, "Groupthink: When Too Many Heads Spoil the Decision," *Management Review*, March 1978, p. 46.

10. C. P. Neck and G. Morehead, "Jury Deliberations in the Trial of U.S. John DeLorean: A Case Analysis of Groupthink Avoidance and an Enhanced Framework," *Human Relations* 45, no. 10 (1992), pp. 1077–91.

11. Robert Towensen, *Up the Organization* (Greenwich, Conn.: Fawcett, 1970), p. 171.

12. P. Slater, "Contrasting Correlates of Group Size," *Sociometry* 21, no. 1 (1958), pp. 129–39.

13. J. M. Levine and R. Moreland, "Progress in Small Group Research," *Annual Review of Psychology* 41 (1990), pp. 585–634.

14. Alan C. Filley, "Committee Management: Guidelines from Social Science Research," *California Management Review* 13, no. 4 (Fall 1970), pp. 13–21.

15. K. G. Stoneman and A. M. Dickinson, "Individual Performance as a Function of Group Contingencies and Group Size," *Journal of Organizational Behavior Management* 10, no. 1 (1989), pp. 131–50.

16. J. R. Hackman and C. G. Morris, "Group Tasks, Group Interaction Process and Group Performance Effectiveness: A Review and Proposed Integration," in *Advances in Experimental Social Psychology*, Vol. 8, I. L. Berkowitz ed. New York, Academic Press, (1975), pp. 1–50.

17. N. Shawchuck, *Taking a Look at Your Leadership Style* (Downers Grove, Il.: Organizational Research Press, 1978).

18. David R. Weibold, "Making Meetings More Successful: Plans, Formats, and Procedures for Group Problem-Solving," *Journal of Business Communication* 16, no. 3 (Summer 1979), p. 8.

19. John Dewey, *How We Think* (Boston: D.C. Heath, 1910).

20. N. R. F. Maier, *Problem-Solving Discussion and Conferences: Leadership Methods and Skills* (New York: McGraw-Hill, 1963), pp. 161–71.

21. Alexander F. Osborn, *Applied Imagination* (New York: Scribners, 1957).

22. A. Meadow, S. J. Parnes, and H. Reese, "Influence of Brainstorming Instructions and Problem Solving on a Creative Problem-Solving Test," *Journal of Applied Psychology* 43, no. 4 (1959), pp. 413–16.

23. Helmut Lamm and Gisela Trommsdorf, "Group versus Individual Performance on Tasks Requiring Ideational Proficiency (Brainstorming): A Review," *European Journal of Social Psychology* 3, no. 2 (1973), pp. 361–88.

24. Marvin E. Shaw, *Group Dynamics*, 3rd ed. (New York: McGraw-Hill, 1981), p. 57.

25. André L. Delbecq, Andrew H. Van De Ven, and David H. Gustafson, *Group Techniques for Program Planning* (Glenview, Il.: Scott, Foresman, 1975).

26. A. H. Van de Ven and A. L. Delbecq, "The Effectiveness of Nominal, Delphi, and Interacting Group Decision-Making Processes," *Academy of Management Journal* 17, no. 4 (December 1974), pp. 605–21.

27. John. E. Jones, "Dealing with Disruptive Individuals in Meetings," *1980 Annual Handbook for Group Facilitators*, ed. J. William Pfeiffer and John E. Jones (San Diego, Calif.: University Associates, 1980), p. 161.

28. M. B. Brewer and R. M. Kramer, "The Psychology of Intergroup Attitudes and Behavior," *Annual Review of Psychology* 36 (1985), pp. 219–43.

29. W. J. Duncan and J. P. Fersal, "No Laughing Matter: Patterns of Humor in the Workplace," *Organizational Dynamics* 17, no. 1 (1989), pp. 18–30.

30. D. J. Isenberg, "Group Polarization: A Critical Review and Meta-analysis," *Journal of Personality and Social Psychology* 50, no. 4 (1986), pp. 1141–51.

31. Lawrence N. Loban, "Questions: The Answer to Meeting Participation," *Supervision*, January 1972, pp. 11–13.

Additional Readings

Forsyth, D. R. *Group Dynamics*. Pacific Grove, Calif. Brooks/Cole, 1990.

Fisher, Aubrey B. *Small Group Decision Making*. New York: McGraw-Hill, 1974.

Hirokawa, Randy Y., and Kathryn M. Rost. "Effective Group Decision Making In Organizations: Field Test of the Vigilant Interaction Theory." *Management Communication Quarterly* 5, no. 3 (1992), pp. 267–88.

Hirokawa, R., and M. S. Poole. *Communication and Group Decision-Making*. Beverly Hills, Calif.: Sage Publications, 1986.

Kelly, Joe. "Surviving and Thriving in Top Management Meetings." *Personnel* 64, no. 6 (June 1987), pp. 24–34.

Larson, Carol E., and Frank M. J. LaFasto. *Teamwork: What Must Go Right: What Can Go Wrong*. Newbury Park, Calif.: Sage Publications, 1989.

Manz, C. C., and H. Angle. "Can Group Self-Management Mean a Loss of Personal Control: Triangulating a Paradox." *Group and Organization Studies* 11, no. 3 (1986), pp. 309–34.

Messeck, D. M., and D. M. Mackie, "Intergroup Relations." *Annual Review of Psychology* 40 (1989), pp. 45–81.

Discussion Questions

1. What are the major advantages and disadvantages of a group? Present a situation in which it would be a good idea to use a group and one in which a group would not be a good idea.

2. What are symptoms of groupthink, and how can you assure groupthink will not become a problem in your meeting?

3. What major considerations should be reviewed when determining who should be included in a meeting?

4. Obviously no correct size exists for a group. What are the limitations of a group that is too small? Too large? Give an example of a group that may be too large.

5. How should an agenda be used? What are the major components of an agenda?

6. What are some guidelines to use when attaching additional materials to the agenda?

7. What are the possible seating arrangements for a meeting? When should each be used?

8. Give an example in which you observed a poor physical arrangement for a meeting. What was wrong with the arrangement? How could it have been improved?

9. Briefly explain the five approaches to a meeting. What factors should be considered when determining which approach should be used?

10. Brainstorming is a beneficial process, but it has inherent limitations. Discuss the limitations of brainstorming and how these limitations may be overcome. Give an example where brainstorming could be used effectively.

11. Give several examples of disruptive behavior that you have observed in a meeting, and explain how they should have been controlled.

12. What are some important factors to keep in mind when dealing with emotional situations in a meeting?

13. What are four types of questions that can be used in a meeting and when is the best time to use each of them?

14. What should be included in a postmeeting memo?

15. Refer back to Chapter 1. Do you think there will be more or fewer meetings in the future? Why?

CASE 13–1
THE REGIONAL RELATIONSHIPS

Jerry Blaire is the regional manager of a national electronic franchise retail store. This franchise has over 200 locally owned stores throughout the eastern United States. As the regional manager, Blaire is responsible for an urban area in which there are eight stores plus the remainder of the state, which has another six stores.

The regional manager is the liaison between the manager-owner of the stores and the corporate offices in Boston. Responsibilities include monitoring the individual stores to assure the provisions of the franchise agreement are maintained, deal with any complaints from managers, take product orders, introduce new products, and manage the regional advertising program.

Blaire has been with this company for seven years, and before that he worked with a home entertainment retail store for three years after he earned his degree in marketing.

Blaire is responsible for coordinating the advertising campaign for all 14 stores in the region. A major part of the campaign involves store hours, which had traditionally been from 10 A.M. to 8 P.M., Monday through Saturday. The minimum number of hours required by the national office is 40 per week. However, several of the managers have been pressuring lately to change the store hours, especially those from inner-city areas. They maintain that their business is minimal after 6 P.M., so they would like to close earlier. Meanwhile, the suburban stores want to stay open later because they do a bigger business in the evening. According to the provisions of the franchise, all the stores in a region must maintain the same store hours.

The problem is getting more attention from the store managers and is a frequent topic of discussion as Blaire makes his visits. Blaire has decided to have a meeting for all the managers so he can systematically analyze the problem of store hours.

Questions

1. What type of a leadership style should Blaire use in this meeting? Why?
2. What meeting format would you recommend?
3. What special problems would you anticipate for this meeting?
4. What preliminary arrangements are particularly important for this meeting?
5. Do you think it is a good idea for Blaire to have a meeting?

CASE 13–2
KEEPING THE MEETING ON THE TOPIC

Waith Manufacturing Company's data processing department was preparing to implement a new computerized production information system at its new Madison plant. The project was divided into two parts. One consisted of the installation of a new computer at the plant and the development of new programs for this computer. The second involved interfacing the new plant computer with the main computer at headquarters to develop production report programs to be run on the main computer.

Kyle Brent was the systems analyst responsible for the development and implementation of the whole project. Janet DeLaura was a lead programmer under Brent working on the plant computer side of the project. Bill Synge was the other lead programmer responsible for the interface system and the development of the programs for the main computer. Brent scheduled a series of weekly status meetings with DeLaura and Synge to ensure the project was moving along as scheduled and to allow for discussion of critical problems. One month before the scheduled implementation of the project, Brent called a special meeting to develop the actual series of tasks needed for the final system conversion. During this meeting, Brent outlined the major tasks concerning the whole project that had to be done on that last day.

Brent then solicited input from DeLaura and Synge. DeLaura spoke up immediately and began talking about several new problems that had surfaced on her side of the project. Brent interrupted her, saying those problems would be discussed at the regular status meeting since this meeting had been called to develop final conversion tasks only. DeLaura became irritated and was silent for a few minutes. Synge said he had a few items to add to the conversion list and covered the first two tasks. Then he said the last task covered reminded him of a current problem he had in the interface program. Brent replied brusquely that only conversion tasks would be discussed at this meeting. Neither DeLaura nor Synge had much to say during the rest of the meeting.

Questions

1. What would you have done to have kept the meeting on the right topic?
2. What techniques might Brent have used to avoid interfering with the flow of ideas?
3. What might DeLaura and Synge have done to improve communications?

14   Strategies in Conflict Management

> *You have just walked out of a meeting with the vice-president of operations in which departmental managers were informed that the salaries of the division's office staff have to be reduced by $100,000 within six weeks. The engineering manager immediately stated that at least four of the employees in your group could be terminated, and this would handle the problem. You became enraged since you believe engineering has to be one of the most padded groups in the company. Unfortunately, the vice-president did not present any concrete ideas, and she said the various managers could work out the reduction among themselves and make a recommendation to her. How would you handle this type of conflict? What is your personal style in conflict situations?*

The world seems to be full of conflict. When the Berlin wall came down in 1989, it appeared that we might have global peace for the first time, but in 1991, two of the world's largest armies went to war. Conflict is also pervasive at the corporate level as demonstrated by Apple Computer. Conflict between company founder Steve Job and CEO John Sculley nearly resulted in disastrous earnings for Apple Computer as they competed for control of the board of directors. Family-owned U-Haul was beset by astronomically high legal fees because of conflict between the brothers and sisters. On a personal level, conflict is among the most common of human experiences and is the basis for such social science theorists as Freud, Marx, and the classical economists.

According to a survey of American Management Association executives, managers are likely to spend about 20 percent of their time dealing with conflict.[1] Conflict may occur as a simple disagreement over the meaning of a work procedure, or it may be an argument over priorities and involve deciding which of two projects should draw from the limited funds available for project development. Or it might bring into focus a long-standing irritation that could result in a work stoppage.

Managers were asked to describe the type of conflicts in which they became involved. One manager described a situation in which four computer programmers wanted to go to a training seminar, but funds were available for only one. Another manager described how both she and a colleague wanted to take their vacations at the same time. Their manager said they could not do that and told them to work out the schedule between them. In both these situations, conflicts had to be resolved.

Organizational conflict is a natural part of the traditional organizational structure because a built-in opposition between units often exists. Increases in conflict correlate positively with such factors as increases in an organization's levels of hierarchy, standardization of jobs, and increases in the number of workers.[2] In fact, organizational conflict is so pervasive that the *Journal of Conflict Resolution* is largely committed to this issue, and a center for research on this subject is located at the University of Michigan.

Conflict generally has a negative connotation; however, conflict is a positive occurrence if managed properly. Conflict requires managers to analyze their goals, it creates dialogue among employees and fosters creative solutions. Without conflict, employees and organizations would stagnate. In 1992, the Saturn division of General Motors provided a typical example of organizational conflict that proved beneficial. Saturn was beginning to develop some momentum and was a leading GM division in sales. Saturn President Richard LeFauve was clamoring for more money from the corporate office to increase assembly capacity. But GM Chairman Robert Stemple didn't believe the division deserved more investment. He saw the Buick division as a higher priority, so a conflict resulted. But this conflict was constructive because it helped GM analyze and establish its corporate strategies and priorities for Saturn.[3]

What causes conflict? When is it functional and when is it not? What methods can be used to resolve conflict? Is any one method best? To assist in conflict management, the following discussion answers these questions. But first we review the relationship between communication and conflict.

The Relationship of Communication to Conflict

As is true with many other terms, conflict has both a colloquial meaning and a long list of specific definitions. However, a quick review of these definitions will help to describe the nature of conflict. Katz and Kahn state that two systems—which could include persons, groups, organizations, or nations—are in conflict when they interact directly in such a way that the actions of one tend to prevent or compel some outcome against the resistance of the other.[4] Another author states that conflict characterizes a situation in which the conditions, practices, or goals of individuals are inherently incompatible.[5]

A third definition presents conflict as a struggle over values or claims to scarce resources, power, or status. In this struggle, opponents aim to neutralize, injure, or eliminate their rivals.[6]

These three definitions help define the nature of conflict and indicate the role of communication in conflict. The first definition uses the word *interact*, implying a communication interaction of some kind. The second definition uses the phrase *inherently incompatible*, and the third definition includes *a struggle over values*. Communication is the method by which managers determine if something is inherently incompatible, and the struggle over values is carried out through communication behaviors. Thus, the ability to communicate effectively may eliminate conflict immediately; however, ineffective communication may cause a situation to appear inherently incompatible and a struggle over values may ensue. The conclusion is that communicative behavior may cause as well as resolve conflict.

Let us examine the specific characteristics of conflict and the corresponding implications for communication. Following are four axioms that are particularly relevant to communication.[7] These axioms are reviewed to ultimately demonstrate how effective communication can make conflict a constructive, positive process.

1. **Conflict involves at least two parties.** Because conflict involves at least two parties, communication is an integral component. Conflict can be generated or resolved only through communication. Consequently, managers must understand the types of communication interactions that can cause conflict and the communication patterns that are most functional after conflict has developed. In fact, a good communicator can bring conflict to the surface and make it a productive process.

2. **Conflict develops due to perceived mutually exclusive goals.** Mutually exclusive goals may exist as a result of objective facts or an individual's values and perceptions. However, the key factor is that the parties involved perceive the objectives as mutually exclusive; frequently, through communication, the involved parties see that the goal is not actually mutually exclusive. But only through communication can the parties in conflict determine the existence of a superordinate goal that may meet both parties' goals. Again, the positive nature of conflict is evident because without conflict the parties may not know about the superordinate goal.

However, the uncertainty and ambiguous information resulting from poor communication can lead two employees to believe their goals are exclusive even though they may not be. For example, an engineering manager and production manager received a poorly written memorandum from the corporate office requiring advance approval for all preventive maintenance work. The ambiguity of the memo caused conflict later when a breakdown developed in the production plant. The engineering manager believed it impossible to correct the breakdown without advance approval while believing the production manager expected the work done immediately. The managers thought they had mutually exclusive goals as a result of ambiguous communications.

3. **Conflict involves parties who may have different value or perceptual systems.** To illustrate how conflictive parties may have different value systems, consider how a first-level supervisor who was once a member of a trade union would have a value system much different from that of a young engineer who has been out of college only two years. This value difference may result in a potential conflict when the two employees consider implementing a computerized production control system. The supervisor could perceive the computerized system as too difficult to learn and as a threat to employees' job security. However, the young engineer might perceive it solely as an engineering challenge. In this case, values affect perception.

The previous example about the engineering manager and the production manager both reading the same memo from the corporate office also provides an example of how perceptual differences may cause conflict. Suppose that the word *emergency* had been used in the memo. An emergency means something quite different to a production manager responsible for production costs than it does to an engineering manager responsible for engineering costs. It is only natural that the engineering manager would want to analyze the problems thoroughly and investigate possible alternatives. As he did so, production costs might climb because of a mechanical failure. Thus, the particular department to which a person belongs in a company may affect values and cause that person to view organizational activity from a frame of reference different from that of someone from another department.

A variant to what has been said about values is the selective attention principle, which holds that we tend to perceive that which is important and pleasing to us and avoid that which is not. The following example shows how differences in perception led to a major conflict.[8] A textile mill allowed a conflict to develop that resulted in big labor turnover. The mill had informed employees when they were hired that it gave automatic raises each year and merit raises for deserving employees after 9 and 18 months. The employees,however, understood this to mean they would receive an automatic raise at *all three* of these periods—9, 12, and 18 months. When they did not obtain their raises, many of them quit because they thought the employer had not maintained the original promise to grant wage increases. In this case, the differences between employee and employer perception led to conflicting views.

Not all the information about the situation ever reaches the perceiver.[9] Also, when the information does reach the perceiver, values affect what is perceived. When conflicting parties have different value or perceptual systems, communication is important in two ways. First, sheer repetition of a positive message about a person may result in greater liking for the person. Exposure and communication between two individuals will likely result in the individuals eventually sharing values and becoming more friendly toward each other.[10] In other words, extensive communication may resolve value differences. Second, as more accurate communication develops between two managers, the perceptual differences will subside, and, hence, the probability of conflict will be reduced.

Chapter 1 mentioned that cultural diversity is increasing in organizations. This diversity will create conflict, but it will be exciting and productive because diverse viewpoints, when managed appropriately, will result in creative outcomes.

4. **Conflict terminates only when each party is satisfied that it has won or lost.** Win–lose situations seem to dominate our culture: for instance, law courts use the adversary system and political parties strive to win elections. Competition to win in sports is so keen that fights between spectators are not uncommon. An example of our culture's fascination with competition and winning is the National Football League's rule limiting the possibility of a tied game. The pervasive win–lose attitude in our culture has made it difficult to imagine that both parties may "win" in any situation labeled a conflict. The labeling process develops a mental set that dictates a particular language pattern such that in our society it seems to say both parties cannot be winners. This problem recalls the first axiom, which states that conflict develops from mutually exclusive goals. However, accurate communication may reveal that a "win" or a "loss" is not the only alternative.

The win–lose attitude develops two-valued thinking, which in turn affects a manager's communication style in a conflict situation. The result may be the inability to perceive a situation accurately and, thus, the failure to discriminate between a win–lose situation and one in which mutual satisfaction is feasible. Such failure to discriminate is common to all of us, and the result is some degree of miscommunication.[11] This miscommunication can often result in managerial conflict. More will be said later about a problem-solving process that helps overcome this weakness and makes conflict positive rather than negative.

An example of conflict between an administrative assistant and a manager helps to clarify this characteristic. The manager and assistant were located across a wide corridor from one another, making it inconvenient to talk. The manager wanted to relocate the assistant's desk next to the manager's office in a small space recently vacated when several copy machines were moved. Conflict developed between the two parties. They had mutually exclusive goals because the assistant liked the bigger, brighter office space, while the manager wanted the assistant to be closer. The manager valued proximity whereas the assistant valued more space, so they perceived the move differently. Both parties viewed the conflict as a win–lose situation.

A Note on Constructive Conflict

While the term *conflict* implies opposing positions with negative results, when properly managed, conflict may be a positive rather than a detrimental force. Some conflict can be seen as essential for the continued development of mature and competent human beings.[12] In fact, a balance among conflict, associated personal stress, and tension is necessary for progress and productivity.[13] Most importantly, conflict may foster creativity. Conflict helps to overcome individual psychological distortions and biases by forcing people out of their traditional modes of thinking. In this way, conflict promotes the unstructured thinking that some see as required for developing good, novel alternatives to difficult problems.[14]

In addition, studies show a higher decision quality when there is open opposition and resistance by subordinates than when the resistance of subordinates is weak or even passive. In one study, high-quality decisions occurred in 45.8 percent of the situations with strong subordinate resistance, but in only 18.8 percent of the situations where the resistance was weak or nonexistent.[15]

Thus, managers who pride themselves in running a smooth ship may not be as effective as they think. The smooth ship may reflect suppressed conflict that could have potential benefit if allowed free play. In fact, the conflict might not be as harmful as its suppression. An appropriate analogy is a procedure used in underground mining at the turn of the century. The miners would periodically leave the mine while one miner would check the entire mine for potential safety hazards. Any walls that had cracks or timbers that appeared weak would be tested with a hammer or even small dynamite charges. Obviously, the procedure was risky for the troubleshooter, but it removed potential hazards. The same is true of conflict. Potential risk is present, but constructive conflict results in improved communications among employees, allowing legitimate differences of interests and beliefs to emerge with productive results.

An important duty of the manager, then, is to identify the potential for destructive or constructive conflict. Would conflict produce creative thought or would it inhibit ideas? Is the developing situation a destructive win–lose one or a constructive win–win environment? Is a problem-solving environment present or is it a defensive one? The remainder of this discussion should help you to identify the nature of conflict and determine the best strategy for managing conflict in a given managerial situation.

A Process Model of Conflict

The conflict process is not static but rather dynamic. When managers understand the process, they are better able to select the appropriate communication strategy. A model developed by Louis Pondy will help. It explains how conflict develops so it can be more effectively managed. Consistent with his model, four stages of a conflict episode are identified in Figure 14–1: latent, perceived, felt, and manifest, all followed by the aftermath.[16] Each stage describes the causes of conflict.

Latent Conflicts

Latent conflicts are the underlying causes or sources of conflict situations. They are of two basic types: functional interdependence and allocational interdependence.

FIGURE 14–1

Stages of a Conflict

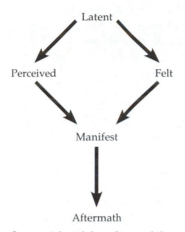

SOURCE: Adapted from Stages of Conflict. Reprinted from Louis R. Pondy, "Organizational Conflict: Concepts and Models," *Administrative Science Quarterly*, 12, no. 2 (September 1967)

Functional Interdependence

Functional interdependence reflects the lines of authority in an organization. For example, the lending and the savings departments are interdependent in all banks. The lending department cannot lend funds until the savings department has collected funds. By the same token, the savings department would be hard pressed if the lending department had no customers. These two areas have common goals within the bank (profit and continued operation of the bank), but their interdependence can lead to conflict over their respective authority. While the savings department would like to give high interest rates to please its customers, the lending department wants to provide low interest rates to please its clientele. When the interdependence of these departments becomes a central issue, conflict will arise over whose authority takes precedence or whose responsibility for the bank's profit goal is more relevant.

Allocation Interdependence

Allocation interdependence arises from the distribution and allocation of the limited resources available in an organization. If resources were unlimited, few conflicts would arise, but this condition seldom exists. When resources are limited, and more than one person or group wants a share, allocational conflict develops. The most obvious allocation conflict occurs during the annual budget review. With funds traditionally limited, it is necessary to decide which department will get what amount. Since each person's goal appears most important from her own perspective, the funds allocated to one department may appear to be funds taken from another. The interdependency of the various departments vying for budget allocations thus can become a major source of conflict.

The example of Saturn presented earlier demonstrates allocation interdependence. GM has a limited amount of resources to allocate to its divisions. If too many funds went to Saturn, Buick may suffer. But no doubt the presidents of both divisions will try to obtain as much as possible, so conflict will inevitably result.

Latent conflict, then, is the set of attitudes and feelings arising from functional and allocational interdependencies in an organization. Latent conflict is dynamic and cumulative. As a group of people works together, each one in the group may develop the notion, "I didn't get what should have been coming to me." This negative reaction does not necessarily lead to immediate conflict; rather, it accumulates and develops into the basis for future conflicts. This is why Pondy calls his model a process model of conflict; it is a dynamic, growing process.

Perceived Conflict

The relationship between conflict and perception has already been briefly discussed. Perceived conflict is present when the parties recognize the latent conditions or when the parties misunderstand one another's true position. Because of the perceptual process, four conditions are possible at this stage.

1. Latent content present, perceived by employees.
2. Latent content present, not perceived by employees.
3. Latent content not present, not perceived by employees.
4. Latent content not present, perceived by employees.

Clearly, failure to identify potentially conflictive situations may prevent conflicts from developing immediately. More often though, the inaccurate or illogical perception of a situation causes conflict when actual latent conflict does not exist. The grid in Figure 14–2 shows why inaccurate perceptions create conflict in the managerial process. Assume two managers are discussing an issue. Two possibilities exist for each manager: each correctly perceives the existence of a latent conflict or incorrectly perceives it. This results in the four possibilities diagrammed. The grid shows that an accurate mutual perception could possibly exist in only one of four occurrences. Of course, this is not always the case, but numerous conflicts not warranted by the actual latent conflict may develop.

Would conflict develop if true latent conflict were present but neither manager perceived it? Conflict would not develop immediately, but productive communication would probably not prevail. In fact, a potential disaster could exist. After being suppressed, the potential conflict might surface as an explosion. The latent conflict conditions may have been worsening, so

FIGURE 14–2

Accuracy of Perceptions and Conflict

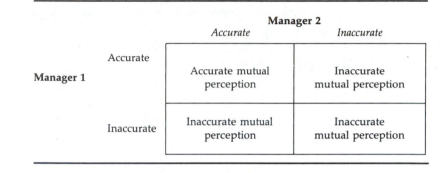

		Manager 2	
		Accurate	*Inaccurate*
Manager 1	Accurate	Accurate mutual perception	Inaccurate mutual perception
	Inaccurate	Inaccurate mutual perception	Inaccurate mutual perception

when the managers finally perceived the true situation, it would probably be beyond repair.

Felt Conflict

The difference between felt and perceived conflict is the difference between seeing and feeling. Two managers may be aware of serious disagreement over a policy, but it may not create any anxiety or affect their feelings toward one another. Let's return to the example of Saturn and Buick. The presidents of these two GM divisions may know they are in conflict, which is perceived conflict. But they don't necessarily need to personalize it. Felt conflict is personalized conflict and should cause managers to be concerned with the dysfunctions of conflict.

Two common explanations prevail for the felt component in conflicts. One is the inconsistency between the demands of an efficient organization and individual growth. Individuals and large organizations find it difficult to meet their needs concurrently, so individuals may frequently feel threatened.[17] The resulting identity crisis may cause anxiety. This anxiety may cause defensive communication on the part of one or both parties involved in a conflict. A second cause of this felt component is that an employee may become totally and personally involved in the organization. The employee's self-image may rely on job successes or failures. The individual may develop such an intimate relationship with his job and the organization that other employees represent a threat to this relationship.

Felt conflict may find expression in fear, threat, mistrust, and hostility. The venting of hostility can be therapeutic, so it is not necessarily detrimental if managed properly. Group discussions can act as a safety valve for this hostility as can periodic meetings between supervisors and subordinates. Effective managers do not become defensive even when they are the focus of the hostile communication. Nondefensive communication is the key to managing felt conflict.

FIGURE 14–3

Ways to Manifest Conflict

Conflict

Aggression ⟵——————————⟶ Integrative problem solving

Manifest Conflict

The observable behavior of the manager, based on latent conditions, perceptions, and feelings, may be either conflict or an attempt to establish mutual goals. The most obvious manifestations of conflict are open aggression at one end of a continuum and integrative problem solving at the other end as depicted in Figure 14–3. A continuum is used because generally neither total open aggression nor completely satisfactory problem solving is manifest. However, the goal is to move as close as possible to integrative problem solving. As the remainder of the discussion shows, managers have numerous ways to manage conflict along this continuum as they attempt to approach the right end of the continuum.

Strategies in Conflict Resolution

Now that we have looked at the relationship of conflict to managerial communication, discussed constructive conflict, and reviewed a process model of conflict, we can review strategies for conflict resolution. Managerial communication strategies for managing conflict could be put into many categories. For our discussion, we use the system presented in Figure 14–4. This figure demonstrates that during a conflict, managers may emphasize interpersonal relations, task production, or a combination. Five possible modes are presented: avoidance, smoothing, forcing, compromise, and maximization.[18]

While reviewing these strategies, the contingency approach to managerial communication should be kept in mind. Various conflict situations require different strategies, so effective communication requires that managers match the strategy to the situation.

Avoidance

The avoidance or withdrawal strategy combines a low concern for production with a low concern for people. The person using this style sees conflict as a hopeless, useless experience. Rather than undergo the tension and frustration of conflict, managers using the avoidance or withdrawal style simply remove themselves from conflict situations. This avoidance or withdrawal may be either physical or psychological. The person using this strategy will comply to avoid disagreement and tension, will not openly take sides in a disagreement among others, and will feel little commitment to any decisions reached.

FIGURE 14-4 **Strategies for Managing Conflict**

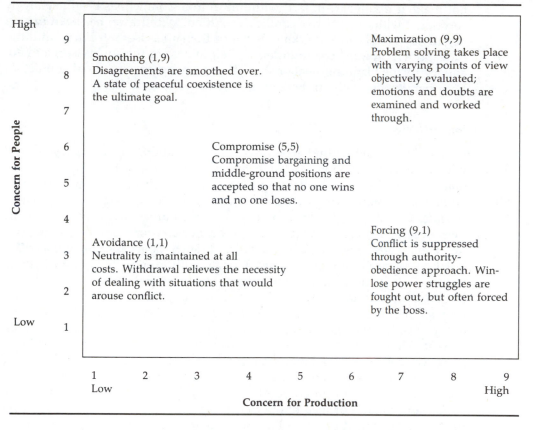

Avoidance need not be dramatic. Many managers avoid by ignoring a comment or quickly changing the subject when conversation begins to threaten. Another way to avoid is to place the responsibility for an issue on a higher manager. The common reply with this strategy is, "I can't really say anything at this level." A third way to withdraw is to use a simple, "I'm looking into the matter." One then hopes the other party will forget the issue.

This avoidance or withdrawal strategy is frequently used in large bureaucracies that have numerous policies. Rather than attempt to resolve the conflict, managers simply blame it on the "policy." This protects the manager from being required to be creative in conflict management; he needs only to withdraw or avoid it.

Conflict resolution requires effective communication skills and involves potential risk, so managers who lack self-confidence in their communication abilities may hope the problem just disappears. However, this usually does not work. The main shortcoming of avoidance is that the manager ignores those very conditions that cause conflict to arise. Simply avoiding conflict will not make it disappear. In fact, withdrawal from conflict has been negatively correlated with constructive conflict resolution. Withdrawal has been further negatively correlated with: knowledge of the supervisor's feelings and attitudes; open, upward communication; helpfulness of the supervisor; and adequacy of the planning relationship. Thus, managers who avoid conflict do not operate effectively in these critical managerial areas.[19]

Smoothing

In smoothing, the second type of conflict resolution, managers try to deal with conflict by making everyone happy. When using this approach, the manager emphasizes maintaining relationships with fellow employees and de-emphasizes achieving productive goals. Since the manager wants others' acceptance, he will give in to others' desires in areas that conflict with his own desires. Managers using this style believe confrontation is destructive.

Typical attempts to smooth may include such things as calling for a coffee break at a tense moment, breaking tension with humor, changing the topic to something nonconflictive, or engaging in some ritual show of togetherness like an office birthday party. Since these efforts are likely to reduce felt conflict, they are more beneficial than simple avoidance. This reduction of felt conflict will probably have short-range effects and may even have some long-range benefit. However, just because someone does not experience a hostile or negative feeling does not mean the real cause of the conflict is resolved. In fact, smoothing is a camouflage approach that can break down at any time and create barriers to progress. Thus, research has found that smoothing is used more in low- or medium-performance organizations than in high-performance organizations. In addition, smoothing correlates negatively with open, upward communication and with participation in goal setting. Managers who want to develop a good communicative relationship with subordinates as well as those higher in the organization would generally not find the smoothing strategy effective.

Forcing

Forcing, the third conflict management tactic, is used by the manager who attempts to meet production goals at all costs, without concern for the needs or acceptance of others. For such a manager, winning or losing is not a mere event; losing is destructive for these people because it is viewed as reduced status, weakness, and the loss of self-image. Winning must be achieved at whatever cost and gives this manager a sense of excitement and achievement. Managers using force feel that for every winner there must be a loser. The forcing manager is willing to sacrifice individuals who refuse to go along with her desires.

A situation characterized by the forcing style will probably have much conflict aftermath and set the stage for later conflicts. The language managers use to describe conflict situations in their organizations often reflects the negative effect this style may have: opposition, battle, fight, conquest, head-to-head, coercion, and smash. Such language and imagery can result in long-lasting emotional wounds.[20]

While force can resolve immediate disputes, the long-term effects will probably include a loss of productivity. Forcing in conflict situations negatively correlates with such factors as adequacy of planning, helpfulness of the supervision, and participation in goal setting. The major difficulty of a forcing strategy is that employees are reluctant to plan or carry out plans when they perceive that the ultimate resolution of the conflict will put them on the losing side of a win–lose position.

Interestingly, while little doubt exists that forcing has limited use, managers consider forcing to be their favorite backup strategy for dealing with conflict.[21] This trend may indicate that managers often lack the communication skills to implement a more effective strategy.

Compromise

Compromise, the fourth style of conflict resolution, assumes that half a loaf is better than none. This approach falls somewhere between forcing and smoothing. Since compromise provides some gain for both sides rather than a unilateral victory, many participants judge this approach as better than the other strategies just discussed.

Compromise is used when one of two conditions exists: (1) neither party involved believes he or she has the power to "force" the issue on the other party, or (2) one or both of the parties believes resolution may not be worth the cost in money, time, or energy that might be needed to win. Compromise is often highly related to negotiations, which is the topic of the next chapter; however, several important points are pertinent here. First, compromise may lead to both parties' perceiving themselves as winners, but they may also both feel like losers. A negative overtone may develop in the working relationship between the employees involved, and any sense of trust may break down. While both parties involved probably entered the negotiations with a cooperative attitude, a sense of competition may be the result of compromise.

A second concern with negotiations is that the party with the most information has the better position. This power of information may restrict open communication among employees. This situation in turn develops the potential for a compromise to become one sided. A third factor to consider in negotiations is the principle of the least-interested party: the party that has the least interest in the outcome is in the more powerful position in the negotiations. In other words, the party that does not really care about the outcome of an issue may actually control it. As a result, an employee who has little concern about the welfare of the company may have an inordinate amount of influence in a compromise.

A Review of These Methods: Win–Lose and Lose–Lose

We have examined four styles of conflict resolution: avoidance, smoothing, forcing, and compromise. Each of these styles or strategies may result in outcomes that we can characterize as win–lose and lose–lose. For instance, a manager may avoid a subordinate's request for a raise by putting it off "for review." Unfortunately, both the manager and subordinate lose because the issue remains, although the manager using this approach may easily perceive it as a win because: "I don't have to discuss the sensitive subject for a while."

A manager may smooth an employee concerned about getting the undesirable jobs in the department; however, until they find a real solution to the problem, a lose–lose or win–lose situation exists. A manager can force an employee to accept an idea, but latent conflict remains. The manager may have forced the issue because he could not detect a way to work out the lose–lose situation. Finally, the compromise concept assumes the desires of both parties cannot be met; hence, there is a need for sacrifices. This is a lose–lose situation even when both parties perceive it to be a win–win outcome since something has obviously been lost.

Maximization: The Win–Win Strategy

Thus far, it may seem that no totally acceptable, productive way exists to manage conflict. Everything has been discussed in terms of loss. Fortunately, this is not the case. Maximization, the last style or strategy to be discussed, is an effective win–win strategy for conflict. This complex, highly effective style requires skillful, strategic managerial communication, but it reaps a big dividend; thus, the remainder of our discussion centers on this strategy. Let us first describe the win–win strategy and then examine specific techniques for implementation.

Description of the Win–Win Strategy

The key to the win–win strategy is that it follows a mutual problem-solving approach rather than a combative one. In contrast to managers who use a forcing or compromising strategy, managers engaged in this type of problem solving assume a high-quality, mutually acceptable solution is possible. The parties direct their energies toward defeating the problem and not each other.

The following example presents a clear description of the problem-solving approach to conflict resolution. It details a meeting in Wisconsin that set out to explore possible prison reforms.

Nine of the state's top prison officials met to design an ideal correctional institution. In the course of the discussion, one group member proposed that uniforms traditionally worn by prison guards be eliminated. The group then began a lengthy argument about whether or not uniforms should be worn. One group member suggested that the issue be resolved democratically by vote. As a result, six people voted against uniforms and three voted in favor of them. The winning members looked pleased while the losing members either got angry or withdrew from further discussion.

A group consultant present at the time suggested that the members take another look at the situation. Then he asked those in favor of uniforms what they hoped to accomplish. Those officials stated that part of the rehabilitative process in correctional institutions is that of teaching people to deal constructively with authority, and saw uniforms as a means for achieving the goal. When asked why they opposed uniforms, the other group members said that uniforms created such a stigma that guards had an additional difficulty laying to rest the stereotypes held by inmates before they could deal with them on a one-to-one basis. The group consultant then asked the group what ways might be appropriate to meet the combined goals, namely, teaching people to deal with authority and avoiding the difficulty of stereotypes held about traditional uniforms. While working on the problem, the group generated 10 possible solutions, including identification of prison personnel by name tags, by color-coded casual dress, or by uniforms for guard supervisors but not for guards in constant contact with prisoners. After discussing the various alternatives, the group decided upon the third solution.

In their first discussion, the group engaged in clear-cut conflict which was only partially resolved by vote. In the discussion led by the consultant, the group turned to problem solving, eventually developing a win–win method which was acceptable to all parties concerned.[22]

Beliefs Necessary to Implement the Win–Win Approach

We are suggesting that the win–win approach is the most desirable; however, a manager wanting to effectively use this approach must possess a series of beliefs. As you review the following four beliefs, keep in mind that resolution of conflict and the entire corporate climate and culture is more pleasant and productive when these beliefs are present.

Belief 1: Cooperation is Better than Competition

The manager must first believe cooperation is better than competition. However, differences of opinion can be an important part of cooperation. American management seems to be based on competition, so it is difficult to envision cooperation as a viable possibility at times.[23] This competition may develop out of Darwin's concept of survival of the fittest: a manager who has a self-image of weakness may fear extinction. Lacking confidence, this person feels a sense of competitiveness with others in the company.

Competition also has an important role in stimulating employees to achieve more. However, as technology becomes more complex and employees more specialized, interdependence is required. Few tasks can be completed without the cooperation of many employees. The group as a whole becomes greater than the sum of all the individuals, so cooperation is required. This is not to say that differences of opinion should be prevented.

Different opinions can lead to new insights and creativity as long as the opinions do not disrupt the group process. A manager must enter the conflict situation believing others' opinions are beneficial. He must be willing to listen. If a manager believes she has the only great ideas, polarization rather than a resolution may result because the manager communicates as if others' ideas are of no value.

As previously mentioned, American management seems to be based on competition. This highly competitive spirit may come from the basis of the American culture. From an early age, sports emphasize a win–lose competitive environment. We must "win" higher grades to get into the best colleges' but the number of winners is limited. And in business, the antitrust laws foster competition. Cooperation is frequently discussed, but the bases of society seem to work against it. But the same is not true in Japan.[24] From an early age cooperation is encouraged. Governmental regulation in Japan encourages cooperation among firms. Conflict is generally discouraged at all levels of business and government. This basic belief about conflict may be one reason Japanese firms have gained a competitive edge in international business during the past decade.

Belief 2: Parties Can Be Trusted

The second belief is that the other parties involved in the conflict can be trusted. Managers who are trusting will not conceal or distort relevant information, nor will they fear stating facts, ideas, conclusions, and feelings that would make them vulnerable.

A researcher compared problem-solving groups. Half the groups were directed to trust other people, to express their views openly, to share information freely, and to aim at a high level of mutual confidence. The other groups were directed to behave in opposite ways. The research found that problem-solving groups with high trust will:

- Exchange relevant ideas and feelings more openly.
- Develop greater clarification of goals and problems.
- Search more extensively for alternative courses of action.
- Have greater influence on solutions.
- Be more satisfied with their problem-solving efforts.
- Have greater motivation to implement conclusions.
- See themselves as closer and more of a team.
- Have less desire to leave their group to join another.[25]

Trusting behavior on the part of one person tends to encourage trusting behavior from the other person. This suggests, conversely, that when a manager convinces others that she does not trust them, the cues to mistrust will evoke mistrustful behavior on the others' part. At the same time, trusting cues will likely evoke trusting behavior from others. So it is best to assume a person can be trusted and to change that view only with evidence to the contrary.

Unfortunately, it is not always easy to accept the assumption that others can be trusted. Everyone enters conflict situations with biases and predispositions toward the other person. The manager who believes in the value of trust and wants to manifest a trusting image must firmly understand his own attitudes, hostilities, antagonisms, and biases. Once a person gets his attitudes in focus, it is possible to keep them from interfering with a solution to the conflict.

The role of trust in resolving conflict is demonstrated by several industries that have dramatically changed management–union relationships. For instance, the General Motors manufacturing facility that produces the Saturn has redefined the relationship between union and management. Management and union had a long tradition of conflict, but the company wanted to revolutionize the relationship to be more competitive with the Japanese. Trust had to be developed before the conflict could be reduced. Specialized team-building and conflict management seminars were conducted for many of the company employees in order to build a trusting environment. The result was one of the most harmonious labor–management relations in the U.S. automotive industry.

Belief 3: Status Differences Should Be Minimized

The third belief that managers must possess is that status differences between parties should be minimized in a conflict situation. Differences in power or status that separate two individuals into a we–they orientation inhibit conflict resolution. A manager who is in a higher status position may yield to the temptation to use the power inherent in the position as the rationale for forcing the solution. The participants, rather than confronting the problem and treating each other as equals, will regress into a win–lose style. This makes communication much easier as interactive listening is not required; however, the result is much less productive.

Managers who do not rely on status will spend time listening to everyone involved.

Belief 4: Mutually Acceptable Solutions Can Be Found

The final belief managers must hold is that a mutually acceptable and desirable solution exists and can be found. Unless both parties believe this is possible, a win–lose strategy will result. Conflict resolution can be extremely frustrating and time consuming unless both parties remain optimistic about finding a mutually acceptable answer. This is not to say that both parties are meeting the same goal. Rather, both parties can reach their different goals in an acceptable manner. If managers do not believe mutual acceptance is possible, they will not take the time needed to implement a win–win strategy. In fact, when a manager does not believe a mutually acceptable and desirable solution to a conflict is present, a win–win effort would be only a facade.

Each of these four beliefs—cooperation, trust, equal status, and mutually acceptable goals—is equally important. A manager must believe in these concepts to implement an effective win–win conflict resolution strategy. But belief in these concepts is not enough; managers must also use the appropriate communication skills in a strategic manner. The next part of this discussion analyzes these skills and the appropriate method for implementing them.

Implementing the Win–Win Strategy

Specific steps should be followed to achieve the win–win strategy. However, before these steps are reviewed, key communication principles that must be used need to be identified.

1. Use neutral rather than emotional terms. "I still tend to prefer my approach" is better than "Your idea is not functional."
2. Avoid absolute statements that leave no room for modification. "I think this is the way . . ." is better than "This is the *only* way."
3. Ask open-ended questions so others will be inclined to offer their viewpoints.
4. Avoid leading questions that lead people to agree verbally even when they disagree. This rule is especially important where status differences are present.
5. Repeat key phrases to make sure all parties are communicating on the same wavelength.
6. Use terms that all parties clearly understand and be sure the conflict is not over the meaning of terms rather than substantive issues.
7. Allow the other person to complete statements. Interruptions only add to the felt conflict and may lead to hostility.
8. Use effective listening skills to ensure the other person's ideas are fully understood.
9. Maintain a pleasant expression. A facial expression that implies a challenge can increase perceived conflict.
10. Use a face-to-face format if possible. Telephoned or written messages are less effective than face-to-face meetings for resolving conflicts.
11. Be aware of the importance of physical arrangements. For instance, sitting in front of a big desk may cause a person to feel defensive.

A sequence of six steps is generally necessary to obtain a win–win outcome.[26] When managers use the communication principles just presented as they follow the sequence given next, they should be able to resolve conflicts successfully.

1. Review and adjust conflict conditions. In the process model of conflict presented earlier, we identified functional and allocational interdependence as the two main causes of latent conflict. When a manager can identify these conditions, it is possible to adjust them to avoid the likelihood of conflict and promote cooperation. This may be accomplished through extensive discussion with clarity as the goal.

2. Review and adjust perceptions. Perceived conflict, the second component of the process model discussed, may exist when there is no latent conflict. Managers can avoid this problem by adjusting and correcting their perceptions through reality testing. Here, individuals objectively and seriously ask themselves, "Am I viewing the situation or the behavior as it actually exists?" Perceptions are more likely to be correct as the number of accurate measures of the situation increases. That is, perceptions become more accurate as an individual learns more facts about the condition and has resulting impressions confirmed by others' perceptions. One way to objectively analyze perceptions is to write down all the pertinent beliefs. This may help a person realize there is no basis for the felt conflict.

3. Review and adjust attitudes. Since a win–win outcome method depends on trust, mutuality, and cooperation, little success will result if the parties are distrustful, hostile, and competitive. Accordingly, one should identify the attitudes and feelings of the parties engaged in the conflict insofar as possible. One person cannot order change in another's attitudes. If a change in attitudes is not immediately possible, the best strategy may be to start with the easily solved problems. Once the easier problems are solved, a more positive attitude may develop for the more complex conflict situation. The trust that results may make cooperative communication easier.

4. Define the problem. For several reasons, a statement of the problem in a conflict situation is usually much more difficult than it seems. First, one must separate attempts to define the problem from a list of solutions. People tend to discuss solutions before they clearly define the problem. Because of this, our inclination is to state the problem as a solution rather than as a goal. This results in ambiguous communication, and it is common for the parties to focus on the solutions without having a clear definition of the problem. The outcome may be increased conflict. Second, managers must state the goals in the form of group goals rather than individual priorities. Third, the problem definition must be specific. One helpful strategy is to clearly write out the problem statement so everyone can see it. When this occurs, the parties involved at least know they agree on the problem.

5. Search jointly for alternatives. All parties, not just one party, should offer potential solutions. If a manager uses effective communication techniques, everyone involved should feel free to offer viewpoints. Also, one idea may stimulate other ideas. The more employees present communicate in an open, trusting environment, the greater the potential for generating effective solutions. Accordingly, it is important that a good listening environment be established to assure that all parties are involved.

6. Evaluate alternatives and develop an ultimate solution. After following the steps and applying the 11 communication principles presented earlier, a manager's evaluation of alternatives is really the easiest step. By this time, attention to the problem is unified, and an open communication environment has been achieved with active participation by all the parties involved.

Conflict and Management Success

The basic nature of organizational dynamics creates conflict.[27] Consequently, organizational managers must understand and learn to manage conflict. And as this chapter has explained, communication is at the foundation of conflict management. Since conflict is a pervasive, vital, but often troublesome aspect of organizational life, effective conflict management has become a major task for training programs in business and industry.[28] Whether one is a college student anticipating a career in management or a practicing manager with years of experience, it is necessary to continually seek constructive communication strategies for conflict management.

Summary

Managers are likely to spend about 20 percent of their time dealing with some kind of conflict, so it is important to understand the causes of conflict and productive methods for resolution. Since miscommunication is an integral element behind conflict, effective managerial communication is one key to resolution.

Conflict can be constructive as well as destructive. The nature of the word *conflict* implies opposing positions with negative results; however, when properly managed, conflict may be a positive force. An important managerial role is to be able to identify the difference between destructive and constructive conflict. This ability is improved by recognizing the four stages of conflict: latent, perceived, felt, and manifest.

Managers may recognize and resolve conflict at any one of these stages. They can then use one of five strategies to resolve conflict: withdrawal, smoothing, forcing, compromising, or maximizing. The first four strategies are termed win–lose or lose–lose because one or both parties in the conflict will lose. However, the maximization strategy is termed a win–win approach because both parties in the conflict are potential winners; consequently, the effective manager should strive for the win–win style.

The win–win strategy can be achieved when the manager believes in cooperation, trusts the other party, believes status differences should be minimized, and believes a mutually acceptable and desirable solution is available. These beliefs are a prerequisite to success, but satisfactory results cannot be obtained unless sound communication principles are used to put the beliefs into action. A sequence of steps should be followed when implementing the win–win strategy: review and adjust conflict conditions, perceptions, and attitudes; develop a problem definition; conduct a joint search for alternatives; and evaluate alternatives and develop an ultimate solution.

When a manager uses strategic communication skills, believes in the win–win approach to conflict resolution, and follows the correct sequence of activities, a constructive approach to conflict resolution can result.

Endnotes

1. Warren H. Schmidt, "Conflict: A Powerful Process for (Good or Bad) Change," *Management Review* 63, no. 12 (December 1974), p. 5.
2. Ronald Corwin, "Patterns of Organizational Conflict," *Administrative Science Quarterly* 14, no. 3 (December 1969), pp. 507–20.
3. "Saturn," *Business Week*, August 17, 1992, p. 86.
4. Daniel Katz and Robert L. Kahn, *The Social Psychology of Organizations*, 2nd ed. (New York: John Wiley & Sons, 1978), p. 613.
5. Clagett G. Smith, "A Comparative Analysis of Some Conditions and Consequences of Intra-Organizational Conflict," *Administrative Science Quarterly* 10, no. 3 (1965–1966), pp. 504–29.
6. K. W. Thomas, "Conflict," in *Organizational Behavior*, ed. S. Kerr (Columbus, Ohio: Grid Publishing, 1979), pp. 151–81.
7. Charles E. Watkins, "An Analytical Model of Conflict: How Differences in Perception Cause Differences of Opinion," *Supervisory Management* 41, no. 3 (March 1974), pp. 1–5; and J. L. Hocker and W. W. Wilmot, *Interpersonal Conflict*, 2nd ed. (Dubuque, Iowa: Wm. C. Brown, 1985).
8. Lewis Benton, "The Many Faces of Conflict: How Differences in Perception Cause Differences of Opinion," *Supervisory Management* 15, no. 3 (March 1970), pp. 7–12.
9. K. E. Weick, "Cognitive Processes in Organizations," in *Research in Organizational Behavior*, vol. 1, ed. B. Staw and L. Cummings (Greenwich, Conn.: JAI Press, 1979), pp. 41–74.
10. Robert Zajonc, "Attitudinal Effects of Mere Exposure," *Journal of Personality and Social Psychology Monograph Supplement* 9, no. 2 (June 1968), pp. 1–27.
11. William V. Haney, *Communication and Interpersonal Relations: Text and Cases*, 6th ed. (Homewood, Ill.: Richard D. Irwin, 1992), pp. 345–58.
12. Robert Kreitner and Angelo Kinicki, *Organizational Behavior* (Homewood, Ill.: BPI Irwin, 1992), p. 375.
13. Kenneth Boulding, *Conflict and Defense* (New York: Harper, 1962), pp. 305–7.
14. L. Putnam and S. Wilson, "Argumentation and Bargaining Strategies as Discriminators of Integrative and Distributive Outcomes," in *Managing Conflict: An Interdisciplinary Approach*, ed. A. Rahim (New York: Praeger Publishers, 1988).
15. L. R. Hoffman, E. Harburg, and N. R. F. Meier, "Differences and Disagreements as Factors in Creative Problem-Solving," *Journal of Abnormal and Social Psychology* 64, no. 2 (1962), pp. 206–24.

16. Louis R. Pondy, "Organizational Conflict: Concepts and Models," *Administrative Science Quarterly* 12, no. 2 (September 1967), pp. 499–506.

17. A. P. Brief, R. S. Schuler, and M. Van Sell, *Managing Job Stress* (Boston: Little, Brown & Co., 1981).

18. This diagram is based on the works of R. R. Blake and J. S. Mouton, "The Fifth Achievement," *Journal of Applied Behavioral Science* 6, no. 4 (1970), pp. 413–26; J. Hall, *How to Interpret Your Scores from the Conflict Management Survey* (Conrole, Texas: Teleometrics, 1986); R. W. Thomas, "Conflict and Negotiation Processes in Organizations" in *The Handbook of Industrial and Organizational Psychology*, 2, ed., M. D. Dunnette and L. Hough (Palo Alto: Consulting Psychologists Press, 1992), pp. 651–718; and K. W. Thomas and R. H. Kilmann, *The Thomas-Kilman Conflict Mode Instrument* (Tuxedo, N.Y.: Xicom, Inc., 1974).

19. W. A. Donohue, M. E. Diez, and R. B. Stahle, "New Directions in Negotiations Research," in *Communication Yearbook* 7, ed. R. N. Bostrom (Beverly Hills, Calif.: Sage Publications, 1983), pp. 249–79.

20. Gareth Morgan, *Images of Organization* (Newbury Park, Calif.: Sage Publications, 1986).

21. Jay W. Lorsch and Paul R. Lawrence, ed., *Studies in Organizational Design* (Homewood Ill.: Irwin-Dorsey, 1970), p. 1.

22. Alan C. Filey, *Interpersonal Conflict Resolution* (Glenview, Ill.: Scott, Foresman, 1975), p. 33.

23. N. J. Adler, *International Dimensions of Organizational Behavior* (Boston: Kent Publishing Co., 1986).

24. Jermiah J. Sullivan, "A Critique of Theory Z," *Academy of Management Review* 8, no. 1 (January 1983), pp. 132–42.

25. D. E. Zand, "Trust and Managerial Problem Solving," *Administrative Science Quarterly* 17, no. 1 (1972), pp. 229–39.

26. Filey, *Interpersonal Conflict Resolution*, p. 23.

27. Daniel Robey, *Designing Organizations* (Homewood, Ill.: Richard D. Irwin, 1986), pp. 176–201.

28. Linda L. Putnam, "Communication and Interpersonal Conflict," *Management Communication Quarterly* 1, no. 3 (February 1988), pp. 293–301.

Additional Readings

Baron, R. A. "Reducing Organizational Conflict: An Incompatible Response Approach." *Journal of Applied Psychology* (1984), pp. 272–79.

Borisoff, Deborah, and David A. Victor. *Conflict Management: A Communication Skills Approach.* Englewood Cliffs, N.J.: Prentice Hall, 1989.

Larson, Frank E., and Frank M. J. LaFrasto. *Teamwork.* Newbury Park, Calif.: Sage Publications, 1989.

Lippitt, Gordon. "Managing Conflict in Today's Organizations." *Training and Development Journal* 37, no. 7 (1982), pp. 66–74.

Rahim, A. *Managing Conflict: An Interdisciplinary Approach.* New York: Praeger Publishers, 1988.

Discussion Questions

1. Give an example in which selective attention has resulted in a conflict.
2. What is your definition of conflict?
3. What are the four axioms of conflict according to Watkins? How is each related to communication?
4. Consider the conflict that developed in the textile mill over raises. Write a note that would clarify the procedure for new employees.
5. Why can conflict be potentially beneficial?
6. What are the four stages of conflict according to Pondy? Briefly distinguish between each stage.
7. What is the difference between functional interdependence and allocational interdependence? Give an example of each.
8. Why can undetected latent conflict be potentially dangerous? Give a specific example.
9. What are two possible causes of felt conflict?
10. Briefly explain each of the styles of conflict resolution as presented in Figure 14-4.
11. List some reasons managers consider forcing to be their favorite backup strategy for dealing with conflict?
12. Why do many managers not have the beliefs necessary for a win–win strategy?
13. Add several other principles to the list of communication principles that are necessary for a win–win strategy.
14. Why is it difficult to adjust attitudes?
15. Briefly list and discuss the steps a manager should follow to implement the win–win strategy.

CASE 14–1
CONFLICT OVER JOB DUTIES

Linda Sims is the manager of the accounting department and Bill Cox is the manager of the purchasing department for a production company. This is a fast-growing company, so a new office wing and lobby were recently added to the administration building. The entire accounting department (11 employees) was moved into new offices next to the new lobby area.

Since the accounting department is located immediately next to the lobby, Ruth Rankin, the receptionist and telephone operator, reports to Sims. Rankin's job responsibilities do not seem to match the duties of any one department. One duty is to greet the vendors and call the purchasing agents the vendors are scheduled to meet. When Rankin is not busy as a receptionist or telephone operator, she works on journal entries assigned to her by Sims.

The company has experienced especially rapid growth over the past six months, which has caused everyone to be busier than usual. It is not uncommon for Rankin to have to make numerous calls to find a particular purchasing agent when he or she was not in the office. Often, Rankin has had to call an agent back two or three times before the agent could come to meet a vendor. She thought this was taking too much of her time, so she complained to Sims. To make matters worse, Sims was also giving Rankin more work.

Sims handled Rankin's complaint by telling Cox that Rankin would make only one call for a purchasing agent from now on and would not attempt to find an agent who was not in the office. She believed the purchasing agents had to be more responsible for meeting the vendors. This complaint upset Cox because he thought Sims was being arbitrary, so he simply told Sims he was not going to tell his employees to do anything differently.

Questions

1. What is the cause of this conflict? Is it functional, allocational, or both? Why?
2. Write a problem statement for this situation.
3. If you were Sims, how would you approach Cox in this situation?
4. What style did Sims initially use?
5. What could Sims do to gain Cox's cooperation rather than make him defensive?

CASE 14–2
CONFLICT BETWEEN THE ASSISTANTS

Rod Edwards, the advertising manager for Waterlite Advertising and Associates, has two assistants. One is Gina Reese, an account executive who gets clients for the company. Edward's second assistant is Mina Shawn, a copywriter. She does the actual writing and designing of the ads for the clients.

Reese and Shawn usually have a close working relationship because they work together on all clients' accounts. Reese gets the clients and discusses their needs with them. Afterward, she tells Shawn about the conversation and the clients' needs so Shawn can design the right ad. Once Shawn finishes the ad, Reese presents it to the client. If the ad is a success, it is usually Reese who gets the praise and recognition because she is the one who presents it to the client.

In the past, Shawn was not bothered by the recognition Reese got because she always knew she was the one who designed the ad. But the last ad Shawn designed brought in a $1 million contract to the firm. Edwards immediately gave Reese a raise for bringing in the client but did not give Shawn any recognition.

Naturally, this caused friction between Reese and Shawn, and their relationship began to deteriorate. Four days after Reese got the raise, their conflict reached a climax.

Reese borrowed Shawn's ruler (a trivial occurrence) and forgot to return it. Shawn caused a scene and refused to talk to Reese for the next few days.

The problem was brought to Edwards' attention because his department was not producing. For the ads to be developed, the assistants had to work together.

Edwards called both employees into his office and immediately started lecturing them. He insisted they start talking and begin working on the next ad. He told them he expected an ad finished by noon the following day. Reese and Shawn walked out of Edwards' office without resolving the problem. They did get some work done the next day, but their close relationship was never resumed.

Questions

1. What kind of conflict resolution strategy did Edwards use? What kind should he have used?

2. This is an example of destructive conflict. Could it develop as a constructive situation?

3. What steps should Edwards have followed to develop a win–win strategy?

15 MANAGERIAL NEGOTIATION

The director of your community agency has just received a special appropriation to be divided among the agency's three major departments. As manager of one of these departments, you can see many worthwhile ways to use the funds. But your director is not certain how to allocate the funds. Obviously, the more funds the other departments receive, the less allocated to your group.

This is where you use your negotiation skills. You have already scheduled a meeting to discuss allocation of the funds. What strategy should you use? Should you make an inordinately high request, knowing that is probably what the other department managers will do? Or should you make a lower request, and tell your manager that you are trying to be conservative and reasonable? Should you be a hard bargainer and make an emotional appeal for funds, or should you use an objective, rational approach? How can you sell your position? What kind of a negotiator is the director? The correct answers to these questions will help you obtain a higher proportion of the funds for your department.

Negotiation is an integral aspect of management. Successful managers negotiate for increased budget allocations, better purchasing prices, higher salaries for themselves and their subordinates, increased time to finish important assignments, more favorable annual objectives, or even better salary offers when starting with a new company. Many managers, however, shy away from negotiation. They do not feel comfortable doing it either because they have not succeeded in previous negotiations or they have not learned the process of dynamic negotiation. Most knowledge about negotiation, unfortunately, comes from limited personal experience.

But negotiation is becoming a more important component of the manager's job.[1] It can be argued that ineffective negotiation reduces organization productivity, demoralizes those involved, and frequently generates hostile feelings among other parties.[2]

Before discussing the dynamic process of negotiation, we should first specify exactly what the term means. The last chapter dealt with conflict resolution in terms of win–lose, lose–lose, and win–win strategies. That discussion urged that every attempt aim at a win–win solution to conflict, and it reviewed the beliefs necessary to implement this approach successfully. To implement the win–win approach, the parties involved must believe (1) cooperation is better than competition, (2) both parties trust each other, (3) status differences between the parties should be minimized, and (4) an acceptable and desirable solution is attainable.

Even though a manager strives to develop an atmosphere that fosters the win–win belief, such an outcome is not always possible. When one or both parties do not hold these four beliefs, a win–win approach is less likely to succeed, so a win–lose or lose–lose strategy is appropriate. When one or both parties see a situation as one in which one party will lose or gain something in exchange for the other party's loss or gain, a negotiation strategy is appropriate. In this situation, one party cannot easily determine the needs or desired outcome of the other party, and one of the parties may not fully trust the other.

The vignette presented at the beginning of this chapter clearly shows how a win–win approach differs from the negotiation approach used in this chapter. Conceivably, a manager could sit down with the director and develop a win–win approach for allocating the funds so each department would benefit. However, suppose the director tries to play one manager against another, or suppose the departments are engaged in dissimilar functions so teamwork is difficult to develop. In these cases, a department may not receive the funds it deserves unless its manager knows how to negotiate.

When managers consider the term *negotiation*, they may often think of collective bargaining between labor and management or a sports agent negotiating for an athlete. These examples are generally termed third-party negotiations. Research indicates managers are more frequently becoming involved in third-party negotiations.[3] However, this discussion emphasizes the type of everyday negotiation situations any manager may face, such as obtaining additional office space for an employee, winning a budget increase, or securing additional support from another department.

A Strategic Model for Negotiations

The best way to approach the negotiation process is through the strategic analysis of managerial communication presented in Chapter 3. To develop a successful negotiation strategy, managers must first be aware of the culture

FIGURE 15–1

Summary of Strategic Analysis for Negotiations

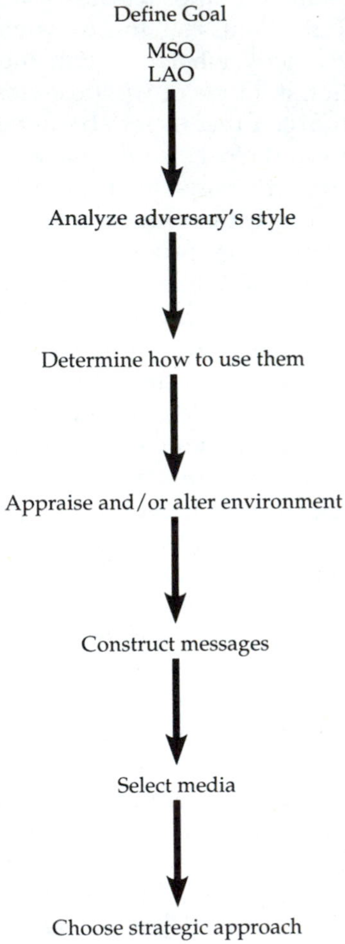

Define Goal

MSO
LAO

↓

Analyze adversary's style

↓

Determine how to use them

↓

Appraise and/or alter environment

↓

Construct messages

↓

Select media

↓

Choose strategic approach

in which they negotiate. Then they need to analyze themselves as negotiators, their adversaries, the purpose or acceptable goal, as well as the most appropriate time, place, channel, message, and strategic approaches. This discussion analyzes each of these components separately, but as in any communication situation, all the variables are interrelated. The general direction this chapter takes is diagrammed in Figure 15–1.

Culture

As mentioned in many places in this book, culture is a primary concern in any communication situation. Both national and organizational culture must be considered when negotiating. Some cultures support an assertive, almost demanding, negotiation style, whereas, in other cultures a more passive approach is expected. A culture may encourage long negotiation sessions that require patience, while others support quick resolution. Some cultures encourage initial offers close to an expected settlement, while in other cultures the initial offer is nowhere near an expected outcome. In some cultures, it is important to develop a personal relationship before negotiating, but in others only a superficial knowledge of others is required. Managers must be thoroughly aware of the other party's national culture to negotiate successfully.

Organizational culture largely determines who has the power within an organization and the extent to which a person can make decisions. There is no reason to negotiate with someone if that person can't make decisions, and this is often the case where power is centralized. Also, in bureaucratic organizations, numerous policies and procedures may preclude flexibility so there is little that can be negotiated. But most organizations are not so highly centralized and bureaucratic that negotiation is of no value. The manager's challenge is to determine what can be negotiated with whom. This challenge is a result of the organizational culture as well as the political structure within the organization.

Personal Negotiation Style

Before entering a negotiation setting, a person also needs to understand his personal approach to negotiation. Just as some people are outgoing and talkative and others are withdrawn and quiet, some managers enter a negotiation with confidence and a positive attitude, while others see defeat from the outset, believing they do not have a chance. Before negotiators can succeed, they must believe in themselves. E. H. Harreman, one of the nation's leading railroad pioneers and a man bubbling with self-confidence, once remarked to a young financier, "Let me be one of 15 men around a table, and I will have my way."[4] Once a manager is aware of the negotiation process, he should feel more confident. In addition, practice in negotiation, if done properly, leads to greater confidence because of the positive results.

Success breeds success! If a person has not succeeded in earlier negotiations, it is important to learn to be a winner. By starting small and applying the principles discussed in this chapter, a person can begin to build confidence.

A manager creates power in negotiations when confident. Being confident, however, is not enough; during negotiations, you must also act and look confident. To begin, do not look as if you are ready for a long fight. One of the poorest practices is to remove your coat, roll up your shirt sleeves, and open your collar so the necktie or scarf hangs sloppily around the neck. In addition, take care not to project a tired, listless image. An adversary's hope and confidence increase dramatically when an opponent looks tired.

In negotiation, vision is an important source of communication; during much of the discussion, negotiators watch one another closely. You can promote success with a neat appearance that suggests you are well organized and a person that cannot easily be exploited. We deal with nonverbal messages in a separate chapter and again later in this chapter, but remember that nervous habits such as tapping a finger on the desk or playing with a pencil can project a nervous, vulnerable image.

Some tension is always part of the negotiation process. This tension generally results from two separate unknowns inherent in any negotiation. The first is whether or not a deal can be struck. A second unknown is how long the negotiations will take. Simply knowing that it is natural to feel these tensions and being aware of their source helps to lessen them considerably, especially once the negotiations have begun. And by recognizing that a certain amount of tension is natural, negotiators will not let the tension hurt their confidence.

Purpose

The purpose of the negotiation process is simple: to maximize your advantage. Initially, that purpose may seem rather obvious, but it is not always simple. In fact, this purpose is one of the most critical elements to consider when developing a negotiation strategy. The purpose of the negotiation may translate to, "know what you want" or, more appropriately, "know what is reasonable to expect." Obviously, wants and expectations are vastly different, but unless you have clearly differentiated between the two, confusion and failure can result.

Negotiation is useless in certain situations. Consider, for example, a production manager who has successfully negotiated personal salary increases in the past. Unfortunately, poor market conditions have affected the company, and nobody is receiving a salary increase. If the manager tries to negotiate now, he will not only fail to get an increase but he also might create resentment because his demands are made during hard times.

In addition, no real negotiation can result when one of the parties has nothing to gain or lose. While this seems obvious, it pays to analyze the situation to determine whether this is the case. Anyone who has tried to negotiate a better price on an item from an individual who was not sure he or she even wanted to sell can appreciate this.

Defining the Maximum Supportable and Least Acceptable Outcomes
If the time is ripe and the other party is committed to the negotiation, then establish the negotiation goal. At this point, two concepts are important: maximum supportable outcome (MSO) and least acceptable outcome (LAO). The maximum supportable outcome is the absolute most one can ask for in the opening position without leaving the realm of reason. A negotiation can be quickly terminated if the MSO is beyond the realm of reason. In one case, a small construction company had some surplus land it wanted to sell. A

transportation firm with a warehouse adjoining the land inquired about the price. The price was so high it was beyond the realm of what the transportation firm believed to be an MSO. The transportation firm incorrectly assumed the construction company was not interested in selling because the price was so high; hence, all communication between the two firms stopped.

The LAO is the least acceptable result one will accept from the negotiation. If the outcome of negotiation is anything less than one's least acceptable outcome, it would be better to terminate the negotiation. Planning is important so the LAO is established before the negotiation. If the LAO is not established before negotiation, the advisory may alter your perception of the LAO.

Of course, both the LAO and MSO also reflect primary, secondary, short-term, and long-term considerations. An outcome frequently is complex and includes more than one aspect. For instance, a purchasing manager is interested in commodity quality, date of delivery, follow-up service, and many other items.

Since these two points—least acceptable outcome (LAO) and the maximum supportable outcome (MSO)—are the guideposts for negotiation, their terms must be clear before one enters negotiation. And it is a critical error (and possibly the most common) for a person to modify either of these two points after negotiation has begun. Doing so suggests the adversary is influencing her opponent unduly.

Naturally, you should keep in mind throughout our discussion of LAO and MSO that the terms are reversed for the other person in the negotiation. Consider the example of a sales manager for a clothing distributor who is negotiating the price of 150 new suits with the purchasing manager of a clothing store. Table 15–1 demonstrates how the two see the terms differently.

In other words, the maximum supportable outcome for one person would be the least acceptable outcome for the other. Also, an MSO may actually be a lower figure than the LAO as demonstrated with the purchasing manager's perceptions.

It is important to keep this "reversal of terms" in mind when studying the following material. One outcome may be desirable to one person, but undesirable to another. In negotiation, as with other aspects of

TABLE 15–1 Reversed Terms

Sales Manager		*Purchasing Manager*
Maximum supportable outcome (MSO)	$15,000	Least acceptable outcome (LAO)
Least acceptable outcome (LAO)	$11,500	Maximum supportable outcome (MSO)

communication, individual perception and frame of reference are important to remember.

Finding the Least Acceptable and Maximum Supportable Outcomes

Because the guidelines provided by the least acceptable outcome and the maximum supportable outcome are so critical, give careful thought to finding these outcomes. The LAO is probably easiest to establish. This is the point below which nothing could be accepted because of the potential loss. In effect, when a negotiator commits to this point, loss is unlikely.

The LAO is both objective and subjective, a combination of the facts surrounding the situation and the value placed on them. Because it is subjective, no magical formula determines the LAO. Thus, make every effort to separate what is acceptable from what is wanted. Remember, the two are vastly different. For instance, a person negotiating salary for a new job may want $47,000 or more per year but would be willing to accept $38,000.

Negotiators can determine their LAO by looking at a few facts. In the example of the job offer, the candidate could have studied what others with similar backgrounds were earning, what the cost of living was in the area, what potential exists for future raises, and what other opportunities were available. Of course, factors other than money, including geographic location, opportunities for advancement, and social climate, are considerations. It is not always easy to determine exactly what one's LAO is, but it is worthwhile to develop some kind of decision work sheet to ensure a systematic and objective process. Table 15–2 presents one possible example for determining the LAO of a job.

Any format that helps the individual to think through the process is of value. The main factor is that development of the LAO requires research and contemplation. A carefully considered LAO lets the manager know when negotiation has slipped beyond the point where acceptance seems to be out of reach.

Of course, we would all prefer to be at the other extreme of the range, the MSO. The MSO is the furthest point from the LAO that the negotiator

---

TABLE 15–2   Establishing the Least Acceptable Outcome

Item	Relative Importance	LAO
Salary	4	$28,000
Location	3	Within 500 miles of hometown near a lake
Company size	1	Member of the Fortune 500
Job duties	5	At least 20% of the job should involve use of computers so I can use these skills
Social climate	2	Several young unmarried people (like me) in the department

can reasonably justify. Some negotiations establish demands that are so un-reasonable they are immediately disregarded. In other words, the demand is beyond that which is supportable.

That area between the MSO and the LAO is the settlement range.[5] Both parties in the negotiation have a conscious (or unconscious) settlement range. To help achieve success, the negotiator must be able to justify the MSO convincingly. Otherwise, the MSO may be set at a point that is beyond the opponent's LAO. And, even though the negotiator might be willing to settle for much less, this possibility may be obviated because the opponent will see no reason to continue the discussion. But the reciprocal of this is also true; the maximum should not be too low, because once the MSO is out, one cannot readjust it. Negotiation will surely cease at that point.

The establishment of the MSO reflects the "one-trip-to-the-well principle." A person gets to state her opening position only once, and it is vital to make the most of it. It is almost impossible to reverse directions and ask for more when the negotiator, after looking more closely at the situation, belatedly realizes her MSO was set too low.

But what is maximum? It is whatever one can support, and this justifi-cation may require some creativity. In developing the maximum supportable outcome, look for unique attributes to include. Do not become so fixed on one or two items that you never consider other possible combinations. Con-sider a marketing manager who is negotiating with the vice-president for an additional employee position in the marketing department. The additional position may not be as big an obstacle to overcome as the salary requested for the position. How can the manager justify a salary of $40,000 for the position? It may be possible to divert attention to something positive like increased sales to distract the vice-president from the salary.

Many people think they do not have the nerve to ask for the limit because they do not want others to consider them unreasonable. Nevertheless, if you can support an outcome, it is not unreasonable, and the opposition should not immediately reject the request. The best way to determine the maximum is to determine what you can support. In doing so, look for new or unique ways to support a position. It will then be much easier to state your maximum request.

Give the opposition clear support for the MSO and use a positive, detailed, and well-structured manner. Consider the simple example of two different managers dealing, at different times, with the same salesperson as they try to buy a similar used photocopier for their department.

Manager 1 says, "I know you are asking $3,200, but all I will give you is $2,300, and that is final."

Although the manager has set $2,300 as his MSO, he would consider other figures, but he has not clearly related this fact to the seller. Instead, it sounds as if this is the only offer. Negotiation seems closed.

Manager 2 says, "The photocopier is four years old and may need repairs in the near future. It copies quite well and looks good, but the side is scratched.

Also, it doesn't have a warranty like a new one. A new photocopier of this class, which has a warranty and no wear or tear, is $4,100. I'll tell you what, I'll give you $2,300 cash so there'll be no receivables to worry about, and I'll take it with me so you won't need to deliver it."

The second manager thoroughly explained her MSO so the seller could understand why she offered $900 less than the asking price. The seller is much more likely to accept the second offer, or at least to continue negotiating. A counteroffer may be made in the settlement range.

So far the discussion has focused on the negotiator's purpose. We also need to look at the different types of adversaries.

The Adversary's Style

Chapter 3 explained that communication style is the approach one uses when communicating. Just as an individual has a communication style, he also has a negotiation style that makes him unique, memorable, and interesting. Think of the recent presidents—Clinton, Bush, Reagan—each has a unique essence.

Thus, managers should consider their own style as well as that of their adversaries in negotiation. Individual style largely determines negotiation strategy, because style is a person's predictable behavior pattern or familiar way of being. An individual's emotional and economic needs as well as her values determine style. However, if a manager is to succeed in negotiations, a style used simply out of habit is inappropriate for the many different situations faced. Consequently, a person can know her own style tendencies, yet make adaptations when appropriate. The manager can be flexible, but only after recognizing the basic style.

Conversely, when one recognizes the adversary's style, one can adapt strategy to fit the situation. Different styles require differing approaches, so the message must be adapted accordingly.

The relationship of power to style is significant and worth considering. Power is the essence of bargaining, and an individual uses a particular style in the conscious or unconscious belief that this style generates the greatest amount of power in a given situation.[6] One's negotiating or bargaining style develops because it is the most effective style for that person. However, an individual's perception of "effective" is highly subjective. Just because a person views his style as effective is not to say it generates the highest level of power or develops the best possible outcome.

Iraqi President Saddam Hussein obviously thought he was using the most effective negotiation strategy with the United States and its allies before they attacked Iraq on January 16, 1991. Later events proved that Hussein did not have the power he thought he had. At any rate, what he did was not as successful as he had anticipated.

The following three negotiation styles reflect a combination of the work of Michael Maccoby and Tessa Warschaw. Maccoby conducted an extensive study of executives in American business and industry and categorized their general managerial styles.[7] Warschaw, as a result of her individual work in interpersonal negotiations and seminars on the subject, has described various styles of negotiation.[8]

Any of the following styles may be effective in generating power in different situations. A manager must determine the most effective style for a given situation rather than use one style habitually. As you review these styles, keep in mind they are only general descriptions. Most people probably use some combination of the basic styles.

The Fast-Flashy Style

People using the fast-flashy style of negotiation are razzle-dazzle negotiators with high volume and quick actions. They generate power by attempting to overwhelm their opponents with quick charm and compelling magic. Such a person constantly smiles, is extremely pleasant to everyone, and has a joke for every occasion along with a brilliant wit. This person gains and holds attention.

This style of negotiation makes for a difficult opponent. She uses flash as a mask either to send double messages, to circumvent an issue, or to change strategy from one minute to the next. This negotiator may also use humor to demean her opposition in public, but the way she states it may take a few minutes to register as a personal attack. These individuals intend jokes to deceive or attack rather than to add humor to a situation. Negotiators of this type are witty and quick and force issues or take over agendas. They interrupt, cut off others, use sarcasm, and toss off flip remarks, but all in a surprisingly charming manner. In the TV series, "M*A*S*H," the character played by Alan Alda often demonstrated this negotiation style.

Used correctly, this style keeps opponents off balance and can be effective. Attempts to outdo this opponent by using the same tactics are usually doomed. After all, this type of negotiator has more practice at using flashy and fast rejoinders. The best defense here is seriousness. When faced with this type of opponent, do not get caught in the game. Do not laugh at a demeaning comical line, and do not try to outwit the person. Rather, keep the discussion on the topic. Do not be overpowered by flashy clothes, extravagance, and grand gestures. Remain positive even when your opponent appears overbearing in her own self-confidence.

The fast-flashy negotiator counts on sweeping the opponent away through false charm and quick wit. In facing this type of opponent, one remains natural and does not let the game follow the fast-flashy set of rules. After all, the purpose is winning the negotiation, not having a witty repartee.

Dictators

In negotiation, the dictator tries to overpower with his subtle demonstration of confidence. This show of confidence results from his being extremely well organized, thorough in his preparation, and continually low key and cool. He presents the image of a totally rational person. Because of his extreme organization and professional image, the dictator can control situations. He keeps close control of the agenda, the flow of communication, and the physical surroundings. The TV character Perry Mason generally portrayed the image of a dictator.

One way in which the dictator maintains control is by regulating the flow of information. In negotiation, dictators often act as the gatekeepers of information; their opponents learn only what the dictator allows them to learn. Dictators will try to control the information by asking a lot of questions while providing only short answers when questioned themselves. They are quick to give directions and commands, but do not provide clues about their own feelings.

When possible, the dictator arranges the physical setting carefully, again, to maintain control. Large spaces, big desks, rich furnishings, and even chairs that seat them higher than others are used to maintain control. They dress to give an image of authority by using dark grays and blues and staying away from the flamboyant attire fast-flashy negotiators might wear. Dictators also control their expressions and gestures. The opponent receives no more non-verbal information than is essential.

Dictators try to obtain power in negotiations by intimidating and controlling their opponents. The dictator's demanding demeanor can be hard to deal with unless the opponent also remains strong and self-confident. Do not be caught in the trap of attire and physical surroundings. Rather than becoming subordinated to the dictator, maintain an attitude of equality, and do not let the dictator verbally control the negotiation.

Parents

Parents represent a third negotiation style. Parents offer comfort, listen intensely, provide a soothing environment, and try to convince opponents that the solution proposed is for the opponent's own good. Similar to the support from a mother or father, this negotiator's offering of love, acceptance, understanding, approval, praise, and tangible rewards is difficult to resist. Through this compassion, the parent generates power knowing that it is difficult for a person to oppose someone so compassionate and supportive.

The parent seems like a nice person. In fact, the parent may even let the other win a small victory, but the win is calculated to appease temporarily. In an attempt to develop a false sense of comfort or apathy, a parent may commend the opposition for positions taken in a negotiation. Just as real-life parents sometimes do, these negotiators want their opponents to develop a sense of commitment and trust so they will not break away.

A real estate agent may use the parent's technique to win over a young couple. She might assure the couple that times are tough and houses expensive; however, if they will just trust her, she will find what they can afford. Later, when the husband or wife balks at what the agent terms the "perfect home for them," the agent sounds hurt or even rejected because the buyers will not accept her deal. She then assures the reticent party that all is well;

FIGURE 15–2

Strategic Managerial Communication Model

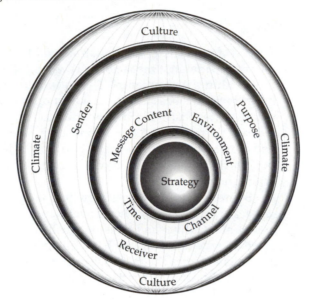

the agent will sell the house in a month or two for the same amount. Buyers involved with these types would do well to consult their own interests—or another agent.

This devious style of negotiation can be difficult to detect, but it must be detected because it is so manipulative. Breaking away from such a supportive environment is difficult. Just as a child no longer needs the total support of parents, a person negotiating with a parent must resist too much tender loving care and recognize the facade to resist the false support.

While these three negotiation styles—fast-flashy, dictator, and parent—are the predominant ones, we can identify many other approaches. The key is to analyze the opponent's style to keep from being manipulated. Naturally, an awareness of the different styles helps managers understand their own style and how to adapt it to fit different situations.

The basic model of strategic managerial communication presented in Chapter 3 is again presented here in Figure 15–2. To use the analogy presented in Chapter 3, we have been peeling away the layers of the onion to develop a strategy. Discussion thus far has focused on the culture, the sender (manager), the purpose or goal of the negotiations, and the receiver's (the adversary's) style. To develop a negotiation strategy systematically, one must also analyze the time, environment, channel, and content of the message. These are the next layer of the onion. Although the following discussion treats these items independently, managers must consider all four simultaneously when developing a negotiation strategy because they all affect each other.

Time

Time is a vital component of strategy.[9] Two questions should be addressed when considering time factors: (1) when to negotiate, (2) how to best use the time within the negotiation. The answer to the second question also provides insights for the best time to make an offer or counteroffer. First, let's look at when to negotiate. Biorhythm addresses those times of the day when individuals perform at their best and their worst. Each individual has his own body metabolism whose traits and habits largely govern his actions. Each person finds the best time of day and day of the week to fit his individual orientation.

Some simple guidelines may help to optimize energy and prevent major setbacks. For instance, when travel is necessary, a wise negotiator allows time to rest after arrival and does not rush right into the discussion. In addition, a person who eats a big lunch is wise not to get involved in a serious discussion immediately after the meal. Digestion will temporarily affect metabolism and may dull thinking. Similarly, do not negotiate when suffering from a headache or any other ailment that does not allow you to concentrate fully. Many individual idiosyncrasies exist, but the consensus seems to be that most people are at peak efficiency about 11 A.M.[10] By this time, they have digested their breakfast, are warmed up but not tired, and their systems are not dulled by a heavy lunch.

Although the ideal is to select the best time to negotiate, such is not always practical. Thus, the savvy negotiator is always fully prepared and never loses an opportunity to negotiate. A quick meeting in the cafeteria, a chance encounter with an opponent in the elevator, or an apparently spontaneous telephone call can represent opportunities for negotiations. To quote Ilich, "Never lose an opportunity to negotiate, but never negotiate until you are certain it's an opportunity."[11]

In any negotiation, the main question to ask is, "When do I have the most power and when is my adversary the weakest?" Naturally, the answer changes. Assume a person wanted to change his work schedule to be able to leave at 4:30 P.M. instead of 5 P.M. to beat the traffic rush. The best time to negotiate this is probably just after the boss has seen the person working before the regular starting time or working during a lunch break. Another opportune time for this negotiation may be immediately after some major accomplishment or even when another department has changed its work schedule. Strategic timing can add significantly to a person's power in negotiation. It is the hidden power of a negotiator.

A second question is how to best use time within the negotiation. Generally, one expects most significant concession behavior and settlement action to occur close to the deadline.[12] An approaching deadline puts pressure on the parties to state their true positions and thus does much to squeeze any elements of bluff out of the latter steps of negotiation. A deadline brings pressure to bear that can actually affect the least acceptable outcome on which each party is willing to settle.[13] A number of major studies verify the power of time limits on the negotiation.[14]

Because of the significance of deadlines, note the following guidelines.

1. **Do not reveal the true deadline.** When an adversary knows the other person's deadlines, negotiations stall until the deadline acts as a pressure for concession. When a person has an extremely tight deadline, she may be wise to extend the deadline rather than to enter the negotiations at a disadvantage. An infamous example of deadlines comes from the negotiations on the Persian Gulf in January 1991. President Bush and the allies continually indicated January 16 was the deadline for any negotiations. A flurry of activities occurred immediately before this date. However, the Iraqis apparently did not think this was the true deadline as the city lights remained on for easy targets the night allies commenced bombing.

2. **Be patient.** This may also be referred to as forbearance.[15] Negotiators should take time to answer questions, provide information, and make decisions. This includes keeping defensive reactions under control as well as avoiding the tendency to take an offensive posture when being verbally attacked. The time provided through patience allows the opportunity to organize, understand issues, test the opponent's strengths and weaknesses, and weigh risks. Also, it creates a sense of pressure in the opponent, especially when the deadline approaches. Forbearance or patience pays.

3. **Use the clock.** Because most Americans are so conscious of time, it is advised that you seek concessions or even provide minor concessions toward the end of a time period. Thus, you might elicit action on the part of the opponent immediately before lunch or dinner because people like to have a sense of accomplishment when taking a break. And a flurry of action can be used to the negotiator's advantage if taken at the right time.

The Environment

In addition to time and timing, the physical environment is important. Environment and location were major concerns when in 1990 Security Pacific Bank and Bank of America negotiated one of the largest bank mergers in U.S. history. First, they had to decide if negotiations would take place in Los Angeles or San Francisco and then the conference facilities and room arrangement were discussed. Negotiations on physical arrangements were conducted before the actual negotiations began. This section explores two aspects of the physical arrangement: site and physical arrangement.

Site selection is often important because it bears directly on the amount of control each party may exercise over the physical arrangements at that site as well as the psychological climate in which the exchange occurs. In negotiations conducted in one's home territory, the host has a legitimate right to assume responsibility for arranging the physical space. This is similar to the home-field advantage in sports; the home team is more likely to come out the winner in both situations.

What is the best way to arrange a conference room or office for negotiations? While no set rules exist because the optimum arrangement could change from one situation to another, a few factors bear stressing. First, prevent distractions such as phone calls. These can be costly if they occur at an awkward time in the negotiation. At the same time, it is acceptable if the opponent is distracted, a clear advantage to being on "home ground" where even daily routine can distract an outsider. Fewer things distract a person when at home. Second, the careful negotiator avoids sitting in a position that suggests subordination or even equality. If in a conference room, sit at the head of the table. If in your office, sit behind the desk. Also, have appropriate equipment such as flip charts, blackboards, or writing tablets ready. Having these items ready underscores the sincerity of your position. And having to hunt for these items can needlessly disturb the communication flow at a critical time.

Observing the physical arrangements of a room and physical position that an opponent takes in a negotiation provides valuable information. Figure 15–3 summarizes several possibilities. For example, a researcher conducted observation and questionnaire studies of seating preferences in several social

FIGURE 15–3

Seating Arrangements

Casual

Cooperative   Competitive

contexts and found that people engaging in casual conversation normally prefer to sit at right angles to each other (if seated at square or rectangular tables), or beside one another when seated at circular tables. He also found that side-by-side seating occurred in cooperative relationships. However, face-to-face seating was the most preferred configuration in competitive relationships, with a moderately wide space separating the parties. He also noted less conversation when people were seated far apart than when they were side by side or opposite one another.[16]

When negotiating, managers can use this information to their advantage. For instance, one wanting to create an impression of cooperation may use a seating arrangement different from that in a competitive atmosphere. Also, a person avoiding interaction wants to move the chairs far apart; when seeking interaction, the person moves the chairs closer together. Other nonverbal elements come into play in negotiations. For example one can use distance to gain power. Birdwhistell found that when two parties are in competitive situations, they find proximity threatening.[17] Consequently, if a manager wants to create stress in an opponent, he might move closer physically, especially to a person who has a combative attitude. Eye contact can also be a strong tool in negotiation. Research indicates people avoid direct visual contact in competitive encounters because it is stressful.[18] Cook hypothesizes that people tend to avoid eye contact in competitive relationships because they find it intimidating, dominating, or overly revealing of motives they wish to keep hidden.[19] In this same regard, other researchers have found that people have greater difficulty telling a convincing lie when they are being watched closely than when not.[20]

Both proximity and eye contact can be valuable tools when managers understand and use them in negotiation. Direct eye contact may keep an opponent from using deception. Also, when a person is competitive, direct eye contact may make the opponent uneasy; consequently, the tactic can be a way for one to gain the upper hand in a negotiation. These topics are discussed more thoroughly in the chapter on nonverbal communication.

A manager is not always able to negotiate on the home territory. In fact, a skillful negotiator may often attempt to catch an opponent off guard by confronting him in a strange place where negotiation is least expected. While effective managers may try this technique on others, they try to avoid having it happen to them.

If you cannot use home ground for negotiation, try for neutral territory. Thus, in a negotiation with a high-level manager, it might be inappropriate to ask her to come to a lower level manager's office. However, one could suggest that both parties meet in a conference room to avoid interruptions by saying, "I know you're busy and get a lot of interruptions. How about meeting in the engineering conference room so we can get away for a few minutes?" Or a meeting at lunch might be an easy way to neutralize a situation. The adversary may be comfortable at lunch, and it may be possible to offset any status advantage.

When you have no alternative to meeting in the adversary's office, you do not need to assume a subordinate role immediately. Typically, the adversary is at a desk and the "visitor" is in a side chair, or worse, in a low-slung occasional chair that causes him to be lower than the adversary at the desk. One can quickly offset the advantage that rests with the person behind the desk merely by standing up and moving around while speaking. With this little nonverbal technique, it is now possible to look down on the adversary.

The Message

Sender, receiver, purpose, time, and environment all help to set the stage for what is really the essence of the negotiation, the message itself. Negotiation revolves around the amount of information that each party decides to relate (or not to relate) about true motives and preferences. Negotiators base such a decision not only on their own standards but also equally on opponents' behavior, openness, and honesty before and during the exchange.

The environmental factors discussed earlier send some of these signals. In addition, negotiators project personal and interpersonal feelings nonverbally through such behavior as head nods, gestures, postures, facial expressions, and eye contact. You can communicate a superior attitude toward another by erect posture, by an unsmiling or haughty facial expression, or by staring another person down; you transmit feelings of anxiety by a tense, rigid posture and wringing of your hands.

Although nonverbal messages are important, the spoken word is the predominant form of communication in negotiation. The major types of verbal messages appropriate for discussion here are making concessions and responding to and presenting questions. But first, we will consider the opening messages.

Opening Messages

Earlier in our discussion we noted that time is a vital component of strategy and power is related to time. The importance of patience was also discussed. Now the question becomes, Should the negotiations begin with an immediate discussion of key issues or is it best to begin with a friendly, neutral conversation? The answer depends on the total time allowed for the negotiations, the type of previous relationship with the parties involved, and whether the general atmosphere is friendly or hostile.

In the United States, the accepted practice is to begin with a general conversation on neutral topics. But the conversation moves rather quickly toward the issues. The same pattern is true with many western Europeans; however, in Mexico and most Asian countries, the initial, neutral conversations are generally much longer. This is why Americans frequently become impatient when negotiating with Asians.

Concessions

We have mentioned that it is important to establish the LAO and MSO before negotiating. But it is not advisable to state these early in the negotiation. Rather, it is best to determine the other person's LAO. You then begin to move away from your MSO toward your LAO and toward the other person's MSO. This is generally accomplished through a series of concessions.

When and how to make concessions is determined by information obtained from questions—our next topic. However, principles of the equality rule can serve as a guideline for making concessions. The first equality principle suggests negotiators generally expect one another to make an equal *number* of concessions from their initial starting point. The second principle is that of equal sacrifice. By this rule, "equality" is judged by *how much* an individual concedes relative to his aspirations—in other words, who makes the bigger sacrifice.

Imagine a situation in which two managers are negotiating a reorganization among several departments. A third manager has retired and has not been replaced; consequently, the duties of her department will be assigned to the two remaining departments. During this negotiation, the two managers must perceive that each has made an equal *number* of concessions as well as an equal *amount*. But numbers and amounts are difficult to quantify when negotiating such items as job duties, reporting relationships, and budgets. Consequently, the manner in which these concessions are made is important. An effective negotiator uses positive language to assure concessions appear frequent and large.

The number and amount of concessions are difficult to determine if the other party is not clear on your starting point. Accordingly, you may want to be nebulous on this point. It is also helpful to find issues that appear to be a major concession to your opponent but only a minor concession to you. In addition, it is often better to make several minor concessions rather than one major concession. Finally, it is best to make these concessions toward the opponent's deadline as little concessions will appear larger then.

Questions

Making concessions is closely related to asking and responding to questions. It is through these questions that an effective negotiator determines when and how much of a concession to offer. The use of questions has been discussed in several other chapters. However, questions are an extremely important tool for the managerial communicator and have a unique role in negotiations so they are reviewed here also.

Asking Questions during the Negotiation

The 17th-century English philosopher Francis Bacon said negotiation was a process of discovery. Negotiators raise questions, give answers, make statements, and offer rebuttals.[21] The process depends heavily on understanding the opponent's needs, motives, and values; and questions can be windows to the mind.

Questions asked in negotiation should reflect three strategic decisions: which questions to ask, how to phrase them, and when to ask them. The appropriate answers to these three questions become a powerful negotiating tool since they can determine the direction in which the conversation moves. Furthermore, questions can control the amount of information likely to be provided and can stimulate an opponent to consider a proposition.[22]

Which Questions to Ask

A negotiator may innocently strike an emotional chord with a question and arouse antagonism; consequently, it may be necessary to prepare the ground before asking questions. One way to accomplish this is by explaining the reason or reasons for asking a question if the potential exists for embarrassment.

Questions serve four purposes:

1. To arouse attention: "When did that change!?"
2. To obtain information: "What is the difference between the two items?"
3. To stimulate thinking: "Could you give me your reaction to the second item?"
4. To bring to a conclusion or summary: "How would you summarize your proposal?" or "Isn't it time to act?"

A question that serves any of these purposes is appropriate in a negotiation. While it is usually a good idea to prepare several questions ahead of time, some people get so involved in asking questions that they stop listening. Also, few people can think of all the right questions during the actual negotiation. Preparation will help to overcome both possibilities.

When preparing questions, do not be afraid to ask ones that show your lack of knowledge. After all, your purpose is to obtain information. Also be willing to ask questions even if you know the answers. This is a good way to obtain useful information about the other person's level of knowledge. However, do not ask too many simple questions, or the opponent may not respect your intelligence.

Also, have the fortitude to ask questions that the opposition may evade. The fact that the opponent evades the questions may provide significant information about him. In some situations, it may be prudent to persist in following up one question with a more probing one when an answer is evasive or poor. Finally, when confused about the proper action or what questions to ask, take a recess to think it out. Few people have the ability to think as quickly and clearly as many of the characters we see in the movies.

How to Phrase the Question

In phrasing questions, do not offend or make an opponent defensive. This rule does not preclude the use of potentially emotional questions, but they must advance—rather than retard—the negotiation. If questions are poorly worded, even the right ones can get the wrong information. A short example shows the importance of phrasing. A sales manager asked his marketing director if it was permissible to take an extra day to go skiing while attending a sales meeting. The request was denied. Another sales manager asked his director if it was acceptable to ski with a potential customer while attending the sales meeting. The request was approved. Was the same question asked by the two sales managers? Yes and no. Yes, the outcome requested was the same, but no, the impact the question had was different.

If you want a particular answer, ask a leading question. A leading question directs the person who is answering from statement to statement until the logic of the questioner's argument is made. Here are two series of leading questions.

> Have you a smaller model? How is that priced? Based on what you say, I can't see how the price of the larger one is justified.

> Is research included in your cost? Where? How is it prorated between jobs? Exactly why do you include it in our charges when you just said that this job requires no research?

In these two examples, the questioner may or may not know the answers, but she had led her opponents to planned conclusions.

When no need exists to lead the opponent in a particular direction, use open-ended questions—questions that usually begin with a how, why, or what. For example, "How would you recommend we close the gap?" "Why is plan A preferable to plan B?" "What is the proposal?" Open questions invite people to express their thinking freely.

Another distinction is that between heated and cool questions. Heated questions may embarrass an adversary or make him defensive, all in violation of earlier suggestions. Consider the statement, "Having already spent *too much* time on one little problem, don't you think we should move on?" That statement will probably cause a heated reaction. Rephrasing it is simple: "Do you think we should move on so we can save time?"

The final type of question, the rhetorical question, is one that is asked not to get an answer, but for effect. Rather than seeking an answer, this type of question attempts to draw attention to a particular item. Examples of rhetorical questions include, "What do you think the vice-president would say to something like that?" or "Do you really want us to believe that?"

The type of question chosen needs to fit the situation. To get the negotiation moving in a specific direction, ask a leading question. The open question is best for general information, but if the purpose is to draw attention, ask a rhetorical question. Finally, be careful not to ask two questions at once.

Such a question as, "Would you prefer a corner office with a typewriter, or would you rather have a larger desk and no extra chair?" needs to be divided into two questions. As the question is presently stated, confusion will result, or the opponent may even ask for both.

When to Ask Questions

A perfectly phrased question at the wrong time is usually worse than no question. Consider an exchange occurring at the headquarters of a small fast-food chain where the manager is working out the terms of a new contract with the representative of a pest control company.

> *Manager:* So we're agreed then. For this price per outlet per month you'll treat each of our outlets and guarantee them against all the pests here (points to list).
> *Exterminator:* (Skimming list) That's right. If any show up between applications, there's no charge for another visit.
> *Manager:* And this price includes termite treatment as well? Great! All the other exterminators charged extra for that.
> *Exterminator:* Termite inspection? No, that shouldn't be on the list (crosses it off). You're right, it is an extra charge.
> *Manager:* Oh.

The moral of the story is to know when to ask questions and when to stop!

Questions can be used for four purposes: to create attention, to obtain information, to start thinking, and to bring discussion to a conclusion or summary. Whenever you need to meet one of these purposes, ask a question. Many negotiators commit a major error in starting out a session with a question that forces an opponent to pick and defend a position. Posed early in negotiations, such questions as, "Where do we all stand before we begin discussion?" or "What do you think of this plan?" tend to immobilize a group because members have to choose a position early and reveal it. Also, a wise negotiator avoids a rapid-fire questioning approach. An opponent needs time to respond, and the questioner needs to listen to the responses.

One effective use of questions is to get negotiations back on track when an opponent has been diverted. A simple question, "How can we relate what you're saying to . . . ?" should get the most recent comments turned in a different, more relevant direction.

Do not ask questions just for the sake of asking a question. Keep the purpose of the question in mind, and then listen for the right time. Then phrase the question to meet the prevailing needs. At the same time, be comprehensive, unlike the kids in Louisiana who came up to a man fishing in a bayou and asked if there were any snakes in the water. The fisherman assured them there were none. After the kids had taken a swim, one asked, "How come there aren't any snakes?" "The 'gators ate 'em all," the man answered.

Answering Questions during the Negotiation

Negotiation is a game of asking and answering questions. The preparation and mental alertness required to ask purposeful questions are just as essential for answering them. Perhaps the most important preparation is to brainstorm and write down in advance questions most likely to arise. Ask an associate to act as devil's advocate and raise a host of hard questions before negotiation. The more time a person has to think about answers, the better those answers will be.

Keep two universal guidelines in mind when answering questions: (1) never answer until the question is fully understood, and (2) take time to think through your answer. Besides applying these two guidelines, you can exercise two options in answering. First, you may answer the question accurately and completely. However, since such directness is not always advisable in many negotiation situations, the second option is to not be totally open when answering.[23] For instance, when negotiating for the salary to go with a new job, it is not wise to directly answer the question, "What is the salary you are looking for?" In this case, it is probably best to respond with a comment something like this, "What do you generally pay for this type of job?" If your MSO is below the other party's lower limits, you will not have revealed your limits too soon.

When a negotiator does not wish to give an answer, several alternatives are available. First, the negotiator may choose to answer only part of the question. For instance, a question may be, "What is required to have this project completed by May 1?" One responds by listing all that is required to have the job done without relating to the date. By receiving complete and detailed information, the interrogator thinks the question has been answered. Meanwhile, the respondent can stay away from potentially damaging information.

Another possibility is to ask for clarification even when the question is fairly clear. Often when people are clarifying a question, they intentionally or unintentionally change the question substantially or provide additional insight into the type of answer sought. Also, the time it takes to restate the question provides additional maneuvering time to consider possible answers. A variation is to ask for clarification for part of the question, thus diverting attention away from the remainder of the question; as a result, one may end up answering only part of the question.

A third possibility is to answer a question different from that asked. In such a ploy, the question being answered is so similar to the one asked that the interrogator actually considers the answer satisfactory. For instance, when asked which budget item would be the best to drop from next year's request, one might answer that inflation is affecting all areas of the budget, and then she might provide a specific example of inflation's effects. This, in turn, could be followed by the next alternative: answering the question with a question. For example, "Where do you think inflation has had the greatest impact on the entire company?" This tactic may or may not divert attention away from the initial question, but is often better than giving a direct answer.

A fourth alternative is to answer a negative question with a positive response. When negotiating salaries, a typical scenario has the opponent asking, "What do you consider the biggest weakness you'll bring to this job?" Naturally, a thorough and accurate answer would put the respondent at a disadvantage. A positive, strategic answer might be, "Well, sometimes I get too caught up in my work and I'll stay until late at night. This really isn't fair to my family, so I have to learn to balance my time between family and work." This answer takes the advantage away from the opponent because it is difficult to fault a hard worker who is also a family person.

Still another possibility is to answer inaccurately. When asked how long a project would take to complete, one might give an inaccurate answer—within reason—in hopes of getting an extension. Since incorrect information may create more problems than no answer in some situations, and ethical questions may develop, a final possibility is to act as if you do not know the answer. For instance, the question may come up when dealing with salary, "How much are you making now?" One possible answer is, "Gee, I really don't know. I recently received a merit raise, then two months later there was a cost of living adjustment, and then the medical and life package recently changed." All this could be followed by, "By the way, could you explain your medical package to me?" This answer avoids the possibility of revealing information that may weaken one's negotiating position.

The real key to answering questions, then, is the ability to think on one's feet. This task becomes easier with experience, but no substitute exists for rehearsing the possible questions and being prepared.

Communication Media

Face-to-face negotiation used to be considered the only viable format, but this is no longer the case. Negotiators today must consider several communication channels when developing their negotiation strategy. Much attention is given to this topic in Chapter 16.

Whether the negotiation is conducted face to face, via the telephone, or in some other way, written media often play a key role.[24] The most common use is the letter of intent, which follows many negotiations. A person's memory is always much better five minutes after a conversation than five days later. The letter or memorandum of intent ensures that all the critical items are mutually agreed on. A letter of intent may reveal that one party made assumptions during negotiation with which the other party did not agree. It is better to have minor differences appear immediately as a result of a letter or memo rather than in the future. Not until the memo is written and accepted can there be confidence that all parties agree on all items.

The person who writes the memo has the advantage, for this person interprets meanings and shapes words to reflect his understanding of the discussion. The question is not one of exploiting the party or catching the opponent in some trap. It is simply getting the area of agreement laid out in one's own way, rather than leaving it to the opponent.

Of course, you do not write the memo in such a tone that it sounds as if the opponent cannot be trusted. You can achieve such tact easily. In one situation, a manager hosted several employees from an out-of-town office. She submitted an expense voucher for $400, but the next paycheck did not cover the expenses. A discussion with her supervisor followed, and after a long negotiation, he agreed to pay $300 of the $400. After the negotiation, the manager sent the following short memo:

TO: Don Averson   Date: March 11, 1994

FROM: Pat Harolds

TOPIC: Expense Voucher

Don, thanks for taking the time to sit down with me and discuss the expenses incurred while hosting the engineers from St. Paul. I'll be looking forward to receiving the $300 with the next paycheck.

This quick note not only confirms the result of the negotiation, but it establishes goodwill.

The letter of intent, then, helps to ensure that the parties agree on all items, and it records the terms of the agreement. Written messages can also be used during negotiation to clarify or restate positions. This tactic is especially important when a negotiation is complicated or drawn out. Also, when numerous parties are involved, a greater possibility exists that some will interpret details differently from others. The elements discussed in Chapters 4, 5, and 6 are important when writing a letter of intent. The message must be concrete, clear, and comprehensive.

Managers can also use written correspondence to de-emphasize an issue or soothe a highly emotional situation. Correspondence brings an issue back into perspective merely by tactfully showing that a matter is not of great importance. Often, the printed word can lend credibility that face-to-face communication lacks since some people are more apt to believe what they see than what they hear. Also, a carefully written memo tends to be less emotional than a face-to-face interaction.

Finally, managers can use written correspondence to present a position when a complex explanation is required. It is difficult to present a complex argument that includes cost figures and diagrams with only an oral presentation. A written statement or even a chart can be helpful when presenting such an argument. In addition, if the opponent has no such aids, counter-arguments might be harder to formulate. Managers who believe that the only negotiating mode is face-to-face severely limit their options.

Strategic Approaches

How a manager acts and looks, how she communicates the maximum supportable outcome, reacts to the adversary's style, uses time, establishes the environmental conditions, and asks and answers questions all constitute the negotiation strategy. Managers combine these communication variables either by design or by accident to develop a strategy. Eight general strategies reviewed in the following paragraphs can assist the negotiator in combining the different aspects of communication systematically. No particular approach is recommended over another; rather, these eight approaches represent possibilities that may best fit a particular situation.[25]

Surprise

The surprise strategy involves unexpectedly introducing a goal or concession into a negotiation. For instance, a manager negotiating budget items with a vice-president might suddenly request a new title. The total surprise may catch the other off guard so the additional request is approved, especially since it does not add additional expense.

A quick concession on a nonessential item is another form of surprise. Once again, this concession may be on an item unrelated to the main focus of the negotiation in hopes that the concession will foster a reciprocal concession by the opponent. Surprise may be particularly valuable with an opponent who is under time pressure, because it may stimulate some quick concessions.

Bluff

A poker player may bluff by placing a large bet even though he does not have a strong hand to back it up. By bluffing, he hopes to scare his opponents. This tactic is also occasionally appropriate in managerial negotiation. Bluffing, the act of creating illusions without the use of lies or outright misrepresentations, is fair play in negotiations because each side is attempting to maximize its own benefit. A difference exists between withholding information and presenting wrong data. For instance, when a person is negotiating to buy an office desk, it is not the same thing to say, "I would like to pay no more than $900" as it is to say, "I have only $900 to spend." A person may want to spend no more than $900 but has additional funds if they are needed.

Diversion

A diversion is an objective established in a negotiation with little hope or desire of actually being achieved. The diversion's purpose is to distract an opponent from the main issue. When diversions are present, one can make concessions on them without losing some of the main objectives of the negotiation. For instance, a manager might ask for a new desk, a table, two chairs, and a bookshelf for his new office when his main objective might really be only a new desk. Naturally, all the items would be nice if they could be achieved. Nevertheless, a manager should not create so many diversions that he loses all credibility—the diversions must be supportable.

Stacking

The stacking strategy is used when one idea is attached to another. For instance, a public relations manager might use this approach when negotiating a new strategy with her administrative vice-president: "I was just reading in *Fortune* that ABC International has changed its approach for its stockholders' meeting. ABC used an approach similar to what I'm suggesting." This manager is stacking her approach on top of ABC's to build credibility.

Legislators also use a form of stacking when presenting bills. They will attach a controversial item as a "rider" onto something that has wide support. Managers use this tactic in negotiations when they stack an undesirable characteristic onto a desirable one. For instance, a person may be asked to take a transfer (undesirable) in combination with a promotion (desirable).

Fait Accompli

The *fait accompli* ploy is a type of bluff that says, in effect, "Here it is, it is accomplished." A person states the terms of an offer and acts as if the terms are acceptable to the opposing party. The expectation is that when an issue is phrased as if it were a negotiated final settlement, the opponent will accept it with little or no protest. Assume an item has been discussed for some time, but no solid agreement has been reached. A manager may write a letter of intent regarding the negotiation and state the issue as settled. Using this approach, real estate agents will occasionally push stubborn buyers into action by jotting down the buyer's tentative terms onto a contract. Once the details are down, the buyer is asked to sign and often does.

Of course, such a unilateral act carries a risk. The opponent may resist "settlement" more because of the ploy itself than the merits of the settlement. This resistance can put the user of *fait accompli* in a difficult, defensive position.

Take It or Leave It

The take-it-or-leave-it position lets an opponent know this offer is the best one; it represents the maximum goal adjustments a person is willing to make. In making a take-it-or-leave-it offer (which is, in fact, an ultimatum) a person takes the risk that the offer will be rejected, so there may be no chance to improve it or even revive the negotiations. One could follow with a different offer if the initial take it or leave it were rejected; however, credibility would be lost because the situation might grow to resemble that of the boy who cried wolf. The full effect is lost after the first time it is used.

Screen

In negotiation, a screen is a third party used by the negotiator as part of the process. The negotiator acts like a screen between the opponent and the final decision maker. For instance, assume a manager is negotiating with an outside contractor. The manager can say that certain conditions proposed by the contractor need to be approved by others in the company. When these conditions are not approved, the adversary may find it necessary to grant concessions to keep the deal going. The third party may actually be a phantom person in the background, but his procedure generates thinking time and may take away some of the opponent's offensive advantage. Instead of negotiating one on one, the opponent has two adversaries, and it is difficult to negotiate through a "barrier" or screen. A typical example of the screen is the car salesperson who always needs to get approval from the nebulous sales manager. After a few minutes (for some reason, the manager is always busy), the salesperson returns and says, "Everything is OK, except the. . . ."

Negotiators often use the screen, but it has a serious drawback: It gives the impression that the negotiator has limited power. A careful manager uses this procedure sparingly when negotiating salaries and budgets with subordinates. It soon appears that the manager has little decision-making authority, and both respect and influence are weakened. In fact, subordinates may bypass the manager thereafter.

If at all possible, do not let an adversary use the third-party technique. Instead, try to get directly to the decision maker. The screen filters out the communications, so much of the strategy used on the adversary is weakened. The effective use of language, of strategically prepared questions and answers, and of nonverbal influence all lose impact when a screen is used.

Emotion

Some negotiators also use a show of emotion, even if the emotion does not exist. A rather calm person might act very upset at a suggestion or offer. Or one might try an emotional appeal that says, "Everything is so tough." Emotions can even serve as a surprise tactic to gain an opponent's attention to an issue or distract it from an issue.

Use this strategy with caution. First, be careful not to become emotional, or your decision-making ability is severely limited. Act emotional without being emotional. This first warning leads to the second caution: Not all people are good actors. When some attempt such a strategy, they either get caught up in the act and do become emotional or give such a poor performance that the opponent easily sees through it.

These eight strategies are only suggestions. Combinations of these or even other strategies are possible. Every strategy has potential drawbacks, strengths, and risks depending on the variables discussed in this chapter. Formulating the appropriate strategy is not an easy task. Good negotiation strategy requires analytical ability, an understanding of communication, a refined set of skills, and creativity. However, after you have studied this chapter, you should be able to enter a negotiation confidently.

Summary

Negotiation is an appropriate tool in conflict resolution in lose–lose or win–lose situations. Before negotiating, the manager should establish the maximum supportable outcome (MSO) and least acceptable outcome (LAO) to know the negotiation range. Both limits must be carefully thought out so managers can protect their best interests while negotiating in a credible manner. The MSO must be one the manager can support convincingly, and the LAO must be one the manager can live with. One should determine the negotiating styles of the adversary so the response can be adjusted accordingly. Responding to the fast-flashy type requires careful concentration on the issues; with the dictator, one needs self-confidence and cannot let one's self be dominated; with parents, the most difficult style to detect, one must resist the false support offered by the adversary.

Negotiators also need to consider when to negotiate, how long to continue, and when to make a counteroffer. Since negotiation is liable to be most fruitful when close to an opponent's deadlines, several suggestions about deadlines are appropriate: (1) do not reveal the true deadlines, if possible; (2) be patient; (3) use the clock. Strategic negotiators should also seek an optimum physical environment that benefits them without giving advantage to the opposition. Successful negotiators occasionally adapt their environment to suit their needs.

Another consideration is language used during the negotiation. Negotiators should use common, basic language, should strive for clarity, should be specific, and should not be apologetic. Questions asked during negotiations have four purposes: to create attention, to obtain information, to stimulate thinking, and to conclude or summarize. In phrasing questions, strategy dictates whether to use open-ended or closed questions. In answering questions, the negotiator must protect his or her interests by taking time to think through the answer and respond only when the question is fully understood. The chapter suggests strategies for adapting answers to suit one's interests.

The medium chosen for negotiation is also important. Which medium is chosen depends on the circumstances. The letter of intent that follows many negotiations requires care in preparation and can work to the advantage of the person preparing it.

Several strategic approaches can be applied in negotiations—surprise, the unexpected introduction of a goal or a concession; bluff, the creation of an illusion without lying; diversion, the distraction of the opponent from the main issue; stacking, the linking of one idea with another for argument's sake;

fait accompli, acting as if terms are acceptable to the opposition before any agreement has occurred; take it or leave it, letting the opponent know that this offer is the last; the screen, using a third party as part of the negotiation; and emotion, acting upset at a suggestion or offer.

Endnotes

1. Max H. Bazerman and Roy J. Lewicki, "Contemporary Research Directions in the Study of Negotiations in Organizations: A Selective Overview," *Journal of Occupational Behavior* 6, no. 1 (1985), pp. 1–17.
2. D. G. Pruitt, *Negotiation Behavior* (New York: Academic Press, 1981).
3. Deborah M. Kolb and Blair H. Sheppard, "Do Managers Mediate, or Even Arbitrate?" *Negotiation Journal*, October 1985, pp. 379–88.
4. John Ilich, *The Art and Skill of Successful Negotiation* (Englewood Cliffs, NJ: Prentice-Hall, 1973), p. 33.
5. Michael Schalzki, *Negotiation: The Art of Getting What You Want* (New York: Signet, 1981), p. 33.
6. Samuel B. Bacharach and Edward J. Lawler, *Bargaining: Power, Tactics, and Outcomes* (San Francisco: Jossey-Bass, 1981), p. 43.
7. Michael Maccoby, *The Gamesman* (New York: Bantam Books, 1978).
8. Tessa Albert Warschaw, *Winning by Negotiation* (New York: Berkley Books, 1980).
9. Peter J. D. Carnevale and Edward J. Lawler, "Time Pressure and the Development of Integrative Agreements in Bilateral Negotiations," *Journal of Conflict Resolution* 30, no. 4 (December 1986), pp. 636–59.
10. David D. Seltz and Alfred J. Modica, *Negotiate Your Way to Success* (New York: New American Library, 1980), p. 52.
11. Ilich, *The Art and Skill of Successful Negotiation*, p. 22.
12. Herb Cohen, *You Can Negotiate Anything* (New York: Bantam Books, 1980), p. 92.
13. Roger Fisher and William Ury, *Getting to Yes: Negotiating Agreement Without Giving In* (New York: Penguin Books), 1981.
14. Jeffrey Z. Rubin and Bert R. Brown, *The Social Psychology of Bargaining and Negotiation* (New York: Academic Press, 1975), p. 122.
15. Gerald I. Nierenberg, *Fundamentals of Negotiating* (New York: Hawthorn, 1973), p. 150.
16. R. Sommer, "Further Studies of Small Group Ecology," *Sociometry* 28, no. 2 (1965), pp. 337–38.
17. R. L. Birdwhistell, *Introduction to Kinesics* (Louisville, K.Y.: University of Louisville Press, 1952).
18. P. A. Andersen and J. F. Andersen, "The Exchange of Nonverbal Intimacy: A Critical Review of Dyadic Models," *Journal of Nonverbal Behavior* 8, no. 12 (1984), pp. 327–49.
19. M. Cook, "Experiments on Orientations and Proxemics," *Human Relations* 23, no. 1 (1970), pp. 62–76.

20. R. V. Exline, J. Thibaut, C. Brannon, and P. Gumpert, "Visual Interaction in Relation to Machiavellianism and Unethical Act," *American Psychologist* 16, no. 3 (1961), p. 396.

21. Chester L. Karras, *Give and Take: The Complete Guide to Negotiating Strategies and Tactics* (New York: Thomas Y. Crowell, 1974), p. 7.

22. Harold Bloom, *Principles and Techniques of Negotiation* (Oradell, N.J.: National Association of Purchasing Management, Inc., 1984).

23. Linda L. Putnam and M. Scott Poole, "Conflict and Negotiation," in *Handbook of Organizational Communication*, by F. Jablin, L. Putnam, K. Roberts, and L. Porter (Newbury Park, Calif.: Sage Publications, 1987), pp. 549–99.

24. Joseph F. Byrnes, "Ten Guidelines for Effective Negotiation," *Business Horizons*, May–June 1987, pp. 7–12.

25. These strategies are partially drawn from Roy J. Lewicki and Joseph A. Littere, *Negotiation* (Homewood, Ill.: Richard D. Irwin, 1985).

Additional Readings

Bazerman, M. H., and R. J. Lewicki. *Negotiating Organizations.* Newbury Park, Calif.: Sage Publications, 1983.

Jandt, F. E. *Win–Win Negotiating: Turning Conflict into Agreement.* New York: John Wiley & Sons, 1985.

Lewicki, R. J., and J. A. Litterer. *Negotiation: Readings, Exercises and Cases.* Homewood, Ill.: Richard D. Irwin, 1985.

Putnam, L. L. and P. Geist. "Argument in Bargaining: An Analysis of the Reasoning Process." *Southern Speech Communication Journal* 50, no. 2 (1985), pp. 225–45.

Wall, James A. *Negotiation: Theory and Practice.* Glenview, Ill.: Scott, Foresman and Company, 1985.

Discussion Questions

1. What is meant by the statement that all the variables are interrelated in a strategic approach to communication?

2. Explain the difference between least acceptable outcome and maximum supportable outcome. Give an example of each.

3. What do you think is your most prevalent negotiation style? Describe some of your personal attributes that support your selection.

4. Briefly describe the three styles of negotiation described in this chapter: fast-flashy, dictator, parent.

5. What are the three guidelines regarding time limits? Explain why they are important.

6. What would be the possible advantages and disadvantages of negotiating during a luncheon engagement?

7. What is the best way to arrange the conference room or office in which negotiations are to take place? Consider not only arrangement but also the distance between items.

8. Assume you are in an adversary's office during a negotiation. What could you do to offset this disadvantage?

9. How is the language used in a negotiation similar to and different from other managerial communication situations?

10. What are four different purposes of a question? Give an example of each purpose.

11. When should a leading question be asked? Give an example where such a question would be appropriate. What is a rhetorical question and how may it be used?

12. What alternatives are available when a complete and accurate answer is not the desired response to a question? Why and when would an accurate answer not be a desirable choice?

13. Why should a letter of intent follow a negotiation and what should it include?

14. Explain the difference between a diversion and a bluff. Give an example of each of these strategies.

15. A number of different potential strategies are presented. Name four strategies and give examples of how each could be used.

CASE 15–1
PURCHASING AND ACCOUNTS PAYABLE

Bill and Mary are both administrative managers in a machine tool company. Mary is the director of purchasing and has four purchasing agents and a secretary reporting to her. Bill is the director of accounts payable and has two people reporting to him. The secretary for the accounts payable group also works for the accounts receivable group, so in effect the accounts payable group has only a part-time secretary.

Bill and Mary both have business degrees and graduated from college three and five years ago, respectively. They are both ambitious, and a high level of competition exists between them. The following discussion occurs in Mary's office, which is down the hall from Bill's. Mary is busy and has a lot of papers spread around on her desk. It is about 45 minutes before the normal quitting time, but it looks as if Mary may not be able to get away on time.

Everything has been rather hectic lately because it is nearing the end of the month. Both Mary and Bill have numerous activities that need to be completed within the next few days.

Analyze the following conversation and indicate what could be done to improve the effectiveness of this interaction.

Bill: Mary, could I use your secretary for a few hours tomorrow? We are really behind, and I've noticed that your secretary doesn't seem to be too busy.

Mary: What do you mean "too busy"? We all have work backing up on us.

Bill: Well, you have one secretary, but we have to share time with accounts payable.

Mary: Well I'm sorry, we're just too busy.

Bill: How about asking her to work some overtime but charge it to our department? Does she like to work overtime?

Mary: She might want to do that. You can ask.

Bill: Would you please ask? That might be better because you're her supervisor.

Mary: No, you go ahead and talk to her. Also, remember you will have to pay the time and a half for overtime.

Bill: I really think you should talk to her.

As Bill says this, the telephone rings, and Bill walks out of the office.

Return to Figure 15–1 and 15–2. What are the major variables presented in these two figures that influence the communication presented in this case?

CASE 15–2
NEGOTIATING A PURCHASE

Reggie Blanchard's delivery van was recently totaled when someone ran a stop sign and struck the van. The other person's insurance company is going to pay Blanchard for the damages to his van, and for a week now Blanchard has been looking at new vans while he temporarily leases one. The following scenario transpired when Blanchard talked to the salesperson who tried to sell him a new van.

Salesperson: Yes, sir, may I be of service to you?

Blanchard: I recently lost my delivery van in an accident. I am temporarily leasing a van, so I would like to get one as soon as possible.

Salesperson: What kind of van did you have?

Blanchard: A 1987 one like this (pointing to a low-priced van). It had low mileage and was in great shape.

Salesperson: I know how you must feel. It is discomforting to lose a service van like that. And then you really don't get enough money from the insurance company to buy a van just like the one you had, do you?

Blanchard: Yes, sir, that's exactly right.

Salesperson: How did the accident happen?

Blanchard then proceeds to explain how the other person ran the stop sign and demolished the passenger side of his van, and as he does this, the salesperson nods his head in agreement at Blanchard's every word.

Salesperson: That sorry old soul must have had mud in his eyes not to have seen you in that intersection.

Blanchard: Ha, Ha, I guess you're right.

Salesperson: Well, now don't worry, because you've come to the right place at the right time. We're making good deals on all this year's models to be ready for the shipment of next year's vans due any week now.

Blanchard: That sounds good. Let me ask you, how much for this one?

Salesperson: Well, these models are going like hotcakes. We find that they have been excellent and the prices are outstanding for the quality in the van. I can let you have this for $17,000.

Blanchard: I hate to say it, but that seems a little high for this model.

Salesperson: Oh, but this van has some great features, including our consumer protection package for $970 (smiling). This includes paint treatment, a sound shield underneath the van, and a three-year rust prevention guarantee. It also includes a membership in our motor club plan, which has some excellent benefits for businesspeople.

This last sentence was spoken while the salesperson put his hand on Blanchard's shoulder.

Blanchard: Is that so?

Salesperson: How much are you looking to spend?

Blanchard: I'm not exactly sure, but judging from what the book value of my old van is, and the amount of the notes that I was paying on it, I'd like to spend not much more than $13,000.

Salesperson: Well, like I say, I can give you this van for $17,000. We've already lowered the sticker price by $2,500. It normally sells for $19,500 (pause). If you can spend $13,000, then $4,000 more won't add that much to your payment. Besides, we're the only dealer in town that offers the consumer protection plan, and we feel that the benefits far outweigh the cost. It's a steal, I tell you.

Blanchard: Oh well, in that case I guess $17,000 is fairly reasonable. Let me think about it, but it sounds good.

Questions

1. What negotiation styles did this salesperson use to move Blanchard toward this sale?
2. List some things Blanchard could do to improve his own position at the beginning of the negotiation.
3. Discuss some negotiation strategies that Blanchard should have used as the negotiation proceeded.

V MANAGERIAL COMMUNICATION IN RAPIDLY CHANGING ENVIRONMENTS

Communicating via technology and across cultures are two challenges for managers that will become more prevalent in the future. Accordingly, these two topics get special attention in Part V. So that present and future managers can better understand technologically mediated communication, Chapter 16 presents a framework for using technology. This is followed by a discussion that indicates how the technology is best matched to the message, followed by a look to the future of technologically mediated communication.

Chapter 17 describes the nature of culture and reviews several intercultural myths. The nature of both verbal and nonverbal intercultural communication is presented. The qualities of a good intercultural communicator are discussed and how intercultural communication may affect managers' careers is reviewed.

16 TECHNOLOGICALLY MEDIATED COMMUNICATION

> Lisa is the manager of the employee development office in a large state government. Now in her mid-40s, she feels good about her achievements, especially the two promotions that have gotten her to her present position. But during her 20 years of experience, things have changed. Everything seems to move much faster and she is having a difficult time keeping up.
>
> Last week, she attended a half-day training session on the use of the new telephone system that allows her to record conference calls. Lisa learned, however, that the technology was not as easy as she had anticipated. And Lisa is not confident about the appropriate time to use a teleconference.
>
> More recently, Lisa received a request for an upgraded word processing graphics package from one of her department heads. She doesn't understand exactly what this new technology will accomplish and if it is worth the extra cost. She just approved $2,000 for several computer-based fax machines even though she was not sure how they would best be used. Finally, she has been told she needs to investigate the possibility of using more video teleconferencing for her training activities to reduce costs.
>
> Lisa believes in the value of communication technology, but all of the new technology is difficult to understand. What are the best ways to use it and can it really be justified? This technology presents Lisa with new complex decisions.

Where does a discussion of technologically mediated communication begin? Technology is changing so quickly that it sometimes seems impossible to get a focus on the topic. Thirty years ago, a communication theorist stated, "Communication is essentially a social affair . . . but life in the modern world is coming to depend, more and more, upon technical means of communication, telephone and telegraph, radio and printing."[1] Think about all the technology that has developed in the past 30 years.

As authors, we appreciate the development of communication technology. When we each wrote our first books, we used only paper and pencil. At times, we nearly developed blisters on our fingers. It was a long, arduous task. But for this book, we used word processors in our offices, fax to coordinate with the publishers, and data bases to review the latest research on managerial communication.

Only a couple of generations ago, the communication revolution was the long-distance telephone. In the 1920s and 1930s, it was a major occasion to place a long-distance phone call. The three-minute station-to-station daytime call from New York to San Francisco costing 75 cents today cost $20.70 in today's dollars in 1915. If the automotive industry had made the same technological advancements as the telecommunications industry, we would all be driving a new Mercedes-Benz that we bought for $500 and that delivers 200 miles per gallon.

Just 10 years ago, the discussion of telecommunication included the definition of "floppy disk" and what was meant by a personal computer. Only five years ago, many textbooks like the one you are now reading would have dedicated much space to an explanation of the difference between hardware and software, the purpose of a modem, and how word processing could soon replace the electrical typewriter. Today, we have moved far beyond that. Now most managers and potential managers are well aware of personal computers, laser printers, videoconferences, and so forth. The present challenge is to determine the most effective and efficient way to use these technologies. As this chapter is written, some of the most rapidly developing communication technologies are probably e-mail systems, cellular telephones, and the fax machine. But again, having access to these technologies does not mean managers maximize their capabilities.[2]

This chapter develops a framework for making strategic decisions in the use of technologically mediated communication. First, however, it is important to establish what we mean by technologically mediated communication. Any system that assists managers to prepare and send messages among senders and receivers can be considered technologically mediated communication. With this definition, smoke signals across the prairie could be considered a technical system because they facilitate sending messages. A typewriter is also a technical system because it helps to prepare messages.

But technology has moved beyond the typewriter or simple telephone with the development of the silicon chip, microprocessor, and satellite. The electric typewriter has given way to the word processor that has sophisticated software graphic packages. Furthermore, hardware development allows the word processor to be networked for electronic mail systems and to draw on huge data bases. The simple telephone was first enhanced with the message recorder, but now call forwarding, conference calls, and voice mail are features of many telephone systems. The telephone and computer integrate to send messages around the world in an economical fashion. All of these systems are part of technologically mediated communication.

A Framework for Using Technologically Mediated Communication

The decision to use a telephone, fax machine, or teleconference can be complicated. To use a telephone is complicated? Surely not! The decision to use a telephone, or fax, or memo, or . . . yes, this is a complicated decision because of the many variables involved.

To understand the many variables involved, refer back to Chapter 3 and the discussion on strategy. With technologically mediated communication, a technological channel transmits the communication. Thus, the main difference is in the channel. However, every other variable is also affected by the technology. It is difficult to discuss one variable—channel—without concurrently discussing all the other variables. However, four concepts are presented here so we can better understand the use of mediated communication: bandwidth, perceived closeness, feedback, and the symbolic interactionist perspective.[3]

Bandwidth

Communication occurs along five sensory channels: visual, auditory, tactile, gustatory, and olfactory.[4] Bandwidth is the information transmission capacity of the available sensory channels. Face-to-face communication between two people within an arm's length of each other has a wide bandwidth because it can use all five channels. When a manager first meets a job applicant, the two people usually shake hands. They are concurrently sharing visual, auditory, tactile, and olfactory cues so this communication has a wide bandwidth.

Mediated communication generally omits one or more of the channels. For instance, a video teleconference omits tactile and olfactory channels or cues. The telephone omits tactile, olfactory, and visual cues.

How many messages sent via different channels can the mind comprehend at one time? This theoretical question has plagued communication researchers for centuries, but it remains a relevant question when considering technologically mediated communication. To help understand this question, imagine a Y. Assume that each communication message or bit is a ball that approaches our brain—the base of the Y—along an arm of the Y. The arms of the Y are different communication channels. What if both balls approach the intersection of the Y concurrently, but there is room for only one ball? Information jamming will occur. In terms of information theory, selective attention results, so the receiver pays attention to only one of the information bits while ignoring the others. In other words, the mind decides which ball can proceed to the base of the Y. This process is diagrammed in Figure 16–1.

The goal is to have as much information as possible processed in the central nervous system without jamming. How many cues from different sources can be processed simultaneously?[5] This leads to the concept of between channel redundancy (BCR).

BCR results in multichannel communication when information is shared among auditory, olfactory, tactile, gustatory, or visual channels. Consider meeting a job applicant. When auditory and visual channels transmit identical information, BCR is complete. This would occur when the person dresses neatly and speaks in an articulate, precise manner. Both of these cues are complementary because they signal that the person is a professional. BCR is mixed or incomplete when different channels transmit conflicting or incongruous information. BCR is zero when each channel transmits completely different information. Other things being equal, information transfer is theoretically most effective when BCR is complete. Interference is highest when BCR is zero.

Information theory has not been able to determine totally what information humans process or how they process it. However, several conclusions

FIGURE 16–1

Information Processing

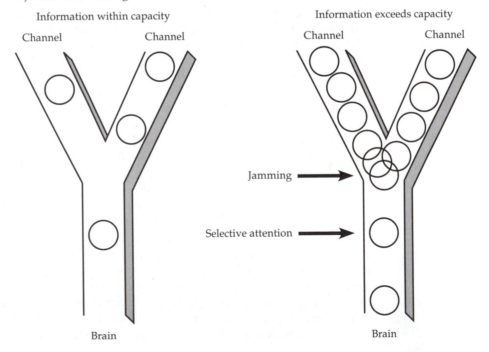

can be stated. First, we can process only a limited amount of information. Second, certain types of information overpower other types of information.[6]

Both of these conclusions have powerful implications for strategic management communication. Managers must determine how much information can be valuable in various situations. Only valuable information—cues—should be provided so a person's information processing capabilities are not overpowered with useless cues.

The choice between videoconferencing and audioconferencing indicates why this is important for technologically mediated communication. Management may be tempted to use videoconferencing because it provides visual cues in addition to audio cues. But the cost for videoconferencing is much higher and it may not be justifiable. The visual cues may be of little value or even distract from the critical audio message that can be provided with the audio only teleconference.

In addition to the concept of bandwidth, the theory of electronic propinquity, or perceived personal closeness, provides a framework for understanding technological mediated communication.

Perceived Personal Closeness

Participants in the communication process can either feel attached or removed from each other. Two people in the same room may feel miles apart, while those on different continents may feel close to each other. Many factors, such as the history of the two people as communication partners, can affect this feeling of closeness. Of particular concern here is how media affects the feeling of closeness, or propinquity. More specifically, the use of mediated communication can make people feel either psychologically closer or more distant.

Much recent research indicates electronic media affect the extent to which people feel close to each other. For instance, some people are much more apprehensive about using the telephone than others and feel less comfortable when making a simple call.[7] When this apprehension exists, telephone conversations would not help a person feel psychologically close to another; psychological distance could be increased because of the accompanying apprehension. No one knows the number of people who are apprehensive about the phone, but a veteran planning and research manager at AT&T has been quoted as saying: "They literally fear making a call."[8] Some suggest it is the inability of the communicator to read nonverbal communication that causes the apprehension.[9]

But others may prefer and enjoy some form of technology over face-to-face communication. Some people actually warm up to the technology. A common phrase used to prepare people for video teleconferences is to be "warm" with the camera. Look at it as if it were a loving person. Some people may feel better with the camera than with a stranger. Some authorities suggested that former President Reagan felt more comfortable in front of a camera than in front of a group of people. When a person feels warm to the technology, psychological distance may be decreased.

A camera or telephone is a rather simple technological device. Other technological devices require more sophistication, so technophobia—the fear of technology—may increase psychological distance among communication partners. For example, electronic mail requires the direct use of the computer. Many people become anxious when required to use a computer. Again, this may seem rather simple, but remember that some people fear the telephone, a much more commonly used instrument.

Telecommunications may increase a person's sense of closeness, also. One research study found that participants in certain situations enjoyed group meetings more when mediated by technology than when everyone was physically present.[10]

Electronic mail also presents some interesting examples. This can provide an economical medium for people to keep in touch and be psychologically close when they are long distances from each other. Frequent electronic mail users commonly say they *talked* to someone when referring to an exchange via a computer. Frequent use, in turn, may result in the user feeling closer to the technology. Others, however, may have technology available but continue to use other, more costly alternatives because of technophobia.

In summary, managers need to determine the extent to which perceived personal closeness is important in different situations. Also, to what extent do various types of technology affect this closeness between the sender and receiver? If this question is not addressed, inappropriately used technology designed to enhance managerial communication may be destructive rather than constructive.

In addition to bandwidth and electronic propinquity, we should consider feedback when discussing technologically mediated communication.

Feedback

The model of communication in Chapter 2 noted that feedback binds the sender and receiver together so they truly communicate with each other. Feedback is always present if it is sought. To understand fully the implications of this statement in relationship to mediated communication, it is important to consider both bandwidth and perceived personal closeness.

With mediated communication, channels for obtaining feedback may be removed. When using the telephone, we do not see the facial expression of our communication partner. Feedback is reduced. Also, when managers are not totally comfortable with a particular medium, they may ignore potential feedback cues. Consider a conference call involving five people at five separate locations. Such a call requires a different set of skills than a normal conversation, and the manager may not be totally comfortable with the situation. Not only are a different set of skills required to monitor feedback, but the manager's anxiety may also reduce attention to feedback.

We have all heard about people who lose their sight because of an accident and gradually enhance the use of their other senses, say hearing. This may be what is necessary for the manager when using various mediated communication systems. For instance, when using the telephone, it may be necessary to sharpen the verbal listening skills since visual abilities are limited.

The same is true when speaking. Articulation and verbal emphasis are more essential if one is attempting to persuade another via the telephone. How many times have you seen a person speaking on the telephone using elaborate hand gestures? The speaker may be using these gestures to make a point rather than verbally emphasizing words or phrases. Or worse, the person may be using facial expression in an attempt to provide feedback to the person thousands of miles away on the other end of the line.

Time is related to feedback. The feedback cycle can be dramatically shortened with technology. This event recently occurred at Arco. A purchasing manager sent a rather long contract via fax to a vendor. The manager used fax because the contract was long and complex—too long to send via electronic mail. Immediately after sending the contract, the sender went to another person's office for a meeting. On returning, the manager checked the voice mail system and found that the receiver of the contract called to indicate it had arrived and was being reviewed. About two hours later, an electronic message was received by the purchasing manager indicating how the vendor wanted the second paragraph changed. This requested revision was sent via electronic mail. This was all done in a matter of a few hours even though the transaction occurred in two cities a thousand miles apart. Also, no busy telephone lines interrupted the process and no secretaries were necessary to draft letters. The time in the feedback loop was reduced tremendously.

Another technology that has significantly decreased the feedback loop is the cellular telephone. Most of us have experienced telephone tag as we call back and forth a number of times trying to contact someone. The cellular telephone has reduced this by making us more accessible. Again, this can reduce the feedback cycle because it is possible to contact others more quickly.

Video teleconferencing affects feedback in several ways. First, although visual feedback is present, it is reduced. As mentioned in the chapter on nonverbal communication, much feedback is received from spacial arrangements and distances. These properties are reduced in the video teleconference. Also, it is not possible to make eye-to-eye contact. However, the time required to arrange for the communication is greatly reduced. The major advantage, and a reason that many companies use videoconferencing, is that travel time for meetings is reduced.[11] A meeting with participants miles apart can be arranged without accounting for travel time. Feedback can be provided immediately among the meeting participants.

At the same time, the reduced time for feedback can cause problems. According to information theory discussed earlier, we have limited capabilities to process information. However, managers may be pressured to decipher information and respond quickly just because the technology allows it. Imagine a manager who receives an electronic message. This medium probably represents speed and suggests the receiving manager should respond quickly. Stress may result. The impression that managers must respond quickly is related to our next discussion.

A Symbolic Interactionist Perspective

Symbolic interactionism is a theoretical framework that can be used to explain sociological and social psychological phenomena. In the imagery of symbolic interactionism, we view society as a dynamic web of communication. Thus, society and every organization in which managers function is an interaction. An interaction is symbolic because, through their interactions, people assign meaning to things and events. Over time, many symbols evolve within the organization and take on agreed on meaning.[12]

The media that managers choose to use for communication may be based partially on symbolic reasons. Some argue that managerial communication behavior represents ritualistic responses to the need to appear competent, intelligent, legitimate, and rational.[13] For example, a face-to-face medium may symbolize concern or caring. Conversely, the manager who congratulates a subordinate on 25 years of service with an electronic mail message may be sending a message symbolizing a lack of personal concern. A handwritten note or a special card would symbolize more personal warmth. A manager wishing to symbolize her authority over a particular matter may use a formal written communication to transmit that message. Computer use is facilitated by a network of supportive relationships. Therefore, choosing to send a message via computer may convey the message that the manager is a member of a particular group.[14]

A recent comprehensive study of managers and their communication media indicates that channel choice was highly symbolic.[15] Managers interviewed in this study said they choose face-to-face media to signal a desire for teamwork, to build trust or goodwill, or to convey informality. Both face-to-face and telephone communication symbolized urgency, showed personal concern, and signaled deference to the receiver who preferred that medium. By contrast, written media were thought to show authority, make a strong impression, and be legitimate and official. Written media were also used to get attention and to comply with protocol.

An interesting story on technologically mediated communication is provided by Harold Geneen the former CEO of ITT. He created ITT-Europe to serve as headquarters for his European operations. No doubt many technological support systems helped him communicate with his European managers; however, for 17 years, Geneen and his senior staff traveled to Europe for one week each month to deal in person with the European managers. Traveling to Europe once a month is an expensive way to communicate. Audio teleconferences would have been much more economical and possibly as effective in communicating the necessary verbal messages. But Geneen's commitment of time and resources to these trips symbolically conveyed the importance of the topics discussed and the need for the managers to work as a team.[16]

Managers should consider four factors when deciding on the most effective and efficient use of mediated communication: bandwidth, perceived closeness, feedback, and symbolism. In short, the choice of technology becomes rather complicated, and it is difficult to generalize from one situation to another. But certain general conclusions can be stated.

Matching Technology and the Message

The discussion so far has emphasized how the channel may vary when communication is mediated by technology. Now consider matching the message and the technology. Not all technology is appropriate for all types of messages. To facilitate this discussion, messages are categorized along these continuum: sensitivity, negativity, complexity, and persuasiveness, as diagrammed in Figure 16–2.[17]

The following discussion considers each of these categories separately. Unfortunately, such a discussion is limited because in reality each category is not independent. For instance, a message may include elements from each of the categories; it may be sensitive, negative, complex, and persuasive. The challenge faced by the manager is to consider the message and how it fits into the various categories and then match it with the appropriate technology.

Message Sensitivity

When considering technology, managers must determine the extent to which the message is sensitive. A sensitive message is one that evokes an emotional

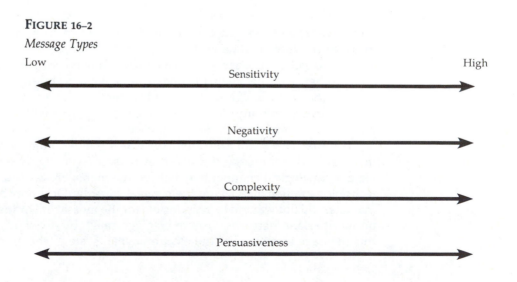

FIGURE 16–2

Message Types

Low   High

                              Sensitivity

                              Negativity

                              Complexity

                              Persuasiveness

reaction from the receiver. Neutral messages convey information that readers process and respond to intellectually but not emotionally. Receivers will not become upset with neutral messages, but neither will they become ecstatic or pleased. Such information is rather mundane.

Sensitive messages should usually be communicated in face-to-face settings to increase the personal element. An extreme example is when a U.S. soldier is killed in battle. A military representative first informs relatives in a personal meeting. Telephone calls are not considered an option. An example at the other end of the continuum is that a meeting agenda could be circulated by electronic mail; however, it would not be appropriate to announce layoffs via this medium.

What if it is not possible to communicate a sensitive message, such as an impending layoff, via a face-to-face setting? Here the technology with the widest bandwidth should be used. Also, an interactive system with an opportunity for feedback should be used if possible. Symbolically this may indicate a high level of concern. For instance, a company that was forced to lay off 5 percent of its employees was geographically decentralized across several states. It was not possible for the CEO to visit all of the departments in a timely manner. The company chose to announce the general plan for the layoffs via an interactive video teleconference. All of the employees throughout the company met in various conference rooms and lunchrooms throughout the company. After the CEO announced the layoffs, the telephone lines were opened for questions.[18]

This technology had one distinct advantage even though it may not have been as personal. It allowed the message to be sent throughout the company concurrently so all the employees received the same message at the same time; thus controlling rumors. This is an advantage that would not have been possible without the technology.

Message Negativity

Messages extend along a continuum from positive to negative. A positive message conveys good news that evokes feelings of satisfaction and pleasure, while a negative message evokes feelings of dismay, anger, and disappointment. When sending a negative message, managers should generally be sensitive to the receiver. Consequently, the extent to which a message is negative and the extent to which it is sensitive are highly related. Some of the same generalities exist for the other categories.

Another important consideration exists when communicating negative messages via technology, however. A person receiving a negative message via a technological channel may believe the manager was hiding behind the technology rather than facing the receiver directly. Or it may appear that the manager did not want to be responsible for the message. For instance, assume no merit salary increases were to be given to all the division's employees. If this message was sent via the electronic mail system, the employees cannot ask any questions. The manager does not have to look directly into the employees' faces as they receive the bad news. The message becomes rather depersonalized; the manager may appear to be less responsible. Employees lose faith in the openness and honesty of management when this method of communication is used.

Most everyone has complained to a large firm about poor service or an incorrect billing. Frequently, the response to the complaint is a form letter from a word processing system. The reaction was probably increased frustration and maybe even hostility. In short, a lack of personalization exists with the technology.

But nothing is ever simple when considering management communication strategy. In one situation, a production manager was complaining to a supplier about the slow delivery of product components. The response from the supplier was a negative message saying material shortages were causing the problem. This was a negative message; however, the response was sent via fax so it indicated the company was concerned and wanted to get the feedback to the production manager as quickly as possible. But let's take this a step further. The telephone might have been even more effective because the diction could have indicated sincerity. But what if the supplier did not want to face potential questions from the production manager. Then the fax rather than the telephone would be the medium of choice. As can be seen again, no easy solution can be presented, as all contingencies must be considered.

Message Complexity

Guidelines for using technology are somewhat clearer when considering message complexity. As the complexity of the message increases managers should attempt to use (1) wider bandwidth, (2) the medium that will add to psychological closeness, (3) the technology that provides for the greatest amount of feedback, and (4) symbolism consistent with the complexity.

Discussion of a complex team project schedule involving a series of dates and figures provides an example. Assume seven managers were involved at four locations. In the past, it may have been necessary to conduct a face-to-face discussion to assure that everyone understood all the complexities. This may have involved expensive travel and project delays just to get everyone together. But today, an even greater danger exists. The managers might have tried to call each other via the telephone and get everything coordinated. This is a danger because it is difficult to convey complex information orally with no visual support. Also, some of the communication partners could have questions, but it could go undetected by others because of the lack of nonverbal feedback.

A number of viable solutions exist for communicating complex messages, however, without getting everyone together face to face. One possibility is for everyone to fax a written statement to each other summarizing the project's main points with appropriate supporting diagrams. This can be done on a word processor, so items can be easily changed. Once everyone has the printed fax messages and has studied them, an audioconference call can be placed. This gives everyone the chance to discuss the written messages. After the discussion, everyone could again fax a revised understanding to all those involved. The revision would not take long to draft because the original written statement would still remain on the word processor. This process can be repeated until everyone agrees. No travel is necessary, but a relatively wide bandwidth is used; feedback is provided, and all the symbols indicate this is a serious, complex communication situation.

Research indicates the communication of complex, detailed information is not necessarily improved by face-to-face interaction.[19] An explanation of a complex engineering formula, for instance, can be just as effective with audio and graphic communication as when the person doing the explanation is physically present. Both teleconferencing and computer conferences, to be discussed next, can facilitate the communication of complex messages because they may stimulate better concentration from the receiver.

Audio-graphic Teleconferences
It is not always necessary for a person to be physically present when explaining complex information. The economies of audio-graphic teleconferencing make this an important consideration. This option includes an electronic writing tablet, a computer terminal and a microphone-speaker system. At one location, a person can explain complex material on a speaker system and concurrently write on the electric tablet. The figures appear on the computer terminal at the receiver end along with the audio explanation. The only thing missing is the facial expression of the sender.

Allstate Insurance has used audio-graphics teleconferencing extensively to explain the complexities of new insurance policies. Before the accessibility of the technical systems, the corporate training staff had to schedule expensive travel agendas to numerous field offices. Now that the audio-graphics system is installed, the training staff can remain in Chicago and explain new policies to those in the field. Limited travel is required. In addition, it is possible to arrange training sessions as problems develop. Again, travel arrangements are not necessary.

Computer Conferencing
Complex information can also be communicated with computer networks. No audio message is used to supplement the written message. This system has been commonly used in companies as diverse as Honeywell and Sears. Frequently, all of the personal computers in these companies are linked much like telephones are connected. This allows the employees to have "meetings" by writing messages on their computers. This can be done by having a "conference call" on the computer. All employees involved work on their computers concurrently and send messages to each other. This is what is termed *interactive computer conferencing*. Research indicates it can be relatively effective

for answering questions when complex, nonsensitive information is involved.[20] However, computer conferencing has been used for relatively controversial activities as well. For instance, managers at Greyhound-Dial hammered out a radically changed corporate mission statement in less than two hours.

Another option is to not have all those involved stationed on their computers concurrently. A person can respond to messages at his convenience. The advantage is that not everyone involved has to be available at the same time. For instance, a manager could work on her computer in the evening at home and respond to messages received during the day. Again, technology adds flexibility.

Complex Data and Graphics

The chapter discussing written reports stresses the importance of visual aids. Much research has investigated the best way to present graphs of complex data via computers and the main finding is that pictures and illustrations enhance comprehension beyond that of text alone. The research generally analyzes only the conversion of statistics into tables or graphs rather than visuals supplementing audio messages.[21] But now with the wide availability and use of graphics packages, graphics are being used with many different applications. This is another reason it is important to understand the best use of graphics.

Message Persuasiveness

Persuasive messages involve an effort to induce a receiver to take a particular action. Persuasion is not an effort to fool, seduce, or manipulate the receiver. Rather, it is an attempt to get employees to comply with behaviors that will meet the goals of the organization. When thinking of persuasion, salespeople probably come to mind; however, managers frequently use persuasion, influence tactics, or compliance-gaining strategies to influence employees to perform in a particular way. Efforts to introduce new work procedures, increase teamwork, or change corporate culture require persuasive communication. The topic of persuasion has been of interest since Aristotle's writings. But a leading researcher recently wrote: "Despite the vast number of pages written and the countless studies undertaken about persuasion, it is difficult to shake the uneasy feeling that we have precious little reliable, socially relevant knowledge about it."[22]

Our understanding of persuasion is further complicated when considering mediated communication. Little research has been conducted in this area; consequently, it is necessary to generalize about what we know from non-mediated communication.

A popular book, *Influence: The New Psychology of Modern Persuasion*, presents three conclusions about persuasion that are particularly pertinent to our discussion.[23] First, managers can more easily persuade those who like them.

Second, people are more easily persuaded when they see the person attempting to influence as an authority. Third, it is easier for managers to persuade others as they get psychologically and physically closer to them.

Persuaded By the One You Like

Few would be surprised to learn that we most prefer to say yes to the requests of someone we know and like. Related to this is that it is difficult to say no to a person we like. In addition, we like people with whom we spend more time. But do we spend time with people because we like them, or do we like people because we spend time with them? Again, research indicates we like people more as we spend time with them—even if we are forced to spend this time together.

This research finding is important to our discussion because the quality of the time we spend with people via technology is generally not the same quality as if the person is physically present. Many romantic relationships have lost intensity because it was necessary to conduct a long-distance courtship. In other words, no matter how much time we spend with people in teleconferences, they cannot substitute for personal presence.

Return to the example of Geneen presented earlier. He may have made his trips to Europe to develop a friendly, supportive relationship with the managers there. Theory holds that the more time he spent with the people, the more everyone would like each other. It would then be easier to persuade his managers to implement new ideas and so forth.

Persuasion is easier when employees like the manager attempting to persuade them. If personal presence is not possible, mediated communication may substitute. But mediated communication cannot substitute completely for personal contact.

Persuaded By the One You Believe

The second principle is not overly surprising either. We listen and are persuaded by those who appear to be authorities on the topic. This point is important among television executives. The newsperson or the special reporter must be believable. Whether it is Peter Jennings or Dan Rather, they succeed partly because they look and sound like authorities. They have special makeup support staff, experts who provide feedback on their articulation, and so forth. Television and radio personnel make a nice living by sounding and looking believable.

But what about average managers who must use video or telephonic technology in an attempt to persuade? It would seem they are at a disadvantage. Again, these technologies should be used for persuasion only when necessary due to time or cost restrictions.

Another point adds to this caveat: It is more difficult to say no when looking a person directly in the eye. Even when we like a person or believe she is an authority, it is easier to say no from a distance. This is one reason sales professionals try to get a person to say yes in their presence.

Let's deviate from managerial communication for a moment and consider a student who is close to getting a B for a course. Unfortunately, the final grade is a C. But the student truly believes a B is the right grade. It is time for all of the persuasive skills to come to the surface. Let's put that managerial communication course to work. Here is one possible strategy for persuading the professor to listen to the student and change the grade.

The first step is to write a well-organized letter asking the professor to consider changing the grade. It is important to write the letter immediately after the grade is received. The letter will probably use an inductive psychological progressive approach asking the professor to reconsider the grade. Timing is important here to assure the professor that the incorrect grade received the student's immediate attention. In other words, it is important that the student present the image of grave concern about the incorrect grade. Also, it is best to use a word processor so changes can be made easily after several friends have looked at the letter. Remember that two or three heads are better than one so it is helpful to have others help with the editing. Also, the spelling and grammar review options on the word processor help to assure everything is correct.

The letter should indicate that a telephone call will follow the letter so an appointment can be arranged. It is important *not* to ask for a decision in the letter. Keep in mind that it is easier to say no from a distance. One consideration may be to send the letter via fax machine. Two reasons exist for this. First, it is important to get the attention of the professor immediately after receiving the grade to show the seriousness of the appeal. Second, use of the technology indicates the student is a professional. But fax may be unnecessary use of technology. The professor may perceive this as being overly dramatic. This is one of those difficult decisions required in strategic communications.

The next step is to call the professor for an appointment. Or better yet, stop by the professor's office. Remember to use technologically mediated communication in persuasive situations only when necessary. But herein also lies the advantage of the technology. This scenario may occur during a semester break, so the student may be out of town. The telephone is necessary to make the appointment in a timely manner. A long-distance call indicates the student is not willing to wait—and the student considers this a serious grade error.

Turn to another student who does not agree with the grade received. Upon returning to campus after the semester break, the student calls the professor to ask that the grade be reconsidered. The professor may quickly forget the request or simply say no. The principles of management communication suggest that the probability of success is much less for the latter student.

Technological Mediated Persuasive Presentations
Much sophisticated work has gone into preparing persuasive audiovisual presentations. But these presentations are not as effective as personal

exposure of the one attempting the persuasion. If possible, it is best to have the person physically present. When physical presence of an authority is not possible, a well-organized presentation by a somewhat less credible source may be a good substitute. But again, a trade-off must be made. Strategic management communication decisions must be reached. How much should be spent on developing a persuasive video or audio presentation compared to a presentation made by one who is physically present but less credible? What is the balance between physical presence and credibility? These questions must be addressed. When considering persuasive managerial communication, however, one principle must always be considered. A person physically present is more persuasive than one who is present only via technologically mediated communication.

A Look to the Future

Electronic mail, fax machines, audio and video teleconferencing, sophisticated word processing systems, voice mail—all of these systems are with us today and are being used more and more frequently. If one were to speculate about what developments would affect managerial communication in the future, any number of possibilities would exist. However, several safe projections can be made. The first is that each one of the technologies mentioned will simply be used more. Just as the telephone is part of life now, electronic mail and videoconferencing will soon be as pervasive. An office without a computer will be like a home without a television—an anomaly.

Several other predictions are relatively safe. First, decision making will be affected; second, job and organizational design will be altered; third, mediated collaborative writing will be common; fourth, group decision support systems (GDSS) will be used in many organizational settings. Both collaborative writing and GDSS are related in that they involve groups interacting with technology. Each of these four future events is discussed here.

Decision Making

Managerial decision making may be defined as the process of identifying and solving problems. Decision making requires that managers scan for pertinent information. Most discussions on this topic generally contain two major stages. One is the problem identification stage. Information about relevant conditions is monitored both to determine if performance is meeting expectations and to diagnose the cause of any shortcomings. The other stage involves problem solution. Alternative actions are considered, and one alternative is selected and implemented. In both stages, the more information available, the greater the probability that effective decisions will be made. And more and more information is becoming available with increased technologies.

Burger King provides an example of the effect of communication technology on decision making. In most metropolitan areas, each Burger King store is networked via computer to a central office where each sale is transmitted and recorded. When one store is running low on a product, without even placing a phone call, the central facility is aware of the shortage and can send supplies. This is comparable to electronic mail except the messages are automatically prepared and transmitted. Stage one in the decision process, the identification stage, is more easily accomplished because of communication technology.

As organizations become larger and as more sophisticated information systems are available, the probability is greater that technological communication systems may be used in many situations. For instance, Intel has several manufacturing and research facilities in Arizona and northern California. Attempts to resolve complex technological problems frequently require experts from different specialties. Teleconferencing facilities, electronic mail, and fax allow employees to exchange information quickly and accurately. In this example, the second stage of the decision process is facilitated.

Let's take the example of Intel a step further. Assume that highly technical information is needed for some especially unique semiconductor research. This information may be available only in the Science Library at Arizona State University. An engineer in California could access the information through a special terminal in her office that is connected to the library in Tempe, Arizona. A copy of the document could be available to the engineer within minutes.

This quick access to information has three apparent implications. First, anyone who wants to remain competitive must know where and how to access the information. And he or she must be able to do it quickly. Those who do not have the information will soon lose their competitive edge. Products will be introduced and replaced so quickly that those without communication technology will have little chance of survival.[24]

But the second result is more negative. Managers who are bombarded with masses of information find the odds of making an effective decision greatly decreased. If managers receive large quantities of both relevant and irrelevant information, the important facts and figures may be overlooked and can create problems. But even when presented with only relevant information, the human mind can process only so much data. As noted earlier in Figure 16–1, a point develops at which the mind blocks out any additional, albeit valuable information. Excessive information is termed *information overload*. As technology allows for rapid acquisition of greater amounts of information, poorer rather than better decisions may result.

Communication technology allows managers to quickly change their decisions. Say a manager writes an analytical report comparing the acquisitions of two pieces of property for a retail outlet. The report's recommendation is finalized and ready for submission to an executive committee. At the last minute, some new information is made available through a data base to which the company subscribes. This allows the manager to alter the recommendation at the last minute. Furthermore, it can be done quickly in the formal report because it was written on a word processor. As presented in Chapter 2, the manager's challenge is to know where to get information, when and how to present it to others, and how and when to use it. In some ways, information technology makes the manager's decision making easier, but in other ways it becomes more complex.

Job and Organizational Design

Before discussing job and organizational design, first consider managerial control. Jobs are designed and organizational relationships created so control can be achieved. First, jobs are *formally* structured so both employees and managers know what standards to expect and can determine when the standards are not being met. Second, many jobs are *standardized* to reduce variability among jobs—again, this allows everyone to know what standards to expect and when deviations from standards occur.

Increasing communication technology will allow managers to monitor more closely the standards expected from a job performance. Take a simple example of a sales representative responsible for calling on furniture stores. The objective is to obtain cooperation in setting up a special display within the stores. The standard of performance is to make 2 calls per day and obtain three displays per 10 calls. The formal requirement is to report the day's activities to the central office at the end of each day. This is done with a phone call and voice mail. The salesperson may leave questions in the voice mailbox and instructions may be waiting from the managers when the person calls in. Interaction can occur even though the salesperson and the manager are not physically in the office at the same time.

In the past, this interaction would not have been possible. It would have been necessary to mail reports to the central office, so feedback may not have been obtained for several days. Interaction via technologically mediated communication allows the manager to maintain control. The standardized and formalized job elements can be monitored more easily. Deviations from standards can be detected quickly, allowing for possible corrections.

In addition to improved control of specific jobs, organizational relationships may change with mediated communication. We generally think of jobs being connected by means of either horizontal or vertical integration. Horizontal communication or integration occurs between people at the same hierarchical level. Managers may meet horizontally to coordinate activities, solve problems, resolve conflicts, or just share information. Regardless of the purpose, more horizontal communication can take place as a result of technology. Assume the board of directors of a hospital system with eight locations directed the personnel managers to implement a sexual harassment training program in each hospital. The managers would probably want to share ideas with each other on the most efficient way to implement the program. Travel would not be necessary for a meeting—a video teleconference or a conference call could meet the purpose. If the only option was a meeting requiring travel, it might not be held due to expenses and inconvenience. Thus, information would not be shared. In this case, technology would allow for greater integration at lower expense.

Vertical integration is the coordination among higher and lower levels within the hierarchy. Unfortunately, it often seems that different levels of the organization typically do not communicate well with each other.[25] But as noted when discussing formalization, mediated communication should assist this process. Managers and subordinates are more accessible with voice mail, telephone recorder machines, electronic mail, and the like. Distance and time are less troublesome.

To improve vertical integration, the goal of one major corporation, Allied Signal, is to make electronic mail accessible to everyone in the company. This way employees have access to managers above them regardless of time constraints. Most of us know how hard it is to get access to top managers just because they are so busy. But electronic mail can get a subordinate into a manager's office at any time. Also, managers can communicate with their subordinates regardless of distance and time barriers.

This improved vertical and horizontal integration will result in dramatically different job and organizational structure. Several reports have indicated that managers' jobs have become more information oriented, while the number of managers required in an organization has decreased.[26] In addition, fewer secretaries are needed to support managers. The old stereotype of a male executive being assisted by a female secretary has long disappeared. The new scenario has a female or male manager being served by a personal computer or a computer-assisted telephone. The bottom line is that more information can be communicated among employees more quickly, meaning that fewer managers are necessary.

Collaborative Writing

Imagine five managers sitting around a special conference table that provides each manager with an individual computer. Rather than having a monitor for each computer, however, they share a large output projector on a wall screen. The computers have special hardware that allows the managers to edit the same document simultaneously. Any changes made to the document are visible to all members as changes occur. Furthermore, no protocols built into the software prevent group members from altering or even deleting each other's work.

Such conference rooms are mostly experimental today, but empirical research indicates this type of a setting may be just around the corner.[27] The potential advantage is that more than one person can be involved in the writing process concurrently. Unfortunately, collaborative writing too often means one person first writes part of the report or memo and then hands it to another person for revision. This person may then pass it on to another and so forth. This can become extremely time consuming and coordination can become difficult, if not impossible. Consequently, the insights of others are frequently not used.

Collaborative writing will allow managers to develop synergy. Different viewpoints and ideas of the participants can quickly be compared and discussed. As versions of the text are compared, a better product results. Because collaborative writing is becoming so important, it is discussed more extensively in Chapter 4.

Group Decision Support Systems—GDSS

GDSS, group decision support systems, is similar to collaborative writing in that it involves group effort mediated by technology. The fundamental goal of a GDSS is to support collaborative work activities such as idea creation, message exchange, project planning, document preparation, mutual product creation, and joint planning and decision making.[28] One GDSS, called SAMM, was developed at the University of Minnesota.[29] SAMM is designed to promote participative, democratic decision making in 3-to-16-person groups. Designed to be operated by the group itself, SAMM provides decision tools such as problem definition, idea or solution evaluation, stakeholder analysis, and nominal group technique. It has been used by a number of groups in government and business and is being adapted for use in computer conferences.

Group decision support systems presently exist for groups whose members are dispersed, working in their separate conference rooms, offices, homes, or other locations. Other systems support face-to-face meetings that occur in one physical setting, such as a conference or board room. The least sophisticated systems provide technical features aimed at removing common communication barriers. With these, it is possible to instantaneously display ideas on large screens, vote on individual preferences, compile anonymous input of ideas and preferences, and electronically exchange ideas between members. As the GDSS becomes more sophisticated, it may include budget models and various quantitative analysis techniques. The most sophisticated systems are characterized by computer-aided group communication and include expert advice in the selecting and arranging of rules to be applied during interpersonal communication.[30]

Group decision support systems have become available within the past three to five years. The progress made during this time indicates that within a few years, most managers in large organizations will have some type of GDSS available. The exact changes that this will bring is unknown; however, some of the information discussed in Chapter 13 will certainly change.

The Management Challenge

What does all this mean for managers? It means they must become sensitive to the correct type of communication channel to use in different situations.

It means managers must learn to use these new technologies. It means another dimension has been added to managerial communication.

Let us expand on each of these points. Several recent studies have indicated a strong correlation exists between a manager's sensitivity to media choice and managerial performance. When a task involved complex information or was highly sensitive, for instance, effective managers were more inclined to use communication channels with a broad bandwidth. Ineffective managers were less sensitive to the relationship between the task and the channel of communication.[31]

But it is not easy to learn how to use these new technologies. The effective use of a videoconference, for instance, requires extensive training.[32] Electronic mail means one must be comfortable with the computer. Some managers still have not learned to type—their speed with the new technology is obviously hindered. Not surprisingly, many companies now offer basic typing for top executives. With the many telephone options now available, elaborate training programs are conducted on how to use the phone. All of this technology is placing new requirements on the manager.

A whole new dimension has been added to the manager's job: understanding and selecting the correct communication technology. Gone is the day that a manager gives a handwritten note to the secretary and asks "her" to type a letter. New alternatives are available requiring strategic decisions.

If managers don't learn how to make these strategic decisions, their jobs could be in jeopardy. In corporate America, over $900 billion has been spent on information technology in the service sector alone. Companies will be expecting their managers to make this pay.[33]

The technology payoff could be increased if managers had a table summarizing when the technology is best used, but such a table is not possible. Too many contingencies must be considered to say which technology should be used when. Figure 16–3 demonstrates some of the questions that must be addressed when selecting a technology.

A manager may be considering sending a message by fax. The initial reason for using the fax was that she wanted to quickly send the message to several people in different locations. Fax seemed like the best alternative, but a review of Figure 16–3 results in a mixed reaction. First, it is a sensitive message to field salespeople indicating that several support staff in the central office may have to be laid off. Although the message could be quickly sent to several people at different locations via fax, the symbolism may convey a cold feeling about a sensitive issue. Even though telephone calls would take longer, and it may be difficult to contact the salespeople due to schedule problems, this may be better communication technology.

Trade-offs frequently may have to be made. A videoconference may allow numerous managers in dispersed locations to participate in a meeting. Although a computer conference allows for less nonverbal feedback, it may be more economical. In another situation, a telephone call may save time, but valuable complex information may be misinterpreted. A detailed fax with a follow-up phone call may be better.

FIGURE 16–3

Technology Choice Contingencies

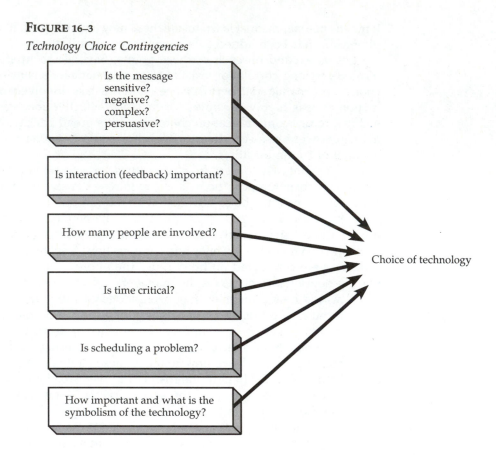

Many examples could be provided, but managers must make their own decisions. Choosing the correct technology will not be easy; however, with the concepts presented in this chapter and use of the strategic model presented in Chapter 3, managers can meet the challenge and make effective strategic decisions.

Summary

To understand better how technology affects managerial communication, four concepts are discussed. First, bandwidth is affected because one channel is generally omitted when technologically mediated communication is used. Perceived closeness, or electronic propinquity, is a consideration because electronic media affect the extent to which people feel close to each other. The feedback cycle is much shorter with technology, so this is also a consideration. Finally, the symbolic interactionist perspective is considered because the use of various technologies has different symbolic meanings.

When matching technology to the message, four categories of messages are considered. First is message sensitivity: Greater bandwidth should generally be used with sensitive messages. The second category is positive and negative messages. Managers must be careful not to hide behind technology when presenting negative messages. The third category is message complexity. Two ways to effectively transmit some complex messages are audio-graphic teleconferencing and computer conferencing. The fourth category is persuasiveness of messages. The extent to which the receiver likes the sender and the extent to which the sender is perceived as an authority must be considered. In general, persuasion is less effective when the communication is mediated by technology.

Technology will probably affect management communication in the future through decision making, job and organizational design, collaborative writing, and group decision support systems. All of these new technologies will be a challenge for future managers as they must learn new technologies and make strategic decisions.

Endnotes

1. C. Cherry, *On Human Communication* (New York: John Wiley & Sons, 1961).
2. Claudia Orr and Karin Stulz, "Teach Technology Skills—Not Button Pushing," *Business Education Forum* 45, no. 5 (1991), pp. 29–32.
3. Selection of these variables is partially based on C. Heeter, "Classifying Mediated Communication Systems," in *Communication Yearbook,* vol. 12, ed. James A. Anderson (Newbury Park, Calif.: Sage Publications, 1988), pp. 477–86.
4. Felipe Korzenny and Connie Bauer, "Testing the Theory of Electronic Propinquity," *Communication Research* 8, no. 4 (1981), pp. 479–98.
5. For further discussion, see Larry R. Smeltzer and Charles M. Vance, "An Analysis of Graphics Use in Audio-Graphic Teleconferences," *Journal of Business Communication* 26, no. 2 (1989), pp. 123–42.
6. Steven H. Chaffee and Charles R. Berger, "What Communication Scientists Do," in *Handbook of Communication Science,* ed. C. Berger and S. Chaffee (Newbury Park, Calif.: Sage Publications, 1987), pp. 99–123.
7. N. L. Reinsch, Cam Monroe Steele, Philip V. Lewis, Michael Stano, and Raymond W. Beswick, "Measuring Telephone Apprehension," *Management Communication Quarterly* 4, no. 2 (1990), pp. 198–221.
8. Sonnly Kleinfield, *The Biggest Company on Earth: A Profile of AT&T* (New York: Holt, Rinehart & Winston, 1981), p. 16.
9. N. L. Reinsch Jr. and Raymond W. Beswick, "Voice Mail versus Conventional Channels: A Cost Minimization Analysis of Individuals' Preferences," *Academy of Management Journal* 23, no. 4 (1990), pp. 801–16.
10. Larry R. Smeltzer, "An Analysis of Receivers' Reactions to Electronically Mediated Communication," *Journal of Business Communication* 23, no. 4 (1986), pp. 37–54.

11. Earl C. Gottschalk, Jr., "Firms are Cool to Meetings by Television," *The Wall Street Journal*, July 26, 1983, p. 1.
12. R. L. Daft and K. E. Weick, "Toward a Model of Organizations as Interpretation Systems," *Academy of Management Review* 9, no. 2 (1984), pp. 284–95.
13. M. S. Feldman and J. G. March, "Information in Organizations as Signal and Symbol," *Administrative Science Quarterly* 26, no. 1 (1981), pp. 171–86.
14. J. Fulk, C. Steinfield, C. Schmitz, and J. Power, "A Social Information Processing Model of Media Use in Organizations," *Communication Research* 14, no. 5 (1987), pp. 171–86.
15. R. L. Daft, R. H. Lengel, and L. K. Trevino, "Message Equivocality, Media Selection and Manager Performance: Implications for Information Systems," *MIS Quarterly* 11, no. 2 (1987), pp. 355–66.
16. H. Geneen, with A. Moscow, *Managing* (Garden City, N.Y.: Doubleday, 1984).
17. This categorization was largely drawn from Ronald E. Dulek and John S. Fielden, *Principles of Business Communication* (New York: Macmillan, 1990).
18. Larry Smeltzer, "Announcing Organization Wide Change," *Group and Organization Study*, March 1991, pp. 5–24.
19. R. E. Rice, "Evaluating New Media Systems," in *Evaluating the New Information Technologies: New Directions for Program Evaluation*, ed. J. Johnson (San Francisco: Jossey-Bass, 1984), pp. 53–71.
20. B. Gallup, B. DeSanctis, and G. W. Dickson, "Computer-Based Support for Group-Problem Finding: An Experimental Investigation," *MIS Quarterly* 12, no. 2 (1988), pp. 277–96.
21. Larry Smeltzer and Charles Vance, "An Analysis of Graphic Use in Audio-Graphic Teleconferences," *Journal of Business Communication* 26, no. 2 (1989), pp. 123–41.
22. Gerald R. Miller, "Persuasion," in *Handbook of Communication Science*, ed. C. Berger and S. Chaffee (Newbury Park, Calif.: Sage Publications, 1987), pp. 446–83.
23. Robert B. Cialdini, *Influence: The New Psychology of Modern Persuasion* (New York: Quill, 1984).
24. Tom O'Flaherty, "The Many Corporate Uses," *Management Technology*, October 1983, p. 54.
25. Gerald M. Goldhaber, *Organizational Communication* (Dubuque, Iowa: Wm C. Brown, 1983), p. 156.
26. "The Portable Executive," *Business Week*, October 10, 1988, pp. 102–12; and Mark Memmott, "Thousands of Good Jobs Gone for Good," *USA Today*, August 21, 1992, p. B1.
27. J. D. Beard and J. Rymer, eds., "Collaborative Writing in Business Communication," special issue of *Bulletin of the Association of Business Communication* LIII, no. 2 (1990); David Kirkpatrick, "Here Comes the Payoff from PCs," *Fortune*, March 23, 1992, pp. 93–102.
28. R. Johansen, *Groupware: Computer Support for Business Teams* (New York: Free Press, 1988).
29. G. DeSanctis, V. Sambamurthy, and R. Watson, "Computer Supported Meetings: Building a Research Environment," *Large Scale Systems* 13, no. 1 (1987), pp. 43–59.
30. Marshall Scott Poole and Geraldine DeSanctis, "Understand the Use of Group Decision Support Systems: The Theory of Adaptive Structuration," in *Organizations and Communication Technology*, ed. J. Fulk and C. Steinfield (Newbury Park,

Calif.: Sage Publications, 1990), pp. 173–93; and "Smart Programs Go to Work," *Business Week*, March 2, 1992, pp. 97–105.

31. Gail S. Russ, Richard L. Daft, and Robert H. Lengel, "Media Selection and Managerial Characteristics in Organizational Communications," *Management Communication Quarterly* 4, no. 2 (November 1990), pp. 151–75.

32. Tracey A. Willmon, "Conceptualizing Organizational Communication Competence," *Management Communication Quarterly* 4, no. 4 (May 1988), pp. 515–34.

33. "Curing a High-Tech Hangover," *Business Week*, June 15, 1992, p. 146.

Additional Readings

Daft, R. L., and R. H. Lengel. "Information Richness: A New Approach to Managerial Information Processing and Organization Design." In *Research in Organizational Behavior*, vol. 6, ed. B. Staw and L. L. Cummings. Greenwich, Conn.: JAI Press, pp. 191–233.

Daft, R., and R. Lengel. "Organizational Information Requirements, Media Richness, and Structural Design." *Management Science* 32, no. 5 (1986), pp. 554–71.

McLeod, R., Jr., and J. W. Jones. "A Framework for Office Automation." *MIS Quarterly* 11 (1987), pp. 86–104.

Sproull, L., and S. Kiesler. "Reducing Social Context Cues: Electronic Mail in Organizational Communication." *Management Science* 32, no. 110 (1986), pp. 1492–1512.

Steinfield, C. W. "Computer-Mediated Communications in the Organization: Using Electronic Mail at Xerox." In *Case Studies in Organizational Communication*, ed. B. Sypher. New York: Guilford Press, 1990.

Tobias, R. L. "Telecommunications in the 1990's." *Business Horizons*, January–February 1990, pp. 82–86.

Discussion Questions

1. Give an example not presented in the book that demonstrates how communication technology has advanced in the past five years. How has this technology affected the management process?

2. Cite an example of how communication technology has changed your activity as a student.

3. Give an example in which you were forced to communicate within a reduced bandwidth when you would have preferred a broader bandwidth.

4. Provide an example in which the communication technology did not greatly affect the propinquity between you and another communicator. Now give an example in which it did affect the propinquity between you and another person.

5. Why do you believe that some people would suffer from greater technophobia than others? Do you have any technophobia in certain situations? Explain.

6. What is the best medium for sending a highly sensitive message to a subordinate in the same city as the manager? Explain your answer.

7. Describe several examples in which you believe that a communication medium was chosen for symbolic reasons.

8. Explain why a sensitive message should be sent on a medium with a wide bandwidth. Why would a contemporary manager be tempted to use a medium with a narrow bandwidth for a sensitive message?

9. What are the disadvantages to categorizing messages in the discussion on matching technology with the message?

10. Speculate why complex information is not necessarily better communicated in a face-to-face format.

11. Give an example in which you could justify the use of communication technology when you are attempting to persuade someone to take an action.

12. Provide an example in which technology has changed a person's job.

13. How has communication technology affected your university?

14. What do you believe would be the greatest difficulty in becoming proficient in collaborative writing?

15. What future changes do you foresee as communication technology makes still more advancements?

CASE 16–1
The Potential for Technology

Bill Emory is the operations vice-president of a large banking firm in California that has 48 branch operations. These operations vary from drive-in facilities with 10 employees to larger facilities employing as many as 150 people. Employee turnover has always been a major problem in these branches, and no employment strategy has been effective in reducing this problem. The high turnover has made employee training a special problem.

The personnel department is responsible for employee training, but personnel charges branch operations for the expenses incurred. The recent expansion in training due to ever-changing services offered by the bank has become extremely costly. Emory has decided it is time to attempt to reduce these costs by implementing some new training strategies. He believes that many of the new communication technologies could be used to save training expenses. In particular, savings could be realized for the branches that are more than 400 miles from the corporate office. (In the past, the training representatives would travel to the branch site, stay overnight, present a one- or two-day training session, and then return. Emory would like to reduce these travel and lodging expenses.)

Emory has casually asked the personnel manager, John Tyson, to investigate communication technology possibilities in training, but no action has been taken; consequently, Emory has decided to write a persuasive letter to Tyson encouraging Tyson's staff to investigate this subject.

Write a letter that could be used for this purpose. Include one or two specific technologies that might be appropriate, their advantages, and the communication impact that could be expected. Special attention should be given to training for the tellers. For instance, the procedures for recording the various transactions and customer communications should be part of the training.

CASE 16–2
Improvements at ServeNow

ServeNow is a grocery store chain that has seven stores in the southeastern United States. ServeNow's strategy is to target smaller towns (under 50,000 population) so it can become the dominant store in the area. The chain is headquartered in the largest town, population 75,000, in which it has a store. Each store is at least 50 miles from another store within the network.

The owner of the stores, Edward Bushley, has found that it is extremely difficult to monitor store activities because of travel logistics. As a result, the manager of each store has traditionally had a lot of latitude. Many of the pricing and inventory decisions are made at the individual locations. However, most purchasing is made through a central purchasing office in the headquarter city.

But during the past two weeks, three managers left ServeNow to start a major grocery brokerage firm. This took Bushley by surprise, but being an entrepreneur himself, he understands their desire to start their own business. In addition, another manager is nearing retirement. Mr. Bushley has found that it is extremely difficult to find qualified replacements for these energetic, creative managers.

Bushley had hoped that potential managers would be available among his present employees, but he discovered the company had been weak in its human resources planning. Current staff members do not seem to have the capabilities nor desire to become store managers. It became obvious that managers would have to be found outside of the present staff.

Bushley retained a small-business consultant who specializes in personnel problems. The consultant agreed that no potential managers were on the present staff. The assistant store managers would be able to manage during the transition, but ultimately new personnel would have to be hired. She stated that Bushley would have to hire managers who were not familiar with the stores' operations and simply spend more time with them than he had with the previous managers. In particular, Bushley would have to spend time training them and answering operational questions.

But Bushley asks, "How can I possibly spend more time at the individual stores? It seems that I am already too busy to maintain a balanced lifestyle." Assume you are a management communication consultant and make several recommendations. Explain your recommendations.

17 STRATEGIES FOR SUCCESS IN INTERCULTURAL COMMUNICATION

George Folse is sitting in his office considering the implications of a major crossroad in his career. When he graduated 15 years ago from a large southwestern university with a degree in management, he had no idea he would ever have to face the choice now before him.

Unlike most graduates, he has stayed with the firm, an oil company, that hired him on graduation. He stayed with this company because it has allowed him to realize the potential he knew he had. The company has done so through a series of promotions, which have brought him to his present position of domestic operations division head. He has been in that position for a year now, and he is just beginning to feel that he has a firm grip on everything the job entails.

Now the company wants him to realize some potential he is not sure he has. This morning the president stopped by his office and made an unexpected request. The operations vice-president for the company's Indonesian subsidiary has been hired by another company, and the president wants George to assume his position.

Flattered but caught off guard, George asked how much time he might have to think about his offer. The president said he was hoping George could leave within two days. He added, that, since George didn't have a spouse and children, he thought the preparation to leave would be minimal. Outside of packing, all he would need to do would be to watch the one-hour film the company had put together to prepare expatriate employees for living and working in Indonesia.

George diplomatically refrained from telling the president that the common impression of people who had watched this film was not very good. He had heard that it does little more than tell viewers how to find housing, how to get a full-time live-in servant for about $50 a month, and where to find the grocery stores that sell American food.

George realizes his future with the company hinges on his acceptance

concluded

of this offer, so he is going to take the job. He is determined, however, to go to Indonesia with more than the film as his source of knowledge about living and working there. Where should he go and what should he try to learn about this country and its people to become the best intercultural communicator he can possibly be? These areas of inquiry, on a more global basis, are the subjects addressed in this chapter.

At first glance, the preceding scenario may seem hard to identify with for a number of reasons. First, readers may have difficulty seeing themselves in that kind of position 15 years from now. Second, they may not think it is likely that they will become international businesspeople. Finally, even if they are able to picture themselves in a career path leading to overseas work, they may think it presumptuous and impractical that this president would expect one to be packed and shipped out in two days.

Put all skepticism aside. This scenario was real life for an executive just a few years ago. Without revealing names, and with a few detail changes to protect the guilty, something very close to this meeting occurred in the offices of a major U.S. oil company not long ago. It is likely that something similar to this dilemma could also happen to the readers of this book at some point in their careers.

First of all, if you are not visualizing that degree of success in your career, perhaps you should. Maybe you ought to start thinking about a career path that has certain milestones along the way. Try to come up with such a hypothetical career path before your last semester in school. You don't want to be at a loss for words when recruiters ask where you see yourself in 5 and 10 years. Many are fond of asking these questions when they come to college campuses to recruit graduates.

Keep in mind, too, that one does not have to be vice-presidential material to be a candidate for an overseas assignment. Depending on the company for which one works, the extent of its overseas operations, and the rules and regulations of the host country, people at various levels may be offered overseas assignments. In fact, some companies with limited operations overseas prefer to send some of their newest people to staff those sites. This point will be addressed in greater detail later in this chapter.

Perhaps you are still skeptical about personalizing the preceding scenario because you just do not think there is much of a chance that you will ever work overseas. But the chances that you will do so are increasing almost daily.

First of all, we have witnessed tremendous growth in international trade in the past two decades. In the United States, for example, the total value of import/export trade in 1990 exceeded $857 billion: almost $494 billion in imports and almost $364 billion in exports.[1]

Second, with all the changes in Europe and the former Soviet Union, trade opportunities should swell to even greater heights. For some years before 1992, firms were being encouraged to establish agents in the eastern bloc countries to be fully prepared to avail themselves of the opportunities to be presented by Europe 1992.[2]

Even if you don't go overseas, you may find yourself working for a firm owned by a company from another country. In the United States, for example, the direct investment of foreign-based companies grew from $9 billion in 1966 to $1,786 billion in 1990.[3] Whether you find yourself in such a position or whether you work in an increasingly culturally diverse work force in your home country, you will probably find numerous opportunities to be an interculturally sensitive communicator.

The last aspect of the opening scenario that you may be skeptical about is the lack of preparation given to that future vice-president of operations. It's a sad fact of multinational corporate life that the quality of the training given to people headed for overseas assignments differs widely by company and by country. It's been estimated that 30 to 50 percent of American managers fail to perform adequately abroad because they have not been sufficiently prepared for adjusting to the foreign culture.[4] Companies in Japan and Australia, on the other hand, are noted for the high quality of training they provide their workers headed overseas.

This chapter will not cover everything anyone ever needed to know about being an intercultural managerial communicator in all parts of the world. That ambitious goal is the subject of thousands of books and articles in any school library and could not possibly be condensed into one chapter. Our goal instead will be an introduction to the types of issues, concerns, and mores one would need to study to prepare for an overseas assignment. Additionally, we will make a number of suggestions about what readers can do now and in the coming years to better prepare themselves to be good intercultural communicators.

What is Culture?

Before we review the many aspects of intercultural communication, we might want to get an idea of the meaning of the word *culture*. Though definitions of this term abound and vary widely in terms of their complexity, Gould defines it in a clear and straightforward manner.

> Culture is what we grow up in. Beginning in childhood, we learn the behaviors, habits, and attitudes that are acceptable to those around us. These are transmitted to us orally, nonverbally, and in writing. As time goes on, we gradually acquire the knowledge, beliefs, values, customs, and moral attitudes of the society in which we mature. A body of common understanding develops with which we feel comfortable. We know what to expect, and we know what is expected of us.[5]

Defined in such a way, culture includes the religious systems to which we are exposed, the educational system, the economic system, the political system, the recreational outlets, the mores governing dress and grooming, the standards of etiquette, the food and how it is prepared and served, the gift-giving customs, the morals, the legal system, the quality and quantity of communication among the people, the greeting practices, the rituals performed, the modes of travel available, as well as the many other aspects of people's lives that they come to take for granted.

When we recognize how pervasive a person's culture is and how much it can differ from country to country, we can then begin to appreciate more fully the difficult job facing a manager in an intercultural environment. The people in another country are quite comfortable with a culture that may seem strange to a visiting businessperson. Yet it is the visitor who will have to make the adjustments and live with the uncertainty and the unusual occurrences and practices. If that visitor wants to succeed in this highly competitive global marketplace, he or she will have to learn to see and accept things as others see and accept them.

Intercultural Myths

Before we examine the various aspects of intercultural communication, we need to dispel a couple of intercultural myths. One is the global village concept, and the other is the universality myth.

The *global village concept* was introduced by Marshall McLuhan in his 1967 book, *The Medium Is the Message.* This concept proposed that advancements in communication and transportation technologies would ultimately shrink the world to a point where we would be one big happy global village. Some believe the global village concept has been realized because we now know instantly of happenings in even the most remote parts of the world.[6]

Others believe we are nowhere near fruition of the global village concept. They contend that the great advancements in communication and transportation technologies have only created a greater proximity among the various peoples of the world, and that proximity has only enhanced the perceived differences among those peoples.[7]

In conjunction with the latter view, it has been suggested that today's students, the future international businesspeople of the world, are going to be responsible for whether or not we ever do see the fruition of the global village concept. To be successful in the global marketplace, they will need to adjust to another culture, and they will need to gain and maintain the trust of their intercultural partner. In other words, they will need to bridge the cultural gap.[8] With each successful international business venture (successful for all parties involved), we move closer to the ultimate realization of the global village concept.

The other myth of which we should be wary is the *universality myth.* This myth is often promoted by people who have spent a short time in a foreign country. Initially, they notice all the differences between their own culture and that of the host country. Then, they start to note all the similarities. They ultimately come away from the experience concluding that, under the skin, we are all alike: brothers and sisters in the common family of man.

The short visit does not provide these people the deeper insight into the culture that would have revealed major differences in beliefs, values, and mores. To illustrate, we might look at some of the results of a survey conducted in a number of countries. One of the questions asked of the respondents was, "Do you agree or disagree with the statement: 'Most people can be trusted?'" The levels of agreement are listed below:

United States	55%
United Kingdom	49%
Mexico	30%
West Germany	19%
Italy	1%

One could argue that language differences might have been responsible for some of the variation. But even if we allow for some margin of error, we would still have a significant variation in a very basic belief. We are truly not all alike under the skin, brothers and sisters in the common family of man. We differ appreciably, and those differences must be recognized and understood and accepted if we are to understand and deal with one another.

Some of the Ways in Which We Differ

One of the most extensive studies of cultural differences was conducted by Geert Hofstede in a very large U.S.-based multinational corporation. He collected more than 116,000 questionnaires from this corporation's employees in 40 countries around the globe. A massive statistical analysis of his findings revealed four dimensions of national culture: power distance, uncertainty avoidance, individualism/collectivism, and masculinity/feminity.[9]

Power distance indicates the extent to which a society accepts the fact that power in institutions and organizations is distributed unequally. It is reflected in the values of both the more powerful and less powerful members of the society. The Philippines, Venezuela, Mexico, and Yugoslavia were a few of the countries with the highest power distances; and Denmark, New Zealand, Austria, and Israel were a few of the countries with the lowest power distances.

A manager in a culture with high power distance is seen as having dramatically more power than a subordinate would have. This manager might favor a controlling strategy and behave like an autocrat. In a culture with a lower power distance, however, a manager would be seen as having little more power than a subordinate and thus might favor more of an equalitarian communications strategy.

Uncertainty avoidance relates to the degree to which a society feels threatened by uncertainty and by ambiguous situations. It tries to avoid these uncertainties and ambiguous situations by providing greater career stability, establishing more formal rules, not allowing odd ideas and behaviors, and believing in absolute truths and the attainment of expertise. Greece, Portugal, Belgium, and Japan were found to have strong uncertainty avoidance; while Singapore, Hong Kong, Denmark, and Sweden had weak uncertainty avoidance.

Uncertainty avoidance is probably going to be a major factor for most intercultural managers to contend with. Most likely, they will be expected to implement change, and uncertainty avoidance is a significant obstacle to change. Such managers ought to remember that using an equalitarian communications strategy to get people involved can greatly help reduce resistance to change.

On the *individualism/collectivism* dimension, individualism suggests a loosely knit social framework in which people are supposed to take care of themselves and their immediate families only. Collectivism, on the other hand, is evidenced by a tight social framework in which people distinguish between in-groups and out-groups. They expect their in-group (relatives, clan, organization) to take care of them; and because of that, they believe they owe absolute loyalty to it. The United States, Australia, and Great Britain were the most individualistic countries; while Pakistan, Colombia, and Venezuela were the most collectivist countries.

Managers from individualistic cultures and collectivist cultures conflict in many ways. In negotiations, for example, managers from collectivist cultures do not want to make decisions. They must first collaborate; consensus must be reached. But managers from individualistic cultures do not collaborate and cannot understand why the other group must spend so much time in conference.

Masculinity/femininity, as a dimension, expresses the extent to which the dominant values in the society are "masculine." This masculinity would include assertiveness, the acquisition of money and things, and not caring for others or the quality of life. These values are labeled masculine because, within nearly all societies, men scored higher in these values. Japan, Austria, Venezuela, and Mexico were among the most masculine societies; and Denmark, Sweden, and Norway were among the most feminine societies.

Consider the following comparison. In the United States, men are judged at least partly on their ability to make a good salary. Frequently, this judgment precludes traditional U.S. feminine values of caring for a baby. In Helsinki, Finland, however, a man may be called away from a meeting to tend to the baby in the childcare center in the next building. Imagine the reaction of a typical U.S. male manager at a meeting in Helsinki when this happens.

Hofstede believed that where a country ranked on these dimensions would affect whether or not leadership, motivation, and organization theories and concepts would be workable in that country. For example, management by objectives, or MBO, is thought to be unworkable in France because of that country's large power distance and strong uncertainty avoidance. Likewise, the French are said to be opposed to the feasibility of matrix organizations because they violate the principle of unity of command. And Germans dislike matrix organizations because they frustrate their need for organizational clarity.

One other cultural difference an intercultural communicator needs to keep in mind is whether the culture is a high-context or low-context culture. In a *high-context* culture, much information is either in the physical context or internalized in the person. In such a culture, people look for meaning in what is not said, in the nonverbal communication or body language, in the silences, the facial expressions, and the gestures. Japan and Saudi Arabia are high-context countries, as are Chinese- and Spanish-speaking countries.

In a *low-context* culture, most information is expected to be in explicit codes, such as words. In such a culture, communicators emphasize sending and receiving accurate messages directly, usually by being highly articulate. Canada and the United States are low-context cultures. As one might suspect, negotiations between low-context and high-context cultures can be fraught with peril when the parties are not warned of the differences in approaches.[10]

Given the globalization of today's marketplace and the increasing pace at which firms are becoming multinational, it has been suggested that organizations around the world will begin to look very much alike. One theory states that as the companies become more similar, the organizational culture might dominate or diminish the effects of the national culture. Research thus far does not support the likelihood of these developments. Laurent found that employees of different nationalities working for a multinational firm maintained and even strengthened their cultural differences. German workers became more German, American workers became more American, and Swedish workers became more Swedish.[11]

Having recognized some of the fundamental dimensions on which the people of the world differ—sometimes considerably—we now turn our attention to the more practical approaches to success as intercultural communicators. More specifically, the rest of this chapter discusses dealing with language differences, being nonverbally sensitive, being a good intercultural communicator, and preparing for assignments or careers in international business.

Should You Learn the Language?

The first decision facing an international business traveler is whether to learn the language spoken in the country to be visited. People who have learned a second language will testify that it can be a long, involved, and tedious task. Furthermore, the difficulty level varies with the language to be learned.

Some have many subtle nuances that non-natives have a hard time capturing. Furthermore, the many dialects that exist within a country complicate the process even more.

For short stays in a country, perhaps just to set up a partnership or sign a contract, most people would agree that one need not learn the language. Since English is the recognized language of business throughout the world, the chances are good that the people one deals with will speak it. If they don't, one can always use an interpreter. Great care, however, should be exercised in selecting an interpreter, for they vary widely in ability.

Additionally, remember that interpreting involves much more than just the translation of words. Biculturalism—sensitivity to cultural and social differences—is often just as important as bilingualism. A good interpreter is sensitive to what is appropriate to the occasion. He or she also needs to know what makes people laugh in the other culture, for humor is very difficult to translate. Political sensitivity, too, is an essential aspect of good interpreting.[12]

As the length of the stay increases, the need to learn, and the wisdom of learning, the language also increases. Most authorities agree that a stay of more than two to three months would justify the time and effort of learning the language of the land. Even if we flounder in our initial attempts to use it, most people will forgive us and appreciate the efforts expended. And besides the obvious business benefits to be gained from learning the language, we get the added advantage of not having to rely on interpreters and/or guides every time we want to go somewhere.

One further advantage of learning the language and learning it well is avoidance of interpretational disasters that have visited other companies in their advertising and product labeling. For example, the Parker Pen Company unwittingly advertised in Latin America that its ink would prevent unwanted pregnancies. Similarly, Otis Engineering claimed on posters at a Russian trade show that its oil equipment would improve people's sex lives.

Sometimes slogans and product names backfire when translated into other languages. For example, Pepsi's slogan, "Come alive with Pepsi," in German read, "Come alive from the grave with Pepsi." GM's "Body by Fisher" became "Corpse by Fisher" in Flemish. Perhaps the most well known dilemma over a product's name was Chevrolet's Nova, which in Spanish means, "It doesn't go." Ford had a similar experience with its truck called the Fiera, which in Spanish means "ugly old woman." Finally, Sunbeam encountered a real problem in Germany where its "Mist Stick" became "Manure Wand."[13]

One last caution is advisable about language usage. Some people choose a middle-of-the-road approach and learn only specific statements that are common or are pertinent to a particular setting. Such people should remember that in some languages, particularly the Eastern languages, the same word can be used to mean many different things. The tone of the voice varies to indicate a specific meaning.

To illustrate, years ago a group of American businessmen signed a contract with a group of Chinese businessmen in Peking. That evening the Chinese businessmen took the American businessmen out to dinner to celebrate the deal. One of the Americans had practiced his expression of appreciation all afternoon. He was going to say, "Thank you for this delicious meal. My stomach is so full that I must loosen my belt." What he actually said was, "The girth of thy donkey's saddle is loose."

The wife of a New Jersey CEO found herself similarly perplexed a few years ago. Her husband had just signed a deal with a Taiwanese firm that afternoon, and a reception was to be held at the CEO's home in honor of the visiting businessmen that evening. She had practiced all day how to say, "How do you do?" in their language, or so she thought. As the first Taiwanese executive came through the reception line, he turned to the CEO and asked, "Why is this woman talking about my mother?" In his language, the word to indicate a question can also be used to mean horse, scold, sesame seed, and mother. She had apparently used the wrong tone in pronouncing the word.[14]

Nonverbal Sensitivity

Whether or not traveling managers choose to learn the verbal language of the land, they should try to learn as much as they can about the nonverbal language common in that culture. Interpretations of gestures, postures, spacial relationships, time, dress, and rituals vary widely among cultures. Business deals have been lost over a seemingly harmless American signal that was interpreted as a grave insult in another part of the world.

In learning about the nonverbal channel of communication in a particular country, remember that nonverbal communication can be almost as evolutionary as verbal communication. In any verbal language, some words get added and some go by the wayside. Additionally, some already existing words take on new and/or different meanings. The same is true of nonverbal cues. They also change over time. Consequently, a manager preparing for work in another country should search for information published within the last 10 years. Additionally, she might consider tapping the personal insight of managers who have lived in the country or have recently visited it.

Greetings

From the start of any business contact, one should be aware that the form of greeting used may vary from culture to culture. Though the handshake is a fairly standard greeting in most parts of the world, the pressure used may differ. The high-pressure grip, which in America is supposed to suggest warmth and confidence, may communicate something else where a lighter grasp is traditional.

In Japan, the bow is still practiced by older businessmen. Sometimes the bow and handshake will both be used to signal respect for both cultures.

Note, too, the different levels of bowing, each with significant meanings. In other parts of the world, the greeting may assume the form of a hug, a nose rub, a kiss, or the placing of the hands in a praying position.[15]

On the subject of greetings, note too that business cards are treated differently in different parts of the world. In Japan, they are handed to the recipient with both hands with the information facing the receiver. Also, they are never put away hastily, but studied carefully and then arranged on the table during a business meeting. Finally, in any non-English-speaking country, getting the information printed on the reverse side of the business card in the host country's language is a courteous and well received practice.[16]

Dress

While the business suit is considered acceptable attire for a business meeting in most parts of the world, it may or may not be totally acceptable for an evening of entertainment. For men in Indonesia, a nice batik shirt over a pair of slacks is considered acceptable at even the most formal occasions. However, it should not be tucked into the slacks.

When dressing in native attire, be sure to note how it is worn and also where it is worn. An associate in charge of family planning for an international human welfare organization found this advice to be painfully true. In Togo, she had found some of the "most beautiful beads (she) had ever seen." She seized the first "grand occasion to flaunt (her) new find." After the laughter subsided, she discovered to her horror that these beads were used to hold up a loincloth worn under the skirt. To everyone there, she had part of her underwear around her neck.[17]

On the subject of dress, we should exercise caution even when we are not in business meetings or at official social functions. Standards of travel and entertainment dressing are much more conservative in some parts of the world than they are in the United States. Shorts and tank tops or tube tops worn in public are considered immodest and offensive in many Arab and eastern countries.

Space, Touch, and Posture

The space maintained, touching practiced, and postures assumed in business and social encounters vary appreciably across the globe. Americans are said to have a spacial bubble of up to several feet into which strangers should not encroach. In Arab countries and Latin America, people speak almost face to face and nose to nose. It has been said that an Arab wants to be close enough to smell your breath and body odor when he communicates with you. Americans not acquainted with that fact tend to back away, sometimes tripping or getting pinned to a wall—and usually offending the oncomer.

In some countries, Iran, China, and Indonesia, for example, it is considered acceptable for two men to walk down the street holding hands as a sign of close friendship. However, in many of these same countries, it is not acceptable for a man and a woman to walk down the street hand in hand. This immodest public display of affection is frowned upon.

Also on the subject of touching, managers should exercise some care about what is touched. In China and Thailand, the head is considered sacred. It should never be touched, and objects should never be passed above it. In Tonga, touching someone's head could get one the death penalty. Finally, in Muslim countries, the left hand is associated with a form of personal hygiene and should not be used to touch food or present a gift.

With regard to posture, a note of caution is in order. In some parts of the world, Arab countries, Thailand, Indonesia, it is considered insulting to show the sole of your shoe to someone else. Businessmen are cautioned never to cross their legs with the ankle at the knee and never to lean back in an office chair with the feet on the desk.

Gestures

In Puwahla, India, an American businessman was trying to establish a partnership with the owner of a manufacturing plant there. Through an interpreter, he was presenting all the benefits that would accrue to the plant owner when the owner started to shake his head from side to side. Down but not out, the American tried to speak with even more enthusiasm. Later, the plant owner repeated the head movements. Discouraged, the American threw his materials into his briefcase, slammed it shut, and stormed out. It was only when he got back to the hotel that he found out that this head movement meant yes in that part of the country.

In Rio, a New Jersey computer salesman was making his first international presentation, and it appeared to be going perfectly. Feeling triumphant, he gave the OK sign to his company's managers in the audience. The chill that immediately swept the room was unmistakable. His colleagues called for a break and ushered him out of the room, explaining to him that he had nonverbally called the audience a group of human posterior orifices. Apologies and an explanation saved the sale but not without some effort.[18]

The victory sign made so famous by Churchill means something entirely different when reversed, with the palm facing the signer. In Britain, it then means the equivalent of the middle-finger gesture in the United States. In some African countries, the gesture we use to say come here, with the palm facing upward and the fingers moving toward us and then away repeatedly, means good-bye. In Ethiopia, pointing and the one-finger come here gesture are considered insulting and are used only with children and dogs.

As demonstrated by the preceding illustrations, the gestures we use in international encounters can be fairly dangerous. A friendly or innocuous gesture can turn out to be a vivid and/or profane insult. And something that very clearly means one thing in one country may mean the opposite in another country.

When we consider the many pitfalls that underlie any intercultural transaction, we might find it amazing that many multinational firms have achieved some degree of success. But if they want to continue and even increase their level of success in the increasingly competitive global marketplace, they are going to have to become more interculturally sensitive than they have been in the past.

Time

Perhaps one of the biggest adjustments that American managers have to make when doing business in some parts of the world is in their view of time. To Americans, time is money and even more important than money some of the time (as when an executive is asked to donate time and offers a check instead). They want things to start when they are supposed to start and end when they are supposed to end.

They don't always get what they want. While Romanians, Japanese, and Germans value punctuality, many of the Latin countries have a more relaxed attitude toward time.[19] In some countries, it is not unusual for a meeting to start 60 to 90 minutes after the scheduled starting time. And when it starts, it doesn't really start. There may be 30 to 45 minutes of "get-to-know-you" time. Often, the meetings will last much longer than Americans expect them to last.

Some of these variations in time perceptions are related to the basis on which the people do business. As opposed to the written contract orientation of the United States, businesspeople in many other countries prefer to build their business relationships on trust—sometimes sealing a deal with a handshake or oral agreement. To establish the necessary trust, they need to get to know the people with whom they are dealing; and that takes time. When Americans insist on getting down to business immediately, they are seen as aggressive and perhaps unworthy of trust.

Food

In some intercultural encounters, if there is a part of the anatomy that may have to summon more courage than would other parts, it may well be the palate. One well traveled businessperson claims that one needs a true spirit of adventure and a cast-iron stomach to be an international businessperson.

Host nationals will want visitors to experience the culinary delights that bring so much pleasure to their taste buds, their national dining treasures. It is hard for them to imagine or understand that these same treats might bring forth horror and revulsion in someone not experienced with them. The beauty truly is in the eye of the beholder. To reject that beauty without even trying it would be seen as rude.

Thus, one might be called on to try sheep's eyes in Saudi Arabia, shark's fin soup in China, a roasted gorilla hand in one part of Africa, a live fish brought to the table and carved in Japan, or a durian in some parts of Southeast Asia. A durian is a spiny fruit about the size of a cantaloupe and has been described as smelling like rotting onions in an outhouse. Yet many people consider it a delicacy. Inside is a slimy whitish-yellowish substance surrounding large seeds. One scoops out some of the substance, pops it into the mouth and spits out the seed.

Depending on the nature of the treat being served, there are a few ways of getting through such dining experiences. One way is to carve the food into very thin slices to minimize the texture and the reminder of whence it came. Another way is to swallow the food quickly so as to get as little of the taste as possible. Another way is to avoid learning what is being served. Do not ask and do not look at any English-language menus. Simply follow the lead of the host.[20]

Gifts

Gift-giving practices vary widely throughout the world. Common and expected in some countries, it is frowned upon in others. For example, while gift giving is important in Japan, it is generally considered inappropriate in Germany. It is likewise not normally practiced in Belgium or the United Kingdom.[21]

Even where it is practiced, the nature and the value of the gifts may differ greatly. Though flowers are often safe if one is invited to dinner at someone's home, chrysanthemums should be avoided in many European countries because of their funereal association. In Japan, white flowers carry the same message, as do purple ones in Brazil and Mexico.[22]

Remember, too, that numbers and shapes might have some significance. The number four is associated with bad luck in Japan, as is seven in Kenya—though seven is seen as lucky in Czechoslovakia. The triangle is considered a negative shape in Hong Kong, Korea, and Taiwan.[23]

Finally, investigate the interpretation of gifts bearing the company logo. While some people may interpret such gifts as a symbol of the business relationship being established or maintained, some might think the giver was simply too cheap to buy a gift on his or her own.

Sexism

While women in the United States are making progress getting jobs formerly held by men and at various organizational ranks, such is not true in many other parts of the world. And in those parts of the world where the men reign supreme in business, those men are not going to want to deal or negotiate with a woman as an equal.

For these reasons, many companies simply do not send women on overseas assignments to such countries. And if ever a woman were to be the most logical candidate, because of her background and knowledge, for such an assignment, the company would probably send a male with her. The man would appear to be doing the negotiating, while he would actually be doing so with her guidance.

While not intended to be complete, the preceding discussion was designed to illustrate the very precarious world of the intercultural communicator. And the dangers of nonverbal slippage are there whether or not a person chooses to learn the verbal language. In the end, the ultimate success of multinational firms will depend on how much effort their people expend toward being interculturally sensitive and thus sidestepping those dangers.

What Is a Good Intercultural Communicator?

While not a comprehensive profile, the following description portrays some of the most important qualities and characteristics of a good intercultural communicator. By a good intercultural communicator, we mean someone who is going to avoid the pitfalls of the job described above, someone who is going to maintain harmonious relations with his intercultural partners, someone who is very likely to achieve success in his international business career.

First and foremost, a good intercultural communicator is *not ethnocentric*. An ethnocentric person sees her country as the best in the world and looks down on others as inferior because they do not have as much to boast about. It might be the freedoms, the conveniences, the technology, the assertiveness, the intellectual wealth, or the sophistication. For whatever reasons, the ethnocentric person looks condescendingly on people of other countries and usually builds resentment rather than good relationships.

There is nothing wrong with national pride. There is nothing wrong with believing that one's country is great and perhaps the best in the world. But a good intercultural communicator realizes that other people have national pride and love for the country they call home. He focuses on the strengths of the host country and refrains from flaunting or even suggesting national superiority. Appropriate behavior is like that of a guest in someone's home. A well behaved guest does not go around saying, "We have more bathrooms at our house. We have a bigger living room and a family room at our house. Why don't you have a three-car garage instead of a carport? Why is your backyard so small?" A well behaved guest is genuinely appreciative of whatever hospitality the host is able to provide.

While good intercultural communicators avoid ethnocentrism, they are also *nondefensive* about their homeland. For example, people in other parts of the world for many years have thought of the United States as some sort of ideal country. When they learn it has problems such as the high divorce rate, drug abuse, gang warfare, child abuse, teen pregnancies, AIDS, race riots, and corrupt politicians, they are naturally curious and eager to hear explanations. A defensive denial or a casual claim that the problems aren't that bad will not do. While one may not be able to explain fully how these problems came to be, a straightforward discussion of the problems and what things are being done about them would be appreciated.

A good intercultural communicator is *curious* about other parts of the world and *brave.* She must have a genuine interest in the people and the places that exist outside her national boundaries. And this interest cannot be faked. One can only guess how many international business deals have been foiled by the attitude: "I'm going to get this guy's signature on the dotted line and get the hell out of this God-forsaken place as soon as I can." Intercultural managers must instead be brave about the conditions they might have to confront. The creature comforts of home are just not always available throughout the world.

Good intercultural communicators are *empathetic* and *understanding.* They are nonjudgmental. They are able to see the world through the eyes of their intercultural partners with some degree of objectivity. They understand that the initially strange behaviors and mores of others have locally very justifiable, long-standing reasons. They do not try to push their culture's ways on people for whom these ways may not work.

Good intercultural communicators are *patient* and *industrious.* They learn to live with ambiguity; they come to expect the unexpected. Meetings will not always go as planned. Businesses will not always be open during the hours posted. Conveniences will not always be readily available. Though much of their coping behaviors will involve riding out the unexpected, they will also sometimes use their industriousness to come up with alternatives to what they expected. If one mode of transportation proves too unpredictable, they simply look for another. If one means of communication fails, they just find another.

Finally, a good intercultural communicator is *genuinely personable* to the people of the other country with whom he is dealing. A good intercultural communicator truly likes and respects those people. It cannot be faked. Some years ago, an international businessperson referred to the people of a particular Third World country as "just having come down out of the trees." Though he never said it in front of anyone from that country, the attitude was reflected in his behavior and caused him significant problems dealing with people from that country. Anyone given to casual and hurtful ethnic stereotyping probably has no place in the international business community.

Career Concerns

As readers look toward the possibility of a temporary or permanent career in international business, they might want to keep some legitimate concerns uppermost in their minds. If they are open to the thought of such a career, they should investigate certain things before they accept employment with a multinational firm.

First, does the firm provide adequate training to employees who are headed overseas? Though some improvement can be noted over the past few decades, many firms still have quite a way to go in developing training programs that truly prepare employees for these assignments. Find out, too, if the training includes the family and if the company provides sufficient support for the move. Such points could logically be addressed during the initial or second employment interview.

Second, are the overseas operations truly important to the company? Or do they represent such a small part of operations or revenues as to be insignificant? In the latter case, some companies prefer to send some of their newest people on overseas assignments because they are so dispensable. While such an assignment may seem very romantic and exotic, you must consider the career ramifications.

You may end up being out of sight and out of mind for several years, away from the people who could influence your career, away from what is happening in the company, away from training opportunities, and away from technological advancements. You might return in several years out of touch with what is happening on the domestic front and out of touch with the people causing things to happen. You might find yourself in a dead-end job with obsolete skills working for someone who wished you would leave voluntarily so that he didn't have to let you go.

Third, even if the overseas operations are important to the company, how do they treat people on overseas assignments? Some companies have programs designed to keep people in touch with what is happening at headquarters and/or in domestic operations. A home-based mentor is sometimes assigned to an expatriate to keep her in touch with the home front in a more personal way. Often, the program includes care packages to the expatriate including, among other things, company newsletters.

Fourth, does the company have a repatriation program? Adjusting to the return to domestic operations from several years on an overseas assignment can be just as traumatic as the adjustment to the assignment itself. Does the company have a program to help such people readjust? A survey of members of the American Society for Personnel Administration International revealed that only 31 percent of the respondents' companies had a repatriation program.[24] The existence or lack of such a program tells a great deal about the value the company places on its human resources.

A career or stint in international business can be an exciting, challenging, exotic, and educational experience when a person has the full support of the company. You owe it to yourself to find out if that support is behind you before you embark on such an adventure.

What Now?

Do you leave an overseas assignment or a career in international business up to fate? If you have a definite or tentative interest in such assignments or such a career, do you have to wait for the job offer to begin preparation? The answer is most definitely *no!* You can do a number of things to better prepare yourself now for an eventual overseas venture.

The first step might be to learn a foreign language. The choice of a particular language is simple if one has a preference for work in a particular company. But even if such a preference cannot be stated, the choice of a language is at least simplified by an interest in a particular part of the world, in which case a predominant language might be identified.

Learning a second language has some obvious and some subtle advantages. Obviously, it would facilitate business dealings in the country in which that language is the native tongue. Perhaps not so obvious is the fact that that language, be it French, German, Spanish, or Dutch, may be spoken as a second language in a number of other countries. In such countries, the traveling businessperson who is not fluent in the native tongue may be able to communicate in a language that is second to both parties.

Perhaps the most subtle advantage of learning a second language is that it may facilitate the learning of a third and a fourth and a fifth. This fringe benefit is especially evident in parts of the world, for example, Southeast Asia, made up of very separate countries with related cultures.

Another step one might take to better prepare for an international assignment or career is to investigate the opportunities available, both social and academic, sponsored by one's academic institution. On the social side, it is not uncommon for schools, perhaps through the international student office, to have programs designed to bring a host-country student and a foreign student together for a half hour or an hour a week.

On the surface, the aim of such programs is to help the foreign student become acculturated by providing him or her a source for explanations of things that may seem strange initially. It also, however, provides the host-country student an opportunity to gain insight into the foreign student's culture. Lastly, it provides the host student a contact, a person in another country who later would probably be happy to return the favor, should the host student ever visit that country. Such contacts can make the job of an international businessperson immeasurably easier and more enjoyable.

Additionally, readers might want to investigate the existence—not always widely advertised—of academic certificates or specializations offered by their schools. Is there an international business certificate they can earn while pursuing the bachelor's degree? Can they earn special recognition for studying specific parts of the world: a Latin American studies emphasis, an Asian studies emphasis, or a Mexican/American business emphasis? Such certificates and specialties could provide the edge one needs in interviewing with multinational firms.

Also, does the school have a chapter of AIESEC? AIESEC is a worldwide organization aimed at providing international internships for its members. For example, a chapter in Los Angeles might arrange through local businesses to set up five internships for five French students from a chapter in Paris. The Paris chapter, in turn, would arrange to set up five internships in Paris for five students from the Los Angeles chapter. These internships can be invaluable learning experiences for students interested in careers in international business.

Finally, stay abreast of business, political, and economic developments throughout the world. Remain aware of the changes taking place and the opportunities becoming available. Read newspapers with an international focus, such as the *Christian Science Monitor* or the *Financial Times*. In the increasingly competitive global marketplace, one shall have to stay in close touch with such developments and opportunities to survive as well as to succeed.

Summary

Given the changes occurring in the world marketplace and the increasingly competitive nature of markets both at home and abroad, firms must become more active internationally to survive and prosper. These trends and developments all suggest that today's students have a noteworthy chance of becoming tomorrow's international businesspeople. To be successful international businesspeople, they will have to be successful intercultural communicators.

A person's culture is pervasive, a body of common understanding with which he or she feels comfortable. But cultures differ appreciably, and those differences must be understood and accepted if cross-cultural business ventures are to succeed. The world has not yet become one big global village, and people are not all alike under the skin. International businesspeople must still work to bridge the cultural gaps that exist among the peoples of the world.

For short business trips to another country, it is probably not necessary to learn the language of that country. For stays of two to three months or more, it might be a good idea to do so. Learning the language frees the businessperson from having to rely on interpreters. It also lessens the chances of encountering the interpretational disasters some companies have experienced in their advertising and product labeling.

Regardless of whether or not the language of the land is learned, international businesspeople need to be as nonverbally sensitive as they can. They need to be aware of greeting rituals and standards of dress. They should be aware that space, touch, and posture are dealt with differently in some cultures. They need to be especially careful about their gestures, for innocent American gestures can become profane and/or insulting in other cultures. They need to accept patiently others' interpretations of time, to be open to culinary adventures, and to be familiar with gift-giving rituals. Finally, they need to recognize that sexism reigns supreme in many parts of the world.

A good intercultural communicator is not ethnocentric, is nondefensive about his or her homeland in the face of questions about its problems, is curious about other people and brave with regard to the conditions he or she might have to confront, is empathetic and understanding and nonjudgmental of intercultural partners, is patient and industrious in living with ambiguity and expecting the unexpected, and is genuinely personable to the people of the other country with whom he or she is dealing.

Before accepting a job with a multinational firm, an applicant should assess (1) the training the company provides for overseas assignments, (2) the philosophy of the company toward its overseas installations, (3) whether or not the company attempts to keep the expatriots in touch with domestic affairs, and (4) whether or not the company has a repatriation program to help returning employees readjust to home operations.

Finally, readers who accept the possibility of an international assignment or career should seize whatever opportunities are available to prepare themselves. They might consider learning a second language. They should investigate the social and academic programs available through their schools. Additionally, they need to stay abreast of business, economic, and political developments throughout the world and the opportunities that arise from them.

Endnotes

1. *Direction of Trade Statistics Yearbook* (Washington, D.C.: International Monetary Fund, 1990), p. 402.
2. Lee Boam, "Doing Business in the Five New German States," *Business America*, December 3, 1990, p. 6.
3. *Statistical Abstracts of the United States*, 110th ed. (Washington, D.C.: National Data Book, U.S. Department of Commerce, Bureau of the Census, 1990), p. 793.
4. C. Glenn Pearce, Ross Figgins, and Steven Golen, *Business Communication Principles and Applications*, 2nd ed. (New York: John Wiley & Sons, 1988), p. 626.
5. Norm Sigband and Arthur Bell, *Communicating for Management and Business*, 4th ed. (Glenview, Ill.: Scott, Foresman, 1986), pp. 69–70.
6. Dale Level and William Galle, *Managerial Communication* (Plano, Texas: Business Publications, Inc., 1988), p. 379.
7. Sigband and Bell, *Communicating for Management and Business*, p. 67.
8. Ibid.
9. Geert Hofstede, "Motivation, Leadership and Organization: Do American Theories Apply Abroad?" *Organizational Dynamics*, Summer 1980, pp. 42–63.
10. Phillip Harris and Robert T. Moran, *Managing Cultural Differences*, 3rd ed. (Houston: Gulf Publishing, 1991), p. 36.
11. A. Laurent, "The Cultural Diversity of Western Conceptions of Management," *International Studies of Management and Organization* XIII, no. 1–2 (Spring–Summer 1983), pp. 75–96.

12. Robert A. Kapp, *Communicating with China* (Chicago: Intercultural Press, 1983), pp. 42–43.
13. Richard D. Steade, James R. Lowry, and Raymond E. Glos, *Business: It's Nature and Environment* (Cincinnati: South-Western Publishing Company, 1984), p. 378.
14. Roger E. Axtell, ed., *Do's and Taboos Around the World* (New York: John Wiley & Sons, 1985), pp. 16–17.
15. M. Katherine Glover, "Do's and Taboos: Cultural Aspects of International Business," *Business America*, August 13, 1990, p. 4.
16. Ibid.
17. Axtell, *Do's and Taboos*, pp. 3–4.
18. Ibid., p. 39.
19. Glover, "Do's and Taboos," p. 3.
20. Axtell, *Do's and Taboos*, p. 9.
21. Glover, "Do's and Taboos," p. 4.
22. Ibid.
23. Ibid., p. 2.
24. Michael G. Harvey, "Repatriation of Corporate Executives: An Empirical Study," *Journal of International Business Studies*, Spring 1989, pp. 36–37.

Additional Readings

Adler, Nancy. *International Dimensions of Organizational Behavior.* (2nd ed.), PWS-Kent, Boston, Mass., 1991, pp. 313

Asante, Molefi Kete, and William B. Gudykunst, eds. *Handbook of International and Intercultural Communication.* Newbury Park, Calif.: Sage Publications, 1989.

Chesanow, Neil. *The World-class Executive.* New York: Rawson Associates, 1985.

Copeland, Lennie, and Lewis Griggs. *Going International: How to Make Friends and Deal Effectively in the Global MarketPlace.* New York: Random House, 1985.

Harris, Phillip, and Robert Moran. *Managing Cultural Differences,* 3rd ed. Houston: Gulf Publishing, 1991.

Terpstra, Vern, and Kenneth David. *The Cultural Environment of International Business,* 3rd ed. Cincinnati: South-Western Publishing Co., 1991.

Thiederman, Sondra. *Bridging Cultural Barriers for Corporate Success.* Lexington, Mass.: Lexington Books, 1990.

Valentine, C. F. *The Arthur Young International Business Guide.* New York: John Wiley & Sons, 1988.

Victor, David. *International Business Communication.* New York: Harper Collins, 1992.

Discussion Questions

1. Do you believe the global village concept has been realized? If you do, why? If you don't, given the nature of developments in the world today, do you have an idea of when we might see the fruition of the global village concept?

2. React to this statement by an international businessperson: "I'm trying to bring some conveniences and comforts and some progress to these people. If they want these things, they are going to have to do business my way and on my terms."

3. Give examples of major differences between two cultures that would seem to contradict the universality myth.

4. If English is the international language of business throughout most of the world, why should you learn a foreign language in preparation for an overseas assignment?

5. Why should an American in a foreign country be concerned with how he or she is dressed when not doing business or attending an official social function?

6. Are there any parts of the United States where touching behaviors are different from what they were where you grew up? Explain.

7. Besides the examples provided in the chapter, are you familiar with any other gestures that are interpreted in a different way in other parts of the world?

8. Argue in favor of the U.S. perception of time in conjunction with its written contract orientation.

9. Argue in favor of the more relaxed attitude toward time found elsewhere in the world where businesspeople prefer to build relationships on trust, which takes time to establish.

10. What culinary oddities originate from particular parts of this country, perhaps associated with a particular subculture?

11. Why should a world traveling businessperson have to force himself or herself to partake of food that is repulsive in smell and/or appearance?

12. Can gifts exchanged between two businesspeople, especially expensive ones, be considered a form of bribe or kickback?

13. An American businesswoman should not allow sexism in another country to keep her from openly engaging in negotiation. Do you agree or disagree?

14. When bribery of government officials in a foreign country is common and expected, the U.S. government has no right to impose its ethical standards on U.S. firms doing business there, thus preventing them from bribing and preventing them from doing business there. Do you agree or disagree with the preceding statement? Why?

15. Do you think you have a future in international business? Why? Why not?

16. Based on the profile presented in the chapter, do you think you would be a good intercultural communicator? Why? Why not?

17. Do you consider it ethical for a corporation with very limited operations overseas to send its newest people to staff these operations because they are the most dispensable personnel?

18. Investigate the certificates, specializations, programs, and clubs available at your school aimed at expanding your global horizons.

19. How does being a high-context or low-context culture relate to whether or not the culture tends to rely heavily upon written contracts?

20. Describe your native homeland using the four dimensions identified by Hofstede.

CASE 17–1

You are a human resources training specialist working for a large automaker. Your company will soon complete construction of a plant in Sonora, Mexico. This plant will specialize in the production of your very popular subcompact, the Chaperone.

Initially, all of the new plant's management will be transferred from various locations in the United States. Later, supervisors will be promoted from the ranks of the Mexican nationals hired to work on the production line. It is hoped that many of these supervisors will eventually rise to the ranks of at least middle management.

The company now faces a twofold problem, however. First, it needs to identify the criteria used to select the managers who are going to be transferred from the United States to the Sonora plant. Second, it needs to train them to function in a different culture.

Because you earned an international business certificate along with your under-graduate degree in human resources management, your boss has decided that this job is right up your alley. She believes this to be true even though your familiarity with Mexico is limited to two coastal vacations there three and four years ago.

She wants a three-page proposal, in memo form, on her desk in two days. The first page should cover the criteria to be used in selecting the managers to be sent to Sonora. She notes that you needn't bother with their technical expertise. Others will screen the candidates on that basis. You should instead focus on the qualifications they should have to be good intercultural managers and communicators and how the company should assess those qualifications.

The remaining two pages of the memo should outline the training program through which the transferrees would go. This program will have to cover, at a minimum, language training, the larger cultural variations, nonverbal sensitivity, managerial philosophies, and organizational cultures in the two countries.

Fortunately, you recently ran across two books that should prove to be good references. One is *Good Neighbors: Communicating with the Mexicans*, by John C. Condon, written in 1985. The other is *Management in Two Cultures: Bridging the Gap between U.S. and Mexican Managers*, by Eva Dras, written in 1988.

Armed with these and any other good sources you may be able to tap, write a memo that will establish the foundation for success in this international venture. Your selection criteria should single out the candidates with the greatest potential for success. Your training program should then ensure the likelihood that they will achieve that success.

EXERCISE 17–1

This exercise is designed to give a class more detailed information on a number of countries throughout the world. The class should be divided into small groups of four of five members each, and each group is assigned a number.

After the group assignments have been made, numbers are drawn from a hat or bag to determine the order of group choice. As a group's number is pulled, it identifies a country that it is interested in researching. The objective is for each group to research a different country.

The topic of this research project is: "What Americans Need to Know about Doing Business in the Country of Choice." The research should focus on the nonverbal aspects of business-related transactions. The group may assume this information is being gathered to benefit an American businessperson who will spend two weeks in this country establishing a business partnership with a local manufacturer.

The research will be two-pronged. First, the group will do some library research on the country. Some of the references and additional readings listed at the end of this chapter might be helpful. The library also will have a number of books and articles that deal with the country the group has chosen. Remember to choose recent citations. The other prong in the research task will be a one-on-one interview with at least two people from the country. If the school has an international student office, this office might serve as a good source of referrals to students from the chosen country.

After all the group members have completed their library and/or survey research, the findings should be analyzed and merged into an 8-to-10 minute group oral presentation before the class. This presentation is then to be followed by a three-to-five-minute question-and-answer session.

The group might wish to begin the presentation by giving about two minutes of background on the country. Its political, socioeconomic, and religious history might help to explain nonverbal communication aspects to be addressed by the group later in the presentation.

The rest of the presentation might deal with such topics as the manner in which the language is spoken (precision, use of accents, etc.); the interpretation of space; the significance of time; aspects of touch, posture, and gestures; differences in social and business dress; and the fine points of etiquette that should be familiar to a person attempting to transact business in the chosen country.

Questions are likely to be generated from specific parts of the presentation, so group members should examine the presentation to identify the parts most likely to generate questions and be prepared to answer them.

1 THE LEGAL DIMENSION OF MANAGERIAL COMMUNICATION

Increased government regulation, higher levels of employee awareness, and a willingness to pursue litigation mean that business professionals need to be aware of the legal implications of their communications. If the business is sued either in a court of law or by an administrative agency, records must be retrieved and made available to the court or agency when subpoenaed. The business records may be entered into evidence. Documents or tapes of internal or external letters, telephone conversations, and minutes of meetings are the records generally sought as evidence. With the increased ability to store and duplicate such documents, these records are now saved for long periods; consequently, the margin of error in communication has been greatly reduced in recent years.

Legal problems that arise in managerial communication can often be traced to problems of perception. If a message is not received in the same light in which it was sent, the message is subject to misinterpretation. Legal problems may arise from misinterpretations. To complicate the situation, the law itself can often lead to misinterpretation.

The many legal problems that may arise from managerial communications are not within the scope of this discussion; the topics covered here are only the major ones with which a manager should be familiar. Legal counsel should be consulted whenever concerned about the legality of a situation. Let's consider several legal areas of which business professionals must be aware.

Defamation

Defamation is a public statement that is injurious to an individual's character or reputation. To be considered a public statement, the words must be communicated to, and understood by, a person other than the one to whom the words were directed.[1] Therefore, an argument between two people, if a third person does not hear it, is not defamatory regardless of what is said. If a third party is present, however, defamation becomes a possibility.

The same holds true for letters, telegrams, faxes, and materials stored in computers. If the letter is seen by a third party, the receiver may have grounds to file defamation charges against the sender. In this case, if the letter were marked "personal," the receiver would have to prove the sender knew the letter would possibly be intercepted. Materials stored on a computer that can be accessed by others are also subject to defamation charges, a new concern in our era of networked computers.

Any written record may contain defamatory statements. Letters, memos, faxes, and other written business records can be subpoenaed and used in court against a company. If such records are in the hands of someone outside the company, such as the company supplier, the court can require the business to produce the records. The court can subpoena the records, and the plaintiff (the person suing) can enter the records as trial evidence. The judge or jury can consider these records against the defendant (the person being sued).

The best defense against defamation is the truth. When the statements in question are true, the plaintiff will have a hard time proving defamation. Truth, however, is sometimes difficult to prove, particularly in a court of law.[2] The exception to the defense of truth is when malice can be proven. The term *malice* refers to a statement made "with the knowledge that it is false or with reckless disregard of whether it is false or not."[3] Even if the statements in question in a defamation case are factual, if they are communicated to at least one other person and malice can be proven, the courts will probably rule in favor of the plaintiff.

In one case involving defamation, the plaintiff, Mr. Bloomfield, was being considered for an insurance agent's position with Puritan Life Insurance Company. Puritan requested an investigative report on Bloomfield from Retail Credit Company, a credit-reporting service and the defendant in the case. The court found that the "reports recommended that plaintiff not be hired partly because of poor health and excessive drinking. Retail credit said that he was temperamental and showed his dislikes. . . . These and other elements of the report, in plain and unambiguous language and without resort to innuendo, clearly had the effect of injuring him in his profession and were properly considered defamatory."[4]

Successful defamation cases show that the words in Table 1 may be considered defamatory and might well be avoided or used with extreme caution.[5]

Defamation can also arise when an employee is being considered for a new position within the company. Suppose a committee is formed to review all the applicants, and during a meeting committee members decide to ask a former supervisor about one applicant's credentials. The supervisor writes a memo to the committee chairperson saying the applicant contradicts himself and cannot be trusted. This may be a defamatory statement because it is a public statement (the entire committee may read the memo); it is potentially injurious to the applicant's reputation; it is a written statement; and it may be difficult to prove the truthfulness of these statements.

TABLE 1 Defamatory Words

bankrupt	inferior
communist	insolvent
corrupt	kickbacks
crook	misappropriation
dishonest	profiteer
disreputable	quack
drug addict	shyster
falsified	swindler
forger	thief
fraud	unchaste
hypocrite	unworthy of credit
incompetent	worthless

The idea that perception would be a factor in defamatory cases is not surprising. Often such statements are not intentional, and meanings are misinterpreted. The statements, however, are no less defamatory when they are unintentional.

Privacy

The Privacy Act of 1974 deals with records kept by federal agencies about individuals. According to this act, individuals have the right to inspect files containing data collected about them by the federal government and to correct any inaccuracies. While such practices are not yet legally required of businesses in the private sector, many organizations have established them voluntarily.

Under the Fair Credit Reporting Act of 1968, employees and applicants for employment must be notified if an investigation about the individual's character, general reputation, personal characteristics, or mode of living is to be conducted.[6] The search may include a review of the credit record and other public information gathered by the credit-reporting agency on the employee or applicant.

The Business Roundtable, a group representing American business, recommends the voluntary incorporation of privacy practices for employees of American business. The American Management Association (AMA) refers to these practices as "employee fair information practices." According to an AMA survey, managers believed the following rights of employees should be protected:

1. The right to inspect personal information as held by their employers, and suggest corrections to their records, and to file written disputes in those records if any item is not resolved to their satisfaction.

2. The right to be told whom an employer will contact to obtain information about them and what sort of questions will be asked.
3. The right to restrict the dissemination of information about them outside their organizations.

In addition, those managers responding to the survey agreed they had experienced two major problems in protecting the confidentiality of employee information. First, was the unauthorized internal release of the information. Second, was the release (whether authorized or not) outside the corporation to persons who had no legitimate business seeing the information.[7]

Although adherence to the practices mentioned here is not regulated by the government, businesses and their managers are still responsible for protecting the privacy of employees. If an employee finds untrue information in the records that could damage his or her reputation, that employee may sue for defamation. Dissemination of highly objectionable, private information about an individual can lead to an invasion of privacy charge. Even if such information is true, the person holding the information is responsible to protect it from disclosure.

Imagine that a claims processor in the benefits department told a friend in the company that a production manager was receiving psychiatric treatment. This friend, who does not work in the company's benefits section and has no legitimate business knowing this information, tells others in the company about the production manager. Such dissemination of information would be an invasion of privacy.

Agency

The principal-agent relationship describes the employment situation in which the employee (the agent) has the power to contract for the employer (the principal). The law of agency deals with questions of contractual liability when an agent enters into a contract on behalf of a principal. The word *contract* here is generally defined as any legal business agreement.

The agency relationship is necessary in business for it permits the manager to act for the company. To qualify as an agent, the individual needs to be authorized by the company to be an agent. Usually these people hold a managerial position. For large organizations, this relationship can become a problem because the law of agency assumes the manager is under the control of the company so the company is liable for the agent's contracts. An especially important feature of the agency concept regarding communications is that the correspondence of the manager is deemed by law to be the company's correspondence.

Use of the company's letterhead is effective in establishing the principal-agency relationship. Company stationery signifies that the company is in agreement with the message. Even if the message contains a statement denying the agency relationship, the agency concept still holds because it is contained in the letterhead. Therefore, only company business, never personal business, should be conducted on the company's letterhead.

The firm's name does not necessarily have to be a part of the signature portion of a letter when using company stationery. The agency concept is established as long as the company letterhead is being used. To establish the agency relationship when using nonletterhead stationery, however, the company name must appear as part of the signature portion of the letter. Once the company name is established, the manager cannot deny responsibility for acting on behalf of the company. The company may be bound by the agency relationship to agree with the correspondence.

Agency or contract law can result in disastrous effects when managers are careless with their communication. An overzealous sales manager may follow up a meeting with a client company by writing a letter to it. In this letter, the manager indicates that 100 cases of a product for $2 per unit can be delivered by the end of the month. The manager, attempting to show what excellent services and prices can be provided by the company, may have made an offer. If the client, surprisingly, accepts the offer, a contract may be established. Problems may result if production cannot deliver on this offer!

The following court case is an example of an agency that resulted from communication problems. The defendant, Tony Greve, was employed by Beltone Hearing Aid Center and entered into a lease agreement for two automobiles with Lou Bachrodt Chevrolet. Greve subsequently left the employment of Beltone and took the automobiles with him. The lessor of the vehicles, Lou Bachrodt Chevrolet, filed suit against both Greve and Beltone Hearing Aid Center.

The basic question presented in this case is whether Beltone communicated to Lou Bachrodt Chevrolet that Greve had apparent or implied authority to conduct official company business with Lou Bachrodt. The court ruled that while it was true that Beltone did not sign the leasing agreement, it is obvious it condoned the lease by making payments on it for four to five months. Consequently, Greve was the apparent agent of Beltone, and even though he was using the automobiles for his private use, the company implied its approval by making the lease payments and not questioning the use of the vehicles.[8]

Specialized services can also result in agency relationship. Insurance and real estate professionals, for example, have agency relationships with their clients. The technical language used in these disciplines is often confusing to laypeople and managers who seek to acquire the services. To avoid confusion and potential future litigation, all parties must be clear on meanings of the specialized language because the agents are acting on behalf of the company.

Harassment

Sexual harassment as an area of discrimination has drawn increased attention in recent years, particularly since the 1991 Supreme Court nomination hearing in which Anita Hill charged Clarence Thomas with sexual harassment. Legal aspects of sexual harassment claims are found in the Civil Rights Act of 1964 and the 1990 amendments.

Part of the managerial communication problem with sexual harassment is its many definitions, particularly since it is not defined in the Civil Rights Act. For example, consider the following:

1. The Working Women's Institute states that sexual harassment is any repeated or unwanted verbal or physical sexual advances; sexually derogatory statements; or sexually discriminatory remarks made by someone in the workplace which are offensive or objectionable to the recipient, or cause the recipient discomfort or humiliation, or interfere with the recipient's job performance.[9]

2. Lin Farley states that sexual harassment is best described as unsolicited nonreciprocal male behavior that asserts a woman's sex role over her function as a worker (according to this definition men cannot be harassed by women!).[10]

3. The Bureau of National Affairs concerned with Labor Relations states that in defining sexual harassment broadly, the (EEOC) guidelines state the "unwelcome sexual advances, requests for sexual favors, and other verbal or physical conduct of a sexual nature" will be considered harassment.[11]

The idea of perception is extremely important in harassment cases. As mentioned in the chapter on nonverbal communication, some incidents of harassment are unconscious acts that are a result of sex roles learned at an early age. According to a survey conducted by the Bureau of National Affairs (NBA), the type of sexual harassment hardest to define consists of subtle comments, innuendos, and jokes of a sexual nature. Conduct of this nature leads to what is called a hostile environment. This type of harassment is also the most often cited by employees. Many claims of sexual harassment that have led to federal court decisions involve suggestive remarks as the offensive activity rather than sexual contact.[12]

Because sexual harassment is so difficult to define, it is open to a variety of interpretations. A physical touch may be meaningless to one person and objectionable to another. A joke may be offensive to one person while humorous to another. The law forbids not only freedom from physical sexual harassment, but also forbids a hostile environment in the workplace.

Some incidents of sexual harassment are unconscious acts, while others are intentional with the purpose of gaining power or forcing compliance. If evil intent can be proved in a sexual harassment case, the employer's position may be impossible to defend. The economic implications of harassment claims are being recognized by employers and steps are being taken to protect organizations and their employees. Extensive corporate training is now conducted for managers on this area of communication because of its far-reaching implications.

Fraud

Fraud is an important legal concept for any businessperson, particularly for those in sales. The intentional misleading of one person by another constitutes fraud. The terms *misrepresentation* or *misleading* are broadly interpreted by the courts to include any word or conduct that causes the innocent person to reach an erroneous conclusion of fact. The fraudulent misstatement must be about a fact. Matters of opinion and prediction of future events are not considered fraudulent misrepresentations.

Several of the communication errors presented in earlier chapters, particularly stating an opinion as a fact, could easily lead to fraud. In the case of *Forrester v. State Bank of East Moline* the court stated in its opinion:

> Whenever a party states a matter which might otherwise be only an opinion but does not state it as the expression of the opinion of his own but as an affirmative fact material to the transaction, so that the other party may reasonably treat it as a fact and rely upon it as such, then the statement clearly becomes an affirmation of the fact within the meaning of the rule against fraudulent misrepresentation.[13]

This statement clearly indicates managers must analyze the consequences of their actions before communicating. Consider a manager who is recruiting for a position that is extremely difficult to fill. While visiting with the potential employee, the manager implies it would be possible to leave work early in the afternoon to take advanced courses at the university. Also, the manager states the company reimburses employees who take courses. If the applicant came to work for the company only to find that both of these actions were against company policy, the manager could be accused of fraud. The manager may be guilty even if nothing more than a misunderstanding existed. Clear, concise communication is critical.

Copyright

Most employees generally know that certain copyrighted material, such as text from books and magazine articles, cannot be duplicated without permission from the author or the publisher. Copyright protection also extends to computer software and to silicon chips, and today, video- and audiocassette duplication is becoming more frequent.

The Copyright Act of 1976 is very specific in regard to photocopying and duplicating material. This act becomes rather complicated, but a few guidelines generally ensure that no law is broken when duplicating copyrighted material:

1. Single copies of material may be made for personal files or posting on a bulletin board.
2. Multiple copies of material may be made if a notice of copyright permission is included on the material, the timing renders it

unreasonable to wait for permission, or it is to be used one time for classroom use.

3. Unlimited use may be made of U.S. government works and "fair use" items such as tables, slogans, formulas, and so on.

4. Publishing an original work, tables, or illustrations requires formal permission from the copyright holder. The simple acknowledgement of the source in the manuscript cannot substitute for formal permission when (*a*) prose of 400 words or more from a full-length book is used or (*b*) a table, diagram, or illustration (including cartoons, photographs, or maps) is reproduced exactly or adapted only slightly.

Copyright decision, however, can be complicated. A manager/owner of a small high-technology company was concerned that the company's engineers were not concerned about service quality. She had a meeting scheduled to discuss service quality when she heard this was going to be the topic of a TV special. Can she record the TV special and show it to her employees? A liberal interpretation of copyright law says yes due to timeliness. However, written permission would be required for future showings.

Managers in a position to do extensive duplicating can avoid potential problems by simply asking the original authors for permission to use the material. Most authors are extremely cooperative and often consider it a compliment to have their materials reproduced. If any doubt exists, permission to reproduce the materials should be sought. Time should be allowed for the publisher to respond since the response time can range from a few days to several months. Often, the publisher will request a modest fee for the right to reproduce the material.

Solutions

Organizations are finding ways to deal with the legal problems of communications. For example, many have developed guide letters for their employees. The writer composes an individual letter from several optional sentences and paragraphs prescribed in the guide. These guide letters may stifle the creativity of a manager, but they keep the organization and its employees out of court.

Every business entity is unique, and each will find its own way of handling communication problems. But managers should consider the follow three concepts in order to avoid legal problems.

A Question of Clarity

Throughout this book, we have been advocating clarity in communication. Clarity is important in agency relationships to assure agents understand their responsibilities and authorities. Clarity will also reduce chances of fraud as misrepresentations are minimized.

Clarity can also prevent legal problems when working with complex regulations. For instance, research has found that the manner in which text is presented can either clarify or magnify complexity of difficult tax law concepts.[14] No manager needs to be reminded of the problems that can result when tax laws are misinterpreted or responded to incorrectly.

Another area in which clarity is important is when attempting to collect debts. Collectors are not allowed to misrepresent the legal status of the debt, the actual intent to take legal action, or the consequences of not paying. They are also required to specify the exact amount of the debt and clearly name the creditor.[15]

But clarity may not be desirable in some situations. In other words, strategic ambiguity as discussed in Chapter 3 may be the desirable alternative in certain situations. Or to use a common phase, "If you aren't certain, don't say anything." For instance, a manager was directed to lay off a large number of employees, but she refused to say how she determined who was to be terminated. She did not want to provide any information that could have led to a potential discrimination suit based on age, sex, or race.

Another example involved American Airlines' attempt to communicate effectively with employees.[16] The company distributed a comprehensive employee manual explaining many company policies and procedures. Later, a California court determined this manual served as a contract and ruled that it implied an employee had an implied contract right to job security.

In a third example, a manager indicated in an employment offer letter that the employer would pay for all employee education. The employer was subsequently responsible for paying for the new employee's education to become a private pilot even though this was not related to the job. The manager should have been more ambiguous by saying the company would pay for *some* education.

When Saying No

Negatives used thoughtlessly or in a mistaken effort to say no gently can create legal problems.[17] Suppose that a Native American student wrote to a firm and asked about summer accounting interim possibilities. A manager responds that no internships were available. But the next week, a white male finance major received an internship. The manager thoughtlessly omitted the word *accounting* when indicating no internships were available. But on the surface, it could appear to be a matter of discrimination against the Native American.

Another problem is that a person may inadvertently commit defamation in a negative letter. A manager may say a proposal was not accepted from a supplier because he had been "unfair" or "unreasonable" in a previous arrangement. Either of these terms could lead to defamation.

Closely related to the negative letter is one that calls for an adjustment or apology. An apology for a product default could end up in a product liability suit. Whenever a letter results in a consumer getting his or her money back or in the user complaining of personal injuries, the law may intervene to provide a remedy for the victim.[18]

Computers and Privacy

When a lawsuit is filed against an organization, the lawyers for the plaintiffs have the right to subpoena documents written by employees. This includes any electronic messages. Unfortunately, employees too frequently use e-mail as if it was oral face-to-face communication. E-mail is written and may easily become a public document.

To add to the complexity, a "common law" of electronic mail is evolving.[19] It is now acceptable to read a message on an electronic network and send it on to another recipient without asking permission of or even telling the person who originally wrote the message. The initial sender may be surprised to find who all ultimately reads the message. Potential legal ramification should be considered when using electronic mail.

Clarity, negative messages, and computer privacy are three contingencies managers must consider to reduce legal problems. And remember that if a lawsuit is filed, reports and letters may be among the documents subpoenaed. The statute of limitations doesn't start to run until a product is known to cause harm. Fifteen years after the introduction of a product, consumers may discover it can cause cancer. All related documents may become evidence. Numerous laws and all kinds of reasons exist for lawsuits. If ever in doubt, seek legal counsel before formally communicating.

Endnotes

1. Alice K. Heom, ed., *The Family Legal Advisor*, 2nd ed. (New York: Greyston Press, 1978), p. 235.
2. Lilian O. Feinberg, *Applied Business Communication* (Sherman Oaks, Calif.: Alfred, 1982), p. 490.
3. H. M. Bohlman and Mary Jane Dundas, *Legal, Ethical, and International Environment of Business* (St. Paul, Minn.: West Publishing, 1993), p. 59.
4. *Bloomfield v. Retail Credit Company*, 302 N.E.2d 88 (1973).
5. Zane K. Quible, Margaret H. Johnson, and Dennis L. Mott, *Introduction to Business Communication* (Englewood Cliffs, N.J.: Prentice Hall, 1981), p. 420.
6. Robert Ellis Smith, *Privacy: How to Protect What's Left of It* (Garden City, N.Y.: Anchor/Doubleday, 1979), p. 81.
7. Jack Lester Osborn, *Fair Information Practices for Managers and Employees* (New York: AMACOM, 1980).
8. *Lou Bachrodt Chevrolet, Inc. v. Greve*, 363 N.E.2d 609 (1977).
9. Dail An Neugarten and Jay M. Shafritz, ed., *Sexuality in Organizations* (Oak Park, Ill.: Moore, 1980), p. 3.

10. Lin Farley, *Sexual Shakedown* (New York: McGraw-Hill, 1978), p. 14.

11. *Sexual Harassment and Labor Relations* (Washington, D.C.: Bureau of National Affairs, 1981), p. 3.

12. Ibid., p. 5.

13. *Forrester v. State Bank of East Moline*, 363 N.E.2d 904, 908 (1977) quoting *Buttitta v. Lawrence*, 178 N.E. 390, 393 (1931).

14. Bobbie C. Martindale, Bruce S. Kock, and Stewart S. Karlensky, "Tax Law Complexity: The Impact of Style," *Journal of Business Communication* 29, no. 4 (1992), p. 383.

15. Kitty O. Locker, *Business and Administrative Communication*, 2nd ed. (Homewood, Ill.: Richard D. Irwin, 1992), pp. 383–400.

16. *Cleary v. American Airlines, Inc.*, 11 Cal. App. 3d443, 163, Cal. Rptr. 722 (1980).

17. Elizabeth A. McCord, "The Business Writer, the Law and Routine Business Communication: A Legal and Rhetorical Analysis," *Journal of Business and Technical Communication* 5, no. 2 (April 1991), pp. 173–99.

18. Robert J. Alberts and Lorraine A. Krajewski, "Claim and Adjustment Letters: Theory Versus Practice and Legal Implications," *ABC Bulletin*, September 1987, pp. 1–5.

19. Locker, *Business and Administrative Communication*, p. 743.

APPENDIX 2

SAMPLE REPORT AND CASE ANALYSIS

SAMPLE REPORT ASSIGNMENT

Read the memo requesting the report, the memo of transmittal, and the sample report on PepsiCo. Walter Barbone has asked you to review the following memo requesting the report and Walter's transmittal memo and report before he submits it to his supervisor, Ellen Johnson. Because of a logistical problem, you will not be able to meet with Walter face to face before the report is due; consequently, you need to write a memo to him suggesting possible ways in which the report could be improved.

One of the first things you noticed was that Walter forgot to include an executive summary. Prepare an executive summary for Walter and attach it to the memo you send him.

CASE STUDY ASSIGNMENT

Assume you are a management trainee at the PepsiCo corporate office in Purchase, New York. As a management trainee, you have a weekly class on some aspect of the company, ranging from the technical aspects of production to understanding the management philosophy. Each week you have an assignment to complete.

Your assignment for the next class is to write a three-to-five-page report to the management trainee coordinator regarding your observations about management communication in the company. In particular, you are to address what you see as potential communication problems you will face and specific areas in which you will try to improve your communication.

Relate the information in the following report to the various topics in the book to prepare your report. For instance, it would seem highly probable that you could become involved in international negotiation. What type of skills will be required to complete these negotiations? Besides this example, a number of other management communication topics should be presented in your report.

ALLENTOWN CHAMBER OF COMMERCE

MEMO

TO: Walter Barbone
       Corporate Liaison trainee

FROM: Ellen Johnson
       Director

RE: PepsiCo

DATE: August 16, 1994

As you know, Alice Hornsby and Jeff Richen from PepsiCo will be in town next week to visit their local production facility. We have information indicating that they may be looking for another plant site. I will be representing the Chamber of Commerce during their visit. We have "heard rumors" that PepsiCo may be looking for another plant site, and Allentown may be a possible candidate. We need to present a good image. Although I am familiar with their local operation, I know little about PepsiCo corporation in general and it is important that I have more background about the company.

Please prepare a report on PepsiCo for me. I am particularly interested in the general management communication philosophy as this is often a good opening topic for general conversation with company representatives.

Please have this report ready for me by Friday so that I can review it over the weekend. I will be out of town the next two days, but if you have any questions we can discuss them Thursday.

Thanks, Walter, for taking on this project under such short notice.

PRODUCTS, STRUCTURE, AND PHILOSOPHY OF PEPSICO

By Walter Barbone

FOR

Ellen Johnson

Director, Allentown Chamber of Commerce

August 15, 1994

Table of Contents

ALLENTOWN CHAMBER OF COMMERCE

M E M O R A N D U M

TO: Ellen Johnson

FROM: Walter

RE: Report on Pepsi

DATE: August 19, 1994

Here is the report on Pepsi that you requested. A brief background
of the company is provided along with several problems it faced a
few years ago.   Also, I briefly touched on the corporation's
management style.

While preparing this report, I had a telephone conversation with a
PepsiCo public relations representative from Purchase, New York.
She sent me a recent list of selected articles on PepsiCo as well
as an annual report and a recent history of the company.   Please
let me know if you would like any of these materials or if I could
address any further questions.

AN OVERVIEW OF PEPSICO

This report presents a brief overview of PepsiCo. It first describes the major segments and history of the company and then indicates the nature of its international operations. This is followed by a brief description of some recent problems the company has faced and then its managerial philosophy is explored.

INTRODUCTION

With its 338,000 employees in the United States and worldwide, and annual sales of $19.6 billion (1991), PepsiCo. Inc., is one of the world's largest companies. Headquartered in Purchase, New York, PepsiCo is a major force in three different markets: soft drinks, fast-food restaurants, and snack foods. The company's respected and internationally known products have generated increasing sales revenues each year. Eight of the company's brands generate $1 billion or more each in annual retail sales.

PepsiCo has been rated as one of the 10 most admired companies for four consecutive years by a Fortune survey of U.S. executives and security analysis. The CEO, Wayne Calloway, was named Executive of the Year in 1991. The company has been cited as a model of excellence in Peters and Waterman's book in Search of Excellence. No doubt this is a well respected company.

PepsiCo's soft drink segment, which boosts such names as Pepsi, Diet Pepsi, Mountain Dew and Slice, commands approximately 33% of the U.S. market and 15% of the international market. The various brand name soft drinks are listed in Table 1. Pepsi is the largest selling soft drink in American grocery stores.

Table 1 PepsiCo Brand Name Soft Drinks	
Diet Mountain Dew	Mountain Dew
Diet Mug	Mountain Dew Sport
Diet Pepsi	Mug
Diet Slice	Pepsi-Cola
Miranda	7 Up (Outside U.S.)
	Slice

Although PepsiCo is probably best known for its soft drinks, it also is the largest group of restaurants in the world. With the purchase of Pizza Hut (1977), Taco Bell (1978), and Kentucky Fried Chicken (1986), PepsiCo built a system of over 18,000 restaurants. In addition, in 1991 the company jumped into the burger business by purchasing Hot'n Now, a 77-unit Midwestern drive-through chain.

The snack food business is also critical to the company's success. However, many consumers probably don't know its many snack food products are related to Pepsi. The company's major snack foods are listed in Table 2.

Table 2 PepsiCo Snack Food Brands	
Chee-tos	Sabritas
Doritos	Santitas
Fritos	Smartfood
Grandma's	Smiths
Lay's	Sun Chips
Rold Gold	Tostitos
Ruffles	Walkers

HISTORY

PepsiCo has an interesting history that can be best understood by highlighting some of the corporation's major events.

1965
- Pepsi-Cola and Frito-Lay are merged to form PepsiCo. The new company has sales of $510 million and 19,000 employees.

1968
- Pepsi-Cola Management Institute formed to train managers.

1970
- PepsiCo sales pass the $1 billion mark and the company has 36,000 employees.

1972
- Pepsi-Cola is the first foreign product sold in the then U.S.S.R.

1974
- PepsiCo sales pass the $2 billion mark and the company has 49,000 employees.

1980
- The company has acquired Pizza Hut and now has 111,000 employees with sales of $7 over billion.

1982

- Taco Bell has been added to the company, which now has 284 international restaurants operating in 24 countries.

1985

- PepsiCo is now the largest company in the beverage industry with sales of $7.5 billion and more than 137 employees.

- There are more that 500 Pizza Hut and Taco Bell restaurants in 35 countries.

- PepsiCo now operates more restaurants than any other system in the world.

1986

- PepsiCo acquires Kentucky Fried Chicken, which is later named KFC.

- The company passes $10 billion in sales.

- Pizza Hut opens its 5,000th restaurant.

1986

- Pepsi-Cola is reorganized along geographic lines.

1989

- PepsiCo is named one of Fortune magazine's top 10 "Most Admired Corporations" for the first of four consecutive years.

- Frito-Lay is decentralized and reorganized along geographical lines.

1992

- The company is now one of the top 25 Fortune 500 companies.

- New Crystal Pepsi, a clear cola is introduced.

- 1,000th KFC restaurant opens in Japan.

ORGANIZATIONAL STRUCTURE

PepsiCo has headquarters in New York, but the corporation is actually a group of independently operating divisions with products produced and sold throughout the world. Surprisingly, the soft drink segment is not the largest unit, rather it is the snack food group that is the largest. The major segments and the percentage of the total operating income contributed by each segment are presented in Figure 1. One reason the snack food segment is so large is that it is made up of the well know Frito-Lay products, which out sell the competitor Eagle Snacks as well as the other many snack foods.

Figure 1

Major Segments and Percentage of Total Revenues

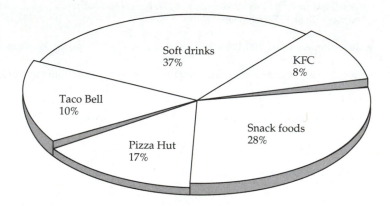

A good indication of the corporation's size is Pepsi-Cola Metro Bottling Company. This is a division of the soft drink segment that is responsible for bottling and distributing within North America. This subsidiary alone has sales of approximately $5 billion which would be the 24th largest food and kindred product company in the United States if it was an independent company. It employs more than 25,000 people with diverse backgrounds and technical skills. It is so large that the division has its own president and CEO, Craig Weatherup. Pizza Hut, Taco Bell, and KFC also have their own presidents.

Although each of these segments runs rather autonomously, it is necessary for the top managers of each segment to communicate with the corporate offices in Purchase, New York. For instance, Pizza Hut's international headquarters is in Wichita, Kansas, but Pizza Hut activities must be coordinated with the PepsiCo offices in New York. Although this may create communication problems between the segments and the corporate office, it allows the segments to remain somewhat autonomous.

Because of the size of the company, each segment is further divided. For instance, Pepsi-Cola North America is made up of several geographical divisions. This makes it difficult to communicate throughout the corporation, but technology is used to support the communication. As an example, communication from the division headquarters to the area units often occurs via videotaping. Also, an internal voice-mail system and electronic mail connect the various units. Pepsi managers have suggested that without technologically mediated communication, it would take weeks for a message to get from the headquarters to the front-line employees. But as with much emerging technology, it takes time for it to be fully implemented. For example, the two main buildings of Pepsi-Cola West are not even connected to each other by e-mail.

AN INTERNATIONAL PERSPECTIVE

PepsiCo has a strong international presence as it lists subsidiaries in the following countries: Argentina, Australia, Bermuda, Canada, Chile, France, Ireland, England, West Germany, Mexico, the Netherlands, Spain, and Turkey. In fact, Pepsi has made international history. In 1958, the United States was invited to participate in a business-culture exhibit in Moscow, and Coca-Cola was invited to attend. U.S. attitude toward the U.S.S.R. at the time was frigid—the cold war was in full swing. Coca-Cola, although conducting business in the U.S.S.R., declined the invitation. Pepsi took the challenge. In the most famous taste test of the 1950s, the CEO of Pepsi offered U.S.S.R. premier Nikita Khrushchev the chance to compare Pepsi bottled in New York to Pepsi bottled in the Soviet Union. Press reporters and photographers had a fantastic time, and Khrushchev and then Vice-President Richard Nixon downed Pepsi after Pepsi. Pepsi went on to become the first American product to be completely manufactured in the U.S.S.R.

But some sophisticated negotiations had to be conducted to make Pepsi's international efforts successful. For instance, the currency of the U.S.S.R., the ruble, is not convertible into currencies such as the U.S. dollar. Selling Pepsi to Soviet citizens for rubles was like giving it away free. So PepsiCo executed an agreement whereby it buys Stolichnaya vodka from the Soviets for dollars and sells it in the United States. Soviet suppliers then use those dollars to buy Pepsi, which they sell at home for rubles. This arrangement took many intercultural negotiation sessions before it was resolved.

Pepsi now deals directly with the distilleries creating Stolichnaya, rather than purchasing through middlepersons, as other vodka importers must. As a result, Pepsi can reduce communication difficulties and time lags. Recently, Pepsi introduced a new, upscale Stolichnaya vodka to the American market. Working directly with factories in Russia, it was able to develop new label and bottle designs and the equipment to create them in only six months—a process that previously would have taken years in the U.S.S.R.

Because of its international experience, PepsiCo has been successful in numerous international efforts. The company plans on having 100 Pizza Huts in Brazil and even opening several in China. But PepsiCo has had to overcome several obstacles. For one, the concept of restaurant chains is unfamiliar to most of the world's population. Second, pizza is unfamiliar, and may seem a luxury in most of the world's nations. An additional problem hinders development of Asian markets: One of the main ingredients of pizza—cheese—would be unwelcome in Asia. Most Asians have grown up without eating dairy products and, therefore, have not developed digestive tolerances for them. However, by listening to the customers and gradually adapting products to meet their concerns, the company has been successful in a wide array of countries in a variety of products. An interesting note is that KFC has its biggest store in China.

But not all are success stories. Craig Weatherup remembers moving to Tokyo at age 30 to run the company's Pepsi business. After a few months, he wanted to launch Diet Pepsi in Japan even though his boss in New York told him it was a dumb idea. Weatherup went ahead anyway. Diet Pepsi sold well for a month and then flopped. The Japanese associate the word *diet* with something medicinal. After the $3 million debacle, Weatherup's boss told him to be more careful next time but not to stop taking risks in the international arena.

DEALING WITH PROBLEMS

PepsiCo is the same as any company in that it has a variety of unexpected problems; however, PepsiCo remains an excellent corporation because it is able to quickly manage these problems. Following is a brief description of three problems that occurred within several month of each other.

The Super Bowl

Every year the Super Bowl represents some of the most expensive advertising time on television. Companies that have purchased this advertising time will put millions of dollars into preparing their advertisements because of their investments in purchasing the time and the huge viewing audience. This has been particularly true for the "cola wars" between Coke and Pepsi.

Diet Pepsi was determined to win the war in 1991 when the company organized a multimillion-dollar, phone-in contest in which three people could win a top prize of $1 million each. Approximately a week before the Super Bowl, concerns from phone companies, local governments, and even the Department of Defense started to arise. They were afraid the contest would create such a response that it could potentially tie up the country's telephone network system. It would be possible that emergency calls could not be placed during the game.

Top marketing managers and the executive staff hurriedly met to discuss the problem. They were all excited about the contest and felt it would be one of the greatest one-day contests ever conducted on television. But quick, difficult decisions had to be made. Numerous intense meetings were held. Less than 72 hours before the game, and after millions of dollars had already been invested, the contest was canceled. Substitute advertisements had to be scheduled for the Super Bowl time.

Magic Johnson

Most people are aware that Ervin "Magic" Johnson announced in November 1991 that he tested positive for HIV, the virus that causes AIDS. But many are not aware that Magic was a substantial investor in Pepsi and was the feature personality in a major ad campaign. Not only was he in one ad campaign when he made the announcement, but the company was also making plans for another major ad featuring the basketball star. Before time was available to even discuss their next move, Craig

Weatherup and other spokespeople were asked about their reaction. Would the company continue to feature the basketball star with HIV? What was the company's position on AIDS? Did the company have a statement regarding homosexuality? Top managers around the country, in addition to the president, had to be ready to respond to these questions from the press. Because of these managers' extensive communication training and experience, they were ready to respond in a tactful manner to these difficult questions.

Rumors

An inexpensive soft drink called Tropical Fantasy is bottled in New York by Brooklyn Bottling. In 1991, a rumor started to circulate that this drink was laced with a mysterious stimulant that made black men sterile. A local district attorney investigated the possibility that the cause was possible sabotage by Pepsi-Cola. Although the involvement of Pepsi-Cola was never substantiated, management had to monitor the rumors carefully and be ready to react immediately. Fortunately, Pepsi was well aware of the rumor long before the district attorney became involved, so the company was able to prepare a communication strategy to defend its position.

SUCCESS THROUGH PEOPLE

Whether it is negotiating a Pizza Hut contract in Spain, working with a bottling plant in Russia, or making a last-minute advertisement decision in the United States, PepsiCo attributes its success to people skills. To quote CEO Wayne Calloway, "It is the three P's: people, people, and people." Described by his colleagues as "tough as nails" Calloway runs a boot camp for managers that makes Paris Island look like Coney Island. Those who can't cut it wash out.

Fast Moving

To prove himself, each manager gets to act like an entrepreneur—risk taking is di rigueur, memos scare, meetings few, and second guessing rare. Sixty-hour workweeks are typical, and managers often work Saturdays and Sundays. But teamwork counts too. As one manager put it, "We believe it's more important to do something than sit around and worry about it."

Informal, quick communication is favored over a formal structure. A few years back, Roger Enrico, then CEO of PepsiCo Worldwide Beverages, decided to sign pop star Michael Jackson for a Pepsi commercial at a record $5 million fee. He didn't telephone PepsiCo CEO Kendall to tell him what he was doing until a few hours before the contracts were to be signed. As Enrico said later, "It didn't occur to me to tell him."

This fast communication was also displayed in 1988 when Coke took Pepsi by surprise during the Super Bowl broadcast. Coke staged a 3-D Diet Coke halftime show claiming that some 2 million people a year were switching from Pepsi, with the lion's share going to Diet Coke. Pepsi believed the numbers were wrong. That week a Pepsi executive was riding up from Manhattan with Phil Dusenberry, the head of Pepsi's ad agency, to see CEO Enrico in Purchase. During the ride, Dusenberry and the Pepsi executive worked out the script for a rebuttal commercial and explained it to Enrico when they arrived at the corporate office. Enrico gave it the OK. The commercial was shot and aired within three days. The advertisement showed a crazed-looking Coke executive in a boardroom staring myopically at this statistics through 3-D glasses as a voice-over says, "Gentlemen, I trust we're all seeing this the same way." Coke watered down its claim in subsequent advertisements. Said Enrico, "If we had sent this up the line for approval, it would have taken a month." This same penchant for quick action is probably why Pepsi was able to introduce a 100 percent NutraSweet formula in 1984 before Coke knew about it.

Development and the Appraisal Systems

Fortune magazine has stated that PepsiCo takes people development more seriously than perhaps any other American corporation. Calloway spends up to two months every year personally reviewing the performance of his top 550 managers, discussing their future with their bosses and with the personnel department. And he expects every manager below him to do the same thing. By the end of each year, every one of the company's 20,000 managers knows exactly where he or she stands.

The company uses performance appraisal interviews to weed out the weak and nurture the strong. The annual performance appraisal pertains to what the manager did to make a big difference in the business, not whether he or she is a nice person. Second, managers then get divided into four categories. Those at the top are promoted. Those in the second group get challenging jobs. Those in the third category continue to be evaluated and rotated. Those in the bottom category are out.

An example of quick promotions is Peter McNally. Soon after joining the company, 24-year-old McNally was given full responsibility for a $500 million segment of the snack business of Frito-Lay. His assignment was to boost the sales of the 1-ounce, single-serving bags of Frito's potato and taco chips. McNally's idea: market larger, 2-ounce bags for teenagers with big appetites. His idea helped boost Frito-Lay's sales by 15 percent a year since 1985. By the age of 30, McNally was vice-president of marketing services for the Taco Bell chain.

Brenda Barnes, a fast-rising, 35-year-old Pepsi-Cola vice-president with 700 people under her control, sums it up best when she says, "We'll never be nor should we be a warm and cuddly environment." There is a merciful side to all this. People tend to get weeded out early in their careers rather than later, when it is harder to find another job.

But such a harsh system has costs. One manager who wasn't considered PepsiCo material found himself walking around the hallways with his face twitching. When the inevitable day of reckoning arrived, he asked the reviewer why he hadn't made it. Looking him straight in the eye, his executioner replied, " You're not enough of a bastard."

But this doesn't mean the "soft side" of management gets completely ignored. Says a manager at Frito-Lay, "We've got a lot of bright people who piss people off." To help remedy that, PepsiCo has a feedback program in which the bosses get evaluated by their subordinates in confidential reports. This gives subordinates an opportunity to be heard and managers a chance to listen to them. Also, throughout the company's management training, much emphasis is placed on two-way communication.

SUMMARY

PepsiCo is a complex $19 billion corporation whose major segments are soft drinks, snack foods, and restaurants. Each segment is managed independently with activities coordinated among divisions from the corporate offices in Purchase, New York. The company has a strong international presence and will probably continue to increase in this area. Although the management style may appear to be rather cut-throat, it also has a soft side to it.

REFERENCES

Brian Dumaine, "Those High-flying PepsiCo Managers," Fortune, April 10, 1989, pp. 78–86.

Thomas J. Peters and Robert H. Waterman, Jr., In Search of Excellence (New York: Warner Books, 1982).

B. Keller, "Does Moscow Mean It This Time?" The New York Times, January 18, 1987, p. F3.

"Pepsi's Marketing Magic: Why Nobody Does It Better," Business Week, February 10, 1986, pp. 52–57.

Hoover Handbook of American Business, 1992, p. 432.

PepsiCo 1992 Annual Report.

"A Different Brand of Leader," Chief Executive, July/August 1991.

INDEX